STRUCTURED ASSEMBLY LANGUAGE PROGRAMMING FOR THE IBM 370

STRUCTURED ASSEMBLY LANGUAGE PROGRAMMING FOR THE IBM 370

JAMES L. SILVER
Indiana University-Purdue University at Fort Wayne

DELLEN PUBLISHING COMPANY
San Francisco

COLLIER MACMILLAN PUBLISHERS
London

Divisions of Macmillan, Inc.

On the cover: "Untitled #11," by Patrick Hogan, 1982; watercolor, 14" x 11". Patrick Hogan is a Los Angeles artist who paints large abstract rope and acrylic paintings as well as intimate water-colors. His work has been shown at the Whitney Museum of American Art and the Solomon R. Guggenheim Museum in Los Angeles. His work is represented by Tortue Gallery in Santa Monica, California.

Interior Design: Rebecca D. Evans, IPS Publishing, Inc.
Composition: IPS Publishing, Inc.
Project Management: Laura Speek Welch, IPS Publishing, Inc.

Permissions: Dellen Publishing Company
400 Pacific Avenue
San Francisco, California 94133

Orders: Macmillan Publishing Company
Front and Brown Streets
Riverside, New Jersey 08075

Collier Macmillan Canada, Inc.

Library of Congress Cataloging in Publication Data

Silver, James L., 1944–
Structured assembly language programming for the IBM 370.

Includes index.

1. IBM 370 (Computer)—Programming. 2. Assembler language (Computer program language)
3. Structured programming. I. Title
QA76.8.I123S45 1986 005.2'25 86-2138
ISBN 0-02-411040-X

Printing: 1 2 3 4 5 6 7 8   Year: 6 7 8 9 0

For Jimmy

CONTENTS

CHAPTER 4 GENERAL INSTRUCTIONS

CHAPTER 5   ARRAYS

APPENDICES

PREFACE

Assembly language is one of the oldest courses in computing curricula. IBM 370 Assembly Language, in particular, is a twenty-year-old subject. In these twenty years, many textbooks have been written to cover this subject. Although the basic architecture of large IBM computers has not changed, the computer environment has changed drastically. Now, a text in IBM 370 Assembly Language needs to directly address the student of the 80s rather than the student of the 60s.

What this text offers is different from the many currently available texts on this topic in its treatment of: (1) the early introduction of structured programming, (2) the use of standard patterns to implement the constructs of structured programming, and (3) extensive use of symbolic constants and the length attribute to create programs that can be easily modified.

Structured programming techniques are an integral part of the text. They are introduced simultaneously with other concepts of assembly language. In particular, they are not relegated to appendices or later chapters, where their position is invariably interpreted by students as indicative of their importance. Rather, structured programming techniques are seen in the development and implementation of every sample program. In addition to creating programs that can be read, understood, and modified with relative ease, this approach allows students to draw on their previous programming experience. They are not expected to adopt a new programming style, but to continue to develop programs as they did in earlier courses using languages such as Pascal.

The provision of patterns for implementing standard constructs of structured programming supports this text's approach. The text provides a schema for each construct, such as IF-THEN-ELSE, and definite and indefinite iterations. These schemata allow students to develop algorithms using these standard constructs, then translate them to assembly language in a straightforward and fairly automatic way. Branch instructions are used only when they are part of one of these constructs. The use of these schemata also imposes strict standards for documentation including labelling conventions and indentation of comments to display the logical structure of a program.

Finally, the text makes extensive use of the length attribute operator and assembler expressions in defining dependent data areas and their exclusive use whenever explicit lengths or displacements are used in instructions. Their use results in programs that are easier to read, especially for the novice programmer. For example, they make a clear distinction between the use of explicit lengths and explicit base registers in SS instructions. This is not the case when lengths and base registers are expressed simply as self-defining terms as in MVC 0(5,8),10(4). The use of these expressions also results in programs that are much more easily modified. For example, it is often possible to accommodate changes in input or output specifications by changing only the storage definitions. Other necessary changes will be made automatically when the program is reassembled.

These techniques provide a number of benefits. As students can translate structured programming constructs to assembly language programs almost automatically, they are able to draw on their previous experience in problem solving and algorithm development. This greatly eases the normally difficult transition from high-level languages to assembly language. The acceptance of the discipline implied by the labelling and indentation conventions and the avoidance of self-defining terms in instructions results in programs which are much easier to read and understand than typical assembly language programs. This is an obvious advantage to the novice programmer struggling with the technicalities of assembly language. The continued use of these techniques by practicing programmers will result in assembly language programs which can be maintained and modified to the same extent as programs written in high-level languages.

It is much easier to write bad programs in assembly language than in high-level languages. Thus, the cost of writing well-structured programs in assembly language is somewhat greater. However, the benefits are still commensurate with the cost. The metaphor of taming the beast is quite prevalent in computer science, but it is nowhere more apt than in the application of structured programming methods to assembly language programming.

Intended Audience

This text is directed to students who have had programming experience in a high-level language, including arrays, procedures, and parameter passing. This experience should have emphasized the use of structured programming techniques and these techniques should be reasonably well-established. In particular, students should view the use of these methods in a language such as Pascal or PL/I as being the "natural" way to program. In languages such as FORTRAN or COBOL, the student should realize that the use of these methods, although awkward at times, results in benefits that are easily worth the cost. Unless these practices are ingrained, it will be difficult to get students to adopt the methods developed in the text. If students harbor doubts about the benefits of structured programming in a high-level language, their programming in assembly language is almost certain to reflect these doubts.

Methods

Given students with the background described above, the text builds as much as possible upon that background. In particular, we adopt conventions and programming standards that allow students to view assembly language programming as an extension of their previous programming experiences, rather than as a new and separate study. In most cases, these conventions do not adversely affect the programs produced. However, we make no apology for the few cases in which the resulting programs could be shortened by abandoning these conventions. Students and faculty should both freely accept these occasional inefficiencies as the cost of writing programs that work consistently.

In considering the order and relative importance of the topics included in the text, we must not lose sight of two important factors. The first is that many of the students in an assembly language course will not be writing assembly language programs on a regular basis after they have completed the course. Second, of those students who do continue to write assembly language programs, a large number will write some or all of those programs for machines with architectures that differ greatly from that of the machine on which they learned.

Curriculum committees have been dealing with these factors for years. The obvious question raised by both students and faculty is "Why not drop assembly language courses from degree requirements?" The answers vary. Some departments and at least one set of national curriculum guidelines have decided either to eliminate assembly language courses or to replace them with lower-level architecture courses in which students write a few assembly language programs. Among those departments which have opted to keep the requirement of an assembly language course, the responses to these two factors are fairly standard. In the first case, students are said to profit from a practical, goal-directed exposure to computer architecture. For students who eventually take a computer architecture course, the benefits are obvious. These students can begin a general study of architecture with a thorough understanding of the architecture of one machine as a foundation. Even those students who do not take architecture courses gain a deeper understanding of the compilers and operating systems they use. Students who subsequently write assembly language programs for other machines are able to transfer the skills they have acquired in their first experience with assembly language programming to their new environment.

In light of these rationales for studying assembly language, such study should concentrate on material that illuminates the architecture of a particular machine or which can be applied to assembly language programming on other machines. Idiosyncrasies of the machine actually used in the course should have minimal influence on the content. (These must be dealt with, but they should be viewed as obstacles rather than objectives.)

In this text, we place special importance upon skills that may be transferred to assembly language programming on other machines; however, the essence of assembly language programming is to take advantage of the intimate relationship between the assembly language and the machine to create programs that are as efficient as possible. Thus, we do utilize such features of IBM 370 programming whenever this can be done without compromising the clarity or modifiability of the programs produced. In doing so, we focus students' attention to those features of 370 architecture that facilitate efficient programming.

We do not attempt to deal extensively with features of the 370 assembly language programming that do not provide either transferrable skills or understanding of 370 architecture. For example, we cover only rudimentary forms of input and output. We do not cover the traditional topics of disk or tape manipulations; these features are highly dependent upon the machine and operating system being used. More to the point, elementary operations such as file updates and merges require the same programming logic as in a high-level language. Students gain little additional insight from their application in assembly language programming. More complex operations such as indexed or direct access methods are beyond the scope of the course for which the text is intended.

Contents

The text consists of eight chapters. In order to cover the entire text in a 15-week semester, it is necessary to complete Chapters 1, and 3 through 8 in two weeks each. Chapter 2 can be covered in one week. This is a rather brisk pace so we will note some topics which can be omitted if necessary.

There is a set of exercises at the end of each section. Students should be expected to complete all of these exercises while reading the section. Most exercises ask students to do such things as trace small groups of instructions, perform type conversions or arithmetic and logical operations, and write short segments of code. In addition to these exercises, each chapter includes four or five programming assignments. These give a complete description of an assembly language program usually including input and output formats. The instructor needs to provide only the sample data for each program. The programs at the end of each chapter are to be approximately equal in coverage so that a student who does one of the programs at the end of each of the chapters covered will receive a reasonably complete introduction to assembly language programming. This allows instructors to assign different programs to different sections of the course or to vary the programming assignments from year to year.

The text begins with a brief overview of IBM 370 architecture and proceeds to cover character and packed decimal instructions in the early chapters. Although the course as a whole should concentrate on binary data types, we begin with packed decimals and use them exclusively while covering structured programming constructs, assembler concepts, and reading hexadecimal dumps. Students are more comfortable with decimal data than binary data types. It is, for example, much easier to learn to read dumps when looking for packed decimal or zoned decimal values than binary data. Once students are confident of being able to find a particular field in a dump, the use of dumps becomes an aid in mastering binary instructions. This approach also allows students to acquire the necessary techniques for input and output used throughout the course.

Instructions to manipulate binary integers and use the 370's registers are introduced after students are more or less at ease with the assembly process. Ideally, students should have had an introduction to binary and hexadecimal arithmetic in earlier courses. Nevertheless, all the necessary details are presented to provide students who have seen the material before with a review and reference source and to allow students with deficiencies in these areas to catch up. In addition to covering all binary arithmetic instructions, register usage guidelines are presented and shift instructions are covered in the same chapter. This selection of topics concludes with an introduction to the use of registers to hold addresses. This is presented in conjunction with the Load Address instruction and the Edit and Mark instruction. This allows the introduction of pointers in a way which minimizes extraneous details. In particular, it allows the use of direct addressing before the complications of array manipulations are introduced.

Chapter 5, on arrays, begins with one-dimensional arrays of full- and halfwords using the RX instructions. Several standard algorithms for array manipulation are implemented in assembly language and the instructions for automatic loop generation are presented. This is followed by a section that implements some multidimensional arrays of binary data using explicit base registers and an introduction to subscript resolution. Arrays of decimal and character types are introduced using DSECTs to describe individual entries. Finally, the chapter discusses general arrays of record structures using DSECTs, this section can be omitted if necessary.

Chapter 6 develops external procedures and reference parameters. The need for independence of procedures and the use of reference parameters are discussed. These factors are used to develop the standard calling sequence. Reference parameters are implemented using DSECTs to describe the arguments. After the techniques have been developed, the system macros, CALL, SAVE, and RETURN, are used for the implementations. This allows the time devoted to these topics to be varied depending on the depth of coverage desired. The last two sections cover input and output from procedures and alternate parameter types. The section on alternate parameter types discusses the problems associated with early generation of the address list and the resulting restrictions on parameters. These last two sections can be omitted if necessary.

The chapter on macros and conditional assembly begins with provisions for writing simple macros involving symbol substitution. It surveys the IBM features for writing more complex macros including set symbols, sequence symbols and conditional assembly instructions. The chapter develops a number of sample macros. One of these provides a procedure calling mechanism that generates the argument address list at execution time. The last section, covering parameter arrays and set symbol lists, can be omitted if necessary.

The last chapter covers floating point data types and instructions. A general discussion of floating point operations and the need for normalization is followed by the peculiarities of the IBM floating point types and hexadecimal normalization. The floating point instructions are presented together with the bit and byte manipulations required for floating point conversions. The chapter develops general purpose macros for the conversions. So, if time becomes a problem, the difficulties associated with conversion can be glossed over and the macros presented without comment.

Finally, the text contains three appendices. The first two contain an instruction summary and a coding table. The third covers several special purpose instructions. These can be presented as needed to illustrate the power and control available to the assembly language programmer. Alternatively, they can be assigned for reading as needed for particular programming projects.

ACKNOWLEDGMENTS

I wish to express my gratitude to the many people who helped in the development and preparation of this text. These include my colleagues who provided support and encouragement. In particular, Bob Leeper first suggested the use of schemata to implement the standard constructs. Linda Rising read the manuscript and used it in the classroom, providing many suggestions and comments. Among the former students who were instrumental in this effort, Susie Bagby deserves special mention; she assisted in the preparation of sample programs and exercises for the text. I would like to thank the following reviewers:

Paul W. Ross	Millersville University of Pennsylvania
Richard Leon Howe	Orange Coast College
Richard Davis	Tulsa Junior College
Steve Treanor	Del Mar College
Ernest Philipp	Northern Virginia Community College
Michael Walton	Miami Dade Community College North
George Rice	De Anza College

IPS Publishing, Inc. and Sally Kostal made the final stages of this project as painless as possible.

Finally, I would like to thank June Fox who convinced me to begin the project.

James L. Silver
January 1986

C H A P T E R 1

INTRODUCTORY CONCEPTS

1.1 MACHINE LANGUAGES AND ASSEMBLY LANGUAGES

Before studying assembly language programming, we will review the concepts of machine languages and assembly languages. It will be particularly helpful to develop a preliminary concept of assembly language programming and to learn what benefits can be derived from studying it.

Originally, the term *machine language* referred to hardware execution of instructions. On most modern, large-scale computers, this definition is not accurate; the so-called machine language programs are interpreted by another program called a *microprogram*. The term *machine language* now refers to the language of a virtual rather than an actual machine. This virtual machine is a model provided by the manufacturer to describe how the actual machine and its microprogram operate. From a user's point of view, it is quite reasonable and useful to deal only with the virtual machine and that is the approach taken in this book. Thus, when we describe an IBM 370, we focus not on a particular collection of hardware components, but on the virtual machine, which has been realized on a large number of IBM computers.

From a practical point of view, the machine language of a particular computer consists of a collection of relatively primitive instructions. Each instruction is assigned a binary code. These codes, called *opcodes*, usually range from 6 to 8 or more bits, depending upon the manufacturer. The opcodes on the IBM 370 computers are 8 bits, or one byte, long. In addition to the opcode, a complete instruction may contain one or more operands, which are also encoded in binary. A single instruction with its operands may easily be 48 bits long. So, when it is necessary to represent machine language instructions, they are usually given in octal or hexadecimal form. (We will see that it is very easy to make conversions between binary and octal and between binary and hexadecimal.) Example 1.1.1 shows the hexadecimal form of an IBM 370 machine language instruction to add two decimal numbers. The example also contains an interpretation of each of the components of this instruction.

Example 1.1.1

| FA | 56 | C2 | 3A | A1 | 35 |

FA The opcode for the Add Packed decimal instruction.

56 The operands are 6 and 7 bytes long respectively.

C23A The address of the first operand may be obtained by adding the contents of register C (12) and the hexadecimal number 23A.

A135 The address of the second operand is obtained by adding the contents of register A and the hexadecimal number 135.

This example shows some of the difficulties of programming in machine language, one being the problem of keeping track of the 256 possible one-byte opcodes. Less obvious, but a great deal more serious is the problem of keeping track of the addresses of data and instructions in memory. Difficult enough when dealing with a single instruction, this problem may well be insurmountable when dealing with a large program and its data.

There was a time when some programs were written entirely in machine language. Even today, occasionally it may be useful to write small segments of code in machine language, for instance, when small changes need to be made in a program available only in a machine language version. However, such a process is at best tedious and repetitive and at worst, mistakes that are difficult to correct are bound to occur.

Assembly Languages

Even when machine language was in common use, programmers who wanted to increase their productivity and the reliability of their programs developed intermediate languages, giving operations short names reminiscent of their functions and using meaningful identifiers for storage areas. When these programmers were reasonably certain that a program was correct, it was a simple matter to convert the mnemonic instruction names to opcodes and to assign addresses to the identifiers. This translation operation known as *assembly* and the intermediate language used was called *assembly language*. For example, the assembly language form of the instruction in Example 1.1.1 might be

AP   X,Y

Although using an intermediate assembly language program was preferable to writing a machine language program directly, the translation process was slow and error prone. Because computers excel at performing tedious, repetitive tasks with great accuracy, it was not long before programs called *assemblers* were developed to automate the translation process.

Early assemblers did little more than translate and keep track of storage areas. Today there are still some assemblers in use, most notably inexpensive versions of assemblers for microcomputers, which provide only simple translation and storage functions. However, over the years, assemblers for larger computers have been greatly enhanced. Most assemblers include "macro" features. Groups of commonly used instructions are assigned a name and the assembler will replace each occurrence of the name in an assembly language program with that group of instructions. These assemblers can replace symbolic parameters in the macro with variable names provided by the programmer. Conditional assemblers can vary the instructions generated depending upon the values assigned to the symbolic parameters on each macro call. Modern assemblers also provide a great variety of mechanisms for allocating and defining storage areas. With these mechanisms, the programmer can describe data structures which may be as complex as those available in high level languages. In some cases, modern assemblers provide a rudimentary form of type checking when the program is assembled.

As assemblers have changed, the environments in which programs are executed have also been altered. The most drastic change has been the transformation from single programming systems to multiprogramming systems. In the latter, it is imperative that concurrently executing programs not interfere with each other. If two concurrently executing programs were both allowed to access a printer whenever they needed to print a line, the printed output would not be useable. In order to ensure noninterference, limits must be placed on the areas of memory that a program may access and the use of input and output devices. Such limits are imposed by a set of instructions that can be accessed only by the operating system. Operating systems were developed in part to allow users to share such resources without interference. But, if user programs were allowed to execute all of the machine's instructions, they could circumvent, accidentally or maliciously, any protection provided by the operating system. So, a number of the instructions are restricted in such a way that they may be executed only by the operating system. Restrictions usually include all input and output instructions.

Because applications programs may not execute input and output instructions on most systems, input and output operations must be performed by the operating system. Typically, the operating system contains subroutines for performing common I/O operations and the assembler provides macros which generate the necessary subroutine calls on behalf of the assembly language programmer. The programmer may use these macros as though they were additional assembly language instructions.

We can now form a preliminary definition of assembly language. Though *machine language* refers not to the actual hardware, but to a hypothetical or virtual machine, in order to submerge unnecessary details, we treat the virtual machine as though it were real. Technical details of the hardware itself need not concern us, for we use a model to determine the effect of executing a particular program. The I/O support provided by the operating system can be viewed in the same light. Assembly language consists of the mnemonic names of those machine-level instructions that our programs will execute, together with the macros and subroutines provided by the operating system and the mechanisms provided by the assembler for structuring data. In this sense, assembly language is defined not by the machine on which the object program is to be executed, but by the operating system and assembler being used. Together, these factors define the virtual machine on which our programs will be executed.

Benefits from Studying Assembly Language

Although programming in assembly language is a great deal easier than programming in machine language, it is still a difficult process and the study of assembly language requires a reasonable commitment of time and effort on the part of the student. The benefits which may be derived from studying assembly language are twofold. First, there are the benefits which result simply from the study itself. The second class of benefits consists of the advantages of writing programs in assembly language. This distinction is especially important for students who do not plan to write assembly language programs even though they successfully complete a required assembly language course.

First, the study of assembly language provides a thorough understanding of computers and programming. Certainly, it enables us to appreciate the limitations of hardware devices, and, more to the point, provides means to circumvent these obstacles. Assembly language also gives a useful introduction to computer architecture. A thorough understanding of the assembly language level of one machine serves as both a practical foundation and a basis for comparison when studying more general concepts of computer architecture. The student of assembly language will have a greater appreciation of the capabilities and limitations of high-level languages. Eventually, the assembly language student will use high-level languages more efficiently and write programs that can utilize specialized features of the machines on which they will be executed. Finally, when determining whether to write a particular program in a high-level language or an assembly language, it will be possible to make an informed decision as to which is more suitable to the task at hand. Clearly, this is an advantage over having to choose a high-level language simply because the programmer does not know how to program in assembly language.

The ability to program in assembly language has other benefits. For many years, the primary benefit was more efficient programs. This is still true to some extent, but it has been greatly mitigated by the increasing capabilities of optimizing compilers, many of which are capable of producing code that competes quite well with code produced by assembly language programmers. Programming in assembly language allows use of machine features that are not available in high-level languages. Most assembly language programs written today are, by their nature and function, closely related to the machine on which they are executed. This includes, for example, portions of operating systems and other programs which interface between a computer and peripheral devices such as printers and disk drives.

Assembly language programming is especially important in view of the continual, rapid evolution of hardware devices. On the one hand, the lack of portability of assembly language is a distinct disadvantage. Because it is so intimately bound to the architecture of a particular computer, any significant change in that architecture results in corresponding change in the assembly language. Each new machine will require operating system routines, compilers, device drivers, and utility programs written in assembly language. Hence, there will always be a need for competent assembly language programmers.

Because the assembly language programmer may be required to adopt new assembly languages from time to time, he needs to learn techniques which can be transferred to new assembly languages, keeping the initial phases of program design relatively independent of the particular assembly language in which the program will be written. This approach is especially useful in learning a first assembly language because the programmer can employ the skills of problem solving and algorithm development acquired in earlier programming courses. The point at which the solution to a problem is bound to a particular assembly language should be postponed as long as possible. When this binding does take place, it should be made as automatic as possible. Of course, a programmer who is experienced in the assembly language of a particular machine will be able to take advantage of the special features of that machine during the design phase, always looking for possible efficiencies in time or space during the coding phase, but resisting the temptation to trade off clarity and reliability for marginal gains in efficiency.

In conclusion, benefits from mastering IBM 370 assembly language programming include a better understanding of computers and programming, an introduction to computer architecture, and the acquisition of skills which can be used in learning other assembly languages. Although the purpose of this book is to teach 370 Assembler, in future years, these other benefits will probably be of much greater value to the reader.

1.2 BITS AND BYTES

Before examining the IBM 370's architecture and instruction set, we need to review the basic properties of binary and hexadecimal numbers. Decimal instructions will be used in our early programs, but it is helpful to know both these non-decimal numeration systems in order to understand the computer itself and the formats of the instructions.

Positional Numeration Systems

Binary, hexadecimal and decimal numbers are all examples of positional numeration systems. In a positional system, the value of a particular symbol depends not only upon the symbol itself but also upon its position. For example, in determining the actual value represented by the decimal number

$$235.83$$

the value of each digit is multiplied by a power of 10 giving the sum

$$2*10^2 + 3*10^1 + 5*10^0 + 8*10^{(-1)} + 3*10^{(-2)} =$$
$$2*100 + 3*10 + 5*1 + 8*(1/10) + 3*(1/100).$$

In each case, the power of 10 used is determined by the position of the digit. If the positions are numbered as shown below, then the value of each digit found at position number i is multiplied by 10^i.

$$\overline{} \quad \overline{} \quad \overline{} \quad \overline{} \quad \cdot \quad \overline{} \quad \overline{} \quad \overline{} \quad \overline{}$$
$$n \quad \ldots \quad 2 \quad 1 \quad 0 \quad \quad -1 \quad -2 \quad -3 \quad \ldots \quad -m$$

This concept can be generalized to any base. If b is a positive integer, in order to write numbers in base b, let b symbols represent the values $0 \ldots (b-1)$. A base b number is any sequence of these symbols and a maximum of one '.'. (The '.' is often called the *radix point* in order to avoid the implication of the name *decimal point*.)

The value represented by a base *b* number such as

$$s_n \qquad s_2 \ s_1 \ s_0 \ . \ s_{-1} \ s_{-2} \ s_{-3} \qquad s_{-m}$$

is given by the sum

$$s_n*b^n + \ldots + s_2*b^2 + s_1*b^1 + s_0*b^0 + s_{-1}*b^{-1} + s_{-2}*b^{-2} + s_{-3}b^{-3} + \ldots + s_{-m}b^{-m}$$

Example 1.2.1 *Determine the decimal form of the base 3 number 102.02.*

$$102.02 \text{ (base 3)} =$$
$$1*3^2 + 0*3^1 + 2*3^0 + 0*3^{-1} + 2*3^{-2} =$$
$$1*9 + 0*3 + 2*1 + 0*(1/3) + 2*(1/9) = 11 \ 2/9.$$

Example 1.2.2 *Give the decimal form of the base 8 (octal) number 537.4.*

$$537.4 \text{ (base 8)} =$$
$$5*8^2 + 3*8^1 + 7*8^0 + 4*8^{-1} =$$
$$5*64 + 3*8 + 7*1 + 4*(1/8) =$$
$$320 + 24 + 7 + 1/2 = 351.5$$

It is not unusual to feel some anxiety when asked to adapt to new number bases, yet we use at least two distinct number bases in day-to-day transactions and convert subconsciously from one to the other with no apparent difficulty. We normally use base 10, but large values are represented in base 1000. The base 1000 digits are the compound symbols 000, 001, 002, . . ., 100, 101, . . ., 999. It is customary to separate these base 1000 digits by commas and to drop any leading zeros. Thus 1,203,126,801 is the base 1000 representation of the number $1*1000^3 + 203*1000^2 + 126*1000^1 + 801*1000^0$. We make the change to base 1000 because our minds tend to resist dealing with more details than absolutely necessary. We are able to make the transition from base 10 to base 1000 subconsciously because every base 1000 digit is precisely equivalent to a three-digit base 10 number. Converting from base 1000 to base 10 is done by replacing each base 1000 digit by its base 10 counterpart and writing these base 10 numbers side by side (i.e., we write the number without the commas.) In the same way, the arithmetic process of converting from base 10 to base 1000 is equivalent to the insertion of commas.

Binary and Hexadecimal Numbers

Because binary numbers require only two digits, they can be represented by sequences of entities capable of being placed in two recognizable states. It is this property which accounts for the ubiquity of binary numbers in computing. Unfortunately, people find it difficult to deal with binary numbers which are longer than 4 or 5 bits long, a real handicap because this includes all numbers greater than or equal to 32. We can, however, adopt the same strategy as that used with large decimal numbers—that is, translate binary numbers to some larger base which is a power of 2. As long as we restrict ourselves to powers of 2, the conversion from one base to another will be easy.

Grouping the bits of a binary number into three's as we do with the digits in a decimal number would be equivalent to translating from binary numbers to octal. There are several computer systems in which this is done. However, IBM 370 architecture tends to use multiples of 16, so it is more convenient to use groups of four bits and translate from binary to hexadecimal.

In order to convert binary numbers to hexadecimal, we begin at the radix point and, going either left or right, group the bits into fours and convert each group of four bits to the corresponding hexadecimal digit. The table below shows all possible groups of four bits together with their decimal and hexadecimal equivalents. Note that because we need 16 different digits to write numbers in base 16, we use 0 through 9 and extend these by using A, B, C, D, E, and F to represent 10, 11, 12, 13, 14, and 15 respectively.

Binary	Hexadecimal	Decimal	Binary	Hexadecimal	Decimal
0000	0	0	1000	8	8
0001	1	1	1001	9	9
0010	2	2	1010	A	10
0011	3	3	1011	B	11
0100	4	4	1100	C	12
0101	5	5	1101	D	13
0110	6	6	1110	E	14
0111	7	7	1111	F	15

Example 1.2.3 *Convert the binary number 1101011.1100101 to hexadecimal.*

1. Group the bits into fours as shown adding 0's at the left or right as necessary to complete a group.

0110 1011 . 1100 1010

2. Replace each group of four bits by the corresponding hexadecimal digit.

6   B . C   A

This gives the hexadecimal form 6B.CA of the binary number 1101011.1100101.

Many of the binary numbers we will use on the IBM 370 are 32 bits long. The following example illustrates the advantage of converting such a number to hexadecimal.

Example 1.2.4 *Convert the following 32 bit binary number to hexadecimal.*

10011101110001011001011101101011

Even if we did not intend to convert this number to hexadecimal, it would be wise to separate bits to make it more readable. For the conversion, we separate the bits into groups of four as above and translate each group to hexadecimal.

$$1001 \quad 1101 \quad 1100 \quad 0101 \quad 1001 \quad 0111 \quad 0110 \quad 1011 \ =$$
$$\ \ 9 \qquad D \qquad C \qquad 5 \qquad 9 \qquad 7 \qquad 6 \qquad B \quad = \ 9DC5976B.$$

Conversion from hexadecimal to binary is simply the reversal of the above process.

Example 1.2.5 *Convert 3A91BF to binary.*

We replace each hexadecimal digit by its 4-bit representation to obtain

$$001110101001000110111111$$

or

$$1110101001000110111111$$

if we drop the leading 0's.

Arithmetic Operations on Binary and Hexadecimal Numbers

Addition and subtraction of binary and hexadecimal numbers are accomplished by employing the same algorithms used for decimal numbers. We simply employ a different set of addition and subtraction tables.

In the case of binary addition, this is especially easy because the addition table has only four entries.

Binary	Addition	Table
+	0	1
0	0	1
1	1	10

Example 1.2.6 *Add the binary numbers 11010111 and 11110010.*

We begin by writing the problem as though it were decimal addition.

$$\begin{array}{r} 11010111 \\ +11110010 \\ \hline \end{array}$$

Starting at the right, add the bits one position at a time, writing the rightmost bit of the sum on the bottom line and the remaining bits, if any, as carries to the left.

$$
\begin{array}{r}
111\ 11 \\
11010111 \\
+11110010 \\
\hline
111001001
\end{array}
$$

(Recall that $1 + 1 + 1 = 10 + 1 = 11$.)

The hexadecimal addition table is more complicated. There are 16 hex-digits, so there are 16*16, or 256, possible combinations of two hex-digits.

Hexadecimal Addition Table

+	0	1	2	3	4	5	6	7	8	9	A	B	C	D	E	F
0	0	1	2	3	4	5	6	7	8	9	A	B	C	D	E	F
1	1	2	3	4	5	6	7	8	9	A	B	C	D	E	F	10
2	2	3	4	5	6	7	8	9	A	B	C	D	E	F	10	11
3	3	4	5	6	7	8	9	A	B	C	D	E	F	10	11	12
4	4	5	6	7	8	9	A	B	C	D	E	F	10	11	12	13
5	5	6	7	8	9	A	B	C	D	E	F	10	11	12	13	14
6	6	7	8	9	A	B	C	D	E	F	10	11	12	13	14	15
7	7	8	9	A	B	C	D	E	F	10	11	12	13	14	15	16
8	8	9	A	B	C	D	E	F	10	11	12	13	14	15	16	17
9	9	A	B	C	D	E	F	10	11	12	13	14	15	16	17	18
A	A	B	C	D	E	F	10	11	12*	13	14	15	16	17	18	19
B	B	C	D	E	F	10	11	12	13	14	15	16	17	18	19	1A
C	C	D	E	F	10	11	12	13	14	15	16	17	18	19	1A	1B
D	D	E	F	10	11	12	13	14	15	16	17	18	19	1A	1B	1C
E	E	F	10	11	12	13	14	15	16	17	18	19	1A	1B	1C	1D
F	F	10	11	12	13	14	15	16	17	18	19	1A	1B	1C	1D	1E

It is possible to memorize this table, especially as commutativity halves the number of entries that need to be learned and we already know some (e.g., 1+1). Nevertheless, it is probably simpler to do hexadecimal addition by mentally converting each pair of hex-digits to decimal, adding the decimal forms, and converting the result to hexadecimal. For example, to find 9 + E, add 9 and 14 in decimal, then convert the decimal result, 23, to its hexadecimal form, 17.

Example 1.2.7 *Add the hexadecimal numbers 7A68BC94 and 5C62A3E1.*

```
  1   111
  7A68BC94
 +5C62A3E1
 ──────────
  D6CB6075
```

Comments: The additions from right to left are

1. 1 + 4 is still 5.
2. 9 + E is done as above.
3. 1 + C + 3 in decimal is 1 + 12 + 3 = 16. In hexadecimal, this is 10.
4. 1 + B + A in decimal is 1 + 11 + 10 = 22 or 16 hexadecimal.
5. 1 + 8 + 2 is 11 decimal or B in hexadecimal.
6. 6 + 6 is 12 in decimal, C in hexadecimal.
7. A + C is the same as 10 + 12 = 22 in decimal. In hexadecimal this is 16.
8. 1 + 7 + 5 is 13 in decimal, D in hexadecimal.

We add binary and hexadecimal numbers by following the same sequence of steps as for decimal values. Subtraction of numbers in other bases is also done analogously to decimal subtraction. Borrowing introduces a slight additional complication, so it is useful to examine the process of decimal subtraction with a view toward generalizing the process to other bases.

For example, consider the operation of subtracting 42597 from 80084.

```
  7  9  9  17 14
  8  0  0  8  4
 -4  2  5  9  7
 ───────────────
  3  7  4  8  7
```

Note that the first need to borrow causes no problem because the next position has a nonzero digit. The second borrow causes the difficulty. As the position from which we would like to borrow has a zero, we must find the first position to the left with a nonzero digit.

After years of grade school exercises, the process becomes automatic: we borrow 1 from the nonzero digit and transport it to the current position, changing all the intervening 0's to 9's. On closer consideration, we realize that we actually use the 1 borrowed from the 8 to make the leftmost 0 into 10. Then we can borrow 1 from that position, leaving the 9. This process is repeated with the next 0, and so on, until we reach the current position. If we repeat the subtraction showing these intermediate steps we have

```
        9  9
  7  10 10 17 14
  8  0  0  8  4
 -4  2  5  9  7
 ───────────────
  3  7  4  8  7
```

Now we see how this can be generalized to binary numbers. If we need to borrow 1 from a position with a 0, we borrow a 1 from the position(s) to the left and use it to make the zero position 10. We can then borrow 1 from this position leaving 1. ($10 - 1 = 1$ in base 2.)

Example 1.2.8 *Subtract 101101 from 1100011.*

```
        10   1   1
      0  10  10  10
  1   1   0   0   0   1   1
 -    1   0   1   1   0   1
 ─────────────────────────
      1   1   0   1   1   0
```

Just as we learned to abbreviate this process in decimal addition, we perform the binary borrowing operation by finding the first nonzero bit to the left, borrowing 1 from that bit, leaving 0, then taking the 1 back to the current position, changing all intervening 0's to 1's.

Example 1.2.9 *Subtract 1 from 10000000.*

```
      1   1   1   1   1   1  10
  1   0   0   0   0   0   0   0
                             -1
 ─────────────────────────────
      1   1   1   1   1   1   1
```

The analog for hexadecimal borrowing is: find the first nonzero position to the left, borrow 1 from that position and take it back to the current position, changing any intervening 0's to F's ($10 - 1$ in base 16.)

Example 1.2.10 *Subtract 3A5B97 from 80005F.*

```
      7   F   F   F  15
      8   0   0   0   5   F
 -    3   A   5   B   9   7
 ─────────────────────────
      4   5   A   4   C   8
```

Although binary and hexadecimal arithmetic are important, binary numbers are used more for encoding non-numeric information than for representing quantities that will be the subjects of arithmetic operations. Character strings, machine instructions, and memory addresses are also coded in binary. Thus, it is important to understand how such information can be encoded.

Coding and Information

The most fundamental problem of coding is to get as much information as possible in a fixed-length representation. In binary, this is equivalent to asking how many different binary numbers we can write with n bits for a fixed n.

Example 1.2.11 *How many different binary numbers can be written with 3 bits?*

The answer is 8 numbers. They are 000, 001, 010, 011, 100, 101, 110, 111 or, in decimal, 0 through 7.

Example 1.2.12 *How many different binary numbers can be written with 8 bits?*

Without listing all of them, we can determine that they are the binary numbers 00000000 through 11111111. In decimal we have 0 through 255, thus, there are 256 such numbers.

Extrapolation of the above examples leads us to the conclusion that we can write 2^n binary numbers with n bits, a factor of crucial importance in dealing with programming on an assembly language level. For example, a machine with only 6 bits in each instruction to encode an operation will be limited to 2^6 (64) different operations. A machine which has room in each instruction for an address of 16 bits will be limited to addressing 2^{16} (65,536) memory cells. Similarly, the standard 7-bit ASCII (American National Standard Code for Information Interchange) code allows 128 different characters whereas the 8-bit EBCDIC coding standard allows 256.

Finally, it is worth noting the effect of the addition or loss of a single bit in the length of a binary code. Because we can encode 2^n different values in n bits and $2^{(n+1)} = 2*(2^n)$ values in $n+1$ bits, the addition of a single bit doubles the number of different values that can be represented and the loss of one bit halves the number of such values.

E X E R C I S E S

1. Convert each of the following binary numbers to decimal.
   a. 1011101
   b. 110101011.001
   c. 1010010.101

2. Convert the following hexadecimal numbers to decimal.
   a. 3E1
   b. AC4
   c. 752

3. Convert each of the following binary numbers to hexadecimal.
   a. 110101011011
   b. 10011010011111.101
   c. 101101110.1101101

4. Convert each of the following hexadecimal numbers to binary.
   a. E35F1
   b. 3AE16.D
   c. 2CB56.E8

5. Perform each of the following binary additions.

   a.   1 0 1 1 0 1 1 0   **b.**   1 0 1 1 1 0 1 1
     +   1 1 0 1 1 0 1   +1 1 1 1 0 1 0 1

   c.   1 0 1 1 1 0 1 0 1 1 1   **d.**   1 1 1 0 0 1 1 0 1 1
     +   1 1 1 0 1 1 1 0 1 0   +1 1 0 1 1 1 0 1 1 0

6. Perform the following hexadecimal additions.

   a.   3 A 1 5 F E 1   **b.**   2 F 4 5 3 E 7 8
     +   4 F 8 D 1 F   +D 4 4 E F 9 3 A

   c.   F B 4 3 2 7 9 A 4 C   **d.**   7 A 9 2 3 E 5 4 B
     +   E 5 2 7 2 C 9 A D   +8 C 5 4 7 2 B 1 A

7. Subtract the following binary numbers.

   a.   1 0 1 1 0 1 1 1 1 0 1   **b.**   1 0 1 1 0 0 0 0 1 0 1 1
     −   1 1 0 1 1 0 0 1 0 0   −   1 1 1 0 1 0 1 0 1 1 0

   c.   1 1 0 1 0 0 0 1 1 0 1   **d.**   1 0 0 1 0 1 1 0 1 1 0 1
     −   1 1 1 0 1 1 0 1 1 0   −   1 0 0 1 1 0 1 0 1 1 0

8. Subtract the following hexadecimals.

   a.   3 A 1 6 F E 7   **b.**   F 5 0 6 9 A E
     −1 8 0 9 7 C 5   −8 A 9 B F 1 F

   c.   C A 4 2 3 1 7 4 B 9   **d.**   9 A C 4 B 7 7 E 4
     −A 7 2 1 6 6 3 B C 2   −6 B F 0 E 2 3 F 1

9. Give the range of values which can be represented in each of the following formats.
   a. 10 bits: _____   **b.** 15 bits: _____
   c. 24 bits: _____   **d.** 5 hex-digits: _____

1.3 INTRODUCTION TO IBM 370 ARCHITECTURE

In this section, IBM 370 architecture is briefly described as it is presented in the IBM publication *IBM System/370 Principles of Operation*. As explained in the first section, we are not describing a piece of hardware, but a model that can be used to predict how the actual hardware will behave under a given set of conditions. For the present, we restrict our attention to two particular aspects of 370 architecture, memory organization and the organization of the Central Processing Unit (CPU).

FIGURE 1.3.1 The Overall Structure of a Computer

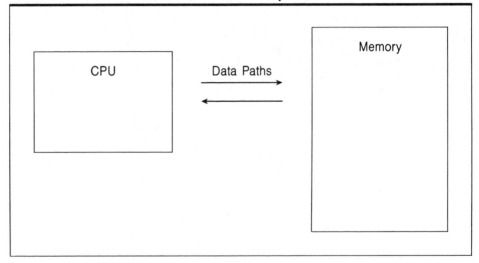

Memory Organization

The memory of any computer consists of a large collection of units, each of which is capable of storing a single bit. Such a collection would be unmanageable without the imposition of some additional structure. This structure is imposed by grouping bits together into units of a fixed size, just as we collect bits into groups of fours when manipulating binary numbers. Each group is assigned a unique number known as its *address*. One of the fundamental characteristics of any computer system is the number of bits in each of these groups. This is the smallest unit of information which can be addressed and, on most systems, all information transferred between the CPU and primary memory must be in integral multiples of the smallest addressable unit. In the case of the IBM 370, this unit is 8 bits long and is called a *byte*. From our discussion of binary and hexadecimal numbers we recall that a byte, or 8 bits, is equivalent to two hexadecimal digits and that we can encode 256 different values in a byte. (Because a byte is the same as two hex-digits, a single hex-digit is sometimes cleverly called a *nibble*. The unbearably cute have even been known to spell it "nybble." We refrain from doing either.)

A related and equally important characteristic is the size of the addresses. The number of bits in each address determines the maximum number of addressable units which can be accessed at one time. This factor, together with the size of each unit, places an absolute maximum on the number of bits in primary memory. IBM System/370 addresses are 24 bits long. This means that the maximum useful memory is $2^{24} = 16,777,216$ bytes. (This value is also known as 16 megabytes.)

FIGURE 1.3.2   Memory Cells and Addresses

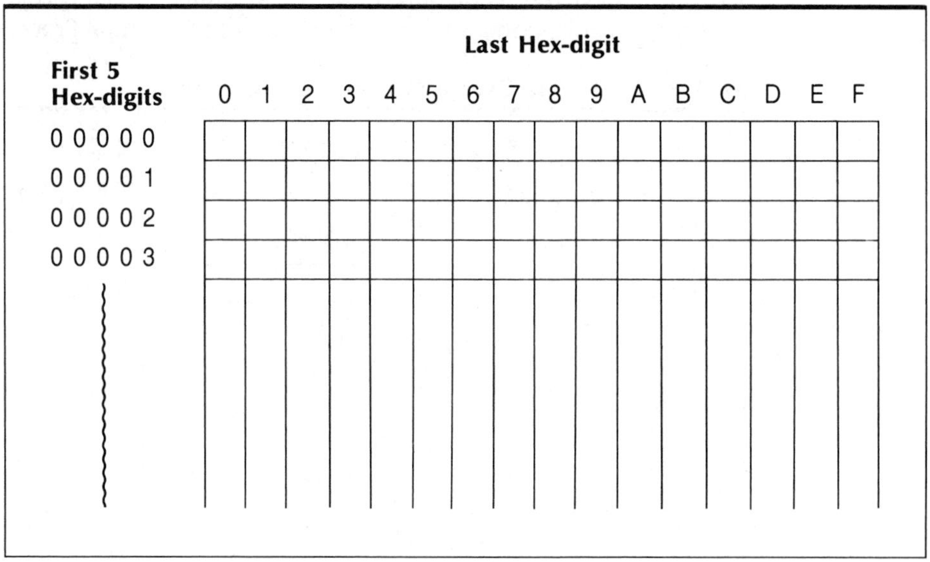

Representation of Character Data

In more practical terms, we are interested in how numbers and strings of characters are stored. In terms of character information, the size of each addressable unit determines the maximum size of the character set, and the number of possible addresses is the maximum number of characters that can be stored. To encode character information the IBM System/370 uses EBCDIC, an acronym for Extended Binary-Coded-Decimal Interchange Code, pronounced *eb'-suh-dic*. EBCDIC uses a one-byte code for each character, which allows for 256 different codes. Not all of these are used and the unused codes are scattered throughout the sequence of possible codes to allow for the orderly addition of new codes for special applications.

The first 64 EBCDIC codes (hexadecimal values 00 through 3F) are reserved for control characters, such things as carriage return, line feed and form feed characters, as well as characters used for applications such as communications. The codes with decimal values 64 through 127 (40 through 7F in hexadecimal) are reserved for special characters such as those in the string '!@#$%&*()', the space character, and punctuation marks. The lower case letters are assigned codes between 80 and BF and the upper case letters have codes between C0 and EF. The digits 0 through 9 are assigned EBCDIC codes F0 through F9 respectively. There is certainly no need to learn the EBCDIC coding sequence, but it is useful to know the approximate order in which the codes are assigned. When we compare two character strings, their relative orders are determined by the EBCDIC codes with which they are represented. For example, it is important to know that the lower case letters are assigned codes smaller than those assigned to the upper case letters, as this may determine the result of a string comparison.

Example 1.3.1 *The string 'IBM System/370' would be stored in 14 consecutive bytes of memory as*

```
 I  B  M     S  y  s  t  e  m  /  3  7  0
C9 C2 D4 40 E2 A8 A2 A3 85 94 61 F3 F7 F0
```

If we assume that the string is stored beginning at address 5C6305, then the codes will appear in memory as shown below.

FIGURE 1.3.3 A String Stored in Memory

	0	1	2	3	4	5	6	7	8	9	A	B	C	D	E	F
5 C 6 3 0						C9	C2	D4	40	E2	A8	A2	A3	85	99	61
5 C 6 3 1	F3	F7	F0													

In order to designate the string in the example above, we could specify the addresses of the fourteen locations which it occupies; but, as strings are always stored in consecutive locations, it is sufficient to specify the address of the first character in the string together with its length. Each byte in a 370 has its own address, so we can examine any individual character in the string by specifying the address of that character. We can also identify a substring by its starting address and the number of characters in the substring. In the example above, the substring 'System' can be identified by its starting address, 5C6309, and its length, 6.

Representation of Decimal Numbers

Numerical information can, of course, be stored as a sequence of EBCDIC codes just as the number 370 in the example above is stored as F3 F7 F0. Numbers stored in this form are called *zoned decimal numbers*. This format is used for numbers which are to be printed. It is also the form in which numbers are stored if they have been read from a card or other human-readable medium. The first hexadecimal digit in the rightmost byte of the representation is used to indicate the sign of the number, F for plus and D for minus.

Example 1.3.2

Decimal Number	Zoned Form
370	F3 F7 F0
84626	F8 F4 F6 F2 F6
−84626	F8 F4 F6 F2 D6

The zoned format is not a very efficient way in which to encode numbers. As a result, the IBM 370 does not provide instructions for performing arithmetic on zoned numbers. The problem is that we are using a byte which is capable of encoding 256 different pieces of information to represent one of 10 possible digits. The 246 unused bit patterns are wasted. This inefficiency can be mitigated by packing two digits into each byte. Numbers represented in this form are called, appropriately, *packed decimal numbers*. In order to represent both positive and negative numbers, the rightmost hexadecimal digit in each number is used to encode a sign and the remaining hexadecimal digits are used to represent their decimal counterparts. As was the case with character strings, both packed and zoned decimal numbers can be represented by a starting address and a length.

Example 1.3.3

Decimal Number	Packed Form
370	37 0F
370	37 0C (*)
84626	84 62 6C
−84626	84 62 6D

* The sign may be encoded in any of the following ways

$$+ \text{ A, C, E, F}$$
$$- \text{ B, D.}$$

Numbers which are the result of an arithmetic operation will always have C for + and D for −.

If −84626 is stored in memory beginning at address 7A623F, then the contents of this byte and the next two bytes will be as shown below.

FIGURE 1.3.4 A Packed Decimal Number Stored in Memory

	0	1	2	3	4	5	6	7	8	9	A	B	C	D	E	F
7 A 6 2 3																84
7 A 6 2 4	62	6D														

The 370 provides a number of instructions for manipulating packed decimal numbers. There are instructions for addition, subtraction, multiplication, and division of packed decimals. These are supplemented by instructions for rounding and converting between zoned and packed formats. It is possible to write programs which deal entirely with decimal numbers and, from this point of view, the IBM 370 may be thought of as a decimal machine. This accounts to some extent for its popularity in commercial applications.

Representation of Binary Numbers

There are a number of applications for which decimal arithmetic is not fast enough or does not provide a sufficient range of values. The predecessor of the IBM 370, the 360, was so-named because it was intended to cover the "full circle" of computing. That is, it was intended to support both commercial and scientific programming. To this end, the 360 and 370 are supplied with a complete set of binary, as well as decimal instructions.

Binary numbers on the IBM 370 come in several different formats. There are binary *integers* and *floating-point* binary numbers. For the present, we shall restrict our attention to the binary integers. The standard binary integers are 32 bits long and are called *fullword binary numbers*. Since approximately half of the potential 2^{32} bit patterns are used to represent negative numbers, the range of fullword binary numbers is $-2,147,483,648$ (-2^{31}) to $2,147,483,647$ ($2^{31} - 1$). As this range of values is not always needed, the 370 also supports a 16-bit binary integer which is called a *halfword*. There are also several circumstances under which a 64-bit quantity may be manipulated as a single binary number.

The table below illustrates the relations between IBM terminology, hexadecimal numbers and binary numbers.

Term	Bytes	Hex-digits	Bits
Byte	1	2	8
Halfword	2	4	16
Fullword	4	8	32
Doubleword	8	16	64

Memory Boundaries

Many IBM 370 implementations transfer data between memory and the CPU in fullwords. In order to simplify the hardware required for memory control, these values are fetched beginning at addresses that are multiples of 4. Such addresses are called *fullword boundaries*. Whenever it is necessary to fetch a fullword which crosses such a boundary, the machine must fetch two fullwords and extract the desired portion. As a result, on most models, performance is degraded significantly unless fullwords are stored beginning at fullword boundaries. Similarly, halfwords should begin at addresses that are multiples of 2 and doublewords at addresses that are multiples of 8. These are called *halfword* and *doubleword boundaries* respectively.

When addresses are expressed in binary, it is easy to recognize these boundaries. Just as multiplication of a decimal number by 10 has the effect of appending a 0 to the right of the number, multiplication of a binary number by 2 is equivalent to the addition of a 0 bit on the right. Multiplication by 4 is equivalent to the addition of two 0 bits and so on. Thus, the halfword boundaries are the addresses that end in a 0, the fullword boundaries are the addresses that end with two 0's and the doubleword boundaries are those ending with three 0's. In hexadecimal form, halfword boundaries end with 0, 2, 4, 6, 8, A, C, or E; fullword boundaries end with 0, 4, 8, or C; and doubleword boundaries end with 0 or 8.

Example 1.3.4 *Identify each of the following as byte, halfword, word, or double-word boundaries.*

(Note that all doubleword boundaries are word boundaries, all word boundaries are also halfword boundaries, and every address is a byte boundary. Therefore, we need only specify the strongest term that is applicable.)

12A43B	Byte
6F8C2E	Halfword
23A3D8	Doubleword
65FF47	Byte
43DE3C	Word

Identifying address boundaries is a useful exercise for gaining familiarity with binary and hexadecimal numbers. But, as a matter of fact, we can instruct the assembler to perform the necessary alignment automatically. We will not need to be aware of alignment problems except on a very few occasions.

Summarizing IBM 370 memory organization: memory is organized into cells, each of which has a 24-bit address and is capable of storing a single byte. When manipulating character data or decimal numbers, we think of a value as consisting of a starting address together with a length. These values may be located at any address. In the case of binary values, data are organized into halfwords of 16 bits, fullwords of 32 bits and, occasionally, doublewords of 64 bits. Although these values may also begin at any address, most models which employ 370 architecture will perform significantly better if they are stored beginning at the appropriate boundary.

Central Processing Unit Organization

The Central Processing Unit (CPU) is responsible for executing the instructions in our programs as well as those in the operating system and in the programs of other users. To this end, it contains hardware for decoding instructions, performing arithmetic and logical operations, and controlling memory accesses. The most visible components of the CPU are 16 General Purpose Registers, 16 Control Registers, 4 Floating Point Registers, and a 64-bit register called the Program Status Word or PSW. The arithmetic and logical operations are performed by hardware components which are referred to collectively as the Arithmetic and Logic Unit (ALU).

FIGURE 1.3.5   The Central Processing Unit

General Purpose Registers ← 32 bits →	Control Registers ← 32 bits →	Floating Point Registers ← 64 bits →
R0	C0	F0
R1	C1	F2
R2	C2	F4
R3	C4	F6
R4	C4	
R5	C5	**PSW** ← 64 bits →
R6	C6	
R7	C7	
R8	C8	
R9	C9	**Arithmetic Logic Unit (ALU)**
RA	CA	
RB	CB	
RC	CC	
RD	CD	
RE	CE	
RF	CF	

The General Purpose Registers may be used to store either binary numbers or addresses. As addresses are 24 bits long and the most common size for a binary number is a fullword, or 32 bits, the registers are designed to store 32 bits. When an address is stored in a register, it is stored in the rightmost 24 bits. The General Purpose Registers are numbered from 0 to 15. Thus, each register can be identified by a single hexadecimal digit 0 - F. IBM 370 Assembly Language allows registers to be referred to by decimal values 0 through 15; however, in this text, we refer to them as R0, R1, . . . , RE, RF in order to make such references clearly identifiable.

The Control Registers are 32 bits long and the Floating Point Registers are 64 bits long. We will not use any instructions which access the Control Registers. The Floating Point Registers will be used when we deal with the floating point instructions in Chapter 8.

The Program Status Word contains information relative to the current state of the program being executed. This information includes the address of the next instruction to be executed, a 2-bit Condition Code and a bit that indicates whether the machine is in the Supervisor State (see Privileged Instructions below) or in the Problem State. The PSW also includes a 4-bit Program Mask which is used to control the action of the machine when one of four conditions occur. These conditions, called Program Exceptions, include Fixed Point Overflow and Decimal Overflow. When one of these exceptions occurs, the Program Mask is checked. If the corresponding bit is 1, then the program is terminated. We will include in our programs instructions to set all of these bits to 1.

Instruction Categories

The IBM 370 instruction set may be divided into five broad categories. IBM refers to these categories as System Control instructions, General instructions, Decimal instructions, Floating Point instructions, and Input/Output instructions. Of these, the System Control and Input/Output instructions are designated Privileged instructions—that is, they may only be executed when the PSW indicates that the machine is in the Supervisor State. The Decimal instructions include all operations that may be performed on packed decimal values. The category of General instructions contains all the instructions for operating on binary integers as well as those for manipulating character information and controlling the flow of execution.

IBM 370 instructions vary from two to six bytes in length. Each instruction consists of a one- or two-byte opcode followed by one or two operands. These operands are classified as Storage (S), Indexed (X), Immediate (I), and Register (R). An Immediate operand is a one-byte value that is stored in the instruction itself. A Register operand is identified by a single hexadecimal digit that usually designates one of the 16 general purpose registers. Storage operands and Indexed operands are identified by a coded representation of the starting address of the operand together with a length that may be included in the instruction or may be implied by the instruction type.

The starting address of a Storage operand is encoded using a technique called base-displacement addressing. As we have observed, addresses on an IBM 370 are 24 bits long. Rather than encoding addresses directly, base-displacement addressing forms addresses by adding a 12-bit displacement to a 24-bit base address contained in a register. The operand is encoded in two bytes, or four hexadecimal digits. The first hexadecimal digit designates the base register and the remaining three hex-digits give the 12-bit displacement. In forming the address, the 370 takes the rightmost 3 bytes from the base register and adds the 12-bit displacement. The leftmost byte of the base register is ignored.

Example 1.3.5 *Suppose registers A, B, and C contain the values shown.*

$$RA : 30739002$$
$$RB : 4073A002$$
$$RC : 7873B002$$

The base-displacement operand A33B would be translated to an actual address by adding the right three bytes of register RA to the displacement 33B. This would yield the address 739002 + 33B = 73933D.

Other base-displacement computations are shown below.

Storage Operand	Base Register	Displacement	Address Computation
A7DE	RA	7DE	739002 + 7DE = 7397E0
B3F0	RB	3F0	73A002 + 3F0 = 73A3F2
BFFF	RB	FFF	73A002 + FFF = 73B001
C000	RC	000	73B002 + 000 = 73B002

The use of base-displacement addressing provides two advantages. The most obvious is that addresses can be stored in two bytes instead of three. This results in a 33% reduction in the space which would be required to represent the addresses of all the operands in a program. Less obvious, but more important, is the fact that a program does not need to be loaded at the same address every time it is executed, as would be the case if direct addresses were used in a program. As long as the correct starting address is placed in the base register, a program which uses only base-displacement addressing can be loaded at any available starting address.

The Indexed operands have an addressing format similar to that of the Storage operands with the addition of the contents of a second register called the *Index Register*. The second register is useful for accessing entries in an array.

Each 370 instruction has fixed operand types. Thus, the instructions may also be classified according to the operand addressing expected. The name of each instruction format consists simply of the one or two letters indicating the operand addressing mechanism. These names are RR (Register-Register), RX (Register-Indexed), RS (Register-Storage), SI (Storage-Immediate), S (Storage), and SS (Storage-Storage). The opcode for the S format is two bytes long. All other formats have a one-byte opcode. In addition to the operand addressing mechanisms, the Storage-Storage instructions include the length of one or both operands. Thus SS instructions may be subdivided into 1-length SS instructions and 2-length SS instructions. The machine language format of each of these instruction formats is shown in Figure 1.3.6.

Symbols: Each symbol below represents a single hexadecimal digit interpreted as follows.

CC or CCCC	Operation Code
L_1	Length for the first operand in an SS2 instruction.
L_2	Length for the second operand in an SS2 instruction.
LL	Length for both operands in an SS1 instruction.
B	Base register for a storage operand.
DDD	Displacement for a storage operand.
I_2I_2	A single data byte.
R	A register operand.
X	An index register.

We deal with each format in more detail when we examine individual instructions. For now, observe that many of the details in the machine language formats can be supplied automatically by the assembler. In particular, this is true of the base register and length fields in the SS instructions. Thus, when we write assembly language programs, the use of these instructions is much simpler than their machine language formats would indicate.

FIGURE 1.3.6 Machine Formats

Byte 1	Byte 2	Byte 3	Byte 4	Byte 5	Byte 6
SS1 Format					
C C	L L	B_1 D_1	D_1 D_1	B_2 D_2	D_2 D_2
SS2 Format					
C C	L_1 L_2	B_1 D_1	D_1 D_1	B_2 D_2	D_2 D_2
S Format					
C C	C C	B_1 D_1	D_1 D_1		
SI Format					
C C	I_2 I_2	B_1 D_1	D_1 D_1		
RS Format					
C C	R_1 R_3	B_2 D_2	D_2 D_2		
RX Format					
C C	R_1 X_2	B_2 D_2	D_2 D_2		
RR Format					
C C	R_1 R_2				

E X E R C I S E S

1. Represent each of the following numbers in both zoned decimal format and packed decimal format.
   a. 39473
   b. −494672
   c. 8566723
   d. −826738

2. Identify each of the following addresses as a byte, halfword, fullword, or doubleword boundary.
   a. 5C9268
   b. 24369E
   c. 307F34
   d. 7A429D
   e. 6822AC
   f. 4642A0

3. Suppose that registers RA, RB, and RC contain the values shown below.

   RA : CC7A2348
   RB : 4071375C
   RC : 907A45AA

   Find the effective address corresponding to each of the following base-displacement operands.
   a. A76C
   b. C664
   c. B99D
   d. AA9E

4. Find the starting and ending addresses for both operands in the following SS2 instructions.
   a. FA4BA1D5BE3A
   b. FAA9C4FEB13A

1.4 INTRODUCTION TO THE ASSEMBLER

Recalling the machine language formats from the last section, it is easy to see why programming directly in machine language is not desirable. For one thing, memorizing the hexadecimal operation codes would be difficult and it would be irritating to have to refer constantly to a list of these opcodes. An even greater and more irritating task would be keeping track of the allocation of storage areas. For each field in memory used, it would be necessary to record the base register, displacement, and length factors for that field. When such a field was used as an operand in an instruction, this information would have to be retrieved and encoded in the proper format. Fortunately, the assembler relieves the programmer of these responsibilities.

Before considering individual details of the assembly process, we view it in the complete context of program development and execution. This sequence of events is shown in the figure below. The source program is provided as input to the assembler. The result of the assembly process is an object program which contains the machine language form of the instructions in the source code, as well as space for data areas. Before it can be executed, this object program must be combined with system-provided routines that perform tasks such as input and output. This combining operation is performed by a program known as a *linker* or a *linkage editor*. The linker produces an executable image which is placed in memory by yet another program called a *loader*. It is at this point that the program produced from the assembly language source code actually begins executing.

FIGURE 1.4.1 The Assemble, Link, Execute Processes

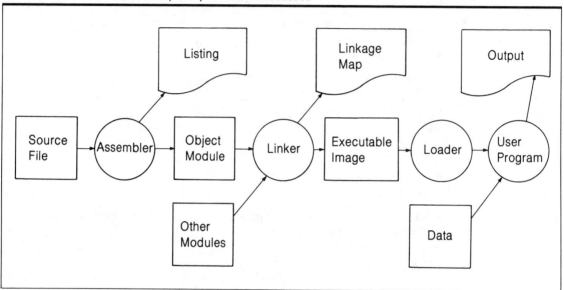

The instructions in the source program are of three types: machine instructions, assembler instructions, and macro instructions. Machine instructions are translated to machine format and become part of the object module. Assembler instructions, sometimes called *assembler directives*, direct the assembler to do something, such as define storage areas, symbolic constants, and instruction labels. Macros are names for predefined groups of instructions. The assembler replaces the macro name with the group of instructions and then processes those instructions as though they were part of the source code.

During the assembly process, the assembler keeps track of where it is in the object module by means of a variable called the *location counter*. Generally speaking, the value of the location counter indicates the position in the object module where the next instruction or variable will be placed. There are a number of instructions which effect the location counter.

The assembler also maintains a data structure called the *symbol table* which contains such things as names for data areas and instruction labels. This is the mechanism by which the assembler keeps track of the base register and displacement, length, and type of each field.

The assembler directives covered in this section will be characterized by their effect on the location counter and the symbol table.

Instruction Formats

Although the instructions in the source program fall into three distinct categories, the format is the same for all three. The possible components of an instruction and their position on a line are shown in the table below.

Entry	Start
Name	1
Operation	10
Operands	16
Comments	30
Continuation	72
Sequence	73

As shown, the instructions are line oriented and are entered in columns 1 through 71. Column 72 is the continuation column. Any character in this column indicates that the instruction will be continued on the next line. Columns 73-80 may be used for sequence numbers or left blank. Although the assembler is fairly liberal about other column positions, it is customary to place components in the position indicated by the standard assembler coding forms. Symbols or labels must begin in column 1. The operation and operand entries usually begin in the columns shown, but it is sufficient to have one blank separating these fields from each other and from the name field. The operand field is terminated by a single blank and the remaining columns through 71 may be used for comments.

The name field may be left blank or may contain a symbolic name consisting of one to eight characters. The first character must be a letter or one of the characters $, #, @. The remaining characters may also include digits.

Example 1.4.1 *The following are examples of valid symbolic names.*

> LENGTH   SIZE1 $LTH   FIELD3   TOTAL

The symbols shown below are *not* valid.

> LTH__A   5ENTRY   SIZE.A

When sample assembly language instructions are shown in this text, they follow the pattern of keywords in upper case and elements to be supplied by the programmer in lower case, surrounded by angular brackets. For example, later in this section we give the EQU directive using the pattern

<name>   EQU   <expression>

Here values for <name> and <expression> would be supplied by the programmer while EQU is a keyword and would be entered as shown.

When a format includes optional fields other than those shown above, these are enclosed in square brackets.

The Location Counter

The final result of the assembly operation will be one or more modules of object code called *control sections* or *CSECTs*. The programs in the first few chapters consist of a single control section. Later, programs may have several control sections.

During assembly, the assembler keeps track of the size and current location in a control section with the aid of a location counter. The largest value assumed by the location counter during the assembly is the size of the control section. At any time, the current value of the location counter represents the next byte in the control section to be allocated or initialized. This is the same as the offset in bytes from the beginning of the control section to the current byte. The current value of the location counter may be referenced by the programmer with the symbol "*".

The location counter is usually initialized to zero at the beginning of the control section by the instruction

```
<name>     START   0
```

The value supplied for the name field will be used as the name of the CSECT. We follow the practice of including a comment on this line that makes it look like a program header. For example

```
SAMPLE     START   0                   PROGRAM SAMPLE
```

Each time the assembler adds an instruction or a piece of data to the object module, it checks the location counter to determine where the new value should be placed. After inserting the value, the assembler increments the location counter by the number of bytes added. In order to reserve space for a field in the object module without initializing the corresponding locations, the assembler simply increments the location counter by the number of bytes to be reserved. Unless the location counter is later reset, this assures that the reserved bytes will not be allocated to other fields.

The EQU Directive

Assembly constants and labels can be defined with the EQU (EQUate) instruction. The format for this instruction is

```
<name>     EQU     <value>
```

When it encounters this directive during assembly, the assembler enters the name in the symbol table together with the indicated value.

Example 1.4.2 *Some typical constant definitions are*

```
LENGTH    EQU    5
NUMENTS   EQU    100
SIZE1     EQU    20
LABEL     EQU    *
```

The last instruction assigns the current value of the location counter as the value of the symbol "LABEL". This symbol may then be used to identify the location in the program where the EQU was placed. In particular, it may be used as the target of a branch instruction.

The EQU instruction has a more general form which allows the use of an expression on the right hand side. The expression may consist of the arithmetic operations +, −, *, / and parentheses, together with constants and previously defined symbols. (The assembler must determine from the context whether the asterisk represents the value of the location counter or the multiplication operation.) The usual order of evaluation of operations is employed (multiplication and division first followed by addition and subtraction proceeding from left to right within classes). The division operation is *integer* division. Any fractional part is discarded.

Example 1.4.3 *The following EQU instructions illustrate the use of expressions.*

Instruction			Value Assigned
SIZE	EQU	6+4	10
DBLE	EQU	2*SIZE	20
LTHA	EQU	DBLE+7	27
HLFLTH	EQU	LTHA/2	13
ALL	EQU	SIZE+DBLE+LTHA	57

All of the symbols shown in Example 1.4.3 are known as *absolute* symbols. They may be used throughout an assembly language program in almost every context in which a number would be allowed. As we shall see, using such symbols in place of numbers often leads to programs which are easier to read and to modify. Symbols that are used to identify storage areas and instructions in a program are called *relocatable* symbols because their values must be adjusted whenever the program containing them is loaded at a different location in memory.

The ORG Directive

In addition to obtaining the value of the location counter using the asterisk, we can actually change the value with the ORG directive. The format is

```
ORG    <exp>
```

The assembler evaluates the expression and assigns the value obtained to the location counter. The expression must be a "relocatable" expression, that is, it must represent a location in the code or data areas of the program.

Example 1.4.4 *The following instruction increments the location counter by 20.*

ORG   *+20

The DS and DC Directives

Relocatable symbols that identify storage areas are defined with the DS and DC assembler directives. Both of these instruct the assembler to reserve storage space for variables to be used in an assembler program. In addition, the DC directive instructs the assembler to initialize the storage area with a value provided in the instruction. DS stands for Define Storage and DC for Define Constant. However, both of these directives define storage areas that may be altered during the execution of the program. Areas that are defined by the DC directive are not constants in the usual sense. They are simply storage areas which are to have an initial value when the program begins execution.

The format for the DC directive is

[<sym>]   DC   [<dup>]<type>[L<lth>]['<val>']

<sym>   An optional character string used to identify the storage area.
<dup>   An optional duplication factor.
<type>   A single letter indicating the type of the field.
<lth>   Length in *bytes*.
<val>   Initialization value (DC) or a prototype value (DS).

The format for the DC directive is identical. If both a length and a value are specified, and if the implicit length determined from the value differs from the explicit length, then the explicit length is used and the value is either padded or truncated to fit.

There are a number of allowable type designators. In the following examples we will use these four.

P   Packed decimal
Z   Zoned decimal
C   Character
X   Hexadecimal

When processing DS and DC directives, the assembler identifies each symbol by the current value of the location counter. This value is stored together with the length factor and the type of the symbol in the symbol table. The location counter is then incremented by the length times the duplication factor.

In order to model this situation accurately, we view the symbol as representing the first byte in the field. The length and type may then be viewed as additional attributes of the symbol. This is in contrast to the view that the symbol represents the entire field. In many situations, these two views seem to be equivalent, and a clear distinction is not always made between them. In the example below, we represent the entire field reserved by each DS or DC directive and attach the symbol to that field. There will, however, be other occasions when it will be useful to make this distinction.

Notation

In our examples, we need to represent both the size of a field in memory and its contents. It is simple to devise a notation that indicates the number of bytes in a field. However, the contents of a field may be interpreted in a number of different ways.

As a packed decimal number,
as a zoned decimal number,
as a character string,
as an unsigned binary or hexadecimal number,
as a signed binary number,
as a floating point number.

Often, we also need a notation that conveys our interpretation of the contents of a field.

In order to satisfy these two requirements, we adopt the following conventions. In our prose, we use the same notation the assembler uses to initialize a field. That is, a type indicator followed by a value in single quotes. For example P'5012' denotes a packed decimal field that contains the number 5012. (We have to remind ourselves that this field requires three bytes of storage.) We use P'003' to denote a two-byte packed field that currently contains 3. In contrast, C'5012' denotes a field that contains the characters 5, 0, 1, and 2. (In this case, we need to remember that the field is four bytes long.) This notation focuses our attention on the meaning of the field. The length of the field must be deduced from our knowledge of the mechanism used to store different types of data.

Whenever we want to refer to the way in which a field is stored in memory, as opposed to the way it is being interpreted, we use the assembler's hexadecimal notation. That is X followed by a hexadecimal number in single quotes. Each pair of hexadecimal digits represents the contents of a single byte. Thus, P'5012' is stored as X'05012C', C'5012' is stored as X'F5F0F1F2', Z'5012' is stored as X'F5F0F1C2'. In describing the effect of the instructions we study, we normally represent field contents in this way.

In our examples, we often show pictures of memory cells, giving their hexadecimal contents. This is especially useful when we want to illustrate relationships between fields and the effect of overlapping fields. In this notation, the packed number P'5012' is shown as

05	01	2C

Finally, we always denote hexadecimal numbers by preceding their values with X and enclosing the values in single quotes. Binary numbers are marked in similar fashion using B to indicate the base. A number without any type indicator is assumed to be decimal. This eliminates any possible confusion between 110, B'110', and X'110'.

Example 1.4.5 *The following DS and DC directives reserve storage as indicated. The length attribute of each symbol is denoted L'<symbol>.*

SUM   DC   P'35'   Reserve 2 bytes and initialize with the packed form of 35. (In hexadecimal, this is 035C.)

SUM: | 03 | 5C | L'SUM = 2

NUSUM   DC   PL3'35'   Reserve 3 bytes and initialize with the hexadecimal 00035C.

NUSUM: | 00 | 03 | 5C | L'NUSUM = 3

TOOBIG   DC   PL3'2341489'   Reserve 3 bytes and initialize with 2341489. (Because this value does not fit into 3 bytes, it will be truncated *on the left*.)

TOOBIG: | 41 | 48 | 9C | L'TOOBIG = 3

HEXSUM   DC   X'00035C'   Reserve 3 bytes of storage and initialize with the same value as NUSUM.

HEXSUM: | 00 | 03 | 5C | L'HEXSUM = 3

PVECTOR DS   4PL3   Reserve 12 bytes to hold 4 packed numbers, each of which is 3 bytes long. The symbol PVECTOR identifies the first of these fields.

PVECTOR: | | | | | | | | | | | | | L'PVECTOR = 3

STRING   DS   CL5   Reserve 5 bytes.

STRING: | | | | | | L'STRING = 5

CSTR   DC   C'NAME: '   Reserve and initialize 6 bytes. In character form, these bytes will contain:

CSTR: | N | A | M | E | : | | L'CSTR = 6

The hexadecimal value stored in each byte will be the EBCDIC code for the appropriate character. Thus, in hexadecimal form, the 6 bytes will contain:

CSTR: | D5 | C1 | D4 | C5 | 7A | 40 |

In the following examples, the character form of each field is shown. The actual values will, of course, be stored in hexadecimal form.

SHORT	DC	CL6'SUM'	Reserve 6 bytes. The string 'SUM' will be stored in the left of the reserved field padded on the right with blanks.

SHORT: | S | U | M | | | | L'SUM = 6

LONG	DC	CL6'ADDRESS'	If the value is too long, it will be truncated on the right.

LONG: | A | D | D | R | E | S | L'LONG = 6

ZNUM	DC	Z'21839'	Initialize 5 bytes with the zoned form of 21839.

ZNUM: | F2 | F1 | F8 | F3 | C9 | L'ZNUM = 5

ZSHORT   DC   ZL5'32'

ZSHORT: | F0 | F0 | F0 | F3 | C2 | L'ZSHORT = 5

ZLONG   DC   ZL4'3463587'

ZLONG: | F3 | F5 | F8 | C7 | L'ZLONG = 4

In all of the examples in which an explicitly specified length differs from the length of the initialization value, the assembler will either truncate or pad the value. Fields of type C will be truncated on the right or padded on the right with blanks. Numerical types will be truncated on the left or padded with zeros on the left. It is important to note that the assembler does not give any warning when truncation occurs.

The Length Attribute

The length attribute of a symbol does not change if the program is loaded at a different location in memory. Thus, it is an absolute quantity and can be used any place an absolute expression can be used. It can be used in other instructions with the notation

L'<symbol>

as in the examples above.

The use of the length attribute is helpful in a number of contexts. For example, suppose we have defined PNUM1 by

PNUM1   DC   P'34223'

and we want PNUM2 to have the same length as PNUM1. We could count the number of bytes in PNUM1 and use this in the definition of PNUM2.

```
PNUM2      DS      PL3
```

This approach leads to several undesirable effects. The first is the necessity of having to examine the number 34223 to determine how many bytes it requires. In addition to wasting time, it is quite possible that we may err in determining the length, resulting in an error when the program is executed. The second problem is that if, at some future time we need to change the initialization value 34223 to 9983457, then the definition of PNUM2 must also be changed. However, the definitions of these two fields do not make their dependency clear and it seems likely that the second change may be missed.

The alternative approach that answers both of these objections is to use the length attribute in the definition of the second field.

```
PNUM1      DC      P'34223'
PNUM2      DS      PL(L'PNUM1)
```

In the first case, the assembler will now look up the length of PNUM1 and use it in the definition of PNUM2. This eliminates the need for determining the length and also guarantees that the correct length is used. In the second case, any time the initialization value is changed, the length of PNUM2 is changed automatically.

In this simple example, the advantage of the second approach is clear. However, there are relationships between fields that are considerably more complex. When complex relationships are hidden in the context of a large program, the approach recommended may well mean the difference between programs that can be modified to fit changing circumstances and programs that must be discarded and rewritten.

Note that when the length attribute was used in the definition of PNUM2 above, it was enclosed in parentheses. Parentheses are necessary whenever length is given by anything other than a number. Similar restrictions apply to the duplication factor when it is used.

Duplication Factors

The use of alternative expressions for the length or duplication factor in a DS or DC is not restricted to cases where two fields are the same size. For example, when using arrays, we normally define an array by first defining a symbol to be used as a duplication factor and then using that symbol in the definition of the array.

```
NUMENTS    EQU     25
PARRAY     DS      (NUMENTS)PL5
```

This is particularly useful because programs that use arrays commonly have several arrays of the same size and also use the array size in other contexts, such as limits for counted loops. If it is always accessed through the symbol NUMENTS, then the program can be modified to allow a different number of entries simply by changing this one EQU directive.

Sample Symbol Definitions

Consider a partial example demonstrating the kinds of relationships that may exist between various fields. Suppose that we are writing a program in which three non-negative packed numbers, A, B, and C, are to be added and their sum stored in a packed field SUM. Finally, the packed value in SUM is to be converted to zoned form and stored in ZSUM. Assuming that the packed numbers to be added are 4 bytes long, how do we define these fields?

We begin by *not* assuming that these fields will always be 4 bytes long. It would be prudent to define a symbol, say PLEN, to be 4 and to use this symbol in the other definitions. It might also be wise to allow an extra byte in SUM since the sum of the three packed numbers may have one more digit than the numbers themselves. Finally, when the packed number is converted to zoned form, we will need 1 byte to store each digit. The sign will be stored as the zone portion of the last byte, so the length of ZSUM should be 2*L'SUM−1. This gives the following definitions.

```
PLEN      EQU    4
A         DS     PL(PLEN)
B         DS     PL(PLEN)
C         DS     PL(PLEN)
SUM       DS     PL(PLEN+1)
ZSUM      DS     ZL(2*L'SUM−1)
```

One other assistance provided by the assembler is the cross-reference listing that may be obtained as part of the listing produced by the assembler when it assembles a program. The cross-reference listing includes all of the symbols used in the program together with the number of the line in which the symbol is defined and the number of every line in which a reference to that symbol occurs. In the case of relocatable symbols, cross-reference listing also gives the displacement from the beginning of the program to the symbol. This is listed in the column labelled VALUE. As an example, the cross-reference listing for the program containing the fields defined above might contain the following entries.

Symbol	Len	Value	Defn	References
A	00004	00013A	00121	0034,0035,0056
B	00004	00013E	00122	0036,0045
C	00004	000142	00123	0037,0039,0056,0078
PLEN	00001	000004	00120	0121,0122,0123,0124
SUM	00005	000146	00124	0034,0035,0036,0067,0125
ZSUM	00009	00014B	00125	0067,0076

Note the lengths of A, B, C, SUM, and ZSUM are as expected. The length of PLEN is unimportant—the assembler always uses length 1 for absolute symbols.

The values given for A, B, C, SUM, and ZSUM represent the number of bytes from the beginning of the program to the given field. Thus A begins X'13A' (314 in decimal) bytes from the beginning of the program. As 4 bytes are reserved for this field, B begins 4 bytes later, at X'13E' (318 in decimal). The value given for PLEN is its defined value of 4.

When the assembler lists the statements in the source code, it assigns a number to each statement. These numbers are used in the last two columns. The values given in the column labelled DEFN assume that PLEN was defined in statement number 120 in the assembly listing and that the definitions occurred exactly as shown above. The values listed in the column labelled 'REFERENCES' give the line numbers of all occurrences of each symbol. As PLEN occurs in the definitions of A, B, C, and SUM, the numbers of each of these definitions are given in the list of references for PLEN. Similarly, as SUM appears in the definition of ZSUM, the reference list for SUM contains 125, the statement number of this definition.

E X E R C I S E S

1. Give the value of the symbol defined by each of the following equates.

a. LENGTH	EQU	5
b. HLEN	EQU	LENGTH/2
c. SLEN	EQU	LENGTH+HLEN
d. PNUM	DC	P'2319'
PLEN	EQU	L'PNUM

2. Give the contents of the field defined by each of the following instructions.

a. ITEM	DC	P'240921'
b. ZDAYS	DC	ZL3'90384'
c. RATE	DC	PL5'12'
d. NAME	DC	C'JOHN ADAMS'
e. COUNT	DC	PL2'98023'
f. NUNAME	DC	CL15'JOHN ADAMS'
g. ZNUM	DC	Z'2849'
h. FNAME	DC	CL4'JOHN ADAMS'
i. ZRATE	DC	ZL8'12'

3. Write the DS or DC assembler directive to create the following storage areas.

   a. An area to hold 3 packed numbers each of which is 5 bytes long.
   b. A character field that is 6 bytes long and initialized with the string 'AVG.'
   c. An area which initialized to the hexadecimal number X'A493C4'.

4. Write the assembler code necessary to create storage space for an array of 20 student names with a maximum of 40 characters per name.

5. Assuming the following EQU instructions and the indicated hexa-decimal starting value for the location counter, give the value of the location counter before each of the following DS or DC instructions.

	PLEN	EQU	5
	ZLEN	EQU	10

Location Counter	**Instruction**		
12E	NUM1	DS	PL(PLEN)
_____	NUM2	DS	PL(PLEN)
_____	NUM3	DS	PL(2*PLEN)
_____	ZNUM	DS	ZL(ZLEN)
_____	PCONST	DC	P'293842'
_____	ZCONST	DC	Z'−38938'
_____	CHCONST	DC	C'LAST ENTRY'
_____			

1.5 SOME SIMPLE INSTRUCTIONS

Now, we examine some assembly language instructions and their corresponding machine language instructions, considering each instruction on both the assembly language level and the machine language level. On the assembly language level, we view the instruction as manipulating logical entities that are identified with symbols defined with DS or DC directives. On the machine language level, we consider the instructions in terms of the changes they effect in memory locations or registers. On this level, the memory locations are identified by a base register, a displacement, and, in the case of the SS instructions, a length.

In order to write assembly language programs, we need to be at ease with both levels and occasionally to deal with additional intermediate levels. For example, when assembling an SS instruction, the assembler needs to include one or two lengths. It uses the defined lengths of both operands for a 2-length SS instruction and the length of the first operand for a 1-length SS instruction. However, the programmer can override these default lengths by explicitly specifying the operand length. In addition, a symbolic operand may include a displacement which changes the starting location of the operand. Examples of both types of operands appear below.

All new instructions are described in a standard format. The instruction name is given with the letters used to form the mnemonic name in upper case. This is followed by the mnemonic itself and the machine language format. We then give the assembly language format using S1 for the first symbolic operand and S2 for the second. We show the format used when one or two explicit lengths are given using L1 and L2 for the lengths. These lengths are optional; when omitted, the assembler will use the defined lengths of the fields involved. Both S1 and S2 may be simple symbols or symbols plus or minus an offset given as an absolute expression. L1 and L2 may similarly be absolute expressions.

The instruction description concludes with a listing of the error conditions that can occur during the execution of the instruction. In IBM terminology, these are called *program exceptions*. These exceptions are listed in the output produced when a program terminates because of an error. After each exception is a brief description of the circumstances that might cause the error.

The MVC Instruction

The simplest instruction is one that simply copies the contents of one set of memory locations to another set of memory locations. The copying operation proceeds one byte at a time and this instruction is called *Move Character*.

MoVe Character *MVC 1-length SS*

```
        MVC     S1(L1),S2
```

The contents of the memory locations designated by the second operand are copied one byte at a time, from left to right, to the corresponding locations of the first operand.

Exception:

Access   Improper address for one or both operands.

Recalling the machine format for a 1-length SS instruction, we see that there is a single byte available to store a length. The value stored must be between 0 and 255. This is interpreted as representing the number of bytes *beyond the first byte* which are to be moved. The actual length of the operand must therefore be between 1 and 256 bytes.

Example 1.5.1 *Suppose FLD1 and FLD2 have been defined by*

```
FLD1        DS      CL5
FLD2        DS      CL5
```

During execution, the memory locations corresponding to FLD1 and FLD2 are as shown below.

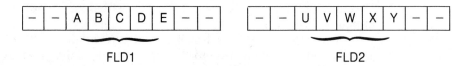

(All memory locations actually contain a byte. For convenience, when we want to view the data stored in a memory location as character data, we show the character whose EBCDIC code is stored there. In this example, a '−' is used to represent the contents of a location whose value does not concern us.)

The instruction

    MVC   FLD1,FLD2

proceeds in the following way. The bytes containing the codes for the characters U, V, W, X, and Y are copied one at a time from FLD2 to FLD1. After the instruction has been completed, FLD2 would be unchanged and FLD1 would be shown as

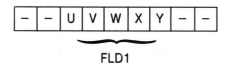

FLD1

    Now let us see how we might use this instruction in a more realistic setting. Suppose the fields NAME, STREET, CITSTAT, and OUT have been defined as follows.

```
NAME      DS      CL30
STREET    DS      CL30
CITSTAT   DS      CL25
OUT       DS      CL30
```

    A typical problem might require us to move the values from NAME, STREET, and CITSTAT, one at a time to the field OUT. (Presumably, these values would be printed once they were moved to OUT, but we will postpone the question of how the printing is to be done.)

    The following instruction would cause the 30 characters in the field identified by NAME to be copied to the field OUT.

    MVC   OUT,NAME

The next instruction will copy 30 characters from STREET to OUT.

    MVC   OUT,STREET

Explicit Lengths and Offsets

In the instruction above, the assembler uses the length of the first operand. This instruction will have the same effect as the following variation in which a length is specified.

    MVC   OUT(30),STREET

The next instruction copies only the first 20 characters of STREET to OUT. The last 10 bytes of OUT are not affected.

    MVC   OUT(20),STREET

Now suppose that we want to copy the contents of CITSTAT to OUT. The instruction

    MVC   OUT,CITSTAT

has the desired effect. Unfortunately, it does more than we want. Because the assembler uses the length of the first operand, this instruction copies 30 bytes. It copies CITSTAT into the first 25 bytes of OUT and then proceeds to copy 5 bytes from whatever field that happens to follow CITSTAT into the last 5 bytes of OUT.

In order to copy only the field CITSTAT we use

    MVC   OUT(L'CITSTAT),CITSTAT

The first operand begins at the same byte as OUT but is only 25 bytes long. Thus the effect is to copy CITSTAT into the leftmost 25 bytes of OUT and leave the last 5 bytes of OUT unchanged. Thus CITSTAT will be left justified in OUT. (The last 5 bytes of OUT may contain garbage. We will shortly see how this can be padded with blanks.)

If we want to copy CITSTAT into the rightmost part of OUT, we add a displacement to the start of OUT. Before considering such an instruction, we need to know how the bytes of OUT are stored in memory. If OUT represents the first byte of this field, OUT+1 must represent the byte whose address is one more than the address of OUT. Other offsets are shown below.

Byte Number

1	2	3	4	5	6	7	8	9	10 . . . .
OUT+0	OUT+1	OUT+2	OUT+3	OUT+4	OUT+5	OUT+6	OUT+7	OUT+8	OUT+9

In order to force the first operand to begin at the sixth byte of OUT, we specify OUT+5 for that operand.

    MVC   OUT+5(L'CITSTAT),CITSTAT

This works, but it requires that the programmer determine how many bytes to skip. If the length of one of the fields is changed, then the offset given in the instruction needs to be changed. The following instruction also right justifies CITSTAT in OUT.

    MVC   OUT+L'OUT−L'CITSTAT(L'CITSTAT),CITSTAT

In spite of its length, the second is preferable. It does not require the programmer to determine the offset and if the lengths of the fields are changed, the assembler will automatically change the instruction when the program is reassembled. The obvious generalization of this instruction

        MVC   FLD1+L'FLD1−L'FLD2(L'FLD2),FLD2

will always right justify FLD2 in FLD1, assuming that FLD2 is not longer than FLD1.

   When a shorter field is copied into a longer field, regardless of where it is placed, there will be bytes of the longer field that contain their original values. In the case of character data, it is desirable to have these bytes filled with blanks. This can easily be done by filling the longer field with blanks before moving in the shorter field. The most direct way to do this is to define a field BLANKS by

BLANKS   DC   CL256' '

then using the instruction

        MVC   OUT,BLANKS

As the assembler uses the length of the first operand in the instruction, this will work whatever the length of OUT may be. (It cannot exceed 256 bytes.)

   A frequently used alternative illustrates an interesting property of the MVC instruction. Suppose we write the storage definition for OUT in the following way.

          DC   C' '
OUT   DS   CL30

During execution, the area of memory that includes the field OUT looks like

```
O  O
U  U
T  T
−
1
```

That is, the byte immediately before the first byte of OUT contains a blank.
   Now, consider the effect of the instruction

        MVC   OUT,OUT−1

Because the assembler uses the length of the first operand, the instruction will move 30 bytes. In fact, it moves the 30 bytes beginning at OUT-1 to the 30 memory locations beginning at OUT. However, this operation proceeds one byte at a time, from left to right. Assuming that OUT is initially filled with X's, let us trace the movement of several bytes.

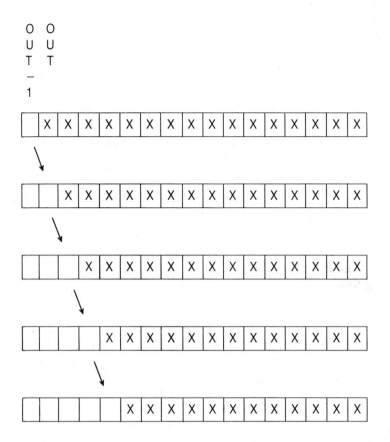

The effect of the way in which the instruction operates on the bytes of overlapping operands is to propagate the single blank from OUT-1 throughout the field OUT. Thus, the following pair of instructions can be used to left justify CITSTAT in OUT and fill out the last 5 bytes of OUT with blanks.

```
MVC    OUT,OUT−1
MVC    OUT(L'CITSTAT),CITSTAT
```

The MVI Instruction

It is sometimes necessary to set the value of a single byte in memory. This can be done by defining a field containing that character and then copying that field to the desired memory location using the MVC instruction. However, there is special instruction provided that accomplishes this called the *Move Immediate* instruction.

MoVe Immediate *MVI SI*

```
MVI    S1,I
```

The one byte immediate datum is moved to the memory location corresponding to the first operand.

Exception:

Access   Improper address for first operand.

The symbol *I* in the instruction description represents a single byte of data represented as a decimal number from 0 to 255 or in the format

<type> '<value>'

where <type> is one of the type designators C, B, or X.

Example 1.5.2 *This instruction places the character $ in the first byte of FLD. (The length of FLD is irrelevant.)*

        MVI   FLD,C'$'

Because the EBCDIC code for $ is 91 (decimal) = X'5B' = B'01011011', the following three instructions have the same effect.

        MVI   FLD,91
        MVI   FLD,X'5B'
        MVI   FLD,B'01011011'

The format used for the immediate datum depends upon the context. In the example above, although any of the four instructions would work, the first would obviously be used if FLD is viewed as containing character data.

The MVI instruction can be used to provide a third alternative for filling a field with blanks (or any other characters). We can use MVI to put the desired character in the first byte of the field, then use a variation of the MVC above to propagate that character through the rest of the field.

        MVI   OUT,C' '
        MVC   OUT+1(L'OUT−1),OUT

AP, SP, and ZAP

The decimal arithmetic instructions are all 2-length SS instructions. Examination of the machine format for SS2 instructions shows that the format allows a single hex-digit for each length. As with the MVC instruction, the length stored there is interpreted as the number of bytes after the starting byte. The assembler actually stores the length minus one. This means that packed decimal fields may range from 1 to 16 bytes or 1 to 31 decimal digits in length. As both lengths are stored, this also implies that the two operands need not have the same length.

In all three instructions, the first field receives the result of the operation and the second field is unchanged. If necessary, the value will be truncated or padded on the left to fit the receiving field. If truncation requires the elimination of non-zero digits, then the Decimal Overflow program exception will be raised. In advanced assembler language programming, it is possible to disable this exception and include code in the program to handle the overflow. On the programs in this text, we treat decimal overflow as a programming error and allow it to terminate the program.

Add Packed decimal *AP 2-length SS*

      AP   S1(L1),S2(L2)

If the operands are of different lengths, the shorter one is extended by adding 0's on the left. The two values are added. The result is stored in the first field, eliminating leading zeros as necessary. If the result will not fit in the first field, a Decimal Overflow exception is raised.

Exceptions:

Access	Improper address for one or both operands.
Data	One or both fields does not contain a valid packed number.
Decimal Overflow	The result is too large for the first operand.

Example 1.5.3 *Suppose that X and Y have been defined by the following.*

```
X           DS      PL3
Y           DS      PL4
```

At execution, the contents of these fields are as shown below.

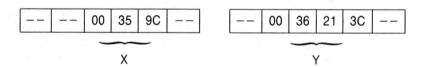

Then, the instruction

      AP   X,Y

performs the addition

$$
\begin{array}{r}
0000359 \\
+0036213 \\
\hline
0036572
\end{array}
$$

The two leading zeros are removed and the result is stored in X. The field Y is not affected.

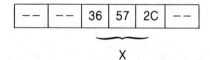

Example 1.5.4 *Assuming that the fields X and Y have lengths and values as shown, the following table gives the result of executing the instruction*

AP   X,Y

X Before	Y	X After
00 | 43 | 2F	00 | 00 | 54 | 2D	00 | 11 | 0D
03 | 15 | 64 | 3D	20 | 32 | 48 | 5D	23 | 48 | 12 | 8D
12 | 83 | 59 | 3C	15 | 9D	12 | 83 | 43 | 4C
23 | 6C	04 | 36 | 5C	Overflow
58 | 9D	72 | 6D	Overflow
99 | 87 | 6C	88 | 9C	Overflow

The Decimal Subtract instruction is the obvious analog of the Add instruction. The result is stored in the first field, being truncated or padded as necessary, and the second field is unchanged. Of course, overflow can occur as in the case of the Add instruction.

Subtract Packed decimal *SP 2-length SS*

SP   S1(L1),S2(L2)

If the operands are of different lengths, the shorter one is extended by adding 0's on the left. The value from the second field is subtracted from the value in the first field. The result is stored in the first field, eliminating leading zeros as necessary. If the result will not fit in the first field, a Decimal Overflow exception is raised.

Exceptions:

Access	Improper address for one or both operands.
Data	One or both fields does not contain a valid packed number.
Decimal Overflow	The result is too large for the first operand.

Example 1.5.5 *Assuming that the fields X and Y have lengths and values as shown, the following table gives the result of executing the instruction*

SP   X,Y

X Before	Y	X After
00 43 2F	00 00 54 2D	00 97 4C
03 15 64 3D	20 32 48 5C	23 48 12 8D
12 83 59 3C	15 9C	12 83 43 4C
23 6C	04 36 5C	Overflow
58 9D	72 6C	Overflow
99 87 6C	88 9D	Overflow

The ZAP instruction is used to copy packed numbers from one field to another. If both fields are the same size, this could be done with the MVC instruction. The ZAP instruction is more general in that it permits the two fields to be of different lengths. If the receiving field is longer than the sending field, the value will be padded on the left with zeros. If the receiving field is shorter than the sending field, then leading zeros will be removed provided this allows the value to fit the receiving field. If the nonzero part of the value is too large for the receiving field, then a Decimal Overflow exception occurs.

Zero and Add Packed decimal *ZAP 2-length SS*

        ZAP   S1(L1),S2(L2)

The effect of this instruction is identical to setting the first field equal to 0 then performing an Add Packed instruction. It takes the value from the second field and adds or removes leading zeros so that it can be placed in the first field. If the nonzero part of this value will not fit in the first field, a Decimal Overflow exception is raised.

Exceptions:

Access	Improper address for one or both operands.
Data	The second field does not contain a valid packed number.
Decimal Overflow	The result is too large for the first operand.

Example 1.5.6 *Assuming that the fields X and Y have lengths and values as shown, the following table gives the result of executing the instruction*

        ZAP   X,Y

X Before	Y	X After
00 | 43 | 2F	00 | 00 | 54 | 2D	00 | 54 | 2D
03 | 15 | 64 | 3D	20 | 32 | 48 | 5C	20 | 32 | 48 | 5C
12 | 83 | 59 | 3C	15 | 9C	00 | 00 | 15 | 9C
23 | 6C	04 | 36 | 5C	Overflow

Example 1.5.7 *Suppose that X, Y, Z and RESULT are defined by the following.*

```
X          DS      PL4
Y          DS      PL3
Z          DS      PL5
RESULT     DS      PL6
```

In order to implement the assignment

RESULT = X + Y − Z

we use

```
        ZAP     RESULT,X
        AP      RESULT,Y
        SP      RESULT,Z
```

We have covered only five of the IBM 370 instructions, yet with these instructions together with some input/output operations, we can write some simple programs. There are a number of other technicalities involved in creating and executing assembler language programs. We will deal with some technical details in the next chapter and defer consideration of other instructions until later chapters.

E X E R C I S E S

1. Given the following storage definitions, write instructions and any additional storage definitions necessary to exchange the values in NAME1 and NAME2.

```
NAMELEN    EQU     20
NAME1      DS      CL(NAMELEN)
NAME2      DS      CL(NAMELEN)
```

2. Given the fields defined above, write an instruction to copy the first character from NAME1 into the field

   INITIAL   DS   CL1

3. Write instructions to fill the field NAME1 with blanks, then move the last five characters of NAME2 into the first five positions of NAME1.

4. Given the field definitions below, write the instructions needed to implement each of the following assignment statements.

ITEM1	DS	PL(PLEN)
ITEM2	DS	PL(PLEN)
ITEM3	DS	PL(PLEN)
SUM	DS	PL(SUMLEN)
ANSWER	DS	PL(ANSLEN)

   a. SUM = ITEM1 + ITEM2 + ITEM3
   b. ANSWER = 2*SUM + ITEM1 − ITEM3

5. Assume that the fields ADDR1 and ADDR2 have lengths and contents as shown below.

   ADDR1 : '457 HIGH STR'   ADDR2: '4922 WASHINGTON BLVD'

   Show the result of executing each of the following instructions.

   a.   MVC   ADDR1,ADDR2
   b.   MVI   ADDR1+(L'ADDR1−1),C'.'

6. Given the above memory locations, describe the adverse effect of executing the following misguided instructions.

   a.   MVC   ADDR2,ADDR1
   b.   MVC   ADDR2(L'ADDR1),ADDR1
   c.   MVI   ADDR1+L'ADDR1,C'.'

7. Assume X, Y, and Z have values and lengths as shown.

   X : X'0012497F'   Y : X'9621321F'   Z : X'013159321D'

   Give the result of executing each of the following instructions.

   a.   AP   X,Y
   b.   SP   Y,X
   c.   ZAP   Z,X
   d.   AP   Z,Y
   e.   SP   X,Y
   f.   SP   Z,X
   g.   AP   Y,Z

C H A P T E R 2

RUNNING ASSEMBLY LANGUAGE PROGRAMS

2.1 INPUT AND OUTPUT

In this chapter, we cover a diverse group of topics which are primarily operating system dependent. These topics include input and output, the Job Control Language instructions for assembling and executing programs, and techniques for debugging programs using hexadecimal dumps. In this book, we concentrate on DOS and use it in sample programs. However, we include the details needed for running programs under OS. Because we limit our coverage of input and output operations, the differences are minimal.

Input/Output is an extremely complicated process. In order to manage the potential complexities of it, physical I/O operations must be performed by the operating system. Users are not allowed to perform their own I/O operations on most modern computer systems. The process is further simplified by the use of system-provided macros. A macro is not an instruction in itself, but a name assigned to a set of assembler instructions. When the assembler interprets these instructions, it generates a sequence of assembly language instructions. The method by which a macro is invoked is designed to look like an assembly language instruction and, until we are ready to begin writing our own macros, we view macros as extensions of the instruction set.

In this section, we cover the basic macros for doing input and output. However, we begin with the machine instructions for converting character to packed decimal data.

The PACK Instruction

We have seen some instructions for performing arithmetic on packed fields, but when numbers are read from a typical character input device, they are read as characters. The character string that represents the digits in a decimal integer is in fact a *zoned decimal number*. For example, the character string '2574' can be interpreted as the zoned decimal number 2574. The distinction between the two types is primarily conceptual. When the assembler creates a zoned number, it uses a C or a D in the last digit to indicate the sign. Otherwise, the character string '2574' and the zoned number 2574 are distinguished only by the instructions used to manipulate the two values. Thus, when performing an input operation, we can read a record into a field of 80 characters and later, without conflict, treat a subfield of that character field as a zoned decimal number.

Assuming that we have read a zoned decimal number, before we can perform any arithmetic involving that number, it must be converted to packed form. The process is quite straightforward. The EBCDIC code for each of the digits consists of the hexadecimal digit F followed by the digit itself, so when we consider the hexadecimal form of the zoned number, the process is equivalent to discarding the F's and packing the digits together. The last F must be retained as the sign indicator of the packed number.

The PACK instruction handles these details and allows the conversion operation to be combined with a move to another field.

PACK *PACK 2-length SS*

      PACK   S1(L1),S2(L2)

The value in the second field is processed one byte at a time from right to left and the resulting bytes are stored in the first field from right to left. The two hex-digits in the rightmost byte of the second field are reversed; the numeric parts of the remaining bytes are extracted and combined in pairs to produce the result bytes. If the values of the second field are exhausted before the first, the remaining positions in the first field are filled with zeros. If the positions in the first field are exhausted before those of the second, the remaining bytes in the second field are ignored.

Exceptions:

Access   Improper address for one or both operands.

Example 2.1.1 *Suppose that ZNUM and PNUM are defined by the following, and that ZNUM contains X'F8F5F9F1F3F6'. (The contents of PNUM are irrelevant.)*

```
ZNUM       DS      ZL6
PNUM       DS      PL4
```

Then, during the execution of the instruction

      PACK   PNUM,ZNUM

the field PNUM will undergo the following transformations as each byte is added to PNUM.

--	--	--	--
--	--	--	6F
--	--	13	6F
--	59	13	6F
08	59	13	6F

Note that the only exception that can be caused by PACK is an Access exception. PACK does *not* validate the number. In particular, it does not check to determine whether the second field contains a valid zoned number, nor does it check the result in the first field at the end of the operation. This operation consists entirely of switching the two hex-digits in the rightmost byte and extracting the right hex-digit from the remaining bytes. This operation can be performed on any type of data. In general, the execution of the instruction

      PACK   PNUM,ANYFLD

does not guarantee that PNUM contains a valid packed number.

Example 2.1.2 *Assuming that the field ZNUM has lengths and values as shown, the following table gives the result of executing the following instruction, given that PNUM has been defined as PL4. (In the character format, a blank is represented as b̸.)*

PACK   PNUM,ZNUM

ZNUM Character	ZNUM Hexadecimal								PNUM After			
0056821	F0	F0	F5	F6	F8	F2	F1		00	56	82	1F
5921858	F5	F9	F2	F1	F8	F5	F8		59	21	85	8F
00351	F0	F0	F3	F5	F1				00	00	35	1F
89728760	F8	F9	F7	F2	F8	F7	F6	F0	97	28	76	0F
b̸b̸b̸3001	40	40	40	F3	F0	F0	F1		00	03	00	1F
−9035	60	F9	F0	F3	F5				00	09	03	5F
00482+	F0	F0	F4	F8	F2	D1			00	04	82	1D
IBMb̸370	C9	C2	D4	40	F3	F7	F0		92	40	37	0F
(*$$*)	4D	5C	5B	5B	5C	5D			0D	CB	BC	D5

The examples above illustrate some of the useful, as well as some of the annoying, aspects of PACK. The lengths of the two fields do not have to be compatible. The PACK instruction will add or remove leading zeros as necessary. Unfortunately, it will also truncate leading nonzero digits.

Because it does not check the zoned number for validity, the PACK instruction will accept numbers that have leading blanks (EBCDIC 40) instead of leading zeros. The operation extracts the 0 from the numeric part and ignores the 4 in the zone part of the leading blanks. Thus, these blanks are treated as though they were zeros. Unfortunately, none of the input values are validated. The result of a PACK instruction can be an invalid packed field or a meaningless number.

Finally, notice that because the EBCDIC code for a minus sign is X'60', placing a minus in front of a zoned number does not result in a negative packed number. The minus is effectively ignored when the numeric portion is extracted. In order to create a negative number, we need to force the PACK instruction to put the hex-digit D in the numeric portion of the rightmost byte. In the days of punched cards, this was done by overpunching the last digit with a minus sign. This punched an 11 zone on the card in the same column as the digit. When this card code was translated to EBCDIC as the card was read, the code consisted of a D followed by the digit. When using an editor on an interactive system, it is necessary to use a hexadecimal input mode to get this effect.

The IBM 370 includes an UNPACK instruction (UNPK) that reverses the steps effected by PACK. This is of limited usefulness, however, as packed numbers that have resulted from arithmetic operations always have a D or a C in the sign position. UNPK does not convert these sign indicators to F.

Example 2.1.3 *Suppose ZNUM has been defined as ZL7 and PNUM has been defined as PL3, and PNUM contains X'05342C'.*

After the execution of

        UNPK   ZNUM,PNUM

ZNUM will contain X'F0F0F0F5F3F4C2'. If this number were printed, it would appear in character form as C'000534B' since X'C2' is the EBCDIC code for the character B.

Because of its limitations, we will not consider UNPK any further.

Editing

The Edit instruction, ED, provides a much more satisfactory way of converting packed numbers to character form. It assumes that the receiving field, its first operand, contains a pattern called an *edit mask*, which directs the execution of the instruction. These masks can be quite complicated, but we will begin with simplified versions which work well enough for our first programs.

EDit *ED 1-length SS*

        ED   S1(L1),S2

The packed number in the second operand is edited one digit at a time, from left to right as directed by an edit pattern, or mask, in the first operand. The result of the edit operation replaces the edit pattern in the first operand.

Exceptions:

Access	Improper address for one or both operands.
Data	The second operand does not contain a valid packed number. (This exception may occur if the edit pattern does not correspond to the packed number.)

The effect of the instruction depends upon the pattern, so we cannot fully explore the possibilities of the Edit instruction until we cover all the possibilities for pattern creation. We shall postpone most of these until later.

A simplified pattern may consist of a fill character followed by an appropriate number of digit selectors. The fill character may be any printable character. The digit selector is an unprintable character assigned the hexadecimal code X'20'. When the Edit instruction is executed, the fill character is left unchanged. Each of the digit selectors should correspond to a digit in the packed decimal number in the second field. Those digit selectors that correspond to leading zeros are replaced by the fill character. The digit selectors corresponding to digits other than leading zeros are replaced by the zoned form of those digits.

Example 2.1.4 *Suppose that OUTNUM contains X'402020202020' and that PNUM contains X'00355C'.*

During execution of the instruction

       ED   OUTNUM,PNUM

the digit selectors in the OUTNUM correspond to digits in PNUM as shown below.

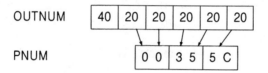

The first two digit selectors are replaced by the fill character (a blank). The last three digit selectors are replaced by the zoned form of the digits 3, 5, 5. Thus, after execution of the instruction, OUTNUM contains X'404040F3F5F5'. In character form, this is C'   355'.

As can be seen from the correspondence in the example above, the pattern always has one digit selector for each digit in the packed decimal number. If the pattern does not have enough digit selectors, then the remaining digits in the packed number will be ignored. If the pattern has too many digit selectors, then a Data exception will be raised when the sign indicator (the C in the last example) is processed.

The pattern above still has several shortcomings. In particular, suppose that PNUM has X'00000C' as its value. In this case, every digit selector would correspond to a leading zero and be replaced by the fill character. After the edit operation, OUTNUM would contain all blanks. A second problem emerges if PNUM contains X'00436D'. With the given edit pattern, the sign indicator, D, would be ignored and OUTNUM would indicate that the number was positive.

We will postpone solution of the second of these two problems and content ourselves with printing positive numbers. The first problem can be overcome by using the *significance starter*, X'21'. The significance starter functions as a digit selector and is replaced by the fill character or the zoned form of a digit. However, all digit selectors to the right of the significance starter will be replaced by the corresponding digits even if they select leading zeros. Example 2.1.5 illustrates the functioning of the significance starter.

Example 2.1.5 *Suppose that before execution of the following instruction, the fields OUTNUM and PNUM have lengths and values as indicated in the table below.*

          ED   OUTNUM,PNUM

The third column of the table gives the value of OUTNUM in both hexadecimal and character form after the instruction has been executed. The value of PNUM is not changed by the instruction.

OUTNUM Before	PNUM	OUTNUM After	
40 20 21 20	15 2C	40 F1 F5 F2	C' 152'
40 20 21 20	03 1C	40 40 F3 F1	C' 31'
40 20 21 20	00 5C	40 40 40 F5	C' 5'
40 20 21 20	00 0C	40 40 40 F0	C' 0'
40 21 20 20	03 1C	40 40 F3 F1	C' 31'
40 21 20 20	00 5C	40 40 F0 F5	C' 05'
40 21 20 20	00 0C	40 40 F0 F0	C' 00'

The fill character is always unchanged; it is not replaced by a digit. Also, it is never possible to force a zero to be printed in the first position. This means that we cannot create an edit pattern to print a PL1 number that prints the number 0.

The table below gives edit patterns for the packed types PL2 through PL6 that force a zero in the last position.

Type	Edit Pattern
PL2	40 20 21 20
PL3	40 20 20 20 21 20
PL4	40 20 20 20 20 20 21 20
PL5	40 20 20 20 20 20 20 20 21 20
PL6	40 20 20 20 20 20 20 20 20 20 21 20

Usually the same print field is used many times in a program. Because the editing operation replaces the edit pattern with the edited number, a new copy of the pattern must be moved into the field before each editing instruction. Thus the edit mask is usually defined in a separate field, also useful because the same mask may be used with several print fields. We might, for example, define all of the masks above with the following DC directives.

```
MASK2     DC     X'40202120'
MASK3     DC     X'402020202120'
MASK4     DC     X'4020202020202120'
MASK5     DC     X'40202020202020202120'
MASK6     DC     X'402020202020202020202120'
```

A field to be used to print a PL4 number would then be defined by

```
OUTFLD    DS     CL(L'MASK4)
```

(Note that the form of the definition assures that the field is exactly the same size as the edit pattern.)

In order to edit a PL4 number, say TOTAL, we use the following pair of instructions.

```
          MVC    OUTFLD,MASK4
          ED     OUTFLD,TOTAL
```

A similar pair of instructions should make up all edit operations. First use MVC to copy the mask into the output field or a work area, then use ED to do the editing operation.

The I/O Macros

IBM's major operating systems provide macros to implement five basic file manipulations. These operations are defining files, opening and closing files, and writing or reading files. These differ from one operating system to another, but have many similarities. We will consider the macros used in the DOS and OS.

DOS Macros for Defining Files

In DOS, file definitions are accomplished by a group of macros called *DTF's* (Define The File). There is a DTF macro for each type of I/O device. We shall consider DTFCD, which describes an input file and DTFPR, which describes a printer.

The DTF macros are assigned labels that are used in the program to identify a particular file. Each macro has a number of potential operands that specify characteristics of the file. The examples given below are fairly general, but may require modification at some installations.

A typical DTF for an input file is

```
Column
1              10      16                                                     72
|              |       |                                                      |
<fname>        DTFCD   DEVADDR=SYSIPT,DEVICE=2501,EOFADDR=<label>,            X
                       IOAREA1=INBUF1,IOAREA2=INBUF2,WORKA=YES
INBUF1         DS      CL80
INBUF2         DS      CL80
```

The operand DEVADDR specifies the system logical unit to be used for this file. DEVICE gives the particular device type—in this case, a model 2501 card reader. IOAREAs 1 and 2 specify two 80-byte fields which may be used by the system for input operations. For convenience, these are defined immediately after the DTF. Specifying WORKA=YES tells the system that each occurrence of the GET macro will provide a work area. The X in column 72 indicates that the DTF is continued on the next line. This must be present as the IBM assemblers are line-oriented and always assume that the end of a line is the end of the instruction unless there is a nonblank character in column 72.

<fname> represents a symbol to be used to identify the file in OPEN, CLOSE, PUT and GET macros. <label> represents a location in the program defined as

```
<label>        EQU     *
```

When reading an input record, if the system detects an End-Of-File, an automatic branch to this label occurs. This can be used to construct loops to read and process input records until the end of a file. We will consider a general pattern for such loops after we have covered the other I/O macros.

The DTF for the printer is similar to DTFCD, a typical instance is

```
Column
1         10     16                                                          72
|         |      |                                                           |
<fname>   DTFPR  DEVADDR=SYSLST,DEVICE=3203,BLKSIZE=133,CTLCHR=ASA,   X
                 IOAREA1=OUTBUF1,IOAREA2=OUTBUF2,WORKA=YES
OUTBUF1  DS      CL133
OUTBUF2  DS      CL133
```

The operand BLKSIZE specifies that we will print records containing 133 bytes each. The operand assignment CTLCHR=ASA indicates that the first character of each line will be interpreted as a printer control character. This character will not be printed, but controls printer spacing as indicated in the following table.

Character	Printer Spacing
blank	Space 1 line before printing.
0	Space 2 lines before printing.
−	Space 3 lines before printing.
+	Suppress line spacing.
1	Skip to line 1 on new page.

OS Macros for Defining Files

OS provides a single macro for defining all types of files. It is called *DCB*, for Data Control Block. As with the DOS macros, the operands used as well as their values are installation dependent.

A typical DCB for an input file is

```
Column
1         10     16                                                          72
|         |      |                                                           |
<fname>   DCB    DDNAME=SYSIN,MACRF=(GM),DSORG=PS,LRECL=80,           X
                 BLKSIZE=80,RECFM=F,EODAD=<label>
```

A typical output DCB is

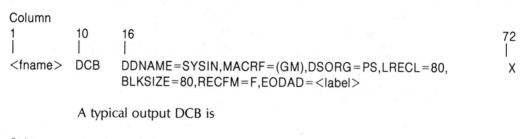

```
Column
1         10     16                                                          72
|         |      |                                                           |
<fname>   DCB    DDNAME=SYSPRINT,MACRF=(PM),DSORG=PS,LRECL=133,       X
                 BLKSIZE=133,RECFM=F
```

In both macro instructions, DDNAME identifies the file to the operating system. MACRF identifies the macros that will be used for operations on the files. DSORG designates the data set organization. LRECL and BLKSIZE designate the record length and block size, respectively. In this case, as the record length and block size are the same for both files, there will be one record per block. RECFM specifies the record format, for example, fixed (F) as opposed to variable. The EODAD value is used in the same way as the EOFADDR in the DTFCD in DOS.

Opening Files in DOS

Both input and output files are opened and closed with the OPEN and CLOSE macros, as in

        OPEN   <fname>[,<fname>. . .]

and

        CLOSE   <fname>[,<fname>. . .]

<fname> is the name on the DTF for the file being opened or closed.

Example 2.1.6

        OPEN   READER,PRINTER
        CLOSE   READER,PRINTER

Opening Files in OS

The OS macros for opening and closing files differ only in the form of the arguments. In both macros, the arguments are given in the form of a list enclosed in parentheses. The list entries for the OPEN macro are pairs consisting of a DCB name and a processing option enclosed in parentheses. The only processing options we will need are INPUT and OUTPUT.

The format for these macros is

        OPEN   (<fname>,(<option>)[,<fname>,(<option>). . .])
        CLOSE   (<fname>[,<fname>. . .])

<fname> is the name on the DCB for the file being opened or closed. We will only use the options INPUT and OUTPUT.

Example 2.1.7

        OPEN   (READER,(INPUT),PRINTER(OUTPUT))
        CLOSE   (READER)

PUT and GET Macros

For input and output operations we can use macros that are the same for both OS and DOS. They are the PUT and GET macros. They take the following forms.

> PUT   <fname>,<symbol>

and

> GET   <fname>,<symbol>

For the GET macro, the symbol identifies an 80-character field and, for the PUT macro, a 133-character field.

In order to process all the records in an input file, we need a loop of the form

```
Open File
Repeat
     Read Record
     Process Record
Until End-of-File
Close File
```

Both OS and DOS will cause an automatic branch to an address specified in the DTFCD or DCB macro when End-Of-File occurs. In our example, this address is a label which marks the end of the loop, say, UNTIL. To successfully implement the loop, we also need a mechanism to force the repeat. This can be done with an *extended mnemonic* "instruction,"

> B   <label>

Although this is not an instruction in itself, the assembler processes it by generating an unconditional branch instruction to the indicated label.

Assuming that INFILE is the symbol attached to the DTFCD and that INREC has been defined as CL80, we can now write instructions to implement the algorithm segment. We will use the DOS form of the OPEN and CLOSE macros.

```
          OPEN   INFILE          Open File
REPEAT    EQU    *               Repeat
          GET    INFILE,INREC        Read Record
          .                          Process Record
          .
          .
          B      REPEAT
UNTIL     EQU    *               Until End-of-File
          CLOSE  INFILE          Close File
```

In general, the code for processing records will extract information from subfields of the record and manipulate that information. Similarly, output must be created by moving items into subfields of a 133-character field, say LINE, and then printing LINE in one operation.

```
PUT     PRINTER,LINE
```

E X E R C I S E S

1. Suppose that before every one of the following instructions the operand field lengths and contents are as shown below. Give the value of the target field after the instruction has been executed.

   ```
   Z    : X'F0F0F0F1F4F9F5'   W: X'00000005341C'
   P1   : X'00013C'           P : X'000354219D'
   P2   : X'003C'             Q: X'000000051C'
   P3   : X'000000000C'
   OFLD: X'402020202020202020'
   SFLD: X'4020202020212020202020'
   ```

   a. PACK   P1,Z
   b. PACK   P2,Z
   c. ED   OFLD,P
   d. PACK   Q,Z
   e. ED   OFLD,Q
   f. ED   OFLD,W
   g. ED   SFLD,P3
   h. ED   OFLD,P3
   i. ED   SFLD,Q

2. Each of the following strings indicates an edit format. The digits are represented by 9's. 0 indicates the position where a leading zero should be forced. All other characters stand for themselves. Write a DC instruction for an edit mask to produce the given format.

   a. ' 99909'
   b. '9999990'
   c. '*99990'
   d. ' 999999999'

3. Write a DC instruction for an edit pattern to print the following fields. In each case, significance should be forced at the rightmost digit.

   a. PNUM   DS   PL7
   b. NUNUM   DS   PL4

4. Write the code and file definition macros to copy 80 column records from INFILE to OUTFILE until the end of INFILE is reached. Assume that these two files are as described in the sample macros given in this section.

2.2 SAMPLE PROGRAM

In this section, we consider a small but complete assembly language program. We have discussed most of the details needed to write this program. A few additional details will be covered as the need for them arises.

Suppose we have a set of input records of 80 characters each. Each record contains three five-digit numbers in the first 15 columns. We will write a program to read these records one at a time until the end of the file is reached. As each record is read, we print a line containing the three numbers and their sum.

The basic algorithm for this program is

```
Open Files
Repeat
      Read a Record
      Find the Sum
      Print the Numbers and the Sum
Until End-of-File
Close Files
```

The numbers will be read in zoned form and they must be packed before we can perform any arithmetic operations on them. After the addition has been performed, the packed sum must be converted to character form before it can be printed.

It is a good idea to edit the packed form of the input values also. We could, of course, simply print the zoned forms that were read from the input record, but editing allows us to do such things as remove leading zeros, if there are any. Later we can also use the Edit instruction to insert commas into the number being printed or to include a minus sign with negative numbers.

For each of the input values, say A, B, C, we need to define a zoned input field, a packed field, and an output field. We will call these fields ZNA, ZNB, and ZNC; PCKA, PCKB, and PCKC; and OUTA, OUTB, and OUTC. For the sum, we need a packed field and an output field, PCKSUM and OUTSUM.

With these facts in mind, we can now add additional details to our algorithm.

```
Open Files
Repeat
      Read ZNA, ZNB, ZNC
      Pack into PCKA, PCKB, PCKC
      PCKSUM = PCKA + PCKB + PCKC
      Edit PCKA, PCKB, PCKC, and PCKSUM into Output
          Line
      Print Line
Until End-of-File
Close Files
```

Before we write the assembly code needed to implement this algorithm, we need to give careful consideration to the definition of the data areas. We begin with the input records. Because we must read an entire record at once, we need a definition such as

```
INREC      DS      CL80
```

However, we also need to be able to access the first 15 columns of this record as ZNA, ZNB, and ZNC. In other words, ZNA must correspond to the first 5 bytes of INREC, ZNB must use the same memory locations as the next 5 bytes of INREC, and ZNC must overlap the third set of 5 bytes of INREC. We can achieve this by using the ORG instruction to manipulate the location counter. Recall that the instruction

```
        ORG     INREC
```

will assign the value of the symbol INREC to the location counter. The effect of this instruction is to reset the location counter to the beginning of INREC, allowing us to reallocate the memory locations that were reserved for INREC.

In order to make it easier to modify our program, we define a constant ZLEN to represent the length of the input values.

```
ZLEN       EQU     5
```

The storage definitions for the input records will be

```
INREC      DS      CL80
           ORG     INREC
ZNA        DS      ZL(ZLEN)
ZNB        DS      ZL(ZLEN)
ZNC        DS      ZL(ZLEN)
```

Because the ORG instruction resets the location counter to the value it had at the beginning of INREC, INREC and ZNA will have the same offset. They begin at the same location in memory. As ZNA is given a length of 5, the DS that defines it will cause the location counter to be incremented by 5. When ZNB is defined, the location counter will be equal to the offset for the beginning of INREC plus 5. Thus, ZNB will be the same as the second 5 bytes of INREC. These fields will overlap in memory as shown below.

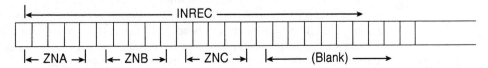

Because of the way these fields overlap, in order to read values for ZNA, ZNB, and ZNC, we only need

```
        GET     INFILE,INREC
```

In reading 80 characters into INREC, the system will simultaneously fill the three fields ZNA, ZNB, and ZNC. The instruction

```
          PACK    PCKA,ZNA
```

will indeed pack the first 5 bytes of INREC into PCKA.

The GET macro will also fill the last 65 bytes of INREC, so we need to complete the definition above. For example, if we used the following storage definitions

```
INREC        DS      CL80
             ORG     INREC
ZNA          DS      ZL(ZLEN)
ZNB          DS      ZL(ZLEN)
ZNC          DS      ZL(ZLEN)
LINE         DS      CL133
```

then the field LINE would overlap the last 65 bytes of INREC. The GET above would also change the first 65 bytes of LINE. It is unlikely that we would want this to happen, so we need to make certain that these two fields do not overlap. This can be done by advancing the location counter to the first byte after INREC with

```
          ORG     INREC+L'INREC
```

The complete definition for INREC and its subfields is

```
INREC        DS      CL80
             ORG     INREC
ZNA          DS      ZL(ZLEN)
ZNB          DS      ZL(ZLEN)
ZNC          DS      ZL(ZLEN)
             ORG     INREC+L'INREC
```

Having defined the input variables, we consider the definition of the variables to be used inside the program. The packed fields PCKA, PCKB, and PCKC must be large enough to contain the zoned numbers that will be read. If these zoned numbers consist of 5 digits, then a packed length of 3 bytes will suffice. However, we used the constant ZLEN in the definitions of the zoned fields so that we could change the input specifications easily. If the input numbers are increased to 7 digits, then PL3 will not be large enough. In order to make our program truly modifiable, the lengths of the packed numbers should be determined from the value assigned to ZLEN. A moment of reflection shows that the integer quotient ZLEN/2 represents the number of bytes needed for the digits that will be packed two to a byte. One more byte will hold the last digit and the sign. Thus

```
PLEN         EQU     ZLEN/2+1
```

gives the correct length for the three packed fields to hold the input values.

The sum may have one more digit than the input values, so it should be 1 byte longer. The storage definitions for all of the packed fields are

```
PCKA       DS      PL(PLEN)
PCKB       DS      PL(PLEN)
PCKC       DS      PL(PLEN)
PCKSUM     DS      PL(PLEN+1)
```

In addition to these internal variables, we also need edit masks to edit the values into the output fields. It is possible to define these edit masks so that they are also functions of the constant ZLEN. However, this is quite cumbersome, so we simply define the masks as constants. The net effect of this decision reduces the modifiability of the program somewhat. Nevertheless, the final program can be adjusted to accommodate different input values by changing only the definitions of ZLEN and the two edit masks.

The mask for printing the input values needs to be appropriate for a PL3 number. The mask for the total must contain a PL4 number. This gives

```
ITMSK      DC      X'402020202120'
SUMMSK     DC      X'4020202020202120'
```

Having defined the input fields and the internal variables to be used in our program, we now need only define the output area that we will use. Printing is done with the PUT macro, which requires a record of 133 characters. It is, in general, good practice to initialize the entire 133-character record with a single DC directive, as an attempt to print an uninitialized field often results in an error that terminates the program. In our case, if we want a blank for the printer control character (normal spacing), we use the following storage definition.

```
LINE       DC      CL133' '
```

This appears to put only one blank into LINE, but when a short string is used to initialize a character field, the assembler pads the string on the right with blanks. In this case, the assembler will put the single blank we give it at the left of LINE and pad it with 132 more blanks.

In order to print the numbers, we must first move them into subfields of LINE and then print the entire line. Suppose we want to print the first number in column 20, leave 5 blank spaces between the fields for the input values, and leave 10 blank spaces before the field for the sum. Because the first character in LINE, found at LINE+0, will be interpreted as a printer control character, for the remaining positions in the line, the offset LINE+i corresponds to print column i. In order to start a field in column 20, we use

```
LINE       DC      CL133' '
           ORG     LINE+20
OUTA       DS      CL(L'ITMSK)
```

In order to skip 5 columns, we add 5 to the location counter with

```
ORG     *+5
```

Observing that the length of each field should be the same as that of the corresponding edit pattern, we get the following definitions.

```
LINE        DC      CL133' '
            ORG     LINE+20
OUTA        DS      CL(L'ITMSK)
            ORG     *+5
OUTB        DS      CL(L'ITMSK)
            ORG     *+5
OUTC        DS      CL(L'ITMSK)
            ORG     *+10
OUTSUM      DS      CL(L'SUMMSK)
            ORG     LINE+L'LINE
```

The complete source code for this program is shown in Sample Program 1. Note that any line with an asterisk in column 1 is treated as a comment. This is useful for separating major sections of code and for long comments.

The source code contains some details that have not been discussed and that will be mentioned only briefly. The first of these details is the instruction

```
PRINT   NOGEN
```

This instructs the assembler to print none of the instructions generated by macro expansions. It should be included in all programs.

The next is the pair of instructions

```
BALR    RC,0
USING   *,RC
```

The first is assembled into a machine language instruction that loads the correct base value into register 12 (RC). The USING is a directive that instructs the assembler to use RC as the base register and to measure the displacements from the current value of the location counter. When we examine the object code produced for this program, we will see that the assembler supplies RC as the base register for all of the data areas and computes the correct displacement for each field.

The next pair of instructions

```
ICM     R0,B'1000',=B'00001111'
SPM     R0
```

sets the Program Mask part of the Program Status Word (PSW) so that overflows will cause the program to terminate with an error message from the operating system. The first instruction puts the bit pattern B'00001111' into the leftmost byte of R0. The second instruction uses the rightmost 4 bits of this byte as the new value for the Program Mask.

Finally, note the EOJ (End-Of-Job) macro, which is the last thing in the code section. Execution of the instruction generated by this macro terminates the program. The end of the source deck is marked by the END directive.

```
**********************************************************************************
*    SAMPLE PROGRAM 1-DOS VERSION                                               *
*                                                                               *
*    A PROGRAM TO READ 80-CHARACTER RECORDS UNTIL EOF.                          *
*    EACH RECORD CONTAINS THREE 5-DIGIT NUMBERS IN THE FIRST                    *
*    15 COLUMNS. THE PROGRAM ADDS THESE THREE NUMBERS AND                       *
*    PRINTS THEM TOGETHER WITH THEIR SUM                                        *
*                                                                               *
**********************************************************************************
          PRINT   NOGEN
SAMPLE01  START   0                   PROGRAM SAMPLE01
          BALR    RC,0                :
          USING   *,RC                :
          ICM     R0,B'1000',=B'00001111'
          SPM     R0                  :
          OPEN    INFILE,PRINTER      OPEN FILES
*
REPEAT    EQU     *                   REPEAT
          GET     INFILE,INREC            READ ZNA, ZNB, ZNC
          PACK    PCKA,ZNA                PACK INTO PCKA, PCKB, PCKC
          PACK    PCKB,ZNB                :
          PACK    PCKC,ZNC                :
          ZAP     PCKSUM,PCKA         PCKSUM = PCKA + PCKB + PCKC
          AP      PCKSUM,PCKB             :
          AP      PCKSUM,PCKC             :
          MVC     OUTA,ITMSK          EDIT PCKA, PCKB, PCKC, PCKSUM
          ED      OUTA,PCKA                   INTO LINE
          MVC     OUTB,ITMSK              :
          ED      OUTB,PCKB               :
          MVC     OUTC,ITMSK              :
          ED      OUTC,PCKC               :
          MVC     OUTSUM,SUMMSK           :
          ED      OUTSUM,PCKSUM           :
          PUT     PRINTER,LINE            PRINT LINE
          B       REPEAT                  :
UNTIL     EQU     *                   UNTIL END-OF-FILE
*
          CLOSE   INFILE,PRINTER      CLOSE FILES
          EOJ                         END SAMPLE01
```

```
********************************************************************************
*      SYMBOL DEFINITIONS                                                      *
********************************************************************************
R0          EQU    0                    SYMBOLIC NAME FOR REGISTER 0
RC          EQU    12                   SYMBOLIC NAME FOR BASE REGISTER
ZLEN        EQU    5                    LENGTH OF INPUT VALUES
PLEN        EQU    ZLEN/2+1             LENGTH OF PACKED NUMBERS
********************************************************************************
*      FILES                                                                   *
********************************************************************************
INFILE      DTFCD  DEVADDR=SYSIPT,DEVICE=2501,EOFADDR=UNTIL,                  X
                   IOAREA1=INBUF1,IOAREA2=INBUF2,WORKA=YES
INBUF1      DS     CL80
INBUF2      DS     CL80
*
PRINTER     DTFPR  DEVADDR=SYSLST,DEVICE=3203,BLKSIZE=133,CTLCHR=ASA,         X
                   IOAREA1=OUTBUF1,IOAREA2=OUTBUF2,WORKA=YES
OUTBUF1     DS     CL133
OUTBUF2     DS     CL133
********************************************************************************
*      CONSTANTS                                                               *
********************************************************************************
ITMSK       DC     X'402020202120'      MASK FOR INPUT VALUES
SUMMSK      DC     X'4020202020202120'  MASK FOR SUM
********************************************************************************
*      VARIABLES                                                               *
********************************************************************************
PCKA        DS     PL(PLEN)             PACKED FORM OF A
PCKB        DS     PL(PLEN)             PACKED FORM OF B
PCKC        DS     PL(PLEN)             PACKED FORM OF C
PCKSUM      DS     PL(PLEN+1)           PACKED SUM
********************************************************************************
*      I/O WORK AREAS                                                          *
********************************************************************************
INREC       DS     CL80                 INPUT RECORD
            ORG    INREC                   :
ZNA         DS     ZL(ZLEN)             A
ZNB         DS     ZL(ZLEN)             B
ZNC         DS     ZL(ZLEN)             C
            ORG    INREC+L'INREC        END INPUT RECORD
*
LINE        DC     CL133' '             OUTPUT LINE
            ORG    LINE+20                 :
OUTA        DS     CL(L'ITMSK)          A
            ORG    *+5                     :
OUTB        DS     CL(L'ITMSK)          B
            ORG    *+5                     :
```

```
OUTC        DS      CL(L'ITMSK)              C
            ORG     *+10                     :
OUTSUM      DS      CL(L'SUMMSK)             SUM
            ORG     LINE+L'LINE      END OUTPUT LINE
*
            END
```

The OS version of this program is shown below. Note that it is essentially the same as the DOS version above. The differences are underlined for emphasis.

```
*********************************************************************************************
*     SAMPLE PROGRAM 1-OS VERSION                                                          *
*                                                                                          *
*     A PROGRAM TO READ 80-CHARACTER RECORDS UNTIL EOF.                                    *
*     EACH RECORD CONTAINS THREE 5-DIGIT NUMBERS IN THE FIRST                              *
*        15 COLUMNS. THE PROGRAM ADDS THESE THREE NUMBERS AND                              *
*        PRINTS THEM TOGETHER WITH THEIR SUM                                               *
*                                                                                          *
*********************************************************************************************


            PRINT   NOGEN
SAMPLE01    START   0                        PROGRAM SAMPLE01
            SAVE    (14,12)                  :
            BALR    RC,0                     :
            USING   *,RC                     :
            ST      RD,SAVE+4                :
            LA      RD,SAVE                  :
            ICM     R0,B'1000',=B'00001111'  :
            SPM     R0                       :
            OPEN    (INFILE,(INPUT))         OPEN INFILE
            OPEN    (PRINTER,(OUTPUT)        OPEN PRINTER
*
REPEAT      EQU     *                        REPEAT
            GET     INFILE,INREC                 READ ZNA, ZNB, ZNC
            PACK    PCKA,ZNA                     PACK INTO PCKA, PCKB, PCKC
            PACK    PCKB,ZNB                     :
            PACK    PCKC,ZNC                     :
            ZAP     PCKSUM,PCKA              PCKSUM = PCKA + PCKB + PCKC
            AP      PCKSUM,PCKB                  :
            AP      PCKSUM,PCKC                  :
            MVC     OUTA,ITMSK               EDIT PCKA, PCKB, PCKC, PCKSUM
            ED      OUTA,PCKA                        INTO LINE
            MVC     OUTB,ITMSK                   :
            ED      OUTB,PCKB                    :
            MVC     OUTC,ITMSK                   :
            ED      OUTC,PCKC                    :
            MVC     OUTSUM,SUMMSK                :
```

```
          ED      OUTSUM,PCKSUM              :
          PUT     PRINTER,LINE                PRINT LINE
          B       REPEAT                     :
UNTIL     EQU     *                  UNTIL END-OF-FILE
*
          CLOSE   (INFILE,,PRINTER)      CLOSE FILES
          L       RD,SAVE+4              :
          RETURN (14,12)             END SAMPLE01
SAVE      DS      18F                    :
************************************************************************
*    SYMBOL DEFINITIONS                                              *
************************************************************************
R0        EQU     0                  SYMBOLIC NAME FOR REGISTER 0
RC        EQU     12                 SYMBOLIC NAME FOR BASE REGISTER
RD        EQU     13                 SYMBOLIC NAME FOR REGISTER 13
ZLEN      EQU     5                  LENGTH OF INPUT VALUES
PLEN      EQU     ZLEN/2+1           LENGTH OF PACKED NUMBERS
************************************************************************
*    FILES                                                          *
************************************************************************
INFILE    DCB     DDNAME=SYSIN,MACRF=(GM),DSORG=PS,LRECL=80,       X
                  BLKSIZE=80,RECFM=F,EODAD=UNTIL
*
PRINTER   DCB     DDNAME=SYSPRINT,MACRF=(PM),DSORG=PS,LRECL=133,   X
                  BLKSIZE=133,RECFM=F
************************************************************************
*    CONSTANTS                                                      *
************************************************************************
ITMSK     DC      X'402020202120'        MASK FOR INPUT VALUES
SUMMSK    DC      X'4020202020202120'  MASK FOR SUM
************************************************************************
*    VARIABLES                                                      *
************************************************************************
PCKA      DS      PL(PLEN)           PACKED FORM OF A
PCKB      DS      PL(PLEN)           PACKED FORM OF B
PCKC      DS      PL(PLEN)           PACKED FORM OF C
PCKSUM    DS      PL(PLEN+1)         PACKED SUM
************************************************************************
*    I/O WORK AREAS                                                 *
************************************************************************
INREC     DS      CL80                   INPUT RECORD
          ORG     INREC                  :
ZNA       DS      ZL(ZLEN)               A
ZNB       DS      ZL(ZLEN)               B
ZNC       DS      ZL(ZLEN)               C
          ORG     INREC+L'INREC      END INPUT RECORD
*
```

```
LINE       DC     CL133' '              OUTPUT LINE
           ORG    LINE+20               :
OUTA       DS     CL(L'ITMSK)           A
           ORG    *+5                   :
OUTB       DS     CL(L'ITMSK)           B
           ORG    *+5                   :
OUTC       DS     CL(L'ITMSK)           C
           ORG    *+10                  :
OUTSUM     DS     CL(L'SUMMSK)          SUM
           ORG    LINE+L'LINE           END OUTPUT LINE
*

           END
```

E   X   E   R   C   I   S   E   S

1. Write a set of definitions to describe an 80-character input record in each of the following formats.

   a. CUSTREC

Information	Columns	Type
Name	1 - 20	Character
Address	21 - 60	Character
Account Number	61 - 66	Numeric
Number of orders	67 - 69	Numeric

   b. STUREC

Information	Columns	Type
Social Security Number	1 - 9	Numeric
Last Name	10 - 24	Character
First Name	25 - 34	Character
Middle Initial	35	Character
Credit Hours	36 - 37	Numeric
Class	38 - 39	Character

   c. PAYREC

Information	Columns	Type
Account Number	1 - 12	Character
Balance	13 - 18	Numeric
Payment	19 - 24	Numeric
Date Paid	25 - 37	Character

2. Write a set of definitions to describe 133-character output line, HEADLINE, using the following format

Start Position	**Contents**
12	'NAME'
24	'ADDRESS'
75	'ACCOUNT NUMBER'
100	'ORDERS'

3. Write a set of definitions to describe a 133-character line, DETAIL, whose fields correspond to the fields in HEADLINE from the last exercise. Assume that the account number is a packed number that will be edited using NUMMSK as the edit mask and that the number of orders will be edited using ORDMSK.

4. Write the definitions for the edit masks and two 80-character fields used to create the heading and detail lines shown below. In the detail line, A is used to indicate a position in a character field. 9 and 0 are used to denote positions in numeric fields. 0 marks the position at which the first leading 0 should be printed.

   ```
   PART NUM.  DESCRIPTION                             QUANTITY  PRICE
   AAAAAA     AAAAAAAAAAAAAAAAAAAAAAAAAAAAAAAAAA  999       999
   ```

5. For each of the following descriptions of zoned fields, write definitions for a packed field to hold the packed form of the number and an edit mask to edit the packed field.

   ```
   ACCTLEN    EQU    7
   SUMLEN     EQU    8
   BALLEN     EQU    9

   a. ZACCOUNT  DS     ZL(ACCTLEN)
   b. ZSUM      DS     ZL(SUMLEN)
   c. ZBALANCE  DS     ZL(BALLEN)
   ```

2.3 ASSEMBLER LISTINGS, EXECUTION AND DUMPS

Having completed the source code for a complete assembly language program, we are now ready to assemble and test it. We will give two JCL (Job Control Language) job streams. The first will execute the assembler and produce a listing. It will not create an executable module for our program. Regardless of how much care we exercise in preparing the source file, it will almost always contain typographical errors and may often contain syntax errors, so it is pointless to attempt to produce an executable version on the first run. The second set of JCL statements creates an executable version and executes it. This job stream should be used when all assembly errors have been eliminated.

Some installations provide a mechanism by which the remainder of the job can be canceled if the assembly operation produces errors. In this case, only one job stream will be needed. The approach used here should be suitable for any DOS installation.

Assembly Job Stream

The following JCL statements show the job stream for an assembly only job.

```
// JOB <jobname>
// OPTION XREF,NODECK
// EXEC ASSEMBLY
```

Source Code

```
/*
/&
```

When this job stream is used, the assembler processes the source code and produces a listing that indicates all errors found. An example appears in Listing 2.3.1. Note that the program contains several typographical errors. The assembler flags each statement containing an error and also lists all of the errors on the last page of the listing.

Listing 2.3.1 Assembler Listing with Errors

```
                          EXTERNAL SYMBOL DICTIONARY                    PAGE    1


SYMBOL     TYPE        ID  ADDR  LENGTH LD-ID

SAMPLE01  SD (CSECT)  001 000000 000409
IJCFZIB3  ER (EXTRN)  002
IJDFAZIW  ER (EXTRN)  003
```

```
LOC   OBJECT CODE    ADDR1 ADDR2  STMT   SOURCE STATEMENT                        DOS/VSE ASSEMBLER 17.03 85-09-10

                                    1 ************************************************************************
                                    2 *     SAMPLE PROGRAM 1                                                 *
                                    3 *                                                                       *
                                    4 *     A PROGRAM TO READ 80 CHARACTER RECORDS UNTIL EOF.                 *
                                    5 *     EACH RECORD CONTAINS 3 5-DIGIT NUMBERS IN THE FIRST               *
                                    6 *     15 COLUMNS. THE PROGRAM ADDS THESE THREE NUMBERS AND              *
                                    7 *     PRINTS THEM TOGETHER WITH THEIR SUM                               *
                                    8 *                                                                       *
                                    9 ************************************************************************
                                   10         PRINT NOGEN
000000                             11 SAMPLE01 START 0              PROGRAM SAMPLE01
000000 05C0                        12         BALR  RC,0                 :
                      00002        13         USING *,RC                 :
000002 BF08 C3FE      00400        14         ICM   R0,B'1000',=B'00001111'
000006 0400                        15         SPM   R0                   :
                                   16         OPEN  INFILE,PRINTER   OPEN FILES
                                   25 *
                      0001A        26 REPEAT  EQU   *                    REPEAT
                                   27         GET   INFILE,INREC     READ ZNA, ZNB, ZNC
00002A 0000 0000 0000              33         PACK  PACKA,ZNA        PACK INTO PCKA, PCKB, PCKC
       *** ERROR ***
000030 F224 C2F9 C308 002FB 0030A  34         PACK  PCKB,ZNB             :
000036 F224 C2FC C30D 002FE 0030F  35         PACK  PCKC,ZNC             :
00003C 0000 0000 0000              36         ZAP   PCKSUM,PCKA      PCKSUM = PCKA + PCKB + PCKC
       *** ERROR ***
000042 0000 0000 0000              37         AP    PCKSUM,PCKB          :
       *** ERROR ***
000048 0000 0000 0000              38         AP    PCKSUM,PCKC          :
       *** ERROR ***
00004E D205 C367 C2E8 00369 002EA  39         MVC   OUTA,ITMSK       EDIT PCKA, PCKB, PCKC, PCKSUM
000054 DE05 C367 C2F6 00369 002F8  40         ED    OUTA,PCKA            INTO LINE
00005A D205 C372 C2E8 00374 002EA  41         MVC   OUTB,ITMSK           :
000060 DE05 C372 C2F9 00374 002FB  42         ED    OUTB,PCKB            :
                                   43         MOVC  OUTC,ITMSK           :
       *** ERROR ***
000066 DE05 C37D C2FC 0037F 002FE  44         ED    OUTC,PCKC            :
00006C D207 C38D C2EE 0038F 002F0  45         MVC   OUTSUM,SUMMSK        :
000072 0000 0000 0000              46         ED    OUTSUM,PCKSUM        :
       *** ERROR ***
                                   47         PUT   PRINTER,LINE     PRINT LINE
000088 47F0 C018      0001A        53         B     REPEAT               :
                      0008C        54 UNTIL   EQU   *                    UNTIL END-OF-FILE
                                   55 *
                                   56         CLOSE INFILE,PRINTER    CLOSE FILES
                                   65         EOJ                    END SAMPLE01
                                   68 ************************************************************************
                                   69 *     SYMBOL DEFINITIONS                                               *
                                   70 ************************************************************************
                      00000        71 R0      EQU   0        SYMBOLIC NAME FOR REGISTER 0
                      0000C        72 RC      EQU   12       SYMBOLIC NAME FOR BASE REGISTER
                      00005        73 ZLEN    EQU   5        LENGTH OF INPUT VALUES
                      00003        74 PLEN    EQU   ZLEN/2+1 LENGTH OF PACKED NYUMBERS
                                   75 ************************************************************************
                                   76 *     FILES                                                           *
                                   77 ************************************************************************
```

```
  LOC   OBJECT CODE     ADDR1 ADDR2  STMT   SOURCE STATEMENT                    DOS/VSE ASSEMBLER 17.03 85-09-10

                                      78 INFILE   DTFCD DEVADDR=SYSIPT,DEVICE=2501,EOFADDR=UNTIL,            X
                                                        IOAREA1=INBUF1,IOAREA2=INBUF2,WORKA=YES
00010A                               119 INBUF1   DS    CL80
00015A                               120 INBUF2   DS    CL80
                                     121 *
                                     122 PRINTER  DTFPR DEVADDR=SYSLST,DEVICE=3203,BLKSIZE=133,CTLCHR=ASA,   X
                                                        IOAREA1=OUTBUF1,IOAREA2=OUTBUF2,WORKA=YES
0001E0                               143 OUTBUF1  DS    CL133
000265                               144 OUTBUF2  DS    CL133
                                     145 ***********************************************************
                                     146 *    CONSTANTS                                            *
                                     147 ***********************************************************
0002EA 402020202120                 148 ITMSK    DC    X'402020202120'    MASK FOR INPUT VALUES
0002F0 4020202020202120             149 SUMMSK   DC    X'4020202020202120' MASK FOR SUM
                                     150 ***********************************************************
                                     151 *    VARIABLES                                            *
                                     152 ***********************************************************
0002F8                               153 PCKA     DS    PL(PLEN)           PACKED FORM OF A
0002FB                               154 PCKB     DS    PL(PLEN)           PACKED FORM OF B
0002FE                               155 PCKC     DS    PL(PLEN)           PACKED FORM OF C
000301                               156 PACKSUM  DS    PL(PLEN+1)         PACKED SUM
                                     157 ***********************************************************
                                     158 *    I/O WORK AREAS                                       *
                                     159 ***********************************************************
000305                               160 INREC    DS    CL80              INPUT RECORD
000355                00305          161          ORG   INREC             :
000305                               162 ZNA      DS    ZL(ZLEN)          A
00030A                               163 ZNB      DS    ZL(ZLEN)          B
00030F                               164 ZNC      DS    ZL(ZLEN)          C
000314                00355          165          ORG   INREC+L'INREC     END INPUT RECORD
                                     166 *
000355 4040404040404040             167 LINE     DC    CL133' '          OUTPUT LINE
0003DA                00369          168          ORG   LINE+20           :
000369                               169 OUTA     DS    CL(L'ITMSK)       A
00036F                00374          170          ORG   *+5               :
000374                               171 OUTB     DS    CL(L'ITMSK)       B
00037A                0037F          172          ORG   *+5               :
00037F                               173 OUTC     DS    CL(L'ITMSK)       C
000385                0038F          174          ORG   *+10              :
00038F                               175 OUTSUM   DS    CL(L'SUMMSK)      SUM
000397                003DA          176          ORG   LINE+L'LINE       END OUTPUT LINE
                                     177 *
                                     178          END
0003E0 5B5BC2D6D7C5D540             179                =C'$$BOPEN '
0003E8 5B5BC2C3D3D6E2C5             180                =C'$$BCLOSE'
0003F0 000000A0                     181                =A(INFILE)
0003F4 00000305                     182                =A(INREC)
0003F8 000001B0                     183                =A(PRINTER)
0003FC 00000355                     184                =A(LINE)
000400 0F                           185                =B'00001111'
```

CROSS-REFERENCE   PAGE   4

```
SYMBOL    LEN   ID VALUE DEFN    REFERENCES                      85-09-10

IJCU0006 00008 001 0000F8 00115  0104
IJCX0006 00008 001 0000C0 00096  0085
IJJC0004 00004 001 000090 00061
IJJ00001 00004 001 00000C 00021
IJJZ0006 00001 001 00010A 00118
IJJZ0007 00001 001 0001E0 00142
INBUF1   00080 001 00010A 00119  0096  0112
INBUF2   00080 001 00015A 00120  0093  0115
INFILE   00006 001 0000A0 00081  0022  0062  0181
INREC    00080 001 000305 00160  0161  0165  0165  0182
ITMSK    00006 001 0002EA 00148  0039  0041  0169  0171  0173
LINE     00133 001 000355 00167  0168  0176  0176  0184
OUTA     00006 001 000369 00169  0039  0040
OUTB     00006 001 000374 00171  0041  0042
OUTBUF1  00133 001 0001E0 00143  0136
OUTBUF2  00133 001 000265 00144  0141
OUTC     00006 001 00037F 00173  0044
OUTSUM   00008 001 00038F 00175  0045  0046
PACKA    ##### UNDEFINED #####   0033
PACKSUM  00004 001 000301 00156
PCKA     00003 001 0002F8 00153  0036  0040
PCKB     00003 001 0002FB 00154  0034  0037  0042
PCKC     00003 001 0002FE 00155  0035  0038  0044
PCKSUM   ##### UNDEFINED #####   0036  0037  0038  0046
PLEN     00001     000003 00074  0153  0154  0155  0156
PRINTER  00006 001 0001B0 00125  0023  0063  0183
RC       00001     00000C 00072  0012  0013
REPEAT   00001 001 00001A 00026  0053
R0       00001     000000 00071  0014  0015
SAMPLE01 00001 001 000000 00011
SUMMSK   00008 001 0002F0 00149  0045  0175
UNTIL    00001 001 00008C 00054  0095  0114
ZLEN     00001     000005 00073  0074  0162  0163  0164
ZNA      00005 001 000305 00162  0033
ZNB      00005 001 00030A 00163  0034
ZNC      00005 001 00030F 00164  0035
=A(INFILE)
         00004 001 0003F0 00181  0029
=A(INREC)
         00004 001 0003F4 00182  0030
=A(LINE) 00004 001 0003FC 00184  0050
=A(PRINTER)
         00004 001 0003F8 00183  0049
=B'00001111'
         00001 001 000400 00185  0014
=C'$$BOPEN '
         00008 001 0003E0 00179  0020
=C'$$BCLOSE'
         00008 001 0003E8 00180  0060
```

```
                    DIAGNOSTICS AND STATISTICS                              PAGE    5

      STMNT ERROR NO.  MESSAGE                                              85-09-10
        33   IPK156   SYMBOL 'PACKA' UNDEFINED
        36   IPK156   SYMBOL 'PCKSUM' UNDEFINED
        37   IPK156   SYMBOL 'PCKSUM' UNDEFINED
        38   IPK156   SYMBOL 'PCKSUM' UNDEFINED
        43   IPK097   UNDEFINED OP CODE 'MOVC', OR MACRO NOT FOUND
        46   IPK156   SYMBOL 'PCKSUM' UNDEFINED


    THE FOLLOWING MACRO NAMES HAVE BEEN FOUND IN MACRO INSTRUCTIONS
       OPEN     GET     MOVC     PUT     CLOSE     EOJ      DTFCD    DTFPR

    OPTIONS FOR THIS ASSEMBLY - ALIGN, LIST, XREF, NOLINK, NORLD, NODECK, NOEDECK

    THE ASSEMBLER WAS RUN IN 65416 BYTES
    END OF ASSEMBLY
```

In most cases, we can detect the error by examining the flagged statement. For example, see statement 33, where the problem is a misspelled identifier. The identifier PCKA has been typed as PACKA. Note that the error message for this statement on page #5 of the listing indicates the problem with the message 'PACKA' UNDEFINED. We correct the spelling of PCKA.

In statement number 43, the mnemonic MVC has been misspelled as MOVC. The assembler diagnostic for this statement describes the error as an undefined OP CODE or unfound MACRO. We change MOVC to MVC.

The statements numbered 36, 37, 38, and 46 appear to be correct and, in fact they are. In this case the error is not in the statements flagged by the assembler, but in the definition of the symbol PCKSUM. The identifier was entered incorrectly in the name field of the definition. The result is a definition for a symbol that we do not want and an undefined symbol PCKSUM. All of these errors can be eliminated by correcting the definition of PCKSUM.

Listing 2.3.2 Assembler Listing with No Errors

```
                         EXTERNAL SYMBOL DICTIONARY                         PAGE    1


    SYMBOL     TYPE        ID  ADDR  LENGTH LD-ID

    SAMPLE01  SD (CSECT)   001 000000 000401
    IJCFZIB3  ER (EXTRN)   002
    IJDFAZIW  ER (EXTRN)   003
```

```
LOC  OBJECT CODE    ADDR1 ADDR2 STMT  SOURCE STATEMENT                           DOS/VSE ASSEMBLER 15.02 85-09-11

                                 1 ***********************************************************************
                                 2 *    SAMPLE PROGRAM 1                                                  *
                                 3 *                                                                      *
                                 4 *    A PROGRAM TO READ 80 CHARACTER RECORDS UNTIL EOF.                 *
                                 5 *    EACH RECORD CONTAINS 3 5-DIGIT NUMBERS IN THE FIRST               *
                                 6 *    15 COLUMNS. THE PROGRAM ADDS THESE THREE NUMBERS AND              *
                                 7 *    PRINTS THEM TOGETHER WITH THEIR SUM                               *
                                 8 *                                                                      *
                                 9 ***********************************************************************
                                10          PRINT NOGEN
000000                          11 SAMPLE01 START 0                   PROGRAM SAMPLE01
000000 05C0                     12          BALR RC,0                 :
                    00002       13          USING *,RC                :
000002 BF08 C406    00408       14          ICM  R0,B'1000',=B'00001111'
000006 0400                     15          SPM  R0                   :
                                16          OPEN INFILE,PRINTER       OPEN FILES
                                25 *
                    0001A       26 REPEAT   EQU  *                    REPEAT
                                27          GET  INFILE,INREC            READ ZNA, ZNB, ZNC
00002A F224 C2FE C30B 00300 0030D 33      PACK PCKA,ZNA               PACK INTO PCKA, PCKB, PCKC
000030 F224 C301 C310 00303 00312 34      PACK PCKB,ZNB              :
000036 F224 C304 C315 00306 00317 35      PACK PCKC,ZNC              :
00003C F832 C307 C2FE 00309 00300 36      ZAP  PCKSUM,PCKA           PCKSUM = PCKA + PCKB + PCKC
000042 FA32 C307 C301 00309 00303 37      AP   PCKSUM,PCKB           :
000048 FA32 C307 C304 00309 00306 38      AP   PCKSUM,PCKC           :
00004E D205 C36F C2F0 00371 002F2 39      MVC  OUTA,ITMSK            EDIT PCKA, PCKB, PCKC, PCKSUM
000054 DE05 C36F C2FE 00371 00300 40      ED   OUTA,PCKA                INTO LINE
00005A D205 C37A C2F0 0037C 002F2 41      MVC  OUTB,ITMSK            :
000060 DE05 C37A C301 0037C 00303 42      ED   OUTB,PCKB             :
000066 D205 C385 C2F0 00387 002F2 43      MVC  OUTC,ITMSK            :
00006C DE05 C385 C304 00387 00306 44      ED   OUTC,PCKC             :
000072 D207 C395 C2F6 00397 002F8 45      MVC  OUTSUM,SUMMSK         :
000078 DE07 C395 C307 00397 00309 46      ED   OUTSUM,PCKSUM         :
                                47          PUT  PRINTER,LINE         PRINT LINE
00008E 47F0 C018    0001A       53          B    REPEAT
                    00092       54 UNTIL    EQU  *                    UNTIL END-OF-FILE
                                55 *
                                56          CLOSE INFILE,PRINTER      CLOSE FILES
                                65          EOJ                       END SAMPLE01
                                68 ***********************************************************************
                                69 *    SYMBOL DEFINITIONS                                               *
                                70 ***********************************************************************
                    00000       71 R0       EQU  0                    SYMBOLIC NAME FOR REGISTER 0
                    0000C       72 RC       EQU  12                   SYMBOLIC NAME FOR BASE REGISTER
                    00005       73 ZLEN     EQU  5                    LENGTH OF INPUT VALUES
                    00003       74 PLEN     EQU  ZLEN/2+1             LENGTH OF PACKED NYUMBERS
                                75 ***********************************************************************
                                76 *    FILES                                                            *
                                77 ***********************************************************************
                                78 INFILE   DTFCD DEVADDR=SYSIPT,DEVICE=2501,EOFADDR=UNTIL,             X
                                             IOAREA1=INBUF1,IOAREA2=INBUF2,WORKA=YES
000112                          119 INBUF1  DS   CL80
000162                          120 INBUF2  DS   CL80
                                121 *
                                122 PRINTER DTFPR DEVADDR=SYSLST,DEVICE=3203,BLKSIZE=133,CTLCHR=ASA,    X
```

```
LOC  OBJECT CODE    ADDR1 ADDR2  STMT  SOURCE STATEMENT                        DOS/VSE ASSEMBLER 15.02 85-09-11

                                            IOAREA1=OUTBUF1,IOAREA2=OUTBUF2,WORKA=YES
0001E8                          143 OUTBUF1  DS    CL133
00026D                          144 OUTBUF2  DS    CL133
                                145 ***********************************************************
                                146 *    CONSTANTS                                            *
                                147 ***********************************************************
0002F2 402020202120            148 ITMSK    DC    X'402020202120'    MASK FOR INPUT VALUES
0002F8 4020202020202120        149 SUMMSK   DC    X'4020202020202120' MASK FOR SUM
                                150 ***********************************************************
                                151 *    VARIABLES                                            *
                                152 ***********************************************************
000300                          153 PCKA     DS    PL(PLEN)           PACKED FORM OF A
000303                          154 PCKB     DS    PL(PLEN)           PACKED FORM OF B
000306                          155 PCKC     DS    PL(PLEN)           PACKED FORM OF C
000309                          156 PCKSUM   DS    PL(PLEN+1)         PACKED SUM
                                157 ***********************************************************
                                158 *    I/O WORK AREAS                                       *
                                159 ***********************************************************
00030D                          160 INREC    DS    CL80               INPUT RECORD
00035D            0030D         161          ORG   INREC              :
00030D                          162 ZNA      DS    ZL(ZLEN)           A
000312                          163 ZNB      DS    ZL(ZLEN)           B
000317                          164 ZNC      DS    ZL(ZLEN)           C
00031C            0035D         165          ORG   INREC+L'INREC      END INPUT RECORD
                                166 *
00035D 4040404040404040        167 LINE     DC    CL133' '           OUTPUT LINE
0003E2            00371         168          ORG   LINE+20            :
000371                          169 OUTA     DS    CL(L'ITMSK)        A
000377            0037C         170          ORG   *+5                :
00037C                          171 OUTB     DS    CL(L'ITMSK)        B
000382            00387         172          ORG   *+5                :
000387                          173 OUTC     DS    CL(L'ITMSK)        C
00038D            00397         174          ORG   *+10               :
000397                          175 OUTSUM   DS    CL(L'SUMMSK)       SUM
00039F            003E2         176          ORG   LINE+L'LINE        END OUTPUT LINE
                                177 *
                                178          END
0003E8 5B5BC2D6D7C5D540        179               =C'$$BOPEN '
0003F0 5B5BC2C3D3D6E2C5        180               =C'$$BCLOSE'
0003F8 000000A8                181               =A(INFILE)
0003FC 0000030D                182               =A(INREC)
000400 000001B8                183               =A(PRINTER)
000404 0000035D                184               =A(LINE)
000408 0F                      185               =B'00001111'
```

CROSS-REFERENCE   PAGE   4

SYMBOL	LEN	ID	VALUE	DEFN	REFERENCES					85-09-11
IJCU0006	00008	001	000100	00115	0104					
IJCX0006	00008	001	0000C8	00096	0085					
IJJC0004	00004	001	000098	00061						
IJJ00001	00004	001	00000C	00021						
IJJZ0006	00001	001	000112	00118						
IJJZ0007	00001	001	0001E8	00142						
INBUF1	00080	001	000112	00119	0096	0112				
INBUF2	00080	001	000162	00120	0093	0115				
INFILE	00006	001	0000A8	00081	0022	0062	0181			
INREC	00080	001	00030D	00160	0161	0165	0165	0182		
ITMSK	00006	001	0002F2	00148	0039	0041	0043	0169	0171	0173
LINE	00133	001	00035D	00167	0168	0176	0176	0184		
OUTA	00006	001	000371	00169	0039	0040				
OUTB	00006	001	00037C	00171	0041	0042				
OUTBUF1	00133	001	0001E8	00143	0136					
OUTBUF2	00133	001	00026D	00144	0141					
OUTC	00006	001	000387	00173	0043	0044				
OUTSUM	00008	001	000397	00175	0045	0046				
PCKA	00003	001	000300	00153	0033	0036	0040			
PCKB	00003	001	000303	00154	0034	0037	0042			
PCKC	00003	001	000306	00155	0035	0038	0044			
PCKSUM	00004	001	000309	00156	0036	0037	0038	0046		
PLEN	00001		000003	00074	0153	0154	0155	0156		
PRINTER	00006	001	0001B8	00125	0023	0063	0183			
RC	00001		00000C	00072	0012	0013				
REPEAT	00001	001	00001A	00026	0053					
R0	00001		000000	00071	0014	0015				
SAMPLE01	00001	001	000000	00011						
SUMMSK	00008	001	0002F8	00149	0045	0175				
UNTIL	00001	001	000092	00054	0095	0114				
ZLEN	00001		000005	00073	0074	0162	0163	0164		
ZNA	00005	001	00030D	00162	0033					
ZNB	00005	001	000312	00163	0034					
ZNC	00005	001	000317	00164	0035					
=A(INFILE)										
	00004	001	0003F8	00181	0029					
=A(INREC)										
	00004	001	0003FC	00182	0030					
=A(LINE)	00004	001	000404	00184	0050					
=A(PRINTER)										
	00004	001	000400	00183	0049					
=B'00001111'										
	00001	001	000408	00185	0014					
=C'$$BOPEN '										
	00008	001	0003E8	00179	0020					
=C'$$BCLOSE'										
	00008	001	0003F0	00180	0060					

DIAGNOSTICS AND STATISTICS

85-09-11

NO ERRORS FOUND

THE FOLLOWING MACRO NAMES HAVE BEEN FOUND IN MACRO INSTRUCTIONS
   OPEN   GET   PUT   CLOSE   EOJ   DTFCD   DTFPR

OPTIONS FOR THIS ASSEMBLY - ALIGN, LIST, XREF, LINK, NORLD, NODECK, NOEDECK

THE ASSEMBLER WAS RUN IN 65416 BYTES
END OF ASSEMBLY

Listing 2.3.2 shows the output of the assembler when no errors have been detected. We will examine this listing in detail. The first column of each page in the main program listing is headed LOC. It gives the value of the location counter before the corresponding statement is processed. The column labelled OBJECT CODE contains the hexadecimal form of each machine language instruction or the hexadecimal form of initialization values provided for data areas. The columns labelled ADDR1 and ADDR2 contain the offset corresponding to the fields in the the offset corresponding to the fields in the instructions or the value assigned to a symbol defined with an EQU. The column labelled STMT contains numbers assigned by the assembler to each statement processed. Note that these numbers are not the same as the numbers of the statements in the source file.

Each offset value given in the address column corresponds to the value found in the LOC column at the point where the symbol is defined. For example, in statement number 33, the first operand is PCKA. The value in ADDR1 is X'00300'. Checking statement number 153, we see that this is indeed the value of the location counter when PCKA is defined. When we examine the cross-reference listing, we will also see that this is listed as the VALUE of PCKA.

Examining the listing line by line, observe that the comment lines, those beginning with an asterisk in column one, contain no entries in the columns at the left. These lines do not affect the location counter and create no object code.

The value listed for the location counter is still zero at the beginning of statement 12. Up to this point, no object code has been produced. The BALR instruction is the first statement that is assembled into a machine language instruction. The hexadecimal form of the machine instruction is given in the OBJECT CODE column. X'05' is the opcode for BALR and X'C0' encodes register RC and register R0. Executing this instruction puts the address of the next machine language instruction into register C.

When the BALR instruction is assembled, the location counter is incremented by 2, the number of bytes in the instruction. Because the next statement, the USING directive, is not a machine instruction, there is no entry in the LOC column. However, as the directive refers to the current value of the location counter, this value does appear in ADDR2 column. There we see that it really is 2.

The USING directive instructs the assembler to measure all displacements from the current value of the location counter and to use RC as the base register for this CSECT. Because the location counter will not be changed before the next machine language instruction is assembled, the displacements used will represent the distance from the address in RC to the referenced field. That is, during execution, RC will contain the address of the first instruction generated by the OPEN macro. This instruction will be 2 bytes into the CSECT. The displacement used by the assembler for each field will be measured from the second byte of the CSECT. The sum of the address in RC and the displacement will yield the address of the appropriate field.

Continuing our examination of the statements in the listing, note that statement number 16 is a macro instruction. As we specified PRINT NOGEN, the assembler does not list the statements produced by the macro. The assembler does, however, assign numbers to each of these statements and by examining the next statement number shown, we see that this macro generated nine statements. From the value of the location counter listed in the ADDR2 column on the next line, we see that the machine language form of these instructions uses X'12' or 18 bytes.

Statement number 26 uses EQU to define a label. The effect of this instruction is to assign the value of the location counter, X'1A', to the symbol REPEAT. This does not change the location counter, so the first instruction generated by the GET macro will be at offset X'1A' in the CSECT. When a branch to REPEAT is executed, the next instruction executed will always be the first instruction in the GET macro expansion.

Statements 27 through 47 constitute the range of the loop. Of these, 33 through 46 are translated directly into machine language instructions, with the object code for each listed on the left. As these are all SS instructions, the object code for each is 6 bytes long. Note that the value of the location counter is increased by 6 bytes on each line.

The machine language form of the instruction in line 33 is

$$\text{F224 C2FE C30B}$$

X'F2' is the operation code for the PACK instruction. The next byte encodes the two lengths as X'24'. The assembler stores the number of bytes beyond the first byte, so the values 2 and 4 in the length byte actually represent field lengths of 3 and 5. These are the correct lengths for the operands PCKA and ZNA. The next pair of bytes contains the operand in base-displacement form. The base register for both is register RC. For PCKA, the next three hex-digits, X'2FE', give the offset from the instruction whose address will be in RC to the field PCKA. As this instruction is 2 bytes into the CSECT, the value is 2 less than the distance from the beginning of the CSECT to PCKA. It is this second number that is referred to as the VALUE of the symbol PCKA. This is the value that is given in the column ADDR1. The same relationship holds for the field ZNA. The "value" of ZNA is X'30D'. This is the value of the location counter when ZNA is defined. The displacement inserted in the instruction is 2 less than this value, X'30B'.

This relationship holds for all the fields in instructions 33 through 46. The assembly time value of each symbol is the distance from the beginning of the CSECT to the symbol. The displacement inserted in the machine instruction is the distance for the second byte of the CSECT to the field. Thus, these values always differ by 2.

The PACK instruction is a two-length SS instruction as are the instructions in 34 through 38. Statement 39 contains a one-length SS instruction, MVC. The machine format of this instruction is

$$\text{D205 C37A C301}$$

In this case, the opcode is X'D2'. The second byte, X'05', contains a single length. The assembler obtained this length from the definition of the first field but it happens to be the same for both fields. When executed, the instruction will move 6 bytes.

In the section labelled CONSTANTS, the hexadecimal values assigned to each field with the DC statement are reproduced in the OBJECT CODE columns. Also, the location counter has been incremented by the number of bytes in each constant.

The section labelled VARIABLES shows no initialization values in the OBJECT CODE column, as these fields are defined with the DS directive. The effect of each of these statements is to increment the location counter and to enter the identifier in the symbol table with the appropriate offset and length.

The definitions of the I/O work areas show the effect of the ORG directive on the location counter. Consider, in particular, the definition of LINE that begins in statement 167. The value of the location counter at this point is X'35D'. Although the assembler lists only the first eight bytes used to initialize LINE, the next value of the location counter, X'3E2', shows that it has been incremented by X'85' = 133 bytes. The instruction ORG LINE+20 resets the location counter to the offset for the beginning of LINE, X'35D', plus 20 = X'14'. The next value shown for the location counter in statement 169 is the resulting sum, X'35D' + X'14' = X'371'. The definition for OUTA places it in column 20 of the part of LINE that will be printed. It also assures that OUTA will be the same size as the edit pattern, ITMSK, even if we later decide to alter the pattern.

In statements 170 and 172, the instruction

```
ORG     *+5
```

adds 5 to the current value of the location counter. In terms of the output line, this means that, regardless of the length or starting point of OUTA, there will be 5 blank spaces between the fields OUTA, OUTB, and OUTC. We can change the length of any of these fields without having to readjust the number of spaces between the fields. In the same way, statement 174 places 10 blank spaces between OUTC and the field OUTSUM.

Looking back at the values of the location counter, we see from the LOC entry in statements 167 and 168 that LINE extends from offset X'35D' up to X'3E2'. Checking the offsets for OUTA, OUTB, OUTC, and OUTSUM, we see that they are all within this range and these fields are therefore subfields of LINE. The fields we skipped over by advancing the location counter have already been initialized to blanks by the definition of LINE itself. Were this not the case, these fields would have contained unknown values and would probably generate error conditions when printed.

The next page of the assembler listing contains the cross-reference listing. We find there all of the symbols defined by our program together with some that are defined by the assembler. Note that the values listed in the column labelled LEN are in decimal. In the case of symbols that represent data areas in our program, the values in the LEN column are the defined lengths of the data areas. The VALUE column gives the hexadecimal offset from the beginning of the program to each field. This is the same as the value found in the LOC column when the symbol was defined. The rightmost columns contain statement numbers. The DEFN column gives the number of the statement in which the symbol was defined and the REFERENCES column lists all statements that refer to each symbol.

The last page of the assembler listing contains a summary of the assembly process including a list of all the errors that occurred and a diagnostic error message for each.

When all assembly errors have been eliminated, we can attempt execution of our program with the following job stream.

```
// JOB <jobname>
// OPTION LINK,PARTDUMP,XREF
   ACTION MAP
// EXEC ASSEMBLY
```

> Source Code

```
/*
// EXEC LNKEDT
// EXEC
```

> Data Records

```
/*
/&
```

Suppose, now that we run our program with the following set of data records.

$$003590027600835$$
$$359 \quad 276 \quad 835$$
$$25836 \quad 526 \quad 782$$

The output begins with an assembler listing identical to the one above. This is followed by output from the linker and the results of executing our program. Listing 2.3.3 contains a link-edit map. The map is included in the output as a result of specifying ACTION MAP in the JCL. The format of this map will depend upon the particular linker that is used, but a typical link-edit map is shown.

Listing 2.3.3 *A Typical Link-Edit Map with Partial Output*

```
09/11/85 PHASE-CSECT-ENTRY  LO-LNK HI-LNK  LO-REL HI-REL  LN-HEX   LN-DEC   XF-LNK XF-REL  G O A L   S Y S T E M S

                    BG      200000 2E0FFF  000000 0E0FFF  E1000    921,600  200078 000078  GETVIS = 3,912K

                    F6      6B3000 6DDFFF  000000 02AFFF  2B000    176,128  6B3078 000078  GETVIS = 128K

                    F5      6FE000 77AFFF  000000 07CFFF  7D000    512,000  6FE078 000078  GETVIS = 252K

                    F4      7BA000 836FFF  000000 07CFFF  7D000    512,000  7BA078 000078  GETVIS = 252K

                    F3      876000 8F2FFF  000000 07CFFF  7D000    512,000  876078 000078  GETVIS = 252K

      LINK PARTITION = F2   932000 9AEFFF  000000 07CFFF  7D000    512,000  932078 000078  GETVIS = 252K

                    F1      9EE000 A61FFF  000000 073FFF  74000    475,136  9EE078 000078  GETVIS = 48K

PHASE    PHASE***           932078 9326D9  000078 0006D9  662      1,634    932078 000078  RELOCATABLE
         SAMPLE01           932078 932480  000078 000480  409      1,033
         IJCFZIB3           932488 9325F6  000488 0005F6  16F      367
         IJDFAZIW           9325F8 9326D9  0005F8 0006D9  E2       226

   NORMAL COMPLETION, LIB BLOCKS USED =    2.


 S T A T U S   R E P O R T            DATE: 09/11/85 (MM/DD/YY)   TIME: 15.02 (HH.MM)        DECIMAL NUMBERS
```

LIBRARIES ON COUNT KEY DATA (CKD) DEVICES:	STARTING ADDRESS C H R	NEXT ENTRY C H R E	LAST ENTRY C H R E	DIRECTORY ENTRIES ACTIVE	LIBRARY BLOCKS ALLOCTD ACTIVE DELETED AVAIL	PERCENT DIR.TRACKS FULL & LIBRARY CYLINDERS

```
F2TOLIB LIB092 X'1DF' 555555 3340-70
CORE IMAGE  DIRECTORY  081 00 01   081 00 02   081 00 16     1                                    6        1
LINK        DIRECTORY  081 01 01               081 01 16                                                   1
            LIBRARY    081 02 01   081 03 06   082 11 07              154    12     0    142       7        2
                       359     276          835              1470
                       359     276          835              1470
```

```
JOB  1CFJLS   09/11/85  15.02.48  F-LE-E  FAST-LINKAGE-EDITOR     FLEE/XP V8.37   VSE3   G O A L   S Y S T E M S

ACTION TAKEN  MAP CLEAR REL STAMP LINK RELA=P LBLTYP=0 BYTES

THE FOLLOWING LIBRARIES ARE ACTIVE FOR THIS RUN
LIBR.TYPE   SEQ.NO  FILENAME   VOLID   CUU  SYSNNN  CYL/BLK  DASD

  OBJECT CIL    0     F2TOLIB  555555  1DF  LIB092    081    3340

  SEARCH RLB    1     PRDRLA   VSERES  160  LIB091    057    3380
  SEARCH RLB    2     PRDRLC   VSEWK1  161  LIB090    017    3380
  SEARCH RLB    3     INSTRLB  555555  1DF  LIB089    099    3340
  SEARCH RLB    4     BRNDXRL  VSEWK1  161  LIB088    168    3380
                                                                        LIBRARY   VER.MOD
LIST   AUTOLINK   IJCFZIB3                                               INSTRLB   35.1
LIST   AUTOLINK   IJDFAZIW                                               INSTRLB   35.1
LIST   ENTRY


        * FLEE MAINTENANCE SUMMARY LOG OF INCLUDED MEMBERS *

                TIMES ........LAST.MAINTENANCE......   ........PREV.MAINTENANCE......   ..LAST.CATAL/CREATE..
MEMBER   LIB    CATAL TYPE   DAY   DATE     TIME    TYPE    DAY   DATE     TIME    DAY   DATE     TIME

IJCFZIB3 INSTRLB   2  COPYR  WED 10/24/84 13.59.13  COPYR  WED 09/19/84 10.33.30  WED 09/19/84 10.33.30
IJDFAZIW INSTRLB   2  COPYR  WED 10/24/84 13.59.13  COPYR  WED 09/19/84 10.33.31  WED 09/19/84 10.33.31
```

This listing contains a lot of information that is of no interest to us at this point. The relevant part of the listing is

```
PHASE      PHASE***          932078  9326D9
           SAMPLE01          932078  932480
           IJCFZIB3          932488  9325F6
           IJDFAZIW          9325F8  9326D9
```

The output produced by the assembler has been linked with routines provided by the operating system to handle I/O. The unpronounceable names of these routines are shown above. The hexadecimal values give the starting and ending addresses of the entire program and of each component. In particular, note that the part of the program created from our source file begins at X'932078' and ends at X'932480'. These addresses are an important aid in debugging when errors occur during execution.

After printing several earlier pages with one or two lines, the system has suddenly become cost-conscious and the output appears on the same page as the link-edit map, Listing 2.3.3. We can fix this with a printer control character in the first line we print.

In the first line of output, we see the advantage of packing and then editing the input values. The leading zeros have been eliminated. One can easily verify that the program has produced the correct result. 1470 is the sum of the input values.

The next output line illustrates that the leading zeros in the input fields are not necessary. The EBCDIC code for a blank is X'40'. As we observed earlier, when this is packed and the 4 eliminated, it is equivalent to the leading 0 with EBCDIC code X'F0'.

The third output line is not seen. The next page of output, shown in Listing 2.3.4, indicates that an error occurred. The error message indicates the error type, a Data exception, but it does not indicate which line in our source code caused the error. Instead, it gives the address of the instruction that was being executed at the time of the error.

Listing 2.3.4 Page Containing Error Message

```
OSO3I PROGRAM CHECK INTERRUPTION - HEX LOCATION 9320BA - CONDITION CODE 2 - DATA EXCEPTION
OSO0I JOB 1CFJLS  CANCELED
OSO7I PROBLEM PROGRAM PSW    076D2F00009320C0
```

The address of the instruction that was being executed when the error occurred is the HEX LOCATION given in Listing 2.3.4, X'9320BA'. By comparing this value with the starting and ending addresses for SAMPLE01 in the link-edit map above, we see that this address is near the beginning of SAMPLE01. In order to translate this offset into an instruction reference, we subtract the starting address of SAMPLE01 from the error offset.

$$\begin{array}{r} \text{X'9320BA'} \\ -\text{X'932078'} \\ \hline \text{X'42'} \end{array}$$

The error occurred at offset X'42' in our program. This is the offset of the instruction that was being executed when the error occurred. Looking back at the location counter values in Listing 2.3.2, we find that the corresponding instruction is the AP in statement 37.

> AP   PCKSUM,PCKB

One of the two fields in this instruction evidently contains an invalid form. The first field, PCKSUM, was assigned a value by the preceding ZAP instruction. If there had been anything wrong with this number, the error would have occurred when the assignment was made. The problem must be the number in PCKB. Notice that the value in this field was placed there by the PACK instruction in statement 34. Unfortunately, the PACK instruction does not check to make sure that the result it produces is a valid packed number.

At this point, we know that the number in PCKB is invalid. This must have resulted from an invalid zoned number in ZNB. In order to verify these assertions, we need to locate these two fields in the hexadecimal dump, which is included with the output.

Reading Dumps

Because we specified the option PARTDUMP, whenever an execution error occurs, DOS will produce a hexadecimal dump of the part of memory occupied by our program. In DOS and in OS, we can request dumps of part of memory at any time during execution. The dump that accompanied the error above is shown in Listing 2.3.5.

Listing 2.3.5 Memory Dump

```
1CFJLS                        09/11/85  15.02.53   CPUID=FF01136043810000                        PAGE    1


ENDING TASK REGISTERS

GR 0-F   00932385 00932120 009AEFFF 00000048   009AEFFF 00000000 00000000 009320E0
         40A73002 D7C8C1E2 00000000 009AEFFF   4093207A 009AF800 BF9320A2 00932488


FP REG   411B7E15 1628AED2 5E945BE2 1628AED2   80000000 80000000 80000000 80000000
CR 0-F   81400C61 0B031980 FFFFFFFF 00000000   00000000 00000000 00000000 00000000
         00000000 00000000 00000000 00000000   00000000 00000000 8F000000 00000200


COMREG   F2 ADDR IS 002210
002210   F0F961F1 F161F8F5 00000000 00000000   00000000 00000000 F1C3C6D1 D3E24040
002230   009AEFFF 009326D9 009326D9 00000060   00BFFFFF FF5F4483 20A04CC0 00000000
002250   17580000 00000000 10381040 157A3CF0   F9F1F1F8 F5F2F5F4 00000FA8 0000FED4
002270   28500000 00000000 00000060 00000060   00005061 000052F0 00000AD0 0F280000
002290   00000000 035011E1 00000000 40600F40   40404040 40404000 40404040 40404000
0022B0   009F1940 C0000000 00BC8FA4 2A040000   00000000 00000000 00033DF4 000F0006
0022D0   09000018 00000000


SYSCOM   ADDRESS IS 000418
000418   00008BEC 00000F00 000090AE 000017C8   00000000 00000000 00000000 00002F50
000438   00036000 06007020 00BB0034 0007E807   00000000 83009C5C 00000000 00000000
000458   C0000CF9 00000000 00000000 0000549C   00000000 00000000 00000023 009EE000
000478   00005FF0 00006028 00000000 00009B98   00000558 00A7C2C8 00001F4A 000009CB
000498   00000000 00000000 00008EC0 00008890   00008E28 00003708 00000000 00000000
0004B8   00000000 00000000 00000000 00000000   00008980 00000000 00000000 00000060
0004D8   00000000 00000000 00000000 07F10006   00031980 00000000 00000000 00008990
0004F8   00000000 001F00D0 00000000 00BFFFFF   000053E0 E4A6E000 00BB8000 00BCCBD0
000518   8000D454 00004F1E 020047B0 00BF0000   00B3F608 00A71000 00000000 00005F88
000538   00000000 0000BA28 00027208 00BB9028


PUBTAB   ADDRESS IS 001758
001758   000CFF00 120000F8 000DFF00 230000F8   001F0F00 B00080F8 004CFF00 100000F8
001778   004DFF00 220000F8 005DFF00 230000F8   000EFF00 400000F8 008EFF00 400000F8
001798   009EFF00 400000F8 01C0FF00 6AFF0000   01C1FF00 6AFF0000 01C2FF00 6AFF0000
0017B8   01C3FF00 6AFF0000 01DFFF00 6AFF00F8   0160FF00 6CFF00FC 0161FF00 6CFF00FC
0017D8   0162FF00 6CFF0004 0163FF00 6CFF0004   01640600 6CFF80FC 0165FF00 6CFF00FC
0017F8   0166FF00 6CFF00FC 0167FF00 6CFF0004   0168FF00 6CFF0004 0380FF00 53D300D0
001818   0381FF00 53D300D0 051EFF00 430000F8   FF000000 00000000 FF000000 00000000
001838   FF000000 00000000 FF000000 00000000   FF000000 00000000 FF000000 00000000
001858   FF000000 00000000 FF000000 00000000   FF000000 00000000 FF000000 00000000
001878   FF000000 00000000 FF000000 00000000   FF000000 00000000 FF000000 00000000
001898   FF000000 00000000 FF000000 00000000   FF000000 00000000 FF000000 00000000
0018B8   FF000000 00000000 FF000000 00000000   FF000000 00000000 FF000000 00000000
0018D8   FF000000 00000000 FF000000 00000000   FF000000 00000000 FF000000 00000000
0018F8   FF000000 00000000 FF000000 00000000   FF000000 00000000 FF000000 00000000
001918   FF000000 00000000 FF000000 00000000   FF000000 00000000 FF000000 00000000
001938   FF000000 00000000 FF000000 00000000   FF000000 00000000 FF000000 00000000
001958   FF000000 00000000 FF000000 00000000   FF000000 00000000 FF000000 00000000
001978   FF000000 00000000 FF000000 00000000   FF000000 00000000 FF000000 00000000
001998   FF000000 00000000 FF000000 00000000   FF000000 00000000 FF000000 00000000
0019B8   FF000000 00000000 FF000000 00000000   FF000000 00000000 FF000000 00000000
0019D8   FF000000 00000000 FF000000 00000000   FF000000 00000000 FF000000 00000000
0019F8   FF000000 00000000 FF000000 00000000   FF000000 00000000 FF000000 00000000
001A18   FF000000 00000000 FF000000 00000000   FF000000 00000000 FF000000 00000000
001A38   FF000000 00000000 FF000000 00000000   FF000000 00000000 FF000000 00000000
001A58   FF000000 00000000 FF000000 00000000   FF000000 00000000 FF000000 00000000
001A78   FF000000 00000000 FF000000 00000000   FF000000 00000000 FF000000 00000000
```

```
001A98  FF000000 00000000 FF000000 00000000    FF000000 00000000 FF000000 00000000
001AB8  FF000000 00000000 FF000000 00000000    FF000000 00000000 FF000000 00000000
001AD8  FF000000 00000000 FF000000 00000000    FF000000 00000000 FF000000 00000000
001AF8  FF000000 00000000 FF000000 00000000    FF000000 00000000 FF000000 00000000
001B18  FF000000 00000000 FF000000 00000000    FF000000 00000000 FF000000 00000000
001B38  FF000000 00000000 FF000000 00000000    FF000000 00000000 FF000000 00000000
001B58  FF000000 00000000 FF000000 00000000    FF000000 00000000 FF000000 00000000
001B78  FF000000 00000000 FF000000 00000000    FF000000 00000000 FF000000 00000000
001B98  FF000000 00000000 FF000000 00000000    FF000000 00000000 FF000000 00000000
001BB8  FF000000 00000000 FF000000 00000000    FF000000 00000000 FF000000 00000000
001BD8  FF000000 00000000 FF000000 00000000    FF000000 00000000 FF000000 00000000
001BF8  FF000000 00000000 FF000000 00000000    FF000000 00000000 FF000000 00000000
001C18  FF000000 00000000 FF000000 00000000    FF000000 00000000 FF000000 00000000
001C38  FF000000 00000000 FF000000 00000000    FF000000 00000000 FF000000 00000000
001C58  FF000000 00000000 FF000000 00000000    FF000000 00000000 FF000000 00000000
001C78  FF000000 00000000 FF000000 00000000    FF000000 00000000 FF000000 00000000
001C98  FF000000 00000000 FF000000 00000000    FF000000 00000000 FF000000 00000000
001CB8  FF000000 00000000 FF000000 00000000    FF000000 00000000 FF000000 00000000
001CD8  FF000000 00000000 FF000000 00000000    FF000000 00000000 FF000000 00000000
001CF8  FF000000 00000000 FF000000 00000000    FF000000 00000000 FF000000 00000000
001D18  FF000000 00000000 FF000000 00000000    FF000000 00000000 FF000000 00000000
001D38  FF000000 00000000 FF000000 00000000    FF000000 00000000 FF000000 00000000
001D58  FF000000 00000000 FF000000 00000000    FF000000 00000000 FF000000 00000000
001D78  FF000000 00000000 FF000000 00000000    FF000000 00000000 FF000000 00000000
001D98  FF000000 00000000 FF000000 00000000    FF000000 00000000 FF000000 00000000
001DB8  FF000000 00000000 FF000000 00000000    FF000000 00000000 FF000000 00000000
001DD8  FF000000 00000000 FF000000 00000000    FF000000 00000000 FF000000 00000000
001DF8  FF000000 00000000 FF000000 00000000    FF000000 00000000 FF000000 00000000
001E18  FF000000 00000000 FF000000 00000000    FF000000 00000000 FF000000 00000000
001E38  FF000000 00000000 FF000000 00000000    FF000000 00000000 FF000000 00000000
001E58  FF000000 00000000 FF000000 00000000    FF000000 00000000 FF000000 00000000
001E78  FF000000 00000000 FF000000 00000000    FF000000 00000000 FF000000 00000000
001E98  FF000000 00000000 FF000000 00000000    FF000000 00000000 FF000000 00000000
001EB8  FF000000 00000000 FF000000 00000000    FF000000 00000000 FF000000 00000000
001ED8  FF000000 00000000 FF000000 00000000    FF000000 00000000 FF000000 00000000
001EF8  FF000000 00000000 FF000000 00000000    FF000000 00000000 FF000000 00000000
001F18  FF000000 00000000 FF000000 00000000    FF000000 00000000 FF000000 00000000
001F38  FF000000 00000000 FF000000 00000000

PUBOWN  ADDRESS IS 001F4A
001F4A  00400000 00710000 00000000 00000040    00400000 00000000 0000007D 007F003D
001F6A  00000000 007F007F 00000000 00000000    00000000 00000000 00000000 00000000
001F8A  00000000 00000000 00000000 00000000    00000000 00000000 00000000 00000000
001FAA  00000000 00000000 00000000 00000000    00000000 00000000 00000000 00000000
001FCA  00000000 00000000 00000000 00000000    00000000 00000000 00000000 00000000
001FEA  00000000 00000000 00000000 00000000    00000000 00000000 00000000 00000000
00200A  00000000 00000000 00000000 00000000    00000000 00000000 00000000 00000000
00202A  00000000 00000000 00000000 00000000    00000000 00000000 00000000 00000000
00204A  00000000 00000000 00000000 00000000    00000000 00000000 00000000 00000000
00206A  00000000 00000000 00000000 00000000    00000000 00000000 00000000 00000000
00208A  00000000 00000000 00000000 00000000    00000000 00000000 00000000 00000000
0020AA  00000000 00000000 00000000 00000000    00000000 00000000 00000000 00000000
0020CA  00000000 00000000 00000000 00000000    00000000 00000000 00000000 00000000
0020EA  00000000 00000000 00000000 00000000    00000000 00000000 00000000 00000000
00210A  00000000 00000000 00000000 00000000    00000000 00000000 00000000 00000000
00212A  00000000 00000000 00000000 00000000    00000000 00000000 00000000

PUB2    ADDRESS IS 032E20
```

```
1CFJLS                    09/11/85  15.02.53   CPUID=FF01136043810000                    PAGE    3

032E20   0000DE20 00000000 00000000 00000020    00000000 00000000 00053E00 00000000
032E40   00000000 00000000 00000010 0000000C    00000000 00000000 00000000 00000020
032E60   00000000 00000000 00000000 00000000    00000000 00004800 00000000 00000000
032E80   00027900 00000000 00000000 00000100    00000000 00000000 00000000 00000100
032EA0   00000000 00000000 00000000 00000100    00000000 00000000 00000000 00000100
032EC0   00000000 00000000 00000000 00091200    00000000 0000F5F5 F5F5F5F5 003E1F00
032EE0   00000000 0000E5E2 C5D9C5E2 0010AB00    00000000 0000E5E2 C5E6D2F1 00000100
032F00   00000000 00000000 00000000 00000100    00000000 00000000 00000000 00324E00
032F20   00000000 0000C1C3 C1E6D2F1 000A2A00    00000000 0000C1C3 C1E6D2F2 00000800
032F40   00000000 0000C1C3 C1E6D2F3 00000100    00000000 00000000 00000000 00000100
032F60   00000000 00000000 00000000 00000010    0000C1C2 00000000 00000000 00000000
032F80   00000000 00000000 00000000 00000000    00000000 00000000 00000000 00000000
032FA0   00000000 00000000 00000000 00000000    00000000 00000000 00000000 00000000
032FC0   00000010 0000C1C2 00000000 00000000    00000000 00000000 00000000 00000000
032FE0   00000000 00000000 00000000 00000000    00000000 00000000 00000000 00000000
033000   00000000 00000000 00000000 00000000    00000000 00000100 00000000 00000000


LUBTAB   F2 ADDR IS 00157A
00157A   03FF03FF 04FF06FF 02FF12FF 0EFFFFFF    FFFFFFFF 13FFFFFF 12FF0EFF FFFFFFFF
00159A   FFFFFFFF FFFFFFFF FFFFFFFF FFFFFFFF    FFFFFFFF FFFFFFFF FFFFFFFF FFFFFFFF
0015BA   FFFFFFFF FFFFFFFF FFFFFFFF FFFFFFFF    FFFFFFFF FFFFFFFF FFFFFFFF FFFFFFFF
0015DA   FFFFFFFF FFFFFFFF FFFFFFFF FFFFFFFF    FFFFFFFF FFFFFFFF FFFFFFFF FFFFFFFF
0015FA   FFFFFFFF FFFFFFFF FFFFFFFF FFFFFFFF    FFFFFFFF FFFFFFFF FFFFFFFF FFFFFFFF
00161A   FFFFFFFF FFFFFFFF 0FFF0EFF 0FFF0DFF    0FFF0DFF 0FFF0EFF 0DFF0DFF 0DFF0DFF
00163A   0FFF0FFF 0EFF0DFF 12FF12FF 12FF12FF    FFFF12FF FFFFFFFF FFFFFFFF FFFFFFFF
00165A   FFFF12FF 0DFF0FFF 12FF12FF 12FF0EFF


DIBTAB   F2 ADDR IS 002850
002850   00000000 00000000 00000000 00000000    00000000 00000000 00000000 00000000
002870   00500000 00000000 00000019 00000000    00000000 00000000 00510000 00000000
002890   00000019 03E80000 00000000 00000000    00790000 00000000 00000013 03E80000
0028B0   00000000 00000000 00500000 00000000    00000000 00000000


PIBTAB   ADDRESS IS 000FA8
000FA8   8000C1D9 80000000 000089B0 00633200    0000C2C7 80200000 00000000 00633200
000FC8   8000C6F6 806B3000 00000000 00632800    0000C6F5 806FE000 00000000 00632800
000FE8   0000C6F4 807BA000 00000000 00631400    0000C6F3 80876000 00000000 00631400
00100B   0082C6F2 80932000 00000000 00631400    0000C6F1 809EE000 00000000 00631400
001028   00000000 00000000 00000000 00000000    00636363 63636363 63322828 14141414
001048   03FF03FF 04FF06FF 02FF12FF 0EFFFFFF    FFFFFFFF 13FFFFFF 12FF0EFF FFFFFFFF
001068   FFFFFFFF FFFFFFFF FFFFFFFF FFFFFFFF    FFFFFFFF FFFFFFFF FFFFFFFF FFFFFFFF
001088   FFFFFFFF FFFFFFFF FFFFFFFF FFFFFFFF    FFFFFFFF FFFFFFFF FFFFFFFF FFFFFFFF


PIB2     ADDRESS IS 000F28
000F28   03500000 00200000 00014F68 00000000    03500000 00210000 00015468 001080FF
000F48   25300000 00270000 000153B0 002080FF    24680000 00260000 000152F8 003080FF
000F68   23A00000 00250000 00015240 004080FF    22D80000 00240000 00015188 005080FF
000F88   22100000 00230000 000150D0 0060B0FF    21480000 00220000 00015018 007080FF
000FA8   8000C1D9 80000000 000089B0 00633200    0000C2C7 80200000 00000000 00633200
000FC8   8000C6F6 806B3000 00000000 00632800    0000C6F5 806FE000 00000000 00632800
000FE8   0000C6F4 807BA000 00000000 00631400    0000C6F3 80876000 00000000 00631400
00100B   0082C6F2 80932000 00000000 00631400    0000C6F1 809EE000 00000000 00631400


SMCB     SVA ADDR IS 014FD8
014FD8   03440000 002B002B 00BB8000 00A6E000    00C00000 000184AC 0002E250


SMCB     BG ADDR IS 0154D8
0154D8   00100000 00200000 802E1000 00200000    006B3000 00036000 0003E000
```

```
1CFJLS                    09/11/85  15.02.53   CPUID=FF01136043810000                     PAGE   4


SMCB     F6 ADDR IS 015420
015420   00020000 006B3000 806DE000 006B3000    006FE000 0003E000 0003F000


SMCB     F5 ADDR IS 015368
015368   00060000 006FE000 8077B000 006FE000    007BA000 0003F000 00042000


SMCB     F4 ADDR IS 0152B0
0152B0   00060000 007BA000 80837000 007BA000    00876000 00042000 00045000


SMCB     F3 ADDR IS 0151F8
0151F8   00060000 00876000 808F3000 00876000    00932000 00045000 00048000


SMCB     F2 ADDR IS 015140
015140   00060000 00932000 809AF000 00932000    009EE000 00048000 0004B000


SMCB     F1 ADDR IS 015088
015088   00200000 009EE000 00A62000 009EE000    00A6E000 0004B000 0005B000


LOADLS   ADDRESS IS 033DF4
033DF4   00033E04 00033E04 00033F30 00000000    D7C8C1E2 C55C5C5C 00932078 00000662
033E14   00BB9AA0 00000000 00000000 00000000    00000000 00000000 00000000 00000000
033E34   00000000 00000000 00000000 00000000    00000000 00000000 00000000 00000000
033E54   00000000 00000000 00000000 00000000    00000000 00000000 00000000 00000000
033E74   00000000 00000000 00000000 00000000    00000000 00000000 00000000 00000000
033E94   00000000 00000000 00000000 00000000    00000000 00000000 00000000 00000000
033EB4   00000000 00000000 00000000 00000000    00000000 00000000 00000000 00000000
033ED4   00000000 00000000 00000000 00000000    00000000 00000000 00000000 00000000


F2


LOADLS   ADDRESS IS 033DF4
         00033E04 00033E04 00033F30 00000000
         D7C8C1E2 C55C5C5C 00932078 00000662    00BB9AA0                      PHASE***
         42114040 1D604040 40C6F140 F0F0F140    F1D8F4F7 C9404040 C6F240F9 C1F6F0F7


F2 PARTITION
932000   D7C8C1E2 C55C5C5C 076D2F00 009320C0    D7C8C1E2 00000000 009AEFFF 4093207A    *PHASE***       PHAS          *
932020   009AF800 BF9320A2 00932488 00932385    00932120 009AEFFF 00000048 009AEFFF    * 8                           *
932040   00000000 00000000 009320E0 40A73002    000099B8 D3F8A685 411B7E15 1628AED2    *                  L8       K*
932060   5E945BE2 1628AED2 80000000 80000000    80000000 80000000 05C0BF08 C4060400    * *S   K               D    *
932080   4110C3E6 4500C016 00932120 00932230    0A025810 C3F65800 C3FA58F1 001045EF    * CW              C6 C  1    *
9320A0   0008F224 C2FEC30B F224C301 C310F224    C304C315 F832C307 C2FEFA32 C307C301    * 2 B C2 C C 2 C C B C B   C C*
9320C0   FA32C307 C304D205 C36FC2F0 DE05C36F    C2FED205 C37AC2F0 DE05C37A C301D205    * C C K C B0  C B K C B0  C C K*
9320E0   C385C2F0 DE05C385 C304D207 C395C2F6    DE07C395 C3075810 C3FE5800 C40258F1    *C B0  C C K C B6  C C   C  D 1*
932100   001045EF 000C47F0 C0180700 4110C3EE    4500C0A2 00932120 00932230 0A020A0E    *      0    C                 *
932120   00008000 0C000001 80932140 00932148    00932488 02C40202 009321DA 0093210A    *                      D      *
932140   0293218A 20000050 47000000 D24FD000    E0000000 00000000 0000C000 0D000001    *       K                     *
932160   80932178 00932180 00932488 02440202    0093218A 0093210A 029321DA 20000050    *                             *
932180   47000000 D24FD000 E000F2F5 F8F3F640    F5F2F640 F7F8F240 40404040 40404040    *   K      25836 526 782      *
9321A0   40404040 --SAME--                                                             *                             *
9321C0   40404040 40404040 40404040 40404040    40404040 40404040 4040615C 40404040    *                         /*  *
9321E0   40404040 --SAME--                                                             *                             *
932220   40404040 40404040 40400000 00000000    00008000 0C000003 00932258 00932260    *                          -*
932240   009325F8 08B60B40 01932261 00000000    07004700 00000000 019322E6 20000084    * 8        /            W    *
932260   40404040 40404040 40404040 40404040    40404040 404040F3 F5F94040 40404040    *                      359    *
932280   4040F2F7 F6404040 40404040 40F8F3F5    40404040 40404040 40404040 4040F1F4    * 276      835             14*
9322A0   F7F04040 40404040 40404040 40404040    40404040 40404040 40404040 40404040    *70                          *
```

```
1CFJLS                    09/11/85  15.02.53   CPUID=FF01136043810000                    PAGE   5

9322C0  40404040 --SAME--                                                    ¢                                    ¢
9322E0  40404040 40404040 40404040 40404040    40404040 40404040 40404040 F3F5F940   ¢                            359 ¢
932300  40404040 404040F2 F7F64040 40404040    4040F8F3 F5404040 40404040 40404040   ¢           276       835        ¢
932320  404040F1 F4F7F040 40404040 40404040    40404040 40404040 40404040 40404040   ¢  1470                          ¢
932340  40404040 --SAME--                                                PCKB         ¢                               ¢
932360  40404040 40404040 40404020 20202120    40202020 20202120 25836F05 26047B20   ¢                               ¢
932380  04002583 6CF2F5F8 F3F640F5 F2F640F7    F8F24040 40404040 40404040 40404040   ¢        25836 526 782          ¢
9323A0  40404040 --SAME--                                ZNB                          ¢                               ¢
9323E0  40404040 40404040 40404040 F3F5F940    40404040 404040F2 F7F64040 40404040   ¢           359       276        ¢
932400  4040F8F3 F5404040 40404040 40404040    404040F1 F4F7F040 40404040 40404040   ¢  835             1470          ¢
932420  40404040 --SAME--                                                            ¢                               ¢
932440  40404040 40404040 40404040 40404040    40404040 40404040 40400000 00000000   ¢                               ¢
932460  5B5BC2D6 D7C5D540 5B5BC2C3 D3D6E2C5    00932120 00932385 00932230 009323D5   ¢$$$BOPEN $$BCLOSE          N¢
932480  0F000000 00000000 0A320000 0A320000    47F0F01A 0A320000 C9D1C3C6 E9C9C2F3   ¢                 00   IJCFZIB3¢
9324A0  71309180 10084710 F0A09140 10154710    F0309640 10150A00 91801002 4710F03A   ¢          0       0          0 ¢
9324C0  0A0750E0 F09C58E0 1020D202 10211019    50E01018 91011004 4780F06E 91401002   ¢    0     K               0   ¢
9324E0  4710F064 58E0F09C 47F0F02E 94BF1015    58E0101C 07FED502 F0BEE000 4770F07C   ¢  0   0  00             N 0   0 ¢
932500  47F0F064 50D0F098 18D04400 102C98DE    F0980A00 07FE615C 400C0010 22000000   ¢ 00    0        0      /¢       ¢
932520  009AF800 BF9320A2 91401015 4710F0B8    947F1008 0A009680 F16E4A10 F16C0A00   ¢  8              0         1  1 ¢
932540  9180F16E 4710F0CE 0A009680 F16E4A10    F16C47F0 F0FC9140 10154710 F0F29640   ¢ 1  0    1  1 00          02   ¢
932560  10154B10 F16C9640 101547F0 F0EA4B10    F16C9780 F16E47F0 F0FC4A10 F16C0A00   ¢  .1      00 .1  1  00   1    ¢
932580  47F0F0E6 91801002 4710F106 0A0796B0    100850E0 F09C58E0 10209101 100447B0   ¢ 00W      1        0         ¢
9325A0  F15C9140 10024710 F13658E0 F09C9180    F16E47E0 F0B84B10 F16C47F0 F0CE94BF   ¢1¢       1   0  1   0 . 1  00 ¢
9325C0  10159180 F16E47E0 F14E4B10 F16C94BF    101547F0 F1564A10 F16C94BF 101558E0   ¢  1  1 . 1       01  1       ¢
9325E0  101C07FE 50D0F098 18D04400 102C98DE    F09807FE 00380000 0A320000 0A320000   ¢    0         0              ¢
932600  0A320000 47F0F01A C9D1C4C6 C1E9C9E6    35119180 10024710 F0240A07 90CEF0B0   ¢    00 IJDFAZIW        0    0 ¢
932620  58E01018 06E018D0 D2001017 D0004BC0    102E44C0 F0BC1BCC 18DC43C0 101741E0   ¢     K             0         ¢
932640  001043DE F0C119DC 4780F05A 46E0F04A    0A3243DE F0D143C0 101619CD 4770F080   ¢  0A   0  0   0J        0   ¢
932660  91801016 4780F080 920B1028 0A009180    10024710 F0800A07 42D01016 42D0102B   ¢     0             0        ¢
932680  0A009180 10024710 F0940A07 92011028    58E01028 D2021029 101950E0 10189BCE   ¢     0             K        ¢
9326A0  F0B00A00 07FE0000 4093207A 009AF800    AF932106 D200E000 D000F2C2 C1F9F8F7   ¢0          8       K    2BA987¢
9326C0  F6F5F4F3 C3F14E60 F04093DB D3CBC3BB    B3ABA39B E38B031B 130B0000 00000000   ¢6543C1 -0   L C     T        ¢
9326E0  00000000 --SAME--                                                            ¢                               ¢

93D000    PAGE(S) NOT USED

940000  00000000 --SAME--                                                            ¢                               ¢

940800    PAGE(S) NOT USED

950000  00000000 --SAME--                                                            ¢                               ¢

950800    PAGE(S) NOT USED

960000  00000000 --SAME--                                                            ¢                               ¢

960800    PAGE(S) NOT USED

9AF000  009AF3E4 00000000 00000000 00000000    00000000 00000000 00000000 00000000   ¢  3U                         ¢
9AF020  00000000 --SAME--                                                            ¢                               ¢
9AF400  009AF800 009EDFFF 00000000 009AF422    009AF51B 009AF422 009AF422 00000000   ¢  8          4    5   4   4  ¢
9AF420  00088000 00000000 00000000 00000000    00000000 00000000 00000000 00000000   ¢                               ¢
9AF440  00000000 --SAME--                                                            ¢                               ¢

9AF800    PAGE(S) NOT USED

9B0000  00000000 --SAME--                                                            ¢                               ¢
```

```
9B0800    PAGE(S) NOT USED

9B2800   00000000 --SAME--                                                    †                        †

9B3000    PAGE(S) NOT USED

9C0000   00000000 --SAME--                                                    †                        †

9C0800    PAGE(S) NOT USED

9C5000   00000000 --SAME--                                                    †                        †

9C5800    PAGE(S) NOT USED
```

A memory dump gives the contents of all pertinent memory locations at the time an error occurred. It also gives the contents of the machine registers as well as information relating to the state of the operating system. This represents the complete state of the computation when the error took place.

We can locate any field in a hexadecimal dump by looking up the VALUE and LEN entries for that field in the cross-reference listing. Adding the VALUE entry to the starting address of our program gives the address of the field in the dump. The LEN entry indicates the number of bytes in the field.

The first page of the dump contains register contents at the point at which our program was interrupted. These appear at the top of the page in the lines beginning GR 0-F. The contents of RC may be seen in the fifth entry on the second of these two lines. RC contained X'4093207A'. Because this is an address, the leftmost byte, X'40', is ignored. The number contained in the remaining 3 bytes, X'93207A', is the address of the second instruction in our program. It was placed in RC when BALR RC,0 was executed and has been used as the base address for all memory references.

The remaining entries of the first page of the dump and all of the second and third pages are of no further interest at this point.

On pages 4 and 5 of the dump, we find the contents of the memory locations occupied by our program listed both in hexadecimal and, when applicable, in character form. They are listed 32 bytes to a line with the address of the first byte on each line appearing at the left. The numbers seen at the extreme left increase by X'20' = 32. Within each line, the values are listed in columns of four bytes each. The address of the first byte in each column is a multiple of four. For example, the addresses of the first bytes in the columns of row 1 are X'932000', X'932004', X'932008', X'93200C', X'932010', X'932014', X'932018', and X'93201C'.

The columns at the extreme right contain the character form of each set of memory locations. If the contents of a particular byte do not represent the EBCDIC code for a printable character, a blank is printed.

From the cross-reference listing, we get the offset and length for PCKB. They are X'303' and 3. In order to find PCKB in the dump, we add X'303' to the starting address X'932078', getting X'93237B'. In the dump, this address is in the line that begins with the address X'932360'. The starting address of the second group of four columns in this line is X'932370'. The field PCKB is marked. It contains

X'052604'. As the last hex-digit is not a valid sign indicator, the number is invalid. This caused the Data exception.

The offset and length for ZNB are X'312' and 5. The starting address for ZNB is X'932078' + X'312' = X'93238A'. This is marked in the dump in the line beginning with address X'932380'. The 5 bytes represented by ZNB contain X'40F5F2F640'. This is the root of the problem. In character form, ZNB is ' 526 '. There is an extra blank at the end—the number was not entered in the correct position.

The table below shows the offset and the corresponding starting address for several other fields. By locating these fields in the dump, we can find their contents at the time the execution error occurred. Fields such as LINE and INREC that contain character strings can also be seen at the right of the dump in character form.

Symbol	Offset	Address
INREC	X'30D'	X'932385'
INBUF1	X'112'	X'93218A'
INBUF2	X'162'	X'9321DA'
LINE	X'35D'	X'9323D5'
OUTBUF1	X'1E8'	X'932160'
OUTBUF2	X'26D'	X'9322E5'
PCKSUM	X'309'	X'932381'

Having found the error in the input records using the information in the dump, we can now get an error-free run by correcting the input. We can also add the instructions to begin the output on a new page. Listing 2.3.6 shows the final version of this program together with the output generated from a larger set of input values.

Listing 2.3.6 Final Version with Output

```
LOC  OBJECT CODE    ADDR1 ADDR2  STMT   SOURCE STATEMENT                          DOS/VSE ASSEMBLER 16.54 85-09-12

                                   1  *****************************************************************
                                   2  *     SAMPLE PROGRAM 1                                          *
                                   3  *                                                               *
                                   4  *     A PROGRAM TO READ 80 CHARACTER RECORDS UNTIL EOF.         *
                                   5  *     EACH RECORD CONTAINS 3 5-DIGIT NUMBERS IN THE FIRST        *
                                   6  *     15 COLUMNS. THE PROGRAM ADDS THESE THREE NUMBERS AND       *
                                   7  *     PRINTS THEM TOGETHER WITH THEIR SUM                        *
                                   8  *                                                               *
                                   9  *****************************************************************
                                  10         PRINT NOGEN
000000                           11  SAMPLE01 START 0                 PROGRAM SAMPLE01
000000 05C0                       12         BALR RC,0                :
                    00002        13         USING *,RC                :
000002 BF08 C49A     0049C        14         ICM  R0,B'1000',=B'00001111'
000006 0400                       15         SPM  R0                  :
                                  16         OPEN INFILE,PRINTER      OPEN FILES
                                  25         PUT  PRINTER,PAGE        START OUTPUT ON A NEW PAGE
                                  31  *
                    0002A        32  REPEAT EQU  *                    REPEAT
                                  33         GET  INFILE,INREC        READ ZNA, ZNB, ZNC
00003A F224 C30E C31B 00310 0031D 39         PACK PCKA,ZNA            PACK INTO PCKA, PCKB, PCKC
000040 F224 C311 C320 00313 00322 40         PACK PCKB,ZNB            :
000046 F224 C314 C325 00316 00327 41         PACK PCKC,ZNC            :
00004C F832 C317 C30E 00319 00310 42         ZAP  PCKSUM,PCKA         PCKSUM = PCKA + PCKB + PCKC
000052 FA32 C317 C311 00319 00313 43         AP   PCKSUM,PCKB         :
000058 FA32 C317 C314 00319 00316 44         AP   PCKSUM,PCKC         :
00005E D205 C404 C300 00406 00302 45         MVC  OUTA,ITMSK          EDIT PCKA, PCKB, PCKC, PCKSUM
000064 DE05 C404 C30E 00406 00310 46         ED   OUTA,PCKA                INTO LINE
00006A D205 C40F C300 00411 00302 47         MVC  OUTB,ITMSK          :
000070 DE05 C40F C311 00411 00313 48         ED   OUTB,PCKB           :
000076 D205 C41A C300 0041C 00302 49         MVC  OUTC,ITMSK          :
00007C DE05 C41A C314 0041C 00316 50         ED   OUTC,PCKC           :
000082 D207 C42A C306 0042C 00308 51         MVC  OUTSUM,SUMMSK       :
000088 DE07 C42A C317 0042C 00319 52         ED   OUTSUM,PCKSUM       :
                                  53         PUT  PRINTER,LINE        PRINT LINE
00009E 47F0 C028     0002A        59         B    REPEAT              :
                    000A2        60  UNTIL  EQU  *                    UNTIL END-OF-FILE
                                  61  *
                                  62         CLOSE INFILE,PRINTER     CLOSE FILES
                                  71         EOJ                      END SAMPLE01
                                  74  *****************************************************************
                                  75  *    SYMBOL DEFINITIONS                                         *
                                  76  *****************************************************************
                    00000        77  R0     EQU  0                    SYMBOLIC NAME FOR REGISTER 0
                    0000C        78  RC     EQU  12                   SYMBOLIC NAME FOR BASE REGISTER
                    00005        79  ZLEN   EQU  5                    LENGTH OF INPUT VALUES
                    00003        80  PLEN   EQU  ZLEN/2+1             LENGTH OF PACKED NYUMBERS
                                  81  *****************************************************************
                                  82  *    FILES                                                      *
                                  83  *****************************************************************
                                  84  INFILE DTFCD DEVADDR=SYSIPT,DEVICE=2501,EOFADDR=UNTIL,          X
                                             IOAREA1=INBUF1,IOAREA2=INBUF2,WORKA=YES
000122                           125  INBUF1 DS   CL80
000172                           126  INBUF2 DS   CL80
                                 127  *
```

```
    LOC  OBJECT CODE    ADDR1 ADDR2  STMT   SOURCE STATEMENT                      DOS/VSE ASSEMBLER 16.54 85-09-12

                                     128 PRINTER  DTFPR DEVADDR=SYSLST,DEVICE=3203,BLKSIZE=133,CTLCHR=ASA,      X
                                                        IOAREA1=OUTBUF1,IOAREA2=OUTBUF2,WORKA=YES
  0001F8                             149 OUTBUF1  DS    CL133
  00027D                             150 OUTBUF2  DS    CL133
                                     151 ***********************************************************************
                                     152 *    CONSTANTS                                                       *
                                     153 ***********************************************************************
  000302 402020202120                154 ITMSK    DC    X'402020202120'     MASK FOR INPUT VALUES
  000308 4020202020202120            155 SUMMSK   DC    X'4020202020202120' MASK FOR SUM
                                     156 ***********************************************************************
                                     157 *    VARIABLES                                                       *
                                     158 ***********************************************************************
  000310                             159 PCKA     DS    PL(PLEN)            PACKED FORM OF A
  000313                             160 PCKB     DS    PL(PLEN)            PACKED FORM OF B
  000316                             161 PCKC     DS    PL(PLEN)            PACKED FORM OF C
  000319                             162 PCKSUM   DS    PL(PLEN+1)          PACKED SUM
                                     163 ***********************************************************************
                                     164 *    I/O WORK AREAS                                                  *
                                     165 ***********************************************************************
  00031D                             166 INREC    DS    CL80               INPUT RECORD
  00036D               0031D         167          ORG   INREC                :
  00031D                             168 ZNA      DS    ZL(ZLEN)             A
  000322                             169 ZNB      DS    ZL(ZLEN)             B
  000327                             170 ZNC      DS    ZL(ZLEN)             C
  00032C               0036D         171          ORG   INREC+L'INREC      END INPUT RECORD
                                     172 *
  00036D F140404040404040            173 PAGE     DC    CL133'1'           NEW PAGE
                                     174 *
  0003F2 4040404040404040            175 LINE     DC    CL133' '           OUTPUT LINE
  000477               00406         176          ORG   LINE+20              :
  000406                             177 OUTA     DS    CL(L'ITMSK)          A
  00040C               00411         178          ORG   *+5                  :
  000411                             179 OUTB     DS    CL(L'ITMSK)          B
  000417               0041C         180          ORG   *+5                  :
  00041C                             181 OUTC     DS    CL(L'ITMSK)          C
  000422               0042C         182          ORG   *+10                 :
  00042C                             183 OUTSUM   DS    CL(L'SUMMSK)         SUM
  000434               00477         184          ORG   LINE+L'LINE        END OUTPUT LINE
                                     185 *
                                     186          END
  000478 5B5BC2D6D7C5D540            187                =C'$$BOPEN '
  000480 5B5BC2C3D3D6E2C5            188                =C'$$BCLOSE'
  000488 000001C8                    189                =A(PRINTER)
  00048C 0000036D                    190                =A(PAGE)
  000490 000000B8                    191                =A(INFILE)
  000494 0000031D                    192                =A(INREC)
  000498 000003F2                    193                =A(LINE)
  00049C 0F                          194                =B'00001111'
```

SYMBOL	LEN	ID	VALUE	DEFN	REFERENCES				
IJCU0007	00008	001	000110	00121	0110				
IJCX0007	00008	001	0000D8	00102	0091				
IJJC0005	00004	001	0000A8	00067					
IJJO0001	00004	001	00000C	00021					
IJJZ0007	00001	001	000122	00124					
IJJZ0008	00001	001	0001F8	00148					
INBUF1	00080	001	000122	00125	0102	0118			
INBUF2	00080	001	000172	00126	0099	0121			
INFILE	00006	001	0000B8	00087	0022	0068	0191		
INREC	00080	001	00031D	00166	0167	0171	0171	0192	
ITMSK	00006	001	000302	00154	0045	0047	0049	0177	0179	0181
LINE	00133	001	0003F2	00175	0176	0184	0184	0193	
OUTA	00006	001	000406	00177	0045	0046			
OUTB	00006	001	000411	00179	0047	0048			
OUTBUF1	00133	001	0001F8	00149	0142				
OUTBUF2	00133	001	00027D	00150	0147				
OUTC	00006	001	00041C	00181	0049	0050			
OUTSUM	00008	001	00042C	00183	0051	0052			
PAGE	00133	001	00036D	00173	0190				
PCKA	00003	001	000310	00159	0039	0042	0046		
PCKB	00003	001	000313	00160	0040	0043	0048		
PCKC	00003	001	000316	00161	0041	0044	0050		
PCKSUM	00004	001	000319	00162	0042	0043	0044	0052	
PLEN	00001		000003	00080	0159	0160	0161	0162	
PRINTER	00006	001	0001C8	00131	0023	0069	0189		
RC	00001		00000C	00078	0012	0013			
REPEAT	00001	001	00002A	00032	0059				
R0	00001		000000	00077	0014	0015			
SAMPLE01	00001	001	000000	00011					
SUMMSK	00008	001	000308	00155	0051	0183			
UNTIL	00001	001	0000A2	00060	0101	0120			
ZLEN	00001		000005	00079	0080	0168	0169	0170	
ZNA	00005	001	00031D	00168	0039				
ZNB	00005	001	000322	00169	0040				
ZNC	00005	001	000327	00170	0041				
=A(INFILE)									
	00004	001	000490	00191	0035				
=A(INREC)									
	00004	001	000494	00192	0036				
=A(LINE)	00004	001	000498	00193	0056				
=A(PAGE)	00004	001	00048C	00190	0028				
=A(PRINTER)									
	00004	001	000488	00189	0027	0055			
=B'00001111'									
	00001	001	00049C	00194	0014				
=C'$$BOPEN '									
	00008	001	000478	00187	0020				
=C'$$BCLOSE'									
	00008	001	000480	00188	0066				

```
                    DIAGNOSTICS AND STATISTICS                          PAGE    5


                                                                   85-09-12

NO ERRORS FOUND


THE FOLLOWING MACRO NAMES HAVE BEEN FOUND IN MACRO INSTRUCTIONS
   OPEN     PUT     GET     CLOSE    EOJ      DTFCD    DTFPR

OPTIONS FOR THIS ASSEMBLY - ALIGN, LIST, XREF, LINK, NORLD, NODECK, NOEDECK

THE ASSEMBLER WAS RUN IN 65416 BYTES
END OF ASSEMBLY


           359       276      835         1470
           178       983      983         2144
          1829      1223    98231       101283
           123        45      341          509
          3422      3342    20056        26820
         98478     57839    82832       239149
```

A good program should not crash when it receives invalid input. Unfortunately, adding reasonable input validation checks would make our programs impossibly large for an introductory course. We will, therefore, continue to assume that our programs have correct input, though such an assumption is not reasonable outside of an introductory programming course.

E X E R C I S E S

Questions 1 through 7 refer to Listing 2.3.6.

1. Give the opcode for the MVC instruction.

2. Give the opcode for the PACK instruction.

3. Find the lengths of the two operands in statement 35.

4. Give the offset of the UNTIL label.

5. Give the number of statements generated by the expansion of the OPEN macro.

6. Give the number of bytes of object code generated by the GET macro.

7. Give the number of times ITMSK is referenced.

Question 8 refers to Listing 2.3.3.

8. Give the starting address of the routines IJCFZIB3 and IJDFAZIW.

Question 9 refers to Listing 2.3.4.

9. The rightmost three bytes of the PSW shown in Listing 2.3.4 contain an instruction address. Which instruction is this?

Questions 10 through 12 refer to Listing 2.3.5.

10. Give the contents of register R6.

11. Find the machine format of the instruction corresponding to statement 40.

12. Find each of the following fields in the dump.
    a. ITMSK
    b. OUTA
    c. ZNA
    d. PCKA
    e. PCKC

CHAPTER 3

DECIMAL INSTRUCTIONS

3.1 DECIMAL MULTIPLICATION AND DIVISION

Now that we have seen a complete assembly language program, we can look in detail at individual instructions and their effects without losing sight of their position as part of a complete program. In addition to learning new machine instructions, we will also encounter new features, provided by the assembler and the operating system, which make programming easier.

In this chapter, we examine additional decimal arithmetic and character manipulation instructions. We also cover instructions for comparing numeric and character fields and effecting branches determined by the results of those comparisons. By the end of the chapter, we will have an instruction set that allows us to write reasonably sophisticated programs for manipulating decimal and character data.

Here and throughout the text, a large part of our efforts are directed toward learning how to use these instructions in well-structured programs, rather than in mastering the details of the instructions themselves. These details can be summarized easily in two or three pages, but learning how to use the instructions is not an easy task.

Assembly language programming is concerned more with binary arithmetic than decimal arithmetic. However, we will postpone our consideration of binary arithmetic until we have gained more familiarity with other aspects of assembly language programming. For example, when writing the programs suggested at the end of this chapter, it is likely that debugging efforts will require increased use of hexadecimal dumps. As we saw in the last chapter, it is a simple matter to recognize and interpret packed and zoned decimal numbers in a dump. It is not so easy to recognize binary data. We will avoid adding that additional complication until we have gained more experience in using dumps.

Decimal Multiplication

The first instruction in this chapter is the Multiply Packed (MP) instruction. Before we examine the details of this instruction, consider the effect of multiplication on the size of the numbers involved.

When two decimal numbers are added, the number of digits in the sum will never be more than one greater than the number of digits in the longer of the two numbers. For example, if we add a five-digit number and a nine-digit number, the sum will never have more than ten digits. It is often the case in programming that the numbers to be added are the same size. For example,

```
X         DS      PL5
Y         DS      PL5
```

The instruction

        AP   X,Y

will only cause an overflow if there is a carry resulting from the addition of the leftmost digits. In general, this can only happen if one or both numbers are near the maximum size.

    On the other hand, when two decimal integers are multiplied, the number of digits in the product is approximately equal to the sum of the number of digits in each of the operands. If X and Y are defined as above,

        MP   X,Y

which, like AP, stores the result in X, would be much more likely to produce an overflow. Because of this situation, a rather severe restriction is placed on the relative sizes of the operands. This restriction makes the instruction above illegal. In fact, the restriction makes overflow impossible. It requires the first field to have as many bytes of leading zeros as the number of bytes in the second field. When the two fields satisfy this requirement, even if both numbers are as large as possible, the product will still fit in the receiving field.

Multiply Packed *MP 2-length SS*

        MP   S1(L1),S2(L2)

The contents of the memory locations designated by the first operand are multiplied by the contents of the field designated by the second operand and the result is stored in the field indicated by the first operand. The signs of both operands are used to determine the sign of the product.

    The second operand may not exceed 8 bytes (15 digits) and must be shorter than the first operand. If either of these conditions is violated, a Specification exception is raised.

    The first operand must have as many bytes of leading zeros as the number of bytes in the second operand. If this condition is violated, a Data exception is raised.

Exceptions:

Access	Improper address for one or both operands.
Data	Invalid packed number in one or both fields or an insufficient number of leading zeros in the first field.
Specification	Improper operand lengths.

Example 3.1.1 *Suppose that M and N are defined by the following.*

```
M          DS     PL7
N          DS     PL4
```

If M contains X'0000000005120D' (−5120) and N contains X '0001203C' (1203) then, after execution of

      MP   M,N

M will contain X'0000006159360D'. N will be unchanged.

Because M is negative and N is positive, the product is negative.

The system checks that restrictions on the sizes of fields are met before an operation is performed. If they have been violated, the appropriate exception will be raised and the program will be terminated, regardless of whether the result would fit in the first operand field. The table below shows several examples where this is the case.

Example 3.1.2 *Assuming that M and N have the lengths and values as shown in the two left-hand columns of the table below, the rightmost column of the table gives the value of M after the completion of the following instruction.*

      MP   M,N

M Before	N	M After
X'000000314C'	X'29701C'	X'009326114C'
X'000000999C'	X'99999C'	X'099899001C'
X'00000002148D'	X'05239D'	X'00011253372C'
X'13209C'	X'237D'	Data Exception
X'0001297C'	X'023C'	Data Exception
X'0007218C'	X'000C'	Data Exception
X'00050C'	X'00060C'	Spec. Exception

As in the case of the second pair of numbers, even when both operands are as large as permitted by the restrictions placed on them by the Multiply instruction, the result will always fit in the first field. In fact, it will always have at least one leading 0.

In the case of the first Data exception above, the multiplication would yield a result of 3130533, which is too long for the field M. If the multiplication had been allowed to take place, the result would have been an overflow. The restrictions imposed on the multiply instruction are designed to prevent this situation.

As the next two Data exception examples show, the error is raised whenever the input restrictions are violated, regardless of the values of the two fields. In both these examples, the product easily fits the first field. Nevertheless, a Data exception will be raised, even when the second field contains 0.

The last of these examples demonstrates the length restriction on the two fields. The second field must be shorter than the first or a Specification exception will be raised.

Decimal Division

The decimal division instruction implements integer division. It provides both a quotient and a remainder. Both of these are stored in the field represented by the first operand. The quotient might be as large as the nonzero part of the dividend and the remainder might be as large as the divisor. As the first field will receive both the quotient and the remainder, the field that holds the dividend may need as many bytes of leading zeros as the number of bytes in the divisor. However, this restriction is not enforced as it is in the case of multiplication. The division will be performed, and, if the quotient and remainder together are too long for the first operand field, a Decimal Divide exception is set.

Divide Packed *DP 2-length SS*

DP   S1(L1),S2(L2)

The contents of the memory locations designated by the first operand are divided by the contents of the field designated by the second operand. The integer quotient is stored in the leftmost bytes of the first operand field and the remainder is stored in the rightmost bytes of the first operand field. The length of the remainder is the same as the length of the second operand. The sign of the quotient is determined according to the rules of algebra and the sign of the remainder is always the same as the sign of the dividend.

The second operand may not exceed 8 bytes (15 digits) and must be shorter than the first operand. If either of these conditions is violated, a Specification exception is raised.

If the quotient is too large to fit in the first operand field together with the remainder or if the divisor is zero, a Decimal Divide exception is raised.

Exceptions:

Access	Improper address for one or both operands.
Data	Invalid packed number in one or both fields.
Specification	Improper lengths.
Decimal Divide	The divisor is zero or the quotient is too large.

Example 3.1.3 *Suppose that M and N are defined by the following.*

```
M          DS       PL6
N          DS       PL4
```

If M contains X'00004612753C' and N contains X'0281293C', then after the execution of

DP   M,N

M will contain X'016C0112065C'. The first two bytes represent the integer quotient, 16. The remaining bytes represent the remainder, 112065.

Both the quotient and remainder occupy an integral number of bytes and the size of the remainder is fixed, even though it may include a number of leading zeros. This means that there are a number of situations in which the quotient does not fit. It is in these situations that a Divide exception is raised. This can be seen in several of the following examples. Note also the rules for determining the sign of the quotient and remainder. These are followed even when the quotient or remainder is zero.

Example 3.1.4 *Assuming that M and N have values and lengths as shown, the table below gives the value of M after execution of the following instruction.*

DP   M,N

Num.	M Before	N Before	M After
1.	X'0352178C'	X'975C'	X'361C203C'
2.	X'0054215C'	X'08369C'	X'6C04001C'
3.	X'0054215C'	X'08369D'	X'6D04001C'
4.	X'0054215D'	X'08369C'	X'6D04001D'
5.	X'0054215D'	X'08369D'	X'6C04001D'
6.	X'0054215C'	X'369C'	X'146C341C'
7.	X'0054215C'	X'00369C'	Divide Excep.
8.	X'54215C'	X'00369C'	Spec. Excep.
9.	X'09213C'	X'00000C'	Divide Excep.

Notes:

1. In the example 1, we see the quotient is 361 and the remainder is 203.
2. The numbers in examples 2 through 5 are the same, only the signs are different. These demonstrate the way in which the signs of the quotient and remainder are determined.
4. In examples 6 and 7, the numbers involved in the operations are the same, but the lengths of the fields are different. In number 6, the division proceeds as expected yielding a quotient of 146 and a remainder of 341. In 7, because the divisor has a defined length of 3 bytes, the remainder will be stored as X'00341C'. As this does not leave enough room for the quotient, a Divide exception is raised.
5. Number 8 demonstrates the result when the defined length of the divisor is greater than or equal to the length of the dividend.
6. Finally, in 9, we see the result of attempting to divide by zero is an error, as one would expect.

In our example and our program documentation, we will use DIV to stand for *integer division* as distinguished from real division. We will use MOD to stand for the remainder operation, that is,

M   MOD   N

represents the remainder obtained when M is divided by N.

Using a Work Area

The restrictions imposed upon the sizes of the fields used in multiplication and division are quite rigorous. This presents the potential for massive confusion. For example, if we are writing a program that contains three fields A, B, and C and need, at various times, to multiply A times B, B times C, and C times A, then no choice of lengths of the three fields will allow all three operations to take place. Rather than force the fields involved in a program to conform to the length rules, we perform expression evaluations involving multiplication and division in temporary work areas, and move the result to the desired field after the operations have been performed.

For example, suppose that we need to implement the assignment

$$M = M \text{ DIV } N$$

We begin by defining a work area in which to carry out the division. In the absence of any knowledge about the relative sizes of M and N, we might use L'M + L'N for the length, assuming that this does not exceed 16.

WORK   DS   PL(L'M+L'N)

In order to perform the operation, we use ZAP to move the contents of M into WORK and pad it with leading zeros. We then divide WORK by N.

```
        ZAP     WORK,M
        DP      WORK,N
```

After the division, the contents of WORK will be

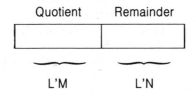

At this point, we need to move the integer quotient from the work area to M with another ZAP instruction. We cannot simply specify WORK as an operand, as this field contains both the quotient and the remainder. Instead, we need to provide both the starting point, which is the same as the beginning of WORK, and the length. In this case, the length of the quotient is the same as the length of M, because of the way in which we defined WORK. Thus we can use

```
ZAP    M,WORK(L'M)
```

In more general situations, we may use a work area whose size is not simply L'M+L'N. This might, for example, be the case if the work area were to be used for a number of different operations. In such cases, we rely on the knowledge that the remainder will have the same length as the divisor. The quotient will occupy the rest of the work area. Its length will always be the length of the work area minus the length of the divisor. Hence,

```
ZAP    M,WORK(L'WORK−L'N)
```

will work correctly, regardless of the definition of WORK.

In order to extract the remainder from a work area, we need to determine the offset from the beginning of the work area to the beginning of the remainder. But, of course, this is just the length of the quotient.

Example 3.1.5 *Suppose we need to divide M by N and store the quotient in Q and the remainder in R. Given a previously defined work area, we use the following.*

```
ZAP    WORK,M
DP     WORK,N
ZAP    Q,WORK(L'WORK−L'N)
ZAP    R,WORK+L'WORK−L'N(L'N)
```

Literal Operands

We conclude this section by considering the assembly code needed to implement the evaluation of several different kinds of expressions. It is not unusual for such expressions to contain constant terms. The use of such terms is facilitated by the *Literal operand*. A literal operand may be used in any situation where a storage operand is permissible.

Literal operands are denoted by an equal sign, '=', followed by a type designator and a value in quotes. The assembler implements Literal operands by reserving a set of storage locations of the correct length and storing the value in those locations. The base register, displacement, and length factors for those locations are then used in instructions in the same way as those of fields defined by the programmer.

Example 3.1.6 *The following are valid Literal operands.*

```
=P'8675'      =P'−019'      =C'ABCDE'      =X'5B0F1A'
```

Literal operands are useful in a number of situations. For example, to set a packed field, X, equal to 0

    ZAP   X,=P'0'

To increment a counter by 1

    AP   COUNT,=P'1'

Like other constants, literals are also susceptible to misuse. They should be used only when we are certain that the value represented will never need to be changed. One should not, for example, use a Literal operand to represent such quantities as field lengths or array dimensions.

Literal and Immediate operands are not interchangeable. Immediate operands may only be used in SI instructions. They are restricted to 1 byte in length and are designated by a decimal number or a type indicator followed by a quoted value. A Literal operand is equivalent to a Storage operand. It may be used as the source (second) operand in SS and RS instructions. Its length is determined implicitly from its value.

In the absence of any other directions, the assembler stores Literal operands at the end of the object module being generated. As it happens, this is probably the worst place for them. Fortunately, we can direct the placement of the literal operands with the LTORG directive. Used as an instruction, this directs the assembler to store literals at the point in the object where the directive is placed. We shall place it immediately after the symbol definitions.

Example 3.1.7 *Write the assembly code to implement the following assignment.*

$$Y = 29*(X^2-Z) \text{ DIV } (X+Z)$$

If we intend to implement this in the same sense that a compiler would, we need to make certain that X and Z are not changed in the process. So, we restrict ourselves from using these variables as work areas. In order to perform a straightforward evaluation of this expression, we need to evaluate both of the parenthesized expressions in work areas, before performing the division.

This requires at least two work areas, say WRK1 and WRK2. WRK1 needs to be large enough to perform the multiplication required to square X and to multiply (X^2-Z) by 29. Plan on using WRK1 as the first operand in the division. WRK2 simply needs to be as large as the larger of X and Z. As the size of this field dictates the number of bytes in WRK1 that will be preempted to store the remainder, we need to make WRK2 as small as possible.

Let us suppose that X and Z are the same size. In order to square X in WRK1, its size needs to be at least 2*L'X. Multiplication of WRK1 by the literal value =P'29' requires another 2 bytes. In the worst case (X+Z equals 1), WRK1 should have enough room to hold $29*(X^2-Z)$ together with a remainder whose length may be 1+L'X. WRK1 should have a length factor of (2*L'X+2) + (1+L'X) = 3+3*L'X. (As a practical matter, it is often simpler to define a work area such as WRK1 to be PL16 and avoid such calculations. Obviously, this approach cannot be used with WRK2 and it is occasionally necessary to carry out the calculations shown above.)

Assuming that WRK1 and WRK2 have been defined with suitable lengths, the code for implementing this assignment is

```
ZAP    WRK1,X              Y = 29*(X^2−Z) DIV (X+Z)
MP     WRK1,X              :
SP     WRK1,Z              :
MP     WRK1,=P'29'         :
ZAP    WRK2,X              :
AP     WRK2,Z              :
DP     WRK1,WRK2           :
ZAP    Y,WRK1(L'WRK1−L'WRK2)
```

It would be appropriate to document the entire sequence of instructions with the single pseudo-assignment statement.

Example 3.1.8 *Suppose that we are writing a program in which a time, given in hours, minutes, and seconds, is to be incremented by the addition of some elapsed time also expressed in hours, minutes, and seconds.*

Assume that we are using 24-hour format for times and that the number of days accrued will be used by another section of code to determine a new date. Assume the following definitions.

```
TIMELEN    EQU    2
HOURS      DS     PL(TIMELEN)
MINUTES    DS     PL(TIMELEN)
SECONDS    DS     PL(TIMELEN)
DHOURS     DS     PL(TIMELEN)
DMINS      DS     PL(TIMELEN)
DSECS      DS     PL(TIMELEN)
DAYS       DS     PL(TIMELEN)
```

When we add DSECS to SECONDS, if the result is greater than 60, we must add the integer quotient SECONDS DIV 60 to the minutes field and return the remainder, SECONDS REM 60, to the field SECONDS. We need to make similar adjustments to MINUTES and HOURS. In this case, we find the decimal divide instruction especially useful.

```
ZAP    WORK,SECONDS              WORK = SECONDS + DSECS
AP     WORK,DSECS               :
DP     WORK,=P'60'              SECONDS = WORK MOD 60
ZAP    SECONDS,WORK+L'WORK−2(2) :
AP     DMINS,WORK(L'WORK−2)     DMINS = DMINS+SECONDS DIV 60
```

```
ZAP     WORK,MINUTES                WORK = MINUTES+MINS
AP      WORK,DMINS                  :
DP      WORK,=P'60'                 MINUTES = WORK MOD 60
ZAP     MINUTES,WORK+L'WORK-2(2)    :
AP      DHOURS,WORK(L'WORK-2)       DHOURS=DHOURS+WORK DIV 60
ZAP     WORK,HOURS                  WORK = HOURS+DHOURS
AP      WORK,DHOURS                 :
DP      WORK,=P'24'                 HOURS = WORK MOD 24
ZAP     HOURS,WORK+L'WORK-2(2)      :
AP      DAYS,WORK(L'WORK-2)         DAYS = WORK DIV 24
```

This example demonstrates one of the disadvantages of using literal operands. That is, we tend to create a very tight bond between our program and the particular values employed. In this case, the value 2, which appears throughout the code, is the length of the literals =P'60' and =P'24'. Suppose, for a moment, that we need to change one of these values and the new value has a different length. We would have to find and change each occurrence of 2 that referred to that particular value. Even in this simple example, it is easy to picture the possibility of missing one of these changes.

Granted, it does not appear to be a serious problem, as these constants are unlikely to change. The only foreseeable change is the possibility that we might decide to adopt a 12-hour format for hours and change the =P'24' to =P'12' (we would also need to change days to halfdays). Such a change would not affect the length factor of 2 used here.

We seem to be reasonably safe. Nevertheless, we must keep in mind that the essence of good programming practice is to protect ourselves against the unforeseen. The problems we can predict cause no serious difficulties. It is the unpredicted problems that become catastrophes.

E   X   E   R   C   I   S   E   S

1. Each of the following instructions will cause an exception if the fields A and B have lengths and values as shown. Identify the exception which will occur and explain why.

   a. MP   A,B   A : X'00099C'   B : X'00018C'
   b. MP   A,B   A : X'00963C'   B : X'023C'
   c. DP   A,B   A : X'93820C'   B : X'000C'
   d. DP   A,B   A : X'0983787C'   B : X'00001C'
   e. DP   A,B   A : X'045C001D'   B : X'093C'
   f. DP   A,B   A : X'0000128C'   B : X'0738821C'

Use the following field definitions for questions 2, 3, and 4.

```
M           DS      PL12
N           DS      PL5
```

2. What is the minimum length which could safely be used to define a field WORK to be used to divide M by N?

3. Give the instruction which would be used to move the quotient to a field named QUOT after the following pair of instructions have been executed.

```
ZAP     WORK,M
DP      WORK,N
```

4. Write an instruction to copy the remainder to a field named REM after execution of the above pair of instructions.

5. Write instruction sequences to accomplish each of the following assignments. Write definitions for any work areas needed.

    a. X = (A+B) * (C−D)
    b. X = 5 * (A^2 − B*C)
    c. X = 3 * A^2 − 2*(B DIV C) + (A−B) MOD 5

6. Write a code segment to simulate the action of an automatic change maker. Given the definitions below, assume CENTS contains a positive integer. The code segment should determine the minimum number of quarters, dimes, nickels, and pennies to equal cents.

```
CENTS       DS      PL2
QUARTERS    DS      PL2
DIMES       DS      PL1
NICKELS     DS      PL1
PENNIES     DS      PL1
```

3.2 COMPARISONS

When we write programs in high-level languages, we control the path of execution through the use of standard constructs such as IF-THEN-ELSE, WHILE loops, and counted loops. On the assembly language level, such constructs are not directly available. Instead, we have primitive instructions that allow us to perform comparisons and then execute branches based on the results of those comparisons.

This gives us two options. We might change the way in which we program and attempt to write algorithms using the primitive assembly language tools, rather than the standard constructs of structured programming. This approach has been tried many times by many programmers, especially during the early days of programming. It has consistently resulted in programs that are harder to write, much harder to read, and almost impossible to modify and maintain. We will adopt a second approach. Rather than try to change the way we design programs, we will learn how to implement the standard constructs with the primitives that are available.

The implementation of any of these constructs, whether by a programmer or by a compiler, involves two steps. They are the evaluation of some condition and a branch that depends upon the result of that evaluation. The IBM 370, like most modern computers, separates these two steps into two types of machine-level instructions. They are the Compare instructions and the Branch instructions, both described in this section. In the next section, we will use these instructions to create the standard constructs of structured programming.

The Condition Code and the Program Status Word

Since the comparison and the branch are separate instructions, it must be possible to record the result of a comparison so that it may be examined by a conditional branch instruction. This is the function of the *Condition Code*.

The Condition Code is stored in a register called the *Program Status Word* (PSW). The PSW is a 64-bit register which contains a number of pieces of information that describe the status of the program. At this time, we are only interested in the Condition Code, which is 2 bits long, and the Instruction Address, which consists of the last 3 bytes of the PSW. (The actual location of the Condition Code in the PSW may vary and need not concern us at this time.)

Since the Condition Code is 2 bits long, it can take on the four values, B'00', B'01', B'10', B'11'. Thus, it can be used to record four distinct states. It is changed by all of the compare instructions and by some of the arithmetic instructions.

The compare instructions have two operands. They set the Condition Code to 0 if the operands are equal. The Condition Code is assigned B'01' if the first operand is less than the second operand or, in IBM's terminology, if the first operand is low. It is assigned B'10' = 2 if the first operand is greater than the second operand (first operand high). The compare instructions never assign a B'11' = 3 to the Condition Code.

When the Condition Code is changed by an arithmetic instruction, its new value indicates the status of the value which resulted from that operation. The Condition Code is assigned B'00', B'01', B'10' to indicate, respectively, that the result was 0 or that its sign was minus or plus. The Condition Code is set equal to B'11' = 3 if the operation produced an overflow.

These settings are summarized in the following table.

| | Condition Code Setting | | | |
	B'00'	B'01'	B'10'	B'11'
After an Arithmetic Instruction	0	Minus	Plus	Overflow
After a Compare Instruction	Equal	1st Op. Low	1st Op. High	------

Of the arithmetic instructions we have seen, AP, SP, and ZAP set the Condition Code. The Edit instruction also sets the Condition Code making it possible to determine whether the edited number was positive, negative, or zero. This information may then be used, for example, to insert a sign before or after the number in the output field.

Example 3.2.1 *Suppose that M contains X'03401D' and N contains X'00215C'.*

Then the instruction

       AP   M,N

stores the sum, X'03186D', in M and sets the Condition Code equal to B'01'.

As we have already seen, a string of bytes may be interpreted in a number of different ways. For example, it might be viewed as a character string, a packed decimal number, a zoned decimal number, or a signed or unsigned binary number. Given any two fields, it is not possible to determine their relative order without knowing how the data in them are to be interpreted. In the case of an IBM 370, a different comparison instruction is provided for each of the possible order relations.

When the values to be compared are to be interpreted as packed decimal numbers, we use the Compare Packed instruction. This instruction checks the sign stored in the last byte when determining the relative orders of the comparands. As character strings and unsigned binary numbers are ordered in the same way, they can be compared with the same instruction, Compare Logical Character (CLC).

Compare Packed

The Compare Packed is a two-length SS instruction, so the two operands need not have the same length. The values stored in the two fields are treated as signed decimal numbers. If their lengths are different, we may view the instruction as padding the shorter one with leading zeros before the comparison. Thus, the defined lengths of the fields will not affect the result of the comparison. This result is determined entirely by the values stored in the fields.

Compare Packed *CP 2-length SS*

       CP   S1(L1),S2(L2)

The contents of the memory locations designated by the two operands are compared and the Condition Code is set to indicate whether the first operand is Low, Equal, or High. The contents of both fields are treated as signed decimal numbers. Neither field is changed by the instruction.

Exceptions:

Access   Improper address for one or both operands.

Data   Invalid packed number in one or both fields.

Example 3.2.2 *Suppose that M contains X'000420259D' and N contains X'0000035C' and X and Y are defined by the following.*

```
M           DS          PL5
N           DS          PL4
```

Then after execution of

```
        CP          M,N
```

the Condition Code will be equal to B'01' indicating that the first operand is lower than the second.

The table in the example below shows the Condition Code setting and its interpretation for various operand fields. In considering the results in the table, it should be observed that all of the details work out as we would like them to. This means that we can use CP without being concerned about things that might go wrong. As long as both fields contain valid packed decimal numbers, no surprises will occur.

Example 3.2.3 *Suppose that M and N are as shown before execution of the following instruction.*

```
        CP          M,N
```

The table gives the value of the Condition Code after the instruction has been executed. Note that the result is not affected by either the lengths of the two fields or by alternative sign indicators.

M Before	N Before	Condition Code After
X'01341C'	X'01340C'	B'10' (M High)
X'00521D'	X'00521C'	B'01' (M Low)
X'032C'	X'00032F'	B'00' (Equal)

Compare Logical Character

When we compare two character strings of equal length, we proceed from left to right. As long as the corresponding characters are the same, we continue to examine the following characters. The first position where the two strings differ determines the relative order of the two strings. If we get to the end of the strings and find all positions to be identical, then the two strings are identical.

If we have two such strings stored as sequences of EBCDIC codes, we can determine the relative orders of the characters represented at each position simply by comparing the codes. In fact, if we interpret the entire sequence of codes as an unsigned binary number, then we can determine the order of the strings simply by comparing these numbers. In order to understand why this is so, consider that codes for the leftmost characters in the string, make up the high order bits of the corresponding number.

Example 3.2.4 *Suppose STR1 contains C'ABC' and STR2 contains C'AEC'.*

These two fields would be represented in EBCDIC as follows.

STR1: X'C1C2C3'   STR2: X'C1C5C3'

In binary form, these are

STR1: B'110000011100001011000011'
STR2: B'110000011100010111000011'

and we can easily see that the larger of the two strings, STR2, is represented by the larger number.

Similar results hold for machines that use other coding schemes such as ASCII. As long as codes are assigned to characters in alphabetical order, only one instruction is needed to compare character strings and unsigned binary numbers.

There are several instructions which perform this comparison. The Compare Logical Character (CLC) instruction can be used to compare character strings of up to 256 characters. Because there are a number of occasions when we need simply to examine a single character, the Compare Logical Immediate (CLI) instruction is provided to augment the CLC instruction. It allows us to compare a single memory byte with an immediate value specified in the instruction.

Compare Logical Character   *CLC 1-length SS*

     CLC   S1(L1),S2

The contents of the memory locations designated by the two operands are compared, one byte at a time, from left to right, until a position is found where the two fields differ or all bytes have been processed. If all bytes are the same, the Condition Code is set equal to B'00'. Otherwise, it is set to indicate the relative order of the leftmost position where the fields differ.

Exception:

Access   Improper address for one or both operands.

Compare Logical Immediate *CLI SI*

     CLI   S1,I2

The content of the memory location designated by the first operand is compared with the immediate byte specified by the second operand. The Condition Code is set to indicate their relative orders.

Exception:

Access   Improper address for first operand.

Example 3.2.5 *Suppose that STR1 and STR2 are defined by the following.*

```
STR1      DC      C'ABCDE'
STR2      DC      C'ABDCE'
```

Execution of the instruction

```
        CLC     STR1,STR2
```

will result in the Condition Code's being set equal to B'01' to indicate that the first operand, STR1, is lower than the second, STR2.
    Execution of the instruction

```
        CLI     STR2,C' '
```

will compare the first character of STR2 to the blank character and set the Condition Code to B'10' since the EBCDIC code for the first character of STR2 is X'C1', which is higher than the EBCDIC code for the blank character, X'40'.
    Because CLC is a one-length SS instruction, the assembler will put the length of the first operand in the instruction and this will determine the number of bytes to be compared. In order for the instruction to work correctly, the operands should represent fields of the same length. If we need to compare two character strings of differing lengths, we must move the shorter one to a work area and pad it with blanks.

Example 3.2.6 *Consider the code needed to compare character strings in the following fields.*

```
SHORT     DS      CL6
LONG      DS      CL20
```

Since their lengths are different, we define a work area

```
WORK      DS      CL20
```

to hold the smaller string during the comparison.
    We could move the shorter string into WORK, and pad it with blanks. In fact, it is easier to first fill WORK with blanks and then move SHORT into the left of WORK.
    The following instructions move a blank into the first byte of WORK with MVI, then use the MVC to propagate the blank throughout WORK. The 6 bytes from SHORT are copied into WORK using MVC with an explicit length. Finally, we use

CLC to compare WORK and LONG and set the Condition Code.

```
MVI     WORK,C' '
MVC     WORK+1(L'WORK−1),WORK
MVC     WORK(L'SHORT),SHORT
CLC     WORK,LONG
```

Branching

Our ultimate objective is to create control structures similar to the ones we use in high-level language. To this point, we have half of the tools necessary. Having set the Condition Code with any of the above instructions, we still need to be able to create instructions that will change the order of execution depending upon the value of the CC.

Using the assembler branch instruction that corresponds to the machine language branch instruction is rather cumbersome. Because of this, the assembler provides additional mnemonics, which it then uses to generate branch instructions for us. We will cover these 'extended mnemonics' and use them in our programming.

In addition to the Condition Code, the Program Status Word also contains a three-byte Instruction Address. Whenever the CPU is ready to execute a new instruction, it checks the Instruction Address in the PSW and fetches an instruction from this location in memory. The Instruction Address is then incremented by the length of the new instruction. In normal processing, this means that it will contain the address of the first memory location after the current instruction. This basic 'Fetch/Execute' cycle is repeated indefinitely and it is this cycle which causes the sequential execution of the part of a program that contains no branch instruction.

A branch instruction is implemented by providing a mechanism for altering the Instruction Address. Then, instead of executing the instruction which follows the current instruction in memory, the CPU will execute the instruction whose address has been placed in the Instruction Address part of the PSW.

At our current level of programming, an address is represented by a label. We have already placed labels in our code with the EQU directive. All that remains is to invoke an instruction to examine the Condition Code and, depending upon its value, to place the address corresponding to a label in the Instruction Address or to leave this part of the PSW unchanged. This can be accomplished with the Branch on Condition (BC) instruction.

The BC instruction uses the RX instruction format, but, as it is not a typical RX instruction, we do not consider the complete format until later, but present here a somewhat restricted form of the instruction.

The instruction has two operands. The first is a 4-bit mask, which determines under what conditions a branch will take place. The second operand determines the branch address. It is usually a label.

The four bits in the mask are interpreted in the following way.

1. Number the bits from left to right beginning with 0.
2. If the value of the Condition Code is i and bit number i is 1, then store the address determined by the second operand in the Instruction Address portion of the Program Status Word (i.e., branch to this location for the next instruction). Otherwise, do nothing.

Branch on Condition *BC RX*

> BC   M1,S2

M1 represents a 4-bit mask in which the bits are numbered from left to right, 0,1,2,3. If the Condition Code is i and bit i is 1, then store the address represented by S2 in the Instruction Address.

Exceptions: None.

Example 3.2.7 *The following instruction will branch to the label TOP if the Condition Code is 1 or 3.*

> BC   B'0101',TOP

If the CC is 0 or 2, no branch will occur and execution would continue with the instruction after this one.

The instruction

> BC   B'1111',TOP

will branch to TOP for any value of the Condition Code. It is equivalent to an unconditional branch instruction.

The instruction

> BC   B'0000',TOP

will not branch under any circumstances. It is referred to as a NOP (No Operation) instruction. Although it may appear to be of little use, we will see that there are situations where it is advantageous to be able to insert an instruction in a program that does not affect the state of the computation.

Example 3.2.8 *Suppose we want to compare two packed fields, COUNT and LIMIT, and branch to STOP if COUNT is greater than or equal to LIMIT.*

We use the CP instruction to set the condition and then write a BC with the appropriate mask.

If we test COUNT and LIMIT with

> CP   COUNT,LIMIT

then we need to branch if the CC is 0 (COUNT = LIMIT) or 2 (COUNT > LIMIT).

Our mask should have a 1 for bits 0 and 1 and 0's for the other two bits. This yields the instruction

BC   B'1010',STOP

We can generate all the branches we need to by using the BC instruction with appropriate masks. However, the task of generating the masks is somewhat tedious and prone to error. In order to alleviate this problem, the assembler can generate the masks for us. This is accomplished by providing a list of 'extended mnemonics' that describe the conditions under which the branch should take place. In order to make these as useful as possible, there is one set of mnemonics which should be used after a comparison and another set to use after an arithmetic operation.

For use after a comparison instruction:

BH   Branch on first operand High
BL   Branch on first operand Low
BE   Branch on operands Equal
BNH   Branch on first operand Not High
BNL   Branch on first operand Not Low
BNE   Branch on first operand Not Equal

For use after an arithmetic instruction:

BP   Branch on Plus
BM   Branch on Minus
BZ   Branch on Zero
BO   Branch on Overflow
BNP   Branch on Not Plus
BNM   Branch on Not Minus
BNZ   Branch on Not Zero
BNO   Branch on No Overflow

In addition to these, we have already used the extended mnemonic for an unconditional branch, B, when we designed a loop to process input records until End-Of-File in Chapter 1. The mnemonic NOP is used to instruct the assembler to generate the BC instruction with all zeros in the mask.

Example 3.2.9 *In Example 3.2.8, after the comparison of COUNT and LIMIT, we needed a branch to STOP if COUNT was greater than or equal to LIMIT. With the extended mnemonics, we are able to write a somewhat more meaningful instruction.*

Paraphrasing the branch condition to correspond to those in the list of extended mnemonics, we need to branch if COUNT is not low. We have the following pair of instructions.

```
CP     COUNT,LIMIT
BNL    STOP
```

Example 3.2.10 *The following set of instructions compares two character strings, ITEM and KEY, then branches to FOUND if they are equal or branches to CONTIN if ITEM is less than KEY.*

```
CLC    ITEM,KEY
BE     FOUND
BL     CONTIN
```

The examples above illustrate one of the advantages in separating the comparison and the branch operations into two distinct instructions. It is not necessary to provide a complete set of branch operations for every possible data type. Each data type needs only to be provided with its own comparison instruction. Once the Condition Code has been set, the same set of branch instructions can be used for all types. In fact, as we have seen, all of these apparently different branches are implemented by means of a single branch instruction, BC.

We have seen that the use of extended mnemonics can help improve the readability of a program. In the next section, we introduce a number of additional techniques for using the branch instructions in a well-structured program.

E X E R C I S E S

1. Give the value of the Condition Code after execution of the instruction CP M,N for each of the following pairs of values of M and N.

M	**N**
a. X'00134F'	X'134C'
b. X'0003859C'	X'0003859D'
c. X'84796C'	X'97856D'
d. X'00001D'	X'00000C'
e. X'09479D'	X'847D'

2. Write the code that would be required to compare each of the following pairs of strings.

a. SNGR1	DC	C'PAUL SIMON'
SNGR2	DC	C'ART GARFUNKLE'
b. STR1	DC	C'CLEESE'
STR2	DC	C'PYTHON'

3. Given operands with the following values, give the result of executing each of the following pairs of instructions.

A : X'0769438C' C : X'0000081C'
B : X'9768345D' D : X'0000000C'

a. CP   A,B
    BNH   LOOP1
b. CP   A,B
    BL   LOOP1
c. CP   D, =P'0'
    BE   DONE
d. AP   B,C
    BP   POS
e. SP   C,B
    BNM   TOP
f. ZAP   D,C
    BNZ   NODIV

3.3 STRUCTURE IN ASSEMBLY LANGUAGE PROGRAMS

The branch instructions seen in the last section are the only mechanisms available for controlling the flow of an assembly language program. However, the fact that we must write programs with explicit branch instructions does not mean that we can disregard the precepts of structured programming stressed in earlier courses. On the contrary, it was for precisely this type of programming that these rules were originally developed.

There are two basic reasons for adhering to the precepts of structured programming. First, they enable us to produce programs with minimal effort, partly because we can use the available constructs to produce code that is adapted to the particular problem being solved, rather than forcing an adaptation to available machine language instructions. The natural relationship between the problem and its solution makes it easier to read and understand the program. This relationship strongly influences the second factor in favor of structured programming techniques; the resulting programs are easier to modify and maintain. If there is a natural relationship between a program and the problem being solved, then any reasonable change in the context of the problem produces a fairly obvious change in the code. In particular, a change of small scope in the problem will require a change of similarly small scope in the solution.

Structured programming played an important part in the development of modern languages such as Pascal. As a result, it is difficult, although not impossible, to write an unstructured Pascal program. The language was designed to make structured programming the path of least resistance.

Unfortunately, it is all too easy to write unstructured assembly language programs. It was, in fact, an environment consisting primarily of assembly language and Fortran 66 programming which Djkstra addressed in his letter, "GO TO Statement Considered Harmful," in 1968.

Obviously, we cannot write assembly language programs without the use of branch instructions. However, we must exercise the discipline needed to avoid the pitfalls of the limitless use of branches referred to by Djkstra. We will do so by adopting this policy: **Never use a branch instruction except as part of the standard constructs of structured programming such as an IF-THEN-ELSE, a counted loop, or an indefinite iteration.**

We adhere to this policy by setting up patterns to implement each of the standard constructs. These patterns include conventions for labelling, comments, and indentation of comments.

In addition to providing the protection afforded by structured programming practices, this approach will allow us to develop algorithmic solutions in the same manner as in earlier courses. This enables us to build upon the programming experience we have already gained, rather than requiring us to adopt new approaches to programming.

IF-THEN-ELSE

Whenever an algorithm calls for an IF-THEN-ELSE construct, we will implement it with the following pattern

```
IFmm       EQU    *              IF <condition        >
           <Instructions  >      :
           <to set up the >      :
           <comparison.   >      :
           C--                   :
           B--                   :
THENmm     EQU    *              THEN
           <Instructions  >          <Comments for  >
           <to implement  >          <THEN clause   >
           <THEN clause.  >          <indented four >
                                     <spaces.       >
           B     ENDIFmm             :
ELSEmm     EQU    *              ELSE
           <Instructions  >          <Comments for  >
           <to implement  >          <ELSE clause   >
           <ELSE clause.   >         <indented four >
                                     <spaces.       >
ENDIFmm    EQU    *              ENDIF
```

Each occurrence of 'mm' in the pattern will be replaced by a two-digit number to distinguish the labels in this construct from those in other IF-THEN-ELSE constructs in the program. C-- and B-- represent the comparison and branch instructions appropriate to the condition and data type involved.

In a number of cases, we can summarize the effect of several assembly language instructions with a single comment. In order to keep logical dependencies clear, we use a properly indented colon as a comment on lines that have no other comments.

The particular comparison instruction used will depend upon the type of data being compared. If we only need to test an arithmetic expression to determine whether it is positive, negative, or zero, then no comparison will be needed if the last arithmetic operation performed is one which sets the Condition Code.

The branch instruction should be formed by negating the condition given in the first comment line. As we want to execute the THEN clause when the condition is true, the branch instruction should be chosen to cause a branch to the ELSE clause when it is false. The choice of this instruction requires some care. The problem is to make certain that we properly negate the condition. For example, if the condition given in the comment is $A <= B$, then the case $A = B$ should be handled by the THEN clause and the branch must occur if $A > B$. If the code for the comparison compares A and B in that order, then the correct branch instruction is BH.

Example 3.3.1 *Suppose that A, B, and C are packed fields and that we need to implement the following algorithm segment.*

```
IF  A < 2*B+C
THEN X = B+C−A
ELSE X = B−2*C+A
```

Assuming this is the third IF-THEN-ELSE in the program, we would use

```
IF03      EQU    *            IF A < 2*B+C
          ZAP    TEMP,B       :
          AP     TEMP,B       :
          AP     TEMP,C       :
          CP     A,TEMP       :
          BNL    ELSE03       :
THEN03    EQU    *            THEN
          ZAP    X,B              X = B+C−A
          AP     X,C          :
          SP     X,A          :
          B      ENDIF03      :
ELSE03    EQU    *            ELSE
          ZAP    X,B              X = B−2*C+A
          SP     X,C          :
          SP     X,C          :
          AP     X,A          :
ENDIF03   EQU    *            ENDIF
```

Again, there are no branch instructions that use the labels IF03 and THEN03 as targets. The presence of these labels, however, does make it much easier to see the logical structure of the program. Their presence is especially important in programs that have nested IF-THEN-ELSEs. The use of such labels is in no way extravagant, as they do not effect the object code at all.

Counted Loops

In designing a construct for a counted loop, we would like to be able to implement the equivalent of one of the counted loop structures from a high-level language. We adopt the following as a basic algorithmic construct.

FOR <loop_counter> = <limit1> TO <limit2> BY <delta>
  .
  .
  .
ENDFOR

Clearly, we want this to be interpreted in a way that is compatible with common loop semantics in high-level languages. This means that the values of limit1, limit2, and delta should be determined before loop entry and their values stored, so that they may not be changed during execution of the loop. We dedicate a separate storage field to each of these values to assure that they will not be changed accidentally.

Our intention to mimic loop semantics common to most high-level languages also implies that our loop should be top-tested. The value of the loop counter should be compared with the value of limit2 before the first and all subsequent entries to the loop range.

With these considerations in mind, we construct the following pattern.

```
FORmm      EQU     *              FOR <ctr> = <lim1> TO <lim2>
           <Instructions to   >       :
           <initialize ctr to  >      :
           <lim1 and to assign >      :
           <the value of lim2  >      :
           <to LIMmm.          >      :
FTESTmm    EQU     *                  :
           C--     <ctr>,LIMmm        :
           BH      ENDFORmm           :
           <Instructions to   >   <Comments describing >
           <implement  loop   >   <loop range indented   >
           <range.            >   <four spaces.          >
                                      :
           <Instruction to    >       :
           <increment ctr.    >       :
           B     FTESTmm              :
ENDFORmm EQU      *              ENDFOR
```

Example 3.3.2 *Suppose that we need to set a field FACT equal to the factorial of the non-negative integer in a packed decimal field, N.*

```
FACT = 1
For I = 1 to N
    FACT = FACT*I
End
```

Using the pattern for a counted loop, we can easily translate this short algorithm to assembly code as

```
          ZAP     FACT,=P'1'          FACT = 1
FOR04     EQU     *                   FOR I = 1 TO N
          ZAP     I,=P'1'               :
          ZAP     LIM04,N               :
FTEST04   EQU     *                     :
          CP      I,LIM04               :
          BH      ENDFOR04              :
          MP      FACT,I              FACT = FACT*I
          AP      I,=P'1'               :
          B       FTEST04               :
ENDFOR04  EQU     *                   ENDFOR
```

Because we implemented a top-tested counted loop, our code will work correctly even for $N = 0$. In this case, the initial value of the loop counter will exceed the upper limit N and the range of the loop will not be executed at all. Nevertheless, the final value of FACT will be 1 or 0-factorial.

Indefinite Iterations

The other primary construct of structured programming is indefinite iteration. This is often found as a top-tested WHILE loop or as a bottom-tested REPEAT-UNTIL loop. We provide patterns for both types, observing that we have already implemented a special purpose REPEAT-UNTIL loop for processing input records until End-Of-File.

```
WHILEmm   EQU     *              WHILE <condition        >
          <Instructions to  >      :
          <test entry cond-  >     :
          <ition and branch  >     :
          <to ENDWHLmm if>         :
          <it is false.      >     :
                                    :
          <Instructions for  >    <Comments for loop  >
          <loop range.       >    <range indented four >
                                  <spaces.             >
          B    WHILEmm              :
ENDWHLmm  EQU     *              ENDWHILE
```

```
REPEATmm  EQU    *                 REPEAT
          <Instructions for  >        <Comments for loop    >
          <loop range.       >        <range indented four  >
                                      <spaces.              >
          <Instructions to   >        :
          <test condition    >        :
          <and branch to     >        :
          <REPEATmm if        >        :
          <it is false.      >        :
UNTILmm   EQU    *                 UNTIL <condition         >
```

Example 3.3.3 *The application of Euclid's Algorithm to find the greatest common divisor of two integers requires repeated integer division until the remainder is zero. If we call the two integers M and N, we have the following.*

```
DVSR = M
RMNDR = N
WHILE RMNDR <> 0
    DVDND = DVSR
    DVSR = RMNDR
    RMNDR = DVDND MOD DVSR
ENDWHILE
GCD = DVSR
```

Using our standard form to translate this to assembly language, we have

```
          ZAP    DVSR,M              DVSR = M
          ZAP    RMNDR,N             RMNDR = N
WHILE03   EQU    *                   WHILE (RMNDR <> 0)
          CP     RMNDR,=P'0'          :
          BE     ENDWHL03             :
          ZAP    DVDND,DVSR           DVDND = DVSR
          ZAP    DVSR,RMNDR           DVSR = RMNDR
          ZAP    DVWRK,DVDND          RMNDR = DVDND MOD DVSR
          DP     DVWRK,DVSR           :
          ZAP    RMNDR,DVWRK+L'DVWRK−L'RMNDR(L'RMNDR)
          B      WHILE03              :
ENDWHL03  EQU    *                   ENDWHILE
          ZAP    GCD,DVSR            GCD = DVSR
```

In this particular case, the use of a top-tested loop is not closely related to the structure of the algorithm itself. If we can assume that the field N is nonzero, then we can safely dispense with the top-tested loop and use the following.

```
               ZAP    DVSR,M                    DVSR = M
               ZAP    RMNDR,N                   RMNDR = N
REPEAT07       EQU    *                         REPEAT
               ZAP    DVDND,DVSR                  DVDND = DVSR
               ZAP    DVSR,RMNDR                  DVSR = RMNDR
               ZAP    DVWRK,DVDND                 RMNDR = DVDND MOD DVSR
               DP     DVWRK,DVSR                  :
               ZAP    RMNDR,DVWRK+L'DVWRK−L'RMNDR(L'RMNDR)
               CP     RMNDR,=P'0'                 :
               BNE    REPEAT07                    :
UNTIL07        EQU    *                         UNTIL RMNDR = 0
               ZAP    GCD,DVSR                  GCD = DVSR
```

Finally, we observe that in both cases the use of the ZAP instruction to move the remainder to the field RMNDR automatically sets the CC to indicate whether RMNDR is 0. The explicit use of a compare instruction is unnecessary. Omitting this from the second example, we have

```
               ZAP    DVSR,M                    DVSR = M
               ZAP    RMNDR,N                   RMNDR = N
REPEAT07       EQU    *                         REPEAT
               ZAP    DVDND,DVSR                  DVDND = DVSR
               ZAP    DVSR,RMNDR                  DVSR = RMNDR
               ZAP    DVWRK,DVDND                 RMNDR = DVDND MOD DVSR
               DP     DVWRK,DVSR                  :
               ZAP    RMNDR,DVWRK+L'DVWRK−L'RMNDR(L'RMNDR)
               BNZ    REPEAT07                    :
UNTIL07        EQU    *                         UNTIL RMNDR = 0
               ZAP    GCD,DVSR                  GCD = DVSR
```

In the next section, we see how to define a work area so that the quotient and remainder can be accessed more easily. This is one of many instances in which we gain additional efficiency by taking advantage of our understanding of assembly language. However, at this time, our main emphasis must be on the production of reliable programs. We are much more likely to succeed by relying upon experience already gained in designing programs. In general, we should attempt to minimize the effects of programming in assembly language. One way to do this is to make the translation from an algorithmic solution to an assembly language program as automatic as possible—the primary purpose of our introduction of the standard structures. Even in those cases where their use leads to code that can be improved upon, they still enable us to produce assembly language programs more quickly and reliably than would otherwise be possible. Once we have gained experience and confidence in our ability to write assembly language programs, we can begin to look for marginal improvements in speed and efficiency.

E X E R C I S E S

Assuming that all fields are packed decimal, write instructions to implement the following constructs.

1. IF 2*A < B−C
   THEN
       X = B+C−2
   ELSE
       X = B−C*A
   ENDIF

2. COUNT = 0
   WHILE COUNT <= NUMGRDS
       COUNT = COUNT+1
       TOTGRD = TOTGRD+STUGRD
   ENDWHILE

3. FOR I = 1 TO EXPONENT
       POWER = POWER*NUMBER
   ENDFOR

4. I = NUMBER
   REPEAT
       I = I DIV 2
       EXPONENT = EXPONENT+1
   UNTIL I = 0

5. REMNDR = NUMBER MOD 2
   IF REMNDR = 0
   THEN
       EVEN = EVEN+1
   ELSE
       ODD = ODD+1
   ENDIF

6. Suppose that an input file consists of employee records and daily time records. The employee record indicates the number of days the employee worked. It is followed in the input file by the appropriate number of daily time records in the format shown below. Assuming that an employee record has been read and the number of days worked has been packed into the field TOTDAYS, write a FOR loop to read the correct number of daily time records and sum the total hours in TOTHOURS.

```
DAYTIME    DS     CL80
           ORG    DAYTIME
INHOURS    DS     ZL5
           ORG    DAYTIME+L'DAYTIME
```

7. Suppose that we have a file, DAYFILE, of daily time records in the following format.

```
DAYTIME    DS      CL20
           ORG     DAYTIME
DAYEMPNM   DS      ZL8
INHOURS    DS      ZL5
           ORG     DAYTIME+L'DAYTIME
```

Assume that the records in DAYFILE are in ascending order of employee numbers and that EMPNUM contains an employee number. Assume also that the file is currently positioned at the first record for the employee whose number is in EMPNUM. Write code to calculate the total hours for this employee.

8. Suppose an input file consists of 12 records, one for each month. Assume that these records are defined by

```
MONTHLY    DS      CL80
           ORG     MONTHLY
INAVG      DS      ZL3
           ORG     MONTHLY+L'MONTHLY
```

Write the code to read these records from TEMPFILE and find the yearly average.

9. A semester average of all students in a class has been calculated and stored in CLSAVG. The number of students in the class is stored in the field NUMSTU. Given an input file, STUAVGS, which contains the average for each student in the class, write the code to read the individual averages and count the number of students above the class average. Assume that the input records are defined by

```
STUDENT    DS      CL80
           ORG     STUDENT
STUAVG     DS      ZL3
           ORG     STUDENT+L'STUDENT
```

10. Assume that two fields, WORD1 and WORD2 contain strings of 20 characters each. Write the code to exchange their values, if necessary, so that WORD1 < WORD2.

3.4 WELL-STRUCTURED DATA

One of our objectives in programming is to develop a natural relationship between a problem and its solution. Attempts to develop and exploit such a relationship cannot succeed if we restrict our attentions to the code produced. We must devote a corresponding amount of effort to the design of the data structures that will be used. If the relationship between the data structures in a program and the "natural objects" of the problem is contrived and artificial, then we cannot possibly produce code that will manipulate these data structures in a natural way.

The problem we face in trying to produce effective data structures in an assembly language program is similar to that faced in producing well-structured code. We have at our immediate disposal only the most primitive of data types. The assembler and the machine language instructions that we have seen so far appear to support only simple scalar variables and character strings. The IBM 370 also provides several instructions for manipulating arrays. It would, however, be a serious error to limit our programs to these simple types. Instead, we will follow a course analogous to the one adopted for structuring code, using the primitive types available together with facilities provided by the assembler to construct more complex types.

In this section, there are several methods for structuring data. The examples presented illustrate how these methods can be used to define data structures, which are both natural and easy to modify. We need to create a natural bond between the data structures and the code, which allows easy modification of both. At this point, we restrict our attention to record structures and variant record structures. In later chapters, we consider arrays of the primitive types and of these structured types.

Using Symbols to Create Modifiable Data Structures

The most common change in problem specification is a simple change in the size of an input field. Regardless of the complexity of the problem being solved, such a change must be viewed as trivial. It is not unreasonable to expect it to be accommodated by an equally trivial change in the program. Unfortunately, this is often not the case. The problem is that the length of one field may have a wide ranging effect on a program.

For example, the length of a zoned number in an input record may determine the length of a packed field to hold the number, the lengths of one or more accumulators, and the lengths of one or more output fields and edit masks. To further complicate matters, any of these lengths may appear as an explicit length in an instruction. If a programmer uses the actual length of the input field and the derived lengths of the other fields, then a change in the input specifications may require extensive changes in the program.

We can protect ourselves from some of these ill effects by never using an actual length in an instruction. Instead, we always use the length attribute, L', perhaps as part of a formula, whenever it is necessary to include an explicit length in an instruction. Suppose QTY is an input field of length 8, and we want to place it in the extreme left of a larger field, OUTFLD. The instruction

```
MVC     OUTFLD(8),QTY
```

would have the desired effect, but its use reduces the ability of the program to respond to changing problem specifications. The instruction

```
        MVC     OUTFLD(L'QTY),QTY
```

is preferable for a number of reasons, but of greater interest is that a change in the field QTY can be accommodated without changing this instruction.

Having gone to some effort to make our code responsive to changes in the problem specifications, we now consider ways to make our storage definitions equally responsive to such changes. The approach is similar. If the length of a particular field depends upon some other quantity, then that dependency should be made explicit in the storage definition.

For example, suppose we are defining two packed fields, QONHND and QONORD, and that the particular application requires that these two fields have the same length. If that length is currently 6 bytes, then we could write the storage definitions as

```
QONHND  DS      PL6
QONORD  DS      PL(L'QONHND)
```

Now, if we change the length of QONHND, we can be assured of maintaining the desired relationship.

This still has the potential for some minor problems. If there are a number of fields with the same length, or related lengths, it may not always be clear which should be given the actual length and which ones should be defined in terms of the length attributes of other fields. If the data areas are large, making a change may necessitate searching a number of instructions before finding where the change should be made. An alternative is to use the EQU directive to define constants that represent lengths and then to use the constants to define the storage areas. These constants may then be grouped together at the beginning of the storage definition section, making it an easy matter to find and change a particular value.

If we adopted this approach in the example above, we would have the EQU instruction

```
QLEN      EQU     6
```

at the beginning of the storage definition section. The storage definitions themselves would become

```
QONHND  DS      PL(QLEN)
QONORD  DS      PL(QLEN)
```

Example 3.4.1 *Suppose we are writing a program to read a set of input records containing two zoned decimal fields named QTY and AMT. Assume these two fields are 5 bytes each. Our program is to multiply the numbers in these two fields and place the packed product in a field named PTOTAL.*

We will write a set of storage definitions for the fields needed for the multiplication, beginning by writing symbol definitions for the required lengths. In the absence of any other information about the problem, we should probably view the fact that the input fields are the same length as being coincidental. Thus we define two symbols

```
QTYLEN     EQU     5
AMTLEN     EQU     5
```

We find the correct length for the two packed fields by evaluating the assembler expression <zoned length>/2+1. As the assembler uses integer division, this expression always computes the correct length, leaving room for the sign indicator. Thus, we have

```
PQTYLEN    EQU     QTYLEN/2+1
PAMTLEN    EQU     AMTLEN/2+1
```

The length of the work area for the multiplication can be defined by

```
WRKLEN     EQU     PQTYLEN+PAMTLEN
```

In the absence of any knowledge about the actual values involved, PTOTAL should be defined with the same length as the work area.

```
TOTLEN     EQU     WRKLEN
```

The storage definitions for the input fields, the packed fields, and the work areas are

```
QTY        DS      ZL(QTYLEN)
AMT        DS      ZL(AMTLEN)
PQTY       DS      PL(PQTYLEN)
PAMT       DS      PL(PAMTLEN)
WORK       DS      PL(WRKLEN)
PTOTAL     DS      PL(TOTLEN)
```

We can now see how easily these fields can be changed to accommodate varying input specifications. If, for example, the length of QTY is changed to 7 bytes, we have only to change the EQU for QTYLEN. All of the other changes required will be made automatically when the program is reassembled. Similarly, if additional information about the values leads us to conclude that the product will always have a byte of leading zeros, then we can reduce the size of the field PTOTAL by rewriting the EQU instruction for TOTLEN.

Creating Record Structures

In a high-level language, a record structure is generally viewed as a single entity that can be divided into subfields. A simple record structure may be referred to by a single name and manipulated as a unit by some instructions, but, when convenient, the fields of the record may also be referenced by name and accessed individually. For example, in Pascal, a record type NAMES may be defined to contain three fields, FIRST, MIDDLE, and LAST. Then, if STUDENT is a variable of type NAMES, we can refer to all three components at once as STUDENT or we can access the three fields separately as STUDENT.FIRST, STUDENT.MIDDLE, and STUDENT.LAST.

In order to implement such a record in assembly language, we need to define a field called STUDENT containing all three names and then three fields, FIRST, MIDDLE, and LAST in such a way that they will occupy the same storage locations as STUDENT. This can be accomplished by defining STUDENT, then using the ORG instruction to reset the location counter to the beginning of the field STUDENT, and writing storage definitions for the three subfields. If we begin by defining symbols for the lengths of these fields, we have

```
FIRSTLEN    EQU     10
MIDLEN      EQU     10
LASTLEN     EQU     20
NAMELEN     EQU     FIRSTLEN+MIDLEN+LASTLEN
```

The storage definitions are

```
STUDENT     DS      CL(NAMELEN)     STUDENT
            ORG     STUDENT         :
FRSTNAME    DS      CL(FIRSTLEN)      FIRST NAME
MIDNAME     DS      CL(MIDLEN)        MIDDLE NAME
LASTNAME    DS      CL(LASTLEN)       LAST NAME
```

In order to understand the effect of these instructions, suppose that, when the first DS is processed, the location counter has X'12A' as its value. The listing below shows the value of the location counter at the beginning of each instruction.

```
LOCATION      INSTRUCTION
COUNTER
12A           STUDENT     DS      CL(NAMELEN)
152                       ORG     STUDENT
12A           FRSTNAME    DS      CL(FIRSTLEN)
134           MIDNAME     DS      CL(MIDLEN)
13E           LASTNAME    DS      CL(LASTLEN)
152
```

The value of the location counter at the beginning of a DS or DC instruction is interpreted as the distance from the beginning of the program to the beginning of the field being defined. STUDENT and FRSTNAME will both begin X'12A' bytes from the beginning of the program. MIDNAME begins 10 bytes after the start of STUDENT and LASTNAME 10 bytes later. Because STUDENT consists of 40 bytes, these fields coincide as desired.

We can easily extend this approach to create more complex record structures. For instance, it is often natural for a field in a record structure to be further subdivided into other fields.

Example 3.4.2 *Suppose we need to create a record structure that will contain employee information for a payroll program. The record will contain an employee number in zoned form (9 digits), the employee's name and address. The name field will contain the employee's last name, first name, and middle initial (in that order). The address field will consist of a street address, city, state, and ZIP code.*

The following storage definitions allow us to access the entire record, the employee number, name and address, or the employee's last name, first name, middle initial, street address, city, state, or ZIP code as needed.

```
ENUMLEN   EQU   9
LASTLEN   EQU   15
FIRSTLEN  EQU   10
MIDLEN    EQU   1
NAMELEN   EQU   FIRSTLEN+MIDLEN+LASTLEN
STRTLEN   EQU   20
CITYLEN   EQU   10
STATELEN  EQU   2
ZIPLEN    EQU   5
ADDRLEN   EQU   STRTLEN+CITYLEN+STATELEN+ZIPLEN
RECLEN    EQU   ENUMLEN+NAMELEN+ADDRLEN
EMPREC    DS    CL(RECLEN)         EMPLOYEE RECORD
          ORG   EMPREC             :
EMPNUM    DS    ZL(ENUMLEN)        EMPLOYEE NUMBER
EMPNAME   DS    CL(NAMELEN)        EMPLOYEE NAME
          ORG   EMPNAME            :
LASTNAME  DS    CL(LASTLEN)          LAST NAME
FRSTNAME  DS    CL(FIRSTLEN)         FIRST NAME
MIDINIT   DS    CL(MIDLEN)           MIDDLE INITIAL
ADDRESS   DS    CL(ADDRLEN)        ADDRESS
          ORG   ADDRESS            :
STREET    DS    CL(STRTLEN)          STREET
CITY      DS    CL(CITYLEN)          CITY
STATE     DS    CL(STATELEN)         STATE
ZIPCODE   DS    CL(ZIPLEN)           ZIP CODE
```

Note that the first ORG will reset the location counter to the beginning of EMPREC, allowing us to subdivide this record. The second ORG allows us to redefine the field EMPNAME. As NAMELEN is equal to the sum of the lengths of the three following fields, the storage areas occupied by these fields will coincide with that allocated to EMPNAME. Similarly, the last ORG instruction permits us to define the subfields of the filed ADDRESS.

As in the example above, we use indentation in the remarks column to illustrate the record structure. This justifies the inclusion of remarks such as STREET, CITY, and ADDRESS, which otherwise appear redundant. In each case, the remark itself conveys no new information, but its position on the line does.

Variant Record Structures

The key mechanism in our definition of a record structure is the ability to assign a value to the location counter, using the ORG instruction. This allows us to define the entire record as a single entity and then to redefine the same set of storage locations to represent the subfields of the record. But, if we like, we can repeat this process and provide other definitions for the same storage area. This allows us to define variant record structures.

We can use variant record definitions to simplify use of the division instruction. Recall that the storage area used for the division assumes two formats. Before the division takes place, it should contain a single packed number. After the division operation, it contains both the quotient and remainder. The ORG instruction allows us to provide both definitions of the storage area as the following example shows.

Example 3.4.3 *Suppose it is required to divide a packed field named TOTAL by a packed field named COUNT and to store the quotient in the field AVERAGE.*

We can define the work area for the division as follows.

```
DIVWORK    DS     XL(L'TOTAL+L'COUNT)
           ORG    DIVWORK
DIVIDEND   DS     PL(L'DIVWORK)
           ORG    DIVWORK
QUOTIENT   DS     PL(L'DIVWORK−L'COUNT)
REMNDR     DS     PL(L'COUNT)
```

With this definition, DIVWORK is simply a byte-field of an appropriate length. The two alternate structures allow us to view DIVWORK as a single packed decimal number, DIVIDEND, or as the pair of packed decimal numbers, QUOTIENT and REMNDR.

When preparing the work area for the division, we view it as a single packed decimal number. After moving the dividend into the work area with a ZAP instruction and performing the division, we use the second alternative, and view the work area as two packed decimal numbers. The quotient is then moved to AVERAGE with another ZAP. This yields the following instruction sequence.

```
ZAP     DIVIDEND,TOTAL
DP      DIVIDEND,COUNT
ZAP     AVERAGE,QUOTIENT
```

The symbol DIVWORK need not be used in the code. We have used it in the storage definitions to emphasize the fact that we are manipulating a single entity that can assume two distinct forms.

Variant record structures are equally useful in problems that allow input records of several different formats. We would like to be able to read such a record as a character string. However, once we have determined what type of record has been read, we would like to access individual fields of the record by names that depend upon the record type. We can achieve this by providing storage definitions that first describe the entire record and then redefine appropriate fields. Typically, the definitions describe a fixed field, which indicates the record type, and varying fields, which correspond to each of the possible types. This is illustrated in the following example.

Example 3.4.4 *Suppose we are writing a program to implement a simple text editor. The available commands are Insert, Delete, and Change, each represented by a single character in column 1. The formats are as shown below.*

Insert	I	Column 1
	Line Number	Columns 2-4
	Text	Columns 5-80
Delete	D	Column 1
	Line Number	Columns 2-4
Change	C	Column 1
	Old String	Columns 2-21
	New String	Columns 22-41

We assume that the line number for the Insert command is the number of the line before which the new text should be inserted. The line number in the Delete command is the number of the line to be deleted. Thus, although they both represent line numbers, their meanings differ so we will give them different names.

```
CODELEN    EQU    1
LNUMLEN    EQU    3
STRLEN     EQU    20
TEXTLEN    EQU    80-CODELEN-LNUMLEN
```

```
COMMAND   DS    CL80                    INPUT RECORD
          ORG   COMMAND                 :
CODE      DS    CL(CODELEN)             COMMAND CODE
VARIANT   DS    CL(80-CODELEN)          VARIANTS
          ORG   VARIANT                     INSERT COMMAND
INSNUM    DS    ZL(LNUMLEN)                     LINE NUMBER
INSTEXT   DS    CL(TEXTLEN)                     TEXT
          ORG   VARIANT                     DELETE COMMAND
DELNUM    DS    ZL(LNUMLEN)                     LINE NUMBER
          ORG   VARIANT                     CHANGE COMMAND
OLDSTR    DS    CL(STRLEN)                      OLD STRING
NEWSTR    DS    CL(STRLEN)                      NEW STRING
          ORG   COMMAND+L'COMMAND       END INPUT RECORD
```

The three possible formats for the resulting storage area are shown below.

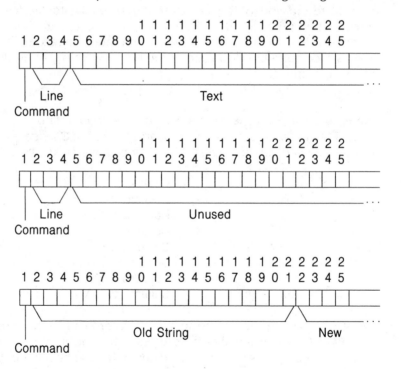

In this example, we see two obvious advantages of using variant record structures. The first is simplicity. Without variant record structures, it would be necessary to determine the type of each input record and move it to a different work area whose format was compatible with the record type. The second advantage is a savings in the space required for the program. We do not need to define a separate storage area for each possible format.

Output Records

Just as we find it convenient to provide alternative structures for input records, it is also useful to be able to describe different formats for an output record. In this case, because these records are typically 133 bytes each, the amount of storage area saved may be substantial.

The ORG instruction can be used in two distinct ways to describe a field in an output record. In the first case, it is often desirable to begin a field in a particular column. This is generally the case when a printer spacing chart has been used to describe the format of the output. To do this, we need to be able to specify the starting position of a field relative to the beginning of the output record. The ORG instruction will be of the form

```
ORG      <record name>+<displacement>
```

When the first byte of the output record is being used as a printer control character, this is particularly simple. The printer control character corresponds to displacement 0, and the displacement for each of the print positions is the same as the column number of that position. To begin a subfield of LINE in column 10, we precede its storage definition by

```
ORG      LINE+10
```

The second use of ORG in defining an output field is to skip a particular number of positions between two output fields. To specify the number of spaces between the end of one field and the beginning of the next we use

```
ORG      *+<skip>
```

The effect is simply to increment the location counter by the number of positions to be skipped as in

```
ORG      *+5
```

Equivalently, if we want to specify the number of spaces from the beginning of the one field to the beginning of the next, we use

```
ORG      <field name>+<skip>
```

Both of these uses of ORG are illustrated in the following example.

Example 3.4.5 *Suppose we want to create a student registration report that has two heading lines and a detail line in the formats shown on the next page.*

```
              CENTRAL HIGH SCHOOL
           FINAL REGISTRATION REPORT

      DEPT    COURSE    CREDIT    PASS/    FEE
              NUMBER    HOURS     FAIL
      AAA     9999      9         A        $999.99
```

We assume that the starting position for the first column is assigned to the symbol FIRSTCOL by an EQU instruction and the common width of all columns is defined as COLWIDTH.

It is possible to reserve space for a single, general purpose output line and define the individual lines above as variants of that line. In order to do this with a heading line in which the contents don't change, we need to describe the non-blank fields in separate DC instructions. These fields must then be moved into the general purpose output line before it is printed. In the example above, this would be a useful approach for dealing with the first two heading lines and the detail line. However, in the case of the lines containing the column headings, the number of instructions required to move individual column headings into the output line tends to outweigh the space saved by using only one storage area for output.

In this example, we will use a single output line for the first two heading lines and the detail line. We will define the two lines of column headings as separate constant records. The symbols FIRSTCOL and COLWIDTH will be used in both definitions. In addition to guaranteeing that the columns and column headings line up, this will allow us to make changes in the output format with minimal code changes.

The necessary storage definitions are as follows.

```
SCHLNAME  DC      'CENTRAL HIGH SCHOOL'
RPTNAME   DC      'FINAL REGISTRATION REPORT'
.
.
.
          DC      C' '                        USED TO CLEAR LINE
LINE      DS      CL133                        GENERAL PURPOSE
*                                              OUTPUT LINE
*
*    SCHOOL NAME LINE
*
          ORG     LINE+(L'LINE−L'SCHLNME)/2    CENTER SCHOOL NAME
OSCHLNME  DS      CL(L'SCHLNAME)               SCHOOL NAME FIELD
*
*    REPORT NAME LINE
*
          ORG     LINE+(L'LINE−L'RPTNAME)/2    CENTER REPORT NAME
```

```
ORPTNME    DS       CL(L'RPTNAME)              REPORT NAME FIELD
*
*    FIELDS FOR DETAIL LINE
*
           ORG      LINE+FIRSTCOL             SKIP TO COLUMN 1
DEPT       DS       CL(DPTLEN)                   DEPARTMENT NAME
           ORG      DEPT+COLWIDTH                :
CRSNUM     DS       CL(CRNUMLEN)                 COURSE NUMBER
           ORG      CRSNUM+COLWIDTH              :
CRHRS      DS       CL(CRHRLEN)                  CREDIT HOURS
           ORG      CRHRS+COLWIDTH               :
PASFAL     DS       CL(PFLEN)                    PASS/FAIL
           ORG      PASFAL+COLWIDTH              :
FEE        DS       CL(FEELEN)                   COURSE FEE
           ORG      LINE+L'LINE                  :

           .
           .
           .

*
*    FIRST LINE OF COLUMN HEADINGS
*
COLHEAD1   DC       CL133' '                  COLHEAD1
           ORG      COLHEAD1+FIRSTCOL            :
DPTHD1     DC       C'DEPT'                      DEPARTMENT HEADING
           ORG      DPTHD1+COLWIDTH              :
CRSHD1     DC       C'COURSE'                    COURSE HEADING
           ORG      CRSHD1+COLWIDTH              :
CRHD1      DC       C'CREDIT'                    CREDIT HOURS HEADING
           ORG      CRHD1+COLWIDTH               :
PFHD1      DC       C'PASS/'                     PASS/FAIL HEADING
           ORG      PFHD1+COLWIDTH               :
  FEEHD1 DC         C'FEE'                       FEE HEADING
           ORG      COLHEAD1+L'COLHEAD1       END COLHEAD1
*
*    SECOND LINE OF COLUMN HEADINGS
*
COLHEAD2   DC       CL133' '                  COLHEAD2
           ORG      COLHEAD2+2*FIRSTCOL          :
CRSHD2     DC       C'NUMBER'                    COURSE HEADING 2
           ORG      CRSHD2+COLWIDTH              :
CRHD2      DC       C'HOURS'                     CREDIT HOURS HEADING 2
           ORG      CRHD2+COLWIDTH               :
PFHD2      DC       C'FAIL'                      PASS/FAIL HEADING 2
           ORG      COLHEAD+L'COLHEAD2        END COLHEAD2
```

The way in which these lines are used depends upon the mechanism used to define them. The two lines of column headings may simply be PUT to the output file. The other lines must be cleared and individual fields filled before printing. For example, the code to print the first two heading lines would be

```
MVC   LINE,LINE−1          FILL LINE WITH BLANKS
MVC   OSCHLNME,SCHLNAME    INSERT SCHOOL NAME
PUT   PRINTER,LINE         PRINT LINE
MVC   LINE,LINE−1          FILL LINE WITH BLANKS
MCV   ORPTNME,RPTNAME      INSERT REPORT NAME
PUT   PRINTER,LINE         PRINT LINE
```

Generally, as in the example above, the use of symbols in storage definitions requires an extra effort. In order to justify this effort, we should be aware of the benefits it provides. There are many.

1. We can shift the entire report left or right by changing the constant FIRSTCOL. Such a change will shift both column heading lines and the detail lines by the same amount.

2. We can spread out or compress the report by changing the value of the symbol COLWIDTH.

3. Since the field definitions are all self-relative, we can add a new column to the report without changing the description of other columns or the code that manipulates those columns.

4. All fields have been defined to be the correct length, so it will not be necessary to encode a length in any of the machine instructions. (We assume that the fields which will be moved into the output line have been defined with the same length symbols.)

5. We can easily change the length of any field provided the new length does not exceed COLWIDTH. For example, suppose we have used P or F as the PASS/FAIL column and PFLEN = 1. If we want to begin using PASS or FAIL, we need only change PFLEN to 4. The length of the field PASFAL and the corresponding move instruction will be changed automatically.

E X E R C I S E S

1. Write an assembly language definition for a payroll information record with the following structure. (The decimal points are implicit.)

Field	Format
Employee Name	
Last Name	AAAAAAAAAAAAAAA
First Name	AAAAAAAAAA
Middle initial	A

Social Security Number	999999999
Hours Worked	
Regular Hours	99.9
Overtime Hours	99.9
Pay Rate	99.99

2. The following record definition allows two types of records. One type includes fields for salespeople who work for commissions. The other type includes fields for hourly salespeople. Write an assembly language definition of a record structure which combines the two types.

Record type 1. Commissioned Employees

Field	**Format**
Classification Code	A (C)
Social Security Number	999999999
Base Salary	9999.99
Budget Code	999
Commission Rate	.99

Record type 2. Hourly Employee

Field	**Format**
Classification Code	A (H)
Social Security Number	999999999
Hourly Rate	99.99
Department Code	999
Job Code	AA

3. Write an assembler definition for a record, LINE, to print the record defined in 1. The information should be centered on the page with 8 spaces between major fields and 1 space between subfields.

4. Write EQU's and storage definitions for all fields needed to read in two zoned numbers of 5 digits each, pack these numbers into two other fields, and add them in a fifth field. In your definitions, use the implied relationships among the lengths of these fields.

5. Change your answer to problem 4 to accommodate input fields of 9 digits each. (If your solution to 4 was correct, you should only need to make one change.)

6. Write symbol and storage definitions to create the following input record structure.

INVREC

Field	**Format**
Item Number	99999
Product Description	AAAAAAAAAAAAAAAAAAAAAAAAAAAA
Quantity on Hand	9999999
Quantity on Order	9999999
Product Cost	999.99 (Decimal implied.)

7. Given the storage definitions in Example 3.4.4, add the storage definitions for the following commands.

Replace	R	Column 1
	Line Number	Columns 2-4
	New Text	Columns 5-80
Move	M	Column 1
	Start Line	Columns 2-4
	End Line	Columns 5-7
	Before Line	Columns 8-10

8. Make the changes necessary in Example 3.4.2 to include the employee's entire middle name, rather than the initial. Assume that the middle name is limited to 12 characters.

9. Write the storage definitions for a variant record structure which describes an input line in either of the following two formats. (All decimals are implicit.)

Field	Format
Policy Type	A (L)
Premium	999.99
Beneficiary	AAAAAAAAAAAAAAAAAAAAAAAAAAAAAAAA
Age	999
Death Benefit	999999.99

Field	Format
Policy Type	A (H)
Premium	9999.99
Deductible	999.99
Coverage	99999999.99

10. Write the code necessary to define an output line to print the information in the record in Exercise 6. The output should be centered in the line with 8 spaces between fields.

3.5 DECIMAL POINTS AND ROUNDING

We have now covered most of the instructions for manipulating decimal numbers. These instructions support only decimal integers. There is no provision for manipulating or even representing decimal numbers that include a fractional part. However, it is possible to use the EDIT instruction to insert a decimal point in a number before it is printed.

In order to make use of this feature, when writing programs that generate results with a fractional part, the programmer must keep track of the position in the number where the decimal point belongs. We call this the *implied decimal point*. When the number is to be printed, the decimal point is inserted in the correct position.

Determining the position of the implied decimal point is a simple matter when adding or subtracting numbers in which the positions of the implied decimal points are the same. Multiplication introduces some additional complications. Addition and subtraction of numbers in which the implied decimal positions differ and division of numbers with implied decimal points introduce additional complications.

In order to deal with these complications, we use a notation to represent the position of the implied decimal and to describe how different operations affect the implied decimal point. We also use this notation in the program documentation to reflect the changes in the position of the implied decimal effected by each arithmetic operation.

Keeping Track of Decimal Points

We will use the notation (d,f) to indicate that a packed decimal number has d digits and that f digits are to the right of the decimal point. Since packed decimal numbers always have an odd number of digits, d should always be odd. f may be any integer. (Readers who have used PL/I will recognize this as the method used to declare FIXED DECIMAL numbers.)

If, for example, we indicate that the packed decimal field AVERAGE has format $(7,3)$ then we mean the AVERAGE has been defined by

```
AVERAGE    DS      PL4
```

and contains 3 fractional positions. Thus, if the field AVERAGE contains X'0361201C', this value should be interpreted as representing 0361.201.

Example 3.5.1 *Using 9 to represent any digit and C for the sign indicator, the table below shows the actual packed representation corresponding to each format. The column labelled Output Format shows how such a number should be printed with the decimal point.*

Format	Packed Form	Output Format
(9,0)	999999999C	999999999.
(7,6)	9999999C	9.999999
(5,5)	99999C	.99999

In the examples above, f ranges from 0 to d. In fact, we can give a reasonable and useful interpretation to format specifications in which f is negative or greater than *d.* For example, the specification (5,7) should be interpreted as representing a number with 5 digits and 7 digits to the right of the decimal point. That is, the number will be stored in the form X'99999C' but should be printed as .0099999. Similarly, a number that is interpreted as (5,−3) would be stored as X'99999C' and printed as 99999000. The example below shows the internal representation and print format for other numbers of this type.

Example 3.5.2

Format	Packed Form	Output Format
(7,9)	9999999C	.009999999
(5,8)	99999C	.00099999
(5,−3)	99999C	99999000.
(5,−7)	99999C	999990000000.

Shifting and Rounding

The IBM 370 provides an instruction that allows us to shift a packed decimal number left or right. A left shift removes leading zeros and adds zeros on the right. A right shift moves the digits in the number to the right. The rightmost digits are lost and an equal number of zeros are added to the left. Since the right shift may lose significant digits, the shift instruction includes a provision for rounding the result.

Shift and Round Packed SRP SS

        SRP   S1(L1),D,I

The digits in the packed decimal number designated by the first operand are shifted right or left as described below. Before performing a right shift, the value of I (0 to 9) is added to the leftmost digit that will be-lost. The sign indicator is not affected.

    If D is specified in the form 64+n, where n is a positive integer, the shift is determined as follows.

+n Shift left n digits. 0's are shifted in on the right, overflow occurs if a nonzero digit is shifted out on the left.

−n Shift right n digits. Before the shift, I is added to the nth digit from the right. Then the number is shifted right n digits. 0's are shifted in on the left.

Exceptions: Access, Data, Decimal Overflow.

Example 3.5.3 *Suppose that M is defined as PL5. Assume that M contains X'000168549C' before each of the following SRP instructions is executed. The table gives the contents of M after the shift has been completed.*

Shift Instruction	M After
SRP M,64+2,0	X'016854900C'
SRP M,64+3,0	X'168549000C'
SRP M,64+5,0	Decimal Overflow
SRP M,64+1,7	X'001685490C'
SRP M,64−2,0	X'000001685C'
SRP M,64−5,0	X'000000001C'
SRP M,64−8,0	X'000000000C'
SRP M,64−1,5	X'000016855C'
SRP M,64−2,5	X'000001685C'
SRP M,64−3,5	X'000000169C'
SRP M,64−2,7	X'000001686C'

Notes:

1. The value of I is ignored on a left shift. (However, the assembler does require that it be present.)

2. The instruction SRP M,64−3,5 proceeds as follows: The value of I (5) is added to the third digit from the right.

$$
\begin{array}{r}
1\\
\text{X'000168549C'}\\
+\quad 5\\
\hline
\text{X'000169049C'}
\end{array}
$$

The carry out of this position is added to the next digit on the left, making it 9. The three digits on the right are shifted out and three zeros are shifted in on the left. The final value of M is X'000000169C'.

In general, the addition of the rounding factor, I, on a right shift will affect the result if it forces a carry into the next position.

When we shift a number with an implied decimal point, if we want the number to represent the same value (perhaps with some loss of significance), then we need to change the format representation. For example, if the field M above is (9,4) and contains X'000168549C' before a shift instruction, then it represents 00016.8549. The implied decimal point is between the 6 and the 8. If we execute the instruction SRP M,64+2,0, then M will contain X'016854900C'.

In order to keep the decimal point between the 6 and the 8, its format should be regarded as (9,6). That is, we add 2 to the number of fractional positions.

In general, suppose a number M has format (d,f) before a shift instruction. If we want the number to represent the same value after a shift instruction, we add the shift factor to f as indicated below.

Shift Instruction	New Format
SRP M,64+n,l	$(d,f+n)$
SRP M,64−n,l	$(d,f-n)$

Addition and Subtraction

Suppose that we have two numbers with formats $(d1,f1)$ and $(d2,f2)$. If we were to add or subtract these numbers by hand, we would write them so that the decimal points line up. When we use AP or SP, the effect is to line up the rightmost digits of the two numbers.

For example, suppose that X and Y are PL4 fields containing X'0012758C' and X'0003712C'. Adding these fields with AP yields the following addition.

$$
\begin{array}{r}
1\ \ 1\ \ \ \ \\
0012758 \\
+0003712 \\
\hline
0016470
\end{array}
$$

Unfortunately, if these fields have implied decimal points as indicated by X:(7,2) and Y:(7,5), then this is equivalent to performing the following operation.

$$
\begin{array}{r}
1\ \ 1\ \ \ \ \\
00127.58 \\
+00.03712 \\
\hline
0016470
\end{array}
$$

which is absurd.

In order to get a correct result, we must have $f1 = f2$. If this is already the case, then we simply perform the operation. The value of f for the result will be the common value $f1$ and $f2$. If $f1 <> f2$, we must shift one of the two numbers so that the decimal points will be aligned.

The alignment can be accomplished by performing a left shift on the number with the smaller f value or a right shift on the number with the larger f value. The choice depends upon the context. However, since a right shift may lose significant digits, we generally shift left.

Example 3.5.4 *Suppose that X and Y are PL5, that SUM is PL6 and that we need to set SUM = X + Y.*

If the formats are X:(9,5) and Y:(9,3), then we need to shift one of these two values in order to align the implied decimal points. In this case, we can move the value of

Y into SUM, then shift SUM left two places, and perform the addition. The instructions to accomplish this are

ZAP	SUM,Y	SUM = Y	SUM:(11,3)
SRP	SUM,64+2,0		SUM:(11,5)
AP	SUM,X	SUM = SUM+X	SUM:(11,5)

Observe that we have tacitly assumed that overflow will not be a problem. If an overflow is possible, we could enlarge the field SUM or shift the value in X to the right and lose some digits.

Example 3.5.5 *Suppose that ITEM is a PL5 field and SUM is PL6. Assume that we need to implement the following assignment.*

$$SUM = SUM+ITEM$$

The names of these two fields seem to imply that SUM is an accumulator. If this is the case, then whenever alignment is necessary, we should probably shift the value in ITEM rather than the value in SUM.

When we do need to shift the value in ITEM, this shift should take place in a work area. There are two compelling reasons for performing a shift in a work area, rather than in the field ITEM. In the first place, the implementation of the assignment above should not change the value stored in ITEM. Second, if a left shift is necessary, performing this operation in ITEM may cause an overflow. If we use a work area, then it would be defined as

WORK   DS   PL(L'SUM)

If the implied decimal points are described by

ITEM : (9,2)
SUM : (11,5)

then, we would move the value from ITEM to WORK, shift WORK three places to the left to align the decimal points and add it to SUM.

ZAP	WORK,ITEM	WORK = ITEM	WORK:(11,2)
SRP	WORK,64+3,0		WORK:(11,5)
AP	SUM,WORK	SUM = SUM+WORK	SUM:(11,5)

Now, suppose that the formats are given by ITEM:(9,6) and SUM:(11,2). In this case, the value from ITEM needs to be shifted right 4 positions to align the decimal points. As we will lose 4 digits, we may want to round the shifted value. The instructions to accomplish this are

ZAP	WORK,ITEM	WORK = ITEM	WORK:(11,6)
SRP	WORK,64−4,5		WORK:(11,2)
AP	SUM,WORK	SUM = SUM+WORK	SUM:(11,2)

Multiplication

For multiplication, we do not need to check the positions of the implied decimal points before performing the operation. After the operation has been completed, the number of fractional positions in the result will be the sum $f1 + f2$.

Example 3.5.6 *Suppose that RATE is PL3 with format (5,4) and HOURS is PL2 with format (3,1). Assume that we need to multiply RATE times HOURS and store the result, rounded to two decimal places, in PAY.*

In order to perform this operation, we need a work area that is 5 bytes long. The result will have 9 digits of which 5 (4+1) are to the right of the decimal point.

The product can be rounded to two decimal places by shifting right three digits with a rounding factor of 5. The required instructions are

ZAP	WORK,HOURS	WORK = HOURS	WORK:(9,1)
MP	WORK,RATE	WORK = WORK*RATE	WORK:(9,5)
SRP	WORK,64−3,5		WORK:(9,2)
ZAP	PAY,WORK		

For example, if RATE contains X'95802C' and HOURS contains X'791C' the first instruction will set WORK equal to X'000000791C' the format indicates that this represents 79.1.

The MP instruction corresponds to performing the multiplication below.

$$\begin{array}{r} 79.1 \\ \times\ \ 9.5802 \\ \hline 757.79382 \end{array}$$

The product would be stored as X'075779382C'. Its implied decimal point is designated by the format (9,5).

The SRP instruction adds 5 to the third digit from the right. Since no carry occurs, the shifted result will be X'000075779C'. The format indicates that this should be interpreted as 757.79.

Example 3.5.7 *Suppose that X is a PL3 field with format (5,7) and that Y is PL2 with format (3,−4). Assuming that WORK is PL5, consider the following instruction sequence.*

ZAP	WORK,Y	WORK = Y	WORK:(9,−4)
MP	WORK,X	WORK = WORK*X	WORK:(9,3)

Suppose that X contains X'83786C' and Y contains X'792C'. After the ZAP instruction, WORK will contain X'000000792C'. The format indicates that this should be interpreted as 7920000. The value in X represents .0083786. Thus the execution of the MP instruction is equivalent to

$$\begin{array}{r} 7920000 \\ \times\ \ .0083786 \\ \hline 66358.5120000 \end{array}$$

The value stored in WORK after the multiplication will be X'066358512C'. We can see that the format specification for the implied decimal point is correct.

Division

When two numbers are divided, the number of fractional digits in the quotient is equal to the number of fractional digits in the dividend minus the number of fractional digits in the divisor. For example, suppose that DIVIDEND is PL5, has format (9,5), and contains X'004569651C' and that DIVISOR is PL3, has format (5,2), and contains X'35234C'. If we divide these fields with DP, we get an integer quotient of 129. Dividing 45.69651 by 352.34 yields .12969435. The quotient obtained with DP does indeed contain 3 (5−2) fractional digits.

The situation is complicated by the fact that, when we perform a division, the number of fractional positions in the quotient is usually predetermined. In order to get the desired number of fractional digits, we often need to perform a shift before the division takes place. If we want to round the result to some specified number of fractional digits, we perform a shift that allows us to compute one more than the desired number of digits. After the division has been performed, we shift the quotient right one position, using a rounding factor of 5.

In general, suppose that $f1$ is the number of fractional digits in the dividend and $f2$ the number of fractional digits in the divisor. The number of fractional digits in the quotient will be $f1-f2$. If we need to compute a quotient with f fractional digits, then we need to adjust this difference by shifting the dividend or the divisor. We can adjust either $f1$ or $f2$. The choice depends upon the problem.

The majority of the time, we need to increase $f1-f2$. That is, we need to increase the number of fractional digits in the quotient. This can be accomplished by increasing $f1$ (shift the dividend to the left) or decreasing $f2$ (shift the divisor to the right). Because shifting the divisor to the right would result in the loss of significant digits, we normally shift the dividend to the left.

Example 3.5.8 *Suppose that DIVIDEND is PL5 with format (9,4) and that DIVISOR is PL3 with format (5,3). Assume we need to divide DIVIDEND by DIVISOR and round the result to 2 decimal places.*

If we simply divide DIVIDEND by DIVISOR, the quotient would have 1 (4−3) fractional digit. In order to round the result to 2 decimal places, we need to compute a quotient with 3 fractional digits. Shifting the dividend 2 digits to the left adds 2 fractional positions.

In defining the work area, the dividend will be shifted 2 digits to the left before the division takes place. The work area must have room for this extra byte. The size of the remainder is still determined by the size of the divisor. The other bytes of the work area are used to hold the quotient. Thus WORK and QUOTIENT should be defined as follows.

```
WORK        DS    PL(1+L'DIVIDEND+L'DIVISOR)
            ORG   WORK
QUOTIENT    DS    PL(L'WORK−L'DIVISOR)
REMNDR      DS    PL(L'DIVISOR)
```

We have the following instruction sequence.

```
ZAP    WORK,DIVIDEND    WORK = DIVIDEND            WORK:(15,4)
SRP    WORK,64+2,0      :                          WORK:(15,6)
DP     WORK,DIVISOR     QUOTIENT = WORK/DIVISOR    QUOTIENT:(9,3)
SRP    QUOTIENT,64-1,5  :                          QUOTIENT:(9,2)
```

After the division has taken place, only the quotient part of the work area should be shifted. (If we attempted to shift the entire work area, a Data exception would be raised because the work area does not contain a single packed decimal number.)

By memorizing the rules for manipulating the implied decimal points, the construction of these instructions can be made quite automatic. If we look more closely at the instructions generated, we find that it is also a fairly automatic process. We can see this by tracing the steps in the example above.

Suppose that DIVIDEND contains X'057120518C' and that DIVISOR contains X'51203C'. Adding the implied decimal points, we need to perform the following division.

$$5\ 1.2\ 0\ 3\ \overline{)\ 5\ 7\ 1\ 2.0\ 5\ 1\ 8}$$

The position of the implied decimal point in the quotient is as shown. Shifting the dividend in the work area 2 places to the left is the equivalent of adding 2 zeros on the right, as we would if we were to do this division by hand. The result is as shown below.

$$5\ 1.2\ 0\ 3\ \overline{)\ 5\ 7\ 1\ 2.0\ 5\ 1\ 8\ 0\ 0}^{\ \ \ 1\ 1\ 1\ 5\ 5\ 6}$$

After the division, the quotient part of the work area will contain X'000111556C'. The implied decimal point is now 3 digits from the right. The second shift instruction adds 5 to the rightmost digit, forcing a carry into the next position, then shifts the number right 1 position. The final value in QUOTIENT is X'000011156C' with format (9,2) as required.

Example 3.5.9 *Suppose that TEMPSUM is PL4 with format (7,1) and DAYS is PL2 with format (3,0). Divide TEMPSUM by DAYS and store the result, rounded to 4 decimal places, in AVTEMP.*

Dividing the fields without shifting would yield one decimal place. In order to round the result to 4 decimal places, we need to compute 5. To do this, we must shift the value from TEMPSUM 4 digits to the left before dividing. The work area must have an extra 2 bytes to accommodate the 4 0's that will be shifted in.

We have

```
ZAP    WORK,TEMPSUM        WORK = TEMPSUM       WORK:(15,1)
SRP    WORK,64+TSHIFT,0                         WORK:(15,5)
DP     WORK,DAYS           WORK = WORK/DAYS     QUOT:(11,5)
SRP    QUOT,64-1,5                              QUOT:(11,4)
ZAP    AVTEMP,QUOT
```

where

```
TSHIFT    EQU    4
WORK      DS     PL(2+L'TEMPSUM+L'DAYS)
          ORG    WORK
QUOT      DS     PL(L'WORK-L'DAYS)
          ORG    WORK+L'WORK
```

Advanced Editing

Some additional mechanisms for creating editing patterns include provisions for inserting decimal points and other characters in printed numbers. We also consider a method for indicating negative numbers.

In the edit patterns in Chapter 1, we used the blank (X'40') as a fill character. In fact, we can use any character. For example, when printing an amount on a check, it is customary to protect the value from alteration by replacing leading zeros with a printing character such as an asterisk.

The following edit pattern can be used to print a PL3 number using the asterisk as a fill character.

```
PAT       DC     X'5C2020202120'
```

In order to create this edit pattern, we need to look up the EBCDIC code for the character '*'. Similarly, on reading a program that contains a pattern like the one above, we may need to look up the code X'5C'. An alternative definition of PAT, which avoids this problem is

```
PAT       DC     XL6
          ORG    PAT
          DC     C'*'
          DC     X'2020202120'
```

Here we use the ORG to allow us to define PAT using a mixture of type specifiers. We can also write mixed type specifiers in a single DC instruction as in

```
PAT        DC    XL6
           ORG   PAT
           DC    C'*',X'2020202120'
```

Example 3.5.10 *Suppose COUNT is a PL3 field containing X'00035C', OCOUNT is a 6-byte field, and PAT is as above.*

Execution of

```
           MVC   OCOUNT,PAT
           ED    OCOUNT,COUNT
```

will result in OCOUNT containing X'5C5C5C5CF3F5'. In character form, this is '****35'.

In addition to the fill character and the digit selectors, an edit pattern may include other character codes called *message characters*. During the edit operation, any message characters encountered before the start of significance are replaced by the fill character. After significance has been started by the occurrence of a nonzero digit or forced by the significance starter X'21', message characters in the pattern are left unchanged.

Typical uses for message characters include putting dashes in social security numbers or phone numbers and inserting commas or decimal points in numeric output fields.

Example 3.5.11 *The following pattern can be used to edit a PL5 number in the format normally used for social security numbers.*

```
SSPAT      DS    CL12
           ORG   SSPAT
           DC    X'40202020',C'−',X'2020',C'−',X'20202020'
```

If SSNUM contains X'198980769C' then execution of the instructions

```
           MVC   OUTNUM,SSPAT
           ED    OUTNUM,SSNUM
```

will set OUTNUM equal to '198−98−0769' (Note that this pattern could not produce a social security number with a leading 0. Even if we use X'21' as the first digit selector, a social security number which begins with 0 would not be printed properly. There is no edit pattern that will force the first zero in a number to be printed.)

Example 3.5.12 *Suppose AMTPAT is defined by the following (X'6B' is the EBCDIC code for a comma) and suppose AMT is a PL4 field.*

```
AMTPAT     DC    X'40206B2020206B202120'
```

Consider the instruction sequence

```
MVC     OAMT,AMTPAT
ED      OAMT,AMT
```

Given various values for AMT, the table below shows the contents of OAMT in both hexadecimal and character form after this pair of instructions has been executed.

AMT	OAMT	OAMT
X'7609761C'	X'40F76BF6F0F96BF7F6F1'	' 7,609,761'
X'0629071C'	X'404040F6F2F96BF0F7F1'	' 629,071'
X'0007720C'	X'4040404040F76BF7F2F0'	' 7,720'
X'0000061C'	X'4040404040404040F6F1'	' 61'
X'0000000C'	X'404040404040404040F0'	' 0'

As long as digit selectors are being replaced by the fill character, we want the message characters to be replaced by the fill character also. However, we would not want this to occur when the message character is a decimal point. So, when creating edit patterns to insert a decimal, we must be certain to include a significance starter before the decimal point.

Example 3.5.13 *Create an edit pattern to edit a PL4 number with format (7,4). (X'4B' is the EBCDIC code for a decimal point.)*

```
PAT        DC     X'402020214B20202020'
```

Note the inclusion of the significance starter immediately before the decimal.
The following table gives the results of editing several PL4 numbers using this pattern.

Number	Hexadecimal	Character
X'7609761C'	X'40F7F6F04BF9F7F6F1'	' 760.9761'
X'0039761C'	X'404040F34BF9F7F6F1'	' 3.9761'
X'0009761C'	X'404040404BF9F7F6F1'	' .9761'
X'0000061C'	X'404040404BF0F0F6F1'	' .0061'
X'0000000C'	X'404040404BF0F0F0F0'	' .0000'

Until now, we have printed only positive numbers. In fact, all of the edit operations we have done so far have ignored the sign indicator. The edit operations in the examples above would have produced the same results if all of the numbers had been negative. It is, nevertheless, possible to create an edit pattern that distinguishes between positive and negative numbers.

When an edit operation processes the last digit in a packed decimal number, the sign indicator is checked. If the number being edited is positive, all following message characters are replaced with the fill character. If the sign indicator is negative, the remaining message characters are unchanged. This feature allows us to include message characters at the right of the pattern that will be printed if the edited number is negative and replaced by the fill character otherwise.

Example 3.5.14 *Consider the following edit pattern.*

```
BALPAT    DS     XL19
          ORG    BALPAT
          DC     C' ',X'2020',C',',X'202021',C'.',X'2020',C' - CREDIT'
```

If this pattern is used to edit the PL4 number X'0005612C', the result will be

$$X'4040404040F5F64BF1F2404040404040404040'$$

In character form, we have

```
C'      56.12               '
```

Using this pattern to edit the number X'0005612D' yields

```
X'4040404040F5F64BF1F2406D40C3D9C5C4C9E3'
C'      56.12 - CREDIT'
```

Conclusions

Having completed our consideration of editing numbers with implied decimal points, note that the position of the decimal point in the edit pattern is fixed when the pattern is created. As the position of the decimal point in the edit pattern is fixed, we must make certain that the position of the implied decimal point in any numeric field is also fixed. Otherwise, when we want to print such a number, it would be difficult to make certain that the decimal point is in the correct position.

There are other reasons for keeping the implied decimal point in a packed field fixed. The most obvious is the difficulty of keeping track of a moving decimal point. If a program changes the position of the implied decimal point in a numeric field, then its current position at any time during execution would depend on the flow of control up to that point. This would usually be quite difficult to determine.

In general, there are too many other difficulties in assembly language programming to add problems of keeping track of where a moving decimal point is at any particular time. We consider the position of an implied decimal point in a packed number to be a fixed attribute of that field, like its length or type. As the assembler will not enforce such a restriction on us, we must police ourselves. The following rules are helpful.

1. The number of fractional positions in any packed field should be described in a remark when the field is defined.

2. The SRP instruction should only be used to move an implied decimal point while a number is in a work area.

3. Whenever a number is to be stored in a packed field other than a work area, the number of fractional positions in the number should be the same as the number of fractional positions specified for the field. If this is not the case, SRP should be used to convert the number to the correct format.

E   X   E   R   C   I   S   E   S

1. For each of the following format descriptions, give the packed representation and the output format showing the implied decimal point.
   a. (5,9)
   b. (3,−3)
   c. (7,7)
   d. (5,0)

2. Assume that there is a 6-byte packed decimal field containing X'00097634228C'. Give the contents of N after each of the following instructions, noting any error conditions.
   a. SRP   N,64−3,9
   b. SRP   N,64+3,9
   c. SRP   N,64−8,0
   d. SRP   N,64+5,0
   e. SRP   4,64−1,5

3. Suppose that A and B are 4-byte packed fields and that TOTAL is a 5-byte packed field. Write the code to set TOTAL = A+B given each of the following pairs of format specifications.
   a. A : (7,4)   B : (7,3)
   b. A : (7,7)   B : (7,−3)
   c. A : (7,0)   B : (7,5)

4. Suppose that A is a 6-byte packed field and B is a 5-byte packed field. Write the instructions and work area definitions to implement each of the following assignment statements. Give the minimum length of the field C.

   a. A : (11,5), B : (9,2), C = A*B
   b. A : (11,7), B : (9,9), C = A*B (Rounded to 3 places.)
   c. A : (11,4), B : (9,5), C = A/B (Truncated to 4 places.)
   d. A : (11,5), B : (9,6), C = A/B (Rounded to 2 places.)

5. Given the following packed fields and formats, write the code to find decimal hours rounded to 6 places and speed rounded to 5 places.

   a. MILES   (7,4)
   b. HOURS   (3,0)
   c. MINUTES   (3,0)
   d. SECONDS   (3,1)

6. Write a definition for an edit pattern to perform each of the following edit operations.

   a. Edit a 5-byte number AVERAGE using an asterisk as a fill character.
   b. Edit a 4-byte packed field PHONE with a dash between the third and fourth digits.
   c. Edit a 7-byte number with format (13,3), inserting commas every three digits to the left of the decimal point.
   d. Edit a (5,4) number with significance forced at the first digit to the right of the decimal point.
   e. Edit a 3-byte number, TEMPERAT, formatted as (5,1). If the number is negative, the string 'BELOW ZERO' should appear to the right of the number.

3.6 SUBROUTINES FOR MODULARIZED PROGRAMMING

The importance of procedures and subroutines in designing and writing programs is addressed from earlier programming courses in high level languages. Such facilities are even more important in assembly language programming. The basic problem is that so many details make it hard to visualize a program as an integrated whole. This problem is even more difficult for a third party trying to read and understand a program.

The standard solution to this problem is to write programs that deal with various levels of abstraction. The top level of the program should be relatively close to the natural structure of the problem at hand. We can insulate this top level from the details of a solution by submerging those details in subsidiary routines. The extent to which such details are hidden depends on the problem and its solution, but the general objective is to attain a top-level program that we can comprehend. There should be no more detail in this top level than we can keep in our heads at one time.

We apply the same principles to the construction of the subsidiary routines simply by viewing each of them as a new, slightly smaller, easier problem. In order to attain this objective, we need to keep these subsidiary problems independent of the main program and of each other. This calls for the ability to pass arguments to the procedures. In this way, we can view each procedure as receiving some collection of input data, processing that data, and generating output. The problem as a whole is simplified because the number of relationships between the components is minimized.

In Chapter 6, we discuss procedures that can accept parameters. For now, we will cover a mechanism for creating subroutines—subprograms that communicate with a calling routine through globally accessible variables. This will allow us to postpone the problem of passing arguments to a procedure.

In order to implement subroutines, we need a mechanism for passing control from the calling program to the subroutine and, at the conclusion of the subroutine, returning to the point from which the call was made.

To illustrate, suppose the overall structure of the program is

```
         .
         .
         .

Instruction a
                    CALL OURSUB

Instruction b
         .
         .
Instruction c
                    CALL OURSUB

Instruction d
         .
         .
         .

OURSUB    EQU    *
         .
         .
         .

                    RETURN
ENDSUB    EQU    *
         .
         .
```

We need a mechanism to get from either point of call to OURSUB. A branch instruction would do that, but at the end of OURSUB, we need to continue execution with the first instruction after the call. If we simply use a branch instruction to invoke the subroutine, we would not be able to determine if the return should be to Instruction b or Instruction d.

The 370 instruction set provides for this contingency with the Branch And Link (BAL) instruction. When used for the call between Instruction a and Instruction b, a BAL instruction would first store the address of Instruction b in a register, then branch to OURSUB. When used for the second call, it would place the address of Instruction d in its register operand before branching to OURSUB. In the routine OURSUB, it would be possible to examine this register to determine the correct return address.

Because of the way the fetch-execute cycle works, this instruction is remarkably easy to implement. By the time the machine begins to execute an instruction, the address of the following instruction is already in the Instruction Address part of the Program Status Word (PSW). This is the desired return address and the implementation simply requires that this value be placed in the register operand. The actual branch is implemented by storing the new address in the Instruction Address portion of the PSW.

The instruction which performs this task, BAL instruction, is an RX instruction. However, we shall use it in a restricted form for now. RX instructions will be discussed in more detail in Chapter 4.

Branch And Link *BAL RX*

BAL $\quad$ R$_1$,S$_2$

The contents of the Instruction Address portion of the PSW is copied into the right 3 bytes of R$_1$. The address determined by the second operand becomes the new Instruction Address.

Condition Code: Unchanged.

Exceptions: None.

When we use the BAL instruction to implement a subroutine call, we need to provide a register to receive the return address. We could use any available register, however, we need coordination between the calling instruction and the subroutine. If the subroutine expects to find the return address in a particular register, then that register must be used every time the subroutine is called. In a sense, it is the code for the subroutine that determines which register will be used in each of the BAL calls.

We might use different registers for different subroutines. This would have the unfortunate effect of increasing the number of details that we need to keep track of in a program. Because the code for the subroutine is often well separated from the call instructions, we need to establish some mechanism for recording which register should be used with which procedure. We also need to make certain that the register to be used was not already in use for some other purpose.

Because of these complications, the only workable solution is to dedicate a single register to hold the return address on all subroutine calls. In order to achieve compatibility with IBM's compilers for high level languages, we always use RE, adopting the following construct for subroutine calls.

BAL $\quad$ RE,\<name\> $\qquad$ CALL \<name\>

Now, our skeletal program becomes

```
        .
        .
        .
Instruction a
            BAL     RE,OURSUB        CALL OURSUB
Instruction b
        .
        .
        .
Instruction c
            BAL     RE,OURSUB        CALL OURSUB
Instruction d
        .
        .
        .
OURSUB      EQU     *
        .
        .
        .
            RETURN
ENDSUB      EQU     *
        .
        .
```

In order to implement the return from a subroutine, we need to be able to branch to a location whose address is in a register. This can be done with the extended mnemonic instruction BR, Branch Register. The assembler creates an instruction which causes an unconditional branch to the address in the register operand. The format of this instruction is

$$BR \qquad R_1$$

If the return address is in RE, then we can implement the return from the subroutine with

$$BR \qquad RE$$

Before establishing a protocol for subroutine calls and returns, we need to clear up one more detail. It is often desirable to be able to call one subroutine from within another. If we simply leave the return address from the last subroutine call in RE, it would be destroyed by the next call. In order to avoid this, we always save the contents of RE as soon as we enter the subroutine and restore the value as part of the return mechanism. This requires that each subroutine have a fullword in which the return address can be stored. We include the definition for this fullword as part of a standard construct for a subroutine heading.

```
          DS      F                    :
<name>    EQU     *                    SUBROUTINE <name>
          ST      RE,<name>−4          :
```

The DS instruction immediately preceding the entry label reserves a fullword of storage to hold the return address. As it has no label assigned to it, we access it by specifying its offset from the subroutine entry point: <name>−4. This has the advantage of making this storage relatively inaccessible and greatly reduces the possibility that we might accidentally change the return value.

Notice that we always save the return address, regardless of whether we expect to make another call from within this subroutine. In this way, we can always add a subroutine call when modifying a program, without making any other changes in the subroutine itself.

The return from the subroutine is implemented by restoring the return address to RE and branching to that address. We use the following instructions and comments.

```
          L       RE,<name>−4          RETURN
          BR      RE                   :
```

Example 3.6.1 *Suppose that we are writing a program which generates a multi-page report.*

A typical approach is to keep count of the number of lines printed per page. Before printing any line, we check the value of this variable. If it has exceeded some constant value, then we start a new page with an appropriate heading and reset the line counter.

Because we may print lines at several different locations in a program, we can greatly simplify the program by writing a subroutine to begin the new page and reset the line counter.

Assume that LINCNT and PGNUM are packed fields with the obvious interpretations—that HEADLINE is a line containing the printer control character for a new page, a subfield named OPGNUM to contain the page number, and any additional information needed—and that PGMSK is an edit pattern for the page number. The following subroutine performs the needed functions.

```
            DS      F                    :
PAGEHEAD    EQU     *                    SUBROUTINE PAGEHEAD
            ST      RE,PAGEHEAD−4        :
            AP      PGNUM,=P'1'          INCREMENT PGNUM
            MVC     OPGNUM,PGMSK         EDIT INTO HEAD1
            ED      OPGNUM,PGNUM         :
            PUT     PRINTER,HEAD1        PRINT HEAD1
            ZAP     LINCNT,=P'0'         INITIALIZE LINCNT
            L       RE,PAGEHEAD−4        RETURN
            BR      RE                   :
```

The code to check LINCNT and invoke PAGEHEAD when necessary is

```
IF05       EQU    *              IF LINCNT > PGLINS
           CP     LINCNT,PGLINS  :
           BNH    ENDIF05        :
THEN05     EQU    *              THEN
           BAL    RE,PAGEHEAD       CALL PAGEHEAD
ENDIF05    EQU    *              ENDIF
```

Before we go on to a more detailed example using subroutines, note a restriction inherent in this approach. While we can call one subroutine from within another, we can never call a subroutine recursively. Each subroutine has a single location for a return address. If a subroutine is invoked before it has returned from a preceding call, the new return address will destroy the pending address, making successful completion of the first call impossible.

We have also restricted communication between the calling routine and a subroutine to globally accessible variables. This greatly simplifies the mechanics involved in creating and invoking subroutines, but it also creates additional burdens for the programmer. We need to make certain that we use the same name for a global variable in a subroutine as in the calling routine. We also need to ensure that the names used for local variables in our subroutines are unique. In debugging a program, if we find that a variable has an incorrect value assigned to it, we need to be able to locate all portions of code where the variable can be accessed, but, with our current approach, every variable can be accessed from any place in the program.

Basically, the problem is that the subroutines are too closely tied to the calling programs. This makes it difficult to view them as independent components. Later, we will learn how to write procedures that are truly independent of the calling program. For now, we try to mitigate the problems mentioned above by establishing standards for accessing global variables.

We will begin each subroutine with a set of comments as shown.

```
****************************************************************************
*      <Subroutine name>                                                  *
*                                                                         *
*      <Description>                                                      *
*                                                                         *
*      INPUT VARIABLES:     <Variables whose values are                   *
*                            used in the subroutine. >                     *
*                                                                         *
*      OUTPUT VARIABLES:    <Variables whose values are                   *
*                            changed by the subroutine. >                  *
*                                                                         *
*      WORK VARIABLES:      <Other variables which are                    *
*                            used by the subroutine. >                     *
*                                                                         *
****************************************************************************
```

Under Register Usage, we will not list the registers RC or RE, which will be used in the same way throughout the program.

The subroutine in the example above would begin with the following preamble.

```
*************************************************************************************
*    PAGEHEAD                                                                     *
*                                                                                 *
*    START A NEW PAGE, PRINT HEADINGS, INCREMENT PGNUM                            *
*    AND INITIALIZE LINCNT.                                                        *
*                                                                                 *
*    INPUT VARIABLES:    LINCNT, PGNUM                                            *
*                                                                                 *
*    OUTPUT VARIABLES: LINCNT, PGNUM, PGHEAD                                      *
*                                                                                 *
*    WORK VARIABLES:    HEAD1                                                     *
*                                                                                 *
*    REGISTER USAGE:    <NONE>                                                    *
*                                                                                 *
*************************************************************************************
```

In our source code, we will place subroutines immediately after the code for the main program.

E   X   E   R   C   I   S   E   S

1. Write a subroutine SKIP which uses a packed input variable, SKPLNS. Assuming that SKPLNS contains a positive integer, n, the subroutine should PUT n blank lines to the file PRINTER.

2. Write the code to invoke the subroutine SKIP to skip 7 lines in the output.

3. Modify the subroutine in exercise 1 so that it accepts two packed input variables, SKPLNS and LINCNT, representing the number of lines to be skipped and the current line. If LINCNT+SKPLNS > PGLINS, it should call the subroutine PAGEHEAD from Example 3.6.1. Otherwise, it should skip the indicated number of output lines as before.

3.7 SAMPLE PROGRAM

In this section, we develop a sample program that uses many of the concepts we have covered in this chapter. In this program and in the exercises and other programs we will consider later, we attempt to deal with a problem of moderate complexity. In order to keep the programs manageable, we make certain simplifying assumptions. The most basic of these is to assume that input data are always correct.

Debugging Aids

Before consideration of the sample program, we note several operating system features which are helpful in debugging programs. These allow us to obtain dumps of selected areas of memory and to force early termination of a program.

DOS allows the programmer to request a dump during execution of a program with the PDUMP macro. The format of this macro is

    PDUMP <starting address>,<ending address>

It generates instructions to print the Program Status Word, the register contents, and a hexadecimal dump of the memory locations between the two addresses. The addresses are normally expressed in symbolic form.

Example 3.7.1

    PDUMP LINE,LINE+L'LINE   DUMP THE CONTENTS OF LINE
    PDUMP PNUM,PNUM+L'PNUM DUMP PNUM

In order to obtain a dump of larger memory areas, we insert labels before and after the areas to be dumped as shown below.

Example 3.7.2

    PDUMP STRTDMP,ENDDMP   DUMP WORK AREAS
            .
            .
            .
    STRTDMP EQU   *
    WORK1   DS   PL(WORKLEN)
    WORK2   DS   PL(WORKLEN)
    WORK3   DS   PL(WORKLEN)
    ENDDMP   EQU   *-1

If necessary, these labels could be situated so that all of the memory locations occupied by a program are dumped.

OS has a similar macro called SNAP, which prints a memory 'snapshot' when the generated instructions are executed. A typical invocation of the SNAP macro has the following format.

```
SNAP    ID=<n>,DCB=PRINTER,PDATA=(PSW,REGS),STORAGE=
        (<addr1>,<addr2>)
```

<n>	An integer to identify the output.
<addr1>	The starting address of the area to be dumped.
<addr2>	The ending address of the area to be dumped.

The two addresses given in the SNAP macro may be used in the same way as the addresses in the DOS PDUMP macro.

Example 3.7.3

```
SNAP    ID=1,DCB=PRINTER,PDATA=(PSW,REGS),STORAGE=
        (LINE,LINE+L'LINE)
SNAP    ID=2,DCB=PRINTER,PDATA=(PSW,REGS),STORAGE=
        (STRTDMP,ENDDMP)
```

In addition to macros for generating partial dumps during execution, both operating systems provide macros which can be used to force early termination of a program. The DOS macro is CANCEL. The format is

```
CANCEL
```

The OS macro is ABEND. It includes an operand to identify the particular ABEND call which caused termination. The format is

```
ABEND  <n>
```

<n>   An integer to identify the terminating instruction.

Problem Statement

Write an IBM 370 Assembly Language program to process order records for the Summit City Sand and Cement Company. The input to this program consists of a set of price records, followed by customer records and order records. The formats for these records will be as shown below.

Price Record	Customer Record	Order Record
Code --------Col. 1 (P)	Code --------Col. 1 (C)	Code --------Col. 1 (O)
Price --------Col. 2-4	Acct. No. ----Col. 2-6	Acct. No. ----Col. 2-6
Item Code ---Col. 5	Name -------Col. 7-26	Item Code ---Col. 7
Blank --------Col. 6-80	Addr. -------Col. 27-66	Qty. ---------Col. 8-10
	Blank -------Col. 67-80	Addr. -------Col. 11-50
		Blank -------Col. 51-80

Notes:

1. The end of the input file is marked by a trailer record with a 'T' in column 1.
2. The Item Codes are S (sand), G (gravel), and C (cement).
3. Quantities are in tons and prices are given in tenths of dollars per ton.
4. A state sales tax, which is currently 4.5%, must be computed on the total cost and rounded to the nearest cent.
5. The address on the Customer Record is the customer billing address. The address on the Order Record is the delivery address.

The customer records and order records have been merged. Thus we can expect to find a record for each customer followed by 0 or more order records for that customer.

As stated in the first chapter, we assume that the input has already been validated; we will not include range checks for input data, nor will we compare the account number on order records with that on the customer records.

Algorithm

We begin with a top-level algorithm that assumes the existence of a number of subroutines to perform individual tasks. This algorithm is shown below. In order to allow the program to be modified easily to accommodate more items, we allow the subroutine that reads prices to read records until it comes to a customer record or the trailer record. Similarly, the routine that processes order cards for each customer will read until it finds the next customer card or the trailer card. Thus, on return from both of these routines, we will have read one record ahead. This is the record whose code is checked at the beginning of the WHILE loop.

```
Open Files
Read Price Records
while Code <> Trailer do
      Print Report Headings
      Read and Process Order Records
      Print Footer Lines
end while
Close Files
```

The code for Print Report Headings and Print Footer Lines is straight-forward.

Processing the price records consists of identifying the item code and packing the price into the corresponding field for later use. We use nested conditional statements for this, although if we had many more items, an implementation of a case statement would be desirable. The algorithm for Read Price Records is

```
Read Price Records
    Read Inrec
    while (Inrec = Price Record) do
        if Item = Sand then
            Sandprce = Price__Rec.Price
        else
            if Item = Gravel then
                Gravprce = Price__Rec.Price
            else
                Cementpr = Price__Rec.Price
            end if
        end if
        Read Inrec
    end while
```

We process each order record by identifying the item and retrieving the price for that item. At the same time, we move a character string that represents that item to the detail line. As these operations are moderately complex, we place them in a separate subroutine. The price is then used in a common set of instructions which compute the cost for all orders. The algorithms for these two subroutines are as follows.

```
Read and Process Order Records
    Subtotal = 0
    Read Inrec
    while Code = O do
        Identify Item and Get Price
        Print Customer Address
        Cost = Quantity * Price
        Print Cost
        Read Inrec
    end while

Identify Item and Get Price
    if Item__Code = S then
        Item = 'SAND'
        Price = Sandprce
    else
        if Item__Code = G then
            Item = 'GRAVEL'
            Price = Gravprce
        else
            Item = 'CEMENT'
            Price = Cementpr
        end if
    end if
```

Before defining the data areas for our program, we use the EQU instructions to assign symbolic names to the lengths and offsets we will use. As we have observed, this allows us to modify our program later. Most of these values can be read directly from the input and output specifications. We determine the lengths of most packed fields from the length of the corresponding zoned fields.

In order to minimize the amount of space required for our program, we define the input records and most output lines as variant record structures. In the case of the input records, we identify a particular record type by the code. The format of the output records is identified by context. In the case of the output records, this decision involves a trade-off. Our approach will reduce the size of the data areas required. But, at the same time, it increases the size of the code. We need to include code to clear the output line a number of times during execution. We need to add instructions to move constant fields, such as labels and headers, into the output line. We mitigate this disadvantage by defining the two lines containing column headings as constant fields.

Finally, we note the shifts involved in the price and tax calculations. The quantity has no decimal places and the price has 1. In order to print a cost with 2 decimal places, the product must be shifted left 1 position. The subtotal used for the tax calculation has 2 decimal places, and the tax rate has 3 places. Thus the product needs to be shifted right 3 places. In this case, the result is rounded when the shift takes place.

```
******************************************************************************
*                                                                            *
*     PROGRAM BILLING                                                        *
*                                                                            *
*     A PROGRAM TO PRODUCE BILLING STATEMENTS FOR THE SUMMIT CITY            *
*     SAND AND CEMENT COMPANY.                                               *
*                                                                            *
*     INPUT:    A SET OF PRICE RECORDS FOLLOWED BY CUSTOMER AND              *
*               ORDER RECORDS. INPUT RECORDS ARE ASSUMED TO BE               *
*               IN THE CORRECT ORDER AND ALL INPUT FIELDS ARE                *
*               ASSUMED TO BE CORRECT.                                       *
*                                                                            *
*     OUTPUT:   A MONTHLY BILLING FOR EACH CUSTOMER.                         *
*                                                                            *
******************************************************************************
           PRINT   NOGEN
BILLING    START   0                    PROGRAM BILLING
           BALR    RC,0                 :
           USING   *,RC                 :
           OPEN    READER,PRINTER       OPEN FILES
*
           BAL     RE,LDPRICES          READ PRICE RECORDS
*
WHILE01    EQU     *                    WHILE CODE <> TRAILER DO
           CLC     CODE,TRAILER         :
```

```
            BE      ENDWHL01                    :
            BAL     RE,PRNTHDS                  PRINT REPORT HEADINGS
            BAL     RE,READORDS                 READ AND PROCESS ORDER RECORDS
            BAL     RE,PRNTFOOT                 PRINT FOOTER LINES
            B       WHILE01                     :
ENDWHL01    EQU     *                           ENDWHILE
*
            CLOSE   READER,PRINTER      CLOSE FILES
*
            EOJ                         END BILLING
****************************************************************************
*                                                                          *
*    LDPRCS                                                                 *
*                                                                          *
*    READ PRICE RECORDS AND STORE CURRENT PRICES.                          *
*                                                                          *
*    INPUT VARIABLES:     <NONE>                                           *
*                                                                          *
*    OUTPUT VARIABLES:  SANDPRCE, GRAVPRCE, CEMENTPR, INREC                *
*                                                                          *
*    WORK VARIABLES:     <NONE>                                            *
*                                                                          *
****************************************************************************
            DS      F                   :
LDPRICES    EQU     *                   SUBROUTINE LDPRICES
            ST      RE,LDPRICES−4       :
            GET     READER,INREC        READ INREC
WHILE02     EQU     *                   WHILE (INREC = PRICE RECORD) DO
            CLC     CODE,PRICECOD       :
            BNE     ENDWHL02            :
IF01        EQU     *                   IF ITEM = SAND
            CLC     PCITEM,SANDCODE     :
            BNE     ELSE01              :
THEN01      EQU     *                   THEN
            PACK    SANDPRCE,PRICE          SANDPRCE = PRICE__REC.PRICE
            B       ENDIF01             :
ELSE01      EQU     *                   ELSE
IF02        EQU     *                       IF ITEM = GRAVEL
            CLC     PCITEM,GRAVELCD     :
            BNE     ELSE02              :
THEN02      EQU     *                       THEN
            PACK    GRAVPRCE,PRICE              GRAVPRCE = PRICE__REC.PRICE
            B       ENDIF02             :
ELSE02      EQU     *                       ELSE
            PACK    CEMENTPR,PRICE              CEMENTPR = PRICE__REC.PRICE
ENDIF02     EQU     *                       ENDIF
ENDIF01     EQU     *                   ENDIF
```

```
          GET     READER,INREC              READ INREC
          B       WHILE02                   :
ENDWHL02  EQU     *                         ENDWHILE
          L       RE,LDPRICES-4    RETURN
          BR      RE                        :
****************************************************************************************
*                                                                                      *
*    PRNTHDS                                                                            *
*                                                                                      *
*    START NEW PAGE AND PRINT HEADING LINES                                            *
*                                                                                      *
*    INPUT VARIABLES:    INREC                                                         *
*                                                                                      *
*    OUTPUT VARIABLES:   <NONE>                                                        *
*                                                                                      *
*    WORK VARIABLES:     OUTLINE                                                       *
*                                                                                      *
****************************************************************************************
          DS      F                         :
PRNTHDS   EQU     *                         SUBROUTINE PRNTHDS
          ST      RE,PRNTHDS-4              :
*
          MVC     OUTLINE,OUTLINE-1         START NEW PAGE
          MVC     CTRLCHAR,NEWPAGE          :
          PUT     PRINTER,OUTLINE           :
*
          MVC     OUTLINE,OUTLINE-1         PRINT COMPANY NAME AND ADDRESS
          MVC     OUTLINE+(L'OUTLINE-L'OUTSMMT)/2(L'OUTSMMT),OUTSMMT
          PUT     PRINTER,OUTLINE           :
          MVC     OUTLINE,OUTLINE-1         :
          MVC     OUTLINE+(L'OUTLINE-L'OUTSTRT)/2(L'OUTSTRT),OUTSTRT
          PUT     PRINTER,OUTLINE           :
          MVC     OUTLINE,OUTLINE-1         :
          MVC     OUTLINE+(L'OUTLINE-L'OUTCTYST)/2(L'OUTCTYST),OUTCTYST
          PUT     PRINTER,OUTLINE           :
*
          MVC     OUTLINE,OUTLINE-1         PRINT CUSTOMER BILLING ADDRESS
          MVC     CTRLCHAR,DBLSPACE         :
          MVC     CUSTINFO(L'CCNAME),CCNAME
          PUT     PRINTER,OUTLINE           :
          MVC     OUTLINE,OUTLINE-1         :
          MVC     CUSTINFO(L'CCSTREET),CCSTREET
          PUT     PRINTER,OUTLINE           :
          MVC     OUTLINE,OUTLINE-1         :
          MVC     CUSTINFO(L'CCCTYST),CCCTYST
          PUT     PRINTER,OUTLINE           :
*
```

```
          MVC     OUTLINE,OUTLINE-1          PRINT CUSTOMER ACCOUNT NUMBER
          MVC     CTRLCHAR,DBLSPACE          :
          MVC     CUSTINFO(L'OUTACTNO),OUTACTNO
          MVC     CSTACTNO,CCACCTNO          :
          PUT     PRINTER,OUTLINE            :
*
          PUT     PRINTER,HDLINE1            PRINT REPORT HEADINGS
          PUT     PRINTER,HDLINE2            :
*
          L       RE,PRNTHDS-4              RETURN
          BR      RE                         :
*****************************************************************************************
*                                                                                       *
*     READORDS                                                                           *
*                                                                                        *
*     READ AND PROCESS ALL ORDER RECORDS FOR CURRENT CUSTOMER.                           *
*     THIS SUBROUTINE ALSO READS IN THE NEXT CUSTOMER RECORD OR                          *
*     THE TRAILER RECORD.                                                                *
*                                                                                        *
*     INPUT VARIABLES:     <NONE>                                                        *
*                                                                                        *
*     OUTPUT VARIABLES:   SUBTOTAL, INREC                                                *
*                                                                                        *
*     WORK VARIABLES:     WORK, COST, PKDPRICE, OUTLINE                                  *
*                                                                                        *
*****************************************************************************************
          DS      F                          :
READORDS  EQU     *                          SUBROUTINE READORDS
          ST      RE,READORDS-4              :
INITACCM  EQU     *                          INITIALIZE ACCUMULATOR
          ZAP     SUBTOTAL,=P'0'             :
          GET     READER,INREC               READ INREC
WHILE03   EQU     *                          WHILE CODE = 0 DO
          CLC     CODE,ORDERCOD              :
          BNE     ENDWHL03                   :
          BAL     RE,FINDPRCE                IDENTIFY ITEM AND GET PRICE
*
          MVC     DTLSTR,OCSTREET            MOVE ADDRESS INFO TO
          MVC     DTLCTYST,OCCTYST           DETAIL LINE
          MVC     DTLQTY,QTYMSK              :
          PACK    PKDQTY,OCQTY               :
          ED      DTLQTY,PKDQTY              :
          MVC     DTLPRICE,PRICEMSK          :
          ED      DTLPRICE,PKDPRICE          :
*
          ZAP     WORK,PKDQTY                COST = PKDQTY*PKDPRICE
          MP      WORK,PKDPRICE              :
```

```
            SRP     WORK,64+1,0                 :
            ZAP     COST,WORK                   :
            MVC     DTLCOST,COSTMSK             MOVE TO DETAIL LINE
            ED      DTLCOST,COST                :
            AP      SUBTOTAL,COST               :
*
            PUT     PRINTER,OUTLINE             :
*
            GET     READER,INREC                READ INREC
*
            B       WHILE03                     :
ENDWHL03    EQU     *                           ENDWHILE
            L       RE,READORDS-4               RETURN
            BR      RE                          :
************************************************************************************************
*                                                                                              *
*    FINDPRCE                                                                                   *
*                                                                                              *
*    IDENTIFY THE ITEM AND RETRIEVE THE PRICE.                                                  *
*                                                                                              *
*    INPUT VARIABLES:     OCITEM, SANDPRCE, GRAVPRCE, CEMENTPR                                   *
*                                                                                              *
*    OUTPUT VARIABLES:  DTLITEM, PKDPRICE                                                        *
*                                                                                              *
*    WORK VARIABLES:    <NONE>                                                                  *
*                                                                                              *
************************************************************************************************
            DS      F                           :
FINDPRCE    EQU     *                           SUBROUTINE FINDPRCE
            ST      RE,FINDPRCE-4               :
            MVC     OUTLINE,OUTLINE-1           CLEAR OUTPUT LINE
IF03        EQU     *                           IF ITEM_CODE = S
            CLC     OCITEM,SANDCODE             :
            BNE     ELSE03                      :
THEN03      EQU     *                           THEN
            MVC     DTLITEM(L'SAND),SAND          ITEM = 'SAND'
            ZAP     PKDPRICE,SANDPRCE             PRICE = SANDPRCE
            B       ENDIF03                     :
ELSE03      EQU     *                           ELSE
IF04        EQU     *                             IF ITEM_CODE = G
            CLC     OCITEM,GRAVELCD             :
            BNE     ELSE04                      :
THEN04      EQU     *                             THEN
            MVC     DTLITEM(L'GRAVEL),GRAVEL      ITEM = 'GRAVEL'
            ZAP     PKDPRICE,GRAVPRCE             PRICE = GRAVPRCE
            B       ENDIF04                     :
ELSE04      EQU     *                             ELSE
```

```
          MVC     DTLITEM(L'CEMENT),CEMENT          ITEM = 'CEMENT'
          ZAP     PKDPRICE,CEMENTPR                  PRICE = CEMENTPR
ENDIF04   EQU     *                                      ENDIF
ENDIF03   EQU     *                                  ENDIF
          L       RE,FINDPRCE−4          RETURN
          BR      RE                     :
```

```
************************************************************************************
*                                                                                *
*    PRNTFOOT                                                                     *
*                                                                                *
*    PRINT FOOTER LINES FOR CUSTOMER STATEMENT.                                  *
*                                                                                *
*    INPUT VARIABLES:    SUBTOTAL                                                *
*                                                                                *
*    OUTPUT VARIABLES:  <NONE>                                                   *
*                                                                                *
*    WORK VARIABLES:    WORK, TAX, TOTAL                                         *
*                                                                                *
************************************************************************************
```

```
          DS      F                      :
PRNTFOOT  EQU     *                          SUBROUTINE PRNTFOOT
          ST      RE,PRNTFOOT−4              :
          MVC     OUTLINE,OUTLINE−1      PRINT UNDERSCORE LINE
          MVC     CUSTINFO(L'UNDERSCR),UNDERSCR
          MVC     CUSTINFO+1(DTLLEN),CUSTINFO
          PUT     PRINTER,OUTLINE       :
*
          ZAP     WORK,SUBTOTAL         TAX = SUBTOTAL * TAXRATE
          MP      WORK,TAXRATE          :
          SRP     WORK,64−3,5           :
          ZAP     TAX,WORK              :
*
          MVC     OUTLINE,OUTLINE−1     PRINT SUBTOTAL FOOTER
          MVC     SUBTLHD,OUTSUBTL      :
          MVC     SUBTLFTR,SUBTLMSK     :
          ED      SUBTLFTR,SUBTOTAL     :
          PUT     PRINTER,OUTLINE       :
*
          MVC     OUTLINE,OUTLINE−1     PRINT TAX FOOTER
          MVC     TAXHD,OUTTAX          :
          MVC     TAXFTR,TAXMSK         :
          ED      TAXFTR,TAX            :
          PUT     PRINTER,OUTLINE       :
*
          MVC     OUTLINE,OUTLINE−1     PRINT TOTAL FOOTER
          ZAP     TOTAL,SUBTOTAL             TOTAL = SUBTOTAL+TAX
```

```
          AP      TOTAL,TAX                    :
          MVC     TOTALHD,OUTTOTAL       PRINT TOTAL FOOTER
          MVC     TOTALFTR,TOTALMSK            :
          ED      TOTALFTR,TOTAL              :
          PUT     PRINTER,OUTLINE             :
*

          L       RE,PRNTFOOT-4          RETURN
          BR      RE                          :
```
****
```
*     SYMBOL DEFINITIONS                                                                                    *
```
****
```
*
*                              REGISTERS
*
RC        EQU     12                     REGISTER 12
RE        EQU     14                     REGISTER 14
*
*                         INPUT FIELD LENGTHS
*
CODELEN   EQU     1                      RECORD TYPE CODE
PRICELEN  EQU     3                      PRICE
ACTNOLEN  EQU     5                      ACCOUNT NUMBER
ITEMLEN   EQU     1                      ITEM CODE
QTYLEN    EQU     3                      QUANTITY
NAMELEN   EQU     20                     CUSTOMER NAME
STRETLEN  EQU     20                        STREET
CTYSTLEN  EQU     20                        CITY, STATE
ADDRLEN   EQU     STRETLEN+CTYSTLEN  ADDRESS
*
*                         PACKED FIELD LENGTHS
*
PKPRCLEN  EQU     PRICELEN/2+1           PRICE
PKQTYLEN  EQU     QTYLEN/2+1             QUANTITY
PKCSTLEN  EQU     PKPRCLEN+PKQTYLEN  COST
PKSUBLEN  EQU     PKCSTLEN+1             SUBTOTAL
PKTAXLEN  EQU     PKSUBLEN-1             CALCULATED TAX
PKTOTLEN  EQU     PKSUBLEN               CALCULATED TOTAL
*
*                  OUTPUT FIELD LENGTHS AND OFFSETS
*
DTLLEN    EQU     110                    LENGTH OF DETAIL LINE
TOTOFFST  EQU     99                     OFFSET TO FOOTER FIELD
ITMOFST   EQU     11                     DETAIL LINE ITEM FLD LEN
DLADOFST  EQU     26                     OFFSET TO DELIVERY ADDRESS
CTYOFFST  EQU     51                     OFFSET TO CITY/STATE FIELD
QTYOFFST  EQU     76                     OFFSET TO QUANTITY FIELD
PRCOFFST  EQU     91                     OFFSET TO PRICE FIELD
```

```
CSTOFFST   EQU    111                      OFFSET TO COST FIELD
HDOFFSET   EQU    11                       OFFSET TO CUSTOMER INFO FLD
LASTCOL    EQU    119                      OFFSET TO LAST COL PRINTED
***********************************************************************************
*                                LITERALS                                      *
***********************************************************************************
           LTORG
***********************************************************************************
*                                FILES                                         *
***********************************************************************************
READER     DTFCD  DEVADDR=SYSIPT,DEVICE=2501,EOFADDR=ENDWHL02,                  X
                  IOAREA1=INBUF1,IOAREA2=INBUF2,WORKA=YES
INBUF1     DS     CL80
INBUF2     DS     CL80
*
PRINTER    DTFPR  DEVADDR=SYSLST,DEVICE=3203,BLKSIZE=133,CTLCHR=ASA,           X
                  IOAREA1=OUTBUF1,IOAREA2=OUTBUF2,WORKA=YES
OUTBUF1    DS     CL133
OUTBUF2    DS     CL133
***********************************************************************************
*                                CONSTANTS                                     *
***********************************************************************************
*
*                         CARRIAGE CONTROL
*
NEWPAGE    DC     C'1'                 :
DBLSPACE   DC     C'0'                 :
SNGLSPCE   DC     C' '                 :
*
*                     CONSTANTS USED IN OUTPUT FIELDS
*
OUTSMMT    DC     C'SUMMIT CITY SAND AND CEMENT' COMPANY NAME AND ADDRESS
OUTSTRT    DC     C'2108 N. CALIFAX STREET'      :
OUTCTYST   DC     C'FORT WAYNE, INDIANA 46823'   :
OUTSUBTL   DC     C'SUBTOTAL'               FOOTER LABELS
OUTTAX     DC     C'TAX'                    :
OUTTOTAL   DC     C'TOTAL'                  :
OUTACTNO   DC     C'ACCOUNT NUMBER: '       ACCOUNT NUMBER LABEL
SAND       DC     C'SAND'                   ITEM NAMES
GRAVEL     DC     C'GRAVEL'                 :
CEMENT     DC     C'CEMENT'                 :
*
*                            EDIT MASKS
*
PRICEMSK   DC     X'4021204B20'             PRICE
COSTMSK    DC     X'4020206B2021204B2020'   COST
SUBTLMSK   DC     X'40202020206B2021204B2020' SUBTOTAL
```

```
TAXMSK     DC    X'4020206B2021204B2020'          TAX
TOTALMSK   DC    X'40206B2020206B2021204B2020'    TOTAL
QTYMSK     DC    X'40202120'                       QUANTITY
*
*                        RECORD CODES
*
TRAILER    DC    C'T'                              TRAILER RECORD
PRICECOD   DC    C'P'                              PRICE RECORD
CUSTCOD    DC    C'C'                              CUSTOMER RECORD
ORDERCOD   DC    C'O'                              ORDER RECORD
SANDCODE   DC    C'S'                              SAND
GRAVELCD   DC    C'G'                              GRAVEL
CEMENTCD   DC    C'C'                              CEMENT
*
*                      SPECIAL CHARACTER
*
UNDERSCR   DC    C'_'                              USED TO CREATE UNDERLINE
*
***********************************************************************************
*                          VARIABLES                                          *
***********************************************************************************
*
*
*                          ITEM PRICES
*
SANDPRCE   DS    PL(PKPRCLEN)                      SAND
GRAVPRCE   DS    PL(PKPRCLEN)                      GRAVEL
CEMENTPR   DS    PL(PKPRCLEN)                      CEMENT
*
*                    PACKED CALCULATION FIELDS
*
COST       DS    PL(PKCSTLEN)                      COST            F(7,2)
SUBTOTAL   DS    PL(PKSUBLEN)                      SUBTOTAL        F(8,2)
TAX        DS    PL(PKTAXLEN)                      TAX             F(7,2)
TOTAL      DS    PL(PKTOTLEN)                      TOTAL           F(9,2)
*
*                     PACKED WORK FIELDS
*
PKDPRICE   DS    PL(PKPRCLEN)                      PRICE           F(3,1)
PKDQTY     DS    PL(PKQTYLEN)                      QUANTITY        F(3,0)
TAXRATE    DC    P'45'                             STATE TAX RATE  F(2,1)
WORK       DS    PL(PKSUBLEN+L'TAXRATE+1)          WORK AREA
***********************************************************************************
*                       I/O WORK AREAS                                        *
***********************************************************************************
***********************************************************************************
*                          INPUT                                              *
***********************************************************************************
```

```
INREC      DS     CL80                       INPUT RECORD
           ORG    INREC                      :
CODE       DS     CL(CODELEN)                INPUT RECORD TYPE CODE
VARIANT    DS     CL(L'INREC-CODELEN)        VARIANTS
           ORG    VARIANT                    PRICE RECORD
PRICE      DS     ZL(PRICELEN)                 PRICE
PCITEM     DS     CL(ITEMLEN)                  ITEM
           ORG    VARIANT                    CUSTOMER RECORD
CCACCTNO   DS     ZL(ACTNOLEN)                 ACCOUNT NUMBER
CCNAME     DS     CL(NAMELEN)                  NAME
CCADDR     DS     CL(ADDRLEN)                  ADDRESS
           ORG    CCADDR                       :
CCSTREET   DS     CL(STRETLEN)                   STREET
CCCTYST    DS     CL(CTYSTLEN)                   CITY, STATE
           ORG    VARIANT                    ORDER RECORD
OCACCTNO   DS     ZL(ACTNOLEN)                 ACCOUNT NUMBER
OCITEM     DS     CL(ITEMLEN)                  ITEM NUMBER
OCQTY      DS     ZL(QTYLEN)                   QUANTITY
OCADDR     DS     CL(ADDRLEN)                  ADDRESS
           ORG    OCADDR                       :
OCSTREET   DS     CL(STRETLEN)                   STREET
OCCTYST    DS     CL(CTYSTLEN)                   CITY, STATE
           ORG    INREC+L'INREC              END INPUT RECORD
****************************************************************************************************
*                                        OUTPUT                                                 *
****************************************************************************************************
           DC     C' '                       BLANK TO CLEAR OUTPUT LINE
OUTLINE    DS     CL133                      OUTPUT LINE
           ORG    OUTLINE                    :
CTRLCHAR   DS     CL1                        CONTROL CHARACTER
           ORG    OUTLINE+HDOFFSET                     :
CUSTINFO   DS     CL(L'OUTLINE-L'HDOFFSET)             CUSTOMER INFO FLD
           ORG    CUSTINFO                             :
ACCTHDNG   DS     CL(L'OUTACTNO)                       ACCOUNT NUMBER FLD
CSTACTNO   DS     CL(ACTNOLEN)                         :
           ORG    CUSTINFO                   DETAIL LINE HEADING 1
DTLITEM    DS     CL(ITMOFST)                  ITEM TYPE
           ORG    OUTLINE+DLADOFST             DELIVERY ADDRESS
DTLSTR     DS     CL(STRETLEN)                   STREET
           ORG    OUTLINE+CTYOFFST               :
DTLCTYST   DS     CL(CTYSTLEN)                   CITY, STATE
           ORG    OUTLINE+QTYOFFST               :
DTLQTY     DS     CL(L'QTYMSK)                 QUANTITY
           ORG    OUTLINE+PRCOFFST             :
DTLPRICE   DS     CL(L'PRICEMSK)               PRICE
           ORG    OUTLINE+LASTCOL-L'COSTMSK    :
DTLCOST    DS     CL(L'COSTMSK)                COST
```

```
              ORG      OUTLINE+TOTOFFST              FOOTER LINES
SUBTLHD       DS       CL(L'OUTSUBTL)                  SUBTOTAL
              ORG      OUTLINE+LASTCOL-L'SUBTLMSK          :
SUBTLFTR      DS       CL(L'SUBTLMSK)                      :
              ORG      OUTLINE+TOTOFFST                    :
TAXHD         DS       CL(L'OUTTAX)                   CALCULATED TAX
              ORG      OUTLINE+LASTCOL-L'TAXMSK            :
TAXFTR        DS       CL(L'TAXMSK)                        :
              ORG      OUTLINE+TOTOFFST                    :
TOTALHD       DS       CL(L'OUTTOTAL)                 TOTAL AMOUNT
              ORG      OUTLINE+LASTCOL-L'TOTALMSK          :
TOTALFTR      DS       CL(L'TOTALMSK)                      :
              ORG      OUTLINE+L'OUTLINE              END OUTLINE
*
HDLINE1       DC       CL133' '                      HEADLINE 1
              ORG      HDLINE1                            :
              DC       C'-'                          DOUBLE SPACE
              ORG      HDLINE1+ITMOFST                    :
              DC       C'ITEM'                       COLUMN HEADINGS
              ORG      HDLINE1+DLADOFST                   :
              DC       C'DELIVERY ADDRESS'                :
              ORG      HDLINE1+QTYOFFST                   :
              DC       C'QUANTITY'                        :
              ORG      HDLINE1+PRCOFFST                   :
              DC       C'PRICE'                           :
              ORG      HDLINE1+CSTOFFST                   :
              DC       C'COST'                            :
              ORG      HDLINE1+(L'HDLINE1)           END HEADLINE 1
*
HDLINE2       DC       CL133' '                      HEADLINE 2
              ORG      HDLINE2+QTYOFFST                   :
              DC       C'(TONS)'                     2ND LINE COL. HEADINGS
              ORG      HDLINE2+PRCOFFST                   :
              DC       C'($ PER TON)'                      :
              ORG      HDLINE2+(L'HDLINE2)          END HEADLINE 2
*
              END
```

A sample input file for testing this program is shown below.

```
P023S
P098G
P123C
C94302BILTWELL CONST. CO. 123 MAIN STREET      FORT WAYNE, IN 46894
094302S453324 NORTH AVENUE    FORT WAYNE, IN. 46893
094302G043324 NORTH AVENUE    FORT WAYNE, IN. 46893
094302G032324 NORTH AVENUE    FORT WAYNE, IN. 46893
```

```
094302C068324 NORTH AVENUE    FORT WAYNE, IN. 46893
094302S067123 MAIN STREET     FORT WAYNE, IN. 46894
094302G104123 MAIN STREET     FORT WAYNE, IN. 46894
C98749XXX PAVING COMPANY  453 EAST CHESTNUT   FORT WAYNE, IN 46845
098749S109453 EAST CHESTNUT   FORT WAYNE, IN. 46845
098749G200453 EAST CHESTNUT   FORT WAYNE, IN. 46845
098749C094123 FREMONT DR.     FORT WAYNE, IN. 46845
T
```

The output produced when the program is executed with this sample data is shown in Listing 3.7.1.

Listing 3.7.1

```
                              SUMMIT CITY SAND AND CEMENT
                                 2108 N. CALIFAX STREET
                               FORT WAYNE, INDIANA 46823


        BILTWELL CONST. CO.
        123 MAIN STREET
        FORT WAYNE, IN 46894

        ACCOUNT NUMBER: 94302


        ITEM        DELIVERY ADDRESS                         QUANTITY    PRICE         COST
                                                             (TONS)      ($ PER TON)

        SAND        324 NORTH AVENUE     FORT WAYNE, IN. 4689    453      2.3          1,041.90
        GRAVEL      324 NORTH AVENUE     FORT WAYNE, IN. 4689     43      9.8            421.40
        GRAVEL      324 NORTH AVENUE     FORT WAYNE, IN. 4689     32      9.8            313.60
        CEMENT      324 NORTH AVENUE     FORT WAYNE, IN. 4689     68     12.3            836.40
        SAND        123 MAIN STREET      FORT WAYNE, IN 46894     67      2.3            154.10
        GRAVEL      123 MAIN STREET      FORT WAYNE, IN 46894    104      9.8          1,019.20
        -----------------------------------------------------------------------------------------
                                                                        SUBTOTAL      3,786.60
                                                                        TAX             170.40


                              SUMMIT CITY SAND AND CEMENT
                                 2108 N. CALIFAX STREET
                               FORT WAYNE, INDIANA 46823


        XXX PAVING COMPANY
        453 EAST CHESTNUT
        FORT WAYNE, IN 46845

        ACCOUNT NUMBER: 98749


        ITEM        DELIVERY ADDRESS                         QUANTITY    PRICE         COST
                                                             (TONS)      ($ PER TON)
        SAND        453 EAST CHESTNUT    FORT WAYNE, IN 46845    109      2.3            250.70
        GRAVEL      453 EAST CHESTNUT    FORT WAYNE, IN 46845    200      9.8          1,960.00
        CEMENT      123 FREMONT DR.      FORT WAYNE, IN 46834     94     12.3          1,156.20
        -----------------------------------------------------------------------------------------
                                                                        SUBTOTAL      3,366.90
                                                                        TAX             151.51
                                                                        TOTAL         3,518.41
```

P R O G R A M M I N G   P R O J E C T S

1. *Monthly Sales Report*   Lo Key's Oriental Grocery uses two formats for their monthly sales personnel records. The records contain a one character code in column one to distinguish between salaried employees (S) and commissioned employees (C). The two formats are shown below.

    Salaried Employees

Field	Columns	Comments/Format
Code	1	S
Salesperson Name	2 - 31	
Soc. Sec. Number	32 - 40	
Annual Salary	41 - 47	(7,2)
Monthly Sales	48 - 54	(7,2)

    Commissioned Employees

Field	Columns	Comments/Format
Code	1	C
Salesperson Name	2 - 31	
Soc. Sec. Number	32 - 40	
Annual Base Pay	41 - 47	(7,2)
Commission Rate	48 - 49	(2,2)
Monthly Sales	50 - 56	(7,2)

    Write a program to prepare a monthly payroll report in the format shown below. Leave the Commission Rate and Commission entries blank for salaried employees.

    ```
                                   LO KEY'S ORIENTAL GROCERY
                                     MONTHLY PAYROLL REPORT

    SALES PERSON                  SOCIAL        MONTHLY      BASE PAY    COMMISSION      TOTAL
                                  SECURITY      SALES                   RATE         COMPENSATION
    AAAAAAAAAAAAAAAAAAAAAAAAAAAAAA  999-99-9999   99,990.99    99,999.09      .09        99,999.09

    ...........................................................................................

                                                               TOTAL COMPENSATION   9,999,999.09
                                                               MONTHLY SALES        9,999,999.09
    ```

2. *Electric Bill*   The Sparky Electric Company uses the following rate schedule. The first 500 kilowatt hours cost 6.105 cents each. Over 500 kilowatt hours, the charge is 5.254 cents per kilowatt hour. In addition, there is a $5.35 per month service charge. The input records for their monthly billing are formatted as follows.

Field	Columns	Comments/Format
Name	1 - 20	
Street Address	21 - 40	
City, State, Zip	41 - 60	
Old Meter Reading	61 - 65	(5,1) Kilowatts
New Meter Reading	66 - 70	(5,1) Kilowatts
Old Balance	71 - 75	(5,2) Dollars
Payment	76 - 80	(5,2) Dollars

Write a program to produce a monthly statement for each customer in the format shown below. (The CR message should only be printed if the amount is negative—i.e., the customer has overpaid.)

```
                         SPARKY  ELECTRIC  COMPANY
                         2837  WEST  MAIN  STREET
                         FRANKLIN,  PA.  15758


<Customer Name    >
<Street Address   >
<City, State, Zip >


CURRENT METER READING: 0999.9   PREVIOUS READING: 0999.9   CONSUMPTION: 0999.9 KWH


    9990.9 KWH @6.105 CENTS    999.09    LAST MONTH'S BALANCE  999.09
    9990.0 KWH @5.254 CENTS    999.09    PAYMENT               999.09
                                                               ......
    MONTHLY SERVICE CHARGE       5.35    UNPAID BALANCE        999.09(CR)
    ------------------------------------
    ELECTRIC SERVICE           999.09    THIS MONTH            999.09
                                                               ......
                                         BALANCE DUE           999.09(CR)
```

3. *Grade Report* Harvey's Law School and Auto Repair has recently acquired a slightly used IBM 370. They need an assembly language program to produce student grade reports. The input for the program will consist of a file of student records and grade records. Each student record will be followed by a set of grade records for that student. These records will be formatted as shown in the following.

Student Record

Field	Columns	Comments/Format
Record Code	1	S
Student Number	2 - 10	
Name	11 - 30	
Street Address	31 - 50	
City State Zip	51 - 70	
Credit Hours Attempted	71 - 73	(3,0)
Total Grade Points	74 - 76	(3,0)

Grade Record

Field	Columns	Comments/Format
Record Code	1	G
Student Number	2 - 10	
Department	11 - 13	
Course Number	14 - 16	
Course Name	17 - 36	
Credit Hours	37	
Grade Points	38	(4,3,2,1,0)

Your program should produce a grade report for each student. The format of this report is shown below.

The GPA is total grade points divided by credit hours. These averages should be rounded to 5 decimal places.

If the student's GPA is less than 2.00000 but greater than or equal to 1.00000, the student is placed on probation and a probation notice is printed at the bottom of the report. If the student's GPA is less than 1.0000, a suspension notice is printed.

Probation notice: YOU ARE HEREBY NOTIFIED THAT YOU ARE ON PROBATION.

Suspension notice: YOU ARE HEREBY NOTIFIED THAT YOU ARE ON SUSPENSION.

```
                          HARVEY'S LAW SCHOOL
                           AND AUTO REPAIR

                         STUDENT GRADE REPORT

STUDENT   < Student Name    >              STUDENT NUMBER 099-99-9999
          < Address         >
          <                 >


DEPT                       COURSE      COURSE NAME              CREDIT   GRADE
                           NUMBER                               HOURS


AAA                         999        AAAAAAAAAAAAAAAAAAAA        0       0


.............................................................................

SEMESTER TOTALS:                        CUMULATIVE TOTALS:
       CREDIT HOURS        990                 CREDIT HOURS      990
       GRADE POINTS        990                 GRADE POINTS      990
       GPA             0.99999                 GPA           0.99999

<Probation or suspension notice when applicable.>
```

4. Write a program to read a file of records each containing a distance in miles, feet and inches. Print each distance and then print the sum in lowest terms. Check the output for page overflow, printing no more than 40 distances per page. Use appropriate input and output formats.

C H A P T E R 4

GENERAL
INSTRUCTIONS

4.1 REPRESENTATION OF SIGNED BINARY NUMBERS

In Chapter 1, we discussed binary and hexadecimal numbers and considered the addition and subtraction of such numbers. The numbers we used in these operations were always assumed to be positive. More precisely, these numbers should be considered unsigned numbers. We need to make a distinction between a signed number whose sign is + and a number that has no sign. In our discussions on representation of these numbers, we simply made no provision for recording a sign.

There are several ways to represent binary and hexadecimal numbers. In later sections, we consider arithmetic operations on signed numbers and various logical operations. The remainder of the chapter covers some of the IBM 370 instructions for manipulating binary numbers.

Signed Binary Numbers

Given a fixed number of bit positions, say n, we can create 2^n bit patterns, B'00 . . . 0' through B'11 . . . 1'. If we interpret these patterns as representing unsigned binary numbers, then they represent 0 through 2^n-1. We are now going to consider three ways in which we can interpret this same set of bit patterns as representing both positive and negative numbers. All three representations are used in various contexts in computing.

The choice of a representation for a particular context is not made by the programmer. Instead, it is made by the computer designers. In making this decision, the primary criterion is the ease of implementation. The choice of a representation is determined more by the operations that need to be provided rather than an intuitive sense of which representation is more natural.

The three representations that we discuss may be used in any number base. However, we concentrate on binary numbers, beginning with a brief description and going on to consider them in more detail.

Of the three representations, the easiest to understand is *sign-magnitude representation*. This format employs an explicit sign together with an unsigned number, which represents the magnitude. From our perspective, this seems the most natural representation, as it is the way we normally write signed decimal numbers. The second, *biased notation*, shifts all numbers by a constant amount. The most widely used representation is *complement notation*, in which positive numbers are represented as usual while negative numbers are replaced by their "complements."

Sign-Magnitude Representation

When we write signed decimal numbers, we write an explicit plus or minus sign together with an unsigned decimal number. The unsigned number represents the size or magnitude of the signed number. It is this mechanism that is used for sign-magnitude representations in computing.

This is the notation which we have been using for packed decimal numbers. A packed decimal with n bytes has room for $2*n$ hexadecimal digits. The rightmost of these is used to encode the sign while the rest are used to encode decimal digits.

Now, suppose we want to represent signed binary numbers in sign-magnitude notation using n bit positions. The obvious choice is to give up one of the bit positions for the purpose of representing the sign. We could use any of the bits for the sign, but, for convenience, the leftmost is usually chosen. Similarly, we could interpret the sign bit in two ways, but it is more common to interpret 0 as + and 1 as −.

We can then use the remaining $n-1$ bit positions to encode the magnitude as an unsigned binary number. The magnitudes we can represent are $0 \ldots 2^{(n-1)}-1$. The signed numbers which can be represented are $+0 \ldots +2^{(n-1)}-1$ and $-(2^{(n-1)}-1) \ldots -0$. (Unfortunately, 0 has two representations in sign-magnitude form. They are $B'00\ldots0'$ and $B'10\ldots0'$. In some implementations, $B'10\ldots0'$ may be declared illegal, to remove this objection.)

To summarize, with the conventions noted above, given an n-bit binary number,

$$B'b_{n-1}b_{n-2} \ldots b_1\, b_0'$$

b_{n-1}, the leftmost bit, would be interpreted as the sign bit. The remaining bits, b_{n-2}, $\ldots$, $b_1\, b_0$, would be interpreted as the magnitude.

Example 4.1.1 *Suppose we have 4 bits available for representing sign-magnitude numbers. If we use the leftmost bit to encode the sign, then we have 3 bits remaining to represent the magnitude. The magnitudes will be $0 \ldots 7(2^3-1)$.*

If we use 0 to represent + and 1 for −, the 16 available bit patterns will be interpreted as shown below.

Bit Pattern	Value	Bit Pattern	Value
0000	+0	1000	−0
0001	+1	1001	−1
0010	+2	1010	−2
0011	+3	1011	−3
0100	+4	1100	−4
0101	+5	1101	−5
0110	+6	1110	−6
0111	+7	1111	−7

Sign-magnitude representation is fairly natural and its obvious advantage is that we can tell at a glance whether a number is positive or negative. Unfortunately, it is not particularly good for implementing arithmetic operations. For example, in order to add two numbers written in sign-magnitude notation, it is first necessary to compare the signs. If they are the same, the magnitudes are added and the result is given the common sign. If the original numbers have different signs, the smaller magnitude must be subtracted from the larger. The difference is given the sign of the number with the larger magnitude. Subtraction of sign-magnitude numbers presents similar complications.

A second objection to sign-magnitude representation is the difficulty of comparing two numbers. If both numbers are positive, we can compare their magnitudes as unsigned binary numbers. If their signs differ, then we need not consider the magnitudes. However, when both are negative, then their relative order must be obtained by comparing their magnitudes and then reversing the order.

As we have seen, sign-magnitude representation is used to represent packed decimal numbers. In binary form, it is used to represent the fractional part, or *mantissa*, in most floating point notations.

Biased Notation

Biased notation alleviates some of the problems associated with sign-magnitude representation. The concept is only slightly more complicated than sign-magnitude. Given unsigned numbers of a fixed size and a number k, we interpret each unsigned number m as representing the signed number $m' = m - k$. Equivalently, given a signed number m', it would be represented by the number $m = m' + k$. This particular representation is also called excess-k notation. Although it is not necessary, since we normally want to represent as many negative numbers as positive, k is usually chosen to be approximately half of the largest number that can be represented. When used in base 2, if there are n bits available, k is usually chosen to be $2^{(n-1)}$.

Example 4.1.2 *Again, suppose we have 4 bits available to represent signed numbers. Letting $k = 8(2^3)$ yields the standard excess-8 notation. The interpretation of each bit pattern as a signed number is shown below.*

Bit Pattern	Value	Bit Pattern	Value
0000	−8	1000	+0
0001	−7	1001	+1
0010	−6	1010	+2
0011	−5	1011	+3
0100	−4	1100	+4
0101	−3	1101	+5
0110	−2	1110	+6
0111	−1	1111	+7

It is still possible to determine whether a number is negative by examining the first bit. In this case negative numbers have a 0 in the leftmost bit position, non-negative numbers begin with 1.

It is quite easy to determine the relative order of two numbers in biased notation. The order of the numbers is the same as the order of their biased representation.

Addition and subtraction using biased notation is much simpler than with sign-magnitude notation. When we add two excess-k representations, the sum will have an extra k. It must be adjusted by subtracting k. Similarly when two excess-k numbers are subtracted, the difference must be adjusted by the addition of k.

Example 4.1.3 *Find the sum and the difference of the excess-64 numbers* B'0001101' *and* B'1001011'.

In order to check the results, we first convert to sign-magnitude form by subtracting $64 =$ B'1000000'.

$$B'0001101' - B'1000000' = -B'0110011' = -51$$
$$B'1001011' - B'1000000' = +B'0001011' = +11$$

We perform the addition by adding B'0001101' and B'1001011' and subtracting B'1000000'.

$$
\begin{array}{r}
1111 \\
B'0001101' \\
+B'1001011' \\
\hline
B'1011000' \\
-B'1000000' \\
\hline
B'0011000'
\end{array}
$$

Converting the result to sign-magnitude notation

$$B'0011000' - B'1000000' = -B'0101000' = -40$$

we see that it is correct.

The subtraction is performed by adding B'1000000' to B'0001101' then subtracting B'1001011'.

$$
\begin{array}{r}
B'0001101' \\
+B'1000000' \\
\hline
B'1001101' \\
-B'1001011' \\
\hline
B'0000010'
\end{array}
$$

The excess-64 result B'0000010' represents

$$B'0000010' - B'1000000' = -B'0111110' = -62$$

Although an adjustment is required for both addition and subtraction, these operations are still simpler than the corresponding operations on sign-magnitude representations. The advantage is that in the case of biased notation, the addition and subtraction operations are the same regardless of the relative signs of the two numbers.

Unfortunately, multiplication and division of excess-k numbers are much more difficult. As a result, biased notation is often used in a context that requires addition and subtraction but not multiplication or division. This is the case with the exponent in floating point number representations. For example, the standard floating point form on the IBM 370 codes the exponent in excess-64 notation.

Complementary Notation

Complementary notation seems, in some sense, to be the least natural of the three. Yet, it greatly simplifies all arithmetic operations and is the most commonly used way of representing signed numbers.

In complementary notation, positive numbers are represented by themselves. Negative numbers are represented by the complements of their magnitudes.

The value used for complementation is usually a power of the base or one less than a power of the base. For example, the b's complement of an n-digit base b number k is the rightmost n digits of $b^n - k$. When the complement is formed by subtracting from $b^n - 1$, it is called $(b-1)$'s complement.

For binary numbers, we have 2's complement or 1's complement. In the case of decimals, we have 10's complement and 9's complement; in hexadecimal, 16's complement and F's complement or 15's complement.

Example 4.1.4 *The 6-digit 10's complement of 807512 is $10^6 - 807512 = 1000000 - 807512 = 192488$. The 6-digit 9's complement of this number is $999999 - 807512 = 192487$.*

Example 4.1.5 *The 4-digit 16's complement of the hexadecimal number X'3AB9' is found by subtracting this number from $16^4 = $ X'10000' as follows.*

$$
\begin{array}{r}
\text{FFF10} \\
\text{X' } 10000' \\
-\text{X' } 3AB9' \\
\hline
\text{X' } C547'
\end{array}
$$

The F's complement is found similarly.

$$
\begin{array}{r}
\text{X'FFFF'} \\
-\text{X'3AB9'} \\
\hline
\text{X'C546'}
\end{array}
$$

The 2's complement of an n-bit binary number is the rightmost n bits obtained from the result of subtracting that number from $2^n = $ B'100...0' (a 1 followed by n

0's.) The 1's complement is formed by subtracting the number from $2^n - 1 = B'111 \ldots 1'$ (n 1's).

Example 4.1.6 *The 1's complement of the 6-bit number B'001011' is found as follows.*

$$\begin{array}{r} B'111111' \\ -B'001011' \\ \hline B'110100' \end{array}$$

Notice what happens when we perform the subtraction. Because the number we are subtracting from is all 1's, every position in the subtrahend that contains a 1 yields a zero in the result. Each position that contains a zero yields a 1. We can, in fact, find the 1's complement of a binary number simply by reversing each bit.

Example 4.1.7 *The 1's complement of the 16-bit number B'1001101101010100' is B'0110010010101011'.*

Example 4.1.8 *Find the 2's complement of the 8-bit number B'01110100'.*

Applying the definition above, we find the 2's complement by subtracting B'01110100' from B'100000000' as follows.

$$\begin{array}{r} 01111110 \\ B'\; \mathit{100000000}' \\ -B'\; 01110100' \\ \hline B'\; 10001100' \end{array}$$

However, as the 2's complement is, by definition, 1 more than the 1's complement, it can be found more easily by taking the 1's complement and adding 1. This gives the following sequence.

$$B'01110100' \rightarrow B'10001011' \rightarrow B'10001100'$$

$$\underbrace{\qquad}_{\text{Form the 1's}} \qquad \underbrace{\qquad}_{\text{Add 1}}$$
$$\text{complement}$$

The 2's complement of B'00000000' may be found in the same way.

$$B'00000000' \rightarrow B'11111111' \rightarrow B'100000000'$$

In this case, the result has one extra bit. But, recall that the 2's complement of an n-bit number includes only the rightmost n bits. Thus, the 2's complement of B'00000000' is B'00000000'.

Because finding the 1's complement is easy, as the examples above show, finding the 2's complement is also simple. We can simplify the process even further by observing how the subtraction operation proceeds. As we process the bits from right to left, the rightmost 0 bits in the subtrahend result in 0's in the 2's complement. The first 1 bit encountered forces a borrow. The borrow must come from the 1 at the extreme left. The result of the borrow is that the position from which we subtract B'1' becomes B'10' while each intervening B'0' is changed to B'1'. Subtracting B'1' from B'10' gives 1. Each of the remaining bit positions will be subtracted from 1, as with 1's complement. Thus, the value in each of these positions will be reversed.

The process can be summarized quite simply: To find the 2's complement of a binary number, proceeding from right to left, leave all bits unchanged up to and including the first B'1'. Reverse all the remaining bits.

Example 4.1.9 *Find the 2's complement of B'010110010'.*

Leaving the rightmost 0 and 1 unchanged, reverse all bits to the left of the 1 giving B'101001110'.

2's Complement in Hexadecimal

Just as it is often convenient to express binary numbers in hexadecimal form, we will find it much easier to work with 2's complement numbers written in base 16. The conversion is as before: each group of four bits corresponds to a single hexadecimal digit. If it is necessary to complement a binary number that has been represented in hexadecimal form, recall that the 2's complement of any binary number can be formed by taking the 1's complement and adding 1. Forming the 1's complement in binary is equivalent to subtracting the number from all 1's. A binary number consisting of all 1's becomes all F's when converted to hexadecimal. (Assuming that the number of bits is a multiple of 4.) Thus, in order to form the 2's complement of a binary number written in hexadecimal, we simply subtract each hexadecimal digit from F and then add 1. (This is, in fact, the equivalent of taking the 16's complement of the hexadecimal representation.)

Example 4.1.10 *Give the 2's complement of each of the following 16-bit numbers written in hexadecimal form.*

$$X'3A6E' \rightarrow X'C591'+1 = X'C592'$$
$$X'FA5B' \rightarrow X'05A4'+1 = X'05A5'$$

Using 2's Complement to Represent Signed Numbers

Suppose we begin with an n-bit number m. Its 2's complement is 2^n-m. This is also an n-bit number, so we can take its 2's complement. When we do this, we have $2^n-(2^n-m) = 2^n-2^n+m = m$. We get m back again. This suggests that we might be able use 2's complement to represent signed numbers so that complementation is equivalent to negation.

If we agree to this, then the rest is fairly natural. Given n bits to represent signed numbers, if we want about as many positive as negative numbers, then only half of these can represent positive values. Suppose we let $0 \ldots 2^{n-1}-1$ represent themselves as positive values. Then we represent the negation of each of these numbers by its complement. The table below illustrates this scheme for $n = 4$.

Bit Pattern	Hex. Form	Value	Binary Comp.	Hex. Comp.	Value
B'0000'	X'0'	0	B'0000'	X'0'	0
B'0001'	X'1'	+1	B'1111'	X'F'	−1
B'0010'	X'2'	+2	B'1110'	X'E'	−2
B'0011'	X'3'	+3	B'1101'	X'D'	−3
B'0100'	X'4'	+4	B'1100'	X'C'	−4
B'0101'	X'5'	+5	B'1011'	X'B'	−5
B'0110'	X'6'	+6	B'1010'	X'A'	−6
B'0111'	X'7'	+7	B'1001'	X'9'	−7

Note that 0 no longer has two representations, as it is its own complement. We can still determine the sign of a number by inspecting the leftmost bit. This bit is usually called the *sign bit.*

One 4-bit number is missing from the list above. It is the number B'1000'. If we decide to use this bit pattern, it should represent a negative number because its first bit is one. Furthermore, when considered as an unsigned number, it is less than the bit patterns used for the other negative numbers. Therefore, it should represent a negative number smaller than the others, −8. Notice that the 2's complement of this number is B'1000'.

In general, the range of signed values that can be represented in n-bit 2's complement notation is -2^{n-1} to $2^{n-1}-1$. -2^{n-1} is represented by a 1 bit followed by $n-1$ 0 bits. −1 is represented by n 1 bits. The values $0 \ldots 2^{n-1}-1$ are represented as usual.

If we assume that the number of bits is a multiple of 4, then, when these numbers are written in hexadecimal form, the range of values is X'800 . . . 0' (-2^{n-1}) to X'FFF . . . F' (-1) and X'000 . . . 0' to X'7FF . . . F' $(2^{n-1}-1)$.

Note that a 2's complement number written in hexadecimal form is still negative if its first bit is 1. When the number of bits is a multiple of 4, as above, this is equivalent to having 8, 9, A, B, C, D, E, or F for the first hexadecimal digit.

Comparing 2's Complement Numbers

Although the order relation for 2's complement representations is not as straightforward as it was in the case of biased notation, it is not terribly complicated. The relative size of two negative numbers can be determined directly from their representations. For example the 2's complement representation of −6, B'1010' is less than the 2's complement representation of −3, B'1101'. In general, to determine the relative order of any two 2's complement representations, first check the signs. If they differ, they determine the order. If they are the same, the orders of the two numbers are the same as that of their representations. This relationship is illustrated in Figure 4.1.1.

FIGURE 4.1.1 Four-bit Numbers Interpreted as Unsigned and as 2's Complement Signed Numbers

Four	0	0	0	0	0	0	0	0	1	1	1	1	1	1	1	1
bit	0	0	0	0	1	1	1	1	0	0	0	0	1	1	1	1
number	0	0	1	1	0	0	1	1	0	0	1	1	0	0	1	1
	0	1	0	1	0	1	0	1	0	1	0	1	0	1	0	1

Unsigned	0	1	2	3	4	5	6	7	8	9	10	11	12	13	14	15
Signed	0	1	2	3	4	5	6	7	-8	-7	-6	-5	-4	-3	-2	-1

Example 4.1.11 *Give the relative order of each of the following pairs of 2's complement numbers.*

$$B'01001100' \text{ and } B'10100101'$$
$$B'10110010' \text{ and } B'10111001'$$
$$B'01011011' \text{ and } B'00101101'$$

In the first case, the signs differ. The second number is negative, so $B'01001100' > B'10100101'$. The numbers in the second pair are both negative. The order is $B'10110010' < B'10111001'$. It is the same as it would be if they were interpreted as unsigned numbers. The third pair are positive numbers and they are ordered as expected: $B'01011011' > B'00101101'$.

Example 4.1.12 *Arrange the following hexadecimal representations of 16-bit 2's complement numbers in ascending order.*

$$X'5FBA' \quad X'A04D' \quad X'0000' \quad X'7F00' \quad X'A08C' \quad X'86A1' \quad X'6A01' \quad X'FFFF'$$

First note that $X'A04D'$, $X'A08C'$, $X'86A1'$, and $X'FFFF'$ are negative. Then separately order the negative and the non-negative numbers as though they were unsigned.

$$X'86A1'<X'A04D'<X'A08C'<X'FFFF'<X'0000'<X'5FBA'<X'6A01'<X'7F00'$$

Converting 2's Complement Numbers to Decimal

In order to convert a 2's complement binary number to a signed decimal number, we first check the sign bit. If it is 0, then the number is positive and we simply convert it as usual. If the sign bit is 1, the number is negative. In order to convert it, we recall that it is the 2's complement of its magnitude. We can find the magnitude by complementing the given number. The magnitude can then be converted to decimal and the minus sign attached.

Example 4.1.13 *Convert the following 8-bit 2's complement numbers to both binary and decimal numbers with an explicit sign.*

$$B'01001100' = +B'01001100' = +76$$
$$B'11101010' = -B'00010110' = -22$$
$$B'10001100' = -B'01110100' = -116$$
$$B'11111111' = -B'00000001' = -1$$

Example 4.1.14 *Convert the following 32-bit 2's complement numbers to signed decimal numbers.*

X'80000000' = B'10000000000000000000000000000000'
→ -2^{31} = −2,147,483,648

X'FFFFF47A' → −(X'00000B85'+X'1') = −X'00000B86'
= −2950

X'EFFFA8D2' → −(X'1000572D'+X'1') = −X'1000572E'
= −268,457,774

X'FFFFFFFF' → −(X'00000000'+X'1') = −X'00000001'
= −1

X'FFFFFED0' → −(X'0000012F'+X'1') = −X'00000130'
= −304

X'0003A0B4' → +237,748

X'7FFFFFFF' → +2,147,483,647

We have seen some of the characteristic features of 2's complement representations. The first bit in any number indicates the sign of the number. 0 has only one representation. It is relatively easy to compare 2's complement numbers. Finally, for our convenience, they can easily be written in hexadecimal form.

Compared with the other two methods of representing signed numbers, none of these characteristics explains why 2's complement numbers are so widely used. Their primary advantage over the other two representations is the ease with which arithmetic operations can be performed on 2's complement numbers. We shall examine these operations in detail in the next section.

E X E R C I S E S

1. Give the value represented by each of the following 5-bit numbers when it is interpreted as (1) an unsigned number, (2) a sign-magnitude number, (3) an excess-16 number, and (4) a signed 2's complement number.

   a. B'10110'   **d.** B'11111'
   b. B'11010'   **e.** B'00101'
   c. B'01101'   **f.** B'01010'

2. Add each of the following pairs of 8-bit numbers assuming that the representation used is (1) sign-magnitude and (2) excess-128.

   a.   B'10110101'
        +B'00110101'

   b.   B'10110101'
        +B'10111010'

3. Give the 2's complement of each of the following numbers.
   a. B'10110101'
   b. B'00101000'
   c. X'A90F3E21'
   d. X'0039FEA1'
   e. X'FFFFFFFF'
   f. X'80000000'

4. Arrange the following 2's complement numbers in ascending order.
   X'7F5B' X'8EF0' X'FFFF' X'59A2' X'315D' X'D4FE' X'D4FF'

5. Convert the following 2's complement numbers to signed decimals.
   a. B'00101111'
   b. B'11101011'
   c. B'11111100'
   d. B'10111111'

6. Write the following as 8-bit 2's complement numbers.
   a. −78
   b. −39

4.2 SIGNED BINARY ARITHMETIC

In this section, we will consider arithmetic operations on 2's complement representations of signed numbers. In general, the usefulness of a representation of signed integers depends upon the simplicity of these operations. As we do each operation, note the ease with which they may be implemented. This will be more apparent if we first consider an alternative description of 2's complement numbers.

An Alternative View of 2's Complement

Suppose that m is a negative number to be represented in n-bit 2's complement form. Then $m = -m'$ for some positive number m'. According to our definitions, the 2's complement representation for m is the complement of m', the rightmost n bits of $2^n - m' = 2^n - (-m) = 2^n + m$. But observe, if m is a positive number that can be written in n bits, then 2^n+m is simply a 1 bit followed by the n-bit representation of m. The rightmost n bits of this sum is the same as n.

To summarize: For any integer m from -2^{n-1} to $2^{n-1}-1$, the n-bit 2's complement representation of m is the rightmost n bits of 2^n+m.

Arithmetic Operations on 2's Complement Numbers

2's complement arithmetic has two advantages over arithmetic operations on other representations of signed numbers. The first is that the operations do not involve special cases with respect to the signs of the numbers, as is the case with sign-magnitude representations. The second advantage is that the results do not have to be adjusted as they do in biased notation.

In the case of addition on n-bit 2's complement numbers, we simply add the representations, ignoring all but the rightmost n bits.

Example 4.2.1 *Consider the effect of adding the 8-bit 2's complement representations of 45 and -18.*

$$45 = B'00101101' \qquad 18 = B'00010010' \qquad -18 = B'11101110'$$

$$\begin{array}{r} 111\ 11 \\ B'\ 00101101' \\ +B'\ 11101110' \\ \hline B'100011011' \end{array}$$

The sum has 9 bits. However, when we consider only the rightmost 8 bits we have the 8-bit 2's complement representation for $+27$.

We can obtain the same result more directly simply by adding the two values and discarding the last carry bit as the following additions demonstrate. For uniformity, we will show all carries (including 0).

	00000110		11100111
38	B'00100110'	-89	B'10100111'
$+(-57)$	$+$B'11000111'	$+117$	$+$B'01110101'
-19	B'11101101'	28	B'00011100'

	11111100		00000011
-36	B'11011100'	67	B'01000011'
$+(-76)$	$+$B'10110100'	$+41$	$+$B'00101001'
-112	B'10010000'	108	B'01101100'

Notice that, in the first two examples, it is actually easier to do the 2's complement addition than the decimal addition. When asked to add $38+(-57)$, we usually reverse the two numbers, computing $57-38$, and then adjust the sign. When performing 2's complement addition, the steps we take are the same, regardless of the relative signs of the two numbers. This is the essential difference between sign-magnitude representation and 2's complement representation.

We do need to exercise some care in performing this addition. In ignoring the last carry bit, we may overlook an overflow. In order to illustrate the problem, consider an example in which an overflow is bound to occur. Suppose we add the 8-bit 2's complement numbers 110 and 75. The sum, 185 is too large to be represented in 8-bit 2's complement.

$$
\begin{array}{rr}
 & 01001110 \\
110 & \text{B'01101110'} \\
+75 & +\text{B'01001011'} \\
\hline
185 & \text{B'10111001'}
\end{array}
$$

We can tell that something has gone wrong. When we try to interpret the sum as a 2's complement number, it is negative.

Similarly, when two negative 2's complement numbers are added, an overflow is indicated by a 0 in the sign bit. An overflow can always be detected by comparing the sign of the result with signs of the operands.

By examining the carry bits, we can develop a more uniform method for detecting overflow. This method does not require examination of the sign bits of the operands.

Suppose we add two positive n-bit 2's complement numbers and get a result with a 1 in the sign bit. Obviously, the 1 must come from a carry into the leftmost or sign position. The addition for this position will then produce 1 for the sum and 0 as the carry out of this position. If we add two negative numbers and obtain a result with a 0 in the sign bit then, because both numbers have a 1 in this position, the 0 can only occur if the carry into this position is 0. The addition will then produce the 0 in the sign position for the sum. The carry out of this position will be 1. Note that the common factor in both cases is that the carry into the sign bit differs from the carry out of the sign bit.

Examining the examples above in which no overflow occurred, note that the carry out of the sign position is always the same as the carry into the sign position. In general, when adding two numbers of the same sign, overflow only occurs if these two carries differ. If the numbers being added have different signs, then one sign bit is 1 and the other is 0. If the carry into this position is 0, the sum of the three bits will be 1 and the carry out of the sign bit will be 0. If the carry into the sign position is 1, the sum of the three bits will be B'10'. Thus, the carry out will also be 1.

When adding 2's complement numbers, an overflow occurs if and only if the carry out of the sign position is different from the carry into this position.

Example 4.2.2 *Add the following 8-bit 2's complement binary numbers indicating which additions cause an overflow.*

Overflow →	1**00**01111	No Overflow →	1**10**01111
	B'10101111'		B'11101101'
	+B'10001011'		+B'11001011'
	B'00111010'		B'10111000'

Overflow →	0**1**111111	No Overflow →	0**0**001110
	B'00110111'		B'00001011'
	+B'01001100'		+B'01101110'
	B'10000011'		B'01111001'

The standard size for binary numbers on the IBM 370 is 32 bits. When it is necessary to perform calculations by hand with these numbers, we certainly want to be able to perform them on the hexadecimal representations of the numbers. In this case, we will usually find it simpler to check the signs. (When written in hexadecimal form, a 32-bit number requires only 8 hexadecimal digits.)

Example 4.2.3 *Add the following 2's complement numbers represented in hexadecimal form indicating whether an overflow occurs.*

$$
\begin{array}{r}
10110100 \\
X'E5AB290C' \\
+X'F0A7B9D0' \\
\hline
X'D652E2DC'
\end{array}
$$

No overflow has occurred even though the carry into the last position differs from the carry out of that position. When the numbers are written in hexadecimal form, this position includes the sign bit and the 3 preceding bits. In binary, the addition for the last hexadecimal position is

$$
\begin{array}{r}
11100 \\
B'1110' \\
+B'1111' \\
\hline
B'1101'
\end{array}
$$

In this form, we see that the carry out of the sign position is the same as the carry into this position.

Example 4.2.4 *Add each of the following pairs of 2's complement numbers indicating which cause an overflow.*

$$
\begin{array}{r}
11000000 \\
X'85A03B14' \\
+X'9F3BC10A' \\
\hline
X'24DBFC1E'
\end{array}
$$
We can detect an overflow since both numbers are negative, but the sum is positive.

11010011	Overflow is impossible since the numbers have different signs.
X'F31B52AC'	
+X'7E4D129A'	
X'71686546'	

01011011	An overflow can be detected since the addends are positive but
X'58AFB0C9'	the sum is negative.
+X'4F0FE1CD'	
X'A7BF9296'	

Before completing our consideration of 2's complement addition, we need to consider one additional complication, the problem of adding two 2's complement binary numbers of different lengths. For example, suppose we need to add the 4-bit 2's complement number B'1011' and the 8-bit 2's complement number B'01101101'. Writing the problem in the following way

$$\begin{array}{r} \text{B'01101101'} \\ +\text{B'}\qquad \text{1011'} \\ \hline \end{array}$$

would probably lead to an incorrect result. If we simply add the 4 bits on the right, add any carry to the next bit, and copy the last 3 bits to the bottom line, then we would get the sum of B'01101101' and B'00001011'. However, the second of these two numbers is positive. It is clearly not the 8-bit 2's complement representation of the negative number B'1011'.

In order to be able to perform this addition, we need to convert the 4-bit 2's complement number B'1011' to its 8-bit 2's complement form. This is a special case of the more general problem of changing the lengths of 2's complements numbers without changing the numbers they represent.

Converting Between 2's Complement Representations

In general, to convert an n-bit 2's complement number to m bits, we extend the sign bit $m-n$ positions to the left. This process is called *sign extension*.

Example 4.2.5 *Convert each of the following 8-bit 2's complement numbers to a 12-bit number.*

$$\text{B'01101100'} = \text{B'000001101100'}$$
$$\text{B'11101010'} = \text{B'111111101010'}$$

If the numbers to be converted are given in hexadecimal form, then we examine the leftmost hexadecimal digit to determine the sign, as usual. If the number is non-negative, we extend on the left with X'0'. If the number is negative, we need to extend it with 1 bits. When grouped in fours, each group of 1 bits becomes X'F'.

Example 4.2.6 *Convert each of the following 16-bit 2's complement numbers, given in hexadecimal form, to 32 bits.*

$$X'6FE3' = X'00006FE3'$$
$$X'7A9B' = X'00007A93'$$
$$X'85A1' = X'FFFF85A1'$$
$$X'E4FA' = X'FFFFE4FA'$$

If we need to convert an *n*-bit 2's complement number to *m* bits and $n > m$, then we must verify that the number can be represented with the smaller number of bits. Clearly, this will be true only if its *n*-bit representation could be obtained by extending the *n*-bit representation as above. That is, the bits to be removed must consist entirely of copies of the sign bit and a correct sign bit must remain after the removal of these bits.

Example 4.2.7

The 8-bit 2's complement number B'00000101' can be represented in 4 bits as B'0101'.

The 8-bit 2's complement number B'00001101' cannot be represented in 4 bits. (B'1101' is negative while the original number is positive.)

The 32-bit 2's complement number X'FFFFA01B' can be written as X'A01B'. (X'A' begins with a 1 bit and we have eliminated only 1 bit.)

X'00006A3B' can be written as X'6A3B'.

X'F3ABF10C', X'FFFF56AB', and X'0000A5C0' cannot be written in 16 bits.

Example 4.2.8 *Add the 2's complement numbers X'008A12FD' and X'9A3B'.*

Before the addition, we must extend the second number to 32 bits.

```
 1111   11
 X'008A12FD'
+X'FFFF9A3B'
 ──────────
 X'0089AD38'
```

Subtraction of 2's Complement Numbers

We have already seen how to subtract unsigned binary numbers. We could adopt an approach similar to the one we normally use for signed decimal numbers. To inspect the signs, perform either a subtraction or addition and determine the correct sign of the result. In fact, our use of 2's complement numbers allows us to simplify this process.

Our definition of the 2's complement representation of signed numbers was motivated by the observation that it made complementation the equivalent of negation. With this in mind, we see that subtraction can be implemented by complementing the subtrahend and adding. Overflow can occur and is detected during the addition step as before.

Example 4.2.9 *Perform the following subtractions by complementing the subtra-hend and adding. (Carries will be shown only when relevant.)*

B'01101011' − B'00101001':
```
              11111111
               B'01101011'
              +B'11010111'
              ───────────
               B'01000010'
```

B'11010011' − B'10101100':
```
               11 1
               B'11010011'
              +B'01010100'
              ───────────
               B'00100111'
```

B'10001011' − B'00111000':
```
              10001000
               B'10001011'
              +B'11001000'
              ───────────
               B'01010011'    (Overflow)
```

X'8F3BA120' − X'013ADE1F':
```
              1111   1
               X'8F3BA120'
              +X'FEC521E1'
              ───────────
               X'8E00C301'
```

X'73A1B904' − X'85A132F0':
```
              1 1111
               X'73A1B904'
              +X'7A5ECD10'
              ───────────
               X'EE008614'    (Overflow)
```

As in addition, if the operands have different lengths, the shorter must be sign extended.

Example 4.2.10 *Subtract X'A3BC' from X'34A10BEE'.*

We can perform the sign extension and complementation in either order.

```
X'A3BC' → X'FFFFA3BC' → X'00005C44'
X'A3BC' → X'5C44'     → X'00005C44'

               111
               X'34A10BEE'
              +X' 00005C44'
              ───────────
               X' 34A16832'
```

Multiplication of 2's Complement Numbers

Multiplication of n-bit 2's complement numbers is similar to addition. If the product can be written in n bits, we can find it simply by multiplying the numbers as unsigned numbers and ignoring all but the rightmost n bits. However, in this case, overflow seems to be much more likely. We can avoid this possibility in the following way. Suppose we need to multiply two n-bit numbers. If we first sign extend the numbers to $2*n$ bits, then, since their product cannot exceed $2*n$ bits in length, we can multiply them without fear of overflow. When we examine the machine instructions for signed binary multiplication, we see that this is equivalent to the approach taken in the design of the IBM 370.

Example 4.2.11 *Multiply the signed binary numbers B'0101' and B'1010'.*

We sign extend the two numbers to 8 bits, B'00000101' and B'11111010'.

$$
\begin{array}{r}
\text{B'11111010'} \\
\times\ \text{B'00000101'} \\
\hline
11111010 \\
111110100 \\
\hline
10011100010 \\
\end{array}
$$

Extracting the rightmost 8 bits from this product, we have B'11100010' as the result.

Converting the three numbers to signed decimals, we have

$$\text{B'0101'} = +5 \qquad \text{B'1010'} = -6 \qquad \text{B'11100010'} = -30$$

allowing us to verify the result. We can also apply this process to 2's complement numbers represented in hexadecimal form.

Example 4.2.12 *Multiply X'8A3F' and X'E3F1'.*

These are 16-bit numbers which we sign extend to 32 bits before multiplying. (Since both are negative we extend with X'F'.) We then employ the same algorithm for multiplication in a positional numeration system which we use for decimal numbers.

```
     X'FFFF8A3F'
   * X'FFFFE3F1'
   ─────────────
      FFFF8A3F     (X'1' * X'FFFF8A3F')
      EFFF919B1    (X'F' * X'FFFF8A3F')
      2FFFE9EBD    (X'3' * X'FFFF8A3F')
      DFFF98F72    (X'E' * X'FFFF8A3F')
     EFFF919B1     (X'F' * X'FFFF8A3F')
    EFFF919B1      (X'F' * X'FFFF8A3F')
   EFFF919B1       (X'F' * X'FFFF8A3F')
  EFFF919B1        (X'F' * X'FFFF8A3F')
  ───────────
```

Note that we need only the 8 hex-digits on the right, so we needn't add all 13 columns. In fact, we can shorten some of the multiplications, and have

```
  X'FFFF8A3F'
* X'FFFFE3F1'
  ───────────
    FFFF8A3F
   EFFF919B1
  2FFFE9EBD
   FFF98F72
    FF919B1
     F919B1
      919B1
       19B1
  ───────────
   0CE8024F
```

The product is X'0CE8024F'.

We would seldom want to carry out such a computation by hand. If the numbers are small enough to make hand computation feasible, it is usually easier to multiply the magnitudes and adjust the sign of the product. Our interest here is not in hand computation, but in demonstrating that with 2's complement representation it is possible to develop an algorithm for multiplication that does not need to check the signs of the numbers.

When this process is implemented in hardware, the numbers are always in binary form. Each positional multiplier is either 0 or 1. Thus, the operation is reduced to a sequence of shifts and additions. If we adjust the sizes of the numbers to make overflow impossible, then we can reduce the number of multiplications and additions required. The following example shows how a binary multiplication might proceed using only shifts and additions.

Example 4.2.13 *Multiply B'11001011'*B'00110100'.*

Extend both numbers to 16 bits and let

$$M = B'1111111111001011'$$
$$N = B'0000000000110100'$$

We can perform the multiplication by examining the bits in N one at a time, from right to left. Each time we move from one bit to another, we shift M left 1 position, discarding the leftmost bit, and add B'0' on the right. Each time we encounter a 1 bit in N, we add the current value of M to an accumulator.

If we denote the accumulator by P, the table below shows how the operation proceeds.

Current Bit of N	M	P
0	B'1111111111001011'	B'0000000000000000'
0	B'1111111110010110'	B'0000000000000000'
1	B'1111111100101100'	B'1111111100101100'
0	B'1111111001011000'	B'1111111100101100'
1	B'1111110010110000'	B'1111101111011100'
1	B'1111100101100000'	B'1111010100111100'
0	B'1111001011000000'	B'1111010100111100'

(As the rest of the bits are zero, P already contains the final product.)

Division of 2's Complement Numbers

As with multiplication, there are algorithms for performing division on 2's complement numbers which do not need to check the sign. However, we are unlikely to perform these operations by hand, so we restrict our attention to division of positive numbers.

Long division of binary numbers can be performed in a way analogous to division of decimals. We will find the process greatly simplified, as the task of finding a "trial divisor" requires us to consider only 0 and 1 as possibilities. When we find that 1 is an appropriate divisor, we subtract the divisor from the appropriate bits of the dividend as usual. This operation can be performed by adding the 2's complement of the divisor.

Example 4.2.14 *Divide B'01101101' by B'0101'.*

Following the usual algorithm for long division, each time we add the 2's complement of the divisor, we compute only as many bits as needed for succeeding operations.

```
               00010101
       0101 ) 01101101
               1011
              ───────
               000111
                1011
               ───────
                001001
                 1011
                ───────
                 0100
```

We have quotient B'00010101' and remainder B'0100'.

In conclusion, note the clear advantage of 2's complement numbers over other representations for signed numbers. Arithmetic operations can be implemented with ease. Thus, although there is some initial awkwardness when performing these operations ourselves, they are much more efficient in machine operations than other possible representations.

E   X   E   R   C   I   S   E   S

1. Add the following 8-bit 2's complement numbers indicating when an overflow occurs.

   a. B'10110101'
     +B'11111110'

   b. B'00101101'
     +B'01110111'

   c. B'10001101'
     +B'11000100'

   d. B'00111011'
     +B'11110110'

   e. B'01100110'
     +B'11011010'

   f. B'11001101'
     +B'11101011'

2. Add the following 32-bit 2's complement numbers indicating when an overflow occurs.

   a. X'FE33A79D'
     +X'FF0A3D41'

   b. X'6F89EA41'
     +X'79F0E1C2'

   c. X'F45D32A1'
     +X'5E36A12B'

   d. X'875D82A0'
     +X'90F032BD'

3. Extend the following 16-bit 2's complement numbers to 32 bits.
   a. X'3F4E'
   b. X'90F1'
   c. X'7A8F'
   d. X'D8E1'

4. Indicate which of the following 32-bit 2's complement numbers can be written in 16 bits and give the 16-bit form.
   a. X'FE902ADE'
   b. X'FFFFFFE4'
   c. X'300ADEF0'
   d. X'000004FE'
   e. X'FFFF9012'
   f. X'FFFF78FE'

5. Subtract the following 8-bit 2's complement numbers indicating when an overflow occurs.

   a. B'10011001'
      −B'10101110'

   b. B'10001101'
      −B'01100101'

   c. B'01001101'
      −B'10110100'

   d. B'01101011'
      −B'10010110'

6. Subtract the following 32-bit 2's complement numbers indicating when an overflow occurs.

   a. X'BD6AA80D'
      −X'EFDA304C'

   b. X'6A46B2D1'
      −X'54D5B891'

   c. X'A472F4A1'
      −X'63FB791A'

   d. X'496B3EF0'
      −X'8E41D1BD'

7. Multiply each of the following pairs of 8-bit 2's complement numbers by first extending them to 16 bits.

   a. B'10011011'
      ×B'01101101'

   b. B'11010110'
      ×B'10110101'

8. Perform the following binary divisions using 2's complements for the subtractions.

   a. B'10110' $\overline{)\,\text{B'110110011'}}$

   b. B'1010' $\overline{)\,\text{B'11010011'}}$

4.3 BINARY NUMBERS AND THE IBM 370

All of the instructions that operate on packed decimal numbers use operands located in primary memory locations. Up to this point, our use of registers has been restricted to providing a base register for programs and loading the correct value into that register with the BALR instruction. In the case of binary numbers, the situation is reversed. Almost all binary integer instructions require that one or both operands be in one of the 16 general-purpose registers.

In this section, we discuss the types of binary numbers supported by the assembler and the 370 architecture and introduce some of the instructions needed to manipulate these numbers.

Binary Machine Types

Recall that the 16 general-purpose registers are 32 bits (4 bytes) each. This size is the basic binary type supported by the IBM 370. It is called a *fullword*. When interpreted as an unsigned binary number, the range of possible values is 0 to $2^{32}-1$. If it is interpreted as a signed binary integer written in 2's complement, the range of values is -2^{31} to $2^{31}-1$. When written in hexadecimal, this value is 8 hex-digits long. In decimal, the range of signed values is $-2,147,483,648$ to $2,147,483,647$.

Because the range of fullword values is so large, the 370 provides limited support for a 16-bit (2 byte) binary integer type called a *halfword*. The range of halfword values is 0 to $2^{16}-1$ or -2^{15} to $2^{15}-1$. Halfword values are used primarily to reduce storage requirements. Instructions are provided that automatically sign-extend halfword values to fullwords when they are loaded into registers. Other instructions remove the high order bits from fullword values in registers and store them in halfword memory fields.

Binary Assembler Types

The assembler provides type designators that correspond to each of the binary machine types. Like the type designators for packed decimals and character strings, these may be used in DS and DC instructions as well as in literal operands. These type designators are

F   Fullword
H   Halfword

As each type implies a length, the DS and DC instructions for these binary types assume the following, restricted form.

[<sym>]   DS   [<dup>]<type>
or
[<sym>]   DC   [<dup>]<type>'<val>'

<sym>   An optional symbol to identify the storage area.
<dup>   An optional duplication factor.
<type>   A type designator (F or H).
<val>   Initialization value.

The initialization value <val> in the DC instruction is given as a signed decimal number. The assembler converts the signed decimal to a 2's complement binary number to use for initialization. This value may be expressed as a simple signed integer. It may also be expressed in scientific notation as shown below.

$$<int1>E<int2>$$

The *int*1 and *int*2 represent integers which may include a sign. The value represented by this notation is $int1*10^{int2}$.

If the value has a fractional part, it will be discarded. If the integer part is too long, it will be truncated on the left and a warning message issued.

Example 4.3.1

SUM	DS	F	Reserve a fullword of storage.
HSUM	DS	H	Reserve a halfword of storage.
RATE	DC	H'357'	Initialize a halfword of storage with the 2's complement form of 357.
LIGHT	DC	F'2.997E8'	Initialize a fullword field with the 2's complement form of the velocity of light (in meters per second).
OFF	DC	F'−9821'	Initialize the field OFF with the 32-bit 2's complement form of −9821.

On many implementations of 370 architecture, values are always fetched from memory in fullwords beginning at a fullword boundary. If a fullword operand begins at some other address, then two memory accesses will be required to get the value. For this reason, fullword values should always begin on fullword boundaries. Similarly, halfwords should begin on halfword boundaries. If the ALIGN option is specified, the assembler will perform these alignments automatically. In order to do this, the assembler skips bytes until it comes to the appropriate boundary. As we can see in the example below, these bytes are wasted.

Example 4.3.2 A portion of an assembler listing showing assembler alignment.

LOC	Object Code	Source Statement			
000340	FFFFFFFF	184	COUNT	DC	F'−1'
000344		185	ITEM	DS	H
000346	0000				
000348	00000000	186	TOTAL	DC	F'0'
00034C	FEAA	187	HRATE	DC	H'−342'
00034E	0000				
000350	FFFFFEAA	188	FRATE	DC	F'−342'

Bytes with offsets 346, 347, 34E, and 34F are skipped in order to accomplish the alignment. Note that the OBJECT CODE columns contain the 2's complement form of each of the constants.

The number of bytes wasted by alignment could be minimized by grouping definitions by type. If a group of storage definitions is organized so that all fullword fields are first, followed by the halfword fields, then the only wasted space would be at the beginning of the group. However, this should only be done when it does not interfere with the logical structure of the data areas. Program clarity should never be traded for a few bytes of storage.

Register Usage

As far as the instructions are concerned, the 16 general-purpose registers in an IBM 370 CPU are, for the most part, interchangeable. There are some exceptions. Registers R0, R1, and R2 are implicit operands in several machine instructions. Register R0 is ignored when it appears as the base register or index register. Furthermore, the operating system assumes some of these registers will be used for particular purposes and we shall adopt additional conventions for register usage.

In this section and throughout the text, we adhere to the practice of referring to the registers as R0, R1, . . ., R9, RA, . . ., RF. We use these names in both our descriptions and our programs. When used in a program, these symbols must be defined with EQU instructions as follows.

```
R0    EQU    0
R1    EQU    1
R2    EQU    2
R3    EQU    3
R4    EQU    4
R5    EQU    5
R6    EQU    6
R7    EQU    7
R8    EQU    8
R9    EQU    9
RA    EQU    10
RB    EQU    11
RC    EQU    12
RD    EQU    13
RE    EQU    14
RF    EQU    15
```

We have already established the convention of using RC as the base register. Registers RD, RE, and RF will also be reserved for special uses. The remaining registers may be used as desired. However, the system uses R0 and R1 during I/O operations. Thus, their values are susceptible to change and they should be used only for temporary work areas. In general, one ought to assume that their values will be changed any time a system macro is used. This leaves registers R2 through RB for general use.

The RX Instruction Format

Many of the instructions for operating on binary numbers are RX instructions. Since we have not used RX instructions previously, we begin by reviewing the RX instruction format.

C	C	R_1	X_2	B_2	D_2	D_2	D_2

Each symbol represents a single hexadecimal digit. The symbols are interpreted as follows.

CC	Operation Code.
B_2	Base register for the storage operand.
$D_2D_2D_2$	Displacement for the storage operand.
R_1	Register operand.
X_2	Index register.

Each RX instruction has a register operand and a storage operand. In contrast to the SS instructions, the placement of the operands does not determine which is the source operand and which the target. Instead, the assembly language format for an RX instruction always places the register operand first and the storage operand second. The source operand and target operand are determined by the particular instruction.

The register operand can be any one of the 16 general-purpose registers. It is encoded as a single hexadecimal digit in the machine instruction format, R_1 in the diagram above. When we write assembly language instructions, we use one of the symbols R0 through RF.

The address computation for the storage operand introduces a variation on the base-displacement addressing scheme called *indexed addressing*. Recall that base-displacement addressing forms the actual address of an operand by adding the contents of a register, called the *base register*, to a displacement encoded as 3 hexadecimal digits. This allows each address to be represented by 2 bytes and it also allows the program to be relocated by changing the value in the base register.

We should, at this point, note an anomaly in the use of base registers. When register 0 is given as the base register, the address computation uses the value 0, not the contents of register 0, as the base address. This provides a mechanism for over-riding the usual base-displacement addressing. It also means we cannot use R0 as a base register.

Indexed addressing adds a third component to base-displacement addressing, that is, an index value. In addition to specifying a register operand and the base register for the storage operand, the RX instruction format includes a third register called the *index register*. If this is register 0, it does not affect the address computation. If the index register is any other register, then the contents of that register are added together with the base address and the displacement in computing the effective address for the storage operand.

In the next chapter, we cover the use of an index register for accessing arrays of binary numbers. For now, we use R0 as the index register, simply by omitting the index register from the assembly language instruction. The assembler will substitute R0 for us. In effect, we use base-displacement addressing as before. We show this restricted form of the assembly language instructions for the rest of this chapter.

Conversion from Decimal to Binary

Although we use binary numbers for many calculations, we want to continue using decimal numbers for input and output. Thus, the first instructions for manipulating binary numbers are those that allow us to convert between decimal and binary.

We have three different numeric types available at this point. They are binary numbers, packed decimal numbers, and zoned decimals. Since conversions may proceed in two directions, there are six distinct conversions we may need to perform. Rather than provide a separate instruction for each possible conversion, the 370 instruction set implements a subset of the total number of possible instructions. We have already seen the instructions for converting between zoned decimals and packed decimals. These are supplemented by instructions to pass from packed decimal numbers to binary numbers. A number can then be converted from zoned decimal to binary in two steps. It is first converted to a packed decimal number using the PACK instruction. Then the packed form is converted to a fullword binary number using the ConVert to Binary (CVB) instruction.

ConVert to Binary *CVB*   *RX*

            CVB   R1,S2

The 8-byte packed decimal number in the doubleword memory location designated by the second operand is converted to 32-bit 2's complement binary and stored in the register operand.

Condition Code: Unchanged.

Exceptions:

Access	Improper address.
Data	The storage operand is not a valid packed number.
Fixed Point Divide	The packed decimal number is outside the allowable range for a 32-bit 2's complement number.

Example 4.3.3

            CVB   R2,DWORK

If DWORK contains X'000000000005440C', then, after this instruction has been executed, R2 will contain X'00001540', the 32-bit 2's complement binary form of the decimal number 5440.

If DWORK contains X'000000009820156D', then this instruction will place X'FF6A2804' in R2.

Finally, if DWORK contains X'000002147483647C', the value placed in R2 will be X'7FFFFFFF'.

Note that the last of the three values above is the largest positive number that can be written in 32-bit 2's complement binary. It is by no means the largest packed decimal that can be represented, as packed decimal numbers may have up to 31 digits. It is not even the largest number that can be stored in the 8-byte field specified as the second operand of the CVB instruction. It is possible for this field to contain a value that cannot be converted to a 32-bit 2's complement number. The fixed point divide exception is raised whenever this occurs.

As we have observed before, the range of signed fullword binary integers is $-2,147,483,648$ to $+2,147,483,647$. In packed decimal form, these values would be stored as X'02147483648D' and X'02147483647C'. Because these largest possible fullword numbers can be stored in 6 bytes, any fullword binary number can be converted to PL6. Thus, although the conversion process itself requires 8 bytes, we usually do not use a full 8 bytes to store each number in decimal form. Rather, we store the decimal form in a field of an appropriate size for the problem and move the number to an 8-byte work area for conversion.

The conversion process requires two fullwords to be fetched from memory, so the work area should be aligned on a doubleword boundary for maximum efficiency. When the ALIGN option has been specified for the assembly, this alignment can be forced by specifying the type designator D (doubleword). The assembler will automatically align the field on a doubleword boundary, just as it aligns F fields on fullword boundaries. As D is actually used to designate the doubleword floating point type, this means we cannot initialize the field, because the initialization value would be stored in floating point form rather than in packed form. However, if we are to use this as a work area for converting input values, initialization would be superfluous.

Example 4.3.4 *Convert the packed number in the field SUM to a fullword binary number in R7.*

```
        ZAP     DWORK,SUM       R7 = SUM
        CVB     R7,DWORK

DWORK   DS      D
```

Converting Input Values to Binary

When the input values are zoned numbers, the conversion process requires two steps. The zoned number must first be converted to packed form using the PACK instruction. The packed number is then converted to binary, using CVB instruction. To illustrate, suppose we read a record containing two test scores in zoned fields named MIDTERM and FINAL, which are to be converted to binary and stored in registers R3 and R4. We define the work area as

```
DWORK       DS      D
```

Each number needs to be in packed and placed in DWORK for the conversion to binary. Assuming that we don't need the packed forms again, we can pack the values directly into DWORK.

```
PACK    DWORK,MIDTERM   R3 = MIDTERM
CVB     R3,DWORK
PACK    DWORK,FINAL     R4 = FINAL
CVB     R4,DWORK
```

Conversion from Binary to Decimal

The instruction for converting fullword binary numbers to packed decimal is symmetrical to CVB. It converts a binary number in a register to an 8-byte packed decimal number. It is an RX instruction so the register operand is given first, but, in this case, the first operand is the source operand and the second is the target.

ConVert to Decimal CVD RX

```
CVD     R1,S2
```

The 32-bit 2's complement number in the register R_1 is converted to an 8-byte packed decimal number in the doubleword memory location designated by the second operand.

Condition Code: Unchanged.

Exceptions:

Access   Improper address.

Example 4.3.5

```
CVD     R5,WORK
```

If R5 contains X'0004CB2F' then, after the instruction has been executed, WORK will contain X'000000000314159C'.

If R5 contains X'FFFCCE6B', then X'000000000209301D' will be placed in WORK.

If R5 contains X'FFFFFFFF' then X'000000000000001D' will be placed in WORK.

Again, as the converted value will never exceed 6 bytes, the conversion is done with an 8-byte work area. We can then use the ZAP instruction to move the value to a smaller storage area.

Printing Binary Numbers

In order to print a binary number stored in a register in decimal form, we first use the CVD instruction to convert the number to packed decimal form. If we were to try to print the number directly from the work area, we would need an edit mask with 15 digit selectors. We know the converted number will not be this long, so we need to move it to a smaller area first. The size of this area can be determined from the application, but will never exceed 6 bytes.

In general, the sequence of instructions for printing a binary number in a register is, CVD to convert the number to decimal in a work area, ZAP to move the number to a smaller field, ED to convert the packed number to printable form, and a PUT to print the line containing the number.

Example 4.3.6 *Suppose register R8 contains the average of the two test scores from the example above. Assuming this value is an integer from 0 to 100, convert it to decimal and print it in the field OUTAV of LINE.*

The code, together with the pertinent definitions, is

```
        CVD     R8,DWORK           OUTAV = R8
        ZAP     PAVG,DWORK
        MVC     OUTAV,AVMSK
        ED      OUTAV,PAVG
        PUT     PRINTER,LINE       PRINT LINE
          .
          .
          .
AVLEN   EQU     2
          .
          .
AVMSK   DC      X'40202120'
          .
          .
PAVG    DS      PL(AVLEN)
DWORK   DS      D
          .
          .
LINE    DS      CL133
          .
          .
OUTAV   DS      CL(L'AVMSK)
          .
          .
```

Load and Store Instructions

Although the instruction for converting decimal numbers to binary leaves the result in a register, as there are only 16 general-purpose registers, these are seldom used for long-term storage. Instead, binary numbers are stored in fullword or halfword memory locations. Nevertheless, virtually all of the binary arithmetic and logical instructions require that one or both operands be in a register. Thus, we need instructions that allow us to move binary numbers between registers and main memory storage locations.

The Load instruction is used to copy a fullword binary number from main memory to a register. It is an RX instruction so we can use it to access arrays of fullwords, but for now, consider a restricted form that allows us to access a single memory location.

Load *L RX*

           L R_1,S_2

The 4 bytes designated by the second operand are copied to the register operand.

Condition Code: Unchanged.

Exception:

Access   Improper address.

Example 4.3.7 *Copy 4 bytes from the memory location indicated by FWORD to register R6.*

           L   R6,FWORD

Values are transferred from registers to main memory locations with the Store instructions. Because it is an RX instruction, its format is identical to that of the Load instruction. However, the direction of movement of the data is reversed. In this case, the value is copied from the first operand to the second.

STore *ST RX*

           ST R_1,S_2

The 4 bytes in the register operand are copied to the memory locations designated by the second operand.

Condition Code: Unchanged.

Exception:

Access   Improper address.

Example 4.3.8 *Copy 4 bytes from register R6 to the memory location indicated by FWORD.*

           ST   R6,FWORD

It is often the case that the values represented in binary can be stored in less than a fullword. If a number is between -32768 and 32767, then it can be represented as a 16-bit 2's complement number requiring only a halfword of storage. As we noted earlier in this chapter, in order to convert a fullword binary number to a halfword, we simply eliminate the 16 high-order bits. If the number can be written as a halfword, these 16 bits will all be copies of the sign bit. This service is provided by the STore Halfword instruction.

STore Halfword *STH RX*

> STH R_1,S_2

The low-order 2 bytes of the register operand R_1 are stored in the memory locations designated by the second operand.

Condition Code: Unchanged.

Exception:

Access   Improper address.

Example 4.3.9 *Copy the low-order 2 bytes from register R6 to the memory locations designated by HWORD.*

> STH   R6,HWORD

If R6 contains X'00005E1A', then X'5E1A' will be copied to the 2 bytes beginning at HWORD.

If R6 contains X'4F09A21B', X'A21B' will be copied to HWORD.

Note that, as the example above indicates, the effect of the instruction is simply to truncate the fullword number on the left. No warning is given if significant bits are lost during this operation. It is the programmer's responsibility to make sure that the operation is meaningful.

The counterpart of the Store Halfword instruction is the Load Halfword instruction. Recall that conversion of a 16-bit 2's complement to 32 bits requires the extension of the sign bit 16 positions to the left.

Load Halfword *LH RX*

> LH R_1,S_2

The 2 bytes designated by the second operand are copied to the low-order 2 bytes of the register operand and the sign bit is then propagated through the high-order 16 bits.

Condition Code: Unchanged.

Exception:

Access   Improper address.

Example 4.3.10 *Copy 2 bytes from the memory location indicated by HWORD to the low-order 2 bytes of register R6 and extend the sign bit through the high-order 16 bits.*

        LH   R6,HWORD

If HWORD contains X'40A1', then this value is copied into the lower half of R6. Then the sign bit (0) is copied into all 16 bits of the high-order 2 bytes of R6. After the instruction has been executed, R6 will contain X'000040A1'.

   If HWORD contains X'A81E', the sign bit will be B'1'. When this is copied into the upper 2 bytes of R6, they will contain X'FFFF'. After execution of the instruction, the contents of R6 will be X'FFFFA81E'.

   In addition to moving numbers between registers and main memory, we may need to move them from one memory location to another or from one register to another. As long as we do not need to change the size, we can move binary numbers from one set of memory locations to another with the MVC instruction.

Example 4.3.11 *To copy a value from one fullword field named SUM to another named TOTAL.*

        MVC   TOTAL,SUM
        .
        .
SUM   DS   F
TOTAL   DS   F

When this instruction is assembled, the assembler will insert the length of TOTAL (4 bytes) in the instruction.

   The instruction in the previous example would also work correctly if both SUM and TOTAL had been defined as halfword fields. When it is necessary to move a value between fields of different sizes, we can use a combination of regular load and store instructions and the halfword instructions.

Example 4.3.12 *Transfer a value from a halfword location, HWORD, to a fullword location, FWORD.*

        LH   R0,HWORD
        ST   R0,FWORD

Transfers from one register to another are accommodated by the Load Register instruction. As this is our first example of an RR instruction, we will first review the format for RR instructions. This is the shortest instruction format, containing only a 1-byte operation code and two register operands encoded in a second byte.
   RR Format:

C C	R_1	R_2

Each symbol represents a single hexadecimal digit interpreted as follows.

CC   Operation Code.
R_1, R_2 Register operands.

As with the SS instructions, operand values may come from both registers. When the effect of the instruction is to change one of the operands, it is always R_1 which is changed.

Load Register *LR   RR*

                    LR R_1, R_2

The contents of R_2 are copied into register R_1.

Condition Code: Unchanged.

Exceptions: None.

Example 4.3.13 *Copy the fullword in register R2 to register R5.*

                    LR   R5,R2

Before moving on to other instructions, note that each of the RX instructions considered moves a predetermined number of bytes. This number depends only upon the instruction type—not the defined length of the storage operands. The instruction formats do not include a length field. Thus, the assembler does not check the lengths of storage operands. It is up to the programmer to make certain that these operations make sense.

Example 4.3.14 *Suppose a program includes the following storage definitions.*

COUNT   DS   PL1
SUM   DS   PL2
TOTAL   DS   PL5

The instruction

                    ST   R5,COUNT

would be assembled and executed without error. Its effect would be to store the first byte of R5 in COUNT, the second and third bytes of R5 in SUM, and the fourth byte of R5 in the first byte of TOTAL. It is the programmer's responsibility to avoid such nonsense.

E X E R C I S E S

1. Write the storage definitions needed to define the following fields.

Field Name	Type	Initialization
TEST	Halfword	(none)
STUDENT	Halfword	(none)
AVERAGE	Fullword	0
TOTAL	Fullword	0
NUMTSTS	Halfword	(none)
CLASSIZE	Fullword	(none)
DWORK	Doubleword	(none)

2. Assuming that the assembler is performing alignment, reorganize the definitions in 1 to minimize wasted storage.

3. Given an input record which contains a 5-digit zoned field named INTEST, write the code needed to convert the value in this field to binary and store it in the field TEST defined in 1.

4. Assume that INSIZE contains a zoned number. Write the code to convert INSIZE to binary and store it in the field CLASSIZE defined in 1.

5. Determine the maximum number of digits needed to represent a halfword binary number in decimal. Write a storage definition for a field PNUMTSTS that is as small as possible, but still capable of holding the decimal form of the binary number in NUMTSTS.

6. Write instructions to convert the number in NUMTSTS to decimal and store the value in the field PNUMTSTS defined in 5.

7. Write the code and storage definitions needed to print CLASSIZE and NUMTSTS in fields of minimal size. The output fields should begin in columns 20 and 50, respectively.

4.4 ADDITION, SUBTRACTION, AND SETTING THE CONDITION CODE

In order to use binary numbers in meaningful computations, we must augment the conversion and Load and Store instructions, with instructions to perform arithmetic operations and to compare numbers. In this section, we cover the instructions for adding and subtracting binary numbers, as well as a group of instructions that test the sign of individual numbers and instructions to compare binary numbers. Together, these allow us to consider program segments using binary numbers.

Binary Addition and Subtraction

The binary addition and subtraction instructions implement the 2's complement operations discussed earlier in this chapter. They come in forms which parallel those of the load and store instructions. That is, each comes in an RR form and full and halfword RX forms. They all perform 32-bit 2's complement arithmetic operations on the two operands and store the result in the first, Register operand. The halfword instructions retrieve a 16-bit value from the Storage operand and sign-extend it to 32 bits before performing the operation.

Add *A RX*

$$A \qquad R_1,S_2$$

The fullword designated by the second operand is added to the fullword in R_1 and the result is stored in R_1.

Condition Code: Reset to

0   If the result is 0.
1   If the result is negative.
2   If the result is positive.
3   If the result exceeds 32 bits.

Exceptions:

Access   Improper address.
Fixed Point Overflow   Sum cannot be represented in 32 bits.

Add Halfword *AH RX*

$$AH \qquad R_1,S_2$$

The two bytes designated by the second operand are sign-extended to 32 bits and added to the fullword in R_1. The result is stored in R_1.

Condition Code: Reset to

0   If the result is 0.
1   If the result is negative.
2   If the result is positive.
3   If the result exceeds 32 bits.

Exceptions:

Access   Improper address.
Fixed Point Overflow   Sum cannot be represented in 32 bits.

Add Register *AR RR*

$$AR \qquad R_1,R_2$$

The fullword in R_2 is added to the fullword in R_1 and the result is stored in R_1.

Condition Code: Reset to

0 If the result is 0.
1 If the result is negative.
2 If the result is positive.
3 If the result exceeds 32 bits.

Exceptions:

Fixed Point Overflow   Sum cannot be represented in 32 bits.

Subtract *S RX*

S R_1,S_2

The fullword designated by the second operand is subtracted from the fullword in R_1 and the result is stored in R_1.

Condition Code: Reset to

0 If the result is 0.
1 If the result is negative.
2 If the result is positive.
3 If the result exceeds 32 bits.

Exceptions:

Access   Improper address.
Fixed Point Overflow   Difference cannot be represented in 32 bits.

Subtract Halfword *SH RX*

SH R_1,S_2

The two bytes designated by the second operand are sign-extended to 32 bits and subtracted from the fullword in R_1. The result is stored in R_1.

Condition Code: Reset to

0 If the result is 0.
1 If the result is negative.
2 If the result is positive.
3 If the result exceeds 32 bits.

Exceptions:

Access   Improper address.
Fixed Point Overflow   Difference cannot be represented in 32 bits.

Subtract Register *SR RR*

SR R_1, R_2

The fullword in R_2 is subtracted from the fullword in R_1 and the result is stored in R_1.

Condition Code: Reset to

0   If the result is 0.

1   If the result is negative.

2   If the result is positive.

3   If the result exceeds 32 bits.

Exception:

Fixed Point Overflow   Difference cannot be represented in 32 bits.

Example 4.4.1 *Suppose that R3 contains X'3A15B204', R4 contains X'F510A24E', R5 contains X'731A294B', FWRD is a fullword memory location containing X'35E92A0C', and HWRD is a halfword memory field which contains X'3A59'.*

When the following sequence of instructions is executed, the value in R3 at the end of each instruction will be as shown to the right of that instruction.

```
A     R3,FWRD    X'3A15B204' +X'35E92A0C' = X'6FFEDC10'
AR    R3,R4      X'6FFEDC10'+X'F510A24E' = X'650F7E5E'
AH    R3,HWRD    X'650F7E5E' +X'00003A59' = X'650FB8B7'
SR    R3,R5      X'650FB8B7' −X'731A294B' = X'F1F58F6C'
SR    R3,R3      X'F1F58F6C' −X'F1F58F6C' = X'00000000'
```

Suppose we need to add the fullword binary numbers in the fields SUBTOTAL and TAX and store the result in TOTAL. The addition operation must take place in a register. If we decide to use R3, we get the following sequence of instructions.

```
L     R3,SUBTOTAL    R3 = SUBTOTAL
A     R3,TAX         R3 = R3+TAX
ST    R3,TOTAL       TOTAL = R3
```

If we are certain that we will not later insert any system macro calls, such as a PUT, in this sequence, then we could use R0 or R1 for the addition. Furthermore, if the documentation makes clear that the register being used is to be treated as a work area, then we could abbreviate the comments. Thus, we might have

```
L     R0,SUBTOTAL    TOTAL = SUBTOTAL+TAX
A     R0,TAX         :
ST    R0,TOTAL       :
```

Setting the Condition Code

The Load and Store instructions covered in the last section do not change the Condition Code. Here, we cover several instructions that do set the Condition Code and note how they can be used to create well-structured programs.

These instructions come in two categories. One set can be used to load a register and, simultaneously, set the Condition Code to indicate whether the value loaded was zero, positive, or negative. The other set of instructions effect a comparison and set the Condition Code to indicate the result of the comparison. In both cases, the value assigned to the Condition Code is the same as that described in the last chapter. Thus, these instructions can be combined with the extended mnemonics for branching to implement the constructs of structured programming as before.

Load Instructions which Set the Condition Code

Load and Test Register *LTR RR*

             LTR R_1,R_2

The fullword value from R_2 is copied into R_1.

Condition Code: Reset to

0   If the value placed in R_1 is 0.

1   If the value placed in R_1 is negative.

2   If the value placed in R_1 is positive.

Exceptions: None.

Example 4.4.2

             LTR   R3,R5

If R5 contains X'24FA1BC0', then after execution, R3 will contain X'24FA1BC0' and the condition code will be 2.

If the value in R5 is X'A02E091B', the instruction will place this value in R3 and set the Condition Code equal to 1.

Similarly, if R5 contains X'00000000', the instruction will place 0 in R3 and assign 0 to the Condition Code.

Notice that the two register operands need not be different. This allows us to use the instruction to test a value already in a register. For example, suppose that we need to implement the following algorithmic construct.

```
If R6 < 0
then
    R7 = R7+R6
else
    R7 = R7−R6
endif
```

We use the same basic pattern we used in the last chapter. The only basic difference is in the instruction used to set the Condition Code.

```
IF03        EQU     *               IF R6 < 0
            LTR     R6,R6           :
            BNM     ELSE03          :
THEN03      EQU     *               THEN
            AR      R7,R6               R7 = R7+R6
            B       ENDIF03         :
ELSE03      EQU     *               ELSE
            SR      R7,R6               R7 = R7−R6
ENDIF03     EQU     *               ENDIF
```

The Load and Test Register instruction is augmented by three other load register instructions, which place a value in a register and set the Condition Code. These three instructions may also be used to change the sign of the value transferred.

The Load Complement Register, LCR, instruction places the 2's complement of the value in its second register operand into the first operand. Its effect is to negate this number. The Condition Code is set to reflect the sign of the negated value. Recall that the 32-bit two's complement representation of -2^{31} is X'10000000'. When this value is complemented, the result is X'10000000'. In fact, $+2^{31}$ cannot be represented as a 32-bit 2's complement number. For this reason, the LCR instruction causes a fixed overflow if X'10000000' is complemented.

Load Complement Register *LCR RR*

      LCR R_1,R_2

The 2's complement of the fullword in R_2 is placed in R_1.

Condition Code: Reset to

0   If the value placed in R_1 is 0.

1   If the value placed in R_1 is negative.

2   If the value placed in R_1 is positive.

3   If the value in R_2 is -2^{31}.

Exception:

Fixed-Point Overflow   Attempt to complement -2^{31}.

Example 4.4.3

      LCR   R5,R7

If R7 contains X'301AB50F', the instruction will place X'CFE54AF1' in R5 and set the Condition Code equal to 1.

If R7 contains X'D4EF678A', X'2B109876' will be placed in R5 and the Condition Code will be set equal to 2.

The Load Positive Register (LPR) instruction places the absolute value of the 2's complement number in its second register operand into the first operand. The Condition Code is set to indicate whether the new value is zero or positive or that an overflow occurred as a result of complementing -2^{31}.

Load Positive Register *LPR* *RR*

      LPR R_1,R_2

The absolute value of the fullword in R_2 is placed in R_1.

Condition Code: Reset to

0   If the value placed in R_1 is 0.

2   If the value placed in R_1 is positive.

3   If the value in R_2 is -2^{31}.

Exception:

Fixed-Point Overflow   Attempt to form 2^{31}.

Example 4.4.4

      LPR   R1,R7

If R7 contains X'FFE29B1A', the instruction will place X'001D64E6' in R1 and set the Condition Code equal to 2.

If R7 contains X'001D64E6', the instruction will place X'001D64E6', its absolute value, in R1 and set the condition code equal to 2.

The Load Negative Register instruction places the negative of the absolute value of its second operand in the register indicated by the first operand and sets the condition code. If the number in the second register is less than or equal to 0, it is transferred unchanged to the first register operand. If it is positive, its complement is placed in the first register.

Load Negative Register *LNR* *RR*

      LNR R_1,R_2

The 2's complement of the absolute value of the fullword in R_2 is placed in R_1.

Condition Code: Reset to

0   If the value placed in R_1 is 0.

1   If the value placed in R_1 is negative.

Exceptions: None.

Example 4.4.5 *Suppose that we need to implement the following algorithmic construct.*

R3 = |R5−R2|
if R3 > 0
then R4 = −R3

We have

	LR	R3,R5	R3 = |R5−R2|
	SR	R3,R2	:
	LPR	R3,R3	:
IF09	EQU	*	IF R3 > 0
	BNP	ENDIF09	:
THEN09	EQU	*	THEN
	LCR	R4,R3	R4 = −R3
ENDIF09	EQU	*	ENDIF

In general, instructions that perform two distinct tasks allow us to create more efficient programs. However, they must be used with caution. This is true of instructions that perform an arithmetic operation and set the Condition Code to reflect the sign of the result, as well as the instructions that transfer a value from one register to another and set the Condition Code. The danger is that, in debugging or modifying such a program, we may insert a new instruction between the one that sets the Condition Code and the instruction that tests the Condition Code.

In the example above, the Condition Code is set by the LPR instruction. It is not tested until the BNP which is used to implement the IF-THEN construct. Suppose that in debugging this program, we insert a set of instructions to print the value in R3. If any of these instructions resets the Condition Code, the test inside the IF-THEN construct becomes meaningless. The situation is complicated by the fact that the Condition Code may sometimes have the correct value. The resulting program may run correctly with some input values and incorrectly with others.

These difficulties can be partially alleviated by minimizing the distance between the instruction that sets the Condition Code and the instruction that checks it. It will still be necessary to watch for potential problems whenever an instruction is inserted in a program. This is somewhat simplified by the fact that we only test the Condition Code as a part of an implementation of a standard construct. At any point in a program, it will be easy to find the next place where the Condition Code is tested. From this point, we can look backwards to determine where it has been set.

Compare Instructions

The compare instructions set the Condition Code to indicate the relative sizes of the two operands. Like the add and subtract instructions, the compare instructions come in both RR and RX formats. There is also an instruction for comparing a sign-extended value from a halfword storage location with a value in a register. In each case, the Condition Code is set as in the decimal compare instructions.

When comparing two bit strings, their relative order depends upon the way in which they are interpreted. For example, consider the two bit strings B'0101' and B'1101'. If these are interpreted as unsigned binary numbers, then

$$B'0101' < B'1101'$$

However, if we view them as 4-bit 2's complement numbers, then B'0101' is positive and B'1101' is negative. Thus,

$$B'1101' < B'0101'$$

We simply have two different order relations defined on the set of all bit strings of a fixed length. The ordering that views each bit string as an unsigned binary number is called the *logical ordering*. The order relation obtained by viewing the bit strings as signed numbers represented in 2's complement notation is called the *arithmetic ordering*. If we denote these as $<_L$ and $<_A$, respectively, then we can remove the apparent ambiguity above by writing

$$B'0101' <_L B'1101'$$
$$B'1101' <_A B'0101'$$

The IBM 370 instruction set provides instructions that implement both the logical and arithmetic order relations. We have, in fact, already seen and used the SS and SI forms of the logical comparison, the CLC and CLI instructions. The CLC instruction can be used to compare sequences of up to 256 bytes, while the CLI instruction compares a single byte in storage with an immediate datum in the instruction. In both cases, the order relation used is the logical ordering. That is, the comparands are treated as unsigned binary numbers. This same logical ordering is implemented as an RX and an RR instruction.

Compare Logical CL RX

> CL R_1, S_2

Compare the fullword value in the register operand with the fullword value beginning at the indicated storage location using a logical comparison and set the Condition Code accordingly.

Condition Code: Reset to

0   If the operands are equal.
1   If the register operand is lower than the storage operand.
2   If the register operand is higher than the storage operand.

Exception:

Access   Improper address for storage operand.

Example 4.4.6

        CL   R4,FWORD

If R4 contains X'3F93BD1A' and FWORD contains X'F29A07C2', the Condition Code will be set equal to 1.

    If R4 contains X'3F93BD1A' and FWORD contains X'1A9B99EF', the Condition Code will be assigned 2.

Compare Logical Register *CLR RR*

        CLR R_1,R_2

Perform a logical comparison of the fullword values in the two register operands and set the Condition Code accordingly.

Condition Code: Reset to

0   If the operands are equal.

1   If the first operand is lower than the second.

2   If the first operand is higher than the second.

Exceptions: None.

Example 4.4.7

        CLR   R7,R3

The values in R7 and R3 will be compared and the condition set as in the example above.

    There are arithmetic comparison instructions which are analagous to the logical comparison instructions.

Compare *C RX*

        C R_1,S_2

Compare the fullword value in the register operand with the fullword value beginning at the indicated storage location using an arithmetic comparison and set the Condition Code accordingly.

Condition Code: Reset to

0   If the operands are equal.

1   If the register operand is lower than the storage operand.

2   If the register operand is higher than the storage operand.

Exception:

Access   Improper address for storage operand.

Example 4.4.8

    C   R4,FWORD

If R4 contains X'3F93BD1A' and FWORD contains X'F29A07C2', the Condition Code will be set equal to 2, as the first number is positive and the second is negative.

If R4 contains X'AF93BD1A' and FWORD contains X'F29A07C2', the Condition Code will be assigned 1. Both values are negative, but the second is higher (closer to zero).

Compare Register *CR RR*

    CR R_1,R_2

Perform an arithmetic comparison of the fullword values in the two register operands and set the Condition Code accordingly.

Condition Code: Reset to

0   If the operands are equal.
1   If the first operand is lower than the second.
2   If the first operand is higher than the second.

Exceptions: None.

Example 4.4.9

    CR   R7,R3

The values in R7 and R3 will be compared and the condition set as in the example above.

These compare instructions are augmented by a halfword compare instruction. A 16-bit 2's complement number from a halfword storage location is extended to a 32-bit 2's complement number for comparison with a fullword value in a register.

Compare Halfword *CH RX*

    CH R_1,S_2

The halfword beginning at the indicated storage location is sign-extended to a fullword value. The fullword in the register operand is then compared with this extended value using an arithmetic comparison and the Condition Code is set accordingly.

Condition Code: Reset to

0   If the operands are equal.

1   If the register operand is lower than the storage operand.

2   If the register operand is higher than the storage operand.

Exception:

Access   Improper address for storage operand.

Example 4.4.10 *Suppose that R4 contains X'0000A24B' and HWORD contains X'A24B'.*

```
          CH      R4,HWORD
```

When the halfword value is extended to a fullword, it will be X'FFFFA24B'. Since this value is negative, the Condition Code will be set equal to 2.

The instructions we have covered to this point are sufficient for writing some short code segments using binary numbers. As an example, suppose we have two halfword storage locations A and B and that we want to compute the product of the two signed binary numbers in these storage locations and store the result in a fullword storage location, PRODUCT. (We cover the multiplication instruction in the next section. However, there are a number of machines, most notably microcomputers, which do not provide a multiplication instruction. Furthermore, when the numbers involved are relatively small, an algorithm such as we will construct here is often faster than a multiplication instruction.)

If A is positive, the following algorithm will obtain the product

```
accumulator = 0
for i = 1 to A
     accumulator = accumulator+B
endfor
PRODUCT = accumulator
```

In order to make it as fast as possible, the values from A and B should be moved to registers and the accumulator should be a register. Assuming that all registers are available, we can assign R2 to hold the value of A, R3 to hold B, and R4 for the product. This change also allows us to change the values obtained from A and B without changing the values in these storage locations. In particular, we can accommodate negative values for A by checking its sign. If it is negative, we can complement both values to get the correct product.

Looking ahead to implementing this algorithm in assembly language, we can simplify the loop construction by counting from |A| down to 1. This allows us to make use of the fact that the subtract instructions set the Condition Code. If we check the Condition Code after the subtraction, we can implement the loop without using an explicit compare instruction. This change also allows us to use R2, the register which gets the original value of A, as a loop counter. Our new algorithm is

```
        R2 = A
        R3 = B
        R4 = 0
        if A < 0
            then R2 = −A
                  R3 = −B
        endif
        for R2 = |A| down to 1
            R4 = R4+R3
        endfor
```

In order to implement the for loop, we need to arrange to subtract 1 from the loop counter. Using Subtract or Subtract Halfword to do this would require a memory access for each loop traversal. The register form of the subtract instruction allows us to eliminate these memory accesses. It does, however, require the use of a register to hold the decrement value. We will use R5.

```
                LH      R2,A                R2 = A
                LH      R3,B                R3 = B
*
*       MULTIPLY R2*R3 PLACING THE PRODUCT IN R4
*
                SR      R4,R4               R4 = 0
IF01            EQU     *                   IF A < 0
                LTR     R2,R2                 :
                BNM     ENDIF01               :
THEN01          EQU     *                   THEN
                LCR     R2,R2                   R2 = −A
                LCR     R3,R3                   R3 = −B
ENDIF01         EQU     *                   ENDIF
*                                             :
FOR01           EQU     *                   FOR R2 = |A| DOWNTO 1
                LH      R5,=H'1'              :
                LTR     R2,R2                 :
FTEST01         EQU     *                     :
                BNP     ENDFOR01              :
                AR      R4,R3                 R4 = R4+R3
                SR      R2,R5                 :
                B       FTEST01               :
ENDFOR01        EQU     *                   ENDFOR
*
                ST      R4,PRODUCT          PRODUCT = R4
```

The code above includes a considerable amount of overhead to implement the loop. In order to be able to decrement the loop counter as quickly as possible, we need to dedicate a register to hold 1. Each traversal of the loop requires a subtraction, an unconditional branch, and a conditional branch that tests the Condition Code. As loops like this one are quite common in programming, the 370 includes an instruction that automates most of the process.

Branch on CounT BCT RX

```
        BCT     R₁,S₂
```

The contents of the register operand, R_1, are decremented by 1. If the result is nonzero, the address represented by the second operand replaces the instruction address portion of the Program Status Word, effecting a branch to this location. If the new value in the register operand is 0, no branch occurs.

Condition Code: Unchanged.

Exceptions: None.

The BCT instruction could be used to construct a loop in the following format.

```
FORmm       EQU     *               FOR <reg> = <ulim> DOWNTO 1
            <Instructions
            to evaluate
            ulim and place
            it in reg       >
FTESTmm     EQU     *
            <Instructions
            to implement
            the range of
            the loop        >
            BCT     <reg>,FTESTmm
ENDFORmm EQU         *               ENDFOR
```

There is, however, a slight problem here. The loop we have just constructed is bottom-tested. When we write algorithms, we tend to assume that loops will be top-tested. In the case of the algorithm we have just implemented, there is a clear distinction when A is 0. The original version of the code correctly exits the loop before the first execution of the range. The final value in R4 will be 0, the correct product. If the first test does not occur until after the range has been executed, then the value in R4 will already have been changed.

This problem is further complicated by the behavior of the BCT instruction. That is, it decrements the register and branches unless the result is zero. If the register contains 0 before the instruction is executed, as would be the case in our algorithm when A = 0, then decrementation will place −1 in the register. Because the result is nonzero, we get a branch back to the top of the loop. The unfortunate outcome is now obvious: the next time through the loop, the new value will be −2, then −3 and so on. It will be quite some time before the register actually contains 0 again.

Rather than forego the use of BCT or attempt to account for its behavior in the design of our algorithms, we can accommodate it by the inclusion of a single test at the beginning of the loop. This gives the following pattern.

```
FORmm      EQU       *              FOR <reg> = <ulim> DOWNTO 1
           <Instructions
           to evaluate
           ulim and place
           it in reg       >
           LTR       <reg>,<reg>
           BNP       ENDFORmm
FTESTmm    EQU       *
           <Instructions
           to implement
           the range of
           the loop        >
           BCT       <reg>,FTESTmm
ENDFORmm EQU         *
```

With the BCT instruction, the code for our multiplication algorithm becomes

```
           LH      R2,A           R2 = A
           LH      R3,B           R3 = B
*
*      MULTIPLY R2*R3 PLACING THE PRODUCT IN R4
*
           SR      R4,R4          R4 = 0
IF01       EQU     *              IF A < 0
           LTR     R2,R2          :
           BNM     ENDIF01        :
THEN01     EQU     *              THEN
           LCR     R2,R2              R2 = −A
           LCR     R3,R3              R3 = −B
ENDIF01    EQU     *              ENDIF
*                                 :
FOR01      EQU     *              FOR R2 = |A| DOWNTO 1
           LTR     R2,R2          :
           BNP     ENDFOR01       :
FTEST01    EQU     *              :
           AR      R4,R3              R4 = R4+R3
           BCT     R2,FTEST01     :
ENDFOR01   EQU     *              ENDFOR
*
           ST      R4,PRODUCT     PRODUCT = R4
```

E X E R C I S E S

1. Suppose that SUBTOTAL and TOTAL are fullword binary fields and that ITEM, is a halfword binary field. Write the instructions needed to implement the following assignment statements.

   a. TOTAL = TOTAL+SUBTOTAL
   b. SUBTOTAL = SUBTOTAL+ITEM

2. Assume that POINT1, POINT2, and DISTANCE are halfwords. Write the code to implement.

   a. DISTANCE = ABS(POINT1−POINT2)
   b. DISTANCE = −DISTANCE

3. Assume that X, Y, and Z are fullword fields. Write properly labelled and commented code to implement the following construct.

   ```
   IF X < 2*Y−Z
   THEN
        R4 = R4+1
   ELSE
        R5 = R5+1
   ```

4. Repeat Problem 3, assuming that X, Y, and Z are halfword fields.

5. Assume that X and Y are fullword fields and implement the following.

   ```
   R2 = 0
   R3 = 0
   WHILE R2 < Y DO
        R2 = R2+X
        R3 = R3+1
   ENDWHILE
   ```

6. Suppose that N and SUM are fullword fields and that N contains a positive integer. Write the assembly language instructions to perform each of the following. Store the result in SUM.

   a. Find the sum of the integers from 1 to N without using BCT.
   b. Find the sum of the integers from 1 to N using BCT.
   c. Find the sum of the odd integers from 1 to N.

4.5 SHIFTING BINARY NUMBERS

An unsigned *n*-digit base *b* number takes the form

$$d_{n-1} \, d_{n-2} \, \ldots \, d_2 \, d_1 \, d_0$$

where each d_i is a symbol representing a number from 0 to $b-1$. This number is interpreted as

$$d_{n-1}{*}b^{n-1} + d_{n-2}{*}b^{n-2} + \ldots + d_2{*}b^2 + d_1{*}b^1 + d_0{*}b^0$$

If we shift each of the digits one position to the left and add a zero at the rightmost position, we get

$$d_{n-1} \, d_{n-2} \, \ldots \, d_2 \, d_1 \, d_0 \, 0$$

which would represent

$$d_{n-1}{*}b^n + d_{n-2}{*}b^{n-1} + \ldots + d_2{*}b^3 + d_1{*}b^2 + d_0{*}b^1 + 0{*}b^0$$
$$(d_{n-1}{*}b^{n-1} + d_{n-2}{*}b^{n-2} + \ldots + d_2{*}b^2 + d_1{*}b^1 + d_0{*}b^0){*}b$$

Thus, this left shift is equivalent to multiplication by the base.

More generally, for $k > 0$, shifting this number k positions to the left with the addition of k 0's on the right is equivalent to multiplication by b^k.

If we want to shift this number to the right without adding fractional digits, we simply drop the rightmost digits. We say these digits have been shifted out. Shifting our original number one position to the right yields

$$d_{n-1} \, d_{n-2} \, \ldots \, d_2 \, d_1$$

which is interpreted as

$$d_{n-1}{*}b^{n-2} + d_{n-2}{*}b^{n-3} + \ldots + d_2{*}b^1 + d_1{*}b^0$$

If we divide the original number by *b*, we get

$$d_{n-1}{*}b^{n-2} + d_{n-2}{*}b^{n-3} + \ldots + d_2{*}b^1 + d_1{*}b^0 + d_0{*}b^{-1}$$

As $0 <= d_0 < b$, the difference between these two numbers, $d_0{*}b^{-1}$, is between 0 and 1. That is, the difference represents the fractional part of the quotient, and the right shift is equivalent to dividing by *b* and rounding the result down to the nearest integer. In general, if $k > 0$, then a right shift of k positions is equivalent to dividing by b^k and rounding the result down to an integer.

The shifts illustrated above assumed that we were manipulating unsigned numbers and that, on the left shift, we could retain all digits. If we try to apply this to binary numbers represented in a computer, we encounter two problems. The number of bit positions is fixed, so when we shift left, we lose the contents of the leftmost positions. On a right shift, we need to provide fill digits for the positions vacated on the left. The possible solutions to these two problems determine two distinct kinds of shift operations.

In this section, we cover the 370 instructions that implement the related operations of shifting, multiplication, and division. Because several of these instructions use the RS format, we begin by considering this machine format together with its varying assembler language formats.

RS Instructions

Recall from Chapter 1 that the machine language format of the RS instructions is

C	C	R_1	R_3	B_2	D_2	D_2	D_2

R_1 and R_3 represent general-purpose register operands. $D_2D_2D_2$ represents the displacement and B_2 the base register for the second operand.

The address computation for the storage operand proceeds as usual. If B_2 is any register other than R0, contents of the base register B_2 are added to the displacement D_2. If B_2 is register R0, then the address is simply D_2. In the following, we will use $c(B_2)$ to denote the contents of B_2.

The general assembly language format for an RS instruction is

   `<mnemonic>`   `<register1>,<register3>,<storage>`

for those instructions which use two register operands. Instructions that do not make use of the extra register operand are written in assembler format as

                                             `<mnemonic>`   `<register>,<storage>`

When the storage operand is a relocatable expression, such as a label, the assembler provides the displacement and the base register specified in the USING instruction. If the storage operand is an absolute expression, for example, a constant, the assembler inserts R0 as the base register. When the instruction is executed, no base value will be added. Thus, the effective value of the operand is the value of the absolute expression.

Logical Shifts

A logical shift ignores any bits shifted out on a left shift and fills with 0's on a right shift. Suppose we have an n-bit binary number. As above, a logical right shift of k bits is equivalent to dividing by 2^k and rounding down to the nearest integer. A logical left shift of k bits is equivalent to multiplication by 2^k modulo 2^n.

All of the shift instructions use the RS format. However, the additional register operand, denoted R_3 above, is omitted. The address computed for the storage operand is not used to fetch a date. Instead, the rightmost 6 bits of this address is used to determine the number of bits to be shifted. The use of the RS format allows the shift amount to be specified as an absolute value or as a variable quantity stored in a register or as the sum of two such quantities.

Shift Left Logical SLL RS

       SLL R_1,N_2
       SLL $R_1,N_2(B_2)$

The second operand is used as in an address computation. The rightmost 6 bits of the result, N_2 or $N_2+c(B_2)$, is interpreted as an unsigned number, s, and the fullword value in R_1 is shifted left s bits. Bits shifted out on the left are discarded and 0's are shifted in on the right.

Condition Code: Unchanged.

Exceptions: None.

Shift Right Logical SRL RS

       SRL R_1,N_2
       SRL $R_1,N_2(B_2)$

The second operand is used as in an address computation. The rightmost 6 bits of the result, N_2 or $N_2+c(B_2)$, is interpreted as an unsigned number, s, and the fullword value in R_1 is shifted right s bits. Bits shifted out on the right are discarded and 0's are shifted in on the left.

Condition Code: Unchanged.

Exceptions: None.

Example 4.5.1

       SLL   R6,5

The contents of R6 will be shifted left by 5 bits. If R6 contains

X'6F09A33B' =
B'0110 1111 0000 1001 1010 0011 0011 1011'

then a logical left shift of 5 bits will result in

B'1110 0001 0011 0100 0110 0111 0110 0000' =
X'E1346760'

While we will continue to show register contents in hexadecimal form, they are actually binary numbers. As the instructions specify bit positions we usually need to write the number in binary form to see the effect of the shift. If the shift amount is a multiple of 4, then it will be equivalent to a hexadecimal shift.

Example 4.5.2

        SLL   R6,2(R3)

The rightmost 6 bits of 2+c(R3) will be used to determine the number of bits to shift. If R6 contains

X'6D35F6CB' =
B'0110 1101 0011 0101 1111 0110 1100 1011'

the table below gives the binary and hexadecimal forms of the new value in R6, given various values in R3.

R3	R6 after the instruction
X'00000001'	B'0110 1001 1010 1111 1011 0110 0101 1000' = X'69AFB658'
X'00000002'	B'1101 0011 0101 1111 0110 1100 1011 0000' = X'D35F6CB0'
X'00000011'	B'1011 0110 0101 1000 0000 0000 0000 0000' = X'B6580000'
X'00000021'	B'0000 0000 0000 0000 0000 0000 0000 0000' = X'00000000'

Example 4.5.3

        SRL   R4,7

The contents of R4 will be shifted right by 7 bits. If R4 contains

X'6F09A33B' =
B'0110 1111 0000 1001 1010 0011 0011 1011'

then a logical right shift of 7 bits will result in

B'0000 0000 0001 1110 0001 0011 0100 0110' =
X'001E1346'

Example 4.5.4

        SRL   R9,7(R4)

The contents of R9 will be shifted right by s bits where s is the rightmost 6 bits of $7+c(R4)$. The positions vacated on the left will be filled with 0's.

Arithmetic Shifts

In effect, a logical shift treats the number being shifted as unsigned and ignores any significant bits that may be lost on a left shift. In contrast, an arithmetic shift treats the number being shifted as a signed number in 2's complement representation and checks bits shifted out on the left for possible overflow.

As implemented in the 370 instruction set, the arithmetic shifts do not move the sign bit, which is the leftmost bit in the number. Only the bits to the right of the sign bit participate in the shift operation. On a right shift, vacated bit positions are filled with copies of the sign bit. On a left shift, an overflow occurs if a bit different from the sign bit is shifted out.

Recall (from our discussions of changing the number of bits in a 2's complement binary number) that we can add or remove copies of the sign bit without changing the value represented by the number. That is, in any 2's complement number, extra copies of the sign bit are not significant. The rule above properly specifies that an overflow occurs on a left shift when a significant bit is shifted out.

In short, a left shift is exactly the same as signed multiplication by a power of 2. A right shift is equivalent to dividing by a power of 2 and rounding the result down to the next integer. (In the case of negative values, this is not the same as the integer quotient.)

The 370 instruction set includes left and right arithmetic shift instructions. Like the logical shift instructions, these instructions use the RS format so the shift amount may be specified as either an absolute value in the instruction or as the sum of an absolute amount and the contents of an explicit base register.

Shift Left Arithmetic *SLA RS*

$$\text{SLA} \quad R_1, N_2$$
$$\text{SLA} \quad R_1, N_2(B_2)$$

The second operand is used as in an address computation. The rightmost 6 bits of the result, N_2 or $N_2 + c(B_2)$, is interpreted as an unsigned number, s, and the rightmost 31 bits of the fullword value in R_1 are shifted left s bits. Bits shifted out on the left are discarded and 0's are shifted in on the right. An overflow occurs if a bit different from the sign bit is shifted out.

Condition Code: Reset to

0   If the value placed in R_1 is 0.

1   If the value placed in R_1 is negative.

2   If the value placed in R_1 is positive.

3   If a significant bit is shifted out.

Exception: Fixed Point Overflow.

Shift Right Arithmetic *SRA RS*

$$SRA \qquad R_1, N_2$$
$$SRA \qquad R_1, N_2(B_2)$$

The second operand is used as in an address computation. The rightmost 6 bits of the result, N_2 or $N_2 + c(B_2)$, is interpreted as an unsigned number, s, and the fullword value in R_1 is shifted right s bits. Bits shifted out on the right are discarded and copies of the sign bit are shifted in on the left.

Condition Code: Reset to

0   If the value placed in R_1 is 0.

1   If the value placed in R_1 is negative.

2   If the value placed in R_1 is positive.

Exceptions: None.

Example 4.5.5

$$SLA \qquad R7,3(R5)$$

The rightmost 6 bits of $3 + c(R5)$ will be used to determine the number of bits to shift. If R7 contains

$$X'FE5F64CB' =$$
$$B'1111\ 1110\ 0101\ 1111\ 0110\ 0100\ 1100\ 1011'$$

the table below gives the binary and hexadecimal forms of the new value in R7, given various values in R5.

R5	R7 after the instruction
X'00000000'	B'1111 0010 1111 1011 0010 0110 0101 1000' = X'F2FB2658'
X'00000002'	B'1100 1011 1110 1100 1001 1001 0110 0000' = X'CBEC9960'
X'00000003'	B'1001 0111 1101 1001 0011 0010 1100 0000' = X'97D932C0'
X'00000004'	Fixed Point Overflow

Example 4.5.6

$$SRA \qquad R6,2(R3)$$

The rightmost 6 bits of $2 + c(R3)$ will be used to determine the number of bits to shift. If R6 contains

$$X'CD35F6CB' =$$
$$B'1100\ 1101\ 0011\ 0101\ 1111\ 0110\ 1100\ 1011'$$

the table below gives the binary and hexadecimal forms of the new value in R6, given various values in R3.

R3	R6 after the instruction
X'00000001'	B'1111 1001 1010 0110 1011 1110 1101 1001' = X'F9A6BED9'
X'00000002'	B'1111 1100 1101 0011 0101 1111 0110 1100' = X'FCD35F6C'
X'00000011'	B'1111 1111 1111 1111 1111 1001 1010 0110' = X'FFFFF9A6'
X'00000021'	B'1111 1111 1111 1111 1111 1111 1111 1111' = X'FFFFFFFF'

Register Pairs

As in decimal multiplication, the number of positions in the product of two numbers may be as large as the sum of the number of positions in each of the multiplicands. In the case of packed decimal multiplication, we were able to accommodate this change in size by defining a work area of an appropriate length. When multiplying binary numbers in registers, we cannot make any such adjustment, because the size of the registers is fixed. Therefore, the fullword multiplication instruction places the product in a pair of registers.

These register pairs consist of an even-numbered register and the following odd-numbered register. Together, the pair is viewed as containing a 64-bit number. The high-order bits of this number are the contents of the even-numbered register and the low-order bits are the contents of the odd-numbered register.

The pair is identified in instructions by the even-numbered register. We shall refer to such a register pair as an even-odd pair.

Example 4.5.7 *Suppose that R4 contains X'A67BE09D' and R5 contains X'88E0AC41'.*

The register pair identified by R4 contains the 64-bit number

$$X'A67BE09D88E0AC41'$$

The number of instructions for directly manipulating register pairs is quite small. For example, there are no instructions for adding, subtracting, or comparing two 64-bit numbers in register pairs. In fact, these operations can all be implemented with combinations of the fullword instructions. For example, to compare two 64-bit numbers in two register pairs, we can compare the even registers. If they are different, then they determine the order of the two numbers. If the high-order bits of the two numbers are the same, then their order can be determined by comparing the odd registers.

The 370 instruction set does include a full complement of doubleword shift instructions. These work in exactly the same way as their singleword counterparts except that the operand is the 64-bit number in a register pair. On a left shift, bits shifted out of the odd register are shifted in on the right of the even register. On a right shift, bits shifted out of the even register are shifted into the odd register.

As these instructions are exact parallels of the fullword shift instructions, which we have covered in detail, we summarize the doubleword shift instructions collectively.

Shift {Left,Right} Double {Arithmetic,Logical} S{L,R}D{A,L} RS

$$<mnemonic> \qquad R_1,N_2$$
$$<mnemonic> \qquad R_1,N_2(B_2)$$

The second operand is used as in an address computation. The rightmost 6 bits of the result, N_2 or $N_2+c(B_2)$, is interpreted as an unsigned number, s. An {arithmetic,logical} {left,right} shift of s bits is performed on the contents of the register pair denoted by the even-numbered register R_1.

Condition Code: Unchanged by logical shifts. Reset by arithmetic shifts to

0   If the shifted value is 0.
1   If the shifted value negative.
2   If the shifted value positive.
3   If a significant bit is lost on a left arithmetic shift.

Exceptions:

Specification exception   (Both) R_1 is not an even register.
Fixed Point Overflow   (Arithmetic only).

Example 4.5.8 *Suppose that R6 contains X'AF09AB23' and R7 contains X'3F1EB65A'.*

After execution of

      SLDL   R6,8

the pair will contain

                X'09AB233F1EB65A00'

R6 will contain X'09AB233F' and R7 will contain X'1EB65A00'. With the same initial contents, the instruction

      SRDA   R6,8

will result in R6 containing X'FFAF09AB' and R7 containing X'233F1EB6'.

A register pair can be loaded or stored using the Load Multiple and Store Multiple instructions. These RS instructions use the second register operand in the RS format to specify a range of registers. The range is determined by viewing the registers as wrapping around so that R0 comes after RF. Thus, R3,R7 specifies the registers R3, R4, R5, R6, R7. RD,R2 specifies RD, RE, RF, R0, R1, R2.

Load Multiple *LM RS*

$$LM \qquad R_1,R_3,S_2$$

The range of registers determined by R_1,R_3 is loaded from the storage locations beginning at S_2.

Condition Code: Unchanged.

Exception:

Access   Improper address for S_2.

STore Multiple *STM RS*

$$STM \qquad R_1,R_3,S_2$$

The range of registers determined by R_1,R_3 is copied to the storage locations beginning at S_2.

Condition Code: Unchanged.

Exception:

Access   Improper address for S_2.

Example 4.5.9

$$LM \qquad R4,R8,FWORDS$$

The 5 fullwords beginning at the memory location determined by FWORDS will be loaded into registers R4, R5, R6, R7, R8.

Example 4.5.10

$$STM \qquad R6,R7,DWORD$$

The contents of the register pair R6,R7 will be stored in the memory locations beginning at DWORD. This 64-bit number can later be reloaded with a LM instruction.

We can use LM to load a 64-bit number into a register pair; however, it is often necessary to load a fullword number into a register pair. If the number is viewed as a signed binary integer, then when it has been extended to 64 bits and loaded into the register pair, the number itself will be in the odd register. The even register will contain 32 copies of the sign bit. The most convenient way to effect this is to load the number into the even register and then use SRDA to shift the register pair 32 bits to the right.

Example 4.5.11 *To load a fullword number from a field named RATE into the register pair R8,R9, we use the following.*

```
        L       R8,RATE              R8,R9 = RATE
        SRDA    R8,32
```

Testing for Overflow

Suppose we have a 64-bit number in a register pair and need to store it in 32-bit form in a fullword location. If we are certain that the number will fit in a fullword, we can simply execute a Store instruction with the odd register of the pair. However, this runs the risk of loosing significant bits. The Store instruction will not check the entire 64-bit number to determine whether it can be stored in a fullword. If we want to include the code for this check, we need to make certain that the even register contains nothing other than copies of the sign bit from the odd register. This can be accomplished by using the SLDA instruction to shift the register pair 32 bits to the left. If the number is too large for a fullword field, this will cause a Fixed Point Overflow. Otherwise, the significant part of the number will end up in the even register and the odd register will be filled with zeros.

When an overflow occurs, the action taken by the machine depends on the current status of the Fixed Point Overflow bit in the Program Mask portion of the Program Status Word. In our sample programs, we have set this bit to 1 so that an overflow would terminate the program. If, instead, we want to have our program handle this condition, we set the bit to 0. Thus, after performing an operation which might cause an overflow, we can use the Branch-on-Overflow or Branch-on-No-Overflow instructions to check the Condition Code.

Example 4.5.12 *Suppose that we need to store a doubleword value in the register pair R2,R3 in a fullword field TAX.*

In order to guard against program termination as a result of an overflow, we turn off the fixed overflow bit, then perform a 32 bit left shift to check the high-order part of the doubleword value. If this shift results in an overflow, the Condition Code will be set accordingly. We assume the existence of an error handling routine which takes some corrective action in the event of an overflow.

```
            ICM     R0,B'1000',=B'00000111'   TURN OFF FIXED OVERFLOW BIT
            SPM     R0                        :
            SLDA    R2,32                     TAX = R2,R3
IF05        EQU     *                         IF OVERFLOW
            BNO     ELSE05                    :
THEN05      EQU     *                         THEN
            BAL     RE,ERROR                      CALL ERROR ROUTINE
            B       ENDIF05                   :
ELSE05      EQU                               ELSE
            ST      R2,TAX                        STORE RESULT
RNDIF05     EQU     *                         ENDIF
            ICM     R0,B'1000',=B'00001111'   TURN ON FIXED OVERFLOW BIT
            SPM     R0                        :
```

E X E R C I S E S

1. Assume that, before each of the following instructions, the operand contents are as shown below.

    R2 : X'003A1F2B'   R3 : X'F903BA12'   R4 : X'0000000C'

    Give the contents of the affected registers after each instruction.

a. SRA	R3,4	**b.** SRA	R3,0(R4)
c. SRL	R3,4	**d.** SRL	R2,4
e. SRA	R2,4	**f.** SLA	R2,8
g. SLA	R3,4	**h.** SLA	R3,8
i. SRDA	R2,16	**j.** SRDA	R2,32
k. SLDA	R2,8	**l.** SLDA	R2,8
m. SLDL	R2,16	**n.** SLDL	R2,4(R4)

2. Write assembly code, including an appropriate shift instruction, to perform each of the following.

    a. Multiply the number in R3 by 32.
    b. Divide the number in R5 by 16.
    c. Implement X = X/8. (Assume integer division.)

3. Write assembly code to convert a fullword binary integer in X to a doubleword binary integer in DWORD.

4. Write the code to convert a fullword in R5 to a halfword in a field named SUM checking for overflow. If an overflow occurs, then SUM should be set equal to X'8000'.

4.6 BINARY MULTIPLICATION AND DIVISION INSTRUCTIONS

The multiplication and division instructions for binary numbers parallel those for packed decimal numbers. Both are integer operations; similar rules are invoked for the lengths of the operands to eliminate overflows, and the division yields both a quotient and remainder. As with decimal operations, if we need to manipulate binary fractions, then we must devise a way to represent the position of an implied binary point.

Binary Multiplication

The fullword multiplication instructions multiply two 32-bit numbers together obtaining a 64-bit product. The first number is obtained from the odd register of an even-odd pair and the result is placed in this register pair. The contents of the even register before the operation are ignored. Note that overflow is not possible; the product will never exceed 64 bits.

Multiply *M RX*

M R_1,S_2

The fullword designated by the second operand is multiplied by the contents of the odd register of the even-odd pair designated by R_1. The result is stored in the register pair.

Condition Code: Unchanged.

Exceptions:

Access   Improper address.

Specification R_1 is not an even register.

Multiply Register *MR RR*

MR R_1,R_2

The fullword designated by the second operand is multiplied by the contents of the odd register of the even-odd pair designated by R_1. The result is stored in the register pair.

Condition Code: Unchanged.

Exceptions:

Specification R_1 is not an even register.

Example 4.6.1

M   R6,COUNT

The 32-bit number in R7 is multiplied by the 32-bit number in the memory locations beginning at COUNT. The 64-bit product is placed in the register pair R6,R7. The contents of R6 before the instruction are ignored.

Suppose that, before the instruction is executed, R6 contains X'00F3B12A', R7 contains X'01005040', and COUNT contains X'00020000'. After execution of the instruction, the register pair R6,R7 will contain

X'00000200A0800000'

R6 will contain the high-order bits, X'00000200', and R7 the low-order bits, X'A0800000'. The field COUNT will be unchanged.

Example 4.6.2 Suppose that R3 contains X'FFFFFFFE' (-2), R4 contains X'00000005', and R5 contains X'FFFFFFFF' (-1) when the following instructions are executed.

MR   R4,R4
MR   R2,R3

The first instruction multiplies the fullword value from R5, the odd member of the even-odd pair designated by the first operand, together with the fullword value in R4, the second operand. The product,

$$X'FFFFFFFFFFFFFFFB'$$

will be stored in the pair R4,R5.

The second instruction also multiplies the fullword from the odd member of the even-odd pair by the fullword designated by the second register operand. In this case, both references are to R3. Thus, the effect of the instruction is to square the fullword value in R3 and store the result in the register pair R2,R3. After execution of this instruction, the pair will contain the 64-bit number

$$X'0000000000000004'$$

Example 4.6.3 *The multiplication instruction provides an alternate method of extending a fullword value to a 64-bit number in a register pair.*

If we place the fullword in the odd register of the pair, then multiply by 1, the result will be the 64-bit equivalent of the original fullword.

```
        L       R5,FWORD
        M       R4,=F'1'
```

This seems more straightforward than our earlier method. However, it should be avoided since the multiplication instructions consume considerably more time than the shift instructions.

Each use of the fullword multiplication instructions requires a pair of registers. Because there are a number of occasions when the numbers being multiplied are known to be relatively small, the fullword instructions are supplemented by a halfword multiplication instruction. This instruction multiplies the fullword contents of its register operand by a halfword storage operand. The result is stored in the register operand. It is possible that the result may not fit in the register. Unfortunately, when this is the case, the high-order bits of the product are lost. No indication of overflow is given.

Multiply Halfword *MH RX*

$$MH \qquad R_1,S_2$$

The contents of the halfword memory location designated by S_2 are sign extended to 32 bits and multiplied by the fullword contents of the register operand R_1. The 64-bit product is truncated on the left to 32 bits and stored in R_1. No indication is given if significant bits are lost.

Condition Code: Unchanged.

Exceptions:

Access   Improper address for second operand.

Example 4.6.4

        MH   R6,HWORD

If R6 contains X'0000143E' and HWORD contains X'13F1', then the product produced by the multiplication will be

                X'000000000193A85E'

The low-order 32 bits of this product will be stored in R6.

If R6 had contained X'00018582' and HWORD had contained X'88C9' the resulting product would have been

                X'FFFFFFFF4A2F5682'

Again, only the low-order 32 bits, X'4A2F5682', would be stored in R6. However, in this case, an undetected overflow would have occurred. Although the high-order part of the product consists of nothing but copies of the sign bit, the leftmost bit of the low-order part is not a copy of the sign bit. In other words, the significant part of the product is 1 bit too long for a register.

Binary Division

The division instructions reflect the operation of the multiplication instructions. Just as the multiplication instructions leave the product in a register pair, the division instructions divide the 64-bit contents of a register pair by a fullword. The integer quotient is stored in the odd register of the even-odd pair and the remainder is stored in the even register. Note that, as compared to the decimal division instruction, the relative order of the quotient and remainder is reversed.

Also observe that the quotient may not fit in a single register. For example, if the dividend is too large to represent in 32 bits and the divisor is 1, the quotient will not fit in a register. Whenever this occurs, a Fixed Point Divide exception is raised.

Divide *D RX*

            D R_1,S_2

The 64-bit contents of the even-odd pair designated by R_1 is divided by the fullword designated by the second operand. The remainder is stored in the even register of the even-odd pair and the quotient is stored in the odd register.

Condition Code: Unchanged.

Exceptions:

Access	Improper address for second operand.
Specification	R_1 is not an even register.
Fixed Point Divide	The quotient exceeds 32 bits (or division by zero).

Divide Register *DR RR*

DR R_1,R_2

The 64-bit contents of the even-odd pair designated by R_1 is divided by the contents of R_2. The remainder is stored in the even register of the even-odd pair and the quotient is stored in the odd register.

Condition Code: Unchanged.

Exceptions:

Specification R_1 is not an even register.

Fixed Point Divide   The quotient exceeds 32 bits (or division by zero).

Example 4.6.5

DR   R4,R7

The 64-bit number in R4 will be divided by the 32-bit number in R7. A 32-bit quotient will be stored in R5 and the remainder in R4. For example, if the pair R4,R5 contains X'0004081000004031B' and R7 contains X'00400000', then this instruction will divide X'0004081000004031B' by X'00400000'. The quotient, X'10204000', will be stored in R5 and the remainder, X'0004031B', in R4.

    The dividend or the divisor may be negative. In this case, the signs of the quotient and remainder are determined in the same way as with packed decimals. A nonzero quotient is negative if the signs of the dividend and divisor are different. Otherwise, the quotient is positive. The sign of a nonzero remainder is the same as the sign of the dividend.

Example 4.6.6

D   R2,=F'487569'

If the pair R2,R3 contains the negative binary number

$$X'FFFFFFCD5B3537F0'$$

then this instruction will divide this number by 487569. Because the signs differ, the sign of the quotient stored in R3 will be negative. As the dividend is negative, the remainder stored in R2 will also be negative.

    After execution of the instruction, R2 will contain X'FFFB7365' and R3 will contain X'FFF9315B'.

    As the number of registers is small, we frequently need to perform arithmetic operations on values stored in memory locations and return results to other memory locations. As we consider some typical examples of expression evaluation we assume that no overflows occur and that the results will always fit in the target fields.

Suppose that X, Y, and Z are fullword fields and that we need to implement the assignment.

$$Z = Y/X$$

In order to perform the division, we need to place a 64-bit version of Y in a register pair and divide by X. We can extend Y to 64 bits by loading it into the even register of the pair and shifting right 32 bits. The code, with an appropriate comment, is

```
L       R6,Y            Z = Y/X
SRDA    R6,32           :
D       R6,X            :
ST      R7,Z            :
```

Expression Evaluation

In evaluating more complicated expressions, we may take advantage of the control provided by coding in assembly language to attempt some optimization. For example, suppose we need to implement the assignment

$$Z = (3*X^2*Y+2*X*Y^2)/(X+Y)$$

We don't have an exponentiation instruction, so the squares must be computed by multiplication. If we write out these multiplications, we can determine the maximum number of operations needed. The expression is

$$(3*X*X*Y+2*X*Y*Y)/(X+Y)$$

Counting operations, we have six multiplications, two additions, and one division. However, noting that the two components of the first parenthesized expression have the term X*Y in common, we can reorganize the expressions as

$$(X*Y)*(3*X+2*Y)/(X+Y) =$$
$$(X*Y)*(X+2*(X+Y))/(X+Y)$$

In this form, we see that we only need to evaluate the subexpression $(X+Y)$ once. Recalling that we can evaluate $2*(X+Y)$ by a left shift, we see that the expression can be evaluated with only 2 multiplications, 2 additions, 1 shift, and a division. In effect, we have eliminated 3 multiplications and replaced a fourth with a shift.

When we implement this expression evaluation, we should also attempt to minimize data movement. Although this is not as important as reducing the number of arithmetic operations, it seems reasonable to try to avoid fetching the same value from memory several times.

One possible implementation of this expression evaluation is shown below. The register pair R4,R5 is used for both multiplications and divisions. In particular, note that after the second multiplication, the pair contains the 64-bit number required for the division. The contents of other registers during the computation are shown below. The entire expression evaluation may be summarized by a single comment.

```
*                                  Z = (X*Y)*(X+2*(X+Y))/(X+Y)
       L      R5,X                  R5    = X
       L      R6,Y                  R6    = Y
       MR     R4,R6                 R4,R5 = X*Y
       A      R6,X                  R6    = X+Y
       LR     R7,R6                 R7    = X+Y
       SLA    R6,1                  R6    = 2*(X+Y)
       A      R6,X                  R6    = X+2*(X+Y)
       MR     R4,R6                 R4,R5 = (X*Y)*(X+2*(X+Y))
       DR     R4,R7                 R5    = (X*Y)*(X+2*(X+Y))/(X+Y)
       ST     R5,Z
```

Rounding with Binary Arithmetic

The operations discussed have been integer operations and fullword binary numbers are used primarily as integers. There is no counterpart of the shift and round instruction for decimal numbers and, in general, the only time rounding is needed is to round a quotient to an integer. This process can be implemented with the instructions we have already covered, as Example 4.6.7 demonstrates.

Example 4.6.7 *Suppose that R5 contains a number to be divided by a fullword number in DIVISOR, the quotient being rounded to the nearest integer.*

In order to accomplish this, we add an extra bit to the right of the number during the set-up for division. After the division, the quotient will have 1 fractional bit. Rounding is effected by adding 1 to the quotient, then shifting right to eliminate the rightmost bit.

```
       LR     R6,R5              R5 = R5/DIVISOR
       SRDA   R6,32              SET-UP FOR DIVISION
       SLDA   R6,1               ADD AN EXTRA BIT FOR ROUNDING
       D      R6,DIVISOR         FIND QUOTIENT WITH EXTRA BIT
       AH     R5,=H'1'           ADD 1 TO RIGHTMOST BIT
       SRA    R5,1               TRUNCATE RESULT
```

E   X   E   R   C   I   S   E   S

1. Suppose that, before each of the following instructions is executed, the operands have the values shown in the list below.
   R2 : X'08800204'   R3 : X'00200407'
   R4 : X'FFFFFFFF'   R5 : X'FFFFFFF8'
   FWORD : X'00000200'   HWORD : X'0040'

Give the new values of all changed operands after the instruction has been executed.

a. MR	R2,R2	b. MR	R2,R3
c. MR	R2,R4	d. MH	R2,HWORD
e. MH	R3,HWORD	f. M	R2,FWORD
g. D	R2,FWORD	h. DR	R2,R4

2. Assuming that all the fields contain fullword binary numbers, write the instructions to evaluate each of the following expressions.

a. (3*A−2*B) DIV C
b. (X+Y) DIV (2*X−Y)

4.7 INSTRUCTIONS THAT MANIPULATE ADDRESSES

Throughout this chapter, we have concentrated on instructions that interpret the contents of the register operands as signed binary numbers. However, these registers are called *general-purpose registers* in part because they can contain either numbers or addresses. This is in contrast to other computer architectures in which certain registers can contain only addresses while others can contain only data. We conclude this chapter by considering several useful instructions that involve the use of addresses stored in registers.

The RX Instruction Format

Recall that the machine addresses on an IBM 370 are 24 bits long. These addresses can be obtained from several sources. The most common mechanism for generating addresses is the base-displacement addressing mechanism. A displacement of three hexadecimal digits is added to a base address in a register. It is possible to arrange to have addresses stored in memory locations during linking and loading. Such addresses can then be moved to a register with a simple Load instruction.

A third alternative is the addressing mechanism available with the RX instructions. Recall that the machine format of the RX instructions is

| C | C | R_1 | X_2 | B_2 | D_2 | D_2 | D_2 |

CC represents the opcode, and R1 the register operand. The remainder of the instruction is used to encode the address of the second operand. As usual, B_2 represents the base register and $D_2D_2D_2$ represents the displacement. The third register, X_2, is called the *Index Register*. Its use introduces the possibility of adding a third component to the address computation for the second operand.

The index register functions in much the same way as the base register. If X_2 is any register other than R0, then the right 3 bytes of the contents of X_2 are added to the address obtained from the base-displacement computation. This last addition is called *indexing*. When X_2 is R0, no indexing takes place.

Example 4.7.1 *Suppose that R0 contains X'400005A0', R1 contains '40000A3C', and RC contains '40314C00'. Consider the following machine instructions.*

X'58A0035C'

X'58'	the opcode for the Load Instruction
X'A'	register operand
X'0'	index register
X'0'	base register
X'35C'	displacement

The address of the second operand is the displacement, X'35C'. As both the base and index registers are R0, no base address is added and no indexing takes place. Execution of this instruction will copy a fullword from X'00035C' to register RA.

X'58A1035C'

X'1'	index register
X'0'	base register

The address for the second operand is obtained by adding the displacement, X'35C' and the right three bytes of the index register, X'000A3C'. The address obtained is X'000D98'. No base value is added, as the base register is register R0.

X'58A0C35C'

X'0'	index register
X'C'	base register

The second operand address is the sum of the displacement and the rightmost three bytes of the base register, X'35C'+X'314C00' = X'314F5C'. No indexing takes place, as the index register is R0.

X'58A1C35C'

X'1'	index register
X'C'	base register

The second operand address is the displacement plus the rightmost three bytes from the index register and the base register. This yields X'35C'+X'000A3C'+X'314C00' = X'315998'.

The full assembler format for an RX instruction allows several variations. If the second operand is a relocatable expression, such as a symbol defined by a DS or a DC, then the assembler insists on supplying the base register. If an absolute expression is given for the displacement of the second operand, the base register may be specified explicitly by the programmer. If it is omitted, the assembler will encode R0 as the base register. Similarly, if the index register, X_2, is omitted, the assembler uses R0 as the index register, which implies that no indexing will take place.

In order to enumerate the possible variations, let S_2 represent an absolute or relocatable expression and X_2 and B_2 registers other than R0. The assembly language format for the second operand of an RX instruction can assume any of the following forms.

Format	S_2 Type	Address Computation
S_2	Relocatable	Displacement(S_2) + Contents(Implied Base Register)
$S_2(X_2)$	Relocatable	Displacement(S_2) + Contents(Implied Base Register) + Contents(X_2)
S_2	Absolute	S_2
$S_2(X_2)$	Absolute	S_2 + Contents(X_2)
$S_2(X_2,B_2)$	Absolute	S_2 + Contents(X_2) + Contents(B_2)
$S_2(,B_2)$	Absolute	S_2 + Contents(B_2)

In the last two instruction formats given above, the base register is called an *explicit base register*. As the examples show, an explicit base register may be used only when the displacement is an absolute expression.

Similar formats are available with SS instructions and with the storage operand of the RS instruction. The exact format for the SS instructions depends upon whether an operand includes a length. The format of the storage operand of an RS instruction is the same as that of an SS operand which does not include the length.

Format	S Type	Address
S	Relocatable	disp(S) + c(Implied Base Register)
S(L)	Relocatable	disp(S) + c(Implied Base Register)
S	Absolute	S
S(B)	Absolute	S + c(B)
S(L,B)	Absolute	S + c(B)

All future instruction descriptions will list the most general form for the assembly language formats. That is, we will show $S_2(X_2,B_2)$ for the second operand of an RX instruction and S(B) or S(L,B) for storage operands. The assembler will supply default values for omitted components.

Example 4.7.2 *Assume a program contains the following assembler instructions.*

```
WRDOFF     EQU     25
  .
  .
  .
WORD       DS      F    ASSUME RC IS THE CURRENT BASE REGISTER
```

The symbol WORD is a relocatable expression since it represents a storage location whose address will change if the program is relocated. WRDOFF is an absolute expression since its value will always be 25, regardless of the location of the program.

These symbols may be used in the following ways.

Instruction	Address of second operand
L R1,WRDOFF	WRDOFF
L R1,WRDOFF(RA)	WRDOFF + c(RA)
L R1,WRDOFF(RA,RB)	WRDOFF + c(RA) + c(RB)
L R1,WRDOFF(,R9)	WRDOFF + c(R9)
L R1,WORD	disp(WORD) + c(RC)
L R1,WORD(RA)	disp(WORD) + c(RC) + c(RA)

Note that each value in the second column represents the address of the second operand. The effect of the corresponding instruction will be to copy a fullword from the locations beginning at this address into register R1.

The Load Address Instruction

The Load Address instruction is an RX instruction. The first operand is a register and the second operand designates an address. This address is computed as in the examples above. However, once the address has been determined, instead of being used to access data, the address itself is placed in the register operand.

Load Address *LA RX*

$$LA \qquad R_1,S_2(X_2,B_2)$$

The address of the second operand is placed in the rightmost 3 bytes of R_1. The leftmost byte of this register is set to 0.

Condition Code: Unchanged.

Exceptions: None.

Example 4.7.3 *Assume WRDOFF and WORD are as in example 4.7.2.*

LA	R5,WORD	Places the address of WORD in R5.
LA	R5,WRDOFF	Places the value of WRDOFF (25) in R5.

Assume that R6 contains X'0003A1CF' and R7 contains X'00002A0E'.

```
LA      R3,1              R3 = 1
LA      R1,5(R6)          R1 = 5+X'03A1CF'
LA      R1,10(R6,R7)      R1 = 10+X'03A1CF'+X'002A0E'
LA      R6,WRDOFF(R6)     Increment R6 by WRDOFF
```

As the examples above indicate, LA can be used in a number of different ways, the most obvious being to place an address in a register. However, it can also be used to place a small positive constant in a register. LA can be used to increment a register or add the contents of two registers with a constant, provided all values are positive. Because register contents are interpreted as addresses, they cannot exceed three bytes. Similarly, if a constant is used, it is interpreted as a displacement. Thus, it cannot exceed three hexadecimal digits.

Using BCTR for Loop Control

In Section 4.4, we covered the use of the BCT instruction to generate counted loops. The use of this instruction results in loops which execute quickly because the decrement and test are performed by the same instruction. However, BCT still requires an address computation for each loop traversal. For example, consider the following code fragment.

```
FOR05     EQU     *                  FOR R5 = 100 DOWNTO 1
          LA      R5,100                :
FTEST05   EQU     *                     :
          .
          ..
          .
          BCT     R5,FTEST05            :
ENDFOR05  EQU     *                  ENDFOR
```

The second argument in the BCT instruction, FTEST05, is represented in base-displacement form. This means that on each of the first 99 loop traversals, the machine must get the address from the base register and add the displacement for FTEST05 in order to generate the branch address. Yet, this computation will always result in the same value.

The redundant address computations can be avoided by using the RR form of the Branch on CounT instruction, BCTR.

Branch on CounT Register BCTR RR

```
          BCTR    R₁,R₂
```

The number in the first register operand, R_1, is decremented by 1.

If the result is nonzero, and R_2 is not register 0, the address in R_2 replaces the instruction address portion of the Program Status Word, effecting a branch to this location.

If the new value in R1 is 0 or if R_2 is register 0, no branch occurs.

Condition Code: Unchanged.

Exceptions: None.

With BCTR, we can use the Load Address instruction to put the branch address in a register before entering the loop. We then use that register as the second operand in a BCTR instruction. The following modification of the loop above illustrates this usage.

```
FOR05      EQU     *                    FOR R5 = 100 DOWNTO 1
           LA      R5,100               :
           LA      RB,FTEST05           :
FTEST05    EQU     *                    :
            .
            .
            .
           BCTR    R5,RB                :
ENDFOR05   EQU     *                    ENDFOR
```

Now the address computation is done only once, by the instruction immediately preceding the FTEST05 label. The address generated is then used without recomputation for all 99 branches.

In addition to its use in loop construction, the BCTR instruction can also be used in another context. Note that, if the second operand is 0, the only effect of the instruction is to decrement its first operand by 1. It happens that this is the quickest way to subtract 1 from a register. Thus, we will often use a construct similar to

```
           BCTR    R5,0                 R5 = R5 - 1
```

We use 0 for the second operand in place of R0, since this is really a dummy operand. Register 0 plays no role in the execution of the instruction.

BALR and BCR

There are two other RR counterparts of RX instruction that expect an address to be in a register. They correspond to the Branch And Link and the Branch on Condition instructions covered earlier.

Branch And Link Register *BALR RR*

```
           BALR    R₁,R₂
```

The contents of the Instruction Address portion of the PSW is copied into the right three bytes of R_1.

If R_2 is not register 0, the right three bytes of R_2 become the new Instruction Address.

If R_2 is register 0, no other action is taken.

Condition Code: Unchanged.

Exceptions: None.

Normally BALR is used to invoke a subroutine whose address is in the second register operand. We will use it in this way in Chapter 6 when we discuss external subroutines. When the second operand is register 0, the instruction has the effect of determining where in memory the program is loaded. We have used it in this way in each of our programs.

```
        BALR    RC,0
```

puts the address of the following instruction in RC. As the second operand is 0, no other action takes place. This is the mechanism we have been using to put the correct value in the base register.

Branch on Condition Register *BCR RR*

```
        BCR     M₁,R₂
```

Branch to the address in R_2 if the value of the bit in M_1 corresponding to the current value of the condition code is B'1'. (The correspondence between mask bits and Condition Code values is the same as the BC instruction.)

Condition Code: Unchanged.

Exceptions: None.

As with the Branch on Condition instruction, the mask in the BCR instruction can be specified by the programmer, but it is much easier to direct the assembler to generate the mask by using one of the extended mnemonics instructions. The mnemonics for the BCR instruction are formed by appending an R to the end of one of the mnemonics for the BC instruction. For example, we might use the extended mnemonic for an unconditional branch to streamline the execution of a while loop as shown below.

```
            LA      RB,WHILE04      :
WHILE04     EQU     *               WHILE R5 < EXPONENT
            C       R5,EXPONENT     :
            BNL     ENDWHL04        :
            .
            .
            .
            BR      RB              :
ENDWHL04    EQU     *               END WHILE
```

The Edit and Mark Instruction

The Edit and Mark instruction provides a final example of a situation in which we need to manipulate an address. We have seen how to use the Edit instruction to perform sign editing. Unfortunately, this requires the sign to be placed after the number. Normally, we prefer to have the sign in front of the number, and, in many situations, would like it to be immediately before the first printable character. A little reflection indicates the problem. We want to place a sign in one byte of the edit field, but we won't know until the program is executed which byte should receive the sign.

The Edit and Mark instruction solves this problem by allowing us to determine the address of the location to receive the sign when the program is executed.

EDit and MarK EDMK SS

$$\text{EDMK} \quad S_1(L_1,B_1),S_2(B_2)$$

An Edit operation is performed using the first and second operands. If a non-zero digit is processed before printing is forced by a significance starter, the address of this digit is placed in R1 otherwise, the value in R1 will be unchanged.

Condition Code: Reset to

0   If the edited value is 0.

1   If the edited value is negative.

2   If the edited value is positive.

Exceptions:

Access   Improper address.

Data   The second operand is not a valid packed number.

Note that, when the value in R1 is changed, the address which is placed there is the address of the first nonzero digit. If we want to insert a sign in front of the number, it should go in the position immediately before this digit. Therefore, we need to decrement this address by 1 before we use it.

If significance is forced by the significance starter, rather than by a nonzero digit, then the value in R1 will be unchanged. We can cope with this difficulty by placing the address of the first digit to be forced in R1 before the EDMK instruction is executed. This is done with the LA instruction.

For example, suppose that we need to edit

```
PNUM        DS        PL3
```

into an edit field named OUTNUM using the edit pattern

```
EDMSK       DC        X'402020212020'
```

Before executing the EDMK instruction, we need to place the address of the byte immediately after the X'21' in R1. After moving EDMSK into OUTNUM, the contents of the OUTNUM together with the offsets from the beginning of the field will be

OUTNUM	40	20	20	21	20	20
Offsets	0	1	2	3	4	5

The first digit to be forced will be at OUTNUM+4. The address of this digit can be placed in R1 with

```
        LA      R1,OUTNUM+4
```

Now, we execute

```
        EDMK    OUTNUM,PNUM
```

If one of the first three digits is nonzero, the address of digit in OUTNUM will replace the value in R1. Otherwise, the value in R1 will be unchanged. In either event, after execution of the EDMK instruction, R1 will contain the address of the first nonblank character in OUTNUM.

We can use the BCTR instruction to subtract 1 from R1.

```
        BCTR    R1,0
```

Then R1 will contain the address of the position where a minus sign should be placed. The instruction

```
        MVI     0(R1),C'—'
```

completes the sequence. The address computation for the first operand adds the displacement, 0, to the address in the explicitly designated base register R1. That is, the address used for the first operand is the address of the location that should receive the minus sign if the edited number is negative.

The complete sequence of instructions is

```
        MVC     OUTNUM,EDMSK    MOVE EDIT PATTERN INTO EDMSK
        LA      R1,OUTNUM+4     PLACE DEFAULT ADDRESS IN R1
        EDMK    OUTNUM,PNUM     PERFORM EDIT OPERATION
IF01    EQU     *               IF PNUM < 0
        BNM     ENDIF01         :
THEN01  EQU     *               THEN
        BCTR    R1,0            ADJUST ADDRESS
        MVI     0(R1),C'—'          INSERT MINUS SIGN
ENDIF01 EQU     *               ENDIF
```

Example 4.7.4 *Rather than include a test after the edit to determine whether a sign needs to be inserted, we can make use of the sign editing facility of EDMK.*

If we include a sign indicator at the end of the pattern, then when the number is positive, this will be replaced by the fill character. When the number is negative, the sign indicator will remain. Without inspecting it, we can then move whatever character is in this position to the appropriate location at the left of the edited number and put a blank in the position on the right.

In designing the data structures and the code for this approach, we face several difficulties. We need to be able to specify several subfields of the edit field, but the actual locations of these fields are determined by the structure of the edit mask. We would like to be able to change the mask as needed without the necessity of making numerous other changes in the program.

The definitions below illustrate one possibility. We include a symbol definition, RCPTFRST, with the definition of the edit mask, RCPTMSK. RCPTFRST gives the offset from the beginning of the mask to the first digit to be forced. It is used to initialize R1 before the EDMK instruction. We assume that the sign will be in the last byte of the mask.

Note that if the mask itself is changed, we need only change the EQU instruction for RCPTFRST. All other needed changes will be made automatically.

```
          MVC     OUTRCPT,RCPTMSK              MOVE PATTERN TO OUTPUT FIELD
          LA      R1,OUTRCPT+RCPTFRST          INITIALIZE POINTER
          EDMK    OUTRCPT,PRECPT               SIGN EDITING
          BCTR    R1,0                         ADJUST R1 (R1 = R1−1)
          MVC     0(1,R1),OUTRCPT+L'OUTRCPT−1  MOVE SIGN TO FRONT
          MVI     OUTRCPT+L'OUTRCPT−1,C' '     PUT A BLANK AT THE END
RCPTMSK   DC      X'402020206B2020206B2021204B202060'
RCPTFRST  EQU     11                                          :
                  .
                  .
                  .
OUTRCPT   DS      CL(L'RCPTMSK)                                :
```

Example 4.7.5 *The EDMK instruction can also be used to put a floating dollar sign at the front of monetary output.*

```
          MVC     OUTCOST,COSTMSK              MOVE PATTERN TO OUTCOST
          LA      R1,OUTCOST+CSTFRST           INITIALIZE R1
          EDMK    OUTCOST,PCKCOST              EDIT THE PACKED COST
          BCTR    R1,0                         DECREMENT R1
          MVI     0(R1),C'$'                   INSERT A '$' IN FRONT OF THE NUMBER
COSTMSK   DC      CL'40206B2021204B2020'
CSTFRST   EQU     5                                           :
          .
          .
          .
OUTCOST   DS      CL(L'COSTMSK)                                :
```

E X E R C I S E S

1. Suppose that R0 contains X'009A8F9D', R5 contains X'00000401', and RC contains X'4032907A'. Give the address generated by each of the following indexed operands.

   a. X'003A1'
   b. X'0C3A1'
   c. X'503A1'
   d. X'5C3A1'

2. Suppose RA contains X'00312A9B' and RB contains X'40203AB1'. Give the value placed in R2 by each of the following instructions.

   a. LA   R2,0(RB)
   b. LA   R2,0(RA,RB)
   c. LA   R2,0(RB,RA)
   d. LA   R2,64(RA)

3. Write a load address instruction to accomplish each of the following.

   a. Set R4 equal to R2 + R3 + 5
   b. Increment R4 by 8.
   c. Set R4 equal to R4 + R6
   d. Set R4 equal to 32.

4. Use BCTR to implement a loop which adds all of the integers from 1 to 500 leaving the result in R4.

5. Use the extended mnemonics associated with BCR to implement the following loop.

   ```
   R2 = 0
   R3 = 1
   R4 = 1
   WHILE R2 < FIB
       R2 = R3+R4
       R3 = R4
       R4 = R2
   END WHILE
   ```

6. Write the instructions and definitions to print a 3-byte packed number stored in PTOTAL using the format $990.99 with a floating dollar sign.

7. Write the instructions and definitions necessary to print a 4-byte packed number in the format −99,999.09 with a floating −.

4.8 SAMPLE PROGRAM

We conclude this chapter by considering a sample program illustrating many of the instructions and techniques we have covered. The program is designed to compute and print tables of all binomial coefficients for various input values.

Recall that the binomial coefficient, C(N,R) represents the number of combinations of N things taken R at a time. It also represents the coefficient of the term $X^R Y^{N-R}$ in the expansion of $(X+Y)^N$. Thus, it has application in a number of areas of mathematics, statistics, and engineering.

The value of C(N,R) is given by the formula

$$\frac{N!}{R! * (N - R)!}$$

The formula can be used directly, however, it entails a lot of computation, and the likelihood of an overflow is quite high. Instead, observe that

$$\frac{N!}{R! * (N - R)!} = \frac{N * (N - 1) * \ldots * (N - R + 1) * (N - R)!}{R! * (N - R)!}$$

$$= \frac{N * (N - 1) * \ldots * (N - R + 1)}{R!}$$

This observation reduces the number of computations necessary and also reduces the probability of overflow. However, when asked to compute a list of all binomial coefficients for a particular value of N, we can make use of the following inductive relationship.

$$C(N,R) = \frac{N * (N - 1) * \ldots * (N - R + 1)}{R!}$$

$$= \frac{N * (N - 1) * \ldots * (N - R) * (N - R + 1)}{R * (R - 1)!}$$

$$= \frac{(N - R + 1)}{R} * \frac{N * (N - 1) * \ldots * (N - R)}{(R - 1)!}$$

$$= \frac{(N - R + 1)}{R} * \frac{N * (N - 1) * \ldots * (N - (R - 1) + 1)}{(R - 1)!}$$

$$= \frac{(N - R + 1)}{R} * C(N, R - 1)$$

Combining this relationship with our knowledge that C(N,0) = 1, we can generate all binomial coefficients by repeatedly multiplying by (N−R+1) and dividing by R, for each new value of R. This gives the following algorithm.

```
COEFFICIENT = 1
R = 0
PRINT R, COEFFICIENT
FOR R = 1 TO N
    COEFFICIENT = (N−R+1)*COEFFICIENT/R
    PRINT R, COEFFICIENT
END FOR
```

This algorithm represents a considerable improvement over evaluating the original formula using factorials. However, its implementation in assembly language can be streamlined by observing that, as R goes from 1 to N, N−R+1 goes from N down to 1. Using this, we can create a countdown loop with N−R+1 as the loop counter.

```
COEFFICIENT = 1
R = 0
PRINT R, COEFFICIENT
FOR MULTIPLIER = N DOWNTO 1
    COEFFICIENT = MULTIPLIER*COEFFICIENT/R
    PRINT R, COEFFICIENT
    R = R+1
END FOR
```

The complete program is shown below. The algorithm above is implemented in the subroutine PRNTBLE. Note that we have minimized the loop overhead by using LA to put the address of the loop top in register RB and using BCTR to decrement R5 and test for 0.

The largest value on N which does not cause a Fixed Point Divide exception is 33. Each input value is compared with 33 and an error message printed if it is too large.

```
*****************************************************************************************
*       SAMPLE4                                                                        *
*       THIS PROGRAM READS A NUMBER, NUM, AND PRINTS A LIST OF THE                     *
*       BINOMIAL COEFFICIENTS FROM C(NUM,0) TO C(NUM,NUM)                              *
*                                                                                      *
*       IT REPEATS THIS PROCESS UNTIL END OF FILE.                                     *
*                                                                                      *
*       THE INPUT VALUES ARE ASSUMED TO BE POSITIVE. THEY MUST NOT                     *
*       EXCEED 33. THE SECOND CONDITION IS CHECKED AND A MESSAGE                       *
*       PRINTED IF IT IS VIOLATED.                                                     *
*                                                                                      *
*****************************************************************************************
```

```
SAMPLE4     START  0                     PROGRAM SAMPLE4
            PRINT  NOGEN                 :
            BALR   RC,0                  :
            USING  *,RC                  :
            ICM    R0,B'1000'=B'00001111'
            SPM    R0                    :
            OPEN   INFILE,PRINTER        OPEN FILES
REPEAT00    EQU    *                     REPEAT
            GET    INFILE,INREC            READ NUM
            PACK   PNUM,INNUM            :
IF00        EQU    *                     IF PNUM > LIMIT
            CP     PNUM,LIMIT            :
            BNH    ELSE00                :
THEN00      EQU    *                     THEN
            MVC    ERRNUM,NUMMSK           PRINT ERROR MESSAGE
            ED     ERRNUM,PNUM          :
            PUT    PRINTER,ERRLINE      :
            B      ENDIF00              :
ELSE00      EQU    *                     ELSE
            BAL    RE,PRNTBLE              PRINT TABLE
ENDIF00     EQU    *                     ENDIF
            B      REPEAT00             :
UNTIL00     EQU    *                     UNTIL END OF FILE
            CLOSE  INFILE,PRINTER       CLOSE FILES
            EOJ
****************************************************************************************
*     PRNTBLE                                                                          *
*                                                                                      *
*     PRINT A TABLE OF THE BINOMIAL COEFFICIENTS C(NUM,0) . . .                        *
*     C(NUM,NUM) USING THE RELATION                                                    *
*                                                                                      *
*                          NUM - R + 1                                                 *
*            C(NUM,R) = -------------- * C(NUM,R-1)                                     *
*                             R                                                        *
*                                                                                      *
*     INPUT VARIABLES   :  PNUM                                                         *
*                                                                                      *
*     OUTPUT VARIABLES :  <NONE>                                                       *
*                                                                                      *
*     REGISTER USAGE    :  R2,R3 - C(NUM,R)                                            *
*                          R4    - R                                                    *
*                          R5    - NUM - R + 1                                          *
*                          RB    - LOOP ADDRESS                                         *
****************************************************************************************
            DS     F                     :
PRNTBLE     EQU    *                     SUBROUTINE PRNTBLE
            ST     RE,PRNTBLE-4          :
```

```
            MVC     OUTNUM,NUMMSK        PRINT HEADLINE
            ED      OUTNUM,PNUM          :
            PUT     PRINTER,HEADLINE     :
            PUT     PRINTER,COLHEADS     :
            MVC     DETAIL+1(L'DETAIL-1),DETAIL
            PUT     PRINTER,DETAIL       :
            L       R3,=F'1'             R3 = 1
            L       R4,=F'0'             R4 = 0
            BAL     RE,PRNTLIN           PRINT R4,R3
FOR00       EQU     *                    FOR R5 = NUM DOWNTO 1
            ZAP     DWORK,PNUM           :
            CVB     R5,DWORK             :
            C       R5,=F'1'             :
            BL      ENDFOR00             :
            LA      RB,FTEST00           :
FTEST00     EQU     *                    :
            LA      R4,1(R4)             R4 = R4+1
            MR      R2,R5                R3 = R3*R5
            DR      R2,R4                R3 = R3/R4
            BAL     RE,PRNTLIN           PRINT R4, R3
            BCTR    R5,RB                :
ENDFOR00    EQU     *                    ENDFOR
            L       RE,PRNTBLE-4     RETURN
            BR      RE                   :
```

```
***********************************************************************************************
*    PRNTLIN                                                                                  *
*                                                                                            *
*    PRINT THE VALUES IN R4 AND R3 WHICH CONTAIN R AND C(NUM,R).                              *
*                                                                                            *
*    INPUT VARIABLES    : R4, R3                                                             *
*                                                                                            *
*    OUTPUT VARIABLES : <NONE>                                                               *
*                                                                                            *
*    WORK VARIABLES    : DETAIL                                                              *
*                                                                                            *
*    REGISTER USAGE    : R3 - BINOMIAL COEFFICIENT (READ ONLY)                              *
*                        R4 - R (READ ONLY)                                                  *
***********************************************************************************************
```

```
            DS      F                    :
PRNTLIN     EQU     *                    SUBROUTINE PRNTLIN
            ST      RE,PRNTLIN-4         :
            CVD     R4,DWORK             PRINT R4, R3
            ZAP     PCKR,DWORK           :
            MVC     OUTR,NUMMSK          :
            ED      OUTR,PCKR            :
            CVD     R3,DWORK             :
            ZAP     PCOEF,DWORK          :
```

```
          MVC    OUTCOEF,COEFMSK        :
          ED     OUTCOEF,PCOEF          :
          PUT    PRINTER,DETAIL         :
          L      RE,PRNTLIN−4           RETURN
          BR     RE                     :
*********************************************************************************
*     SYMBOL DEFINITIONS                                                        *
*********************************************************************************
*
*     REGISTER EQUATES
*
R0        EQU    0                      :
R1        EQU    1                      :
R2        EQU    2                      :
R3        EQU    3                      :
R4        EQU    4                      :
R5        EQU    5                      :
R6        EQU    6                      :
R7        EQU    7                      :
R8        EQU    8                      :
R9        EQU    9                      :
RA        EQU    10                     :
RB        EQU    11                     :
RC        EQU    12                     :
RD        EQU    13                     :
RE        EQU    14                     :
RF        EQU    15                     :
*
*     LENGTHS AND OFFSETS
*
ZNUMLEN   EQU    3                      LENGTH FOR INPUT NUMBERS
PNUMLEN   EQU    ZNUMLEN/2+1            LENGTH FOR PACKED FORM
COEFLEN   EQU    11                     LENGTH FOR COEFFICIENT
PCOEFLEN  EQU    COEFLEN/2+1           LENGTH FOR PACKED FORM OF COEFFICIENT
HEADOFF   EQU    20                     OFFSET FOR HEADING LINE
ROFF      EQU    30                     OFFSET FOR FIRST COLUMN ENTRY
*********************************************************************************
*     LITERALS                                                                  *
*********************************************************************************
          LTORG
*********************************************************************************
*     FILES                                                                     *
*********************************************************************************
INFILE    DTFCD  DEVADDR=SYSIPT,DEVICE=2501,EOFADDR=UNTIL00              X
                 IOAREA1=INBUF1,IOAREA2=INBUF2,WORKA=YES
INBUF1    DS     CL80
INBUF2    DS     CL80
```

```
*
PRINTER    DTFPR  DEVADDR=SYSLST,DEVICE=3203,BLKSIZE=133,CTLCHR=ASA,      X
                  IOAREA1=OUTBUF1,IOAREA2=OUTBUF2,WORKA=YES
OUTBUF1    DS     CL133
OUTBUF2    DS     CL133
************************************************************************************
*    CONSTANTS                                                                    *
************************************************************************************
NUMMSK     DC     X'40202120'                 USED FOR NUM AND R
COEFMSK    DC     X'40202020202020202020202120' USED FOR COEFFICIENT
*
LIMIT      DC     P'33'                    UPPER LIMIT FOR NUM
************************************************************************************
*    VARIABLES                                                                    *
************************************************************************************
PNUM       DS     PL(PNUMLEN)          PACKED FORM OF NUM
DWORK      DS     D                    WORK AREA FOR CONVERSIONS
PCKR       DS     PL(PNUMLEN)          PACKED FORM OF R
PCOEF      DS     PL(PCOEFLEN)         PACKED FORM OF COEFFICIENT
************************************************************************************
*    I/O WORK AREAS                                                               *
************************************************************************************
INREC      DS     CL80                 INPUT RECORD
           ORG    INREC                   :
INNUM      DS     ZL(ZNUMLEN)             NUMBER
           ORG    INREC+L'INREC        END INREC
*
*    HEADLINE LINE
*
HEADLINE   DC     CL133' '             HEADLINE LINE
           ORG    HEADLINE                :
           DC     C'1'                    NEW PAGE CHARACTER
           ORG    HEADLINE+HEADOFF        :
           DC     C'BINOMIAL COEFFICIENTS C(N,R) FOR N ='
OUTNUM     DS     CL(L'NUMMSK)            NUMBER
           ORG    HEADLINE+L'HEADLINE  END HEADLINE
COLHEADS   DC     CL133' '             COLUMN HEADINGS
           ORG    COLHEADS                :
           DC     C'0'                    CONTROL CHARACTER
           ORG    COLHEADS+ROFF+L'NUMMSK-1
           DC     C'R'                 R HEADING
           ORG    *+L'COEFMSK-3           :
           DC     C'C(N,R)'            N HEADING
           ORG    COLHEADS+L'COLHEADS  END COLUMN HEADINGS
*
*    ERROR MESSAGE
*
```

```
ERRLINE    DC     CL133' '                ERROR LINE
           ORG    ERRLINE                 :
           DC     C'1'                     NEW PAGE CHARACTER
           ORG    ERRLINE+HEADOFF          :
ERRNUM     DS     CL(L'NUMMSK)             NUMBER
           DC     C' IS TOO LARGE'         :
           ORG    ERRLINE+L'ERRLINE  END ERROR LINE
*
*     DETAIL LINE
*
DETAIL     DC     CL133' '                DETAIL LINE
           ORG    DETAIL+ROFF             :
OUTR       DS     CL(L'NUMMSK)            R
           DC     C' I'                   :
OUTCOEF    DS     CL(L'COEFMSK)           C(NUM,R)
           ORG    DETAIL+L'DETAIL    END DETAIL LINE
*
           END
```

If this program is run with the following input

```
012
089
023
005
```

the output produced is

BINOMIAL COEFFICIENTS C(N,R) FOR N = 12

R	C(N,R)
0	1
1	12
2	66
3	220
4	495
5	792
6	924
7	792
8	495
9	220
10	66
11	12
12	1

89 IS TOO LARGE

BINOMIAL COEFFICIENTS C(N,R) FOR N = 23

R	C(N,R)
0	1
1	23
2	253
3	1771
4	8855
5	33649
6	100947
7	245157
8	490314
9	817190
10	1144066
11	1352078
12	1352078
13	1144066
14	817190
15	490314
16	245157
17	100947
18	33649
19	8855
20	1771
21	253
22	23
23	1

BINOMIAL COEFFICIENTS C(N,R) FOR N = 5

R	C(N,R)
0	1
1	5
2	10
3	10
4	5
5	1

P R O G R A M M I N G   P R O J E C T S

1. Recall that the Fibonacci numbers are defined by the following inductive relationships.

   $F(1) = 0$ $F(2) = 1$ $F(N) = F(N-1) + F(N-2)$ for $N > 2$

Write a program to read a number MAX and, using binary arithmetic, compute and print F(1) . . . F(MAX).

2. Binary multiplication is usually implemented in hardware by repeated shifting and addition. Write a subroutine that multiplies two halfwords in fields M1 and M2 in this way. Your subroutine should perform the multiplication by examining bits in M1 and, when appropriate, adding another copy of the M2 to the product. Simultaneously, it should shift the product one bit to the left as each bit in M1 is examined.

Leave the product in register R2 for the calling routine.

Test your subroutine by writing a program to read pairs of integers, convert them to halfwords, multiply them using the subroutine and print the product.

(Note: To examine the bits in a register, you can use SLL to move each bit to the sign position, then examine it by using LTR.)

3. Write a subroutine, PRNTBIN, to convert a binary number in register R2 to a character string. Assume the address of the character string is in R3. Examine successive bits of R2 by using SLL and LTR. For each bit position, move C'0' or C'1' to a position in the target string indicated by the address in R3. Increment R3 as each bit is processed.

Test your subroutine in a program that reads a positive integer N and prints the 32 bit signed binary numbers from −N to N along with their decimal equivalents.

4. Many computer applications involve simulation of real world phenomena. This often requires the generation of sequences of apparently random numbers, usually referred to as pseudo-random numbers. One technique for generating such numbers involves selecting an initial SEED value and two other values, MULT and MODULUS. The sequence of numbers is generated by repeatedly performing

SEED = (SEED * MULT) mod MODULUS

This will result in values of SEED between 0 and MODULUS −1.

The apparent randomness of the numbers generated depends very much upon the choices of MULT and MODULUS and, to a smaller extent, upon the initial choice of SEED.

The value of SEED can be manipulated to obtain numbers in a desired range. The results are more satisfactory if MODULUS is a great deal larger than the desired range of values.

Write a program that reads values for SEED, MULT, MODULUS, and a number THROWS. The program should use the pseudo-random number generator above to simulate THROWS tosses of a pair of dice. Print the results of the throws one per line.

C H A P T E R 5

ARRAYS

5.1 ONE-DIMENSIONAL ARRAYS

In this section we introduce arrays. 370 architecture provides special mechanisms to facilitate the manipulation of fullword and halfword arrays, and we begin with those. In later sections, we will see how to access arrays containing other types of data, as well as multidimensional arrays.

Suppose that we have the following instructions.

```
NUMENTS    EQU    25
VECTOR     DS     (NUMENTS)F
```

Recall from our discussion of the DS and DC directives in Chapter 1 that the term (NUMENTS) in the second instruction represents a duplication factor. In this case, the directive instructs the assembler to reserve storage for 25 fullwords. The symbol VECTOR represents the beginning of this storage area. The length factor recorded for VECTOR is 4, the length of a full word. Thus, in a sense, VECTOR actually represents the first of these 25 fullwords.

In order to access other entries, we must specify an offset from the first one. The second entry of VECTOR begins at VECTOR+L'VECTOR, the third one at VECTOR+2*L'VECTOR.

Logically, we view VECTOR as a one-dimensional array, but before exploring this concept, we need to resolve a problem associated with the notation used in RX instructions. As an operand in an RX instruction, VECTOR(R3) represents the indexed operand obtained by adding the contents of R3 to the starting address of VECTOR. There are other circumstances in which we may want to view a number in a register as a subscript for the array. In order to distinguish this from an indexed operand, we will represent a subscripted operand as VECTOR<R3>.

If we think of VECTOR as a one-dimensional array with subscripts beginning at 0, then the entry corresponding to subscript I begins at VECTOR+I*L'VECTOR. The figure below illustrates this relationship.

FIGURE 5.1.1 An Array of Fullwords

Entry	Offset
VECTOR<0>	VECTOR
VECTOR<1>	VECTOR+1*L'VECTOR
VECTOR<2>	VECTOR+2*L'VECTOR
.	.
.	.
.	.
VECTOR<I>	VECTOR+I*L'VECTOR

In a more general context, if we want to view the subscripts as beginning at some other value, say LOWER, then the element VECTOR<I> will begin at VECTOR+(I−LOWER)*L'VECTOR.

At the assembly language level, we can access elements of an array with RX instructions. For example, suppose that VECTOR is addressed with base register RC and consider the effect of the RX instruction

```
L       R2,VECTOR(R3)
```

The address generated for the second operand will be

$$displacement(VECTOR) + contents(RC) + contents(R3)$$

Under the usual storage addressing mechanism, the sum of the first two terms will be the beginning of VECTOR. If R3 contains 0, then the first fullword in VECTOR will be loaded into R2. If R3 contains 4, the second fullword will be loaded into R2.

In general, we can use this instruction to load an entry of VECTOR into R2 by first placing the offset from the beginning of VECTOR to the desired entry into R3 and then executing the instruction above.

Suppose we think of VECTOR as an array with subscripts LOW . . . HIGH and we need to load VECTOR<I> into R2. Assuming that LOW and I are fullword fields, we have

```
L       R3,I            R3 = L'VECTOR*(I−LOW)
S       R3,LOW          :
SLA     R3,2            :
L       R2,VECTOR(R3)   R2 = VECTOR<I>
```

As most of the instructions that manipulate binary numbers are RX instructions, we can perform a number of operations on an array in an analagous manner.

Example 5.1.1 *Given the following symbol and storage definitions, write the instructions to add the entries in the fullword array SCORE and store the sum in SUM.*

```
NUMSTU    EQU    25
SCORE     DS     (NUMSTU)F
SUM       DS     F
```

Beginning with an algorithmic construct using subscripts, we have

```
FOR STUDENT = 1 TO NUMSTU
   SUM = SUM+SCORE<STUDENT>
END
```

But, note that the addition operations must involve a register, so we keep the sum in a register until the loop is completed. If we use R2 for the sum, we have

```
R2 = 0
FOR STUDENT = 1 TO NUMSTU
    R2 = R2+SCORE<STUDENT>
END
SUM = R2
```

In order to implement this loop in assembly language, we use a register, R3, to hold the upper limit. As above, we also need a register, R4, to hold the index value. This gives

```
            SR      R2,R2           R2 = 0
FOR00       EQU     *               FOR STUDENT = 1 TO NUMSTU
            LA      R3,NUMSTU           (RECALL THAT NUMSTU IS
            MVC     STUDENT,=F'1'       DEFINED WITH AN EQU . . .
            LA      RB,FTEST00          NOT A DC)
FTEST00     EQU     *                   :
            C       R3,STUDENT          :
            BL      ENDFOR00            :
            L       RA,STUDENT      R2 = R2+SCORE<STUDENT>
            SH      RA,=H'1'            :
            SLA     RA,2                :
            A       R2,SCORE(RA)        :
            L       R4,STUDENT          :
            LA      R4,1(R4)            :
            ST      R4,STUDENT          :
            BR      RB                  :
ENDFOR00    EQU     *               ENDFOR
            ST      R2,SUM          SUM = R2
```

Note the effect of several special purpose instructions. SR R2,R2 is used to set R2 equal to 0. LA R3,NUMSTU places the value of the symbolic constant NUMSTU in R3. Then, SLA RA,2 effectively multiplies the contents of RA by 4. Finally, LA R4,1(R4) increments R4 by 1.

Examining this code, we see some ways in which it can be improved. On each loop traversal, STUDENT is incremented by 1. RA is then set equal to 4*STUDENT and used as an index into the array. It would clearly be more to the point to increment RA directly, dispensing with STUDENT entirely. This alteration gives the following algorithm.

```
R2 = 0
FOR RA = 0 TO L'SCORE*(NUMSTU−1) BY L'SCORE
    R2 = R2 + SCORE(RA)
ENDFOR
SUM = R2
```

The expression that represents the upper limit for the FOR loop involves only absolute symbols. Thus, its value can be computed by the assembler and placed in a register with the Load Address instruction. The resulting code is

```
          SR    R2,R2                    R2 = 0
FOR00     EQU   *                        FOR RA = 0 TO L'SCORE *
          LA    R3,L'SCORE*(NUMSTU-1)       (NUMSTU-1) BY
          SR    RA,RA                       L'SCORE
          LA    RB,FTEST00               :
FTEST00   EQU   *                        :
          CR    RA,R3                    :
          BH    ENDFOR00                 :
          A     R2,SCORE(RA)             R2 = R2+SCORE(RA)
          LA    RA,L'SCORE(RA)           :
          BR    RB                       :
ENDFOR00  EQU   *                        ENDFOR
          ST    R2,SUM
```

Here, we have used LA RA,L'SCORE(RA) to increment RA by the length of an entry of SCORE. The effect is to move this index register to the next entry of SCORE.

Once we have become more familiar with the use of the RX instructions for accessing arrays, we will be able to write algorithms like the second form above. Until that time, we can continue to write algorithms using the subscript notation and use the subscript resolution formulas to convert these algorithms to assembly language, as we did in the first version.

We conclude with a slightly more complex example.

Example 5.1.2 *Write the code needed to sort the array SCORE in the example above into ascending order.*

Using a selection sort, we begin with the following algorithm.

```
FOR STUDENT = 1 TO NUMSTU-1

    {Find student with lowest score in STUDENT . . . NUMSTU}

    MINSTU = STUDENT
    FOR NXTSTU = STUDENT+1 TO NUMSTU
        IF SCORE<NXTSTU> < SCORE<MINSTU>
        THEN
            MINSTU = NXTSTU
    ENDFOR

    {Exchange SCORE<STUDENT> and SCORE<MINSTU>.}

    TMPSCORE = SCORE<STUDENT>
    SCORE<STUDENT> = SCORE<MINSTU>
    SCORE<MINSTU> = TMPSCORE
ENDFOR
```

Now, as above, we will be using index registers to access the entries in SCORE. We can streamline the code by using the index registers as loop counters. Similarly, we can use an index register to keep track of the position of the lowest grade on each pass through the array. Finally, the binary comparison instruction requires that one of the arguments be in a register. We keep the value of the smallest score in a register for this purpose. This will simplify the exchange at the bottom of the loop.

```
FOR RB = 0 TO L'SCORE*(NUMSTU−2) BY L'SCORE
      R9 = RB
      R2 = SCORE(R9)
      FOR RA = RB +L'SCORE TO L'SCORE*(NUMSTU−1) BY L'SCORE
            IF SCORE(RA) < R2
            THEN
                  R9 = RA
                  R2 = SCORE(R9)
            ENDIF
      ENDFOR
      SCORE(R9) = SCORE(RB)
      SCORE(RB) = R2
ENDFOR
```

At the end of each traversal of the inner loop, R9 contains the index of the smallest score seen in SCORE(RB) through SCORE(RA) and R2 contains a copy of this score. When the loop has completed, R9 indexes the minimum score in SCORE(RB) through the end of score and R2 contains the minimum score.

```
FOR00     EQU     *                                    FOR RB = 0 TO L'SCORE*(NUMSTU−2)
          LA      ULIM00,L'SCORE*(NUMSTU−2)              BY L'SCORE
          SR      RB,RB                                    :
          LA      R8,FTEST00                               :
FTEST00   EQU     *                                        :
          C       RB,ULIM00                                :
          BH      ENDFOR00                                 :
          LR      R9,RB                                  R9 = RB--MINIMUM INDEX
          L       R2,SCORE(R9)                           R2 = SCORE(R9)--MIN. SCORE
FOR01     EQU     *                                    FOR RA = RB+L'SCORE TO
          LA      ULIM01,L'SCORE*(NUMSTU−1)              L'SCORE*(NUMSTU−1)
          LA      RA,L'SCORE(RB)                         BY L'SCORE
          LA      R7,FTEST01                               :
FTEST01   EQU     *                                        :
          C       RA,ULIM00                                :
          BH      ENDFOR01                                 :
IF00      EQU     *                                    IF SCORE(RA) < R2
          C       R2,SCORE(RA)                             :
          BNH     ENDIF00                                  :
THEN00    EQU     *                                    THEN
          LR      R9,RA                                    R9 = RA
```

```
            L       R2,SCORE(R9)                              R2 = SCORE(R9)
ENDIF00     EQU     *                                  ENDIF
            LA      RA,L'SCORE(RA)                        :
            BR      R7                                    :
ENDFOR01    EQU     *                                  ENDFOR
            L       RA,SCORE(RB)                       SCORE(R9) = SCORE(RB)
            ST      RA,SCORE(R9)                          :
            ST      R2,SCORE(RB)                       SCORE(RB) = R2
            LA      RB,L'SCORE(RB)                        :
            BR      R8                                    :
ENDFOR00    EQU     *                          ENDFOR
```

Note that, since SCORE(R9) and SCORE(RB) are both indexed operands, the only way to effect the assignment SCORE(R9) = SCORE(RB) is to copy SCORE(RB) to a register and then store it in SCORE(R9). We use the index register from the inner loop, RA, for this operation because its value is no longer needed.

As a final note, we will be using a number of registers for various purposes. One of the difficulties we must confront is keeping track of which registers are in use at any time. As registers are a scarce resource, we should use them carefully. In general, we should not keep a value in a register for an extended period unless it is used frequently. It is better to have a few extra loads and stores in a program than to risk the possibility of using the same register for conflicting purposes. To help us keep track of which registers are in use at any time, we shall try to use R2, R3, R4 and up, to hold binary numbers. We will select index registers and address registers beginning with RB and going down, RA, R9, R8 and so on.

E   X   E   R   C   I   S   E   S

Use the following symbol and storage definitions with exercises 1-4.

```
NUMTSTS    EQU     10
SCORES     DS      (NUMTSTS)F
TOTAL      DS      F
HIGH       DS      F
LOW        DS      F
AVG        DS      F
ABOVE      DS      F
```

1. Write the instructions to add the entries in SCORES and store the result in TOTAL. Find the average and store it in AVG.

2. Assuming that the average of SCORES has been computed and stored in AVG, write the instructions to count the number of scores which are greater than or equal to the average and store the result in ABOVE.

3. Write the instructions to find the highest and lowest scores and store them in the fields HIGH and LOW.

4. Assume that SCORE is addressed using RC and displacement X'31C' and that RC contains X'40768B078'. Find the address of the fifth entry of SCORE.

For exercises 5-8, modify your answers to exercises 1-4 assuming that all of the fullword fields (including the array) are changed to halfword fields. Use the following symbol and storage definitions.

```
MONTHS    EQU    12
TEMPS     DS     (MONTHS)F
ABOVE70   DS     F
BELOW32   DS     F
```

9. Assuming that average temperatures for the last 12 months are stored one per record as 3 digit numbers, write the code and any storage definitions necessary to read the records and store the temperatures in TEMPS.

10. Write the instructions to count the number of months in which the average was above 70 degrees and the number of months in which the average was below 32 degrees.Store these counts in the appropriate fields.

11. Modify the code in 5.1.2 to sort an array of halfwords.

5.2 SEARCHING AND LOOPING

In this section, we examine the common search algorithms and cover some special purpose looping instructions. The search algorithms we will implement are linear search, linear search with a sentinel, and binary search. The looping instructions are designed to combine the incrementation of an array index with a test for end of loop. We find that they are somewhat awkward to use, but they provide loops that execute much more quickly than those using separate increment and compare steps.

Linear Search

Suppose that X represents an array of fullwords and that the number of entries currently in X is stored in a fullword field named NUMENTS. KEY is a fullword field containing a value which may be in the array. If KEY is in X, we want to place its index in INDEX. Otherwise, we will set INDEX equal to −1.

A standard linear search algorithm, using indexing instead of subscripts, is shown below. Note that we quit searching when INDEX gets to the end of the array. This requires us to make an additional check at the end to determine whether the key was found. If not, we set INDEX equal to −1.

```
INDEX = 0
WHILE (X(INDEX) <> KEY) AND (INDEX < (NUMENTS*L'X) DO
    INDEX = INDEX+L'X
END WHILE
IF INDEX = NUMENTS*L'X
THEN
    INDEX = -1
ENDIF
```

Notice that the loop above will terminate if KEY is found. If KEY is not in the array, INDEX will eventually become NUMENTS * L'X. This index value designates the first byte after the array. If this value is achieved, then INDEX is set equal to -1 at the end of the loop.

In order to implement this in assembly language, we must provide a register for the value INDEX during loop execution. The comparison also requires that KEY be in a register. Finally, we will need a register to hold the value NUMENTS-L'X for the second comparison in the WHILE condition. Using RB, R2, and R3 for these three purposes, the algorithm becomes

```
R2 = KEY
RB = 0
R3 = NUMENTS*L'X
WHILE (X(RB) <> R2) AND (RB < R3) DO
    RB = RB+L'X
END WHILE
IF RB = R3
THEN
    INDEX = -1
ELSE
    INDEX = RB
ENDIF
```

Translating this to assembly language, we have

```
                L       R2,KEY          R2 = KEY
                L       RB,=F'0'        RB = 0
                L       R3,NUMENTS      R3 = NUMENTS*L'X
                MH      R3,=H'4'        :
                LA      RA,WHILE01      :
WHILE01         EQU     *               WHILE (X(RB) <> R2)
                C       R2,X(RB)            AND (RB < R3) DO
                BE      ENDWHL01        :
                CR      RB,R3           :
                BNL     ENDWHL01        :
                LA      RB,L'X(RB)      RB = RB+L'X
                BR      RA              :
ENDWHL01        EQU     *               END WHILE
```

```
IF00      EQU    *               IF RB = R3
          CR     RB,R3           :
          BNE    ELSE00          :
THEN00    EQU    *               THEN
          MVC    INDEX,=F'-1'        INDEX = -1
          B      ENDIF00             :
ELSE00    EQU    *               ELSE
          ST     RB,INDEX            INDEX = RB

ENDIF00   EQU    *               ENDIF
```

Linear Search with a Sentinel

In a high-level language, we implement a linear search with a sentinel on an array, X[1] . . . X[N], by adding an extra position, X[N+1], to the array. Before beginning the search, we set X[N+1] equal to the search key. During the search itself, we are guaranteed that the key will be found. This allows us to simplify the loop entry condition. Using indexing, we have the following algorithm.

```
X(NUMENTS*L'X) = KEY
INDEX = 0
WHILE (X(INDEX) <> KEY) DO
    INDEX = INDEX+L'X
END WHILE
IF INDEX = NUMENTS*L'X
THEN
    INDEX = -1
ENDIF
```

Adding registers as above, we have

```
R2 = KEY
RA = NUMENTS*L'X
X(RA) = R2
RB = 0
WHILE (X(RB) <> R2) DO
    RB = RB+L'X
END WHILE
IF RB = RA
THEN
    INDEX = -1
ELSE
    INDEX = RB
ENDIF
```

The code to implement this algorithm is

```
            L       R2,KEY              R2 = KEY
            L       RA,NUMENTS          RA = NUMENTS*L'X
            MH      RA,=H'4'
            ST      R2,X(RA)            X(RA) = R2
            L       RB,=F'0'            RB = 0
            LA      R9                  :
WHILE01     EQU     *                   WHILE (X(RB) <> R2) DO
            C       R2,X(RB)            :
            BE      ENDWHL01            :
            LA      RB,L'X(RB)          RB = RB+L'X
            BR      R9                  :
ENDWHL01    EQU     *                   END WHILE
IF00        EQU     *                   IF RB = RA
            CR      RB,RA               :
            BNE     ELSE00              :
THEN00      EQU     *                   THEN
            MVC     INDEX,=F'-1'        INDEX = -1
            B       ENDIF00             :
ELSE00      EQU     *                   ELSE
            ST      RB,INDEX            INDEX = RB
ENDIF00     EQU     *                   ENDIF
```

Binary Search

When searching for an element in an array which has been sorted, we can considerably reduce the search time by using a binary search. Using index values, the search proceeds as follows.

```
LOINDEX = 0
HIINDEX = (NUMENTS-1)*L'X
REPEAT
    MIDINDEX = ((LOINDEX+HIINDEX) DIV (2*L'X))*L'X
    IF KEY < X(MIDINDEX)
    THEN
        HIINDEX = MIDINDEX-L'X
    ELSE
        LOINDEX = MIDINDEX+L'X
    ENDIF
UNTIL KEY = X(MIDINDEX) OR (HIINDEX < LOINDEX)
IF KEY = X(MIDINDEX)
THEN
    INDEX = MIDINDEX
ELSE
    INDEX = -1
ENDIF
```

Note the computation of MIDINDEX. The indices must be multiples of L'X. In order to find the middle index, we divide by both L'X and 2. The result is the number of the middle entry (counting from 0). This is converted to an index by multiplying by L'X.

Before generating the assembly code, we replace the indices with registers R9, RA, and RB. We also place the value of KEY in a register for the comparison. This yields the following code segment.

```
          L      R2,KEY              R2 = KEY
          SR     RA,RA               RA = 0
          L      RB,NUMENTS          RB = (NUMENTS−1)*L'X
          BCTR   RB,0                  :
          SLA    RB,2                  :
          LA     R8,REPEAT00           :
REPEAT00  EQU    *                   REPEAT
          LA     R9,0(RA,RB)           R9 = ((RA+RB) DIV (2*L'X))*L'X
          SRA    R9,3                  :
          SLA    R9,2                  :
IF00      EQU    *                   IF R2 < X(R9)
          C      R2,X(R9)              :
          BNL    ELSE00                :
THEN00    EQU    *                   THEN
          LR     RB,R9                  RB = R9−L'X
          SH     RB,=H'4'               :
          B      ENDIF00                :
ELSE00    EQU    *                   ELSE
          LA     RA,L'X(R9)             RA = R9+L'X
ENDIF00   EQU    *                   ENDIF
          C      R2,X(R9)              :
          BE     UNTIL00               :
          CR     RB,RA                 :
          BNLR   R8                    :
UNTIL00   EQU    *                   UNTIL R2 = X(R9) OR (RB < RA)
IF01      EQU    *                   IF R2 = X(R9)
          C      R2,X(R9)              :
          BNE    ELSE01                :
THEN01    EQU    *                   THEN
          ST     R9,INDEX               INDEX = R9
          B      ENDIF01                :
ELSE01    EQU    *                   ELSE
          MVC    INDEX,=F'−1'           INDEX = −1
ENDIF01   EQU    *                   ENDIF
```

This code illustrates the use of LA to add the values in two registers and place the result in a third register. Because it uses the address computation mechanism, it can only be used if it is certain that the sum will not exceed 3 bytes. That is certainly the case here, where the sum is an index into an array.

Looping Instructions

Since the manipulation of arrays often requires both the use of an index register and a looping construct, the System 370 instruction set provides several instructions that combine these two operations. The first of these instructions, BXLE, increments an index register and branches if the new value is less than or equal to a specified value. The second instruction, BXH, branches if the result is greater than the specified value.

Branch on indeX Low or Equal *BXLE RS*

$$\text{BXLE} \qquad R_1, R_3, S_2(B_2)$$

If R_3 is even, then it designates an even-odd pair of registers. The even register contains an increment and the following odd register contains a value for comparison. If R_3 is odd, then the value in R_3 is used for both incrementation and comparison.

The instruction adds the increment to the value in R_1 and stores the result in R_1. If the new value in R_1 is less than or equal to the comparison value, the address determined by the storage operand is placed in the Instruction Address part of the PSW. This causes a branch to the indicated address. If the new value in R_1 is greater than the comparison value, then no branch occurs.

Example 5.2.1

```
BXLE    RA,R4,FTEST00
```

As the second register operand is an even register, its value is used as the increment. The comparison value is taken from the following odd register, R5. This instruction is equivalent to the following sequence of instructions.

```
AR      RA,R4
CR      RA,R5
BNH     FTEST00
```

Example 5.2.2

```
BXLE    RA,R5,FTEST00
```

The second register operand is an odd register, so its value is used as both the increment and the comparison value. This instruction is equivalent to the following sequence of instructions.

```
AR      RA,R5
CR      RA,R5
BNH     FTEST00
```

In order to see the advantages of using BXLE to create a looping construct, recall the following loop from the selection sort in 5.1.

```
FOR01      EQU  *                              FOR RA = RB+L'SCORE
           LA   ULIM01,L'SCORE*(NUMSTU−1)         TO L'SCORE *
           LA   RA,L'SCORE(RB)                     NUMSTU−1) BY
FTEST01    EQU  *                                 L'SCORE
           C    RA,ULIM01                          :
           BH   ENDFOR01                           :

     <Range of loop>

           LA   RA,L'SCORE(RA)                     :
           B    FTEST01                            :
ENDFOR01   EQU  *                              ENDFOR
```

We can recreate this loop using BXLE by putting the increment value, L'SCORE, in an even register, say R4, and the upper limit, L'SCORE*(NUMSTU−1), in R5.

```
FOR01      EQU  *                              FOR RA = RB+L'SCORE
           LA   R5,L'SCORE*(NUMSTU−1)             TO L'SCORE *
           LA   R4,L'SCORE                        (NUMSTU−1) BY
           LA   RA,L'SCORE(RB)                    L'SCORE
FTEST01    EQU  *                                 :

           <Range of loop>

           BXLE RA,R4,FTEST01                      :
ENDFOR01   EQU  *                              ENDFOR
```

Note that the loop is bottom-tested rather than top-tested. We can remedy this deficiency if necessary by including the instructions

```
           CR   RA,R5                              :
           BH   ENDFOR01                           :
```

immediately before FTEST01. This adds two instructions to the overall program, but within the loop itself, the incrementation, comparison, and branch are still effected by the single BXLE instruction.

The alternate form of BXLE uses the same register for both the increment and the limit. This can be employed to create a loop which begins at the upper limit and counts down to zero by using a negative increment. For example, suppose that we want to process the SCORE array from 4.1 with the following loop.

FOR RA = L'SCORE*(NUMSTU−1) TO 0 BY −L'SCORE

    <Range of loop>

ENDFOR

This loop can be implemented by placing −L'SCORE in an odd register and using that register as the second register operand in a BXLE instruction. As the branch will only take place when the value in RA is not greater than −L'SCORE, we use the

BXLE instruction to test for the exit condition. We initialize the counter with the proper initial value, so the loop must be executed one time before the BXLE instruction is invoked. Thus, we place the instruction at the bottom of the loop and use an unconditional branch to return to the top of the loop.

```
FOR01       EQU   *                              FOR RA = L'SCORE *
            LH    R5,=H'-4'                       (NUMSTU-1) TO 0 BY
            LA    RA,L'SCORE*(NUMSTU-1)           -L'SCORE
FTEST01     EQU   *                                   :

            <Range of loop>

            BXLE  RA,R5,ENDFOR01                      :
            B     FTEST01                             :
ENDFOR01    EQU   *                              ENDFOR
```

This loop has the disadvantage of an additional branch instruction. There is an instruction that allows us to create a count-down loop without the additional branch. This new instruction branches if the new value of the first register operand is greater than the comparison value.

Branch on indeX High *BXH RS*

$$\text{BXH} \quad R_1, R_3, S_2(B_2)$$

If R_3 is even, then it designates an even-odd pair of registers. The even register contains an increment and the following odd register contains a value for comparison. If R_3 is odd, then the value in R_3 is used for both incrementation and comparison.

The instruction adds the increment to the value in R_1 and stores the result in R_1. If the new value in R_1 is greater than the comparison value, the address determined by the storage operand is placed in the Instruction Address part of the PSW. This causes a branch to the indicated address. If the new value in R_1 is less than or equal to the comparison value, then no branch occurs.

Using BXH, we can recreate the last loop construct in the following way.

```
FOR01       EQU   *                              FOR RA = L'SCORE *
            LH    R5,=H'-4'                       (NUMSTU-1) TO 0 BY
            LA    RA,L'SCORE*(NUMSTU-1)           -L'SCORE
            CR    RA,R5                               :
            BNH   ENDFOR01                            :
FTEST01     EQU   *                                   :

            <Range of loop>

            BXH   RA,R5,FTEST01                       :
ENDFOR01    EQU   *                              ENDFOR
```

Finally, we observe that we can use BXH to create a second version of the original loop.

```
FOR01     EQU  *                          FOR RA = RB+L'SCORE
          LA   R5,L'SCORE*(NUMSTU−1)        TO L'SCORE *
          LA   R4,L'SCORE                   (NUMSTU−1) BY
          LA   RA,L'SCORE(RB)               L'SCORE
FTEST01   EQU  *                            :

          <Range of loop>

          BXH  RA,R4,ENDFOR01               :
          B    FTEST01                      :
ENDFOR01  EQU  *                          ENDFOR
```

E   X   E   R   C   I   S   E   S

Use the following symbol and storage definitions for Exercises 1-3

```
NUMSTU   EQU   100
STUNO    DS    (NUMSTU)F
STUSUB   DS    F
LOOKUP   DS    F
```

1. Assuming that subscripts for STUNO begin with 1, write instructions to perform a linear search of STUNO for LOOKUP. If it is found, store the corresponding subscript in STUSUB. If it is not found, set STUSUB to 0.

2. Repeat Exercise 1, using a linear search with a sentinel.

3. Repeat Exercise 1, using a binary search.

Write code segments using BXLE or BXH to implement each of the following counted loops.

4. FOR R4 = 0 TO 90 BY 1

5. FOR R7 = 25 TO −1 BY −1

6. FOR R6 = 0 TO 30 BY 5

7. FOR R7 = 100 TO 0 BY −10

5.3 TWO-DIMENSIONAL ARRAYS

The usual model for a computer memory is a large one-dimensional array. The addresses are the subscripts and the contents of the addressed memory locations are the values stored in the array. It is not surprising that implementing one-dimensional arrays in assembly language is relatively straightforward. As we do not think of computer memories in two-dimensional terms, we need to put more effort into creating two-dimensional arrays.

The simplest approach is to view a two-dimensional array as *an array of one-dimensional arrays*. For example, if the array is stored row by row (row major order), we can view the entire array as a one-dimensional array of rows. In order to form the address of a particular entry, we first find the starting address of the row containing the entry. Then we find the offset from the beginning of the row to the entry we want. Both of these steps are one-dimensional addressing operations.

In order to clarify this view of two-dimensional arrays, suppose we have the following set of generic definitions.

```
ROW1      EQU    1                 FIRST ROW SUBSCRIPT
ROWN      EQU    10                LAST ROW SUBSCRIPT
COL1      EQU    1                 FIRST COLUMN SUBSCRIPT
COLN      EQU    4                 LAST COLUMN SUBSCRIPT
ROWS      EQU    ROWN-ROW1+1       NUMBER OF ROWS
COLS      EQU    COLN-COL1+1       NUMBER OF COLUMNS
ENTRYLN   EQU    4                 LENGTH OF EACH ENTRY
ROWLEN    EQU    COLS*ENTRYLN      LENGTH OF A ROW
   .
   .
   .
ROW       DS     F
COL       DS     F
TABLE     DS     (ROWS*COLS)F
```

Assuming that the entries are stored in row major order, we consider the problem of addressing TABLE<ROW,COL>.

Viewing TABLE as a one-dimensional array of rows, we find the starting address of row number ROW. As we saw in the last section, this is the starting address of TABLE plus (ROW−ROW1) times the length of each row. This gives

$$\text{TABLE}+(\text{ROW}-\text{ROW1})*\text{ROWLEN}$$

In order to find the desired entry in this row, we add the starting address of the row and (COL−COL1) times the length of each entry in the row.

$$\text{TABLE}+(\text{ROW}-\text{ROW1})*\text{ROWLEN}+(\text{COL}-\text{COL1})*\text{ENTRYLN}$$

This relationship is illustrated in Figure 5.3.1

FIGURE 5.3.1   Locating an Entry in a Two-Dimensional Array

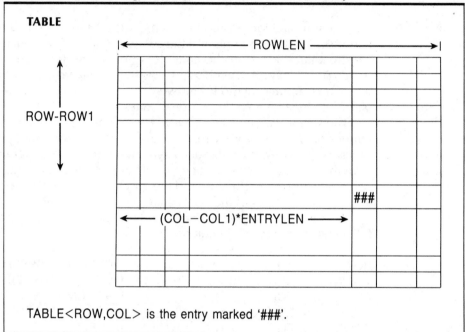

TABLE<ROW,COL> is the entry marked '###'.

If TABLE is stored in column major order, we simply reverse the rolls of rows and columns in the formula above. TABLE<ROW,COL> begins at

$$TABLE+(COL-COL1)*COLLEN+(ROW-ROW1)*ENTRYLN$$

Assuming once again that TABLE is in row major order, suppose we need to load TABLE<ROW,COL> into a register. Referring to the first formula, the most direct approach is to compute the value

$$(ROW-ROW1)*ROWLEN+(COL-COL1)*ENTRYLN =$$
$$(ROW-ROW1)*COLS*ENTRYLN+(COL-COL1)*ENTRYLN =$$
$$((ROW-ROW1)*COLS+(COL-COL1))*ENTRYLN$$

and place it in a register. We can then use the register as the index register in a Load instruction.

The only difficulty we encounter is that, because ROW1 and COL1 are defined with EQUs, there is no convenient way to subtract them from ROW and COL. We encounter similar difficulties with ROWLEN and ENTRYLN. These absolute symbols cannot be used in arithmetic computations during execution. Fortunately, the assembler provides a mechanism that allows us to put the value of an absolute symbol in a fullword field.

Address Constants

An A-type address constant is intended to allow us to set up fields containing addresses. We use them for this purpose in the next chapter, when we implement procedure calls with reference parameters. At this point, we will take advantage of the fact that the assembler views the address of an absolute expression as being the value of the expression itself. Thus, it will store that value in a fullword field.

The format of an A-type address constant is

```
<label>      DC       A(<expression>[,<expression> . . . ])
```

The expressions may be absolute or relocatable. When a relocatable expression is used, the address can not be determined until it is known where the program will be loaded. In this case, the assembler simply reserves a fullword. The address is filled in later. When an absolute expression is used, the value of that expression is used to initialize the field.

The A-type address constant is supplemented by a Y-type address constant. The Y-type constant is manipulated in the same way by the assembler. In this case, however, the value is stored in a halfword rather than a fullword. This is often useful when we want to use a small constant as the second operand in an MH instruction.

Both the A- and Y-type address constants can appear as literal operands.

Accessing Tables in Assembly Language

The assembly language instructions below show how this expression can be evaluated in RB. RB is then used as an index register to load the desired entry of the array into R3.

```
         L       RB,ROW          R3 = TABLE<ROW,COL>
         S       RB,FROW1        :
         MH      RB,=Y(COLS)     :
         A       RB,COL          :
         S       RB,FCOL1        :
         MH      RB,=Y(ENTRYLN)  :
         L       R3,TABLE(RB)    :
```

When the array dimensions begin with (0,0), the code can be abbreviated.

```
         L       RB,ROW          R3 = TABLE<ROW,COL>
         MH      RB,=Y(COLS)     :
         A       RB,COL          :
         MH      RB,=Y(ENTRYLN)  :
         L       R3,TABLE(RB)    :
```

Example 5.3.1 *Write the code to print the following array in row major order, one entry per line together with the row and column number for each entry.*

```
MAXROW    EQU    5
MAXCOL    EQU    6
TABLE     DS     ((MAXROW+1)*(MAXCOL+1))F
```

An algorithm to solve this problem is

```
FOR ROW = 0 TO MAXROW
    FOR COL = 0 TO MAXCOL
        PRINT ROW, COL, TABLE<ROW,COL>
    ENDFOR
ENDFOR
```

In order to implement this algorithm, we need the following field and symbol definitions.

```
PSUBLEN    EQU    2                              SYMBOLIC CONSTANTS
PENTLEN    EQU    5                              :
ROWOFF     EQU    20                             :
COLOFF     EQU    25                             :
ENTRYOFF   EQU    35                             :
COLS       EQU    MAXCOL+1                        :
*
SUBMSK     DC     X'40202120'                    EDIT MASKS
ENTRYMSK   DC     X'40202020202020202120'        :
*
*
DWORK      DS     D                              VARIABLES
PCKSUB     DS     PL(PSUBLEN)                     :
PCKENTRY   DS     PL(PENTLEN)                     :
*
LINE       DC     CL133' '                       OUTPUT LINE
           ORG    LINE+ROWOFF                     :
OUTROW     DS     CL(L'SUBMSK)                    :
           ORG    LINE+COLOFF                     :
OUTCOL     DS     CL(L'SUBMSK)                    :
           ORG    LINE+ENTRYOFF                   :
OUTENTRY   DS     CL(L'ENTRYMSK)                  :
           ORG    LINE+L'LINE                     :
```

We will use the code developed above to access an arbitrary entry of this array. As the loop itself requires a large number of operations, the amount of time saved by the use of the special branch instructions would be negligible. Thus, we implement the loops with explicit comparisons and the Branch on Condition mnemonics instead of the BCR mnemonics.

```
FOR00      EQU    *                    FOR ROW = 0 TO MAXROW
           MVC    ROW,=F'0'            :
FTEST00    EQU    *                    :
           LA     R3,MAXROW            :
           C      R3,ROW               :
           BL     ENDFOR00             :
FOR01      EQU    *                    FOR COL = 0 TO MAXCOL
           MVC    COL,=F'0'            :
FTEST01    EQU    *                    :
           LA     R3,MAXCOL            :
           C      R3,COL               :
           BL     ENDFOR01             :
           L      R2,ROW               OUTROW = ROW
           CVD    R2,DWORK             :
           ZAP    PCKSUB,DWORK         :
           MVC    OUTROW,SUBMSK        :
           ED     OUTROW,PCKSUB        :
           L      R2,COL               OUTCOL = COL
           CVD    R2,DWORK             :
           ZAP    PCKSUB,DWORK         :
           MVC    OUTCOL,SUBMSK        :
           ED     OUTCOL,PCKSUB        :
           L      RB,ROW               OUTENTRY =
           MH     RB,=Y(COLS)          TABLE<ROW,COL>
           A      RB,COL               :
           MH     RB,=Y(L'TABLE)       :
           L      R2,TABLE(RB)         :
           CVD    R2,DWORK             :
           ZAP    PCKENTRY,DWORK       :
           MVC    OUTENTRY,ENTRYMSK    :
           ED     OUTENTRY,PCKENTRY    :
           PUT    PRINTER,LINE         PRINT LINE
           L      R3,COL               :
           LA     R3,1(R3)             :
           ST     R3,COL               :
           B      FTEST01              :
ENDFOR01   EQU    *                    ENDFOR
           L      R3,ROW               :
           LA     R3,1(R3)             :
           ST     R3,ROW               :
           B      FTEST00              :
ENDFOR00   EQU    *                    ENDFOR
```

Although the last example uses the code developed for random access, if the array is stored in row major order, we are actually proceeding through the elements in the order in which they are stored. Under these circumstances, we can simplify the address computations. We initialize an index register to 0, and print the entire array by incrementing this register by L'TABLE as each entry is printed.

Example 5.3.2 *Find the sum of all entries in the array, TABLE, in Example 5.3.1.*

In this case, we do not need the variables ROW and COL. We can process the entire array with a single loop. This is equivalent to viewing TABLE as a one-dimensional array with (MAXROW+1) * (MAXCOL+1) entries.

```
R2 = 0
FOR RB = 0 TO ((MAXROW+1)*(MAXCOL+1)−1)*L'TABLE BY L'TABLE
    R2 = R2+TABLE(RB)
ENDFOR
SUM = R2
```

We will use registers R4 and R5 to support the BXLE instruction. The resulting assembly language code is

```
              LA     R2,0                      R2 = 0
FOR00         EQU    *                         FOR RB = 0 TO ((MAXROW+1)*
              LA     RB,0                          (MAXCOL+1)−1)*L'TABLE BY
              LA     R5,((MAXROW+1)*(MAXCOL+1)−1)*L'TABLE     L'TABLE
              LA     R4,L'TABLE                :
FTEST00       EQU    *                         :
              A      R2,TABLE(RB)              R2 = R2+TABLE(RB)
              BXLE   RB,R4,FTEST00             :
ENDFOR00      EQU    *                         ENDFOR
              ST     R2,SUM                    SUM = R2
```

Explicit Base Registers

Although we can perform all necessary operations on a two-dimensional array with a single index register, it is, in a sense, unnatural. It would seem more natural if we could specify two index registers, one to find the beginning of a row and the other to specify a particular entry in the row. Unfortunately, this is not possible. There is, however, a reasonable alternative in which we specify both a Base register and an Index register.

In the assembly language format for any RX or SS instruction, we can specify an explicit base register provided that the displacement symbol is absolute. This provides several additional operand formats.

First operand in a SS instruction:	$A_1(L_1,B_1)$ or $A_1(,B_1)$
Second operand in an SS_1 instruction:	$A_2(B_1)$
Second operand in an SS_2 instruction:	$A_2(L_2,B_2)$ or $A_2(,B_2)$
Second operand in an RX instruction:	$A_2(B_2)$ or $A_2(B_2,X_2)$ or $A(,X_2)$

A_i represents an absolute symbol, L_i a length, B_i a base register, and X_2 an index register. When a base register or index register is omitted, the assembler uses register 0. When R0 is used as a base register, no base address is added to the displacement. When R0 is used as an index register, no indexing takes place.

In the RX instructions, we can specify both a base register and an index register. For example,

L   R1,0(RA,RB)

RA is an explicit base register and RB an index register. The address computation is as usual,

Address = 0 + contents(RA) + contents(RB)

This allows us to deal with two-dimensional arrays in a more natural way. If RA contains the address of the beginning of a row and RB the number of bytes from the beginning of that row to a desired entry, then this instruction will load that entry into R1.

Recalling the generic table we considered at the beginning of this section, in order to load TABLE<ROW,COL> into a register, we place the address of the beginning of row ROW in one register, the distance from the beginning of that row to TABLE<ROW,COL> in a second register, and write a Load instruction like the one above.

```
L      RA,ROW          PUT ADDRESS OF TABLE<ROW,COL1>
SH     RA,=Y(ROW1)     INTO RA
MH     RA,=Y(ROWLEN)   :
LA     RA,TABLE(RA)    :
L      RB,COL          PUT INDEX FROM TABLE<ROW,COL1>
SH     RB,=Y(COL1)     TO TABLE<ROW,COL> INTO RB
MH     RB,=Y(ENTRYLN)  :
L      R3,0(RA,RB)     R3 = TABLE<ROW,COL>
```

The first three instructions compute, in RA, the index from the beginning of TABLE to the beginning of the desired row. The LA instruction adds this index to the starting address of TABLE to get the address of TABLE<ROW,COL1>. This address is returned to RA. In order to represent this relationship, we adopt the notation A'<field name> to represent the address of a field. In the example above, we would write RA = A'TABLE. (Note that this is a notation we shall use for documentation only—it is not recognized by the assembler.)

We conclude this section with an example that illustrates the use of an explicit base register to access a two-dimensional array.

Example 5.3.3 *Suppose that we have a two-dimensional array, SCORE, which contains test scores for a class of NUMSTU students on NUMTEST tests. Find each student's average, rounded to the nearest integer, and store the averages in a one-dimensional array, AVERAGE.*

The algorithm to solve this problem is routine.

```
FOR STUDENT = 1 TO NUMSTU
    SUM = 0
    FOR TEST = 1 TO NUMTEST
        SUM = SUM+SCORE<STUDENT,TEST>
    ENDFOR
    AVERAGE<STUDENT> = SUM/NUMTEST
ENDFOR
```

We assume that, as may often be the case, the arrays have been defined to be large enough to accommodate the maximum number of students and tests anticipated. Thus, we provide symbolic constants, MAXSTU and MAXTEST to be used in defining the arrays, but we assume that the actual number of students and tests are stored in fullword fields NUMSTU and NUMTEST.

```
MAXSTU     EQU    50
MAXTEST    EQU    10
ENTRYLN    EQU    4
ROWLEN     EQU    ENTRYLN*MAXTEST
*
NUMSTU     DS     F
NUMTEST    DS     F
*
AVERAGE    DS     (MAXSTU)F
SCORE      DS     (MAXSTU*MAXTEST)F
```

Before we implement the algorithm, we need to determine register usage. We will use R2 for STUDENT, R3 for TEST, R4 for SUM, and the register pair R4,R5 for the division. On each pass of the outer loop, we assign the address of SCORE <STUDENT,1> to RB and use this as an explicit base register to access the test scores in this row. RA will be used to index individual test scores. Finally, being somewhat extravagant, we shall use one more register, R9, to index entries in AVERAGE. With these clarifications, our algorithm becomes

```
R9 = 0
FOR R2 = 1 TO NUMSTU
    R4 = 0
    RB = A'SCORE<R2,1>
    RA = 0
    FOR R3 = 1 TO NUMTEST
        R4 = R4+0(RB,RA)
        RA = RA+L'SCORE
    ENDFOR
    AVERAGE(R9) = R4/NUMTEST
    R9 = R9+L'AVERAGE
ENDFOR
```

```
              LA      R9,0              R9 = 0
FOR00         EQU     *                 FOR R2 = 1 TO NUMSTU
              LA      R2,1              :
FTEST00       EQU     *                 :
              C       R2,NUMSTU         :
              BH      ENDFOR00          :
              LA      R4,0              R4 = 0
              LR      RB,R2             RB = A'SCORE<R2,1>
              BCTR    RB,0              :
              MH      RB,=Y(ROWLEN)     :
              LA      RB,SCORE(RB)      :
              LA      RA,0              RA = 0
FOR01         EQU     *                 FOR R3 = 1 TO NUMTEST
              LA      R3,1              :
FTEST01       EQU     *                 :
              C       R3,NUMTEST        :
              BH      ENDFOR01          :
              A       R4,O(RB,RA)       R4 = R4+0(RB,RA)
              LA      RA,L'SCORE(RA)    RA = RA+L'SCORE
              LA      R3,1(R3)          :
              B       FTEST01           :
ENDFOR01      EQU     *                 ENDFOR
              SRDA    R4,32             AVERAGE(R9) = R4/NUMTEST
              SLDA    R4,1              :
              D       R4,NUMTEST        :
              LA      R5,1(R5)          :
              SRA     R5,1              :
              ST      R5,AVERAGE(R9)    :
              LA      R9,L'AVERAGE(R9)  R9 = R9+L'AVERAGE
              LA      R2,1(R2)          :
              B       FTEST00           :
ENDFOR00      EQU     *                 ENDFOR
```

E   X   E   R   C   I   S   E   S

Use the following symbol and storage definitions for the exercises below.

NUMSTU	EQU	25
NUMTST	EQU	6
ENTLEN	EQU	4
TOTAL	DS	F
MAXSCORE	DS	F
KEY	DS	F
STUDENT	DS	F
TEST	DS	F

```
CLASSAVG   DS      (NUMTST)F
STUDAVG    DS      (NUMSTU)F
HIGHEST    DS      (NUMTST)F
SCORES     DS      (NUMSTU*NUMTST) F
```

Assume that the table SCORES has been loaded in row major order. Each row contains all the test scores for one student. Each column contains the test scores for the entire class on one test.

1. Write the instructions to find the highest test score in the table and store it in MAXSCORE. Store the corresponding test number in TEST and the student's number in STUDENT.

2. Write the code to find the highest score on each test and store it in the appropriate entry of HIGHEST.

3. Write the code to find each student's average on all tests. Store these averages in STUDAVG.

4. Write the code to find the class average on each test and store it in the correct position in CLASSAVG.

5. Assuming that STUDENT contains a value from 1 to NUMSTU and that TEST contains a value from 1 to NUMTST, write the code to print SCORES<STUDENT,TEST>.

6. Assuming that STUDENT contains a value from 1 to NUMSTU, write the code to print all the test scores for that student one per line.

7. Assuming that TEST contains a value from 1 to NUMTST, write the code to print the score of every student on that test. Print the values one per line.

8. Write the code to find each student's average on all tests, omitting that student's lowest score. Store these averages in STUDAVG.

5.4 GENERAL ARRAYS

Now that we have covered arrays of fullwords and halfwords, we turn our attention to more general arrays. We will be concentrating on arrays of packed decimal numbers and character strings. However, the methods are easily generalized to arrays containing other types of data. In the next section, we consider arrays of record structures.

Suppose that we have the following instructions.

```
ENTRYLEN   EQU     6
NUMENTS    EQU     25
PVECTOR    DS      (NUMENTS)PL(ENTRYLEN)
```

The DS directive instructs the assembler to reserve storage for 25 entries each of which is ENTRYLEN bytes long. PVECTOR represents the beginning of this storage area. The length factor recorded for PVECTOR is 6. We can use the reserved data area to store up to 25 packed decimal numbers.

As we did with arrays of fullwords, we use angular brackets to denote subscripts. The relationship between a subscripted entry and an offset from the beginning of PVECTOR is analogous to the case of arrays of fullwords. If we view the subscripts as beginning with 0, this relationship is as shown below.

FIGURE 5.4.1 An Array of Packed Decimal Numbers

Entry	Offset
PVECTOR<0>	PVECTOR
PVECTOR<1>	PVECTOR+1*L'PVECTOR
PVECTOR<2>	PVECTOR+2*L'PVECTOR
.	.
.	.
.	.
PVECTOR<I>	PVECTOR+I*L'PVECTOR

If we view the subscripts as beginning at another value, LOWER, then the element PVECTOR<I> will begin at PVECTOR+(I−LOWER)*L'PVECTOR.

Because the RX instructions only manipulate binary data, we cannot use them to access the array PVECTOR directly. The SS instructions that do manipulate packed decimal and character data cannot be indexed. However, we can use the LA instruction with an index register to place the address of an indexed entry of PVECTOR in a second register, then use that register as an explicit base register in an SS instruction. For example, suppose that R3 contains an index into PVECTOR and that we need to add the entry PVECTOR(R3) to a packed field SUM. The instruction

        LA   RB,PVECTOR(R3)

places the address of the indexed entry in RB. We may think of RB as a pointer to the desired entry of PVECTOR. The instruction

        AP   SUM,0(L'PVECTOR,RB)

will add the correct entry to SUM. As AP is a two length SS instruction, it is necessary to include the length factor in the second operand.

While this works correctly, it is not entirely satisfactory. It is not obvious from reading the instruction that the second operand is actually an entry in PVECTOR. We need some mechanism that makes this reference obvious. That is, we are looking for a way to give a meaningful name to the operand 0(L'PVECTOR,RB). This can be accomplished through the use of DSECTs and the USING instruction.

Control Sections and Dummy Sections

A DSECT is a section of code that describes a storage area without allocating any space. This is in contrast to a CSECT or Control Section, in which space is allocated both for instructions and for data. All of the programs we have considered to this point have consisted of a single CSECT. In general, an assembler program can contain several CSECTS and DSECTS. Each DSECT can be used to describe a storage area that is allocated elsewhere. In the case of arrays, we can use a DSECT to describe each entry. The space for the array will be allocated in a CSECT. As the definition of the array entry is not bound to a particular location, it can be used to describe and access any entry of the array.

A CSECT is initiated by a CSECT directive or by the START directive. START is used to begin the main CSECT in a program. Thus, the instruction

```
GRADER     START   0
```

begins a CSECT named GRADER. Other CSECTS are initiated or continued with the CSECT directive. The format is

```
<name>     CSECT
```

A DSECT is initiated by the assembler directive DSECT. It is terminated by the beginning of another DSECT, a CSECT, or the END directive. When the assembler encounters the beginning of a new DSECT or CSECT, it saves the current value of the location counter and reinitializes the location counter to 0. Throughout the definition of the DSECT, the location counter is manipulated as usual. The offset entered as each field is defined is the distance from the beginning of the DSECT to that field.

The format of the DSECT directive is

```
<name>     DSECT
```

To describe the entries in the array PVECTOR, assuming that the name on the START instruction was ARRAYPRG, we might use

```
PVSECT     DSECT
PVENTRY    DS      PL(ENTRYLEN)
ARRAYPRG   CSECT
```

In processing this DSECT, the assembler records PVENTRY as having offset 0 and length indicated by ENTRYLEN. The last instruction terminates the DSECT definition and continues definition of the main program.

If we place this DSECT before the data areas in our program, then the array itself can be defined with the instruction

```
PVECTOR    DS      (NUMENTS)PL(L'PVENTRY)
```

In our sample programs, we place DSECTs immediately after the symbolic constant definitions. Each DSECT will be terminated by the beginning of another DSECT or by the continuation of the main CSECT, as in the example above.

Accessing Arrays Using DSECTs

In order to access an array entry using a DSECT, we place the address of the desired entry in a register. We must also tell the assembler to use that register as the base register for any field defined in the DSECT. This is done with the USING instruction in the following format.

        USING   <DSECT name>,<register>

For example,

        USING   PVSECT,RB

While this USING instruction is in effect, the assembler will supply RB as the implied base register with every field name from PVSECT. The displacement used will be the offset from the beginning of PVSECT to the indicated field. When a length is required, the assembler will use the defined length of the field.

In this case, the only field in PVSECT is PVENTRY. Any reference to this field will be assembled with an offset of 0 and the defined length of PVSECT. The assembler will use RB as the base register as long as the USING instruction is in effect. Thus

        AP   SUM,PVENTRY

will result in the same code as the original instruction:

        AP   SUM,0(L'PVECTOR,RB)

Note that a reference to PVENTRY only makes sense if RB contains the address of an entry in the array. Unfortunately, there is no way for the assembler to check this. The USING instruction is effective at the time the program is assembled. The assembler cannot predict what value will be in RB when the AP instruction above is executed. This also implies that the order in which the USING instruction and the instruction to load the address into RB appear in the program is irrelevant.

Once established, a USING instruction remains in effect until the base register is explicitly dropped by a DROP instruction or used in another USING instruction. The format of the DROP instruction is

        DROP   <register>[,<register> . . .]

as in

        DROP   RB

or

    DROP   R9,RA,RB

The part of the program that is textually between the USING and DROP instructions is called the domain of the USING instruction. The DSECT itself is called the range of the USING instruction. This relationship is illustrated in Figure 5.4.2.

FIGURE 5.4.2   The Domain and Range of a USING Instruction.

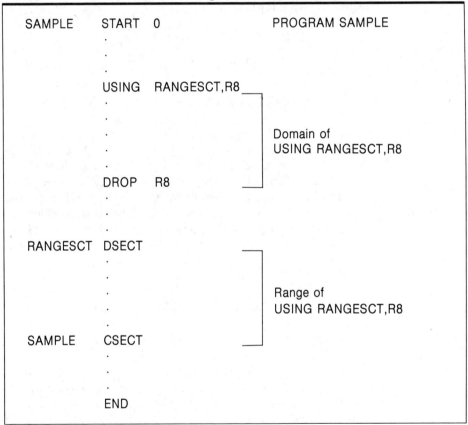

Within the domain of a USING instruction, any field in the range may be referenced. Outside of the domain, such references will be flagged by the assembler as addressability errors.

It is possible to have different USING instructions in effect that provide base registers for the same DSECT. In this case, the assembler used the highest numbered base register. As this may cause confusion, it is good practice to drop a base register whenever it is no longer needed. This eliminates the possibility of error if another base register is later specified for the same DSECT.

Random Access Using DSECTs

If we think of PVECTOR as an array with subscripts LOW . . . HIGH and we need to add PVECTOR<I> to SUM, we can first compute the index value, then use it to compute the address of the desired entry. Assume that LOW and I are fullword fields. We find the displacement from the beginning of PVECTOR to PVECTOR<I> in register RB. At this point, RB indexes the desired entry of PVECTOR. We then use an LA instruction to place the address of PVECTOR(RB) in RB. After this instruction has been completed, we should view RB as a pointer register. It now contains the actual address of an entry of PVECTOR. We access the entry at which RB points by writing a USING instruction that associates RB with the DSECT PVSEC. The desired entry is then referred to as PVENTRY

```
        L      RB,I                  RB = L'PVECTOR*(I−LOW)
        S      RB,LOW          :
        MH     RB,=Y(L'PVECTOR) :
        LA     RB,PVECTOR(RB)   RB = A'PVECTOR<I>
        USING  PVSECT,RB        USE RB WITH PVENTRY
        AP     SUM,PVENTRY      SUM = SUM+PVENTRY
        DROP   RB               RELEASE RB
```

When accessing the entire array, we can use methods which are analogous to those developed for accessing arrays of fullwords. We set up a loop structure that maintains an index register. Before each access, we use an LA instruction to generate the desired address. Finally we give a USING instruction which assigns the pointer register containing the address to a DSECT which describes the entry.

Example 5.4.1 *Suppose the following symbol and storage definitions are part of a program named GRADER. Write the instructions to add the entries in the packed array SCORE and store the sum in SUM.*

```
GRADER     START  0                  PROGRAM GRADER
NUMSTU     EQU    25
SCORELEN   EQU    2
SUMLEN     EQU    3
  .
  .
  .
SCRSECT    DSECT
SCORE      DS     PL(SCORLEN)
GRADER     CSECT
  .
  .
  .
SUM        DS     PL(SUMLEN)
SCORLST    DS     (NUMSTU)PL(SCORELEN)
```

Using subscripts, we have the following algorithm

```
SUM = 0
FOR STUDENT = 1 TO NUMSTU
    SUM = SUM+SCORLST<STUDENT>
END
```

As in the case of the analagous fullword array, before implementing this algorithm in assembly language, we can adapt it to manipulate an index register as part of the loop control mechanism. This alteration gives the following algorithm.

```
SUM = 0
FOR RA = 0 TO L'SCORE*(NUMSTU−1) BY L'SCORE
    SUM = SUM+SCORELST(RA)
ENDFOR
```

We will use BXLE to implement the loop, choosing the pair R2, R3 to hold the increment and upper limit.

```
            ZAP      SUM,=P'0'          SUM = 0
FOR00       EQU      *                  FOR RA = 0 TO L'SCORE*(NUMSTU−1)
            SR       RA,RA                  BY L'SCORE
            LA       R2,L'SCORE             :
            LA       R3,L'*(NUMSTU−1)       :
            CR       RA,R3                  :
            BH       ENDFOR00               :
FTEST00     EQU      *                      :
            LA       RB,SCORELST(RA)    RB = A'SCORELST(RA)
            USING    SCRSECT,RB         USE RB WITH SCORE
            AP       SUM,SCORE          SUM = SUM+SCORE
            DROP     RB                 RELEASE RB
            BXLE     RA,R2,FTEST00          :
ENDFOR00    EQU      *                  ENDFOR
```

Reconsidering the code in the above example, we see that the index register can be eliminated. On each traversal of the loop, the index register is incremented by L'SCORE. The new address placed in RB is the address of the beginning of score, plus the new value of RA. The net effect of these two operations is to increase the value in RB by L'SCORE. We can streamline the program, by incrementing RB directly. RB can also be used to control the loop. We will use subscripts beginning with 1 for the remarks. We can make the range of the loop seem more manageable by moving the USING and DROP instructions outside the loop. In a sense, this more accurately depicts the situation, as RB is pointing to some entry of PVECTOR throughout the loop.

With these changes, we have

```
          ZAP    SUM,=P'0'          SUM = 0
          USING  SCRSECT,RB         USE RB WITH SCORE
FOR00     EQU    *                  FOR RB = A'SCORELST<1> TO
          LA     RB,SCORLST            A'SCORELST<NUMSTU>
          LA     R2,L'SCORE            :
          LA     R3,L'*(NUMSTU-1)     :
          LA     R3,SCORELST(R3)      :
          CR     RB,R3                :
          BH     ENDFOR00             :
FTEST00   EQU    *                    :
          AP     SUM,SCORE          SUM = SUM+SCORE
          BXLE   RB,R2,FTEST00        :
ENDFOR00  EQU    *                  ENDFOR
          DROP   RB                 RELEASE RB
```

As we observed at the beginning of this section, we can use the same techniques for accessing arrays containing other types of data, such as character strings. To illustrate this, suppose that the array of scores above is accompanied by an array that contains names corresponding to the scores. Now, if we want to sort the scores into ascending order, we will need to reorder the student names along with the scores.

Example 5.4.2 *Write the code needed to sort the array SCORELST into ascending order and make the corresponding changes in NAMELST. Assume that the data structures and constant definitions above are augmented by*

```
NAMELEN   EQU    20
          .
          .
          .
NMESECT   DSECT
NAME      DS     CL(NAMELEN)
          .
          .
          .
NAMELST   DS     (NUMSTU)CL(NAMELEN)
TMPNAME   DS     CL(NAMELEN)
TMPSCORE  DS     PL(SCORELEN)
```

Using a selection sort, we have the following algorithm.

```
FOR STUDENT = 1 TO NUMSTU −1

    {Find student with lowest score in STUDENT . . . NUMSTU}

    MINSTU = STUDENT
    FOR NXTSTU = STUDENT+1 TO NUMSTU
        IF SCORELST<NXTSTU><SCORELST<MINSTU>
        THEN
            MINSTU = NXTSTU
    ENDFOR

    {Exchange SCORELST<STUDENT> and SCORELST<MINSTU>.}

    TMPSCORE = SCORELST<STUDENT>
    SCORELST<STUDENT> = SCORELST<MINSTU>
    SCORELST<MINSTU> = TMPSCORE

    {Exchange NAMELST<STUDENT> and NAMELST<MINSTU>.}

    TMPNAME = NAMELST<STUDENT>
    NAMELST<STUDENT> = NAMELST<MINSTU>
    NAMELST<MINSTU> = TMPNAME
ENDFOR
```

Before we proceed further, we need to decide whether we will implement the loops with subscripts, as above; with index registers, as we did with the fullword array in Section 5.1; or with pointers. We can use any of the three approaches, but as we saw in Example 5.4.1, it is easier to manipulate the pointer registers directly.

The use of pointer registers introduces a complication in the exchange of NAMELST<STUDENT> and NAMELST<MINSTU>. After the inner loop is completed, we will have the addresses of SCORELST<STUDENT> and SCORELST <MINSTU>. Before the second exchange can be performed, these addresses must be transformed to the addresses of the corresponding entries of NAME.

The transformation is straightforward but cumbersome. Suppose that the pointer to SCORELST<MINSTU> is in R9. Subtracting the starting address of SCORE from this value gives the offset from the beginning of SCORE to SCORELST <MINSTU>. Dividing this value by L'SCORE yields the number of entries from the beginning of SCORELST to SCORELST<MINSTU>. If this value is multiplied by L'NAME and added to the starting address of name, the result is the address of NAMELST<MINSTU>. Thus, if we want R8 to point to NAMELST<MINSTU>, we need

$$R8 = (R9−A'SCORELST)/L'SCORE*L'NAME+A'NAMELST$$

It would be nice to simplify the calculations, by computing the conversion factor L'NAME/L'SCORE ahead of time. Unfortunately, this is not possible because L'NAME may not be evenly divisible by L'SCORE. R9−A'SCORE will always be divisible by L'SCORE.

Rather than perform this operation for both entries in NAMELST, we will maintain a separate pointer for NAMELST<STUDENT>. We assign registers as follows.

RB   Pointer to SCORELST<STUDENT>
RA   Pointer to NAMELST<STUDENT>
R9   Pointer to SCORELST<MINSTU>
R8   Pointer to SCORELST<NXTSTU>
R7   Pointer to NAMELST<MINSTU>
R6   Used for division

As we will have three registers pointing to SCORELST, we will need two additional DSECTS describing entries in this array. Similarly, we will need one more DSECT to describe entries in NAMELST. We will use

```
NXSCRSCT  DSECT
NXTSCORE  DS      PL(SCORELEN)
MNSCRSCT  DSECT
MINSCORE  DS      PL(SCORELEN)
MNNMESCT  DSECT
MINNAME   DS      CL(NAMELEN)
```

This gives the following, more detailed, algorithm.

```
RA = A'NAMELST<1>
FOR RB = A'SCORELST<1> TO A'SCORELST<NUMSTU-1>

    {Find address of lowest score in the rest of SCORELST}

    R9 = RB
    FOR R8 = RB+L'SCORE TO A'SCORELST<NUMSTU>
        IF NXTSCORE < MINSCORE
        THEN
            R9 = R8
        ENDIF
    ENDFOR

    {Exchange the scores addressed by RB and R9.}

    TMPSCORE = SCORE
    SCORE = MINSCORE
    MINSCORE = TMPSCORE

    {Find the address of the entry of NAMELST corresponding to MINSCORE.}

    R7 = (R9-A'SCORELST)/L'SCORE*L'NAME+A'NAMELST

    {Exchange NAMELST<STUDENT> and NAMELST<MINSTU>.}

    TMPNAME = NAME
    NAME = MINNAME
    MINNAME = TMPNAME

    {Move RA to the next entry of NAME.}

    RA = RA+L'NAME
ENDFOR
```

We will implement the two loops with BXLE, using the following registers.

R4,R5   Increment and upper limit for outer loop.
R2,R3   Increment and upper limit for inner loop.

The assembly language version of this algorithm is

```
          USING   SCRSECT,RB        USE RB WITH SCORE
          USING   NMESECT,RA        USE RA WITH NAME
          USING   MNSCRSCT,R9       USE R9 WITH MINSCORE
          USING   NXSCRSCT,R8       USE R8 WITH NXTSCORE
          USING   MNNMESCT,R7       USE R7 WITH MINNAME
          LA      RA,NAME           RA = A'NAME<1>
*
FOR00     EQU     *                 FOR RB = A'SCORELST<1> TO
          LA      RB,SCORELST          A'SCORELST<NUMSTU−1>
          LA      R4,L'SCORE           :
          LA      R5,L'SCORE*(NUMSTU−2)
          LA      R5,SCORELST(R5)      :
          CR      RB,R5                :
          BH      ENDFOR00             :
FTEST00   EQU     *                    :
*
*                                   FIND ADDR OF LOWEST SCORE
*                                   IN THE REST OF SCORELST
*
          LR      R9,RB             R9 = RB
FOR01     EQU     *                 FOR R8 = RB+L'SCORE
          LA      R8,L'SCORE(RB)       TO A'SCORELST<NUMSTU>
          LA      R2,L'SCORE           :
          LA      R3,L'SCORE*(NUMSTU−1)   :
          LA      R3,SCORELST(R3)      :
          CR      R8,R3                :
          BH      ENDFOR01             :
FTEST01   EQU     *                    :
*
IF00      EQU     *                 IF NXTSCORE <
          CP      NXTSCORE,MINSCORE    MINSCORE
          BNL     ENDIF00              :
THEN00    EQU     *                 THEN
          LR      R9,R8                R9 = R8
ENDIF00   EQU     *                 ENDIF
          BXLE    R8,R2,FTEST01        :
*
ENDFOR01  EQU     *                 ENDFOR
```

```
*
*
*                                              EXCHANGE THE SCORES
*                                              ADDRESSED BY RB AND R9.
*
         ZAP    TMPSCORE,SCORE          TMPSCORE = SCORE
         ZAP    SCORE,MINSCORE          SCORE = MINSCORE
         ZAP    MINSCORE,TMPSCORE       MINSCORE = TMPSCORE
*
*                                              FIND THE ADDRESS OF ENTRY
*                                              OF NAME CORRESPONDING TO
*                                              MINSCORE
*
         LR     R6,R9                   R7 = (R9−A'SCORELST)/L'SCORE
         LA     R7,SCORELST                  * L'NAME+A'NAMELST
         SR     R6,R7                   :
         SRDA   R6,32                   :
         D      R6,=A(L'SCORE)          :
         MH     R7,=Y(L'NAME)           :
         LA     R7,NAMELST(R7)          R7 = A'NAMELST(R7)
*
*                                              EXCHANGE NAME AND MINNAME
*
         MVC    TMPNAME,NAME            TMPNAME = NAME
         MVC    NAME,MINNAME            NAME = MINNAME
         MVC    MINNAME,TMPNAME         MINNAME = TMPNAME
*
*                                              MOVE RA TO THE NEXT
*                                              ENTRY OF NAMELST
*
         LA     RA,L'NAME(RA)           RA = RA+L'NAME
         BXLE   RB,R4,FTEST00           :
*
ENDFOR00 EQU    *                ENDFOR
         DROP   R7,R8,R9,RA,RB
```

Arrays for Input and Output

Even when a program is manipulating primarily arrays of fullwords or halfwords, it is still likely to need arrays of character strings or zoned numbers in the input and output fields. For example, in the exercises in the last section, we considered a program that manipulated a table containing test scores for an entire class. The input records for that program might well consist of a student name followed by all of the test scores for that student. These scores should be defined as an array within the input record. This input array would be accessed using DSECTs as described above.

Example 5.4.3 *Assuming the names are 30 characters long and the test scores are 3 digits long, the input record should be defined by adding the following symbol and storage definitions to those given for the exercises in 5.3. (We assume that the names would also be stored in an array.)*

```
SCORELEN   EQU      3
NAMELEN    EQU      30
 .
 .
 .
INSCRSCT   DSECT
INSCORE    DS       ZL(SCORELEN)
NMESCT     DSECT
NAMENTRY   DS       CL(NAMELEN)
GRADER     CSECT
 .
 .
 .
INREC      DS       CL80                    INPUT RECORD
           ORG      INREC                        :
INNAME     DS       CL(NAMELEN)             STUDENT NAME
INSCORES   DS       (NUMTST)ZL(L'INSCORE)   ARRAY OF TEST SCORES
           ORG      INREC+L'INREC           END INPUT RECORD
 .
 .
 .
NAMES      DS       (NUMSTU)CL(L'NAMENTRY)  STUDENT NAMES
```

The array SCORES can then be filled with the following nested loop. RB is used as a pointer to the array of input scores. RA is a pointer to the array of names. R9 is used as an index register with SCORES. Because we have assumed that the array will be stored in row major order and as the scores will be read in row by row, we simply initialize R9 to 0 and increment it by 4 until all scores are read. When it gets to the end of one row, the next value assumed will be the index for the beginning of the next row.

```
           USING    INSCRSCT,RB      USE RB WITH INSCORE
           USING    NMESCT,RA        USE RA WITH NAMENTRY
           LA       RA,NAMES         RA = A'NAMES<1>
           LA       R9,0             R9 = 0
FOR00      EQU      *                FOR R5 = NUMSTU DOWNT0 1
           LA       R5,NUMSTU             :
           LA       R7,FTEST00            :
FTEST00    EQU      *                     :
           GET      INFILE,INREC     READ INREC
           MVC      NAMENTRY,INNAME  (RA-->NAMENTRY) = INNAME
```

```
            LA      RA,L'NAMENTRY(RA)      MOVE RA TO NEXT NAME ENTRY
            LA      RB,INSCORES            RB = A'INSCORES<1>
FOR01       EQU     *                      FOR R4 = NUMTST DOWNTO 1
            LA      R4,ANUMTST             :
            LA      R8,FTEST01             :
FTEST01     EQU     *                      :
            PACK    DWORK,INSCORE          SCORES(R9) =
            CVB     R2,DWORK                   (RB-->INSCORE)
            ST      R2,SCORES(R9)          :
            LA      RB,L'INSCORE(RB)       MOVE RB TO NEXT ENTRY
            LA      R9,L'SCORES(R9)        MOVE R9 TO NEXT ENTRY
            BCTR    R4,R8                  :
ENDFOR01    EQU     *                      ENDFOR
            BCTR    R5,R7                  :
ENDFOR00    EQU     *                      ENDFOR
```

E X E R C I S E S

1. Write the symbol and storage definitions needed to create a one-dimensional array PNUMS to contain up to 50 packed numbers of 5 bytes each. Define a DSECT to be used to access the array.

2. Calculate the offset from the beginning of the array PNUMS to the eighteenth entry.

3. Suppose that R3 contains an index to an entry in the array PNUMS of Exercise 1. Write the instructions to add this entry to a packed field named TOTAL.

4. A character string can be viewed as a one-dimensional array in which the entries are single characters. From this point of view, write the code find the position of the first nonblank character in an 80 character input record, INREC.

5. Write instructions to eliminate all leading blanks from the record INREC of Exercise 4.

6. Modify the code in Example 5.4.3 to handle the situation in which not all entries of the array are to be used. Suppose that the actual number of students and tests are stored in two fullword fields, NUMSTU and NUMTST. Write the code to read NUMSTU records each containing NUMTST tests.

7. Add any symbol and storage definitions necessary to print the names and test scores stored in the arrays in Example 5.4.3. Print each name and the corresponding test scores on one line.

8. Suppose that the field KEYNAME contains the name of one of the students in the array NAMES of Example 5.4.3. Write the instructions to search the array for KEYNAME and print the test scores for that student.

9. Rewrite the definitions and the code in Example 5.4.3 to store the scores in packed form rather than converting them to binary.

10. Assuming the modification in Exercise 9, write the code to average the grades for each student and store the averages in a packed array named STUAVG.

11. Assuming the modification in Exercise 9, write the code to average the class grades on each test and store the averages in a packed array named CLSAVG.

5.5 ARRAYS OF RECORD STRUCTURES

We saw, in the example of Section 5.4, the increased complexity which results from several arrays containing related data. In that example, the complexity resulted from the need to keep both the names and the scores in the same order. If the information on each student had included other items, such as student number, address, or age, the sort would have been considerably more difficult. In order to control this complexity, we need to be able to manipulate arrays of records. In the example at hand, we would need to access individual fields, as in comparing two scores, and move complete records when making an exchange.

We can implement arrays of record structures in the same way as arrays of packed numbers or character strings, that is, by writing a DSECT to describe a single entry in the array. The DSECT can be used as before to manipulate complete entries, but it can also include definitions for fields within the records. These field names can be used to access components of array entries.

We begin with an example of a record structure involving only two fields.

Example 5.5.1 *Suppose we need to create an array of records containing both student names and scores. Assume the following constant definitions.*

```
MAXSTU    EQU    25
SCORELEN  EQU    2
NAMELEN   EQU    20
```

We want to create an array in which each entry consists of a student's name followed by the score for that student. The length of each entry is given by

```
STRECLEN  EQU    NAMELEN+SCORELEN
```

A complete entry can be described by the following DSECT. We again assume that the containing program is named GRADER. This name is used in a CSECT instruction to terminate the definition of the DSECT.

```
STUSECT     DSECT
STDREC      DS      STRECLEN
            ORG     STDREC
NAME        DS      CL(NAMELEN)
SCORE       DS      PL(SCORELEN)
GRADER      CSECT
```

We noted earlier that when the assembler encounters a DSECT instruction, it saves the current value of the location counter and reinitializes the location counter to 0. Throughout the definition of the DSECT, the location counter is manipulated as usual. When a symbol is defined, the current value of the location counter is stored in the symbol table along with the symbol and its length. The location counter is incremented by the length of the field. The values stored in the symbol table represent the offsets of these symbols from the beginning of the DSECT. If the DSECT definition is terminated by a CSECT with the name of the original CSECT, then the original value of the location counter is restored and definition of the CSECT continues.

The DSECT directive above would define the following symbols with offsets and lengths as indicated below.

Symbol	Offset	Length
STUSECT		1
STDREC	0	22
NAME	0	20
SCORE	22	2

In order to access an entry in this array, we proceed as before, placing the address of the desired entry in a register specified as the implied base register for the DSECT.

If we place the DSECT definition before the data areas in our program, then the array itself can be defined with the instruction

```
STDLIST     DS      (MAXSTU)XL(L'STDREC)
```

The same approach will allow us to define more complex record structures as the following example demonstrates.

Example 5.5.2 *Suppose that we are writing a program that will use the following two record structures.*

Student Record

Field	Type	Length
Student Number	Zoned Decimal	9
Name	Character	20
Address	Character	40
Class	Zoned	1 (1,2,3,4)

Grade Record

Field	Type	Length
Student Number	Zoned Decimal	9
Department	Character	3
Course Number	Zoned Decimal	3
Course Name	Character	20
Credit Hours	Packed Decimal	1
Grade	Character	1

If the program containing these structures is named GRADER, then DSECTs describing the structures would be placed as follows.

```
GRADER     START  0                    PROGRAM GRADER
  .
  .
  .
           EOJ
****************************************************************************************************
*     SYMBOLIC CONSTANTS                                                                          *
****************************************************************************************************
STNUMLEN EQU    9                     STUDENT NUMBER LENGTH
NAMELEN  EQU    20                    NAME LENGTH
ADDRLEN  EQU    40                    ADDRESS LENGTH
CLASSLEN EQU    1                     CLASS LENGTH
STRECLEN EQU    STNUMLEN+NAMELEN+ADDRLEN+CLASSLEN
DEPTLEN  EQU    3                     DEPARTMENT LENGTH
CRSNUMLN EQU    3                     COURSE NUMBER LENGTH
CRSNAMLN EQU    20                    COURSE NAME LENGTH
CRHRSLEN EQU    1                     CREDIT HOURS LENGTH
GRADELEN EQU    1                     GRADE LENGTH
GRRECLEN EQU    STNUMLEN+DEPTLEN+CRSNUMLN+CRSNAMLN+CRHRSLEN+GRADELEN
  .
  .
  .
****************************************************************************************************
*     DSECTS                                                                                      *
****************************************************************************************************
```

```
STUSECT   DSECT
STUDREC   DS      XL(STRECLEN)        STUDENT RECORD
          ORG     STUDREC             :
STNUMBER  DS      ZL(STNUMLEN)        STUDENT NUMBER
STNAME    DS      CL(NAMELEN)         NAME
STADDR    DS      CL(ADDRLEN)         ADDRESS
STCLASS   DS      ZL(CLASSLEN)        CLASS (1, 2, 3, 4)
*

GRDSECT   DSECT
GRADEREC  DS      XL(GRRECLEN)        GRADE RECORD
          ORG     GRADEREC            :
GSTDNUM   DS      ZL(STNUMLEN)        STUDENT NUMBER
GRDEPT    DS      CL(DEPTLEN)         DEPARTMENT
GRCRSNUM  DS      ZL(CRSNUMLN)        COURSE NUMBER
GRCRSNAM  DS      CL(CRSNAMLN)        COURSE NAME
GRCRHRS   DS      PL(CRHRSLEN)        CREDIT HOURS
GRGRADE   DS      PL(GRADELEN)        GRADE
*

GRADER    CSECT
```

The first DSECT, STUSECT, is terminated by the DSECT directive, which initiates the second DSECT, GRDSECT. This DSECT is terminated by the CSECT directive, which marks the continuation of the main CSECT, GRADER.

When we use a DSECT to describe the entries in an array of records, we still need to reserve storage area for the array itself. If the array is relatively small, we may place it at the end of the main CSECT. If the array is large, or if there are several arrays, we can define new CSECTs to hold one or more arrays. Placing arrays in separate CSECTs reduces the likelihood that the program will need multiple base registers, but it also restricts the ways in which the arrays can be accessed.

Example 5.5.3 *Suppose the definitions in Example 5.5.2 are augmented by*

```
MAXSTU    EQU     50
MAXGRCRD  EQU     200
```

Assume we need to define two arrays to hold up to MAXSTU student records and MAXGRCRD grade records.

In order to place these arrays inside the CSECT, GRADER, we place the definitions immediately before the END directive. Thus, the last three records in the program source file will be

```
STDLIST   DS      (MAXSTU)XL(L'STUDREC)
GRDLIST   DS      (MAXGRCRD)XL(L'GRADEREC)
          END
```

Alternatively, these arrays can be defined in a second CSECT by preceding their definitions with a CSECT directive. If we name this CSECT ARRAYS, the program source file would then end with

```
ARRAYS     CSECT
STDLIST    DS      (MAXSTU)XL(L'STUDREC)
GRDLIST    DS      (MAXGRCRD)XL(L'GRADEREC)
           END
```

Finally, we could place each array in its own CSECT with the following code at the end of the program source.

```
STDARRAY   CSECT
STDLIST    DS      (MAXSTU)XL(L'STUDREC)
GRDARRAY   CSECT
GRDLIST    DS      (MAXGRCRD)XL(L'GRADEREC)
           END
```

Accessing Arrays of Records

Arrays of records are accessed in the same way as the arrays in the last section. We give a using instruction that associates a register to the fields in the DSECT and put the address of an array entry in the register. Again, the order in which these two instructions occur is irrelevant.

Suppose we need to access the array STDLIST, defined above. If STDLIST was defined in the main CSECT as in the first option, then its address can be loaded into a register with a simple Load Address instruction,

```
        LA      R8,STDLIST
```

If STDLIST was defined in another CSECT, as in the second two options, then it cannot be addressed directly from the main CSECT. Instead, we must use an address constant to hold the address of the array. For this purpose, we can use a literal operand, as in

```
        L       R8,=A(STDLIST)
```

We bracket the instructions that will refer to the array entries with a USING instruction and a DROP instruction. For example,

```
        USING   STUSECT,R8

        < Instructions which >
        < access STDLIST >

        DROP    R8
```

Throughout the domain of this USING instruction, the assembler will supply R8 as the implied base register with every field name from STUSECT. The displacement used will be the offset from the beginning of STUSECT to the indicated field. When a length is required, the assembler will use the defined length of the field.

Given the USING instruction above,

```
MVC     STNAME,NUNAME
```

will be assembled with R8 as the base register for STNAME. The displacement will be the offset from the beginning of STUSECT to STNAME. (This is the length of STNUMBER or 9.) The length used in the instruction will be the defined length of STNAME, 20. The effective address of the first operand will be 9 plus the address in R8. If R8 points to the beginning of an entry in STDLIST, the address generated will indeed designate the name field in this entry. The instruction will move 20 bytes. The net effect of this instruction is to copy a new value, NUNAME, into the subfield, STNAME, of the record addressed by R8. The relationship between the array and the DSECT is shown in Figure 5.5.1.

FIGURE 5.5.1   Using a DSECT to Access an Array

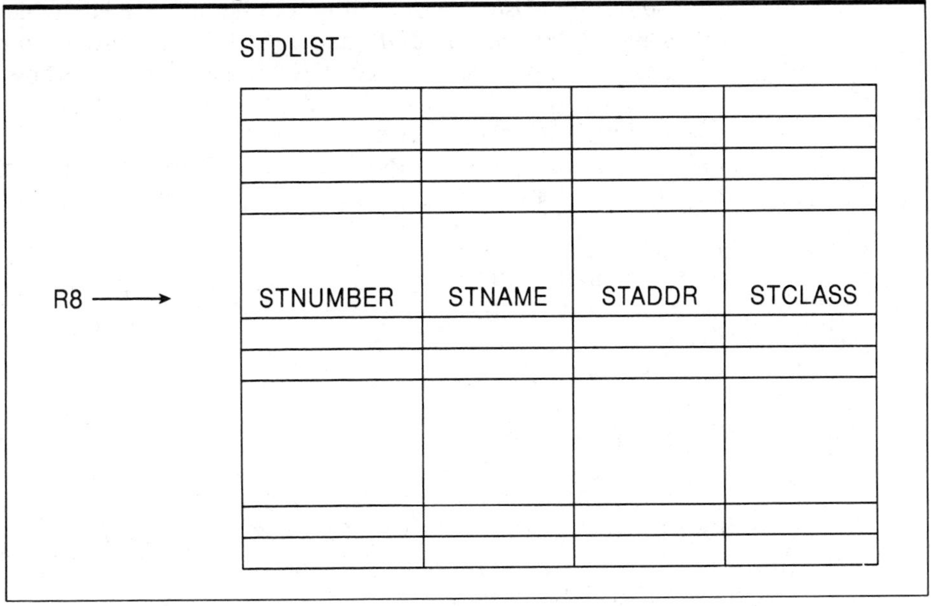

Note that the field names from the DSECT apply to whichever entry of STDLIST is indicated by the address in R8. If R8 is incremented by the instruction

```
LA      R8,L'STUDREC
```

then the same field names will refer to fields in the next entry of STDLIST. In our programs, we will try to emphasize that relationship in the remarks by using the notation

$$(<register> \rightarrow <record\ name>.<field\ name>)$$

to denote a field that is determined by a register address and a USING instruction. In the example above, we would denote the designated fields by

(R8 → STUDREC.STNUMBER)
(R8 → STUDREC.STNAME)

and so on.

In order to illustrate these instructions and documentation conventions, we consider a short example of code that manipulates the array STDLIST defined above.

Example 5.5.4 *Using STUSECT and STDLIST above, write the code to search STDLIST for the student whose name is in KEYNAME. (We assume that the name is in the array.) When found, print all fields in the corresponding student's record.*

We assume the existence of a print field named STLINE, which contains fields ONUMBER, ONAME, OADDR, and OCLASS. We also assume that the array STDLIST was defined in a different CSECT, as in the second two options above.

Given the assurance that the student's name is in the array, the algorithm is straightforward. We choose a pointer register and initialize it to the starting address of STDLIST. We then enter a loop in which this record is incremented by the length of a record until it points to a record containing KEYNAME in the name field.

```
R8 = A'STDLIST
WHILE (R8 → STUDREC.STNAME) <> KEYNAME DO
    R8 = R8+L'STUDREC
END
PRINT (R8 → STUDREC)
```

The code is

```
            L      R8,=A(STDARRAY)      R8 = A'STDLIST
            USING  STUSECT,R8           USE R8 WITH STDREC
WHILE00     EQU    *                    WHILE (R8 -> STUDREC.STNAME)
            CLC    STNAME,KEYNAME           <> KEYNAME
            BE     ENDWHL00                 :
            LA     R8,L'STUDREC(R8)         R8 = R8+L'STUDREC
            B      WHILE00                  :
ENDWHL00    EQU    *                    END WHILE
            MVC    ONUMBER,STNUMBER     PRINT (R8 -> STUDREC)
            MVC    ONAME,STNAME             :
            MVC    OADDR,STADDR             :
            MVC    OCLASS,STCLASS           :
            DROP   R8                   RELEASE R8
```

These conventions and techniques will be further illustrated in a sample program in the next section. We conclude this section by considering a problem that may occur in a program containing several arrays.

Multiple Base Registers

In our discussion of base-displacement addressing, we noted that the instruction formats allow 3 hexadecimal digits for encoding displacements. The displacements range from X'000' to X'FFF'. The largest displacement is 4095. This means that, with a single base register, we can address at most 4096 bytes. This is called the *range of the base register.*

In order to access an array in the main CSECT, we put the address in a register using

> LA   <register>,<array name>

The only requirement for this to work is that the beginning of the array lie within the range of the existing base register. It is, however, quite often the case that a single array is so large that any fields that come after it will lie outside the range of the base register. The assembler will indicate an addressability error on any reference to such a field. It is for this reason that, if a large array is to be included in the main CSECT, it should be last. Unfortunately, this doesn't help if the program requires two or more arrays. It may be that, no matter how their definitions are ordered, at least one will always lie outside the range of the base register.

When a program is too large to be addressed by a single base register, we must provide additional base registers. Fortunately, the assembler handles most of the complications involved. Our responsibility is limited to telling the assembler which registers to use and placing the correct base addresses in these registers before execution.

We inform the assembler about the extra base registers with a more general form of the USING instruction.

> USING   <location>,<register list>

<location>   A relocatable expression. (Usually a symbol or *.)

<register list>   One or more registers separated by commas.

This form of the instruction tells the assembler to use the registers in the register list as base registers and to begin measuring displacements from the indicated location. The first register in the list will be used as the base register for the first 4096 bytes. The second register will be used to address the next 4096 bytes and so on.

Example 5.5.5

> USING   *,RA,RB,RC

This instruction directs the assembler to use registers RA, RB, and RC as base registers and to begin measuring displacements from the current value of the location counter. That is from the location in the program immediately following the USING instruction.

The effect of the USING instruction above is illustrated in Figure 5.5.2. It shows a skeletal assembler listing that contains the USING instruction above, shows the value of the location counter at each point, and defines some labels.

FIGURE 5.5.2   A Program with Multiple Base Registers.

```
LOC                       Source Statement

000000                    BALR    RA,0
000002                    USING   *,RA,RB,RC
000002    BASE    EQU     *                    — BASE+0
000002                                    ┐
                                          │
                                          │   — The range of RA.
000A1E    LABELA  EQU     *               │
                                          │
                                          │
001001                                    │   — BASE+4095
001002                                    ┘   — BASE+4096
                                          ┐
                                          │   — The range of RB.
0013C2    LABELB  EQU     *               │
                                          │
                                          │
002001                                    │   — BASE+8191
002002                                    ┘   — BASE+8192
                                          ┐
                                          │   — The range of RC.
002E13    LABELC  EQU     *               │
                                          │
003001                                    ┘   — BASE+12287
```

As the figure shows, RA is used to address locations from BASE+0 to BASE+4095. Locations from BASE+4096 through BASE+8191 will be addressed using RB as the base register and locations from BASE+8192 to BASE+12287 will be addressed using RC.

This means that a reference to LABELA, any place in the program, will be coded with RA as the base register. The displacement will be the distance from BASE to LABELA, X'000A1E' − X'000002' = X'000A1C'. In the format of an operand in an SS instruction, this will be X'AA1C'. The first X'A' represents the base register and X'A1C' the displacement.

A storage reference to LABELB will have RB as the base register. The displacement will be the distance from BASE+4096 to LABELB, X'0013C2'−X'001002' = X'0003C0'. As an SS operand, LABELB will be represented by X'B3C0'. Similarly, LABELC will be encoded as X'CE11'.

In order for all this to work when the program is executed, RA must contain the address of BASE, RB must contain the address of BASE+4096, and RC the address of BASE+8192. As before, the correct address will be placed in RA by the BALR RA,0 instruction at the beginning of the program. This instruction does not place any value in RB or RC. These registers must be initialized with the correct value *before* the occurrence of any reference to memory locations beyond the range of RA.

This presents a rather interesting problem. We can request the operating system to put these addresses in storage areas in our program when the program is loaded. This is accomplished with the following instruction.

```
BASEADS    DC      A(BASE+4096,BASE+8192)
```

This instruction will reserve two fullwords of storage identified by the symbol BASEADS. When the program is loaded, the actual addresses of BASE+4096 and BASE+8192 will be placed in these locations.

These addresses can be loaded into registers RA and RB with the Load Multiple instruction.

```
           LM      RA,RB,BASEADS
```

The problem is this: Where should we place the addresses represented by BASEADS? Until the LM instruction has been executed, we can only address locations in the range of RA. So, we must make certain that these addresses are within the range of RA. We also want to make sure that they remain within the range of RA even if we later modify the program by adding new code or data areas. Thus, we really need to place these addresses at the top of the program.

This solution presents a second problem. The addresses will be located among the instructions for our program. We need to make sure that the machine does not try to interpret these addresses as instructions. In order to do this, we must direct it to branch around the addresses. This gives the following sequence of instructions.

```
<name>     START   0
           BALR    RA,0
           USING   *,RA,RB,RC
BASE       EQU     *
           LM      RB,RC,BASEADS
           B       ENDADS
BASEADS    DC      A(BASE+4096,BASE+8192)
ENDADS     EQU     *
```

E   X   E   R   C   I   S   E   S

In exercises 1-4, write symbol definitions and DSECTs to describe the record structures for array entries.

1. Describe an employee record containing a name field of length 25, a 6-digit employee number, and a 37-character address field.

2. Modify the DSECT from Exercise 1 to divide the employee address field into a street address (20 characters), a city (15 characters), and a state (2 characters).

3. Describe a university standing record, UNVREC, which contains a university name (30 characters), its location (20 characters), and a ranking (3 digits).

4. Define a pair of record structures consisting of an inventory record and an item description record. The inventory record should contain a 6-digit item number in zoned form and three 4-byte packed numbers which give the quantity on hand, the reorder point, and the quantity on order. The item description record should contain the item number, an item description (30 characters), the supplier (30 characters), and the wholesale and retail prices as 3-byte packed numbers.

5. Write instructions to reserve storage areas for two arrays whose entries were described in Exercise 4. Assume that the number of entries is given by the constant MAXENT and place the definitions in two separate CSECTs.

6. Write the instructions necessary to access the arrays defined in Exercise 5, using R8 as the base register for the inventory record array and R9 as the base register for the item description array.

7. Assume that the arrays described in Exercise 5 are filled and sorted on item number. Write the code to compare the reorder point of each item with the sum of the quantity on hand and the quantity on order. If the sum is less than the reorder point, print the item number and description.

The following exercises refer to the arrays STDLIST and GRDLIST defined as separate CSECTS in the discussions in this section.

8. Write the instructions to sort STDLIST into ascending order on STNUMBER.

9. Modify the code from Exercise 8 to sort STDLIST into ascending order on STNAME.

10. Assuming that GRDLIST is ordered by GSTDNUM, modify the code in Example 5.5.4 to print a list of the grade records for the student whose name is in KEYNAME.

11. Assuming that both STDLIST and GRDLIST have been ordered on the student number fields, write the code to print a list of all student records together with the grade records for each student.

12. Suppose the program, SAMPLE, contains the instructions below.

```
SAMPLE      START   0
            BALR    RA,0
            USING   *,RA,RB,RC
BASE        EQU     *
            LM      RB,RC,BASEADS
            B       ENDADS
BASEADS     DC      A(BASE+4096,BASE+8192)
ENDADS      EQU     *
```

Assuming that SAMPLE was loaded into memory at address X'9B6878', give the actual address of the following storage operands.

a. X'B5CA'

b. X'A9F6'

c. X'C9AD'

5.6 SAMPLE PROGRAM

We conclude this chapter with a sample program which includes most of the types of arrays we have considered. Suppose we have a set of temperature records that contain daily highs and lows for the last 12 weeks. We will write a program that reads these records and produces a report giving the average high and low temperatures for each of the 12 weeks. It will also print a histogram that indicates the number of days of high temperature, in each of the various ranges.

Array Structures

We assume that there is an input record for each of the 12 weeks. Each record contains 7 pairs of temperatures, the low and high temperatures for the corresponding day. Each temperature is a zoned number with three digits.

We view each input record as an array with 7 entries. Each entry is itself a record consisting of a high temperature and a low temperature. In order to find the weekly averages, we simply process the records in this array, keeping a sum of the highs and the lows. The processing will involve packing each temperature and adding it to an appropriate accumulator.

In order to keep track of the number of high temperatures in each range, we will need two arrays. The first array will contain the upper limit for each of the ranges. Because the high temperatures will already be packed to compute the average, the limits in this array should also be packed. The counters for each range will also form an array. These will be incremented by 1 whenever a temperature falls in the indicated range. When all the data have been read, the counters will be used as loop counters as the histogram is printed. Thus, the counters should be stored as fullwords.

Finally, in order to print the histogram, we view a portion of the output line as an array of characters. When printing the line for each range, we load the counter for that range into a register and use it as a loop counter while filling positions of this output array with asterisks. The remaining positions of the array will be left blank.

Our program will include an array of records, an array of packed numbers, an array of fullwords, and an array of characters. In manipulating all of these arrays, we will follow the same pattern: We write a DSECT that describes each entry of the array. We define space for the arrays separately. (In this case, one of the arrays will be part of the input record definition and one part of an output line.) When accessing a particular array, we designate a register and the DSECT for the array in a USING instruction. This DSECT is bound to various entries in the array by the choice of the address in the register.

Algorithm

We divide the program into three components, yielding the following top-level algorithm.

```
Open files.
Setup data structures.
Read input data and print weekly averages.
Print histogram.
Close files.
```

The first component is straightforward. We initialize the accumulators and set up the array of bracket limits. Note that the number of brackets and the range of each bracket can be changed easily.

The algorithm for the subroutine to read the input data and print the weekly averages is shown below. It indicates which registers will be used to access the arrays.

Print headings for weekly averages.
for WEEK = 1 to NUMWEEKS
    Read record containing the data for the week and initialize accumulators for weekly totals.
    Point RB to weekly data record.
    for R3 = 7 downto 1
        PTEMP = (RB → WEEKDATA.HIGH)
        HIGHSUM = HIGHSUM+PTEMP

            {Search the array of range limits for the first value that is greater than or equal to PTEMP. RA will be used to point to an entry in the array of limits and R4 as an index into the array of counters.}

            Point RA to array of range limits.
            Set R4 = 0
            SENTINEL = PTEMP
            while PTEMP > limit indicated by RA
                Move RA to next bracket.
                Move R4 to next counter.
            end while
        COUNT(R4) = COUNT(R4)+1
        PTEMP = (RB → WEEKDATA.LOW)
        LOWSUM = LOWSUM+PTEMP
        Advance RB to record for next day.
    endfor
Print weekly averages.
endfor

The algorithm for printing the histogram is shown below.

Print heading.
Point RB to array of range limits.

{R2 is used to index the array of counters. It is also used to control the loop for printing a line for each range.}

    for R2 = 0 T0 4*(number of ranges−1) by L'COUNT
        Fill the star field with blanks.
        Point RA to the beginning of the star field.
        for R4 = COUNT(R2) downto 1
            (RA → STARPOS) = '*'
            Move RA to NEXT STAR
        endfor
        Print the range. (Print the limit indicated by RB, increment RB, then print the new limit −1.
        Print the stars.
    endfor

The resulting program is shown below.

```
*****************************************************************************************
*     SAMPLE PROGRAM 5                                                                  *
*                                                                                       *
*     THIS PROGRAM READS A SET OF RECORDS TEMPERATURE DATA FOR                          *
*     12 WEEKS. IT PRODUCES A STATISTICAL SUMMARY OF THE                                *
*     TEMPERATURES READ.                                                                *
*                                                                                       *
*     INPUT: 12 RECORDS CONTAINING THE HIGH AND LOW TEMPERATURE                         *
*            FOR EACH OF SEVEN DAYS.                                                     *
*                                                                                       *
*     OUTPUT: 12 WEEKLY HIGHS AND LOWS AND A HISTOGRAM THAT                             *
*             GIVES THE NUMBER OF HIGHS IN EACH OF VARIOUS                              *
*             RANGES.                                                                   *
*****************************************************************************************
SAMPLE5   START  0                    PROGRAM SAMPLE5
          PRINT  NOGEN                 :
          BALR   RC,0                  :
          USING  *,RC                  :
          OPEN   INFILE,PRINTER        OPEN FILES
          BAL    RE,SETUP              CALL SETUP
          BAL    RE,READDATA           CALL READDATA
          BAL    RE,PRNTHIST           CALL PRNTHIST
EOFADDR   EQU    *                     :
          CLOSE  INFILE,PRINTER        CLOSE FILES
          EOJ                          END SAMPLE5
*****************************************************************************************
*     SETUP                                                                             *
*                                                                                       *
*     INITIALIZE THE ARRAY OF RANGE COUNTERS AND ARRAY OF                               *
*     UPPER LIMITS.                                                                     *
*                                                                                       *
*     INPUT VARIABLES: LOWLIM                                                           *
*                                                                                       *
*     OUTPUT VARIABLES: RNGETOP, COUNT                                                  *
*                                                                                       *
*     LOCAL VARIABLES: RANGELIM                                                         *
*                                                                                       *
*     REGISTER USAGE: R2,R3,R4,RB                                                       *
*****************************************************************************************
          DS     F                     :
SETUP     EQU    *                     SUBROUTINE SETUP
          ST     RE,SETUP-4            :
          ZAP    RANGELIM,LOWLIM       RANGELIM = LOWLIM
          LA     RB,RNGETOP            RB = A'RNGETOP<1>
          USING  RTOPSCT,RB            USE RB WITH RTOPNTRY
```

```
              LA      R2,0                    R2 = 0
FOR00         EQU     *                       FOR R3 = 0 TO L'COUNT*NUMRNGS
              LA      R3,0                        BY L'COUNT
              LA      R4,L'COUNT*NUMRNGS          :
FTEST00       EQU     *                           :
              CR      R3,R4                       :
              BH      ENDFOR00                    :
              ZAP     RTOPNTRY,RANGELIM       (RB -> RTOPNTRY) = RANGELIM
              LA      RB,L'RNGETOP(RB)        MOVE RB TO NEXT BRACKET
              AP      RANGELIM,TMPRNGE          RANGELIM = RANGELIM+TMPRNGE
              ST      R2,COUNT(R3)             COUNT(R3) = 0
              LA      R3,L'COUNT(R3)           :
              B       FTEST00                  :
ENDFOR00      EQU     *                       ENDFOR
              ST      R2,COUNT(R3)            COUNT(R3) = 0
              DROP    RB                      RELEASE RB
              L       RE,SETUP-4      RETURN
              BR      RE                  :
*****************************************************************************************
*     READDATA                                                                         *
*                                                                                      *
*     READ INPUT VALUES AND PRINT THE AVERAGE HIGH AND LOW FOR                         *
*     EACH WEEK. COUNT THE NUMBER OF DAYS IN EACH TEMPERATURE                          *
*     RANGE.                                                                           *
*                                                                                      *
*     INPUT VARIABLES: RNGETOP, COUNT                                                  *
*                                                                                      *
*     OUTPUT VARIABLES: COUNT                                                          *
*                                                                                      *
*     LOCAL VARIABLES: HIGHSUM, LOWSUM, AVGHIGH, AVGLOW, WEEK,                         *
*                        WEEKDATA                                                      *
*                                                                                      *
*     REGISTER USAGE: R2,R3,R4,RA,RB                                                   *
*****************************************************************************************
              DS      F                       :
READDATA      EQU     *                       SUBROUTINE READDATA
              ST      RE,READDATA-4           :
              PUT     PRINTER,WEEKHEAD        PRINT HEADINGS FOR WEEKLY AVS
              PUT     PRINTER,SPACE           :
FOR01         EQU     *                       FOR WEEK = 1 TO NUMWEEKS
              ZAP     WEEK,=P'1'              :
FTEST01       EQU     *                       :
              CP      WEEK,NUMWEEKS           :
              BH      ENFOR01                 :
              GET     INFILE,WEEKDATA         READ WEEKDATA
              ZAP     HIGHSUM,=P'0'           HIGHSUM = 0
              ZAP     LOWSUM,=P'0'            LOWSUM = 0
```

```
              LA      RB,WEEKDATA                      RB = A'WEEKDATA
              USING   TMPSECT,RB                       USE RB WITH TMPNTRY
FOR02         EQU     *                                FOR R3 = 7 DOWNTO 1
              LA      R3,7                                 :
FTEST02       EQU     *                                    :
              PACK    PTEMP,HIGH                           PTEMP = (RB -> TMPNTRY.HIGH)
              AP      HIGHSUM,PTEMP                        HIGHSUM = HIGHSUM+PTEMP
              LA      RA,RNGETOP+L'RNGETOP                 RA = A'RNGETOP<1>
              USING   RTOPSCT,RA                           USE RA WITH RTOPNTRY
              LA      R4,0                                 R4 = 0
              ZAP     SENTINEL,PTEMP                       SENTINEL = PTEMP
WHILE00       EQU     *                                    WHILE PTEMP >
              CP      PTEMP,RTOPNTRY                           (RA -> RTOPNTRY)
              BNH     ENDWHL00                                :
              LA      RA,L'RNGETOP(RA)                        MOVE RA TO NXT BRCKT
              LA      R4,L'COUNT(R4)                          R4 = R4+L'COUNT
              B       WHILE00                                 :
ENDWHL00      EQU     *                                    END WHILE
              DROP    RA                                   RELEASE RA
              L       R5,COUNT(R4)                         COUNT(R4) = COUNT(R4)+1
              AH      R5,=H'1'                                 :
              ST      R5,COUNT(R4)                            :
              PACK    PTEMP,LOW                            PTEMP = (RB -> TMPNTRY.LOW)
              AP      LOWSUM,PTEMP                         LOWSUM = LOWSUM+PTEMP
              LA      RB,L'TEMPS(RB)                       ADVANCE RB TO NEXT DAY
              BCT     R3,FTEST02                              :
ENDFOR02      EQU     *                                    ENDFOR
              DROP    RB                                   RELEASE RB
              MVC     OUTWEEK,WEEKMSK                      EDIT WEEK INTO WKLINE
              ED      OUTWEEK,WEEK                            :
              ZAP     DIVWORK,HIGHSUM                      EDIT AVG. HIGH INTO WKLINE
              SRP     DIVWORK,64+2,0                          :
              DP      DIVWORK,=P'7'                           :
              SRP     AVERAGE,64-1,5                          :
              MVC     OHIGHAVG,AVGMSK                         :
              LA      R1,OHIGHAVG+AVGFRST                     :
              EDMK    OHIGHAVG,AVERAGE                        :
              BCTR    R1,0                                    :
              MVC     0(1,R1),OHIGHAVG+L'OHIGHAVG-1
              MVI     OHIGHAVG+L'OHIGHAVG-1,C' '   :
              ZAP     DIVWORK,LOWSUM                       EDIT AVG. LOW INTO WKLINE
              SRP     DIVWORK,64+2,0                          :
              DP      DIVWORK,=P'7'                           :
              SRP     AVERAGE,64-1,5                          :
              MVC     OLOWAVG,AVGMSK                          :
              LA      R1,OLOWAVG+AVGFRST                      :
              EDMK    OLOWAVG,AVERAGE                         :
```

```
          BCTR    R1,0                        :
          MVC     0(1,R1),OLOWAVG+L'OLOWAVG-1
          MVI     OLOWAVG+L'OLOWAVG-1,C' '    :
          PUT     PRINTER,WKLINE              PRINT WKLINE
          AP      WEEK,=P'1'                  :
          B       FTEST01                     :
ENDFOR01  EQU     *                           ENDFOR
          L       RE,READDATA-4               RETURN
          BR      RE                          :
**********************************************************************************
*    PRNTHIST                                                                   *
*                                                                              *
*    PRINT A HISTOGRAM GIVING THE DISTRIBUTION OF DAILY HIGHS.                  *
*                                                                              *
*    INPUT VARIABLES: RNGETOP, COUNT                                           *
*                                                                              *
*    OUTPUT VARIABLES: <NONE>                                                  *
*                                                                              *
*    LOCAL VARIABLES: DETAIL                                                   *
*                                                                              *
*    REGISTER USAGE: R2,R3,R4,RB                                               *
*                                                                              *
**********************************************************************************
          DS      F                           :
PRNTHIST  EQU     *                           SUBROUTINE PRNTHIST
          ST      RE,PRNTHIST-4               :
          PUT     PRINTER,HISTHEAD            PRINT HEADING
          PUT     PRINTER,SPACE               :
          LA      RB,RNGETOP                  RB = A'RNGETOP
          USING   RTOPSCT,RB                  USE RB WITH RTOPNTRY
FOR03     EQU     *                           FOR R2 = 0 TO L'COUNT*(NUMRNGS-1)
          LA      R2,0                           BY L'COUNT
          LA      R3,L'COUNT*(NUMRNGS-1)      :
FTEST03   EQU     *                           :
          CR      R2,R3                       :
          BH      ENDFOR03                    :
          MVC     STARS,STARS-1               STARS = BLANKS
          LA      RA,STARS                    RA = A'STARS
          USING   CHSECT,RA                   USE RA WITH STARPOS
FOR04     EQU     *                           FOR R4 = COUNT(R2) DOWNTO 1
          L       R4,COUNT(R2)                :
          C       R4,=F'0'                    :
          BNH     ENDFOR04                    :
FTEST04   EQU     *                           :
          MVI     STARPOS,C'*'                (RA -> STARPOS) = '*'
          LA      RA,L'STARPOS(RA)            MOVE RA TO NEXT STAR
          BCT     R4,FTEST04                  :
```

```
ENDFOR04   EQU       *                              ENDFOR
           MVC       ORNGBOT,LIMMSK                 EDIT (RB -> RTOPNTRY) INTO
           LA        R1,ORNGBOT+LIMFRST                  HISTLINE
           EDMK      ORNGBOT,RTOPNTRY               :
           BCTR      R1,0                           :
           MVC       0(1,R1),ORNGBOT+L'ORNGBOT-1
           MVI       ORNGBOT+L'ORNGBOT-1,C' '       :
           LA        RB,L'RNGETOP(RB)               MOVE RB TO NEXT BRACKET
           ZAP       LIMWORK,RTOPNTRY               EDIT (RB -> RTOPNTRY)-1 INTO
           SP        LIMWORK,=P'1'                      HISTLINE
           MVC       ORNGTOP,LIMMSK                 :
           LA        R1,ORNGTOP+LIMFRST             :
           EDMK      ORNGTOP,LIMWORK                :
           BCTR      R1,0                           :
           MVC       0(1,R1),ORNGTOP+L'ORNGTOP-1
           MVI       ORNGTOP+L'ORNGTOP-1,C' '       :
           PUT       PRINTER,HISTLINE               PRINT HISTLINE
           LA        R2,L'COUNT(R2)                 :
           B         FTEST03                        :
ENDFOR03   EQU       *                              ENDFOR
           L         RE,PRNTHIST-4                  RETURN
           BR        RE                             :
*********************************************************************************
*     SYMBOL DEFINITIONS                                                        *
*********************************************************************************
           REGEQU
*
TEMPLEN    EQU       3                              INPUT TEMPERATURE LENGTH
PTMPLEN    EQU       TEMPLEN/2+1                    PACKED TEMPERATURE LENGTH
AVGLEN     EQU       5                              AVERAGE LENGTH
PAVGLEN    EQU       AVGLEN/2+1                     PACKED AVERAGE LENGTH
NUMRNGS    EQU       8                              NUMBER OF RANGES
PWKLEN     EQU       2                              LENGTH FOR NUMBER OF WEEKS
*     OFFSETS FOR OUTPUT LINES
WEEKOFST   EQU       20                             OFFSET FOR WEEK IN WKLINE
HIGHOFST   EQU       40                             OFFSET FOR AVERAGE HIGH
LOWOFST    EQU       60                             OFFSET FOR AVERAGE LOW
RBOTOFST   EQU       10                             OFFSET FOR RANGE START
RTOPOFST   EQU       20                             OFFSET FOR RANGE END
STAROFST   EQU       40                             OFFSET FOR STARS IN HISTOGRAM
MAXSTARS   EQU       84                             LENGTH OF STARS
*********************************************************************************
*     DSECTS FOR ACCESSING ARRAYS                                               *
*********************************************************************************
RTOPSCT    DSECT                                    RANGE TOP ENTRIES
RTOPNTRY   DS        PL(PTMPLEN)                     :
```

```
TMPSECT    DSECT                              TEMPERATURE ENTRIES
TMPNTRY    DS      ZL(2*TEMPLEN)                TEMPERATURE RECORD
           ORG     TMPNTRY                        :
LOW        DS      ZL(TEMPLEN)                    DAILY LOW
HIGH       DS      ZL(TEMPLEN)                    DAILY HIGH
CHSECT     DSECT                              CHARACTER POSITION IN HIST. LINE
STARPOS    DS      CL1                            ONE STAR
SAMPLE5    CSECT                                  :
****************************************************************************************
*     LITERALS                                                                        *
****************************************************************************************
           LTORG
****************************************************************************************
*     FILES                                                                           *
****************************************************************************************
INFILE     DTFCD   DEVADDR=SYSIPT,DEVICE=2501,EOFADDR=EOFADDR              X
                   IOAREA1=INBUF1,IOAREA2=INBUF2,WORKA=YES
INBUF1     DS      CL80
INBUF2     DS      CL80
*
PRINTER    DTFPR   DEVADDR=SYSLST,DEVICE=3203,BLKSIZE=133,CTLCHR=ASA,      X
                   IOAREA1=OUTBUF1,IOAREA2=OUTBUF2,WORKA=YES
OUTBUF1    DS      CL133
OUTBUF2    DS      CL133
****************************************************************************************
*     CONSTANTS                                                                       *
****************************************************************************************
NUMWEEKS   DC      P'12'                      NUMBER OF WEEKS IN REPORT
LOWLIM     DC      P'-30'                     START OF FIRST RANGE
TMPRNGE    DC      P'20'                      SIZE OF RANGE
*     EDIT MASKS AND OFFSETS
WEEKMSK    DC      X'40202020'                WEEK NUMBER IN AVERAGE REPORT
AVGMSK     DC      X'40202020214B2060'        AVERAGE HIGH AND LOW
AVGFRST    EQU     5                          LOCATION OF SIGN
LIMMSK     DC      X'4020212060'              RANGE LIMITS IN HISTOGRAM
LIMFRST    EQU     3                          LOCATION OF SIGN
****************************************************************************************
*     VARIABLES                                                                       *
****************************************************************************************
LIMWORK    DS      PL(PTMPLEN)                USED TO DETERMINE UPPER LIM IN HIST.
RANGELIM   DS      PL(PTMPLEN)                USED TO FILL THE ARRAY OF RANGES
WEEK       DS      PL(PWKLEN)                 CURRENT WEEK NUMBER
PTEMP      DS      PL(PTMPLEN)                PACKED TEMPERATURE
HIGHSUM    DS      PL(PTMPLEN+1)              SUM OF THE DAILY HIGHS
LOWSUM     DS      PL(PTMPLEN+1)              SUM OF THE DAILY LOWS
DIVWORK    DS      PL(PAVGLEN+1)              WORK AREA FOR FINDING AVERAGE
```

```
         ORG    DIVWORK           :
AVERAGE  DS     PL(PAVGLEN)       AVERAGE
         ORG    DIVWORK+L'DIVWORK :
********************************************************************************
*    I/O WORK AREAS                                                           *
********************************************************************************
WEEKHEAD DC     CL133' '          HEADING FOR WEEKLY AVERAGES
         ORG    WEEKHEAD          :
         DC     C'1'              START NEW PAGE
         ORG    WEEKHEAD+WEEKOFST :
         DC     C'WEEK'           :
         ORG    WEEKHEAD+HIGHOFST :
         DC     C'AVERAGE HIGH'   :
         ORG    WEEKHEAD+LOWOFST  :
         DC     C'AVERAGE LOW'
         ORG    WEEKHEAD+L'WEEKHEAD END HEADING
*
HISTHEAD DC     CL133' '          HEADING FOR HISTOGRAM
         ORG    HISTHEAD          :
         DC     C'1'              START NEW PAGE
         ORG    HISTHEAD+RBOTOFST :
         DC     C'TEMP. RANGE'    :
         ORG    HISTHEAD+STAROFST :
         DC     C'NUMBER OF DAILY HIGHS'
         ORG    HISTHEAD+L'HISTHEAD END HISTHEAD
*
SPACE    DC     CL133' '          BLANK LINE
*
WEEKDATA DS     CL80              WEEKDATA INPUT RECORD
         ORG    WEEKDATA          :
TEMPS    DS     (7)CL(2*TEMPLEN)  ARRAY OF HIGH-LOW PAIRS
         ORG    WEEKDATA+L'WEEKDATA END WEEKDATA
*
WKLINE   DC     CL133' '          WEEK LINE
         ORG    WKLINE+WEEKOFST   :
OUTWEEK  DS     CL(L'WEEKMSK)      OUTPUT WEEK
         ORG    WKLINE+HIGHOFST   :
OHIGHAVG DS     CL(L'AVGMSK)       AVERAGE HIGH
         ORG    WKLINE+LOWOFST    :
OLOWAVG  DS     CL(L'AVGMSK)       AVERAGE LOW
         ORG    WKLINE+L'WKLINE   END WEEK LINE
*
HISTLINE DC     CL133' '          HISTOGRAM LINE
         ORG    HISTLINE+RBOTOFST :
ORNGBOT  DS     CL(L'LIMMSK)       RANGE BOTTOM
         ORG    HISTLINE+RTOPOFST :
```

```
ORNGTOP    DS      CL(L'LIMMSK)              RANGE TOP
           ORG     HISTLINE+STAROFST        :
STARS      DS      CL(MAXSTARS)             STARS
           ORG     HISTLINE+L'HISTLINE   END HISTOGRAM LINE
***************************************************************************************************
*     ARRAYS                                                                                     *
***************************************************************************************************
RNGETOP    DS      (NUMRNGS+1)PL(PTMPLEN)   ARRAY OF RANGE LIMITS
SENTINEL   DS      PL(PTMPLEN)              SENTINEL FOR BRACKET SEARCH. . .
*                                           THIS MUST BE PLACED IMMEDIATELY
*                                           AFTER RNGETOP TO TERM. SEARCH.
COUNT      DS      (NUMRNGS+1)F             NUMBER OF DAYS IN EACH RANGE
           END
```

If the input data contains negative numbers, it must be entered in hexadecimal form. A sample of such an input file is shown below.

```
F0F2D0F0F0D8F0F2D2F0F1D8F0F3D0F0F1D1F0F1D5F0F0F0F0F0D2F0F1F5F0F1F0F0F2F0F0F1F2F0F2F8
F0F1F0F0F2F7F0F1F2F0F3F1F0F1F0F0F1F9F0F0F5F0F1F5F0F0F5F0F1F8F0F0F6F0F2F2F0F0F7F0F3F3
F0F1F5F0F2F5F0F1F8F0F3F0F0F1F7F0F3F2F0F1F9F0F2F5F0F1F9F0F2F8F0F1F5F0F3F7F0F2F3F0F3F8
F0F2F4F0F3F9F0F2F2F0F3F5F0F2F8F0F3F7F0F3F1F0F4F0F0F2F8F0F3F6F0F2F7F0F3F2F0F2F1F0F3F9
F0F2F6F0F4F0F0F2F2F0F3F8F0F2F5F0F4F1F0F2F9F0F4F2F0F2F7F0F4F3F0F3F1F0F4F4F0F2F2F0F3F3
F0F2F4F0F3F7F0F2F7F0F3F5F0F2F1F0F3F9F0F2F8F0F4F1F0F2F9F0F4F4F0F2F6F0F4F7F0F3F2F0F4F9
F0F3F3F0F4F2F0F3F5F0F4F9F0F3F7F0F5F0F0F3F2F0F4F0F0F2F8F0F4F2F0F3F4F0F4F8F0F3F7F0F5F1
F0F3F9F0F4F7F0F3F8F0F5F5F0F3F8F0F5F9F0F3F9F0F5F8F0F3F2F0F5F7F0F4F0F0F6F1F0F4F5F0F6F2
F0F3F7F0F5F6F0F4F0F0F5F8F0F4F4F0F6F2F0F4F1F0F6F3F0F4F5F0F6F4F0F4F2F0F6F1F0F4F5F0F6F6
F0F4F0F0F6F6F0F4F2F0F6F8F0F4F5F0F7F0F0F4F6F0F6F9F0F4F1F0F6F5F0F5F0F0F7F1F0F5F1F0F6F8
F0F5F2F0F6F7F0F5F5F0F6F1F0F5F1F0F6F2F0F5F4F0F6F4F0F4F9F0F6F8F0F4F8F0F7F0F0F5F2F0F6F9
F0F5F8F0F7F2F0F5F6F0F7F0F0F5F7F0F7F3F0F5F9F0F7F4F0F5F8F0F7F3F0F5F6F0F6F8F0F5F7F0F6F9
```

When executed with this data as input, our program produces the output shown below.

WEEK	AVERAGE HIGH	AVERAGE LOW
1	3.7	−9.6
2	23.6	7.9
3	30.7	18.0
4	36.9	25.9
5	40.1	26.0
6	41.7	26.7
7	46.0	33.7
8	57.0	38.7
9	61.4	42.0
10	68.1	45.0
11	65.9	51.6
12	71.3	57.3

TEMP.	RANGE	NUMBER OF DAILY HIGHS
−30	−11	**
−10	9	**
10	29	************
30	49	*************************************
50	69	******************************
70	89	*****
90	109	
110	129	

P R O G R A M M I N G   P R O J E C T S

1. Using the arrays of records, STDLIST and GRDLIST, described in Examples 5.5.2 and 5.5.3, write a program to read an input file that contains the information to be stored in the arrays and print a grade report for each student.

   The input file will contain a set of student records followed by a trailer card that contains all zeros in the student number field. This will be followed by a set of grade report records with a similar trailer record. Assume that the student records are ordered by student number, but that the grade report records are not in any particular order.

   The grade report for each student should include all the information in the student record as well as the information on all the grade reports for that student. (It is possible that a student may have no grade reports.) The report should also give the student's semester Grade Point Average, counting A as 4 points, B as 3 points, and so on.

2. Write a program to process semester grades for a class of up to 50 students who have taken up to 9 tests. The first input record will contain the number of students (2 digits) and the number of tests (1 digit). The remaining records will contain a 30-character student name and the scores of that student on the tests (3 digits each). The output should list the student names in alphabetical order together with the test scores, average and rank in class for each student.

3. The We Never Sleep Bedding Company has devised a new scheme for computing commissions for their sales personnel. Each sales person will receive a basic commission of 10% of their own gross sales. In addition, the sales person will receive another 10% of daily sales for each day that their personal sales were higher than the average daily sales for the entire sales force in the past week. Finally, the sales person with the highest average daily sales for the past week will receive a $150.00 bonus.

   The input will consist of a set of records which contain a sales person's name (20 characters) and their daily sales for each of the past 5 days. (The We Never Sleep Bedding Company is closed on weekends.) The output report should contain this information together with the average daily sales and the total compensation (commission plus any bonus) for each employee. At the end of the report, give the total compensation, the overall average daily sales, and the total sales for the past week.

4. The Mercury Messenger Company needs a program to process shipping orders. The input to this program will be a rate table and a list of shipping orders. The output will be a report listing all of the input information together with the cost for each shipment.

   The rate table information will begin with a record which gives the number of distance brackets and the number of weight brackets (2 digits each). The next record will give the upper limit for each distance bracket (3 digits each). (Packages to be shipped beyond the upper limit for the last bracket will not be accepted.) There will be one record for each weight bracket. It will give the upper limit for that bracket (2 digits) and the price per pound (format 9.99 with an implied decimal point) for each of the distance brackets. Packages that exceed the weight limit for the last bracket will also be rejected.)

   The information for each package will contain the shipper's name (20 characters), the destination address (40 characters), the weight to the nearest pound (2 digits), and the distance (3 digits).

   The output report should include a copy of the rate table with headings giving the lower and upper limits for each weight and distance bracket. It should print a line for each package giving the input information on that package and the shipping cost, rounded to the nearest cent. At the end of the report, give the number of packages in each weight bracket and in each distance bracket.

5. A two-dimensional array of fullwords can be described by giving its starting address, the number of rows and the number of columns. This information can be packaged in a record structure that we call a *matrix descriptor*. Given such a descriptor, the matrix can be accessed by loading the starting address into a register. That register can then be associated with a DSECT, which describes one entry of the array. All entries can be accessed using a second register as an index register.

   Write a subroutine MATMULT which gets three such descriptors, DESCRPTA, DESCRPTB, and DESCRPTC describing matrices A, B, and C. Assuming that the dimensions are compatible, the subroutine should set C = A*B, using normal matrix multiplication.

   Test your subroutine in a program that reads two arrays specified by giving their dimensions in one record and giving the row entries in succeeding records. Have the program determine the dimensions of the product and call MATMULT to do the multiplication. Print the product in row major order.

   In order to use space as efficiently as possible, your program should allocate a large memory area to hold all three arrays and allocate space to each as needed.

CHAPTER 6

EXTERNAL PROCEDURES AND PARAMETER PASSING

6.1 PROCEDURES AND PARAMETERS

In this chapter, we develop techniques for implementing procedures and reference parameters in assembly language. In addition to using these techniques in our assembly language programs, our approach will prepare us for similar constructs in high-level languages.

First is a review of arguments in favor of using procedures and parameters, as opposed to internal subroutines and global variables. As we review, note the functional characteristics of these constructs, which will be used to guide our implementations.

An implementation of a procedure call and return mechanisms concludes this section. This will provide for saving the state of the calling computation. The particular mechanisms we adopt will allow our assembly language procedures to be interfaced with high-level language programs and procedures.

In later sections, we consider several mechanisms for passing parameters to procedures and for performing input and output operations from procedures.

The Value of Independent Procedures

The most basic characteristic of a general construct for procedures is *independence*. Complete independence implies the ability to take a procedure used in one program and transfer it unchanged to another program. The design of a procedure should be determined by the task it is required to perform. It should not be influenced by the program that involves the procedure. If the same task is required in another program, then it should be possible to use the same procedure in the new program.

This portability of procedures provides an easily applied test for independence, but portability is not the primary argument in favor of independence. There are many procedures that are so small, it is relatively easy to recreate them as needed. Other procedures perform tasks that are so closely related to the particular program in which they are found that these procedures are unlikely to be of use in other programs. Yet, it is still important that these procedures exhibit independence, because independence is the best way of controlling complexity. The basic problem in writing reliable programs is the control of complexity. The primary source of complexity in a particular program is the number of relationships existing among its components. Independence keeps a minimal number of relationships between the calling program and the procedure.

Independence also allows changes to be made in the way a procedure is implemented, without necessitating changes in the calling program. For example, this kind of independence allows us to make improvements in individual procedures in a program. As long as the new procedure accomplishes the same task as the old one, the particular method of implementation used is irrelevant.

Independence of procedures is especially important when testing and debugging programs, making it possible to test procedures separately. It also allows us to make corrections in a particular procedure without having to change other procedures or the calling program.

All of these desirable traits of independence apply to procedures implemented in any language. Procedures implemented in assembly language should display one additional type of independence, that is, independence of the language in which the calling program is written. We would like to be able to create assembly language procedures that can be called from programs written in any major language. Although this may also be desirable in other programming systems, it is especially useful in assembly language. It is this capability that allows us to write assembly language procedures to improve the performance of time-critical sections in a program or to access special hardware features without having to write the entire program in assembly language.

Achieving Independence of Procedures

The objective of independent procedures imposes a number of restrictions on the method of implementation. These relate to the means of providing communication between the calling program and the procedure, while at the same time, allowing the procedure to use local variables and registers without interfering with the calling program.

The communication between the calling program and the procedure must not depend upon a name correspondence between variables. Such a dependence would clearly make it impossible to move a procedure from one program to another. Perhaps more important, it would restrict a procedure to working with one particular set of variables. A procedure written to sort an array named *A* cannot be used to sort another array named *B*. This restriction prohibits the use of global variables for communicating between the procedure and the calling program. We shall, instead, implement an argument-parameter correspondence. The calling program will determine which arguments are to be passed on each procedure call. The correspondence between arguments and parameters will be determined by the position of the arguments in the call.

The argument-parameter correspondence must provide for two-way communication between the calling program and the procedure. Sufficient information must be provided to the procedure to allow it to access the values of the arguments. In order to return information to the calling program, the procedure must be able to change the values of variables in the calling program. The simplest way to provide such communication is to pass the addresses of the arguments to the procedure when it is invoked. This allows the caller to pass different addresses on different invocations, thus changing the argument-parameter correspondence between calls.

We need to provide local data areas in each procedure. In describing the data areas, we should be able to use identifiers that are meaningful in the context of the procedure, without having to determine whether the same identifier is being used in the calling program or in another procedure. Local data areas are certainly necessary in order to move procedures between programs, a capacity that turns out to have a profound effect on the implementation of procedures. Because the assembler has no capacity for limiting the scope of an identifier, procedures must be assembled separately. Because locations in the calling program will be unknown when the procedure is assembled, each procedure must be provided with its own base register during execution.

Similar to the need for local data areas, an assembly language procedure must be able to use the general-purpose registers freely. In fact, our implementation of procedure parameters will require the use of additional registers. Nevertheless, independence of procedures requires that the procedure not destroy any values that might be needed by the caller. As the coding of the procedure should not depend on any knowledge of the operation of the calling program, we adopt the course of saving all register values on procedure entry and restoring them at the conclusion of the procedure.

IBM Standard Calling Sequence

In order to implement all of the features described above in a uniform way, we need to establish a protocol for invoking procedures, the mechanism to be used to pass argument addresses to the procedure, the saving and restoration of register values, and, in the case of functions, a mechanism for returning a value from the function to the calling program. There are many options available for such a protocol, however, IBM has established a protocol that is used by all major IBM compilers. If we adopt this standard, then we can write assembly language procedures that can be called from programs written in other languages.

Under Standard Calling Sequence, the main program and each procedure that will invoke another procedure must provide 18 fullwords of storage to be used for saving the caller's register contents together with other information. This collection of 18 fullwords is called the *save area*. As the procedure is assembled separately from the calling program, it cannot access the caller's save area unless the address of the save area is passed to the procedure by the caller. Register RD (13) is designated for this purpose. Typically, the caller places the address of its save area in RD as part of its own initialization. This address remains in RD throughout the execution of the caller so that it is available whenever a procedure is invoked.

The 18 fullwords of the save area are allocated for use as follows.

Fullword Number	Use
1	Status of the PL/I error handler. The contents of this location are only pertinent when a procedure has been called from a PL/I program.
2	Address of the next higher level program's save area. This location will hold the address that was in RD on procedure entry.
3	Address of the next lower level programs save area. We will not use this location.
4-18	The contents of registers RE, RF, R0, R1, R2, R3, R4, R5, R6, R7, R8, R9, RA, RB, and RC in that order.

The layout of the save area, as we shall use it, is shown below.

SAVE+0	PL/I Error Handler Status
SAVE+4	Address of Caller's Save Area
SAVE+8	Not used
SAVE+12	Contents of RE on procedure entry
SAVE+16	Contents of RF on procedure entry
SAVE+20	Contents of R0 on procedure entry
SAVE+24	Contents of R1 on procedure entry
SAVE+28	Contents of R2 on procedure entry
SAVE+32	Contents of R3 on procedure entry
SAVE+36	Contents of R4 on procedure entry
SAVE+40	Contents of R5 on procedure entry
SAVE+44	Contents of R6 on procedure entry
SAVE+48	Contents of R7 on procedure entry
SAVE+52	Contents of R8 on procedure entry
SAVE+56	Contents of R9 on procedure entry
SAVE+60	Contents of RA on procedure entry
SAVE+64	Contents of RB on procedure entry
SAVE+68	Contents of RC on procedure entry

In addition to specifying the location and format of the save area, the standard calling sequence prescribes uses for several registers. These are listed below.

Register	Use
R0	Return value from function calls.
R1	Pointer to list of argument addresses.
RD	Pointer to caller's save area.
RE	Return address.
RF	Subroutine entry address.

Procedure Invocation

The calling sequence specifies that the address of the called procedure be placed in RF. As the procedure will be separately assembled, its address will not be known to the assembler. The actual address of the procedure cannot be determined until the program is linked. Placing the address in RF requires the use of the V-type address constant. This constant is used only to reserve storage for an external procedure address. The format is

V(<symbol>)

The assembler reserves a fullword for an address and fills it with zeros. When the program is linked, the linker substitutes the address of the symbol in the executable program.

The V-type address constant can be used in a DC or in a literal operand. The procedure address can be placed in RF by the instruction

L   RF,=V(<procedure name>)

The procedure is then invoked with a BALR instruction specifying RF as the second operand.

Procedure Entry

The first instruction in each procedure should save the register contents in the assigned locations in the caller's save area, using RD as a pointer register. Because RD contains the address of the beginning of SAVE, the fullword receiving the contents of the first register, RF, can be designated by an offset of 12 from the address in RD. This can be accomplished with the following Store Multiple instruction.

STM   RE,RC,12(RD)

The relationship between the caller and the procedure is shown below.

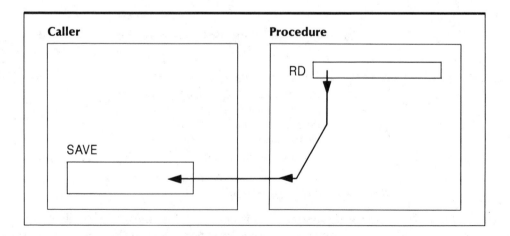

Notice that RD is not included in the registers to be saved. In fact, it would be pointless to save RD in the caller's save area, as the address in RD is the procedure's

only link to that save area. As long as the address in RD is preserved, the procedure makes use of all other registers. Note, in particular, that the return address in RE has also been saved in the caller's save area. We do not need to make separate provisions for saving RE.

Once the procedure has saved the caller's registers, it must establish a base register for its own use. We continue to use RC as the primary base register. Thus, the next instructions in the procedure should be

```
BALR    RC,0
USING   *,RC
```

If the procedure is to invoke other procedures, it should also save the current contents of RD and load RD with the address of its own save area. RD will be saved in the second fullword of the procedure's save area. The new value will then be loaded with a load address instruction.

```
ST      RD,SAVE+4
LA      RD,SAVE
```

These two instructions must follow the BALR-USING sequence in the procedure. None of the procedure's storage areas can be accessed until the base register has been loaded with the procedure's base address.

At this point, the relationship between the procedure's save area and the caller's save area is as shown below.

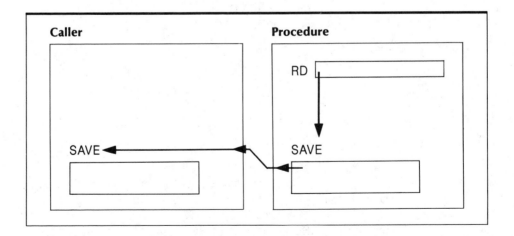

Procedure Exit

Before returning control to the caller, the procedure must restore all of the caller's registers. If RD has been changed to allow other procedures to be invoked, then its value must first be restored with

```
L       RD,SAVE+4
```

When RD contains the address of the caller's save area, the remaining register values can be restored with

```
LM      RE,RC,12(RD)
```

The return to the caller is effected with

```
BR      RE
```

We can now specify the complete entry and exit code for a procedure. If the procedure does not invoke any other procedures, then it need not provide a save area and the address of the caller's save area can be left in RD. The structure of such a procedure is

```
<name>    CSECT  PROCEDURE <name>
          STM    RE,RC,12(RD)
          BALR   RC,0
          USING  *,RC
            .
            .
            .
          <Procedure code>
            .
            .
            .
          LM     RE,RC,12(RD)
          BR     RE
            .
            .
            .
          <Symbol definitions, local data, etc.>
            .
            .
            .
          END
```

When the procedure is to invoke other procedures, the addition of the instructions to change the address in RD creates the following structure.

```
<name>    CSECT  PROCEDURE <name>
          STM    RE,RC,12(RD)
          BALR   RC,0
          USING  *,RC
          ST     RD,SAVE+4
          LA     RD,SAVE
            .
```

```
          .
          .
          .
          <Procedure code>
          .
          .
          .
          L      RD,SAVE+4
          LM     RE,RC,12(RD)
          BR     RE
SAVE      DS     18F
          .
          .
          .
          <Symbol definitions, local data, etc.>
          .
          .
          .
          END
```

SAVE and RETURN Macros

DOS provides two macros to implement the instructions needed to save and restore registers. The SAVE macro generates an instruction to save one or more register values in the save area addressed by RD. The format of this macro is

```
          SAVE   (<reg1>,<reg2>)
```

or

```
          SAVE   (<reg>)
```

(Unfortunately, both forms require the registers to be specified as 0 . . . 15. They do not permit the use of symbolic names.)

If r_1 and r_2 are numbers that represent registers, then the macro call

```
          SAVE   (r₁,r₂)
```

will generate the instruction

```
          STM    r₁,r₂,12+4*(r₁+2-(r₁+2)/16*16)(13)
```

The expression $12+4*(r_1+2-(r_1+2)/16*16)$ determines the offset in the save area corresponding to r_1. The 12 represents the 3 fullwords at the beginning of the save area. The expression $r_1+2-(r_1+2)/16*16$ represents the number of registers stored in the save area before register r_1. Its correctness depends on the fact that the division operation is integer division. The table below shows how this expression is evaluated for several values of r_1.

r_1	$(r_1+2)/16*16$	$r_1+2-(r_1+2)/16*16$	$12+4*(r_1+2-(r_1+2)/16*16)$
14	16	0	12
15	16	1	16
0	0	2	20
1	0	3	24
2	0	4	28

We will use this form of the macro as

          SAVE   (14,12)

The generated instruction will save the contents of all registers except RD in the correct locations of the save area.

The second form of the SAVE instruction generates an instruction to save a single register in the proper location of the save area. The correct offset is determined as above.

The RETURN macro comes in similar forms.

          RETURN (<reg1>,<reg2>)

or

          RETURN (<reg>)

It generates an instruction to restore the indicated registers from the save area addressed by RD. It also generates the instruction to return control to the calling program

          BR   RE

Formats for Procedures and Functions

When the SAVE and RETURN macros are used, the structure of a procedure that will invoke another procedure is

```
<name>    CSECT                        PROCEDURE <name>
          SAVE    (14,12)
          BALR    RC,0
          USING   *,RC
          ST      RD,SAVE+4
          LA      RD,SAVE
            .
            .
            .

          <Procedure code>
            .
            .
            .

          L       RD,SAVE+4
```

```
            RETURN (14,12)
SAVE        DS      18F
            .
            .
            .
            <Symbol definitions, local data, etc.>
            .
            .
            .
            END
```

If the procedure will not invoke other procedures, the instructions to point RD at a new save area on procedure entry and reset RD before exiting can be omitted. However, it is better to use this format for all procedures, making it easy to add a procedure call later, without having to change anything else in the calling procedure.

The format for a function is only slightly different. As we noted in our discussion of register usage, the standard calling sequence specifies that a function should return a value by placing it in register R0. However, if we store a value in R0, then use the RETURN macro as in the code above, the value computed by the function will be replaced by the original value of R0 from the caller's save area. This can be remedied in a number of ways, but the cleanest solution is to have the function code put the value in R0. Immediately before the RETURN macro, we can use SAVE (0) to save the new contents of R0 in the caller's save area. Then, the RETURN macro will not effect the value in R0.

With these considerations, we have the following framework for a function. The order of the instructions shown is crucial.

```
<name>      CSECT                       FUNCTION <name>
            SAVE    (14,12)
            BALR    RC,0
            USING   *,RC
            ST      RD,SAVE+4
            LA      RD,SAVE
            .
            .
            .
            <Code to compute >
            <a value in R0.      >
            .
            .
            .
            L       RD,SAVE+4
            SAVE    (0)
            RETURN (14,12)
SAVE        DS      18F
            .
```

.

.

.

<Symbol definitions, local data, etc.>

.

.

.

END

Assembling Programs Using External Procedures

Among other things, one value of separately assembled procedures is preventing accidental changes in data areas or unintentional side effects. Separately assembled procedures also avoids any potential name conflicts between procedures.

In order to provide these benefits, the job stream will be somewhat more complicated and we will make greater demands upon the services of the operating system. The basic idea is to execute the assembler a number of times. Each such execution assembles one procedure, written as an independent CSECT, and stores the resulting object module. When this is completed, we call on the linker to put these separate modules together to create an executable program. A DOS job stream to assemble, link, and execute a program with two independent procedures is shown below.

```
// <JOB Jobname>
// OPTION LINK,PARTDUMP,XREF
   ACTION MAP
// EXEC ASSEMBLY
```

        Source code for main program.

```
/*
// EXEC ASSEMBLY
```

        Source code for first procedure.

```
/*
// EXEC ASSEMBLY
```

        Source code for second procedure.

```
/*
// EXEC LNKEDT
// EXEC
```

            Data records.

```
/*
/&
```

E X E R C I S E S

1. Why is it necessary to save the contents of RD before calling another procedure? Why is it saved in the current procedure's save area instead of the caller's save area?

2. Write the entry and exit code for a procedure FINDAVG which will invoke another procedure.

3. Use the formula employed by the SAVE macro to calculate the offset in the caller's save area for the value of R8. Write the instructions that will be generated when each of the following macros is expanded.
   a. SAVE (10)
   b. SAVE (14)
   c. SAVE (0)
   d. SAVE (14,5)
   e. RETURN (14,7)

4. Write a procedure to open the standard output file and print the message "Procedural Programming is Easy!"

5. Write a function to open the standard input and output files and copy records from input to output until End-Of-File. Return the number of records read as the function value.

6.2 REFERENCE PARAMETERS

As discussed in the last section, in order to write procedures that are independent of the calling program, we must have some mechanism, other than global variables, for communicating between the calling program and the procedures. In this section, we discuss how to implement reference parameters in 370 Assembly Language.

The use of reference parameters allows two-way communication between the calling program and the procedure. Reference parameters are implemented by passing the argument addresses to the called procedure. Because the procedure knows the address of the argument, it can obtain its value. If necessary, the procedure can also change the value of the argument, passing information back to the caller by means of the change.

Recall the distinction between reference and value parameters. In a high-level language that supports value parameters, a procedure can obtain the value of the corresponding argument, but is prevented from changing the argument. In general, reference parameters should be used only when it is the proper function of the procedure to change the argument value. If the procedure merely needs to know the initial value of the argument, then value parameters would be used. This prevents unexpected errors, which may occur if an argument value is accidentally changed.

Although we use reference parameters in our sample programs, value parameters can be implemented by copying the argument value into a local variable on procedure entry and, thereafter, accessing only that local variable. The advantage is that the calling procedure passes arguments in the same way, regardless of whether they correspond to reference or value parameters. The distinction between the two parameter types is made by the procedure, not by the caller.

In implementing reference parameters, we must address two issues: providing a mechanism for passing addresses from the caller to the procedure, and, once in the procedure, providing a mechanism that allows us to access the parameters in a natural way.

Argument Address Lists

In the last section, we noted that each procedure would be provided with its own base register. We also observed that, in order to avoid possible name conflicts between variables and labels in the procedures and the calling program, procedures should be separately assembled. As a result of these two decisions, none of the locations in the caller can be directly accessed by the procedure. This provides a great deal of protection against accidental changes by the procedure, but it also restricts the amount of communication available. The procedure cannot access any locations in the part of memory occupied by the calling program, unless the procedure is given the addresses of those locations. The only direct communication between the caller and the procedure is through the general-purpose registers. Thus, the address passing needed to implement reference parameters must involve the registers.

If the number of arguments is relatively small, we could place the address of each argument in a register using the LA instruction. As the registers to be used are determined by the procedure rather than the calling program, there would undoubtedly be times when the caller would find it necessary to save the contents of some registers before the subroutine call and restore them afterwards. Further, this mechanism will not work if the number of arguments exceeds the number of available registers.

We need a method that will work for any number of parameters and one that will not require the dislocation of a large number of register values. Our solution is to set up a list of argument addresses in the memory occupied by the calling program, then place the address of this list of addresses in register R1 immediately before the call. This allows the argument list to be as long as necessary.

The value in R1 will represent the address of the first argument address. Thus, the procedure can obtain the address of the argument with an instruction such as

```
L       R5,0(R1)
```

If the addresses in the list are stored in fullword fields, then the address of the second argument could be placed in R6 with

       L   R6,4(R1)

In general, the procedure can obtain the address of the n'th argument in the list by specifying an offset of $4*(n-1)$ from the address in R1.

   The implementation of the address list is simplified by the use of A-type address constants. These constants direct the assembler and the linker to store addresses in the indicated locations. The general format is

DC   A(<expression>)

We used these constants, in the last chapter, with absolute expressions to store the values of expressions in fullword fields. When the expression is relocatable, the linker places the address corresponding to the expression in the fullword field. Thus, if ARG1 is a label in a program, the

       DC   A(ARG1)

will direct the assembler to reserve a fullword field. When the program is linked, the linker will place the address of ARG1 in this field.

   In order to set up a list of addresses for several arguments, say ARG1, ARG2, ARG3, we use

       DC   A(ARG1)
       DC   A(ARG2)
       DC   A(ARG3)

or equivalently,

       DC   A(ARG1,ARG2,ARG3)

These instructions create three successive fullword fields, which will contain the addresses of the three arguments when the program is executed.

   Having established a mechanism for defining the argument address list, we next determine where this address list should be placed. The two options are: (1) placing it in the portion of the source module reserved for data areas; and (2) placing it at the point of the call. The second alternative seems at first glance to be a bit awkward, as it requires the address lists to be interspersed with the code. However, we find that this difficulty is easily overcome. There are several advantages to having the address list at the point of the call, the most compelling one being that it makes the program easier to read. We can determine the arguments on any procedure invocation without referring to the data areas of the source module.

To understand how we circumvent the problem of placing the argument address list in the code, suppose we place the list immediately after the branch to the procedure. (Recall that the standard calling sequence specifies that the address of the procedure should be placed in RF.) We then invoke the procedure with a BALR instruction. The code would be

```
L       RF,=V(<subroutine>)
BALR    <reg>,RF
DC      A(<argument₁>)
DC      A(<argument₂>)
  .
  .
  .
DC      A(<argumentₙ>)
```

The BALR instruction places the address of the following instruction in the first register. In this case, the address of the following "instruction" is, in fact, the address of the argument address list. The register specified as the first operand in the BALR instruction would be R1. That is, we use the link aspect of the BALR instruction to establish the address of the argument address list.

In order to fulfill the requirements of the standard calling sequence, we must separately place the correct address in RE. In this case, we want to return control to the first instruction after the argument address list. We should be able to compute this return address relatively easily. As we know the number of addresses in the address list, we ought to be able to determine the length of this list and the location of the first instruction after the list. However, there is a slight complication. The assembler normally aligns fullword fields on fullword boundaries. If the location counter is not on a fullword boundary when the first address constant is processed, the assembler will skip 2 bytes to get to the next fullword boundary. Thus, we cannot be sure of the distance from the BALR instruction to the end of the address list. The only way to avoid this problem is to make certain that the location counter is on a fullword boundary when the first address constant is processed. For this, we need the CNOP directive.

Conditional NOP *CNOP*

```
CNOP    <byte>,<boundary>
```

This directive instructs the assembler to insert sufficient NOP's to set the location counter to byte <byte> of the field type indicated by <boundary>.

Example 6.2.1

CNOP 0,4   Advance the location counter to a fullword boundary.

CNOP 2,4   Advance the location counter to the second byte of an aligned fullword.

CNOP 6,8   Advance the location counter to byte 6 of an aligned doubleword.

The complete subroutine call will consist of an appropriate CNOP followed by the instruction sequence

```
L       RF,=V(<subroutine>)
LA      RE,<return location>
BALR    R1,RF
DC      A(<argument₁>)
DC      A(<argument₂>)
  .
  .
  .
DC      A(<argumentₙ>)
```

The L and the LA instructions are 4 bytes long and the BALR instruction is 2 bytes long. In order to avoid any skipped bytes, the location counter must be at a fullword boundary when the first address constant is processed. As the preceding instructions occupy 10 bytes, the location counter should be positioned at the second byte of a fullword before the L instruction. This yields

```
CNOP    2,4
L       RF,=V(<subroutine>)
LA      RE,<return location>
BALR    R1,RF
DC      A(<argument₁>)
DC      A(<argument₂>)
  .
  .
  .
DC      A(<argumentₙ>)
```

Now we can calculate the correct return address. To the location counter value at the beginning of the LA instruction, we must add 4 bytes for the LA instruction, 2 bytes for the BALR instruction, and 4 bytes for each of the arguments. The result is a procedure call as follows.

```
CNOP    2,4
L       RF,=V(<subroutine>)
LA      RE,*+6+4*(<number of arguments>)
BALR    R1,RF
DC      A(<argument₁>)
DC      A(<argument₂>)
  .
  .
  .
DC      A(<argumentₙ>)
```

The CALL Macro

Once they are understood, the instructions above for invoking a procedure are straightforward. However, the sequence is long and must be repeated for every procedure call. Fortunately, the operating system provides a macro the *call* macro, that will generate the instructions for us.

The format of the call macro is

CALL   <procedure name>,(<argument list>)

Note that the list of arguments must be separated from the procedure name by a comma and enclosed in parentheses.

Example 6.2.2 *To invoke a procedure named PRO1 with arguments A, B, and C, we would use the following.*

CALL   PRO1,(A,B,C)

This macro call would generate the following sequence of instructions.

```
CNOP    2,4
L       15,=V(PRO1)
LA      14,*+6+4*3
BALR    1,15
DC      A(A)
DC      A(B)
DC      A(C)
ORG     *-4
DC      X'80'
ORG     *+3
```

Note the last three instructions generated by the macro. After defining the address constants for the three parameters, the instruction

ORG   *-4

moves the location counter back 3 bytes to the first byte of the last address constant. The next instruction stores X'80' in this byte and the last instruction resets the location counter to the end of the address list. Recall that the addresses are 3 bytes long. As each address constant occupies 4 bytes, the first byte is set to 0. The last three instructions change the first byte of the last parameter address to X'80' = B'10000000'. That is, they turn on the sign bit in the last fullword in the address list.

If the called procedure examines the sign bit of each argument, it can recognize the last argument in the list. This device allows us to write procedures that can accept a variable number of parameters. An example of such a procedure is shown in a later section.

Accessing Reference Parameters

We now turn to the question of how reference parameters can be accessed from within the procedure. We have access to the addresses of the corresponding arguments. By placing the address of an argument in a register, if we use the register as an explicit base register with 0 displacement, we can access the argument value itself.

Example 6.2.3 *Suppose we have a procedure with 3 fullword parameters and that this procedure is called with arguments A, B, C. A correct call of that procedure creates a list of the three addresses and places the address of that list in R1. The diagram below illustrates the situation once the procedure has been entered.*

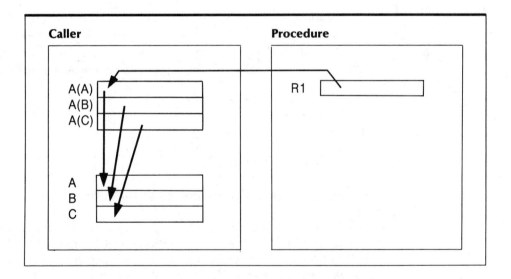

The instruction

        L   R8,0(R1)

will place the fullword at which R1 is pointing, the address of A, in R8. In the same way, the instructions

        L   R9,4(R1)
        L   RA,8(R1)

will load the addresses of B and C into R9 and RA respectively. This is illustrated in the diagram below.

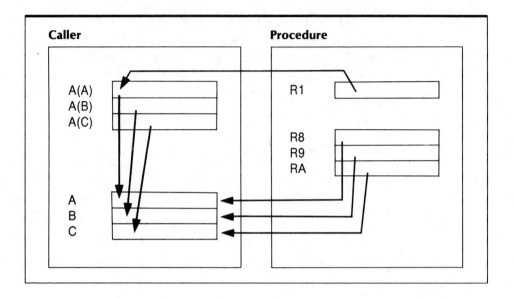

This will allow us to manipulate the arguments as necessary. For example,

```
L       R5,0(R9)
```

will place the value of the argument B in R5.

```
ST      R3,0(RA)
```

would store the contents of register R3 in the fullword field C in the calling program.

Specifying an explicit base register with 0 displacement is general enough to allow us to perform all necessary operations on the arguments. However, it is somewhat primitive. If we needed to copy the value of the third argument into the second, we would use an MVC instruction. Because this instruction requires a length, we code it as

```
MVC     0(4,R9),0(RA)
```

This is not a good way to program. It requires the programmer to keep track of the lengths of the fields involved and the registers that contain the addresses of these fields. These are precisely the kinds of tasks that are supposed to be performed by the assembler. We need a mechanism for accessing arguments that allows the assembler to fulfill this function. Such a mechanism is available through the use of DSECTs and USING instructions.

We will write a DSECT to describe each parameter. In the example above, the DSECTs are used by the assembler to determine the lengths of the arguments. In general, this approach will allow us to manipulate parameters with complicated record structures. In these cases, the assembler would use the DSECT to determine the length and offset of each field in such a structure.

We provide a USING instruction for each parameter, which tells the assembler which register will contain the address of the corresponding argument. When the number of parameters is relatively small, we establish these USING instructions for the entire procedure. If the number of parameters is large or if the procedure needs a large number of registers, the USING instruction for a particular parameter may be in effect for only part of the procedure. Three steps will then be required to access the argument corresponding to a parameter. We write a DSECT describing the parameter. We place the address of the corresponding argument in a register. This address is accessed using the pointer to the address list in R1. We tell the assembler to use the appropriate register by specifying it in a USING instruction with the DSECT for the parameter. Any reference to a field in this DSECT will be assembled with the correct register as long as the USING instruction is in effect. If we need to use the register for another purpose in the procedure, we first break its association with the DSECT, using a DROP instruction.

Example 6.2.4 *Consider a short procedure, SUMMER, which accepts three fullword arguments ITEM1, ITEM2, and SUM. Its function will be to place the sum of ITEM1 and ITEM2 in the fullword SUM.*

```
SUMMER     CSECT                       PROCEDURE SUMMER
           SAVE    (14,12)                 :
           BALR    RC,0                    :
           USING   *,RC                    :
           ST      RD,SAVE+4               :
           LA      RD,SAVE                 :
           LM      R9,RB,0(R1)         PLACE ADDRESSES OF THE THREE ARGUMENTS
*                                      IN R9, RA, AND RB
           USING   ITEM1SCT,R9         ESTABLISH PARAMETER ADDRESSABILITY
           USING   ITEM2SCT,RA             :
           USING   SUMSCT,RB               :
*
           L       R2,ITEM1            SUM = ITEM1+ITEM2
           A       R2,ITEM2                :
           ST      R2,SUM                  :
*
           L       RD,SAVE+4               :
           RETURN  (14,12)            RETURN
SAVE       DS      18F                     :
*
*      REGISTER NAMES
R0         EQU     0                  REGISTER 0
R1         EQU     1                  REGISTER 1
R2         EQU     2                  REGISTER 2
R3         EQU     3                  REGISTER 3
R4         EQU     4                  REGISTER 4
R5         EQU     5                  REGISTER 5
R6         EQU     6                  REGISTER 6
R7         EQU     7                  REGISTER 7
```

```
R8          EQU     8           REGISTER 8
R9          EQU     9           REGISTER 9
RA          EQU     10          REGISTER A
RB          EQU     11          REGISTER B
RC          EQU     12          REGISTER C
RD          EQU     13          REGISTER D
RE          EQU     14          REGISTER E
RF          EQU     15          REGISTER D
*
ITEM1SCT    DSECT
ITEM1       DS      F
ITEM2SCT    DSECT
ITEM2       DS      F
SUMSCT      DSECT
SUM         DS      F
            END
```

The LM instruction places the addresses of the three arguments in registers R9, RA, and RB. The first USING instruction tells the assembler that ITEM1, the only field in ITM1SCT, should be assembled with R9 as the base register. As ITEM1 occurs at the beginning of its DSECT, the displacement will be 0. The object code generated by the instruction

```
        L       R2,ITEM1
```

will specify 0 displacement and R9 as the base register. The effect will be to load the value of the first argument, addressed by R9, into R2.

In the same way,

```
        A       R2,ITEM2
```

will add the value of the second argument to R2 and

```
        ST      R2,SUM
```

will store the sum as the new value of the third argument.

Example 6.2.5 *Consider a function that accepts a variable number of fullword arguments and returns the average of the values of those arguments.*

In order to determine when the last argument has been processed, we check the sign bit of each address after it has been processed.

We do not know how many arguments there will be, so we use a single DSECT to describe them all. We access the different values by changing the address in the corresponding base register.

R2 is used to accumulate the values and R4 to count the parameters. The register pair R2,R3 is used for the division and the average is returned in R0.

```
MEAN        CSECT                    FUNCTION MEAN
            SAVE    (14,12)              :
            BALR    RC,0                 :
            USING   *,RC                 :
            ST      RD,SAVE+4            :
            LA      RD,SAVE              :
            USING   PARMSECT,R9          :
            LA      R2,0                 R2 = 0
            LA      R4,0                 R4 = 0
REPEAT01    EQU     *                    REPEAT
            L       R9,0(R1)                R9 = ARGUMENT ADDRESS
            LA      R1,4(R1)                POINT R1 AT NEXT ADDRESS
            A       R2,PARM                 R2 = R2+PARM
            LA      R4,1(R4)                R4 = R4+1
            LTR     R9,R9                   :
            BNM     REPEAT01                :
UNTIL01     EQU     *                    UNTIL R9 0
            SRDA    R2,32                R3 = R2/R4
            DR      R2,R4                :
            L       R0,R3                MEAN = R3
            L       RD,SAVE+4            :
            SAVE    (0)                  :
            RETURN  (14,12)           RETURN
SAVE        DS      18F                  :
*    REGISTER NAMES
R0          EQU     0                 REGISTER 0
R1          EQU     1                 REGISTER 1
R2          EQU     2                 REGISTER 2
R3          EQU     3                 REGISTER 3
R4          EQU     4                 REGISTER 4
R5          EQU     5                 REGISTER 5
R6          EQU     6                 REGISTER 6
R7          EQU     7                 REGISTER 7
R8          EQU     8                 REGISTER 8
R9          EQU     9                 REGISTER 9
RA          EQU     10                REGISTER A
RB          EQU     11                REGISTER B
RC          EQU     12                REGISTER C
RD          EQU     13                REGISTER D
RE          EQU     14                REGISTER E
RF          EQU     15                REGISTER D
*
PARMSECT    DSECT
PARM        DS      F
            END
```

Observe that the mean is transferred from R3 to R0 by the instruction

LR   R0,R3

As we noted in 6.1, this does not suffice to return the value in register R0 as required by the standard calling sequence. If this instruction were followed immediately by the RETURN macro, then the average in R0 would be replaced by the original contents of R0 from the caller's save area. The instruction

SAVE   (0)

replaces this value with the average, so the RETURN macro places the average in R0 when it restores the original contents of the other registers.

E   X   E   R   C   I   S   E   S

For Exercises 1-3, using the following location counter values, describe the effect of the accompanying CNOP instructions.

1. LOC : X'54A01C'
   a. CNOP 0,4
   b. CNOP 6,8

2. LOC : X'793B26'
   a. CNOP 2,4
   b. CNOP 0,4

3. LOC : X'643616'
   a. CNOP 2,4
   b. CNOP 2,8

4. Write the instructions generated by each of the following invocations of the CALL macro.
   a. CALL DIVIDE,(DIVISOR,DIVIDEND,QUOTIENT,REMAINDR)
   b. CALL MULTIPLY,(FACTOR1,FACTOR2,PRODUCT)

5. Assuming that all fields are 6 byte packed decimals, write the DSECTS, USING, and Load instructions needed to access the parameters in Exercise 4.

6. Write a function BINMULT which has two fullword arguments. It should multiply their values and return the product as its value. Assume that the product will fit in a fullword.

7. Suppose that X, Y, and Z are fullword fields. Write the code needed to set Z = X*Y using the function BINMULT from problem 6.

8. Write a procedure, MULTIPLY, which accepts three fullword arguments, X, Y, and Z and sets Z = X*Y. Assume the product will fit in a fullword.

9. Write a function CVTDTOB which has a 6-byte packed decimal field as its only argument and returns the fullword binary form of the number in that field.

10. Write a function MIN which returns the smallest value of a variable number of fullword parameters.

6.3 SAMPLE PROGRAM

In order to see how the various mechanisms for creating procedures with reference parameters fit together, consider a sample program that contains several procedures and a function. As we do this, we will discover several deficiencies in the techniques that we have developed to this point. These will be corrected in the next section.

Problem

Assume that our input file contains a list of student names and the grades these students have received on, at most, 6 tests. The first record will contain a 1-digit number in column 1 that gives the actual number of tests taken. The remaining cards will have student's name in columns 1 through 30 and test scores in adjacent 3-column fields, beginning in column 31.

The program should read each card, find the student's average, and print the average together with the input data for that student. It should continue this process until the end of the input file.

A sample input file together with the corresponding output is shown below.

Input
```
5
Smith, H. L.      087078088067089
Jones, J. Paul    076100078087081
Harris, David L.  087098078088086
```

Output

Smith, H. L.	87	78	88	67	89	82
Jones, J. Paul	76	100	78	87	81	84
Harris, David L.	87	98	78	88	86	87

We begin by considering a top-level algorithm for this problem. After opening the files, printing the headings, and reading the number of tests, we enter a loop to read and process student cards until End-Of-File. In order to modularize our program as much as possible, we convert the entire set of test scores to binary in one procedure, then invoke a function to find the average.

```
Open files Read Number_of_tests
Print headings
Repeat
    Read Student_Record
    Convert_Scores(Student_Record.Scores,Binary_scores,Number_of_Tests)
    Average = Find_Average(Binary_Scores,Number_of_Tests)
    Print Student_Record.Name
    For Test = 1 to Number_of_Tests
        Print Binary_Scores[Test]
    Endfor
    Print Average
Until End_Of_File
Close files
```

Before filling in the details of this algorithm, we design the data structures for the main program. We will need a fullword field to store the number of tests, this is called *NUMSCR* below. As we will convert all the scores at once, we will also need an array of fullwords to store the scores in binary form. This is called *BINSCRS*. Finally, we will need a fullword field to hold the average and a doubleword work area to use for converting the number of test scores to binary.

```
MAXSCR    EQU    6              MAXIMUM NUMBER OF SCORES
DWORK     DS     D              WORK AREA FOR CONVERSIONS
NUMSCR    DS     F              NUMBER OF SCORES
BINSCRS   DS     (MAXSCR)F      ARRAY OF SCORES
AVERAGE   DS     F              STUDENT AVERAGE
```

The input records are as described above. Notice that the input scores are defined as an array within the student record.

In order to format the output records, we define constant offsets for the beginnings of fields and a constant to represent the number of spaces between columns. These constants are used both in the definition of the heading line and the detail line. In defining the output line, the individual scores are again treated as an array. A line of blanks is defined to provide spacing between the heading line and the first detail line.

```
NAMELEN    EQU    30              LENGTH OF STUDENT NAME
MAXSCR     EQU    6               MAXIMUM NUMBER OF SCORES
SCORLEN    EQU    3               LENGTH OF INPUT SCORES
CHSCRLEN   EQU    4               LENGTH OF OUTPUT SCORES
COLSKIP    EQU    4               SPACES TO SKIP BETWEEN COLUMNS
NAMEOFF    EQU    20              OFFSETS FOR PRINT LINE
SCOROFF    EQU    NAMEOFF+NAMELEN+COLSKIP
AVGOFF     EQU    SCOROFF+MAXSCR*(SCORLEN+1+COLSKIP)+COLSKIP
```

```
*********************************************************************************************
*      I/O WORK AREAS                                                                      *
*********************************************************************************************
INREC      DS     CL80                          INPUT RECORD
           ORG    INREC                           :
INNUMSCR   DS     ZL1                           NUMBER OF SCORES
           ORG    INREC                           :
STUREC     DS     CL80                          STUDENT RECORD
           ORG    STUREC                            :
INNAME     DS     CL(NAMELEN)                      STUDENT NAME
SCORES     DS     (MAXSCR)ZL(SCORLEN)             ARRAY OF SCORES
           ORG    STUREC+L'STUREC               END STUDENT RECORD
*                                               END INPUT RECORD
HEADER     DC     CL133' '                      HEADING LINE
           ORG    HEADER                          :
           DC     C'1'                          CONTROL CHARACTER
           ORG    HEADER+NAMEOFF                 :
           DC     C'NAME'                       NAME HEADING
           ORG    HEADER+SCOROFF                 :
           DC     C'TEST SCORES'                SCORE HEADING
           ORG    HEADER+AVGOFF                  :
           DC     C'AVERAGE'                    AVERAGE HEADING
           ORG    HEADER+L'HEADER               END HEADER
*
BLANKS     DC     CL133' '                      BLANK LINE
*
OUTREC     DC     CL133' '                      OUTPUT RECORD
           ORG    OUTREC                          :
CTRLCHR    DS     CL1                           CONTROL CHARACTER
           ORG    OUTREC+NAMEOFF                 :
OUTNAME    DS     CL(NAMELEN)                   STUDENT NAME
           ORG    OUTREC+SCOROFF                 :
PRTSCRS    DS     (MAXSCR)CL(CHSCRLEN+COLSKIP)
           ORG    OUTREC+AVGOFF                 ARRAY OF STUDENT SCORES
OUTAVG     DS     CL(CHSCRLEN)                  STUDENT AVERAGE
           ORG    OUTREC+L'OUTREC              END OUTPUT RECORD
```

Returning to our top-level algorithm, we note that both the individual scores and the average will have to be edited for printing. We can perform these editing operations in a single procedure, which gets a binary number and a character field as parameters and edits the decimal form of the number into the character field. Unfortunately, we will encounter a problem if we attempt to pass a single entry of the array BINSCRS as an argument in a procedure call. We have implemented our procedure calls with the CALL macro. Recall from our consideration of that macro that the addresses in the address list are filled in by the linker before program execution. In the algorithm at hand, we need to postpone the determination of the address until execution. The address of the individual entries of the array

BINSCRS will not be known until run-time. Furthermore, the address of the desired element changes on each loop traversal. We have to choose between using the CALL macro and not passing an array element. In this program, we copy the array element into a simple variable before the procedure call. This allows us to pass the same variable on each call. In the next section, we will consider the instructions necessary to pass individual elements from an array.

The procedure to perform the conversion and editing is shown below. Notice that the SAVE macro appears first in the procedure. The instruction it generates must be executed before the base register is established in the BALR-USING sequence. Access to the parameters FWORD and CHRFORM is achieved by the two USING instructions and the LM instructions. The USING instructions tell the assembler to use the indicated registers with the DSECTS FULSECT and CHRSECT. The LM instruction puts the addresses of the corresponding arguments into these registers.

The remaining instructions perform a convert to decimal and an edit operation, treating the DSECT fields FWORD and CHRFORM as though they were local variables.

After the RETURN macro, which restores the caller's registers and branches back to the calling program, the format of this procedure is identical to that of an independent program. As it will be assembled separately, it must provide definitions for the symbolic register names. It may contain other symbol definitions, followed by constant definitions and storage definitions for any local variables. Last of all, we include the DSECTS that describe the parameters.

```
CONVERT   CSECT
**********************************************************************************************
*     CONVERT (FWORD,CHRFORM)                                                               *
*                                                                                           *
*     CONVERT THE FULLWORD IN FWORD TO CHARACTER FORM IN CHRFORM.                            *
**********************************************************************************************
          SAVE    (14,12)              PROCEDURE CONVERT
          BALR    RC,0                    :
          USING   *,RC                     :
          ST      RD,SAVE+4                :
          LA      RD,SAVE                  :
          USING   FULSECT,RA               :
          USING   CHRSECT,RB               :
          LM      RA,RB,0(R1)              :
          L       R2,FWORD             CHRFORM = FWORD
          CVD     R2,DWORK                 :
          MVC     CHRFORM,EDMSK            :
          ED      CHRFORM,DWORK+L'DWORK-CHSCRLEN/2
          L       RD,SAVE+4                :
          RETURN (14,12)               END AVG
SAVE      DS      18F
**********************************************************************************************
*     SYMBOL DEFINITIONS                                                                     *
**********************************************************************************************
```

```
*     REGISTER NAMES
R0            EQU     0               REGISTER 0
R1            EQU     1               REGISTER 1
R2            EQU     2               REGISTER 2
R3            EQU     3               REGISTER 3
R4            EQU     4               REGISTER 4
R5            EQU     5               REGISTER 5
R6            EQU     6               REGISTER 6
R7            EQU     7               REGISTER 7
R8            EQU     8               REGISTER 8
R9            EQU     9               REGISTER 9
RA            EQU     10              REGISTER A
RB            EQU     11              REGISTER B
RC            EQU     12              REGISTER C
RD            EQU     13              REGISTER D
RE            EQU     14              REGISTER E
RF            EQU     15              REGISTER D
*
CHSCRLEN      EQU     4               LENGTH OF CHARACTER FORM
****************************************************************************************
*     CONSTANTS                                                                       *
****************************************************************************************
EDMSK         DC      X'40202120'     EDIT MASK
****************************************************************************************
*     VARIABLES                                                                       *
****************************************************************************************
DWORK         DS      D               WORK AREA FOR CONVERSIONS
****************************************************************************************
*     DSECTS FOR PARAMETERS                                                           *
****************************************************************************************
FULSECT       DSECT                   :
FWORD         DS      F               FULLWORD TO BE CONVERTED
*                                     :
CHRSECT       DSECT                   :
CHRFORM       DS      CL(CHSCRLEN)    FIELD TO RECEIVE CHARACTER FORM
              END
```

The procedure CVTSCRS, seen below, is somewhat more complicated than CONVERT. It is also more interesting. Whereas CONVERT has two simple variables as parameters, CVTSCRS includes a record structure and a fullword array. The record structure, STUDREC, contains an array of zoned numbers as one of its fields. As we see in this example, the general approach is as above. We simply write DSECTS describing the parameters, specify those DSECTS in USING instructions, load the corresponding argument addresses into the appropriate registers, then manipulate the parameters as though they were local variables.

In this case, the body of the procedure consists of a single loop in which the zoned scores are packed into a local work area, then converted to binary and stored in the appropriate entry of BINSCRS. As above, the procedure must define all of the symbols it will use, as well as provide for any local constants and variables.

```
CVTSCRS    CSECT
*************************************************************************************
*       CVTSCRS (STUREC,BINSCRS,NUMSCR)                                            *
*                                                                                  *
*       CONVERT NUMSCR SCORES TO BINARY AND STORE IN THE                           *
*       FULLWORD ARRAY BINSCRS.                                                    *
*************************************************************************************
           SAVE    (14,12)                 PROCEDURE CVTSCRS
           BALR    RC,0                      :
           USING   *,RC                      :
           ST      RD,SAVE+4                 :
           LA      RD,SAVE                   :
           USING   STUSECT,R9                :
           USING   BINSECT,RA                :
           USING   NUMSECT,RB                :
           LM      R9,RB,0(R1)               :
           LA      R8,SCORES                 :
FOR00      EQU     *                       FOR R7 = 0 TO 4*(NUMSCR−1) BY 4
           LA      R7,0                      :
           L       R2,NUMSCR                 :
           BCTR    R2,0                      :
           SLA     R2,2                      :
FTEST00    EQU     *                         :
           CR      R7,R2                     :
           BH      ENDFOR00                  :
           PACK    DWORK,0(L'SCORES,R8)    BINSCRS(R7) = (R8−>SCORES)
           CVB     R3,DWORK                  :
           ST      R3,BINSCRS(R7)            :
           LA      R8,L'SCORES(R8)         MOVE R8 TO NEXT ENTRY
           LA      R7,4(R7)                  :
           B       FTEST00                   :
ENDFOR00   EQU     *                       ENDFOR
           L       RD,SAVE+4                 :
           RETURN  (14,12)                 END CVTSCRS
SAVE       DS      18F                       :
*************************************************************************************
*       SYMBOL DEFINITIONS                                                         *
*************************************************************************************
*       REGISTER NAMES
R0         EQU     0                       REGISTER 0
R1         EQU     1                       REGISTER 1
R2         EQU     2                       REGISTER 2
R3         EQU     3                       REGISTER 3
```

```
R4          EQU      4                REGISTER 4
R5          EQU      5                REGISTER 5
R6          EQU      6                REGISTER 6
R7          EQU      7                REGISTER 7
R8          EQU      8                REGISTER 8
R9          EQU      9                REGISTER 9
RA          EQU      10               REGISTER A
RB          EQU      11               REGISTER B
RC          EQU      12               REGISTER C
RD          EQU      13               REGISTER D
RE          EQU      14               REGISTER E
RF          EQU      15               REGISTER D
*
NAMELEN     EQU      30               LENGTH OF STUDENT NAME
MAXSCR      EQU      6                MAXIMUM NUMBER OF SCORES
SCORLEN     EQU      3                ZONED LENGTH OF SCORES
**************************************************************************************************
*      VARIABLES                                                                                *
**************************************************************************************************
DWORK       DS       D                WORK AREA FOR CONVERSIONS
**************************************************************************************************
*      DSECTS FOR PARAMETERS                                                                    *
**************************************************************************************************
NUMSECT     DSECT                     :
NUMSCR      DS       F                NUMBER OF SCORES
*                                     :
BINSECT     DSECT                     :
BINSCRS     DS       (MAXSCR)F        FULLWORD ARRAY OF SCORES
*                                     :
STUSECT     DSECT                     :
STUREC      DS       CL80             STUDENT RECORD
            ORG      STUREC              :
STUNAME     DS       CL(NAMELEN)         STUDENT NAME
SCORES      DS       (MAXSCR)ZL(SCORLEN)  ARRAY OF SCORES
            ORG      STUREC+L'STUREC  END STUDENT RECORD
            END
```

The third and final procedure that we will use in this program is the function FINDAV, which accepts the fullword array BINSCRS and the number of scores, NUMSCRS, as arguments. FINDAV returns as its value the average of the entries in BINSCRS. Once argument addressability has been established, the code consists of a single loop to accumulate the scores in R2. The sum is then divided by NUMSCRS, the quotient being rounded to the nearest integer. The result is stored in R0 to be returned as the function value. However, as we noted earlier, the RETURN macro will replace the contents of R0 with the fullword from the SAVE area location reserved for R0. In order to return the correct value, we use SAVE (0) to save the new R0 value in this location.

```
FINDAV      CSECT
***********************************************************************************
*      FINDAV (BINSCRS,NUMSCR)                                              *
*                                                                          *
*      RETURN THE AVERAGE OF THE NUMSCR SCORES IN THE FULLWORD             *
*      ARRAY BINSCRS.                                                      *
***********************************************************************************
            SAVE     (14,12)            FUNCTION FINDAV
            BALR     RC,0               :
            USING    *,RC               :
            ST       RD,SAVE+4          :
            LA       RD,SAVE            :
            USING    BINSECT,RA         :
            USING    NUMSECT,RB         :
            LM       RA,RB,0(R1)        :
            LA       R2,0               R2 = 0
FOR00       EQU      *                  FOR R9 = 0 TO 4*(NUMSCR−1) BY 4
            LA       R9,0               :
            L        R3,NUMSCR          :
            BCTR     R3,0               :
            SLA      R3,2               :
FTEST00     EQU      *                  :
            CR       R9,R3              :
            BH       ENDFOR00           :
            A        R2,BINSCRS(R9)        R2 = R2+BINSCRS(R9)
            LA       R9,4(R9)           :
            B        FTEST00            :
ENDFOR00    EQU      *                  ENDFOR
            SRDA     R2,32              R0 = ROUND(R2 DIV NUMSCRS)
            SLA      R3,1               :
            D        R2,NUMSCR          :
            LA       R3,1(R3)           :
            SRA      R3,1               :
            LR       R0,R3              :
            SAVE     (0)                :
            L        RD,SAVE+4          :
            RETURN (14,12)             END AVG
SAVE        DS       18F                :
***********************************************************************************
*      SYMBOL DEFINITIONS                                                   *
***********************************************************************************
*      REGISTER NAMES
R0          EQU      0                  REGISTER 0
R1          EQU      1                  REGISTER 1
R2          EQU      2                  REGISTER 2
R3          EQU      3                  REGISTER 3
R4          EQU      4                  REGISTER 4
```

```
R5          EQU     5              REGISTER 5
R6          EQU     6              REGISTER 6
R7          EQU     7              REGISTER 7
R8          EQU     8              REGISTER 8
R9          EQU     9              REGISTER 9
RA          EQU     10             REGISTER A
RB          EQU     11             REGISTER B
RC          EQU     12             REGISTER C
RD          EQU     13             REGISTER D
RE          EQU     14             REGISTER E
RF          EQU     15             REGISTER D
*
MAXSCR      EQU     8              MAXIMUM NUMBER OF SCORES
**************************************************************************************
*     DSECTS FOR PARAMETERS                                                         *
**************************************************************************************
NUMSECT     DSECT                  :
NUMSCR      DS      F              NUMBER OF SCORES
*                                  :
BINSECT     DSECT                  :
BINSCRS     DS      (MAXSCR)F      FULLWORD ARRAY OF SCORES
            END
```

We are now ready to consider the structure of the main procedure in this program. The code, shown below, is a straightforward adaptation of the algorithm constructed at the beginning of this section. We read in each student's record and call CVTSCRS to convert the set of zoned scores to binary. We then call FINDAV to compute the average. Since FINDAV was implemented as a function, the average is returned in register R0. This value is stored in AVERAGE. The student's name is then moved to the output line. Using RA as an index to BINSCRS and RB as a pointer to PRTSCRS, the scores are edited by the procedure CONVERT and moved to the output line. The line is then printed. This process is repeated until all student records have been processed.

```
PROCSAMP    START   0                   PROGRAM PROCSAMP
            PRINT   NOGEN               :
            BALR    RC,0                :
            USING   *,RC                :
            ICM     R0,B'1000',=B'00001100'  :
            SPM     R0                  :
            LA      RD,SAVE             :
            OPEN    INFILE,PRINTER      OPEN FILES
            PUT     PRINTER,HEADER      PRINT HEADING
            PUT     PRINTER,BLANKS      SKIP A LINE
            GET     INFILE,INREC        READ NUMBER OF SCORES
            PACK    DWORK,INNUMSCR      CONVERT TO BINARY AND STORE
            CVB     R2,DWORK            :
```

```
            ST      R2,NUMSCR               :
REPEAT00    EQU     *                       REPEAT
            GET     INFILE,STUREC           READ RECORD
            CALL    CVTSCRS,(STUREC,BINSCRS,NUMSCR)   CNVRT SCORES TO BINARY
            CALL    FINDAV,(BINSCRS,NUMSCR)  AVERAGE =
            ST      R0,AVERAGE              FINDAV(BINSCRS,NUMSCR)
            MVC     OUTNAME,INNAME          PRINT STUDENT NAME
            USING   CHRSECT,RB              :
            LA      RB,PRTSCRS              :
FOR00       EQU     *                       FOR RA = 0 TO
*                                               4(NUMSCRS−1)
            LA      RA,0                    BY 4
            L       R2,NUMSCR               :
            BCTR    R2,0                    :
            SLA     R2,2                    :
FTEST00     EQU     *                       :
            CR      RA,R2                   :
            BH      ENDFOR00                :
            L       R3,BINSCRS(RA)          BINSCORE =
*                                               BINSCRS(RA)
            ST      R3,BINSCORE             :
            CALL    CONVERT,(BINSCORE,CHRSCORE)   CONVERT TO CHAR
            MVC     OUTSCORE,CHRSCORE       PRINT SCORE
            LA      RB,L'PRTSCRS(RB)        MOVE RB TO NEXT POS
            LA      RA,4(RA)                :
            B       FTEST00                 :
ENDFOR00    EQU     *                       ENDFOR
            CALL    CONVERT,(AVERAGE,CHRSCORE)   CONVERT AVERAGE TO CHAR
            MVC     OUTAVG,CHRSCORE         PRINT AVERAGE
            PUT     PRINTER,OUTREC          :
            B       REPEAT00                :
UNTIL00     EQU     *                       UNTIL END OF FILE
            CLOSE   INFILE,PRINTER          CLOSE FILES
            EOJ                             END PROCSAMP
```

E X E R C I S E S

1. Write a function FINDMIN, which accepts the same arguments, BINSCRS and NUMSCR, as the function FINDAV. FINDMIN should return the smallest score as its value.

2. Modify the function FINDAV to accept a third fullword argument, MINSCR. FINDAV should subtract this value from the sum of the scores in BINSCRS and then divide the sum by NUMSCR−1 to find the average.

3. Modify the code in the main CSECT to have it call the function FINDMIN from Exercise 1 and send the value returned as the third argument to the new version of FINDAV from Exercise 2.

4. Write DSECT and storage definitions to create an array of student records. Each record should contain a student name and that student's average. Modify the main CSECT in PROCSAMP to add names and averages to the array in the main loop and count the number of students in the class. After the last record has been read, PROCSAMP should call a procedure SORT, sending the array and the number of students as arguments. Assuming that SORT sorts the array in descending order of averages, print the rank of each student in the class.

5. Write the procedure SORT described in Exercise 4.

6.4 INPUT AND OUTPUT FROM PROCEDURES

We have postponed dealing with input and output operations from an external procedure because there are several options available. In this section, we examine some of the options.

The possibilities for performing I/O operations from external procedures are constrained by the fact that any procedure to perform an operation on a file must have access to an opened DTF for that file. Our choices are: (1) to perform all operations in a single procedure; (2) to implement global access to the DTF for all procedures that will access a particular file; or (3) to pass the address of the DTF as a parameter to each procedure which will access the file.

The simplest approach is to confine operations on a particular file to a single procedure. In this case, the DTF which describes the file can be included in the procedure. This is appropriate whenever all operations on the file will be accomplished by a single procedure call, as would be the case in a procedure whose function is to copy one file to another. In this context, this approach is logically equivalent to performing all I/O operations in the main program. This approach would not be appropriate if operations were disbursed among several calls on the same procedure. In this case, it would be necessary either to recognize the first invocation of the procedure so that the file could be opened or to open the file on each procedure call.

Global DTFs

The second option also has some disadvantages, but it is still of interest. It provides a practical example of a situation in which we may want to allow several procedures to share access to a set of memory locations. In this case, the procedures may collectively access the DTF for a file as well as variables related to the file operations. However, in order to prevent indiscriminant access to these variables, we restrict access to procedures that need to operate on the file. This can be accomplished by grouping these procedures into a single CSECT, which includes the DTF for the file and any variables which are used to access that file. The beginning of each procedure is denoted by a label defined with an EQU. However, in order to call these procedures from outside the CSECT in which they are defined, their names must be specified as entry points in an ENTRY instruction.

The format of the ENTRY instruction is

```
ENTRY   <name>,<name>,. . .
```

The names listed in this instruction are then made known to the linker, so they can be invoked in a CALL instruction from other CSECTs in the program. Any name not given in an ENTRY instruction will be unknown outside the CSECT. It is this mechanism that allows us to protect variables inside a CSECT from indiscriminant access.

Assuming that the procedures will be relatively short and few in number, we use a single base register to access both the procedures and the data area. Such a CSECT will have the following structure.

```
<name>     CSECT
************************************************************************************************
*                                                                                            *
*      <Comment describing the collective function>                                          *
*      <of the procedures in this CSECT.             >                                        *
*                                                                                            *
************************************************************************************************
*

           ENTRY  <Names of procedures called from outside of the CSECT.>
*
<pname>    EQU     *
************************************************************************************************
*                                                                                            *
*                    <Comment describing this procedure.>                                     *
*                                                                                            *
************************************************************************************************
           SAVE    (14,12)             PROCEDURE <pname>
           BALR    RC,0                    :
           USING   *,RC                    :
           ST      RD,SAVE+4               :
           LA      RD,SAVE                 :
                    .
                    .
                    .

           L       RD,SAVE+4               :
           RETURN (14,12)                END <pname>
```

```
SAVE        DS      18F                 :
*
                        .
                        .
                        .
            <Additional procedures.>
                        .
                        .

            <Symbols, constants, DTFs and buffers,>
            <variables, I/O work areas and DSECTs.>
                        .
                        .
                        .
            END
```

As these procedures are all to be assembled at the same time, all labels must be unique. In particular, any of these procedures that will invoke another procedure should have its own save area. Save areas may be defined anywhere in the CSECT, but each should have a unique name. We place the save areas immediately after the return instruction for the procedure.

As an example, in the solution presented in the last section, we performed all output operations in the main program. A better approach would be to perform these operations in procedures. In order to add interest to the problem, suppose that, in addition to printing detail lines, we also want to print a heading line. If we add procedures to open and close the file, we will have four externally called procedures. We will call them OPENOUT, HEADING, PRNTLINE, and CLOSEOUT. We will also have a procedure to convert fullword values to character form, which will be invoked only by PRNTLINE. We can include this procedure in the CSECT, but, as it is not called from outside the CSECT, it will not be listed in the ENTRY instruction. The CSECT must also include the DTF for the output file and the output work areas. This requires that we also include the symbol definitions that specify field widths and offsets.

The complete CSECT is shown below.

```
PRNTRTS   CSECT
***********************************************************************************
*                                                                               *
*      PROCEDURES TO PERFORM OUTPUT FOR PROCSAMP                                 *
*                                                                               *
***********************************************************************************
*
          ENTRY OPENOUT,HEADING,PRNTLINE,CONVERT,CLOSEOUT
*
OPENOUT   EQU     *
```

```
****************************************************************************************************
*     OPENOUT                                                                                    *
*                                                                                                *
*     OPEN THE PRINTER FOR OUTPUT.                                                               *
*                                                                                                *
****************************************************************************************************
              SAVE    (14,12)                PROCEDURE OPENOUT
              BALR    RC,0                      :
              USING   *,RC                      :
              ST      RD,OPSAVE+4               :
              LA      RD,OPSAVE                 :
              OPEN    PRINTER                  OPEN PRINTER
              L       RD,OPSAVE+4               :
              RETURN (14,12)                  END OPENOUT
OPSAVE        DS      18F                       :
*
HEADING       EQU     *
****************************************************************************************************
*     HEADING                                                                                    *
*                                                                                                *
*     START A NEW PAGE AND WRITE PAGE HEADINGS TO OUTFILE.                                       *
*                                                                                                *
****************************************************************************************************
              SAVE    (14,12)                PROCEDURE HEADING
              BALR    RC,0                      :
              USING   *,RC                      :
              ST      RD,HDSAVE+4               :
              LA      RD,HDSAVE                 :
              PUT     PRINTER,HEADER           PRINT HEADINGS
              PUT     PRINTER,BLANKS           PRINT A BLANK LINE
              L       RD,HDSAVE+4               :
              RETURN (14,12)                  END HEADING
HDSAVE        DS      18F                       :
*
PRNTLINE      EQU     *
****************************************************************************************************
*     PRNTLINE(INNAME,BINSCRS,NUMSCR,AVERAGE,OUTFILE)                                            *
*                                                                                                *
*     WRITE THE STUDENT'S NAME, SCORES, AND AVERAGE TO OUTFILE.                                  *
*                                                                                                *
****************************************************************************************************
              SAVE    (14,12)                PROCEDURE PRNTLINE
              BALR    RC,0                      :
              USING   *,RC                      :
              ST      RD,PLSAVE+4               :
              LA      RD,PLSAVE                 :
```

```
               USING   NMESCT,R7                 ESTABLISH PARAMETER ADDRESSES
               USING   SCRSCT,R8                 :
               USING   NUMSCT,R9                 :
               USING   AVGSCT,RA                 :
               LM      R7,RA,0(R1)               :
               MVC     OUTNAME,INNAME            PRINT STUDENT NAME
               USING   CHRSECT,R5                :
               LA      R5,PRTSCRS                :
FOR00          EQU     *                         FOR R6 = 0 TO
*                                                    4(NUMSCRS−1)
               LA      R6,0                      BY 4
               L       R2,NUMSCR                 :
               BCTR    R2,0                      :
               SLA     R2,2                      :
FTEST00        EQU     *                         :
               CR      R6,R2                     :
               BH      ENDFOR00                  :
               L       R3,BINSCRS(R6)            BINSCORE =
*                                                    BINSCRS(R6)
               ST      R3,BINSCORE               :
               CALL    CONVERT,(BINSCORE,CHRSCORE)   CONVERT TO CHAR
               MVC     OUTSCORE,CHRSCORE         PRINT SCORE
               LA      R5,L'PRTSCRS(R5)          MOVE R5 TO NEXT POS
               LA      R6,4(R6)                  :
               B       FTEST00                   :
ENDFOR00       EQU     *                         ENDFOR
               MVC     TEMPAVG,AVERAGE           COPY AVERAGE TO PASS TO CONVERT
               CALL    CONVERT,(TEMPAVG,                                         X
                       CHRSCORE)                 CONVERT AVERAGE TO CHAR
               MVC     OUTAVG,CHRSCORE           PRINT AVERAGE
               PUT     PRINTER,OUTREC            :
               L       RD,PLSAVE+4               :
               RETURN (14,12)                    END PRNTLINE
PLSAVE         DS      18F                       :
*
CONVERT        EQU     *
****************************************************************************************
*      CONVERT (FWORD,CHRFORM)                                                         *
*                                                                                      *
*      CONVERT THE FULLWORD IN FWORD TO CHARACTER FORM IN CHRFORM.                     *
*                                                                                      *
****************************************************************************************
               SAVE    (14,12)                   PROCEDURE CONVERT
               BALR    RC,0                      :
               USING   *,RC                      :
               ST      RD,CVSAVE+4               :
```

```
          LA       RD,CVSAVE                :
          USING    FULSECT,R9               ESTABLISH PARAMETER ADDRESSES
          USING    CHFRMSCT,RA              :
          LM       R9,RA,0(R1)              :
          L        R2,FWORD                 CHRFORM = FWORD
          CVD      R2,DWORK                 :
          MVC      CHRFORM,EDMSK            :
          ED       CHRFORM,DWORK+L'DWORK−CHSCRLEN/2
          L        RD,CVSAVE+4              :
          RETURN (14,12)                    END CONVERT
CVSAVE    DS       18F                      :
*
CLOSEOUT  EQU      *
*********************************************************************************************************
*    CLOSEOUT                                                                                          *
*                                                                                                      *
*    CLOSE THE PRINTER FOR OUTPUT.                                                                     *
*                                                                                                      *
*********************************************************************************************************
          SAVE     (14,12)                  PROCEDURE CLOSEOUT
          BALR     RC,0                     :
          USING    *,RC                     :
          ST       RD,CLSAVE+4              :
          LA       RD,CLSAVE                :
          CLOSE    PRINTER                  CLOSE PRINTER
          L        RD,CLSAVE+4              :
          RETURN (14,12)                    END CLOSEOUT
CLSAVE    DS       18F                      :
*
*
*********************************************************************************************************
*    SYMBOL DEFINITIONS                                                                                *
*********************************************************************************************************
*    REGISTER NAMES
R0        EQU      0                        REGISTER 0
R1        EQU      1                        REGISTER 1
R2        EQU      2                        REGISTER 2
R3        EQU      3                        REGISTER 3
R4        EQU      4                        REGISTER 4
R5        EQU      5                        REGISTER 5
R6        EQU      6                        REGISTER 6
R7        EQU      7                        REGISTER 7
R8        EQU      8                        REGISTER 8
R9        EQU      9                        REGISTER 9
RA        EQU      10                       REGISTER A
RB        EQU      11                       REGISTER B
```

```
RC          EQU     12              REGISTER C
RD          EQU     13              REGISTER D
RE          EQU     14              REGISTER E
RF          EQU     15              REGISTER D
*
NAMELEN     EQU     30              LENGTH OF STUDENT NAME
MAXSCR      EQU     6               MAXIMUM NUMBER OF SCORES
CHSCRLEN    EQU     4               LENGTH OF OUTPUT SCORES
SCORLEN     EQU     3               LENGTH OF INPUT SCORES
COLSKIP     EQU     4               SPACES TO SKIP BETWEEN COLUMNS
NAMEOFF     EQU     20              OFFSETS FOR PRINT LINE
SCOROFF     EQU     NAMEOFF+NAMELEN+COLSKIP
AVGOFF      EQU     SCOROFF+MAXSCR*(SCORLEN+1+COLSKIP)+COLSKIP
****************************************************************************
*     LITERALS                                                           *
****************************************************************************
      LTORG
****************************************************************************
*     CONSTANT                                                           *
****************************************************************************
EDMSK       DC      X'40202120'     EDIT MASK
****************************************************************************
*     FILE DEFINITON                                                     *
****************************************************************************
*
PRINTER     DTFPR   DEVADDR=SYSLST,DEVICE=3203,BLKSIZE=133,CTLCHR=ASA,   X
                    IOAREA1=OUTBUF1,IOAREA2=OUTBUF2,WORKA=YES
OUTBUF1     DS      CL133
OUTBUF2     DS      CL133
****************************************************************************
*     VARIABLES                                                          *
****************************************************************************
BINSCORE    DS      F               SINGLE SCORE IN BINARY
TEMPAVG     DS      F               AREA TO PASS AVERAGE TO CONVERT
CHRSCORE    DS      CL(CHSCRLEN)    SCORE OR AVERAGE IN CHAR FORM
DWORK       DS      D               WORK AREA FOR CONVERSIONS
*
****************************************************************************
*     I/O WORK AREAS                                                     *
****************************************************************************
*
HEADER      DC      CL133' '        HEADING LINE
            ORG     HEADER              :
            DC      C'1'            CONTROL CHARACTER
            ORG     HEADER+NAMEOFF      :
            DC      C'NAME'         NAME HEADING
```

```
          ORG     HEADER+SCOROFF       :
          DC      C'TEST SCORES'       SCORE HEADING
          ORG     HEADER+AVGOFF        :
          DC      C'AVERAGE'           AVERAGE HEADING
          ORG     HEADER+L'HEADER  END HEADER
*
BLANKS    DC      CL133' '             BLANK LINE
*
OUTREC    DC      CL133' '             OUTPUT RECORD
          ORG     OUTREC               :
CTRLCHR   DS      CL1                  CONTROL CHARACTER
          ORG     OUTREC+NAMEOFF       :
OUTNAME   DS      CL(NAMELEN)          STUDENT NAME
          ORG     OUTREC+SCOROFF       :
PRTSCRS   DS      (MAXSCR)CL(CHSCRLEN+COLSKIP)
          ORG     OUTREC+AVGOFF        ARRAY OF STUDENT SCORES
OUTAVG    DS      CL(CHSCRLEN)         STUDENT AVERAGE
          ORG     OUTREC+L'OUTREC  END OUTPUT RECORD
*
*****************************************************************************************
*     DSECTS FOR ARRAYS                                                              *
*****************************************************************************************
CHRSECT   DSECT                        DSECT FOR ACCESSING PRTSCRS
OUTSCORE  DS      CL(CHSCRLEN)         :
*****************************************************************************************
*     DSECTS FOR PARAMETERS                                                          *
*****************************************************************************************
NMESCT    DSECT
INNAME    DS      CL(NAMELEN)          STUDENT NAME
SCRSCT    DSECT                        :
BINSCRS   DS      (MAXSCR)F            ARRAY OF SCORES
NUMSCT    DSECT                        :
NUMSCR    DS      F                    NUMBER OF SCORES
AVGSCT    DSECT                        :
AVERAGE   DS      F                    STUDENT AVERAGE
FULSECT   DSECT                        :
FWORD     DS      F                    FULLWORD TO BE CONVERTED
CHFRMSCT  DSECT                        :
CHRFORM   DS      CL(CHSCRLEN)         :
          END
```

The main procedure is now much cleaner and easier to read. The code is simplified because it does not perform any output operations. The data areas are also more concise as they do not contain the definitions required for the output lines. The complete code for this procedure is shown below. Note that it calls OPENOUT as part of its initial code and calls CLOSEOUT at the end.

```
PROCSAMP  START    0                              PROGRAM PROCSAMP
          PRINT    NOGEN                               :
          BALR     RC,0                                :
          USING    *,RC                                :
          ICM      R0,B'1000',=B'00001100'             :
          SPM      R0                                  :
          LA       RD,SAVE                             :
          OPEN     INFILE                          OPEN INPUT FILE
          CALL     OPENOUT                         OPEN OUTPUT FILE
          CALL     HEADING                         PRINT HEADING
          GET      INFILE,INREC                    READ NUMBER OF SCORES
          PACK     DWORK,INNUMSCR                  CONVERT TO BINARY AND STORE
          CVB      R2,DWORK                            :
          ST       R2,NUMSCR                           :
REPEAT00  EQU      *                                   REPEAT
          GET      INFILE,STUREC                       READ RECORD
          CALL     CVTSCRS,(STUREC,BINSCRS,NUMSCR)     CNVRT SCORES TO BINARY
          CALL     FINDAV,(BINSCRS,NUMSCR)             AVERAGE =
          ST       R0,AVERAGE                          FINDAV(BINSCRS,NUMSCR)
          CALL     PRNTLINE,(INNAME,BINSCRS,                               X
                   NUMSCR,AVERAGE)                 PRINT OUTPUT LINE
          B        REPEAT00                            :
UNTIL00   EQU      *                               UNTIL END OF FILE
          CALL     CLOSEOUT                        CLOSE OUTPUT FILE
          CLOSE    INFILE                          CLOSE INPUT FILE
          EOJ                                      END PROCSAMP
SAVE      DS       18F                                 :
****************************************************************************************
*    SYMBOL DEFINITIONS                                                             *
****************************************************************************************
*    REGISTER NAMES
R0        EQU      0                              REGISTER 0
R1        EQU      1                              REGISTER 1
R2        EQU      2                              REGISTER 2
R3        EQU      3                              REGISTER 3
R4        EQU      4                              REGISTER 4
R5        EQU      5                              REGISTER 5
R6        EQU      6                              REGISTER 6
R7        EQU      7                              REGISTER 7
R8        EQU      8                              REGISTER 8
R9        EQU      9                              REGISTER 9
RA        EQU      10                             REGISTER A
RB        EQU      11                             REGISTER B
RC        EQU      12                             REGISTER C
RD        EQU      13                             REGISTER D
RE        EQU      14                             REGISTER E
RF        EQU      15                             REGISTER D
```

```
*
NAMELEN    EQU     30                    LENGTH OF STUDENT NAME
MAXSCR     EQU     6                     MAXIMUM NUMBER OF SCORES
SCORLEN    EQU     3                     LENGTH OF INPUT SCORES
*********************************************************************************
*     LITERALS                                                                  *
*********************************************************************************
           LTORG
*********************************************************************************
*     FILE                                                                      *
*********************************************************************************
INFILE     DTFCD   DEVADDR=SYSIPT,DEVICE=2501,EOFADDR=UNTIL00            X
                   IOAREA1=INBUF1,IOAREA2=INBUF2,WORKA=YES
INBUF1     DS      CL80
INBUF2     DS      CL80
*********************************************************************************
*     VARIABLES                                                                 *
*********************************************************************************
DWORK      DS      D                     WORK AREA FOR CONVERSIONS
NUMSCR     DS      F                     NUMBER OF SCORES
BINSCRS    DS      (MAXSCR)F             ARRAY OF SCORES
AVERAGE    DS      F                     STUDENT AVERAGE
*********************************************************************************
*     I/O WORK AREA                                                             *
*********************************************************************************
INREC      DS      CL80                  INPUT RECORD
           ORG     INREC                   :
INNUMSCR   DS      ZL1                     NUMBER OF SCORES
           ORG     INREC                   :
STUREC     DS      CL80                    STUDENT RECORD
           ORG     STUREC                    :
INNAME     DS      CL(NAMELEN)                STUDENT NAME
SCORES     DS      (MAXSCR)ZL(SCORLEN)        ARRAY OF SCORES
           ORG     STUREC+L'STUREC         END STUDENT RECORD
*                                        END INPUT RECORD
           END
```

The procedure CVTSCRS and the function FINDAV are unchanged.

File Parameters

We have seen how we can implement I/O operations on a file by making the DTF globally accessible to all procedures that perform these operations. This method works reasonably well if the number of operations on a file is relatively small and if the number of files accessed is small. In other circumstances, it can become awkward. For example, if the number of operations to be performed on the file is large or if the operations are complicated, then the CSECT that contains these procedures can become unmanageably large. The situation is also complicated if one procedure needs to access several files.

The third alternative mentioned in the introduction, passing the DTF as a parameter, avoids these complications. However, its use depends on the way the I/O macros are implemented. In order to see why this is so, we need to review the mechanisms we have been using for file access.

Our input and output operations are all being performed by macros that generate calls on system subroutines. An example of a typical macro instruction is

```
PUT     PRINTER,LINE
```

PRINTER is the name of the DTF which describes the print file and LINE is the name of the field to be sent to this file. The PUT macro provides the addresses of these two fields to the routine which performs the actual operation. The address of the DTF, PRINTER, is passed in R0, and the address of LINE is passed in R1. If this is accomplished by the following instructions,

```
LA      R0,PRINTER
LA      R1,LINE
```

then, because the LA instruction is used, the addresses of PRINTER and LINE will be computed at run time through the usual base-displacement address computation. This means that either PRINTER or LINE can be a procedure parameter. In this case, the only restriction would be that the PUT must occur after the USING instruction establishes the base register for the parameter and the address of the argument is loaded into that register.

There is an important distinction to be made here. Suppose the addresses of PRINTER and LINE are passed using address constants,

```
L       R0,=A(PRINTER)
L       R1,=A(LINE)
```

In this case, the addresses of PRINTER and LINE are filled in by the linker before the program begins execution. PRINTER and LINE cannot be parameters, as the addresses of parameters cannot be determined until the program is executed and may change during execution.

If the available I/O macros use the second method for accessing their operands, then it is not feasible to implement file parameters. In fact, it is not even possible to pass a parameter as an input or output field to a GET or PUT macro. The only reasonable alternative is to replace the system macros with macros which use the appropriate LA instructions instead of using A-type address constants. This can be done quite easily with the material presented in the next chapter. In the following, we assume that such macros are available.

In implementing file parameters, we could write a DSECT that contains a DTF. However, none of the offsets defined by the DTF would be used in the program.

Thus, all the DSECT really needs to do is to define a label at offset 0, which can be used in macro calls. We describe it as

```
<dsname>    DSECT
<fname>     DS      F
```

The <dsname> is used to identify the DSEC in a USING instruction, and the corresponding register is loaded with the address of the DTF passed by the calling program. Throughout the procedure, we refer to the file by <fname>.

For example, we can modify the procedure HEADING, from the example above, to accept the output file as a parameter. If we place this procedure in a CSECT by itself, it becomes

```
HEADING    CSECT
*******************************************************************************
*       HEADING (OUTFILE)                                                     *
*                                                                             *
*       START A NEW PAGE AND WRITE PAGE HEADINGS TO OUTFILE.                  *
*******************************************************************************
           SAVE    (14,12)             PROCEDURE HEADING
           BALR    RC,0                :
           USING   *,RC                :
           ST      RD,SAVE+4           :
           LA      RD,SAVE             :
           USING   FILESCT,RB          ESTABLISH PARAMETER ADDRESS
           L       RB,0(R1)            :
           PUT     OUTFILE,HEADER      PRINT HEADINGS
           PUT     OUTFILE,BLANKS      PRINT A BLANK LINE
           L       RD,SAVE+4           :
           RETURN (14,12)              END HEADING
SAVE       DS      18F                 :
*******************************************************************************
*       SYMBOL DEFINITIONS                                                    *
*******************************************************************************
*       REGISTER NAMES
R0         EQU     0                   REGISTER 0
R1         EQU     1                   REGISTER 1
R2         EQU     2                   REGISTER 2
R3         EQU     3                   REGISTER 3
R4         EQU     4                   REGISTER 4
R5         EQU     5                   REGISTER 5
R6         EQU     6                   REGISTER 6
R7         EQU     7                   REGISTER 7
R8         EQU     8                   REGISTER 8
R9         EQU     9                   REGISTER 9
```

```
RA          EQU     10                  REGISTER A
RB          EQU     11                  REGISTER B
RC          EQU     12                  REGISTER C
RD          EQU     13                  REGISTER D
RE          EQU     14                  REGISTER E
RF          EQU     15                  REGISTER D
*
NAMELEN     EQU     30                  LENGTH OF STUDENT NAME
MAXSCR      EQU     6                   MAXIMUM NUMBER OF SCORES
CHSCRLEN    EQU     4                   LENGTH OF OUTPUT SCORES
SCORLEN     EQU     3                   LENGTH OF INPUT SCORES
COLSKIP     EQU     4                   SPACES TO SKIP BETWEEN COLUMNS
NAMEOFF     EQU     20                  OFFSETS FOR PRINT LINE
SCOROFF     EQU     NAMEOFF+NAMELEN+COLSKIP
AVGOFF      EQU     SCOROFF+MAXSCR*(SCORLEN+1+COLSKIP)+COLSKIP
************************************************************************************
*     I/O WORK AREAS                                                              *
************************************************************************************
*
HEADER      DC      CL133' '            HEADING LINE
            ORG     HEADER                  :
            DC      C'1'                CONTROL CHARACTER
            ORG     HEADER+NAMEOFF          :
            DC      C'NAME'             NAME HEADING
            ORG     HEADER+SCOROFF          :
            DC      C'TEST SCORES'      SCORE HEADING
            ORG     HEADER+AVGOFF           :
            DC      C'AVERAGE'          AVERAGE HEADING
            ORG     HEADER+L'HEADER     END HEADER
*
BLANKS      DC      CL133' '            BLANK LINE
************************************************************************************
*     DSECT FOR PARAMETER                                                         *
************************************************************************************
FILESCT     DSECT
OUTFILE     DS      F
            END
```

The argument corresponding to OUTFILE should be a DTF that has been opened for output. In our example, this DTF is contained in the main program. If the DTF is called PRINTER, the code to invoke the procedure heading is

```
        CALL    HEADING,(PRINTER)
```

In the next section, we consider a complete example, which includes a file parameter.

E   X   E   R   C   I   S   E   S

1. Write the code for a CSECT containing a group of procedures that implement a stack. (The elements in the stack could be anything, but use fullwords for this exercise.) The CSECT should contain the three procedures described below and all necessary data structures.

    function ISMT ()
       Returns −1 in R0 if the stack is empty, 0 if it is not empty.

    procedure PUSH (ITEM)
       Pushes ITEM on top of the stack.

    procedure POP (ITEM)
       Removes the top

    Note that only the function and procedure names will be known outside the CSECT. The names of the data structures used to implement the stacks will not be known elsewhere. This reduces the chance that one of these locations will be changed accidently.

2. Write the code for a CSECT that contains four procedures. These procedures will be used to write output to a special file used for diagnostic messages. Assuming the file is called BUGOUT, these procedures should function as follows.

    procedure OPENBUG ()
       Open BUGOUT.

    procedure PRTSTR (STRING)
       Print a 132-character string from STRING to BUGOUT.

    procedure PRTPCK (IDSTR, PNUM)
       Print a 40-character string from IDSTR followed by a 16-byte packed number from PNUM to BUGOUT.

    procedure PRTFULL (IDSTR, FNUM)
    Print a 40-character string from IDSTR followed by a 16-byte packed number from PNUM to BUGOUT.

    procedure CLOSBUG ()
       Close BUGOUT.

3. Write a procedure READ (RECORD, FILE) that reads records from FILE until it finds a nonblank record or end of file. If it gets to the end of FILE, set the first three positions of RECORD equal to EOF. Otherwise, return the record read in RECORD.

4. Write a procedure RDFULL (FILE, FNUM) to read a zoned number from FILE, convert it to a fullword, and store it in FNUM. Assume that the records in the file contain zoned numbers entered in columns 1 through 9.

6.5 ALTERNATE PARAMETER FORMS

We noted earlier that there is a problem with the mechanism employed by the CALL macro to pass parameter addresses. The difficulty is that, as the values in the address lists are filled in before the program begins executing, the arguments cannot be changed from one call to another. This means that we cannot pass a single element from an array to a procedure unless the index or subscript of that element is determined before execution begins. It also means that a procedure cannot pass one of its parameters as an argument to another procedure.

Both of these conditions occurred in the example in the last section. Recall the following lines from PRNTLINE.

```
        L     R3,BINSCRS(R6)          BINSCORE =
*                                       BINSCRS(R6)
        ST    R3,BINSCORE             :
        CALL  CONVERT,(BINSCORE,CHRSCORE)   CONVERT TO CHAR
        MVC   OUTSCORE,CHRSCORE   PRINT SCORE
        LA    R5,L'PRTSCRS(R5)    MOVE R5 TO NEXT POS
        LA    R6,4(R6)            :
        B     FTEST00             :
```

and

```
        MVC   TEMPAVG,AVERAGE     COPY AVERAGE TO PASS TO
        CALL  CONVERT,(TEMPAVG,   CONVERT AVERAGE TO CHR  X
              OUTAVG)
```

In the first case, we needed to call CONVERT to convert the fullword entry BINSCRS(R6) to character form and store the result in OUTSCORE. Both these elements were varying entries in arrays. (Recall that OUTSCORE was a field in a DSECT being used to access the array of output scores in the output line.) Neither could be passed as an argument using the CALL macro. Instead, we found it necessary to copy the value from BINSCRS(R6) into a temporary location, BINSCORE, which could be passed. The result, returned in a second temporary location, CHRSCORE, then had to be copied to the field OUTSCORE.

In the second case, we needed to convert the fullword value in the parameter, AVERAGE, to character form. AVERAGE could not be passed as the argument, as its address could not be determined until the procedure PRNTLINE was called. Thus, we again had to copy the value from this field into a temporary storage location that could be passed to CONVERT.

In this section, we consider a more general mechanism for generating address lists, which allows both array elements and parameters as arguments in procedure calls.

Dynamically Generated Address Lists

In order to create an argument address list in which argument addresses can vary during execution, our program must contain the instructions to generate the addresses and place them in the list. The addresses must be regenerated each time a particular procedure invocation is executed.

The addresses themselves can be computed with the Load Address instruction.

```
            LA        R0,<argument>
```

This instruction will compute the address of the argument and place it in R0. It will work correctly whether the argument is a simple variable, an indexed array name, or the name of a field in a DSECT that is being used to access a parameter or an array.

Once the address has been computed and placed in R0, we need to store it in the correct location in the address list.

As far as possible, we pattern these instructions on those generated by the CALL macro. We begin with a CNOP instruction to assure correct alignment. We then include the instructions to generate the addresses and store them in the address list. This is followed by the actual call instructions and the address list itself. Assuming N arguments, we have the following pattern.

```
        CNOP    _____
        LA      R0,<argument_1>
        ST      R0,*+_____
        LA      R0,<argument_2>
        ST      R0,*+_____
          .
          .
          .
        LA      R0,<argument_i>
        ST      R0,*+_____        4 bytes
          .
          .
          .
        LA      R0,<argument_N>
        ST      R0,*+_____        8 bytes
        L       RF,=V<pname>
        LA      RE,*+6+4*__          10 bytes
        BALR    R1,RF
        DS      F                    4 bytes
        DS      F
          .
          .
          .
```

```
        DS      F
        .
        .

        .
        DS      F
```

The CNOP instruction is required to assure that the first DS F occurs at a fullword boundary. However, except for the BALR instruction, the intervening instructions are all 4 bytes long. The BALR instruction is 2 bytes long. In order to guarantee that the first DS instruction occurs on a fullword boundary, we need to align to the second halfword of a fullword at the beginning of the sequence. Thus, the operands of the CNOP instruction should be 2,4 as before.

For each STore instruction, we must determine the number of bytes from the beginning of the instruction to the fullword entry in the address list that corresponds to the argument. This is a relatively simple calculation. Between the STore instruction for argument i and the address list entry for argument i, there are $N-i$ pairs of Load and Store instructions for the remaining arguments. Each pair is 8 bytes long. The instructions

```
        L       RF,=V<pname>
        LA      RE,*+6+4*__
        BALR    R1,RF
```

require 10 bytes. The address of argument i in the address list is preceded by $i-1$ addresses each of which occupies 4 bytes. Adding the 4 bytes for the STore instruction for argument i, we have

$$4+8*(N-i)+10+4*(i-1)$$
$$= 14+8*N-8*i+4*i-4$$
$$= 10+8*N-4*i$$

With N arguments, the instruction sequence becomes

```
        CNOP    2,4
        LA      R0,<argument__1>
        ST      R0,*+10+(8*N)-(4*1)
        LA      R0,<argument__2>
        ST      R0,*+10+(8*N)-(4*2)
        .

        .

        .
        LA      R0,<argument__i>
        ST      R0,*+10+(8*N)-(4*i)     4 bytes
        .

        .

        .
```

```
LA     R0,<argument_N>        ⎫
ST     R0,*+10+(8*N)-(4*N)    ⎬  8 bytes
L      RF,=V<pname>           ⎫
LA     RE,*+6+4*N             ⎬  10 bytes
BALR   R1,RF                  ⎭
DS     F                         4 bytes
DS     F
 .
 .
 .
DS     F
 .
 .
 .
DS     F
```

Note that we must substitute the actual value for N in each instruction. Note also that we have not evaluated the expressions. We can leave that task to the assembler.

For example, suppose we want to use this sequence of instructions to implement the first call on convert described above. There are two arguments, BINSCRS(R6) and OUTSCORE. The instructions are

```
CNOP   2,4                           CONVERT(BINSCRS(R6),
LA     R0,BINSCRS(R6)                     OUTSCORE)
ST     R0,*+10+(8*2)-(4*1)    :
LA     R0,OUTSCORE            :
ST     R0,*+10+(8*2)-(4*2)    :
L      RF,=V(CONVERT)         :
LA     RE,*+6+4*2             :
BALR   R1,RF                  :
DS     F                      :
DS     F                      :
```

This new calling mechanism is a generalization of the CALL macro. That is, the calls we have been performing with the CALL macro can be performed by dynamic generation of the address list. For example, consider the invocation of the procedure PRNTLINE in the example in Section 6.4. The call

```
CALL   PRNTLINE,(INNAME,BINSCRS,NUMSCR,AVERAGE)
```

would be implemented as

```
CNOP   2,4                           PRNTLINE(INNAME,BINSCRS,
LA     R0,INNAME                         NUMSCR,AVERAGE)
ST     R0,*+10+(8*4)-(4*1)    :
```

```
        LA      R0,BINSCRS              :
        ST      R0,*+10+(8*4)−(4*2)     :
        LA      R0,NUMSCR               :
        ST      R0,*+10+(8*4)−(4*3)     :
        LA      R0,AVERAGE              :
        ST      R0,*+10+(8*4)−(4*4)     :
        L       RF,=V(PRNTLINE)         :
        LA      RE,*+6+4*4              :
        BALR    R1,RF                   :
        DS      F                       :
        DS      F                       :
        DS      F                       :
        DS      F                       :
        DS      F                       :
```

Note that the use of the dynamic address generation appears to require more from the programmer. However, in the next chapter, we learn how to write our own macros to generate the list of instructions above. If we call this new macro CALLD, then that list of instructions would be generated by the single macro instruction

```
        CALLD   PRNTLINE,(INNAME,BINSCRS,NUMSCR,AVERAGE)
```

Example

We conclude this section and chapter by returning, one last time, to the example from Section 6.3. In this final treatment, we pass the output file as a parameter to the routines that perform output. The DTF for PRINTER is included in the main program and the file is opened and closed in the main program. PRINTER is then added as a parameter to the calls on HEADING and PRNTLINE. As the file is to be passed to the procedures that perform the output, we can once again write each procedure in its own CSECT and assemble the procedures separately.

We use dynamic generation of the address list for all procedure calls. This allows us to pass the array elements BINSCR(R6) and OUTSCR to CONVERT. It also permits us to pass the parameter AVERAGE to CONVERT.

The program with these changes is shown below.

```
PROSCAMP START   0                       PROGRAM PROCSAMP
        PRINT   NOGEN                   :
        BALR    RC,0                    :
        USING   *,RC                    :
        ICM     R0,B'1000',=B'00001100' :
        SPM     R0                      :
        LA      RD,SAVE                 :
        OPEN    INFILE,PRINTER          OPEN FILES
        CNOP    2,4                     CALL HEADING(PRINTER)
```

```
            LA      R0,PRINTER              :
            ST      R0,*+10+(8*1)-(4*1)     :
            L       RF,=V(HEADING)          :
            LA      RE,*+6+4*1              :
            BALR    R1,RF                   :
            DS      F                       :
            GET     INFILE,INREC            READ NUMBER OF SCORES
            PACK    DWORK,INNUMSCR          CONVERT TO BINARY AND STORE
            CVB     R2,DWORK                :
            ST      R2,NUMSCR               :
REPEAT00    EQU     *                       REPEAT
            GET     INFILE,STUREC               READ RECORD
            CNOP    2,4                         CALL CVTSCRS(STUREC,BINSCRS,
            LA      R0,STUREC                       NUMSCR)
            ST      R0,*+10+(8*3)-(4*1)     :
            LA      R0,BINSCRS              :
            ST      R0,*+10+(8*3)-(4*2)     :
            LA      R0,NUMSCR               :
            ST      R0,*+10+(8*3)-(4*3)     :
            L       RF,=V(CVTSCRS)          :
            LA      RE,*+6+4*3              :
            BALR    R1,RF                   :
            DS      F                       :
            DS      F                       :
            DS      F                       :
            CNOP    2,4                     AVERAGE =
            LA      R0,BINSCRS              FINDAV(BINSCRS,NUMSCR)
            ST      R0,*+10+(8*2)-(4*1)     :
            LA      R0,NUMSCR               :
            ST      R0,*+10+(8*2)-(4*2)     :
            L       RF,=V(FINDAV)           :
            LA      RE,*+6+4*2              :
            BALR    R1,RF                   :
            DS      F                       :
            DS      F                       :
            ST      R0,AVERAGE              :
            CNOP    2,4                     CALL PRNTLINE(INNAME,BINSCRS,
            LA      R0,INNAME                   NUMSCR,AVERAGE,
            ST      R0,*+10+(8*5)-(4*1)         PRINTER)
            LA      R0,BINSCRS              :
            ST      R0,*+10+(8*5)-(4*2)     :
            LA      R0,NUMSCR               :
            ST      R0,*+10+(8*5)-(4*3)     :
            LA      R0,AVERAGE              :
            ST      R0,*+10+(8*5)-(4*4)     :
            LA      R0,PRINTER              :
```

```
              ST       R0,*+10+(8*5)-(4*5)            :
              L        RF,=V(PRNTLINE)               :
              LA       RE,*+6+4*5                    :
              BALR     R1,RF                         :
              DS       F                             :
              DS       F                             :
              DS       F                             :
              DS       F                             :
              DS       F                             :
              B        REPEAT00                      :
UNTIL00       EQU      *                          UNTIL END OF FILE
              CLOSE    INFILE,PRINTER              CLOSE FILES
              EOJ                                 END PROCSAMP
SAVE          DS       18F                           :
*****************************************************************************************
*      SYMBOL DEFINITIONS                                                              *
*****************************************************************************************
*      REGISTER NAMES
R0            EQU      0                          REGISTER 0
R1            EQU      1                          REGISTER 1
R2            EQU      2                          REGISTER 2
R3            EQU      3                          REGISTER 3
R4            EQU      4                          REGISTER 4
R5            EQU      5                          REGISTER 5
R6            EQU      6                          REGISTER 6
R7            EQU      7                          REGISTER 7
R8            EQU      8                          REGISTER 8
R9            EQU      9                          REGISTER 9
RA            EQU      10                         REGISTER A
RB            EQU      11                         REGISTER B
RC            EQU      12                         REGISTER C
RD            EQU      13                         REGISTER D
RE            EQU      14                         REGISTER E
RF            EQU      15                         REGISTER D
*
NAMELEN       EQU      30                         LENGTH OF STUDENT NAME
MAXSCR        EQU      6                          MAXIMUM NUMBER OF SCORES
SCORLEN       EQU      3                          LENGTH OF INPUT SCORES
*****************************************************************************************
*      LITERALS                                                                        *
*****************************************************************************************
              LTORG
*****************************************************************************************
*      FILES                                                                           *
*****************************************************************************************
INFILE        DTFCD    DEVADDR=SYSIPT,DEVICE=2501,EOFADDR=UNTIL00                      X
```

```
                      IOAREA1=INBUF1,IOAREA2=INBUF2,WORKA=YES
INBUF1      DS        CL80
INBUF2      DS        CL80
*
PRINTER     DTFPR     DEVADDR=SYSLST,DEVICE=3203,BLKSIZE=133,CTLCHR=ASA,         X
                      IOAREA1=OUTBUF1,IOAREA2=OUTBUF2,WORKA=YES
OUTBUF1     DS        CL133
OUTBUF2     DS        CL133
**********************************************************************************
*      VARIABLES                                                                 *
**********************************************************************************
DWORK       DS        D                    WORK AREA FOR CONVERSIONS
NUMSCR      DS        F                    NUMBER OF SCORES
BINSCRS     DS        (MAXSCR)F            ARRAY OF SCORES
AVERAGE     DS        F                    STUDENT AVERAGE
**********************************************************************************
*      I/O WORK AREAS                                                            *
**********************************************************************************
INREC       DS        CL80                 INPUT RECORD
            ORG       INREC                  :
INNUMSCR    DS        ZL1                    NUMBER OF SCORES
            ORG       INREC                  :
STUREC      DS        CL80                   STUDENT RECORD
            ORG       STUREC                   :
INNAME      DS        CL(NAMELEN)              STUDENT NAME
SCORES      DS        (MAXSCR)ZL(SCORLEN)      ARRAY OF SCORES
            ORG       STUREC+L'STUREC        END STUDENT RECORD
*                                          END INPUT RECORD
            END
HEADING     CSECT
**********************************************************************************
*      HEADING (OUTFILE)                                                         *
*                                                                                *
*      START A NEW PAGE AND WRITE PAGE HEADINGS TO OUTFILE.                      *
*                                                                                *
**********************************************************************************
            SAVE      (14,12)              PROCEDURE HEADING
            BALR      RC,0                   :
            USING     *,RC                   :
            ST        RD,SAVE+4              :
            LA        RD,SAVE                :
            USING     FILESCT,RB           ESTABLISH PARAMETER ADDRESS
            L         RB,0(R1)               :
            PUT       OUTFILE,HEADER       PRINT HEADINGS
            PUT       OUTFILE,BLANKS       PRINT A BLANK LINE
            L         RD,SAVE+4              :
```

```
              RETURN (14,12)                 END HEADING
SAVE          DS    18F                      :
****************************************************************************************************
*       SYMBOL DEFINITIONS                                                                        *
****************************************************************************************************
*       REGISTER NAMES
R0            EQU   0                         REGISTER 0
R1            EQU   1                         REGISTER 1
R2            EQU   2                         REGISTER 2
R3            EQU   3                         REGISTER 3
R4            EQU   4                         REGISTER 4
R5            EQU   5                         REGISTER 5
R6            EQU   6                         REGISTER 6
R7            EQU   7                         REGISTER 7
R8            EQU   8                         REGISTER 8
R9            EQU   9                         REGISTER 9
RA            EQU   10                        REGISTER A
RB            EQU   11                        REGISTER B
RC            EQU   12                        REGISTER C
RD            EQU   13                        REGISTER D
RE            EQU   14                        REGISTER E
RF            EQU   15                        REGISTER D
*
NAMELEN       EQU   30                        LENGTH OF STUDENT NAME
MAXSCR        EQU   6                         MAXIMUM NUMBER OF SCORES
CHSCRLEN      EQU   4                         LENGTH OF OUTPUT SCORES
SCORLEN       EQU   3                         LENGTH OF INPUT SCORES
COLSKIP       EQU   4                         SPACES TO SKIP BETWEEN COLUMNS
NAMEOFF       EQU   20                        OFFSETS FOR PRINT LINE
SCOROFF       EQU   NAMEOFF+NAMELEN+COLSKIP
AVGOFF        EQU   SCOROFF+MAXSCR*(SCORLEN+1+COLSKIP)+COLSKIP
****************************************************************************************************
*       I/O WORK AREAS                                                                            *
****************************************************************************************************
*
HEADER        DC    CL133' '                  HEADING LINE
              ORG   HEADER                     :
              DC    C'1'                        CONTROL CHARACTER
              ORG   HEADER+NAMEOFF              :
              DC    C'NAME'                     NAME HEADING
              ORG   HEADER+SCOROFF              :
              DC    C'TEST SCORES'              SCORE HEADING
              ORG   HEADER+AVGOFF               :
              DC    C'AVERAGE'                  AVERAGE HEADING
              ORG   HEADER+L'HEADER    END HEADER
*
```

```
BLANKS     DC      CL133' '                    BLANK LINE
*************************************************************************************************
*     DSECT FOR PARAMETER                                                                      *
*************************************************************************************************
FILESCT    DSECT
OUTFILE    DS      F
           END
CVTSCRS    CSECT
*************************************************************************************************
*     CVTSCRS (STUREC,BINSCRS,NUMSCR)                                                          *
*                                                                                              *
*     CONVERT NUMSCR SCORES TO BINARY AND STORE IN THE                                        *
*     FULLWORD ARRAY BINSCRS.                                                                  *
*************************************************************************************************
           SAVE    (14,12)                     PROCEDURE CVTSCRS
           BALR    RC,0                        :
           USING   *,RC                        :
           ST      RD,SAVE+4                   :
           LA      RD,SAVE                     :
           USING   STUSECT,R9                  :
           USING   BINSECT,RA                  :
           USING   NUMSECT,RB                  :
           LM      R9,RB,0(R1)                 :
           LA      R8,SCORES                   :
FOR00      EQU     *                           FOR R7 = 0 TO 4*(NUMSCR−1) BY 4
           LA      R7,0                        :
           L       R2,NUMSCR                   :
           BCTR    R2,0                        :
           SLA     R2,2                        :
FTEST00    EQU     *                           :
           CR      R7,R2                       :
           BH      ENDFOR00                    :
           PACK    DWORK,0(L'SCORES,R8)        BINSCRS(R7) = (R8−>SCORES)
           CVB     R3,DWORK                    :
           ST      R3,BINSCRS(R7)              :
           LA      R8,L'SCORES(R8)             MOVE R8 TO NEXT ENTRY
           LA      R7,4(R7)                    :
           B       FTEST00                     :
ENDFOR00   EQU     *                           ENDFOR
           L       RD,SAVE+4                   :
           RETURN  (14,12)                     END CVTSCRS
SAVE       DS      18F                         :
*************************************************************************************************
*     SYMBOL DEFINITIONS                                                                       *
*************************************************************************************************
*     REGISTER NAMES
R0         EQU     0                           REGISTER 0
```

```
R1        EQU    1              REGISTER 1
R2        EQU    2              REGISTER 2
R3        EQU    3              REGISTER 3
R4        EQU    4              REGISTER 4
R5        EQU    5              REGISTER 5
R6        EQU    6              REGISTER 6
R7        EQU    7              REGISTER 7
R8        EQU    8              REGISTER 8
R9        EQU    9              REGISTER 9
RA        EQU    10             REGISTER A
RB        EQU    11             REGISTER B
RC        EQU    12             REGISTER C
RD        EQU    13             REGISTER D
RE        EQU    14             REGISTER E
RF        EQU    15             REGISTER D
*
NAMELEN   EQU    30             LENGTH OF STUDENT NAME
MAXSCR    EQU    6              MAXIMUM NUMBER OF SCORES
SCORLEN   EQU    3              ZONED LENGTH OF SCORES
************************************************************************
*    VARIABLES                                                        *
************************************************************************
DWORK     DS     D              WORK AREA FOR CONVERSIONS
************************************************************************
*    DSECTS FOR PARAMETERS                                            *
************************************************************************
NUMSECT   DSECT                 :
NUMSCR    DS     F              NUMBER OF SCORES
*                               :
BINSECT   DSECT                 :
BINSCRS   DS     (MAXSCR)F      FULLWORD ARRAY OF SCORES
*                               :
STUSECT   DSECT                 :
STUREC    DS     CL80           STUDENT RECORD
          ORG    STUREC           :
STUNAME   DS     CL(NAMELEN)        STUDENT NAME
SCORES    DS     (MAXSCR)ZL(SCORLEN)   ARRAY OF SCORES
          ORG    STUREC+L'STUREC  END STUDENT RECORD
          END
FINDAV    CSECT
************************************************************************
*    FINDAV (BINSCRS,NUMSCR)                                          *
*                                                                     *
*    RETURN THE AVERAGE OF THE NUMSCR SCORES IN THE FULLWORD          *
*    ARRAY BINSCRS.                                                   *
*                                                                     *
************************************************************************
```

```
                SAVE    (14,12)                 FUNCTION FINDAV
                BALR    RC,0                     :
                USING   *,RC                     :
                ST      RD,SAVE+4                :
                LA      RD,SAVE                  :
                USING   BINSECT,RA               :
                USING   NUMSECT,RB               :
                LM      RA,RB,0(R1)              :
                LA      R2,0                     R2 = 0
FOR00           EQU     *                        FOR R9 = 0 TO 4*(NUMSCR−1) BY 4
                LA      R9,0                     :
                L       R3,NUMSCR                :
                BCTR    R3,0                     :
                SLA     R3,2                     :
FTEST00         EQU     *                        :
                CR      R9,R3                    :
                BH      ENDFOR00                 :
                A       R2,BINSCRS(R9)            R2 = R2+BINSCRS(R9)
                LA      R9,4(R9)                 :
                B       FTEST00                  :
ENDFOR00        EQU     *                        ENDFOR
                SRDA    R2,32                    R0 = ROUND(R2 DIV NUMSCRS)
                SLA     R3,1                     :
                D       R2,NUMSCR                :
                LA      R3,1(R3)                 :
                SRA     R3,1                     :
                LR      R0,R3                    :
                L       RD,SAVE+4                :
                SAVE    (0)                      :
                RETURN  (14,12)                 END AVG
SAVE            DS      18F                      :
*********************************************************************************************************
*       SYMBOL DEFINITIONS                                                                             *
*********************************************************************************************************
*       REGISTER NAMES
R0              EQU     0                        REGISTER 0
R1              EQU     1                        REGISTER 1
R2              EQU     2                        REGISTER 2
R3              EQU     3                        REGISTER 3
R4              EQU     4                        REGISTER 4
R5              EQU     5                        REGISTER 5
R6              EQU     6                        REGISTER 6
R7              EQU     7                        REGISTER 7
R8              EQU     8                        REGISTER 8
R9              EQU     9                        REGISTER 9
RA              EQU     10                       REGISTER A
```

```
RB          EQU      11                      REGISTER B
RC          EQU      12                      REGISTER C
RD          EQU      13                      REGISTER D
RE          EQU      14                      REGISTER E
RF          EQU      15                      REGISTER D
*
MAXSCR      EQU      6                       MAXIMUM NUMBER OF SCORES
***********************************************************************************************
*     DSECTS FOR PARAMETERS                                                                  *
***********************************************************************************************
NUMSECT     DSECT                            :
NUMSCR      DS       F                       NUMBER OF SCORES
*                                            :
BINSECT     DSECT                            :
BINSCRS     DS       (MAXSCR)F               FULLWORD ARRAY OF SCORES
            END
*
*
PRNTLINE    CSECT
PRINT       NOGEN
***********************************************************************************************
*     PRNTLINE(INNAME,BINSCRS,NUMSCR,AVERAGE,OUTFILE)                                        *
*                                                                                            *
*     WRITE THE STUDENT'S NAME, SCORES, AND AVERAGE TO OUTFILE.                              *
*                                                                                            *
***********************************************************************************************
            SAVE     (14,12)                 PROCEDURE PRNTLINE
            BALR     RC,0                    :
            USING    *,RC                    :
            ST       RD,SAVE+4               :
            LA       RD,SAVE                 :
            USING    NMESCT,R7               ESTABLISH PARAMETER ADDRESSES
            USING    SCRSCT,R8               :
            USING    NUMSCT,R9               :
            USING    AVGSCT,RA               :
            USING    FILESCT,RB              :
            LM       R7,RB,0(R1)             :
            MVC      OUTNAME,INNAME          PRINT STUDENT NAME
            USING    CHRSECT,R5              :
            LA       R5,PRTSCRS              :
FOR00       EQU      *                       FOR R6 = 0 TO
*                                                   4(NUMSCRS-1)
            LA       R6,0                    BY 4
            L        R2,NUMSCR               :
            BCTR     R2,0                    :
            SLA      R2,2                    :
```

```
FTEST00    EQU     *                               :
           CR      R6,R2                           :
           BH      ENDFOR00                        :
           CNOP    2,4                             CONVERT(BINSCRS(R6),
           LA      R0,BINSCRS(R6)                      OUTSCORE)
           ST      R0,*+10+(8*2)-(4*1)             :
           LA      R0,OUTSCORE                     :
           ST      R0,*+10+(8*2)-(4*2)             :
           L       RF,=V(CONVERT)                  :
           LA      RE,*+6+4*2                      :
           BALR    R1,RF                           :
           DS      F                               :
           DS      F                               :
           LA      R5,L'PRTSCRS(R5)                MOVE R5 TO NEXT POS
           LA      R6,4(R6)                        :
           B       FTEST00                         :

ENDFOR00   EQU     *                               ENDFOR
           CNOP    2,4                             CONVERT(AVERAGE,OUTAVG)
           LA      R0,AVERAGE                      :
           ST      R0,*+10+(8*2)-(4*1)             :
           LA      R0,OUTAVG                       :
           ST      R0,*+10+(8*2)-(4*2)             :
           L       RF,=V(CONVERT)                  :
           LA      RE,*+6+4*2                      :
           BALR    R1,RF                           :
           DS      F                               :
           DS      F                               :
           PUT     OUTFILE,OUTREC                  :
           L       RD,SAVE+4                       :
           RETURN (14,12)                          END PRNTLINE
SAVE       DS      18F                             :
*********************************************************************************************
*      SYMBOL DEFINITIONS                                                                   *
*********************************************************************************************
*      REGISTER NAMES
R0         EQU     0                               REGISTER 0
R1         EQU     1                               REGISTER 1
R2         EQU     2                               REGISTER 2
R3         EQU     3                               REGISTER 3
R4         EQU     4                               REGISTER 4
R5         EQU     5                               REGISTER 5
R6         EQU     6                               REGISTER 6
R7         EQU     7                               REGISTER 7
R8         EQU     8                               REGISTER 8
R9         EQU     9                               REGISTER 9
```

```
RA          EQU    10                      REGISTER A
RB          EQU    11                      REGISTER B
RC          EQU    12                      REGISTER C
RD          EQU    13                      REGISTER D
RE          EQU    14                      REGISTER E
RF          EQU    15                      REGISTER D
*
NAMELEN     EQU    30                      LENGTH OF STUDENT NAME
MAXSCR      EQU    6                       MAXIMUM NUMBER OF SCORES
CHSCRLEN    EQU    4                       LENGTH OF OUTPUT SCORES
SCORLEN     EQU    3                       LENGTH OF INPUT SCORES
COLSKIP     EQU    4                       SPACES TO SKIP BETWEEN COLUMNS
NAMEOFF     EQU    20                      OFFSETS FOR PRINT LINE
SCOROFF     EQU    NAMEOFF+NAMELEN+COLSKIP
AVGOFF      EQU    SCOROFF+MAXSCR*(SCORLEN+1+COLSKIP)+COLSKIP
*********************************************************************************************
*      VARIABLE                                                                            *
*********************************************************************************************
DWORK       DS     D                       WORK AREA FOR CONVERSIONS
*********************************************************************************************
*      I/O WORK AREAS                                                                      *
*********************************************************************************************
*
OUTREC      DC     CL133' '                OUTPUT RECORD
            ORG    OUTREC                  :
CTRLCHR     DS     CL1                     CONTROL CHARACTER
            ORG    OUTREC+NAMEOFF          :
OUTNAME     DS     CL(NAMELEN)             STUDENT NAME
            ORG    OUTREC+SCOROFF          :
PRTSCRS     DS     (MAXSCR)CL(CHSCRLEN+COLSKIP)
            ORG    OUTREC+AVGOFF              ARRAY OF STUDENT SCORES
OUTAVG      DS     CL(CHSCRLEN)              STUDENT AVERAGE
            ORG    OUTREC+L'OUTREC         END OUTPUT RECORD
*
CHRSECT     DSECT                          DSECT FOR ACCESSING PRTSCRS
OUTSCORE    DS     CL(CHSCRLEN)            :
*********************************************************************************************
*      DSECTS FOR PARAMETERS                                                               *
*********************************************************************************************
NMESCT      DSECT
INNAME      DS     CL(NAMELEN)             STUDENT NAME
SCRSCT      DSECT
BINSCRS     DS     (MAXSCR)F               ARRAY OF SCORES
NUMSCT      DSECT
NUMSCR      DS     F                       NUMBER OF SCORES
AVGSCT      DSECT
```

```
AVERAGE    DS      F                       STUDENT AVERAGE
FILESCT    DSECT
OUTFILE    DS      F
           END
CONVERT    CSECT
PRINT      NOGEN
********************************************************************************
*     CONVERT (FWORD,CHRFORM)                                                  *
*                                                                              *
*     CONVERT THE FULLWORD IN FWORD TO CHARACTER FORM IN CHRFORM.              *
*                                                                              *
********************************************************************************
           SAVE    (14,12)                 PROCEDURE CONVERT
           BALR    RC,0                         :
           USING   *,RC                         :
           ST      RD,SAVE+4                    :
           LA      RD,SAVE                      :
           USING   FULSECT,RA                   :
           USING   CHRSECT,RB                   :
           LM      RA,RB,0(R1)                  :
           L       R2,FWORD                CHRFORM = FWORD
           CVD     R2,DWORK                     :
           MVC     CHRFORM,EDMSK                :
           ED      CHRFORM,DWORK+L'DWORK-CHSCRLEN/2
           L       RD,SAVE+4                    :
           RETURN (14,12)                  END AVG
SAVE       DS      18F                          :
********************************************************************************
*     SYMBOL DEFINITIONS                                                       *
********************************************************************************
*     REGISTER NAMES
R0         EQU     0                       REGISTER 0
R1         EQU     1                       REGISTER 1
R2         EQU     2                       REGISTER 2
R3         EQU     3                       REGISTER 3
R4         EQU     4                       REGISTER 4
R5         EQU     5                       REGISTER 5
R6         EQU     6                       REGISTER 6
R7         EQU     7                       REGISTER 7
R8         EQU     8                       REGISTER 8
R9         EQU     9                       REGISTER 9
RA         EQU     10                      REGISTER A
RB         EQU     11                      REGISTER B
RC         EQU     12                      REGISTER C
RD         EQU     13                      REGISTER D
RE         EQU     14                      REGISTER E
```

```
RF          EQU     15              REGISTER D
*
CHSCRLEN EQU       4               LENGTH OF CHARACTER FORM
*************************************************************************************************
*    CONSTANTS                                                                                 *
*************************************************************************************************
EDMSK       DC      X'40202120'     EDIT MASK
*************************************************************************************************
*    VARIABLES                                                                                 *
*************************************************************************************************
DWORK       DS      D               WORK AREA FOR CONVERSIONS
*************************************************************************************************
*    DSECTS FOR PARAMETERS                                                                     *
*************************************************************************************************
FULSECT     DSECT                   :
FWORD       DS      F               FULLWORD TO BE CONVERTED
*                                   :
CHRSECT     DSECT                   :
CHRFORM     DS      CL(CHSCRLEN)    FIELD TO RECEIVE CHARACTER FORM
            END
```

E   X   E   R   C   I   S   E   S

1. A procedure, to sort an array of fullwords, named VECTOR will invoke a
    procedure named SWAP to exchange the values in two entries of the
    array. Write the code to invoke SWAP, sending the array entries indexed
    by R9 and RA as arguments.

2. Modify the code from Exercise 1 to send two entries from an array of
    records. Assume the two elements are being accessed with DSECTs
    EMPREC and MINREC, using R9 and RA as base registers.

3. Suppose the entries in an array of student records are defined by the
    following DSECT.

    ```
    STUREC      DSECT
    STUNMAME DS     CL(NAMELEN)
    STUNUM      DS     CL(NUMLEN)
    STUSCORS DS     (MAXTST)PL(SCORLEN)
    STUAVG      DS     PL(SCORLEN)
    ```

    Write the code to invoke a procedure FINDAVG sending STUSCORS,
    STUAVG, and MAXTST as parameters. Assume that MAXTST is defined
    by an EQU.

4. Modify the code for Exercise 3, assuming the number of tests is stored in a fullword field named NUMTST.

   The standard method for sending an expression as an argument corresponding to a reference parameter is to evaluate the expression in the calling procedure and store the value in a temporary storage area used only for the call. The address of this temporary storage area is then passed to the procedure. The procedure accesses the parameter in the usual way.

In Exercises 5 and 6, write the code to implement the procedure calls. Place the temporary storage area in the code between the address list and the return location.

5. REALPRO (X: FULLWORD)
   CALL REALPRO (2*X−Y)

6. PCKPRT (FILE : DTF; PNUM : 5 BYTE PACKED NUMBER)
   CALL PCKPRT (OUTFILE, 3*PNUM1+PNUM2)

P R O G R A M M I N G   P R O J E C T S

1. Write a program to grade a multiple-choice test. The input will begin with a record containing the number of questions on the test (up to 80), followed by a record containing the correct answers to the questions. (The possible answers are A through E.) The remainder of the file will consist of an identification record for each student, followed by that student's answers. The student identification record will contain the student number (9 digits) and the student name (25 characters). The program should grade the tests and print a report containing the student's grades.

   Your solution should be modularized through the use of procedures. Among others, you should have a procedure to read the correct answers, a procedure to read and check the answers for one student, and a procedure to print a detail line for each student.

2. Do the program from Problem 1, but store each student's name, number, and score in an array of records. Include space in the record for student rank. Write a procedure to find each student's rank and enter the ranks in the array. Write a second procedure to sort the records into ascending order of student names. Finally, add a third procedure to print all the information in the sorted array.

3. Write a set of procedures to support rational arithmetic. Assume that a rational number is represented by a record structure that contains two 16-byte packed decimal numbers, the numerator and the denominator. The sign of the numerator will determine the sign of the rational number. The sign of the denominator should always be "+".

The procedures to be implemented are

procedure ADD (ARG1, ARG2)
    Set ARG1 = ARG1 + ARG2 reduced to lowest terms.

procedure SUBTRACT (ARG1, ARG2)
    Set ARG1 = ARG1 − ARG2 reduced to lowest terms.

procedure MULTIPLY (ARG1, ARG2)
    Set ARG1 = ARG1 * ARG2 reduced to lowest terms.

procedure DIVIDE (ARG1, ARG2)
    Set ARG1 = ARG1 / ARG2 reduced to lowest terms.

procedure REDUCE (ARG)
    Reduce ARG to lowest terms.

procedure READ (FILE, ARG)
    Read a record from FILE which contains two 31-digit zoned numbers, the numerator and the denominator. The first number will be preceded by a blank, a "+", or a "−". This value should be checked and used to code the sign of the resulting rational. This rational number should be returned in ARG, reduced to lowest terms.

procedure PRINT (FILE, ARG)
    Print the rational number in ARG to FILE. Print the sign, the numerator, a "/", and the denominator.

Test your procedures in a program that reads pairs of rational numbers into variables R1 and R2 until the end of the input file is reached. As each pair is read, print the input values followed by the value of the expression (R1*R2)+((R1+R2)/(R1−R2))

4. Write a program to perform a file update on a collection of employee records. Each record will contain an employee number (9 digits), the employee name (20 characters) and address (30 characters), the number of dependents (2 digits), and the pay rate (4 digits with an implied decimal 2 places from the right). The input records will indicate one of the following transactions by the code in column 1. The rest of the record will contain the information needed for the transaction.

Transaction	Code	Other Information
Change Name	N	Employee Number, New Name
Change Address	A	Employee Number, New Address
Change Dependents	D	Employee Number, Number of Dependents
Change Pay Rate	P	Employee Number, New Pay Rate
Insert Record	I	Name, Address, Dependents, Pay Rate
Remove Record	R	Employee Number

The input file will contain the current employee records in order of employee number. These should be read and stored in an array. The end of the employee records will be indicated by a trailer record that contains a "T" in column 1 and the next available employee number in the next 9 columns. The remainder of the file will consist of a collection of transaction records in random order.

Each transaction record should be processed when it is read. Use a separate procedure for each transaction, sending the record to be changed and the information from the transaction record as parameters. To locate an employee number, use a binary search function that gets the array of employee records and an employee number as parameters and returns the address of the desired record as its value. (Return 0 if the record is not found.)

When the End-Of-File has been reached, print the updated list of employee records followed by the new value of the next available employee number.

5. Read the section in Appendix C on the EXecute and TRanslate and Test instructions. Then write a set of procedures to support free-form input of character strings and packed decimal numbers. The procedures should maintain a buffer in which the unused part of an input record is stored together with a pointer to the current location in the record.

The system should provide four basic procedures. These are described below.

procedure READSTR (STRING, LENGTH)

Transfer LENGTH characters from the input file to STRING. If the end of the current record is reached during the transfer, then fill the remaining positions of STRING with blanks.

procedure READNUM (PNUM, LENGTH)

Scan the input until a "+", "−" or digit is found. If a "+" or "−"is found, scan the input until a digit is found. Read the next LENGTH characters and use them to form a packed number to be placed in PNUM. If a "−" was scanned, negate the value in PNUM. If the end of the input record is reached during the scanning, read another record.

procedure READLN ()

Discard the rest of the existing input record and read another.

function EOF ()

Return −1 in R0 if the end of the file has been reached, 0 otherwise.

C H A P T E R 7

MACROS AND CONDITIONAL ASSEMBLY

7.1 SIMPLE MACROS

There are a number of situations in programming, especially assembly language programming, in which the same set of instructions may occur many times, perhaps with a change in the names of the variables involved. If the number of instructions is large, then we may place them in a procedure and pass the variables as arguments. However, if the number of instructions is relatively small, then the overhead of invoking the subroutine and passing the arguments may not be justified.

For this reason, most assemblers provide a mechanism that allows programmers to assign a name to a group of instructions called a *macro*. Whenever the name appears in an assembly language program, the assembler inserts the instructions. The appearance of the macro name in the code is a *macro call* and the insertion of the predefined instructions is called a *macro expansion*.

For example, all of our programs begin with the following pair of instructions.

```
BALR    RC,0
USING   *,RC
```

Using macro facilities, it is possible to define a macro, say BEGIN, which generates these two instructions for us. If a source program contains the lines

```
PROCSAMP START  0                  PROGRAM PROCSAMP
         BEGIN
         OPEN   INFILE,OUTFILE
```

the assembler will insert the instructions that make up the macro BEGIN at the point in the program where the macro name occurs. The resulting code will be

```
PROCSAMP START  0                  PROGRAM PROCSAMP
         BALR   RC,0
         USING  *,RC
         OPEN   INFILE,OUTFILE
```

In this chapter, we consider the facilities provided by the IBM assemblers for creating and using macros.

Macro Calls

In order to make the use of macros as natural as possible, macro calls are designed to look like assembly language instructions. This allows the programmer to view macros as extensions of the instruction set.

We have been using macros since Chapter 1; all of our input and output operations have been performed by macros provided by the operating system. These are examples of typical macro calls.

The PUT macro looks exactly like an instruction with two operands, as in

```
        PUT     PRINTER,LINE
```

The name of the macro is used as though it were an instruction and the two operands are passed to the macro to be used during the expansion.

The DTF macros, which describe the files, display a similar format. In this case, the macro call usually includes a label. The arguments to be passed to the macro are given in a different format, known as *keyword parameters*. In this case, the name of each parameter is specified in the macro call together with the value to be passed to that parameter. For example,

```
PRINTER    DTFPR   DEVADDR=SYSLST,DEVICE=3203,BLKSIZE=133,CTLCHR=ASA,      X
                   IOAREA1=OUTBUF1,IOAREA2=OUTBUF2,WORKA=YES
```

Values are passed to the parameters DEVADDR, DEVICE, and so on, in a format that resembles an assignment statement. Keyword parameters are often used when a macro has a large number of parameters and not all parameters are used in each call.

If we restrict ourselves to the use of positional parameters, then all our macro calls will be of the following form.

```
[<label>]    <macro name>        <argument>,<argument>,. . .        <comments>
```

The label is optional and would normally be used only if the macro is being called to define a storage area.

As in the case of the DTF macros, macro calls can be continued from line to line by beginning the continuation line at column 16 and placing a character in column 72 of the line to be continued.

The instructions generated by the macro are placed in the code at the point at which the macro call occurs. These instructions are then assembled into object code along with the instructions written by the programmer.

Macro Definitions

A macro definition contains four components: (1) a header statement; (2) a prototype statement; (3) a body; and (4) a trailer statement. The macro definition is placed at the beginning of the source module, before the START instruction or the first CSECT instruction.

The header statement contains the word MACRO in the operation field. The trailer statement contains the keyword MEND in the operation field.

A complete macro definition looks like

```
MACRO
<Prototype statement.        >
<                            >
<           Macro body.      >
<                            >
          .
          .
          .
MEND
```

Prototype Statement

The format of the prototype statement is

<nparm>   <mname>   <parmlist>

<nparm>   An optional name parameter.
<mname>   The macro name.
<parmlist> List of symbolic parameters.

Both the name parameter and the symbolic parameters are identified by a string of up to 8 characters, the first of which is an ampersand (&). The macro name follows the usual rules for identifiers. It may contain up to 8 characters.

Example 7.1.1 *The prototype statement for a macro to generate the instructions needed to add 2 fullword fields might be of the following form.*

          AF   &FWRD1,&FWRD2

The name of this macro is AF. The symbolic parameters are &FWRD1 and &FWRD2.

The prototype statement for a macro to generate an edit mask from a character string might be

&MSKNAME EDITMASK   &FORMAT

EDITMASK is the name of the macro. &MSKNAME is a parameter whose value can be a name. &FORMAT is a symbolic parameter.

Macro Body

The body of a macro consists of two kinds of statements, model statements and conditional assembly statements. It is the model statements that describe the code generated by the macro. The conditional assembly statements can be used to direct the way in which the macro is expanded. Conditional assembly statements will be considered in the next section.

A model statement may consist of any assembly language instruction, including a macro invocation. The instruction may contain a name parameter in the label field and symbolic parameters in the operand fields. Each time the model statement is expanded, the parameters are replaced by their values as assigned by the call, and the resulting instruction is inserted in the code. If a model statement is a macro invocation, then the new macro is immediately expanded. When the MEND for this macro is reached, the assembler will continue the expansion of the original macro.

Example 7.1.2

The model statement

        MVC   &TARGET,&SOURCE

generates an MVC instruction in which &TARGET and &SOURCE have been replaced by their values in the current macro call. The resulting instruction is then assembled along with the rest of the code.

Example 7.1.3

The model statement

        PUT   &FILE,&RECORD

causes the PUT macro to be expanded. The resulting instructions cause the field represented by the current value of &RECORD to be put to &FILE.

The macro body may also contain comment lines. A line that begins with an asterisk (*) is treated as a model statement and placed in the code as part of every macro expansion. The macro body itself can be documented with lines that contain '.*' in columns 1 and 2. These lines are treated as comments and are only printed when the macro definition is listed; they are not inserted in macro expansions.

Printing Macro Expansions

In debugging macros, we need to be able to see the instructions being generated. However, if we want to view working macros as extensions of the instruction set, then the generated instructions should not appear in the program listing. In order to satisfy these two conflicting needs, the assembler allows the programmer to control the listing of macro expansions with the PRINT instruction.

The assembler instruction

        PRINT   GEN

causes the instructions generated by macro expansions to be listed.

PRINT   NOGEN

suppresses this listing.

By using these two instructions, which can be inserted in the macro definition itself, we control the listing of individual macro expansions.

Sample Macros

Macros provide a means for extending the effective set of the available instructions. We begin by considering some macros that provide useful generalizations of existing instructions.

For example, using binary integers, all operations require that at least one of the operands be in a register. It would be convenient to have an additional set of instructions that allow both operands to be in memory. If we view these as generalizations of the packed decimal instructions, we give them names and interpretations as follows.

Name	Operation
AF	Add Fullword
SF	Subtract Fullword
MF	Multiply Fullword
DF	Divide Fullword

We expect these new instructions to accept two fullword fields as operands, perform the indicated operation on the values stored in those fields, and store the result in the first field.

In order to bring this about, we must write macro definitions that generate the necessary instructions. That is, it will still be necessary to create the instructions to load one of the operands in a register, perform the operation, and store the result in the first operand field.

There is a conflict here between our desire to make the generated instructions transparent to the programmer and our need to use one or more registers to implement these operations. We could save and restore the contents of these registers as we do when a procedure is invoked. Unfortunately, this would increase the number of instructions required, making the use of these macros less attractive. Instead, following the precedent set by the operating system macros, we adopt the practice of using R0 and R1 freely in our macro instructions. As a precaution, we forgo the use of R0 and R1 in any other context.

Example 7.1.4 *The instructions to define the macro AF are as follows.*

```
        MACRO
        AF      &FWRD1,&FWRD2
.*
.*      ADD FULLWORD
.*
```

```
.*       GENERATE THE INSTRUCTIONS TO ADD &FWRD1 AND &FWRD2
.*       AND STORE THE RESULT IN &FWRD1.
.*
.*       USES REGISTER R0 FOR THE ADDITION.
.*
         L       R0,&FWRD1
         A       R0,&FWRD2
         ST      R0,&FWRD1
         MEND
```

In order to use the macro AF in the main CSECT of a program, we place this definition at the beginning of the module, before the start instruction. Throughout the module, we can invoke this macro to generate the appropriate instructions to add 2 fullword fields and store the result in the first field. If we have selected PRINT GEN, then the generated instructions will be shown in the listing. They can be distinguished from other instructions since the assembler places a + in front of them.

The following partial listing illustrates the placement of the macro and the use of the PRINT instruction to control the listing of generated instructions.

```
1             MACRO
2             AF        &FWRD1,&FWRD2
3 .*
4 .*    ADD FULLWORD
5 .*
6 .*    GENERATE THE INSTRUCTIONS TO ADD &FWRD1 AND &FWRD2
7 .*    AND STORE THE RESULT IN &FWRD1.
8 .*
9 .*    USES REGISTER R0 FOR THE ADDITION.
10 .*
11            L        R0,&FWRD1
12            A        R0,&FWRD2
13            ST       R0,&FWRD1
14            MEND
15 *
16 *******************************************************************************************
17 *
18 MACTST START   0                      PROGRAM MACTST
19            PRINT  NOGEN                   :
20            BALR   RC,0                    :
21            USING  *,RC                    :
22            OPEN   INFILE,PRINTER       OPEN FILES
38            PRINT  GEN
    .
    .
    .
```

```
55          AF      TOTAL,ITEM          TOTAL = TOTAL+ITEM
56+         L       R0,TOTAL
57+         A       R0,ITEM
58+         ST      R0,TOTAL


76          AF      COUNT,=F'1'         COUNT = COUNT+1
77+         L       R0,COUNT
78+         A       R0,=F'1'
79+         ST      R0,COUNT
            .
            .
            .
105         PRINT   NOGEN
106         CLOSE   INFILE,PRINTER          CLOSE FILES
114         EOJ     END MACTST
```

Notice that the PRINT instruction allows us to list only the expansions of the macro we are testing. In particular, the listing does not include the instructions generated by the OPEN and CLOSE macros, although the increment in line numbers gives evidence of their presence in the program.

The instructions generated by the AF macro appear in the listing preceded by a + sign. They are duplicates of the model instructions in which the symbolic parameters have been replaced by their values on each call.

The value that corresponds to a symbolic parameter can be a literal operand. In fact, during the expansion of the macro, the value is not checked at all. The parameter itself is treated as a string of characters. This allows us to provide any argument value desired. If the substitution of the value for the parameter causes an assembly error, this is not detected until after the macro expansion has been completed.

Example 7.1.5 *Definitions of the other fullword macros are shown below. Note that the multiply and divide macros do not do any error checking. Overflows would not be detected and division by zero would result in an exception.*

```
***********************************************************************************************
*
            MACRO
            SF      &FWRD1,&FWRD2
.*
.*      SUBTRACT FULLWORD
.*
.*      GENERATE THE INSTRUCTIONS TO SUBTRACT &FWRD1
.*      FROM &FWRD2 AND STORE THE RESULT IN &FWRD1.
.*
.*      USES REGISTER R0 FOR THE SUBTRACTION.
```

```
.*
          L       R0,&FWRD1
          S       R0,&FWRD2
          ST      R0,&FWRD1
          MEND
*
**********************************************************************************************
*
          MACRO
          MF      &FWRD1,&FWRD2
.*
.*   MULTIPLY FULLWORD
.*
.*   GENERATE THE INSTRUCTIONS TO MULTIPLY &FWRD1
.*   BY &FWRD2 AND STORE THE RESULT IN &FWRD1.
.*
.*   USES REGISTERS R0 AND R1 FOR THE MULTIPLICATION.
.*
          L       R1,&FWRD1
          M       R0,&FWRD2
          ST      R1,&FWRD1
          MEND
*
**********************************************************************************************
*
          MACRO
          DF      &FWRD1,&FWRD2
.*
.*   DIVIDE FULLWORD
.*
.*   GENERATE THE INSTRUCTIONS TO DIVIDE &FWRD1
.*   BY &FWRD2. THE RESULT IS ROUNDED TO THE
.*   NEAREST INTEGER AND STORED IN &FWRD1.
.*
.*   USES REGISTERS R0 AND R1 FOR THE DIVISION.
.*
          L       R0,&FWRD1
          SRDA    R0,32
          SLDA    R0,1
          D       R0,&FWRD2
          A       R1,=F'1'
          SRA     R1,1
          ST      R1,&FWRD1
          MEND
*
```

Macros That Require Work Areas

The macros we considered above needed to use registers. Frequently, a macro may need to use a work area in memory. For example, one of the burdens of using binary integers is the need to convert between decimal and binary. We could simplify this task by providing macros to convert directly from a packed decimal field to a fullword field and back. However, the conversion requires the use of a doubleword work area. For now, we will simply assume the existence of such a work area, named DWORK. This means that, in order to use these macros in a program, the programmer must assume the responsibility of defining this work area. In Section 7.2, we will learn how a macro may define its own work areas.

Example 7.1.6

```
*
********************************************************************************
*
          MACRO
          CVTZF   &FWRD,&ZNUM
.*
.*   CONVERT ZONED DECIMAL TO FULLWORD
.*
.*   GENERATE THE INSTRUCTIONS TO CONVERT THE
.*   ZONED DECIMAL NUMBER IN THE SECOND FIELD TO
.*   A FULLWORD BINARY INTEGER IN THE FIRST FIELD.
.*
.*   USES REGISTER R0 FOR THE CONVERSION.
.*
          PACK    DWORK,&ZNUM
          CVB     R0,DWORK
          ST      R0,&FWRD
          MEND
*
********************************************************************************
*
          MACRO
          CVTFP   &PNUM,&FWRD
.*
.*   CONVERT FULLWORD TO PACKED
.*
.*   GENERATE THE INSTRUCTIONS TO CONVERT THE
.*   FULLWORD BINARY INTEGER IN THE SECOND FIELD
.*   TO A PACKED DECIMAL NUMBER IN THE FIRST FIELD.
.*
.*   USES REGISTER R0 FOR THE CONVERSION.
.*
          L       R0,&FWRD
```

```
        CVD     R0,DWORK
        ZAP     &PNUM,DWORK
        MEND
*
************************************************************************************
```

E   X   E   R   C   I   S   E   S

1. Write the BEGIN macro described at the beginning of this section.

2. Modify the BEGIN macro from Exercise 1 to include instructions to set the program mask bits.

3. Write a macro named REGEQU, which generates the 15 definitions for the symbolic register names R0 through RF.

4. Write a macro named RMF, which accepts 2 fullword operands and generates the instructions to set the first operand equal to the remainder obtained when it is divided by the second.

5. Write a complete set of macros to perform arithmetic operations on halfword fields. Call these macros AHW, SHW, MHW, and DHW. Use R0 and R1 for any calculations.

6. Assuming the existence of a field named BLANKS, which contains 256 blanks, write a macro named BLANK that accepts a single field and generates the instruction to fill the field with blanks.

7. Write two macros DIV and MOD, which accept two packed decimal fields as operands and generate the instructions to set the first operand equal, respectively, to the quotient and remainder obtained when the number in the first field is divided by the number in the second field. Assume the existence of a 16-byte field named DWORK, which may be used for the division.

8. Write a set of macros to implement three operand instructions for packed decimal arithmetic. The first of the three operands should be the target of the operation and the second and third operands the source. For example, if we call the addition macro AP3, then

```
        AP3     X,Y,Z
```

should generate the instructions to set X equal to Y+Z.

7.2 CONDITIONAL ASSEMBLY

Macro definitions can contain all the components of a typical programming language. This includes the ability to define variables, to define labels within a macro, to perform arithmetic and string operations, and to test conditions and execute branches during macro expansion. The instructions that allow us to perform these operations are called *conditional assembly* instructions.

Variables used within a macro are called *set symbols*. Labels in a macro definition are called *sequence symbols*. Conditional assembly instructions can be separated into three classes, those which define set symbols, those which assign values to set symbols, and those which effect tests and branches.

In this section we define set symbols and sequence symbols. We describe the instructions that allow us to assign values to set symbols and consider the operations used in those assignments. Finally, we cover the branching instructions and consider some macros that make use of these facilities.

When we describe these facilities, we are describing an auxiliary programming language. The programs written in this language are the macro definitions themselves. It is important to realize that such a program is "executed" when the macro is expanded. This occurs before the program using the macro is executed. In fact, it takes place before the 370 Assembler program is even assembled.

In order to make this distinction clear, pause to reconsider and expand on the steps involved in the assembly and execution of a program. The assembly and execution of our programs are divided into several distinct phases: assembly, linkage, and execution. In the case of a program with several source modules, the distinction should be clear. The modules are assembled separately, producing object modules. These object modules are then linked together into a load module. It is at this time that address constants used in our programs are filled in by the linker. Finally, the load module is loaded and the program executed. When we view macros as programs, we must realize that they are programs executed by the assembler long before the 370 Assembly Language program that contains them is executed.

In fact, the action of the assembler can be divided into two distinct phases: preassembly and assembly. The macro definitions are interpreted by the assembler during the preassembly phase. This results in the generation of instructions from the model statements. The following table shows the complete sequence of events from coding through execution of a program.

Coding	The programmer writes macro definitions, assembly language instructions, and macro calls.
Preassembly	Macro calls cause the assembler to interpret macro definitions and generate instructions from model statements. These are interspersed with the coded instructions.
Assembly	Both coded and generated instructions are assembled into object code. Relocatable and external address constants are set to zero.

Linkage   Object modules are combined to form a load module. Address constants are assigned the appropriate values.

Execution   The machine language instructions that correspond to both the coded and generated assembly language instructions are executed.

Set Symbols

Set symbols are categorized in two ways: according to scope and according to type. The scopes are local and global. Local set symbols are known only within the macro definition in which they are declared. They are initialized on each macro invocation. A global set symbol is known in all macro definitions that contain a global declaration of that symbol. A global set symbol is initialized only once and maintains its value between macro calls. The three types of set symbols are arithmetic, Boolean, and character.

The six possible combinations of scope and type are selected by six different declaration operators. The declarations must appear at the beginning of the macro definition. Global set symbols must be declared before local set symbols. The six operators used in these declarations are:

Operator	Variable Type/Scope	Initialization Value
GBLA	Global Arithmetic	0
GBLB	Global Boolean	0
GBLC	Global Character	Null String
LCLA	Local Arithmetic	0
LCLB	Local Boolean	0
LCLC	Local Character	Null String

The identifiers used for set symbols follow the same rules as those for symbolic parameters. They must begin with an ampersand (&) and a letter and may contain up to 6 additional letters or digits.

Example 7.2.1 *The following are valid set symbol declarations.*

```
GBLA    &CALLCNT,&DEFNUM
GBLB    &CALL1
GBLC    &WORKA
LCLA    &LENGTH,&POSITN,&COUNTER
LCLB    &DONE
LCLC    &FLDNAME
```

Each declaration may include a list of set symbols or the set symbols may be declared one at a time. This allows for a comment describing the set symbol on the line containing the declaration.

Example 7.2.2

```
LCLA    &LENGTH         LENGTH OF THE STRING
LCLA    &POSITN         CURRENT POSITION IN THE STRING
```

Assigning Values to Set Symbols

The set symbols in 370 Assembly Language are unique in that there is a different assignment operator for each set symbol type. The operators are SETA, SETB, and SETC. The format of each assignment is

\<set symbol\> \<operator\>   \<expression\>   \<comment\>

The type of the expression must be compatible with the set symbol. The SET operators cannot be used to assign new values to symbolic parameters.

In the case of the SETA instruction, the arithmetic expression may be a constant or another arithmetic set symbol. It may contain constants, arithmetic set symbols, symbolic parameters, parentheses, and the operators +, −, *, /. It may not contain any blanks. The precedence of operators is as usual. The division operator represents integer division in which the remainder is discarded.

Example 7.2.3

```
&POSITN    SETA    &POSITN+12              &POSITN = &POSITN+12
&CALLCNT   SETA    &CALLCNT+1             INCREMENT &CALLCNT
&AVERAGE   SETA    (&ITEM1+&ITEM2+&ITEM3)/3  COMPUTE &AVERAGE
```

The expression used with the SETB operator can be a 0 (false), a 1 (true), a Boolean set symbol enclosed in parentheses, or a logical expression enclosed in parentheses. The logical expressions are formed using the logical operators AND, OR, and NOT and the relational operators shown below.

```
EQ    Equal to
NE    Not Equal to
LE    Less than or Equal to
LT    Less Than
GE    Greater than or Equal to
GT    Greater Than
```

Both the logical and relational operators must be separated from letters and digits by at least 1 blank. These logical expressions are unique among assembler expressions in that they can contain blanks.

Example 7.2.4

```
&FALSE     SETB    0
&TRUE      SETB    (NOT &FALSE)
&DONE      SETB    (&TRUE)
&FLAG      SETB    (&POSITN GT &LENGTH)
&EMPTY     SETB    (&STRING EQ '')
&BOOL      SETB    ((NOT &EMPTY) AND (&A LE 10))
```

SETC is used to assign a value to a character set symbol. The expression may consist of a literal string enclosed in quotes or a character set symbol enclosed in quotes. It may also be an arithmetic set symbol enclosed in quotes. In this case, the numeric value is represented as a string omitting the sign and leading zeros. Finally, it may be obtained through the substring and concatenation operations described in the next section.

Example 7.2.5

```
&STRING    SETC    'ABCDE'
&DUPLICA   SETC    '&STRING'     NOTE THAT THE QUOTES ARE REQUIRED
&ARTHSYM   SETA    −034
&STRFORM   SETC    '&ARTHSYM'    '34' IS ASSIGNED TO &STRFORM
```

Sequence Symbols

Sequence symbols are represented by up to 8 characters. They must begin with a period (.) and an alphabetic character, and may contain an additional 6 letters or digits. They may be defined in a number of ways, but we always use the Assembler No OPeration as shown below

```
<seq. sym.> ANOP                    <comments>
```

As its name implies, this instruction does not perform any operation. It simply provides a place to attach a label in a macro definition. We use this facility, together with the branching instructions, to implement the constructs of structured programming in our macro definitions.

Example 7.2.6

```
.IF0       ANOP                    IF &A < 5
.ENDIF0    ANOP                        END IF
.WHILE4    ANOP                        WHILE &POSITN <= &LENGTH
```

Branching Instructions

The conditional assembly instructions include two instructions for branching. One is an unconditional branch instruction, the Assembler GO, AGO. The other is a conditional branch instruction, Assembler IF or AIF.

The format of the AGO instruction is

AGO   \<sequence symbol\>   \<comment\>

Example 7.2.7

```
AGO    .WHILE0
AGO    .ENDIF1
```

The format of the AIF instruction is

AIF   (\<logical expression\>)\<sequence symbol\> \<comments\>

The logical expression is evaluated. If the value is true (1), then the macro expansion continues at the indicated sequence symbol. Otherwise, it continues at the instruction following the AIF.

Note that the logical expression must be enclosed in parentheses and that no blanks may appear between the right parenthesis and the sequence symbol.

Example 7.2.8

```
AIF    (&COUNT GT &UPPER).ENDFOR3
AIF    ((&POSITN GT &LENGTH) OR &DONE).ENDWHL0
AIF    ((&CALL EQ 1) AND (TYPE NE 'P')).ELSE5
```

Structured Macros

Using these branch instructions, we can implement constructs for structured macro definitions similar to those we use for assembly language. In this case, the labels should be sequence symbols. As these must begin with a period, and as macros are relatively short, we use only a single digit to distinguish similar labels.

The AIF simplifies the constructs themselves, as it combines the test and the branch in a single instruction.

The example below contains a skeleton for a typical loop construct. The other constructs are formed in a similar way. We continue our practice of indenting comments to display the logical structure of the code.

Example 7.2.9

```
.WHILE4    ANOP                               WHILE &POSITN <= &LENGTH
           AIF    (&POSITN GT &LENGTH).ENDWHL4
```

        .   .

       .

```
              AGO     .WHILE4
.ENDWHL4  ANOP                              END WHILE
```

Sample Macros

We now consider some simple macro definitions that make use of the capabilities of conditional assembly. In the next two sections, we discuss more complex examples.

    We begin with a macro that defines a vector of 100 fullwords and initializes the entries to 1,2,3,4, and so on. This can be effected by creating 100 DC instructions of the form

```
        DC      F'<number>'
```

In order to generate these instructions, our macro needs a loop. The loop counter can be inserted in a model statement to provide the initialization values.

    We can allow the calling program to supply a name for the vector by providing a symbolic label in the prototype statement. This label can be used with the first DC instruction or we can provide a separate DS. The second option is used in Example 7.2.10.

Example 7.2.10

```
***************************************************************************************************
          MACRO
&LABEL    DEFVEC &NUMPARM
.*
.*    DEFINE VECTOR
.*
.*    DEFINE A VECTOR OF &NUMPARM FULLWORDS. INITIALIZE TO 1,2,3. . .
.*
.*
          LCLA    &ENTNUM          NUMBER OF CURRENT ENTRY
.*
.*                                 DEFINE THE COMPLETE VECTOR
&LABEL    DS      (&NUMPARM)F
          ORG     &LABEL
.*
.*                                 INITIALIZE VECTOR
.*
.FOR0     ANOP                     FOR &ENTNUM = 1 TO &NUMPARM
&ENTNUM   SETA    1                        :
.FTEST0   ANOP                             :
          AIF     (&ENTNUM GT &NUMPARM).ENDFOR0
```

```
      .*
      .*                            .            GENERATE DC INSTRUCTION
      .*
              DC      F'&ENTNUM'
      .*
&ENTNUM       SETA    &ENTNUM+1                    :
              AGO     .FTEST0                      :
.ENDFOR0      ANOP                        END FOR
      .*
MEND
      .*
```

****

This macro could be used to define and initialize vectors of different lengths using the macro calls shown below.

```
VECTOR1    DEFVEC 10            DEFINE A VECTOR WITH 10 ELEMENTS
VECTOR2    DEFVEC 8             DEFINE A VECTOR WITH 8 ELEMENTS
```

When executed, these two macro calls will produce the generated instructions shown in the following partial listing.

```
                              68 VECTOR1   DEFVEC     10
000608                        69+VECTOR1   DS        (10)F
000630           00608        70+          ORG        VECTOR1
000608 00000001               71+          DC         F'1'
00060C 00000002               72+          DC         F'2'
000610 00000003               73+          DC         F'3'
000614 00000004               74+          DC         F'4'
000618 00000005               75+          DC         F'5'
00061C 00000006               76+          DC         F'6'
000620 00000007               77+          DC         F'7'
000624 00000008               78+          DC         F'8'
000628 00000009               79+          DC         F'9'
00062C 0000000A               80+          DC         F'10'
                              81 VECTOR2   DEFVEC     8
000630                        82+VECTOR2   DS        (8)F
000650           00630        83+          ORG        VECTOR2
000630 00000001               84+          DC         F'1'
000634 00000002               85+          DC         F'2'
000638 00000003               86+          DC         F'3'
00063C 00000004               87+          DC         F'4'
000640 00000005               88+          DC         F'5'
000644 00000006               89+          DC         F'6'
000648 00000007               90+          DC         F'7'
00064C 00000008               91+          DC         F'8'
```

The next example shows how global set symbols can be used to provide communication between separate macros and between different invocations of the same macro. Recall that, in writing conversion macros in the last section, we had to rely on the calling program to provide a work area for the conversion. In addition to placing a burden on the calling program, this raises the possibility that a value in the work area may be accidentally destroyed by one of the generated instructions. A better approach is to have the macros themselves define the work area and use a name that is not likely to be duplicated in the calling program.

There are several occasions in which a macro needs to generate a name that will not duplicate a name in the program. The problem we are considering is one example. Another is when the macro needs to define a label to be used as a target of a branch. In order to generate names that will not duplicate names in the program, we make use of the fact that the assembler permits the use of the characters $, #, and @ in identifiers. We can prevent conflicts between program names and macro-generated names by using one of these characters, say $, in macro names and avoiding its use in program names. There remains the possibility of conflict between independent macros, which we will address in other ways.

In this case, we use an abbreviation of the macro's function to reduce the likelihood of conflict with other macros. We call the work area CV$DWORK.

We provide two macros, one to convert a zoned number to binary and another to convert a binary number to packed form. These two macros can use the same work area, however, the work area can only be defined once. We need to be able to recognize the first invocation of one of these macros so that the work area can be defined. Succeeding invocations would simply use the previously defined work area. This approach requires a mechanism for communicating between the two macros and between calls on each of the macros.

Communication can be provided by a global Boolean set symbol, &DEFINED, which is defined in both macros. This symbol would be initialized to *false* by the assembler, however, it would retain its value between macro calls. Each macro can check &DEFINED. If it is false, then the macro can write the definition for CV$DWORK and set &DEFINED to *true*. Otherwise, it can use the previously defined work area.

The definition for CV$DWORK will occur in the middle of the code. As with the address lists used in procedure calls, we must provide for a branch around the work area during execution. We must also address alignment problems similar to those connected with the use of address lists. When the assembler processes the instruction

```
CV$DWORK DS      D
```

it may skip some bytes in order to align this field on a doubleword boundary. An attempt to perform a self-relative branch such as

```
         B       *+8
```

would have to consider this possibility. Alternatively, we could define a label immediately after CV$DWORK and branch to that label. But, rather than introduce the complication of defining another label, we will use

B   CV$DWORK+L'CV$DWORK

This will cause a branch to the first byte after CV$DWORK. The resulting macro definitions are shown in Example 7.2.11.

Example 7.2.11

```
***********************************************************************************************
*
          MACRO
          CVTZF &FWRD,&ZNUM
.*
.*     CONVERT ZONED TO FULL
.*
.*     GENERATE THE INSTRUCTIONS TO CONVERT THE ZONED
.*     NUMBER IN THE SECOND FIELD TO A FULLWORD BINARY
.*     INTEGER IN THE FIRST FIELD.
.*
.*     THE MACRO USES THE WORK AREA CV$DWORK.
.*     IF THIS IS THE FIRST CALL OF A CONVERT MACRO,
.*     IT GENERATES CV$DWORK.
.*
.*     R0 IS USED FOR THE CONVERSION.
.*
          GBLB    &DEFINED           INDICATES THAT CV$DWORK IS DEFINED
.*
.IF0      ANOP    IF NOT &DEFINED
          AIF     (&DEFINED).ENDIF0
.THEN0    ANOP    THEN
.*
.*                                   GENERATE DEF FOR CV$DWORK AND
.*                                   BRANCH AROUND IT.
.*
          B       CV$DWORK+L'CV$DWORK
CV$DWORK  DS      D
.*
&DEFINED  SETB    (NOT &DEFINED)     NEGATE &DEFINED
.*
.ENDIF0   ANOP                       ENDIF
.*
.*                                   GENERATE THE INSTRUCTIONS TO PERFORM
.*                                   THE CONVERSION USING CV$DWORK.
```

```
.*
          PACK    CV$DWORK,&ZNUM
          CVB     R0,CV$DWORK
          ST      R0,&FWRD
.*
          MEND
*
**********************************************************************************************
*
          MACRO
&LABEL    CVTFP   &PNUM,&FWRD
.*
.*   CONVERT FULL TO PACKED
.*
.*   GENERATE THE INSTRUCTIONS TO CONVERT THE FULLWORD
.*   BINARY INTEGER IN THE SECOND FIELD TO A PACKED DECIMAL
.*   NUMBER IN THE FIRST FIELD.
.*
.*   THE MACRO USES THE WORK AREA CV$DWORK.
.*   IF THIS IS THE FIRST CALL OF A CONVERT MACRO,
.*   IT GENERATES CV$DWORK.
.*
.*   R0 IS USED FOR THE CONVERSION.
.*
          GBLB    &DEFINED        INDICATES THAT CV$DWORK IS DEFINED
.*
.IF0      ANOP                    IF NOT &DEFINED
          AIF     (&DEFINED).ENDIF0
.THEN0    ANOP                    THEN
.*
.*                                GENERATE DEF FOR CV$DWORK AND
.*                                BRANCH AROUND IT.
.*
          B       CV$DWORK+L'CV$DWORK
CV$DWORK  DS      D
.*
&DEFINED  SETB    (NOT &DEFINED)  NEGATE &DEFINED
.*
.ENDIF0   ANOP                    ENDIF
.*
.*                                GENERATE THE INSTRUCTIONS TO PERFORM
.*                                THE CONVERSION USING CV$DWORK.
.*
          L       R0,&FWRD
          CVD     R0,CV$DWORK
          ZAP     &PNUM,CV$DWORK
```

```
.*
        MEND
*
***************************************************************************************************
```

The following partial listing shows the result of several invocations of these two macros. Because CVTFP was invoked first, it defined CV$DWORK. Had CVTZF been called first, then it would have generated the definition of the work area.
Note also that the assembler has indeed skipped several bytes in defining CV$DWORK, but the address listed for the branch instruction is correct.

```
                                        90              CVTFP       PTOTAL,TOTAL
000002 47F0 C00E        00010          91+              B           CV$DWORK+L'CV$DWORK
000008                                 92+CV$DWORK DS   D
000010 5800 C03E        00040          93+              L           R0,TOTAL
000014 4E00 C006        00008          94+              CVD         R0,CV$DWORK
000018 F837 C038 C006 0003A 00008 95+               ZAP         PTOTAL,CV$DWORK


                                        96              CVTZF       ITEM,INITEM
00001E F276 C006 C046 00008 00048 97+               PACK        CV$DWORK,INITEM
000024 4F00 C006        00008          98+              CVB         R0,CV$DWORK
000028 5000 C042        00044          99+              ST          R0,ITEM


                                        100             CVTFP       PSUM,SUM
00002C 5800 C052        00054          101+             L           R0,SUM
000030 4E00 C006        00008          102+             CVD         R0,CV$DWORK
000034 F837 C04D C006 0004F 00008 103+              ZAP         PSUM,CV$DWORK
```

E   X   E   R   C   I   S   E   S

1. Determine when each of the following events occurs—at preassembly, assembly, linkage, or execution.

   a. Translating a mnemonic to an object code.
   b. Assigning a value to a set symbol.
   c. Transferring to a label defined with an EQU.
   d. Reading a data card into a field named INREC.
   e. Storing a value in an external address constant.
   f. Transferring to a sequence symbol.
   g. Printing the assembler listing.
   h. Executing a BALR instruction.
   i. Specifying a register to be used with a DSECT.

2. Write set symbol declarations for each of the following.

    a. A local arithmetic set symbol named &LOOPCTR.

    b. An arithmetic set symbol called &NUMCALS which will be used to count the number of times the including macro has been invoked.

    c. A local arithmetic set symbol named &LNGTH and a global Boolean set symbol named &FIRST.

    d. A character set symbol named &PARMINT.

3. Write a set instruction to accomplish each of the following.

    a. Increment the arithmetic set symbol, &LTH by 3.

    b. Initialize the character set symbol &SENTNCE to the string "THIS IS".

    c. Assign the Boolean set symbol &EMPTY, a value which indicates whether &STRING contains the empty string.

4. Write conditional assembly instructions to implement each of the following segments from macro definitions. Assume that all set symbols are arithmetic.

    a. IF   &COUNT<&LIMIT
       THEN
          &DONE = &LIMIT−&RMENDR
       ELSE
          &LIMIT = &LIMIT+1
       ENDIF

    b. FOR &CTR = 1 TO &EXPONENT
          &POWER = 2 * &POWER
       ENDFOR

5. Modify the macro DEFVEC in Example 7.2.10 to initialize all entries of the vector to the same value. This value should be passed as a second parameter, &INIT.

6. Write a macro CVTPF to convert a packed number to a fullword binary number. Share the work area CF$DWORK with the other conversion macos.

7. Write conversion macros CVTPH and CVTHP to convert between packed decimal and halfword data types. Use CV$DWORK as in Exercise 6.

8. Modify the macro REGEQU from Exercise 1-c in Section 7.2 to use a loop to generate the definitions for R0 through R9.

9. Modify the macros DIV and MOD from Exercise 1-g in Section 7.2 to allow them to share a work area named DIV$WORK. This work area should be defined by the first invocation of either macro.

10. Write three operand versions of DIV and MOD. (See Exercise 8 in Section 7.1.)

7.3 ATTRIBUTES AND STRING OPERATIONS

The conditional assembly instructions covered in the last section are augmented by several other features that increase their power. The first of these is a pair of instructions to print warning messages from within a macro definition and to provide early termination of macro expansion when error conditions occur. The second is a collection of attribute operators that allow us to determine various characteristics of the values of symbolic parameters. Finally, there is a facility for string manipulation, which includes concatenation and substring extraction. We describe these features in this section and consider some sample macros that make use of them.

MNOTE and MEXIT

The MNOTE instruction allows us to print a message from within a macro. The distinction between this facility and the comment facility is that comments are only printed if PRINT GEN is enabled. An MNOTE message will always appear in this listing. This instruction may be used to print warning messages when an error condition occurs or to print informational messages.

The format for MNOTE is

MNOTE '<message>'

Example 7.3.1

MNOTE 'INCORRECT NUMBER OF ARGUMENTS'

When it is determined that an unrecoverable error has occurred, macro expansion can be terminated early by executing the MEXIT instruction. This instruction does not have any operands. Its format is

MEXIT

Attribute Operators

In order to write macros that are as general as possible, we need to be able to allow reasonable variation in the operands. At the same time, when variations are permitted, we may need to determine the characteristics of a symbolic parameter on a particular call. For example, we may want to write a macro that permits input values of different types. In each expansion, we might need to determine the type of the current value of that parameter.

In order to satisfy this need, there are a number of attribute operators available. Of these, we are already familiar with the length attribute, L'. In this section, we introduce four new attributes, type, scaling, integer, and count. A sixth operator will be discussed in the next section.

Type: The type attribute, T', returns a single character that indicates the type of the current value of the symbolic parameter to which it is applied. For data fields, this is the same as the type designator used in the DS or DC instruction. A partial list of these values with their interpretation is given in the following table.

Type Attribute Values

Value Returned	Current Value of Symbolic Parameter
C	Character field.
D	Doubleword field.
F	Fullword field.
H	Halfword field.
P	Packed decimal field.
X	Hexadecimal field.
Z	Zoned decimal field.
U	Undefined (includes literal operands and symbols defined by an EQU instruction).

Example 7.3.2

Suppose we have the storage definitions

```
HERE      EQU     *
PNUM      DS      PL4
BNUM      DS      F
```

and the macro definition

```
          MACRO
          FINDTYPE &PARM
          LCLC    &TYPE
&TYPE     SETC    T'&PARM
          MEND
```

The list below shows the value which will be assigned to &TYPE by each macro call.

```
FINDTYPE   HERE      &TYPE = 'U'
FINDTYPE   PNUM      &TYPE = 'P'
FINDTYPE   BNUM      &TYPE = 'F'
FINDTYPE   =P'34'    &TYPE = 'U'
```

Scaling: The scaling attribute, S', can be applied to numeric fields. It returns the position of the implied decimal point in the field. The way in which this value is determined depends upon the type of the field.

In providing an initialization value or a prototype value for a packed decimal field, we can include a decimal point. The decimal point is ignored when determining the length of the field or forming the initialization value. However, its position is recorded by the assembler as the scaling factor for that field. If the scaling attribute is applied to a packed decimal field, this scaling factor is the value returned.

Example 7.3.3 *Suppose that &PARM1 is PNUM1 and &PARM2 is PNUM2.*

If these two fields were defined by

```
PNUM1      DS      P'999.99'
PNUM2      DC      P'2.33423'
```

Then S'&PARM1 will return 2 and S'&PARM2 will return 5.

Integer: The integer attribute, I', is the complement of the scaling attribute. It returns the number of digits to the left of the implied decimal point.

Note that both S' and I' can be used only in arithmetic expressions, for example, in a SETA instruction.

Example 7.3.4 *With &PARM1 and &PARM2 as in Example 7.3.3, I'&PARM1 will return 3. I'&PARM2 will return 2. (PNUM2 will be stored in hexadecimal form as X'0233423C'.)*

Count: The count attribute, which is vulgarly denoted K', can be applied to a symbolic parameter. It returns the number of characters in the string that comprises the current value of the parameter. Recall that the symbolic parameters in a macro are essentially character strings, normally representing an identifier or label in the program, however, we may also pass numbers and quoted character strings as values.

The count attribute may only be used in an arithmetic expression inside a macro.

Example 7.3.5 *The macro below illustrates the characteristics of the count attribute.*

```
****************************************************************************************************
*
           MACRO
           COUNT  &PARM
.*
.*    PRINT AN MNOTE WHICH GIVES K'&PARM
.*
           LCLA   &COUNT                   ARITH. SET SYMBOL TO HOLD COUNT
.*
&COUNT     SETA   K'&PARM
```

```
        MNOTE 'THE COUNT IS &COUNT'
  *
        MEND
  *
***********************************************************************************************************
```

The following partial listing shows the effect of K' on various values for &PARM. Note that the count of the character string includes the quotes. This is an annoyance. In order to pass a string that contains blanks or commas, the string must be enclosed in quotes. Then the assembler passes the quotes to the parameter as part of the string.

```
37             COUNT  PSUM
38+THE COUNT IS 4
39             COUNT  PITEM
40+THE COUNT IS 5
41             COUNT  'THIS IS A STRING'
42+THE COUNT IS 18
43             COUNT  -1234
44+THE COUNT IS 5
  .
  .
  .

78 PSUM    DC     P'000234.332'
79 PITEM   DC     P'3.2'
```

As an example of the way in which these attribute operators may be used, we develop a macro, APF, to add two packed decimal fields.

```
        APF    PNUM1,PNUM2
```

should generate the instructions to add PNUM1 and PNUM2 and store the result in PNUM1. However, we assume that the fields have an implied decimal point determined by the DS or DC instructions that defined them. The macro must check the positions of the implied decimal points and determine whether a shift must be performed before the addition.

This is accomplished by using the scaling factor S' to determine the position of the implied decimal. When the two fields have the same number of fractional positions, no shifting is necessary and the macro simply generates an AP instruction to add the second field to the first. If the decimal positions are different, the second value is moved into a work area and shifted either left or right to align the decimal points. Using the SRP instruction, we do not need to determine the direction of the shift; we simply specify 64 plus the number of fractional positions in the first field minus the number of fractional digits in the second field. We specify a rounding factor of 5 in case the value is shifted right. This value is ignored on a left shift.

In order to avoid generating meaningless instructions, the APF macro uses the type attribute, T', to check the types of the arguments. In this case, its use can also prevent an assembly error, which occurs if the scaling attribute is applied improperly.

This macro also uses a global Boolean set symbol to determine whether the work area has been defined. In this case, the symbol is not accessed by any other macros. It is declared global so that it will maintain its value from one invocation to the next.

```
*****************************************************************************************************
*
                 MACRO
                 APF          &PNUM1,&PNUM2
*
.*       ADD PACKED DECIMAL FRACTIONS
.*
.*       GENERATE THE INSTRUCTIONS TO ADD TWO PACKED DECIMAL
.*       NUMBERS, SHIFTING AS NECESSARY.
.*
.*       THE MACRO USES THE WORK AREA APF$WORK WHICH IS
.*       GENERATED ON THE FIRST CALL
.*
                 GBLB         &DEFINED             INDICATES THAT APF$WORK IS DEFINED
                 LCLA         &SCALE1              NUMBER OF FRACT. DIGITS IN &PNUM1
                 LCLA         &SCALE2              NUMBER OF FRACT. DIGITS IN &PNUM2
                 LCLC         &TYPE1               TYPE OF FIRST OPERAND
                 LCLC         &TYPE2               TYPE OF SECOND OPERAND
*
.IF0             ANOP                              IF NOT &DEFINED
                 AIF          (&DEFINED).ENDIF0
.THEN0           ANOP                              THEN
.*
.*       GENERATE DEF FOR APF$WORK AND
.*       BRANCH AROUND IT.
.*
                 B            APF$WORK+L'     APF$WORK
APF$WORK         DS           PL16
.*
&DEFINED         SETB         (NOT &DEFINED)       NEGATE &DEFINED
.*
.ENDIF0          ANOP         ENDIF
.*
.*       CHECK THE SCALING FACTORS FOR SHIFT
.*
&TYPE1           SETC         T'&PNUM1             CHECK FOR VALID OPERAND TYPES
&TYPE2           SETC         T'&PNUM2
```

```
.*
.*
.IF1          ANOP                              IF &TYPE1 <> 'P' OR &TYPE2 <> 'P'
              AIF     (NOT (('&TYPE1' NE 'P') OR ('&TYPE2' NE 'P'))).ENDIF1
.THEN1        ANOP                              THEN
.*                                              PRINT WARNING AND EXIT
              MNOTE 'ERROR IN OPERAND TYPES.'
              MEXIT
.ENDIF1       ANOP                              ENDIF
.*
.*
&SCALE1       SETA    S'&PNUM1          FIND SCALING FACTORS
&SCALE2       SETA    S'&PNUM2
.*
.*
.IF2          ANOP                      IF &SCALE1 = &SCALE2
              AIF     (NOT (&SCALE1 EQ &SCALE2)).ELSE2
.THEN2        ANOP                              THEN
.*
.*    USE AP TO ADD DIRECTLY
.*
              AP      &PNUM1,&PNUM2
.*
              AGO     .ENDIF2
.ELSE2        ANOP                      ELSE
.*
.*    GENERATE INSTRUCTIONS TO MOVE &PNUM2 INTO WORK AREA, SHIFT AND ADD
.*    TO &PNUM1
.*
              ZAP     APF$WORK,&PNUM2
              SRP     APF$WORK,64+&SCALE1-&SCALE2,5
              AP      &PNUM1,APF$WORK
.*
.ENDIF2       ANOP
.*
              MEND
.*
```

****

The following partial listing shows the effect of invoking macro APF with various fields. The MNOTE does not terminate assembly. Furthermore, as no instructions are generated, it will not prevent execution of the program, although the results would probably be meaningless.

```
123           APF     PSUM,PITEM
124+          B       APF$WORK+L'APF$WORK
```

```
125+APF$WORK  DS      PL16
126+          ZAP     APF$WORK,PITEM
127+          SRP     APF$WORK,64+3-1,5
128+          AP      PSUM,APF$WORK
129           APF     PTOTHRS,PHRS
130+          ZAP     APF$WORK,PHRS
131+          SRP     APF$WORK,64+5-6,5
132+          AP      PTOTHRS,APF$WORK
133           APF     PWORK,PTEMP
134+          AP      PWORK,PTEMP
135           APF     PWORK,=P'1'
136+ERROR IN OPERAND TYPES.


193 PSUM      DC      P'000234.332'
194 PITEM     DC      P'3.2'
195 PTOTHRS   DC      P'0999.99999'
196 PHRS      DC      P'9.999999'
197 PWORK     DC      P'6.99'
198 PTEMP     DC      P'1.99'
```

String Operations

The concatenation operator is a period (.). It can be used both in model statements and in character expressions in SETC instructions or logical expressions.

Concatenation can be used to generate various components in model statements. In fact, the substitution of the value of a parameter or a set symbol in a model statement is equivalent to implicit concatenation. Implicit concatenation is permitted any time it does not result in ambiguity. When implicit concatenation would cause ambiguity, the concatenation operator may be used. On the other hand, the explicit concatenation operator cannot be used whenever an ordinary character precedes a symbolic parameter or a set symbol. If used in this situation, the period will be reproduced in the generated statement.

Example 7.3.6 *In the following fragment of a macro definition, assume that &LENGTH and &COUNT are arithmetic set symbols.*

```
&LENGTH    SETA   4
.FOR0      ANOP                          FOR &COUNT = 1 TO 5
&COUNT     SETA   1
.FTEST0    ANOP
                  AIF (&COUNT GT 5).ENDFOR0
.*   GENERATE DEFINITION
PCK&COUNTDC       PL&LENGTH'&COUNT'
&COUNT     SETA   &COUNT+1
           AGO    .FTEST0
.ENDFOR0   ANOP                          END FOR
```

The implicit concatenation in the model statement results in the following expansion.

```
25+PCK1    DC      PL4'1'
26+PCK2    DC      PL4'2'
27+PCK3    DC      PL4'3'
28+PCK4    DC      PL4'4'
29+PCK5    DC      PL4'5'
```

Although the concatenation used in the name field in the model statement used 9 positions and pushed the DC operand into column 11, the assembler correctly places it in column 10 in the generated instructions.

There are several positions in the model statement where the optional concatenation operator may be included if desired. The model statement

```
PCK&COUNTDC       PL&LENGTH.'&COUNT'
```

would generate the same instructions as the original. However, the model statement

```
PCK.&COUNT      DC      PL.&LENGTH'.&COUNT'
```

would generate instructions of the form

```
PCK.1           DC      PL.4'.1'
```

In a SETC instruction, concatenation can be used to construct new strings to be assigned to a character set symbol. Because a symbol can appear on both sides of a SETC operator, concatenation can also be used to add characters to a string.

Example 7.3.7

```
&CHRFLD     SETC    &FLD1.&FLD2
&EXP        SETC    '('.&SUBEXP.')'
&STRING     SETC    &STRING.&NUCHAR
```

The substring operation is similar to that found in high-level languages. It has the following format.

'<string>'(<start position>,<length>)

<string>   A character string, a symbolic parameter or a set symbol. The string must be enclosed in quotes, even if it is not a literal string.

<start position> An arithmetic expression that designates the position of the first character to be extracted. If the starting position is less than or equal to 0, an error occurs. If it is greater than the length of the string, the assembler prints a warning and returns the null string.

<length> An arithmetic expression that designates the number of characters to extract. An error occurs if the length is negative. If it goes beyond the end of the string, only the characters up to the end of the string are returned.

Example 7.3.8 *Suppose that the value of &STRING is "ABCDEFG". The following table gives the value returned by various invocations of the substring operation.*

Substring Operation	Value Returned
'&STRING'(1,4)	"ABCD"
'&STRING'(3,1)	"C"
'&STRING'(2,5)	"BCDEF"
'&STRING'(3,10)	"CDEFG"
'&STRING'(4,0)	""
'&STRING'(0,5)	ERROR

Example 7.3.9 *Suppose that &STRING is a character set symbol and that &POS and &LTH are arithmetic symbols.*

If &LTH represents the length of &STRING, and &POS is greater than zero and less than &LTH, then the instruction

```
&STRING    SETC    '&STRING'(1,&POS−1).'&STRING'(&POS+1,&LTH−&POS)
```

will remove the character indicated by &POS from &STRING.

We conclude this section with an example of a very useful macro, which employs most of the features we have described. It is a macro that accepts a character string describing an edit format and generates an edit pattern to implement that format. The input argument will be a character string that uses a '9' for normal digit positions, a '0' for the position where the first 0 should be forced, and any fill characters or message characters desired.

For example, given the string

' 99,999.09'

this macro should produce the edit mask

X'4020206B2020214B2020'

This places several requirements on the macro. It must have a label parameter to identify the edit mask. It should have one symbolic parameter to accept the character string. As the character string may contain blanks and commas, it must be enclosed in quotes, which will be a part of the parameter's value.

The basic operation of the macro is examining the string, a character at a time, and generating character fields (containing the fill character or message characters) or hexadecimal fields containing digit selectors.

The only real difficulty is in handling the significance starter. If the string contains a 0, the significance starter should be inserted in the position occupied by the first 9 to the left of the 0. In order to accomplish this, we first scan the string from right to left, looking for a 0. If one is found, we look back to the left for the first 9 we come to. If we find a 9, we change it to a 0 and change the original 0 to a 9. Otherwise, if no 9 is found, we leave the string alone.

Having performed this preliminary processing on the string, we then scan it again from left to right generating the characters in the pattern as we go. Now, we create an X'20' when we see a 9 and an X'21' when we see a 0. Otherwise, we assume the character is a fill character or a message character and place it in a character field.

The macro definition itself is shown below. As we need to change the string, we must copy it into a local character set symbol. It is not permitted to change a symbolic parameter. We leave the quotes attached so that we do not have to treat a change in the first or last character as a special case.

```
********************************************************************************************
               MACRO
&LABEL         EDITPAT &PARM
.*
.*     EDIT PATTERN
.*
.*     ACCEPT A CHARACTER DESCRIPTION OF AN EDIT FORMAT
.*     AND PRODUCE AN EDIT MASK WHICH CAN BE USED TO EDIT
.*     NUMBERS IN THE GIVEN FORMAT.
.*
.*     CHARACTERS IN INPUT DESCRIPTION:
.*        9      - DIGIT
.*        0      - FIRST DIGIT TO BE FORCED
.*        CHAR - ANY MESSAGE CHARACTER OR FILL CHARACTER
.*
               LCLA    &LTH                 LENGTH OF CHARACTER PATTERN
               LCLA    &POS                 POSITION IN STRING
               LCLA    &LFT                 POSITION TO LEFT OF THE 0
               LCLB    &DONE                FLAG TO INDICATE 0 FOUND
               LCLB    &FALSE
               LCLB    &TRUE
               LCLC    &FORM                CHARACTER PATTERN
               LCLC    &CHR                 EXTRACTED CHAR FOR MODEL STMNT
.*
.*
&TRUE          SETB    1                    INITIALIZE CONSTANT
.*
&FORM          SETC    '&PARM'              &FORM = &PARM
```

```
&LTH          SETA   K'&FORM                    &LTH = LENGTH(&FORM)
.*
.*     IF &FORM CONTAINS A 0, THEN CHANGE FIRST 9 TO
.*     ITS LEFT TO 0 AND CHANGE THE ORIGINAL 0 TO 9
.*
&POS          SETA   2                          POS = 2
&DONE         SETB   (&FALSE)                   DONE = FALSE
.WHILE0       ANOP                              WHILE POS < LTH AND NOT DONE
              AIF    (&POS GT &LTH).ENDWHL0        :
              AIF    (&DONE).ENDWHL0               :
.IF0          ANOP                               IF FORM(POS) = '0'
              AIF    ('&FORM'(&POS,1) NE '0').ELSE0
.THEN0        ANOP                                  THEN
&LFT          SETA   &POS−1                          LFT = POS−1
.WHILE1       ANOP                                  WHILE FORM(LFT) <> '9'
              AIF    ('&FORM'(&LFT,1) EQ '9').ENDWHL1      AND LFT <> 1
              AIF    (&LFT EQ 1).ENDWHL1               :
&LFT          SETA   &LFT−1                          LFT = LFT−1
              AGO    .WHILE1                          :
.ENDWHL1      ANOP                                  ENDWHILE
.IF1          ANOP                               IF FORM(LFT) = '9'
              AIF    ('&FORM'(&LFT,1) NE '9').ENDIF1    :
.THEN1        ANOP                                  THEN
.*                                                      CHANGE 9 TO 0
&FORM         SETC   '&FORM'(1,&LFT−1).'0'.'&FORM'(&LFT+1,&LTH−&LFT)
.*                                                 FORM(POS) = '9'
&FORM         SETC   '&FORM'(1,&POS−1).'9'.'&FORM'(&POS+1,&LTH−&POS)
.ENDIF1       ANOP                                  ENDIF
&DONE         SETB   (&TRUE)                     DONE = TRUE
              AGO    .ENDIF0                       :
.ELSE0        ANOP                              ELSE
&POS          SETA   &POS+1                         POS = POS+1
.ENDIF0       ANOP                              ENDIF
              AGO    .WHILE0                        :
.ENDWHL0      ANOP                            END WHILE
.*
.*     CREATE EDIT PATTERN - INSERT X'20' FOR '9' AND X'21' FOR '0'
.*
&LABEL        DS     XL(&LTH−2)
              ORG    &LABEL
.FOR0         ANOP                              FOR POS = 2 TO LTH−1
&POS          SETA   2                            :
.FTEST0       ANOP                               :
              AIF    (&POS GT &LTH−1).ENDFOR0     :
&CHR          SETC   '&FORM'(&POS,1)             CHR = FORM(POS)
.IF2          ANOP                              IF CHR = '9'
```

```
          AIF    ('&CHR' NE '9').ELSE2              :
.THEN2    ANOP                                  THEN
.*                                                   GENERATE X'20'

          DC     X'20'
          AGO    .ENDIF2                            :
.ELSE2    ANOP                                  ELSE
.IF3      ANOP                                      IF FORM(POS) = 0
          AIF    ('&CHR' NE '0').ELSE3             :
.THEN3    ANOP                                      THEN
.*                                                       GENERATE X'21'

          DC     X'21'
          AGO    .ENDIF3                            :
.ELSE3    ANOP                                      ELSE
.*                                                       GENERATE CHAR

          DC     C'&CHR'
.ENDIF3   ANOP                                        ENDIF
.ENDIF2   ANOP                                    ENDIF
&POS      SETA   &POS+1                           :
          AGO    .FTEST0                          :
.ENDFOR0  ANOP                               ENDFOR
.*
          MEND                               END EDITPAT
```
****

The lines below show the instructions produced by this macro for several possible input patterns.

```
                              204 PAT1    EDITPAT   ' 9,990.99'
000706                        205+PAT1    DS        XL(11-2)
00070F              00076 206+            ORG       PAT1
000706 40                     207+        DC        C' '
000707 20                     208+        DC        X'20'
000708 6B                     209+        DC        C','
000709 20                     210+        DC        X'20'
00070A 21                     211+        DC        X'21'
00070B 20                     212+        DC        X'20'
00070C 4B                     213+        DC        C'.'
00070D 20                     214+        DC        X'20'
00070E 20                     215+        DC        X'20'
                              216 PAT2    EDITPAT   ' 999.09'
00070F                        217+PAT2    DS        XL(9-2)
000716              0007F 218+            ORG       PAT2
00070F 40                     219+        DC        C' '
000710 20                     220+        DC        X'20'
000711 20                     221+        DC        X'20'
000712 21                     222+        DC        X'21'
```

000713 4B	223+	DC	C'.'
000714 20	224+	DC	X'20'
000715 20	225+	DC	X'20'
	226 PAT3	EDITPAT	'#0999.99CR'
000716	227+PAT3	DS	XL(12−2)
000720	00016 228+	ORG	PAT3
000716 7B	229+	DC	C'#'
000717 21	230+	DC	X'21'
000718 20	231+	DC	X'20'
000719 20	232+	DC	X'20'
00071A 20	233+	DC	X'20'
00071B 4B	234+	DC	C'.'
00071C 20	235+	DC	X'20'
00071D 20	236+	DC	X'20'
00071E C3	237+	DC	C'C'
00071F D9	238+	DC	C'R'
	239 PAT4	EDITPAT	' 99990'
000720	240+PAT4	DS	XL(8−2)
000726	00020 241+	ORG	PAT4
000720 40	242+	DC	C' '
000721 20	243+	DC	X'20'
000722 20	244+	DC	X'20'
000723 20	245+	DC	X'20'
000724 21	246+	DC	X'21'
000725 20	247+	DC	X'20'

E X E R C I S E S

1. Modify the macros AF and SF from Section 7.1 to check the types of the operands. Print a warning message and exit if they are incorrect.

2. Write a macro named AB (Add Binary), which will accept either full or halfword fields as operands and generate the instructions to add the fields and store the result in the first field. If the type of either field is not full or halfword, print an error message and exit.

3. Write a macro named SB (Subtract Binary) like the AB macro in Exercise 2.

4. Write a macro named BAM (Blank And Move), which performs the string equivalent of ZAP. It should receive two character fields as arguments and generate the instructions to fill the first field with blanks and then copy the second field, or as much of it as will fit, into the left of the first field.

5. Modify BAM so that it only blanks out any unused bytes in the first field.

6. Write a set of conditional assembly instructions to determine whether the current value of the character set symbol &STRING includes any blanks.

7. Write a set of conditional assembly instructions to remove any leading blanks from the character set symbol &STRING.

8. Suppose that the character set symbol &LINE contains 0 or more words separated by blanks. Write a set of conditional assembly instructions to remove the first word from &LINE and assign it to &WORD. (If &LINE contains no words, set &WORD equal to the empty string.)

9. Write a macro named MAKEPAT, which accepts a packed field as an argument and generates an edit pattern appropriate for the field. Use the scaling factor to determine whether the pattern should include a decimal point. If the scaling factor is 0, put a significance starter immediately before last digit selector. Otherwise, place it before the decimal point. Insert commas every 3 digits to the left of the decimal point.

10. Write a macro called *INDEX*, which accepts two arguments, a register and a subscripted array reference. The macro should generate the instructions to determine the index from the beginning of the array to the subscripted entry. Assume that the subscripts begin with 1, that the subscript is delimited by angular brackets, and that the subscript is a single variable. For example, a typical call on the macro would be

        INDEX   R4,TABLE<I>

Assume that the array and the subscript are fullwords.

11. Write a new version of the REGEQU macro, which uses the string "0123456789ABCDEF" to generate the register equates.

7.4 ARGUMENT LISTS AND SET SYMBOL ARRAYS

We conclude this chapter by considering three features for advanced macro definition: (1) the ability to send a list of arguments which correspond to a single parameter; (2) the ability to define and manipulate arrays of set symbols; and (3) the use of the symbol &SYSNDX to define unique labels within a macro. Finally, note how some of the general facilities provided for macro writing may also be used outside of macros.

Argument Lists

Whenever a collection of related arguments are to be passed to a macro or when the exact number of arguments is unknown before the call, argument lists may be used. In fact, a list may be passed to any symbolic parameter, as this mechanism is distinguished by the form of the call, rather than the way in which the parameter is declared.

In order to pass a list of values to a symbolic parameter, the entire list is enclosed in parentheses. The elements in the list are separated by commas.

From within the macro, it is not possible to tell directly whether the value that corresponds to a parameter is a list. However, the system does provide an attribute operator that returns the number of entries in a list—the number attribute, N'. If it is applied to a parameter whose value is not a list, it returns 1 as its value. Otherwise, it returns the number of entries in the list.

Example 7.4.1

Given the macro header

```
MACRO
LISTEX       &ARG1,&ARG2,&ARG3
```

and the macro call

```
LISTEX       NOLIST,(ENTRY1,ENTRY2,ENTRY3),(ENTRY1)

             N'&ARG1 = 1
             N'&ARG2 = 3
             N'&ARG3 = 1
```

The number attribute is also useful in another context. It is permitted to omit any argument or any entry in a list, in a macro call. If the omitted argument is not at the end of the argument list, then its position is indicated with commas. The number attribute can be used to detect an argument omission, as it returns 0 when applied to the corresponding parameter.

Example 7.4.2

With the macro LISTEX from the last example, the call

```
LISTEX   (),,VAL3
```

will result in the following number attributes.

```
             N'&ARG1 = 0
             N'&ARG2 = 0
             N'&ARG3 = 1
```

Individual entries in a list are referenced by a subscript notation. The name of the symbolic parameter is followed by a pair of parentheses enclosing an arithmetic expression which represents the position of the desired argument in the list.

<parameter name>(<position>)

If the subscript is greater than the value returned by N', then the system substitutes the empty string.

Example 7.4.3

Given the following call on the LISTEX macro above,

LISTEX   (A,B,C),(1,2,3,4),ONEVAL

individual list entries will have the following values:

&ARG1(3) = C
&ARG2(2) = 2
&ARG2(5) = "
&ARG3(1) = ONEVAL
&ARG3(2) = "

It is also possible to treat a parameter that receives a list as a character string. When treated in this way, the count attribute will return the number of characters in the string and the substring notation can be applied to extract part of the string.

Example 7.4.4

Given the following call on LISTEX

LISTEX   (VAL1,VAL2,VAL3)
K'&ARG1 = 16

'&ARG1'(3,7) = 'AL1,VAL'
K'&ARG2 = 0

As an example of a macro that uses lists of arguments, consider a macro to implement procedure calls with dynamic address generation, as described in Chapter 5. This is called *CALLD*. It will receive two arguments. The first is the name of the procedure to be called. The second is a list of address references to be placed in the address list to be passed to the procedure. (If the procedure gets no arguments, then the second operand may be omitted on the macro call. The system will substitute an empty list.)

The macro extracts names from the argument list and generates the instructions to create dynamically a list of the addresses corresponding to those arguments. The macro itself is shown below.

```
                 MACRO
                 CALLD   &SUBRT,&ARGLIST
.*
.*       CALL DYNAMICALLY
.*
.*       GENERATE THE INSTRUCTIONS TO CREATE A DYNAMICALLY GENERATED
.*       ADDRESS LIST AND PASS TO AN EXTERNAL SUBROUTINE.
.*
.*
.*
                 LCLA    &NUMARGS            NUMBER OF ENTRIES IN &ARGLIST
                 LCLA    &ARGCTR             INDEX FOR &ARGLIST
.*
                 CNOP    2,4                 ADJUST ALIGNMENT
.*
&NUMARGS SETA    N'&ARGLIST                  &NUMARGS = NUMBER OF ARGS IN &ARGLIST
.FOR0    ANOP                                FOR &ARGCTR = 1 TO &NUMARGS
&ARGCTR  SETA    1                                :
.FTEST0  ANOP                                     :
                 AIF     (&ARGCTR GT &NUMARGS).ENDFOR0
.*
                 LA      R0,&ARGLIST(&ARGCTR)                PLACE ADDRESS IN
                 ST      R0,*+10+(8*&NUMARGS)-(4*&ARGCTR)    ARGUMENT LIST
.*
&ARGCTR  SETA    &ARGCTR+1                         :
                 AGO     .FTEST0                          :
.ENDFOR0 ANOP                                ENDFOR
.*
                 L       RF,=V(&SUBRT)               PERFORM THE CALL
                 LA      RE,*+6+(4*&NUMARGS)
                 BALR    R1,RF
.*
.FOR1    ANOP                                FOR &ARGCTR = 1 TO &NUMARGS
&ARGCTR  SETA    1                                :
.FTEST1  ANOP                                     :
                 AIF     (&ARGCTR GT &NUMARGS).ENDFOR1
.*
                 DS      F
.*
&ARGCTR  SETA    &ARGCTR+1                         :
                 AGO     .FTEST1                          :
.ENDFOR1 ANOP                                ENDFOR
.*
                 MEND                        END CALLD
.*
```

We designed the instructions generated by this macro in order to allow us to pass two types of arguments in a procedure call: individual entries from an array and parameters. The example presented in Chapter 6 had a procedure in which both types of arguments occurred. We see below how this procedure is changed to make use of the CALLD macro. Although there will be more instructions in the object program, from a programmer's point of view, this is no more complicated than the original call instruction. It provides a more general calling mechanism, which is essentially transparent to the user.

The procedure which needs this calling mechanism is shown below. The parameters that necessitate the new calling macro are BINSCRS(R6) and OUTSCORE in the first call and AVERAGE in the second. BINSCRS(R6) is an indexed array element. OUTSCORE is an array entry designated by a DSECT entry. AVERAGE is a parameter accessed by a DSECT.

```
PRNTLINE   CSECT
****************************************************************************
*     PRNTLINE(INNAME,BINSCRS,NUMSCR,AVERAGE,OUTFILE)                     *
*                                                                         *
*     WRITE THE STUDENT'S NAME, SCORES, AND AVERAGE TO OUTFILE.           *
*                                                                         *
****************************************************************************
           SAVE      (14,12)          PROCEDURE PRNTLINE
           BALR      RC,0                :
           USING     *,RC                :
           ST        RD,SAVE+4           :
           LA        RD,SAVE             :
           USING     NMESCT,R7        ESTABLISH PARAMETER ADDRESSES
           USING     SCRSCT,R8           :
           USING     NUMSCT,R9           :
           USING     AVGSCT,RA           :
           USING     FILESCT,RB          :
           LM        R7,RB,0(R1)         :
           MVC       OUTNAME,INNAME   PRINT STUDENT NAME
           USING     CHRSECT,R5          :
           LA        R5,PRTSCRS          :
FOR00      EQU       *                FOR R6 = 0 TO
*                                        4(NUMSCRS-1)
           LA        R6,0             BY 4
           L         R2,NUMSCR           :
           BCTR      R2,0                :
           SLA       R2,2                :
FTEST00    EQU       *                   :
           CR        R6,R2               :
```

```
            BH          ENDFOR00                        :
            CALLD       CONVERT,(BINSCRS(R6),       CONVERT(BINSCRS(R6),          X
                        OUTSCORE)                       OUTSCORE)
            LA          R5,L'PRTSCRS(R5)            MOVE R5 TO NEXT POS
            LA          R6,4(R6)                        :
            B           FTEST00                         :
ENDFOR00    EQU         *                           ENDFOR
            CALLD       CONVERT,(AVERAGE,           CONVERT(AVERAGE,OUTAVG)       X
                        OUTAVG)                         :
            PUT         OUTFILE,OUTREC                  :
            L           RD,SAVE+4                       :
            RETURN      (14,12)                     END PRNTLINE
```

The following partial listing shows the instructions generated by the two calls on the CALLD macro.

```
35      CALLD   CONVERT,(BINSCRS(R6),   CONVERT(BINSCRS(R6),              X
                OUTSCORE)                   OUTSCORE)
36+     CNOP    2,4                     ADJUST ALIGNMENT
37+     LA      R0,BINSCRS(R6)          PLACE ADDRESS IN
38+     ST      R0,*+10+(8*2)−(4*1)     ARGUMENT LIST
39+     LA      R0,OUTSCORE             PLACE ADDRESS IN
40+     ST      R0,*+10+(8*2)−(4*2)     ARGUMENT LIST
41+     L       RF,=V(CONVERT)          PERFORM THE CALL
42+     LA      RE,*+6+(4*2)
43+     BALR    R1,RF
44+     DS      F
45+     DS      F
52      CALLD   CONVERT,(AVERAGE,       CONVERT(AVERAGE,OUTAVG)          X
                OUTAVG)                     :
53+     CNOP    2,4                     ADJUST ALIGNMENT
54+     LA      R0,AVERAGE              PLACE ADDRESS IN
55+     ST      R0,*+10+(8*2)−(4*1)     ARGUMENT LIST
56+     LA      R0,OUTAVG               PLACE ADDRESS IN
57+     ST      R0,*+10+(8*2)−(4*2)     ARGUMENT LIST
58+     L       RF,=V(CONVERT)          PERFORM THE CALL
59+     LA      RE,*+6+(4*2)
60+     BALR    R1,RF
61+     DS      F
62+     DS      F
63      PRINT   OFF                         :
```

As a final note on the use of lists as symbolic parameters, observe that all of the values in a macro call can be accessed through the system parameter &SYSLIST. This system parameter can be accessed from within any procedure, but is particularly useful in a macro in which no symbolic parameters are specified. This allows macros that can receive and access any number of arguments.

Example 7.4.5

Assuming the macro header

```
MACRO
NOPARMS
```

suppose the following invocation occurs.

```
NOPARMS    A,B,(4,6,8)
```

These values can all be obtained from &SYSLIST as the following list of values illustrates.

> N'&SYSLIST = 3
> K'&SYSLIST = 11 The number of characters in the string 'A,B,(4,6,8)'.
> &SYSLIST(1) = A
> &SYSLIST(2) = B
> &SYSLIST(3) = (4,6,8)

The entries in &SYSLIST(3) can be accessed with two subscripts:

> &SYSLIST(3,1) = 4
> &SYSLIST(3,2) = 6

Set Symbol Arrays

It is also possible to define arrays of set symbols that are then accessed in the same way as lists of parameter values. These arrays are declared simply by specifying a dimension in a local or global declaration. The subscripts themselves may be arithmetic expressions. However, due to space limitations, if the expression is complex, we normally evaluate it ahead of time and assign its value to an arithmetic set symbol.

As an example of a macro that uses a set symbol array, we return to our edit pattern macro. The mechanism for extracting substrings and the concatenation operator allow us to change an individual character in a string. However, this is a cumbersome operation. This macro definition can be simplified by copying the characters from the pattern into an array, one character in each position. The code to look for a '0', then find the first 'X' to its left, and change them both is simplified considerably. This new version of the macro is shown below.

```
****************************************************************************************
           MACRO
&LABEL     EDITPAT &PARM
.*
```

```
.*       EDIT PATTERN
.*
.*
.*       ACCEPT A CHARACTER DESCRIPTION OF AN EDIT FORMAT
.*       AND PRODUCE AN EDIT MASK WHICH CAN BE USED TO EDIT
.*       NUMBERS IN THE GIVEN FORMAT.
.*
.*       CHARACTERS IN INPUT DESCRIPTION:
.*            9     – DIGIT
.*            0     – FIRST DIGIT TO BE FORCED
.*          CHAR – ANY MESSAGE CHARACTER OR FILL CHARACTER
.*

              LCLA    &LTH                    LENGTH OF CHARACTER PATTERN
              LCLA    &POS                    POSITION IN STRING
              LCLA    &LFT                    POSITION TO LEFT OF THE 0
              LCLB    &DONE                   FLAG TO INDICATE 0 FOUND
              LCLB    &FALSE
              LCLB    &TRUE
              LCLC    &CHR(64)                INDIVIDUAL CHARACTERS FROM PAT.
.*
.*
&TRUE         SETB    1                       INITIALIZE CONSTANT
.*
&LTH          SETA    K'&PARM−2               &LTH = LENGTH(&PARM)
.*
.FOR0         ANOP                            FOR &POS = 1 TO &LTH
&POS          SETA    1                            :
.FTEST0       ANOP                                 :
              AIF     (&POS GT &LTH).ENDFOR0       :
&CHR(&POS)SETC       '&PARM'(&POS+1,1)             &CHR(&POS) = &PARM(&POS+1)
&POS          SETA    &POS+1                       :
              AGO     .FTEST0                      :
.ENDFOR0      ANOP                            ENDFOR
.*
.*
.*    IF THE PATTERN CONTAINS A 0, THEN CHANGE FIRST 9
.*    TO ITS LEFT TO 0 AND CHANGE THE ORIGINAL 0 TO 9
.*
&POS          SETA    1                       POS = 1
&DONE         SETB    (&FALSE)                DONE = FALSE
.WHILE0       ANOP                            WHILE POS < LTH AND NOT DONE
              AIF     (&POS GT &LTH).ENDWHL0       :
              AIF     (&DONE).ENDWHL0              :
.IF0          ANOP                            IF &CHR(&POS) = '0'
              AIF     ('&CHR(&POS)' NE '0').ELSE0  :
.THEN0        ANOP                            THEN
&LFT          SETA    &POS−1                      &LFT = &POS−1
```

```
.WHILE1     ANOP                                      WHILE &CHR(&LFT) <> '9'
            AIF      ('&CHR(&LFT)' EQ '9').ENDWHL1        AND LFT <> 1
            AIF      (&LFT EQ 1).ENDWHL1                  :
&LFT        SETA     &LFT−1                               &LFT = &LFT−1
            AGO      .WHILE1                              :
.ENDWHL1    ANOP                                      ENDWHILE
.IF1        ANOP                                      IF &CHR(&LFT) = 'X'
            AIF      ('&CHR(&LFT)' NE '9').ENDIF1         :
.THEN1      ANOP                                      THEN
&CHR(&LFT)  SETC     '0'                                  CHANGE 9 TO 0
&CHR(&POS)  SETC     '9'                                  CHANGE 0 TO 9
.ENDIF1     ANOP                                      ENDIF
&DONE       SETB     (&TRUE)                          &DONE = &TRUE
            AGO      .ENDIF0                              :
.ELSE0      ANOP                                      ELSE
&POS        SETA     &POS+1                               &POS = &POS+1
.ENDIF0     ANOP                                      ENDIF
            AGO      .WHILE0                              :
.ENDWHL0    ANOP                                   END WHILE
*
*      CREATE EDIT PATTERN − INSERT X'20' FOR '9' AND X'21' FOR '0'
*
&LABEL      DS       XL&LTH
            ORG      &LABEL
.FOR1       ANOP                                   FOR &POS = 1 TO &LTH
&POS        SETA     1                                  :
.FTEST1     ANOP                                       :
            AIF      (&POS GT &LTH).ENDFOR1             :
.IF2        ANOP                                   IF &CHR(&POS) = '9'
            AIF      ('&CHR(&POS)' NE '9').ELSE2         :
.THEN2      ANOP                                   THEN
*                                                          GENERATE X'20'
            DC       X'20'
            AGO      .ENDIF2                            :
.ELSE2      ANOP                                   ELSE
.IF3        ANOP                                      IF &CHR(&POS) = 0
            AIF      ('&CHR(&POS)' NE '0').ELSE3         :
.THEN3      ANOP                                      THEN
*                                             GENERATE X'21'
            DC       X'21'
            AGO      .ENDIF3                            :
.ELSE3      ANOP                                      ELSE
*                                                          GENERATE CHAR
            DC       C'&CHR(&POS)'
.ENDIF3     ANOP                                      ENDIF
.ENDIF2     ANOP                                   ENDIF
```

```
&POS        SETA    &POS+1                              :
            AGO     .FTEST1                             :
.ENDFOR1    ANOP                            ENDFOR
.*
            MEND                            END EDITPAT
```
****

&SYSNDX

Though we have considered some fairly complicated macros, to this point, none
of our macros have generated code that includes branch instructions. Before we
can write such a macro, we must confront a problem. That is, how can a macro
create a label which is unique? Suppose a macro contains the model instruction

```
LABEL       EQU     *
    .
    .
    .
            B       LABEL
```

This works fine on the first call, assuming that the programmer has not used the
name "LABEL" in the code. The problem occurs on the second and succeeding
invocations of the macro. Each time the model instruction is placed in the code, it
will cause an error, as LABEL has already been defined. A possible solution might
be to define a global arithmetic set symbol, say &CALLS, which we increment on
each invocation.

```
            GLBA    &CALLS
    .
    .
    .
&CALLS      SETA    &CALLS+1
```

We can generate labels unique to a particular call by concatenating the current
value of &CALLS with LABEL.

```
LABEL&CALLS EQU     *
    .
    .
    .
            B       LABEL&CALLS
```

On the first invocation of this macro, the references to the label would be
LABEL1, on the second, they would be LABEL2, and so on.

As a matter of fact, the assembler provides such a feature for us. It maintains a
globally accessible symbol &SYSNDX, which is initialized to 0 and incremented by

1 at the beginning of each macro call. It returns a 4-digit string that can be appended to labels to assure uniqueness.

For example, suppose we want to write a macro, ADDFV, which accepts as arguments two vectors of fullwords and a symbol that gives the number of entries in the two vectors.

```
ADDFV   VECTOR1,VECTOR2,NUMENTS
```

generates the instructions to add corresponding entries in VECTOR1 and VECTOR2 and store the result in VECTOR1. In order to accomplish this task, the macro needs to generate instructions for a counted loop. It will use &SYSNDX to assure that labels used in this loop are unique.

To make this macro as general as possible, we will allow NUMENTS to be either a fullword or halfword field or an absolute symbol. The macro will use the type attribute to determine the type of this parameter.

The definition for this macro is shown below. Like several of the other examples we have considered, it uses a global Boolean set symbol to control the definition of a private work area. We have used the standard FOR construct, but, as &SYSNDX is 4 characters long, we have had to shorten some of the label names. An alternative is to extract the last two characters of &SYSNDX.

```
***************************************************************************************************
        MACRO
        ADDFV   &VECTOR1,&VECTOR2,&NUMENTS
.*
.*   ADD FULLWORD VECTORS
.*
.*   GENERATE THE INSTRUCTIONS TO ADD THE ENTRIES IN &VECTOR1
.*   AND &VECTOR2 AND STORE THE RESULTS IN &VECTOR1.
.*
.*   &NUMENTS GIVES THE NUMBER OF ENTRIES IN THE TWO VECTORS.
.*   IT MAY BE A FULLWORD, A HALFWORD, OR AN ABSOLUTE SYMBOL.
.*
        GBLB    &DEFINED            INDICATES AV$ULIM IS DEFINED
.*
.IF0    ANOP                        IF FIRST CALL
        AIF     (&DEFINED).ENDIF0   :
.THEN0  ANOP                        THEN
.*                                      DEFINE AV$ULIM AND BRANCH
        B       AV$ULIM+L'AV$ULIM
AV$ULIM DS      F
&DEFINED SETB   (NOT &DEFINED)          &DEFINED = FALSE
.ENDIF0 ANOP                        ENDIF
.*
.*   DETERMINE TYPE OF &NUMENTS AND STORE
.*   4*&NUMENTS IN AV$ULIM
```

```
.*
.IF1         ANOP                                    IF T'&NUMENTS = 'H'
             AIF      (T'&NUMENTS NE 'H').ELSE1
.THEN1       ANOP                                    THEN
.*                                                       USE LH TO GET &NUMENTS
             LH       R0,&NUMENTS
             AGO      .ENDIF1                             :
.ELSE1       ANOP                                    ELSE
.IF2         ANOP                                       IF T'&NUMENTS = 'F'
             AIF      (T'&NUMENTS NE 'F').ELSE2           :
.THEN2       ANOP                                       THEN
.*                                                           USE L TO GET &NUMENTS
             L        R0,&NUMENTS
             AGO      .ENDIF2                                :
.ELSE2       ANOP                                       ELSE
.*                                                           USE LA TO GET &NUMENTS
             LA       R0,&NUMENTS
.ENDIF2      ANOP                                       ENDIF
.ENDIF1      ANOP                                    ENDIF
.*     MULTIPLY &NUMENTS BY 4
.*     AND STORE IN AV$ULIM
             SLA      R0,2
             ST       R0,AV$ULIM
.*
.*     GENERATE LOOP TO ADD ELEMENTS
.*
FOR&SYSNDX   EQU      *
             LA       R1,0
FTST&SYSNDX  EQU      *
             C        R1,AV$ULIM
             BNL      ENFR&SYSNDX
             L        R0,&VECTOR1.(R1)
             A        R0,&VECTOR2.(R1)
             ST       R0,&VECTOR1.(R1)
             LA       R1,4(R1)
             B        FTST&SYSNDX
ENFR&SYSNDX  EQU      *
             MEND
```

In the model instructions, the explicit concatenation operator, (.) is required before (R1). Without it, the assembler would incorrectly interpret this as a list reference.

Following, we see the instructions generated by several calls on this macro. In the first instance, the third argument, ABENTS, is an absolute symbol so the macro generates an LA instruction to get its value. The third argument in the second call is a fullword field, so the L instruction is used.

```
105              ADDFV  VECTOR1,VECTOR2,ABENTS
106+             B      AV$ULIM+4
107+AV$ULIM     DS     F
108+             LA     R0,ABENTS
109+             SLA    R0,2
110+             ST     R0,AV$ULIM
111+FOR0005     EQU    *
112+             LA     R1,0
113+FTST0005    EQU    *
114+             C      R1,AV$ULIM
115+             BNL    ENFR0005
116+             L      R0,VECTOR1(R1)
117+             A      R0,VECTOR2(R1)
118+             ST     R0,VECTOR1(R1)
119+             LA     R1,4(R1)
120+             B      FTST0005
121+ENFR0005    EQU    *


139              ADDFV  LVECT1,LVECT2,FENTS
140+             L      R0,FENTS
141+             SLA    R0,2
142+             ST     R0,AV$ULIM
143+FOR0012     EQU    *
144+             LA     R1,0
145+FTST0012    EQU    *
146+             C      R1,AV$ULIM
147+             BNL    ENFR0012
148+             L      R0,LVECT1(R1)
149+             A      R0,LVECT2(R1)
150+             ST     R0,LVECT1(R1)
151+             LA     R1,4(R1)
152+             B      FTST0012
153+ENFR0012    EQU    *
```

Conditional Assembly Instruction in Open Code

We have introduced the conditional assembly instructions as a mechanism for writing macro definitions, certainly the most common use of conditional assembly instructions. Nevertheless, they may also be used in the program itself, outside of macro definitions. This part of a program is referred to as "open code."

Such a feature allows for the selection of individual instructions for assembly. For example, it is possible to include debugging instructions in the source program and use a Boolean set symbol to determine whether those instructions are assembled or bypassed.

Example 7.4.6

```
          LCLB   &DEBUG
&DEBUG    SETB   1
AVERAGE   START  0                    PROGRAM AVERAGE
     .
     .
     .

          AIF    (NOT &DEBUG).SKIP1
          PDUMP  GRADE,GRADE+L'GRADE
.SKIP1    ANOP
     .
     .
     .

          AIF    (NOT &DEBUG).SKIP2
          PDUMP  NAMES,NAMES+(MAXENTS)*L'NAMES
.SKIP2    ANOP
     .
     .
     .
          AIF    (NOT & DEBUG).SKIP3
          PUT    PRINTER,DETAIL
.SKIP3    ANOP
     .
     .
     .

          EOJ
```

The debugging statements in this program will be assembled and executed. When the program is working correctly, the instruction that sets &DEBUG equal to true can be changed or omitted so that &DEBUG is false. Then, when the program is assembled, all of the debugging instructions will be skipped. They will not affect the final code. However, they can be left in the source code to be used if an error shows up later or if it becomes necessary to modify the program.

E   X   E   R   C   I   S   E   S

1. Write a macro named ZERO, which accepts a list of packed fields as its only argument. It should generate ZAP instructions to assign 0 to each field in the list.

2. Write a macro named INCR, which accepts a list of numeric fields as its argument. It should check the type of each field in the list and generate the instructions necessary to increment each field by 1.

3. Modify the macro INCR to accept an optional second argument that gives the increment amount. For example, the call

    INCR   (P1,P2),2

    should generate the instructions to increment P1 and P2 by 2. If the second argument is omitted, the macro should use 1 as the increment.

4. Write the instructions that will be generated by the following invocation of the CALLD macro.

    CALL D PRNTRTE,(I,TABLE (R3))

5. Write three macros named LOOP, EXITLP, and ENDLP, which implement a general looping construct such as that found in ADA. LOOP should create a label of the form Lmmmmmm to mark the top of the loop. ENDLP should cause a branch to the top of the current loop and create a label of the form Xmmmmmm to mark the end of the loop. EXITLP should branch to the Xmmmmmm label for the current loop.

    In order to allow nesting of loops and still keep track of the current loop, these three macros should share a global array and pointer that can be used as a stack. When a new loop is created, use &SYSNDX to determine mmmmmm and push that value on top of the stack. EXITLP should look at the top of the stack to determine which Xmmmmmm label to branch to. ENDLP should also use the value on top of the stack to branch back to the beginning of the loop and to create its own label. It should then pop the value off the top of the stack.

6. Modify the macro ADDFV to manipulate arrays of packed numbers. Call the new macro ADDPV. Assume that &NUMENTS is a packed field.

P R O G R A M M I N G   P R O J E C T S

The macros described in the following projects should be tested by writing programs that generate a variety of macro invocations.

1. Write a general conversion macro, CVT, which accepts two fields as arguments and generates the instructions to convert the value in the second field to the type of the first field. The result should be stored in the first field. The supported types should include character, packed decimal with implied decimal point, zoned decimal, and full and halfword binary numbers. When dealing with packed decimal fields, the macro should take account of the scaling factor. This may require shifting when the result type is packed decimal, truncation if the result type is a binary integer type, or the inclusion of a decimal point in the edit mask if the

result type is character. As we have not really dealt with character string manipulations, the macro need not support character-to-numeric conversions.

2. Write a macro, INDEX, to generate instructions for converting a subscripted array reference to an index. A typical invocation might be

   INDEX   R5,GRADES,(STUDENT,TE ST)

   The first operand specifies the register to receive the index value. The second operand is the name of the array. (In this case a two-dimensional array.) The third operand is a list of the subscript variables. You may assume that the subscripts are simple variables rather than expressions. However, the macro should check the type of the subscripts and perform any conversions necessary.

3. Write a set of macros, ADD, SUB, MUL, DIV (quotient), REM (integer remainder), and COM (compare), to perform conformable arithmetic and comparison operations. That is, each macro should check the types of the two fields involved. If the second type is not the same as the first, then the macro should generate instructions to convert the value from the second field to the type of the first field before performing the operation. The converted value should be stored in a temporary work area. The macro should then generate the instruction appropriate to the type.

   It might be desirable to write procedures to perform some of the conversions. In general, the conversions for all of the new macros should probably be performed by a set of subsidiary macros such as those in Examples 7.1.5 and 7.1.6.

4. Write a macro named DUMPIT, which accepts a filename and a list of field names. The macro should generate instructions to print the name of each field in the list followed by the current value of that field. If the field is a packed decimal number, then edit its value for printing. Use the scaling factor to determine the location of the implied decimal. If the field is a character field, then give its value in character form. (Print a blank for every position with an EBCDIC code less than X'40'.) In all cases, give the contents of the field in hexadecimal. Print the field name on one line and other values on succeeding lines.

   Several of these operations will require you to access the field as an array of bytes.

C H A P T E R 8

FLOATING
POINT
NUMBERS

8.1 INTRODUCTION TO FLOATING POINT NUMBERS

In this final chapter, we consider the floating point data types available on the IBM 370. We recall from Chapter 4, that the binary arithmetic instructions implement integer arithmetic. It is possible to represent fractions with full or halfword integers by providing a mechanism to keep track of an implied binary point, as we did in the case of decimal fractions. This approach works fairly well in a number of situations. In particular, if the numbers are of approximately the same magnitude, then we can perform addition and subtraction without risking large errors. We can also use binary integers if the number of digits of accuracy required is relatively small. However, if the calculations involve numbers of different magnitudes, if the calculations involve a large number of multiplications or divisions, or if the problem requires more than 10 digits of precision, then the results obtained with binary integers may not be satisfactory. Hence, most computer systems provide some form of binary floating point data type.

As an introduction to the concept of floating point numbers, consider a possible representation for floating point numbers in decimal form. Observe the ways in which this decimal form representation interacts with various arithmetic operations. We then introduce the IBM floating point format and describe the features of 370 architecture that support floating point operations. In later sections, we cover a group of bit-manipulation instructions that are required for conversion between the floating point types and other types, the actual conversions, and the floating point operations available.

Floating Point Decimal Numbers

Floating point numbers are represented by a signed fixed point number and a signed exponent. In order to minimize the storage necessary, the fixed point portion is stored without a decimal point. It is usually called the *mantissa* of the floating point number. The "decimal" point is more generally called the *radix* point, as the number base is usually not 10. The signed exponent is often called the *characteristic*. The number of digits in the characteristic determines the magnitudes available, while the number of digits in the mantissa determines the precision.

Example 8.1.1 *A typical representation of a decimal floating point number is*

$$-5.4893 * 10^{+43}$$

Suppose we want to encode this number as efficiently as possible. If we agree that the decimal point will always be placed to the right of the first digit, then there is no need to include it in the representation. Similarly, if the base for the exponent will always be 10, then this can be omitted from the representation. We only need to store the sign for the number itself, the digits 54893, and the exponent +43. The entire number can be represented by $-54893, +43$. The mantissa is -54893 and the characteristic is $+43$.

This representation scheme would encode each number as a pair of signed decimal numbers: a signed 5-digit mantissa and a signed characteristic. The following table gives the representation for some more decimal numbers in this format together with the corresponding value in the usual scientific notation.

Encoded Form	Number
+45631,−12	$+4.5631 * 10^{-12}$
+01023,+18	$+0.1023 * 10^{+18}$
−99999,−99	$-9.9999 * 10^{-99}$

Arithmetic Operations on Floating Point Numbers

Although we will not be performing arithmetic operations on these representations ourselves, we need to know how they are performed in order to understand some of the peculiarities of floating point representations.

Example 8.1.2 *Give the representation of the sum of the decimal numbers represented by +34857,−12 and −49584,−12.*

We first convert these numbers to scientific notation, add them, and then give the representation of the sum.

$$+34857,-12 \text{ represents } +3.4857 * 10^{-12}$$
$$-49584,-12 \text{ represents } -4.9584 * 10^{-12}$$

The sum is

$$(+3.4857 * 10^{-12} + -4.9584 * 10^{-12})$$
$$= (+3.4857 - 4.9584) * 10^{-12} = -1.4727 * 10^{-12}$$

This number would be represented by −14727,−12. Note that the representation can be obtained directly from the representations of the two numbers by adding their mantissas.

Example 8.1.3 *Give the representation of the sum of the decimal numbers represented by +34857,−12 and −49584,−10.*

In this case, we have

$$(+3.4857 * 10^{-12} + -4.9584 * 10^{-10})$$

As the two powers of 10 are different, we cannot factor them both out of the expression. The largest power of 10 we can factor out is 10^{-10}. This gives us

$$(+3.4857 * 10^{-2} - 4.9584) * 10^{-10}$$
$$= (+0.034857 - 4.9584) * 10^{-10}$$
$$= -4.923543 * 10^{-10}$$

Notice that the result has two extra digits. In order to represent it in the format adopted, we need to get rid of two digits, which can be done by rounding the number to 4 decimal places. This yields

$$-4.9235 * 10^{-10}$$

which is represented as $-49235, -10$.

In this case, it would not have been possible to obtain this representation by adding the mantissas of the two original numbers. However, there is a relatively simple relationship between the three representations.

Immediately before the addition, the first number has taken the form $+0.034857 * 10^{-10}$. If we temporarily add an extra digit to our format, this value can be approximated by the representation $+003485, -10$. The characteristic of this number is the same as that of the second number and we can find their sum as in the first example: by adding the mantissas.

$$
\begin{array}{r}
73 \\
-495840 \\
003485 \\
\hline
-492355
\end{array}
$$

As this number is negative, it rounds to -49235, the expected mantissa.

As the examples show, we can always obtain the representation of the sum of two floating point numbers directly from their representations. If their characteristics are the same, we simply add their mantissas. If their characteristics are different, then we adjust the number with the smaller characteristic. For each unit added to its characteristic, we shift the mantissa right one position, adding a 0 on the left. When the characteristics are the same, we can add the mantissas directly. As we will round the result to the number of digits specified by the format, we only need to retain one extra digit in the shifting process.

Example 8.1.4 *Add the numbers represented by* $+48371, +07$ *and* $+63734, +04$.

As the characteristics are not the same, we must adjust the second number, the one with the smaller characteristic. We need to add three to the characteristic, so we shift the mantissa 3 places to the right. This yields $+00063734, +07$. The mantissa of the result must be shortened to 5 digits, so we can drop the 34 on the right. The addition now becomes

$$
\begin{array}{r}
+483710 \\
+000637 \\
\hline
+484347
\end{array}
$$

Rounding to 5 digits, the representation for the sum is $+48435,+07$.

The example above illustrates one of the peculiarities of floating point representations. A number may not have a unique representation. In the format we are using for decimal floating point numbers, the number 34 may be written in several different ways, corresponding to the following exponential notations.

$$3.4 * 10^1 \qquad +34000,+01$$
$$.34 * 10^2 \qquad +03400,+02$$
$$.034 * 10^3 \qquad +00340,+03$$
$$.0034 * 10^4 \qquad +00034,+04$$

Of these four representations, the first is called normal form. It is characterized by the fact that the first digit in the mantissa is nonzero.

Any floating point representation can be converted to normal form through a process known as *normalization*. This is shifting the mantissa left until the first digit is nonzero. The characteristic must be decremented by 1 for each position shifted.

Example 8.1.5 *Normalize* $-00456,+34$.

The mantissa must be shifted left two positions and the characteristic decremented by 2. The normal form of this representation is $-45600,+32$.

Subtraction of floating point representations is entirely analogous to addition. If two representations have different characteristics, the number with the larger characteristic must be adjusted by shifting the mantissa left and decrementing the characteristic until the two characteristics are the same. Then the mantissas may be subtracted. If necessary, the result may be normalized or left in unnormalized form.

Multiplication and division of floating point representations are actually simpler than addition and subtraction. Consider an example in which we multiply two numbers and examine the relation between the representation of the product and the representations of the original numbers.

Example 8.1.6 *Multiply the numbers represented by* $+83904,-10$ *and* $-58003,+23$.

The multiplication is

$$(+8.3904 * 10^{-10}) * (-5.8003 * 10^{+23})$$
$$= (+8.3904 * -5.8003) * (10^{-10} * 10^{+23})$$
$$= -48.66683712 * 10^{(-10 + 23)}$$
$$= -48.66683712 * 10^{+13}$$

In order to fit the result into our floating point representation, we need to make some changes in the number. However, the result can be obtained by multiplying the characteristics and adding the exponents. The remaining manipulations involve shifting the mantissa right one position and incrementing the exponent. We also need to round the mantissa to 5 digits. The result is $-4.8667 * 10^{+13}$, which is represented by $-48667, +13$.

Similarly, two floating point representations can be divided by dividing the mantissas and subtracting the characteristic of the divisor from that of the dividend.

IBM Floating Point Representations

The floating point numbers provided by the IBM 370 are stored in binary form. However, they are more accurately viewed as hexadecimal numbers. We can view the mantissa as a hexadecimal number in the usual way. The exponent is interpreted as a power of 16.

These floating point numbers come in three sizes, but the formats are similar. They consist of a mantissa stored in sign-magnitude form and a characteristic stored in excess-64 notation. The sign of the mantissa is always stored in the leftmost bit of the number. The next seven bits are used to encode the characteristic. The remaining bits hold the magnitude of the mantissa.

Since the characteristic is stored in 7 bits using excess-64 notation, the largest characteristic that can be stored is represented as X'7F'. This represents an exponent of X'3F'. The largest magnitude is of order 16^{63}. The smallest magnitude, corresponding to a characteristic of X'00', has exponent $-X'40' = -64$. A number with this characteristic is of order 16^{-64}.

Short-Form Floating Point Numbers

The short-form floating point numbers, E-type, have a fraction that consists of 6 hexadecimal digits. The entire number fits in a fullword. The format is shown below.

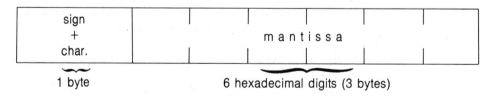

1 byte   6 hexadecimal digits (3 bytes)

The leftmost byte contains the sign in the first bit and the excess-64 characteristic in the next 7 bits. The mantissa uses the remaining 3 bytes, or 6 hexadecimal digits. The precision is equivalent to approximately 7 or 8 decimal digits, and the magnitude is between 16^{-64} and 16^{63}.

Example 8.1.7 *Assume the following fullword represents an E-type floating point number.*

$$X'433B00100'$$

In binary form, X'43' = B'01000011'. Thus, the sign of the mantissa is B'0' or '+'.

The characteristic is X'43'. Since this is in excess-64 notation, we must subtract 64 to determine the exponent. The result is X'43' − X'40' = X'03'.
The number represented, in hexadecimal exponential form, is

$$X'.3B00100' * X'10'^{X'03'}$$

Multiplying a hexadecimal fraction by a power of 16 has the same effect as multiplying a decimal fraction by a power of 10. It is equivalent to a shift in the radix point. This number can be written in fixed point hexadecimal form as

$$X'3B0.0100' = 944.01563$$

Example 8.1.8 *Consider the E-type number X'B83D1000'.*

The binary form of the leftmost byte is B'10111000'. Thus, the sign of the number is B'1' or '−' and the characteristic is B'0111000' = X'3E'. Subtracting 64 = X'40', we discover that the exponent is −X'02'. The number is

$$-X'.3D1000' * X'10'^{-X'02'} = -X'.003D1000' = .00073242$$

The following table gives some other E-type floating point numbers and their equivalents.

E-type	Hexadecimal Exponential	Hexadecimal Fixed Point	Decimal Fixed Point
X'C45C01D6'	$-X'.5C01D6' * X'10'^{X'04'}$	−X'5C01.D6'	−23553.836
X'3C3B1420'	$X'.3B1420' * X'10'^{-X'04'}$	X'.00003B1420'	.0000029359944
X'C610DE11'	$-X'.10DE11' * X'10'^{X'06'}$	−X'10DE11'	−1105425.
X'482D4F01'	$X'.2D4F01' * X'10'^{X'08'}$	X'2D4F0100'	760152320
X'482D4F02'	$X'.2D4F02' * X'10'^{X'08'}$	X'2D4F0200'	760152576

The last two rows in the table above illustrate a problem inherent in floating point representation. The numbers given differ by only one unit in the mantissa. Yet, their decimal counterparts differ by 256. In fact, none of the integers between 760152320 and 760152576 can be represented exactly by an E-type floating point number. Thus, the last two digits of these decimal numbers are not really significant. We should, more accurately, write these numbers as 760152300 and 760152600.

Long-Form Floating Point Numbers

In order to provide more precision than the short-form floating point numbers, the IBM 370 provides a long form, D-type, floating point format. This type occupies two fullwords. The first fullword is in the same format as the short form. It contains the sign bit at the extreme left followed by the 7-bit characteristic. The remaining 3 bytes contain the first 6 hexadecimal digits of the fraction. All 8 hexadecimal digits in the second fullword are used to hold fractional digits. Thus, the D-type floating point format has a 14 hexadecimal digit fraction. This is roughly equivalent to 16 or 17 decimal digits.

As the size of the characteristic of the D-type floating point numbers is the same as the E-type characteristic, the magnitude is not changed appreciably. Rather, it is the precision which is increased by the use of the second fullword.

The format of the long floating point type is shown below.

sign + char.	mantissa
1 byte	14 hexadecimal digits (7 bytes)

The following table gives some examples of D-type floating point numbers and their equivalent in hexadecimal exponential form.

Floating Point Form	Exponential Form
X'D3254E670A123D01'	$-$X'.254E670A123D01' * X'10'$^{X'13'}$
X'2577E00A12B1001F'	X'.77E00A12B1001F' * X'10'$^{-X'1B'}$
X'7F1B00121CAE0900'	X'.1B00121CAE0900' * X'10'$^{X'3F'}$

Because the characteristics are the same, an E-type floating point number can be converted to a D-type number simply by appending a fullword of 0's. A D-type number can be converted to E-type by truncation, eliminating the second fullword, or by rounding.

Example 8.1.9 *Convert the short floating point number X'3F190F0E' to a long floating point number.*

The number is equivalent to X'.190F0E' * X'10'$^{-X'1'}$. This expression is the same as X'.190F0E00000000' * X'10'$^{-X'1'}$ which would be coded as X'3F190F0E00000000'.

Extended Floating Point Numbers

The extended format for floating point numbers allows for 28 hexadecimal digits in the mantissa. The extended numbers actually consist of 2 long-form floating point numbers. However, the first byte of the second number is ignored. The overall format is shown below.

First Doubleword

sign + char.	mantissa
1 byte	14 hexadecimal digits (7 bytes)

Second Doubleword

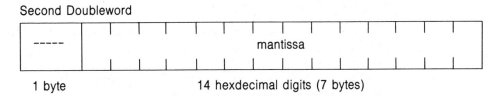

1 byte   14 hexdecimal digits (7 bytes)

Again, the characteristics allowed for an extended floating point number are the same as those permitted for the short and long forms. The only difference is the number of digits in the mantissa. Long floating point numbers may be converted to extended form by appending a doubleword of zeros. Extended form numbers can be converted to long form by deleting the second doubleword or by rounding.

Zero, Overflow, and Underflow

As in all floating point representations, 0 can be written in many ways. Any number in which the mantissa is 0 could be interpreted as representing 0 regardless of the value of the characteristic. However, the floating point number in which the sign, the characteristic, and mantissa are all zero is called a *true zero*.

Whenever the mantissa resulting from an operation is too large to fit in a particular format, the radix point can be moved to the extreme left by adjusting the characteristic. Then the mantissa can simply be truncated on the right. However, if this operation results in an exponent larger than 63, then an exponent overflow has occurred.

An exponent underflow occurs if the exponent is less than −64. In this case, the action to be taken depends upon the application, but most often the result should simply be interpreted as 0.

Normalization

IBM 370 floating point numbers are normalized if the leftmost hexadecimal digit in the mantissa is nonzero. This allows the greatest possible precision, as it maximizes the number of nonzero digits that can be retained.

Most of the arithmetic instructions in the 370 floating point instruction set yield a normalized result. The only exception is a set of addition and subtraction instructions that specify the result be left in unnormalized form. Thus, the normalization of results is determined by the selection of the instruction to perform an operation, rather than the application of a specific normalization instruction.

Example 8.1.10 *Normalize the E-type floating point number X'2A0007A5'.*

The mantissa, X'0007A5' must be shifted 3 hexadecimal digits to the left in order to achieve normalization. This requires that the characteristic, X'2A' be decremented by 3. The normalized result is X'277A5000'.

Floating Point Registers

The IBM 370 instruction set contains a number of floating point instructions. None of these operate on values stored in main memory or in the general-purpose registers. Instead, the CPU contains 4 registers specifically designed to hold floating point numbers. These are aptly named *floating point registers*. Each is 64 bits long, the size of a long floating point number.

The floating point registers are numbered 0, 2, 4, and 6. However, we use EQU to establish symbols, F0, F2, F4, and F6, to identify these registers.

When a short floating point number is loaded into a floating point register, it uses only half the register. The remaining half cannot be used. The long form floating point numbers use an entire floating point register. The extended floating point numbers use a pair of registers. The pair may consist of F0 and F2 or F4 and F6.

E   X   E   R   C   I   S   E   S

1. Give the scientific notation for the following decimal numbers encoded as described in Example 8.1.1.

   a. +39821,−5
   b. −00763,+7
   c. −47639,+14
   d. +84359,−11

2. Give the normal form of the representation of the sum of each of the following pair of numbers. Assume the representation described in Example 8.1.1.

   a. +73942,−13 and −42691,−11
   b. +56391,+6 and −56912,+6
   c. −11487,+1 and −65743,−11
   d. +59376,−24 and +32448,−27

3. Multiply the following floating point numbers represented as in Example 8.1.1.

   a. +47899,−13 * +76653,+10
   b. +83736,+18 * −39382,−12

4. Divide the following floating point numbers represented as in Example 8.1.1.

   a. +88372,−12 / +38444,+10
   b. +76763,−13 / −19362,−15

5. Write each of the following E-type floating point numbers in exponential form.
   a. X'73846100'
   b. X'C8A897E1'
   c. X'F54D9A13'
   d. X'3A925AF7'

6. Give the exponential form of each of the following D-type floating point numbers.
   a. X'B8A2587C910E3634'
   b. X'6A7FA9336820C57F'

7. Round the D-type floating point numbers from Exercise 6 to E-type numbers.

8. Normalize each of the following E-type floating point numbers.
   a. X'B40000A1'
   b. X'4E01DF0A'

8.2 FLOATING POINT INSTRUCTIONS

It seems natural to deal with conversions from decimal and fixed point binary types to floating point types before dealing with the operations on floating point types. Unfortunately, the 370 does not provide instructions to perform these conversions directly. In order to implement the conversions ourselves, we need to use several of the floating point instructions. We have no choice but to cover these instructions before we learn how to input or output floating point numbers. The necessary conversions will be discussed in the next two sections.

These instructions come in various forms corresponding to the possible operand types and locations. The Load instructions allow short and long floating point numbers to be moved from memory locations to floating point registers and from one floating point register to another. The Store instructions allow short and long floating point numbers to be moved from the floating point registers to memory locations. Extended floating point numbers must be moved in two separate operations.

The arithmetic instructions come in forms that support all three types of operand.

Whenever possible, in the descriptions following, we group together related instructions that manipulate different data types. The instruction mnemonics indicate the type of data. E denotes a short operand, D a long operand, and X an extended operand. As with the fixed binary instructions, an R indicates that the second operand is in a register, a floating point register in this case, and that the instruction is an RR instruction. Otherwise, the instructions are RX format.

Load and Store Instructions

Load

LER RR, Short operands.

LER F_1, F_2

LE RX, Short operands.

LE $F_1, D_2(X_2, B_2)$

LDR RR, Long operands.

LDR F_1, F_2

LD RX, Long operands.

LD $F_1, D_2(X_2, B_2)$

Four (short operand) or 8 (long operand) bytes are copied from the second operand location to the floating point register indicated by the first operand location. When the instruction designates a short operand, the second 4 bytes of the target register operand are unchanged.

Condition Code: Unchanged.

Exceptions:

Access   Improper address for the second operand in the RX instructions.

Specification F_1 or F_2 not 0, 2, 3, or 6.

Example 8.2.1 *Suppose that before each of the following instructions the floating point registers and fields contain the values indicated below.*

F0	: X'AAAAAAAAAAAAAAAA'
F2	: X'BBBBBBBBBBBBBBBB'
F4	: X'4444444444444444'
F6	: X'6666666666666666'
SHORT	: X'77777777'
LONG	: X'8888888888888888'

LE	F0,SHORT	will set F0 = X'77777777AAAAAAAA'
LD	F2,LONG	will set F2 = X'8888888888888888'
LER	F4,F6	will set F4 = X'6666666644444444'
LDR	F4,F6	will set F4 = X'6666666666666666'

Store

STE RX, Short operands.

STE $F_1, D_2(X_2, B_2)$

STD RX, Long operands.

STD $F_1, D_2(X_2, B_2)$

Four (short operand) or 8 (long operand) bytes are copied from the register operand to the storage operand.

Condition Code: Unchanged.

Exceptions:

Access   Improper address for the second operand.

Specification F_1 not 0, 2, 3, or 6.

Example 8.2.2 *Suppose that before each of the following instructions the floating point registers and fields contain the values indicated below.*

F0	: X'AAAAAAAAAAAAAAAA'
F2	: X'BBBBBBBBBBBBBBBB'
SHORT	: X'77777777'
LONG	: X'8888888888888888'

    STE F0,SHORT   will set SHORT = X'AAAAAAAA'
    STD F2,LONG   will set LONG = X'BBBBBBBBBBBBBBBB'

As was the case with the fixed point instructions, there is a special set of RR load instructions that set the condition code and allow changes in sign while they copy values from one register to another. This group of instructions is described below.

Load and Test *RR*

LTER Short operands.

        LTER F_1,F_2

LTDR Long operands.

        LTDR F_1,F_2

Copy the value from F_2 to F_1 and set the Condition Code.

Load Complement *RR*

LCER Short operands.

        LCER F_1,F_2

LCDR Long operands.

        LCDR F_1,F_2

Copy the value from F_2 to F_1, inverting the sign bit, and set the Condition Code.

Load Negative *RR*

LNER Short operands.

        LNER F_1,F_2

LNDR Long operands.
> LNDR   F₁,F₂

Copy the negative of the absolute value of the number in F_2 to F_1 and set the Condition Code.

Load Positive *RR*

LPER Short operands.
> LPER   F₁,F₂

LPDR Long operands.
> LPDR   F₁,F₂

Copy the absolute value of the number in F_2 to F_1 and set the Condition Code.

Condition Code:

0   If the result is 0.

1   If the result is negative.

2   If the result is positive.

Exception:

Specification   Register operands not 0, 2, 4, or 6.

Example 8.2.3 *To take the absolute value of the short operand in F2, we can use the instruction*

> LPER   F2,F2

Example 8.2.4 *To check the sign of the double word operand in F4, we can use*

> LTDR   F4,F4

The last load instruction we shall consider allows us to convert a floating point number to a shorter form. It is the Load Rounded instruction.

Load Rounded *RR*

LRER F₁ short, F₂ long.
> LRER   F₁,F₂

LRDR F₁ long, F₂ extended.
> LRDR   F₁,F₂

The magnitude of the mantissa of the second operand is rounded to the appropriate number of hexadecimal digits for the first operand. Exponent overflow may occur.

Condition Code: Unchanged.

Exceptions:

Exponent Overflow

Specification   Invalid value for F_1 or F_2.

Comparisons

The compare instructions set the Condition Code to indicate the relative sizes of the two operands. We can then test the condition as before, allowing us to continue using the constructs for structured programming, which were developed in Chapter 3.

Compare

CER RR, Short operands.

        CER F_1,F_2

CE RX, Short operands.

        CE $F_1,D_2(X_2,B_2)$

CDR RR, Long operands.

        CDR F_1,F_2

CD RX, Long operands.

        CD $F_1,D_2(X_2,B_2)$

The values are compared and the Condition Code set as shown below.

Condition Code:

0   If the operands are equal.

1   If the first operand is low.

2   If the first operand is high.

Exceptions:

Access   Improper address for the second operand in an RX instruction.

Specification   Register operand not 0, 2, 4, or 6 for short or long operands. Register operands not 0 or 4 for long operands.

Addition and Subtraction

The addition and subtraction instructions support all three floating point types. The instructions for manipulating short or long forms are available in RX format, allowing the second operand to be in a memory location, and an RR form which allows the second operand to be in a floating point register. The extended operations are only available in the RR format. Finally, there are instructions to add and subtract short and long forms that do not attempt to normalize the result.

Add Normalized

AER RR, Short operands.

     AER F_1, F_2

AE RX, Short operands.

     AE $F_1, D_2(X_2, B_2)$

ADR RR, Long operands.

     ADR F_1, F_2

AD RX, Long operands.

     AD $F_1, D_2(X_2, B_2)$

AXR RR, Extended operands.

     AXR F_1, F_2

The characteristics of the two floating point operands are compared. If they differ, the mantissa of the number with the smaller characteristic is shifted right with corresponding additions to the characteristic until the characteristics are the same. During this shift operation, the positions of the mantissa are filled on the left with 0's. The last hexadecimal digit shifted out is saved as a guard digit. The mantissa of any unshifted operand has a 0 appended to its right so that the values to be added always have an extra hexadecimal digit called the guard digit. The two mantissas are then added, producing an intermediate sum that has an extra hexadecimal digit on the right.

If the addition produces a carry, the intermediate sum is shifted right 1 position, the carry is inserted in its leftmost position and the characteristic is increased by 1. This may produce an exponent overflow.

If the intermediate sum contains all zeros, including the guard digit, and the significance bit in the program status word is 0, the stored result is a true 0.

If the intermediate sum is not all zeros and there is no carry, then it is shifted left 1 hexadecimal digit at a time, with a corresponding decrease in the characteristic, until the leftmost hexadecimal digit is nonzero. The guard digit participates in this shift and 0's are shifted in on the right. This may cause an exponent underflow. When the normalization is complete, the guard position is dropped and the result stored.

Condition Code:

0   If the result is 0.

1   If the result is negative.

2   If the result is positive.

Exceptions:

Access   Improper address for the second operand in an RX instruction.

Exponent Overflow

Exponent Underflow — Normalization would result in a negative characteristic (exponent < -64) and the exponent underflow bit in the program mask is 1.

Significance — The intermediate mantissa is 0 and the significance bit in the program mask is 1.

Specification — Register operand not 0, 2, 4, or 6 for short or long operands. Register operand not 0 or 4 for AXR.

Example 8.2.5 *We consider the effect of the following instruction for various initial values of F0 and F2.*

            AER   F0,F2

(Since this instruction manipulates short operands, the rightmost 4 bytes of these two registers are irrelevant and will not be shown.)

F0 : X'3F21487B'		F2 : X'3FA21B73'	
Sign	: +	Sign	: +
Characteristic	: X'3F'	Characteristic	: X'3F'
Mantissa	: X'21487B'	Mantissa	: X'A21B73'

Since the characteristics are already the same, both mantissas have a guard digit of 0 appended to the right. These extended values are then added to produce the intermediate sum

$$
\begin{array}{r}
1 \\
\text{X'21487B0'} \\
+\text{X'A21B730'} \\
\hline
\text{X'C363EE0'}
\end{array}
$$

This addition produces no carry and needs no normalization. The guard digit is dropped and the result is stored in F0.

After the instruction has been executed, F0 will contain X'3FC363EE'.

F0 : X'3F21487B'		F2 : X'3FE21B73'	
Sign	: +	Sign	: +
Characteristic	: X'3F'	Characteristic	: X'3F'
Mantissa	: X'21487B'	Mantissa	: X'E21B73'

Again the characteristics are already the same, so both mantissas have a guard digit of 0 appended to the right. The extended values are then added.

$$
\begin{array}{r}
1 \ 1 \\
\text{X'21487B0'} \\
+\text{X'E21B730'} \\
\hline
\text{X'0363EE0'}
\end{array}
$$

This addition produces a carry. The characteristic is increased by 1 and the intermediate sum shifted one position to the right with the carry being inserted on the left. This yields X'10363EE'. The guard digit is dropped and the result, X'3F10363E', stored in F0.

F0 : X'3F21487B'   F2 : X'3BA2EB73'

Sign	: +		Sign	: +
Characteristic	: X'3F'		Characteristic	: X'3B'
Mantissa	: X'21487B'		Mantissa	: X'A2EB73'

The number in F2 has the smaller characteristic. Before the addition takes place, its mantissa will be shifted right 4 positions (X'3F' − X'3B' = 4). The last digit shifted out will be retained as the guard digit. The addition takes place as shown.

$$
\begin{array}{r}
1 \\
\text{X'21487B0'} \\
+\text{X'0000A3E'} \\
\hline
\text{X'21491EE'}
\end{array}
$$

This addition produces no carry and needs no normalization. The guard digit is dropped and the result, X'3F21491E', is stored in F0. Note that the shifting operation described above does not take place in F2. The value in F2 will not be changed.

F0 : X'3F21487B'   F2 : X'BF2146D5'

Sign	: +		Sign	: −
Characteristic	: X'3F'		Characteristic	: X'3F'
Mantissa	: X'21487B'		Mantissa	: X'2146D5'

The characteristics are the same, so no shifting is needed. Because the signs are different, the magnitude of the smaller mantissa is subtracted from the larger. The sign of the result will be determined by the rules of algebra. In this case, it will be +.

$$
\begin{array}{r}
7 \\
\text{X'21487B0'} \\
-\text{X'2146D50'} \\
\hline
\text{X'0001360'}
\end{array}
$$

The resulting mantissa must be normalized. In this case, it will be shifted left 3 positions with a corresponding decrease in the characteristic. The shifted intermediate mantissa will be X'1360000' and the new characteristic will be X'3C'. The value stored in F0 will be X'3C136000'.

Add Unnormalized

AUR RR, Short operands.

       AUR F_1, F_2

AU RX, Short operands.

       AU $F_1, D_2(X_2, B_2)$

AWR RR, Long operands.

       AWR F_1, F_2

AW RX, Long operands.

       AW $F_1, D_2(X_2, B_2)$

The values are added as described under the Add Normalized instructions. However, the intermediate mantissa is not normalized. The guard digit is dropped and the result stored in the first operand.

Condition Code:

0   If the result is 0.

1   If the result is negative.

2   If the result is positive.

Exceptions:

Access	Improper address for the second operand in an RX instruction.
Exponent Overflow	
Significance	The intermediate mantissa is 0 and the significance bit in the program mask is 1.
Specification	Register operand not 0, 2, 4, or 6 for short or long operands.

Example 8.2.6 *Consider the instruction*

       AUR   F0,F2

Suppose that F0 and F2 contain the values used in the last part of example 8.2.5.

F0 : X'3F21487B'   F2 : X'BF2146D5'

The addition of the mantissas will proceed as before.

$$
\begin{array}{r}
7 \\
\text{X'21487B0'} \\
-\text{X'2146D50'} \\
\hline
\text{X'0001360'}
\end{array}
$$

In this case, however, the intermediate sum will not be shifted. The value stored in F0 will be X'3F000136'.

The subtraction instructions are completely analagous to the addition instructions. The result is equivalent to negating the value stored in the second operand, then performing the corresponding addition. We list these instructions without comment.

Subtract Normalized

SER RR, Short operands.

        SER F_1, F_2

SE RX, Short operands.

        SE $F_1, D_2(X_2, B_2)$

SDR RR, Long operands.

        SDR F_1, F_2

SD RX, Long operands.

        SD $F_1, D_2(X_2, B_2)$

SXR RR, Extended operands.

        SXR F_1, F_2

Condition Code:

0   If the result is 0.

1   If the result is negative.

2   If the result is positive.

Exceptions:

Access	Improper address for the second operand in an RX instruction.
Exponent Overflow	
Exponent Underflow	Normalization would result in a negative characteristic (exponent < -64) and the exponent underflow bit in the program mask is 1.
Significance	The intermediate mantissa is 0 and the significance bit in the program mask is 1.
Specification	Register operand not 0, 2, 4, or 6 for short or long operands. Register operand not 0 or 4 for SXR.

Subtract Unnormalized

SUR RR, Short operands.

      SUR F_1, F_2

SU RX, Short operands.

      SU $F_1, D_2(X_2, B_2)$

SWR RR, Long operands.

      SWR F_1, F_2

SW RX, Long operands.

      SW $F_1, D_2(X_2, B_2)$

Condition Code:

0   If the result is 0.

1   If the result is negative.

2   If the result is positive.

Exceptions:

Access	Improper address for the second operand in an RX instruction.
Exponent Overflow	
Significance	The intermediate mantissa is 0 and the significance bit in the program mask is 1.
Specification	Register operand not 0, 2, 4, or 6 for short or long operands.

Multiplication and Division

In order to multiply two numbers in exponential form, we simply add the exponents and multiply the fractions. For example, consider the following multiplication of decimal exponential numbers

$$(.3422 * 10^{13}) * (.4532 * 10^5) = (.15508504 * 10^{(13+5)}) = .15508504 * 10^{18}$$

Multiplication of floating point numbers is done in essentially the same way. The mantissas are multiplied and the characteristics are added. However, as each characteristic is equal to the corresponding exponent plus 64, the sum of the characteristics is too large. It includes both 64's, so it must be reduced by 64.

The multiply instructions normalize both operands before the operation takes place. The result is always normalized. These instructions provide for a variety of operand sizes. The product is always computed to the greatest precision possible, then, when necessary, the result is truncated to the size specified for the target operand.

Multiply

MER RR, Short operands, long result.

    MER F_1,F_2

ME RX, Short operands, long result.

    ME $F_1,D_2(X_2,B_2)$

MDR RR, Long operands.

    MDR F_1,F_2

MD RX, Long operands.

    MD $F_1,D_2(X_2,B_2)$

MXDR RR, Long operands, extended result.

    MXDR F_1,F_2

MXD RX, Long operands, extended result.

    MXD $F_1,D_2(X_2,B_2)$

MXR RR, Extended operands.

    MXR F_1,F_2

If necessary, the two operands are normalized. The characteristics are added and the sum reduced by 64. This is the characteristic of the intermediate product. The mantissas are multiplied and, if necessary, the product is normalized. If the intermediate product is longer than the result needed by the instruction, it is truncated to the appropriate length. The result is stored in F_1.

Condition Code: Unchanged.

Exceptions:

Access	Improper address for the second operand in an RX instruction.
Exponent Overflow	
Exponent Underflow	
Specification	Register operand not 0, 2, 4, or 6 for short or long operands. Register operands not 0 or 4 for long operands.

Example 8.2.7 *Suppose that F0 contains X'5A21B93C————' and F4 contains X'47321AF6————' (The last 4 bytes of these two registers are irrelevant.)*

The execution of

        MER   F0,F4

proceeds as follows.

1. The characteristics are added and the sum reduced by 64:
    $$X'5A'+X'47'-X'40' = X'A1'-X'40' = X'61'$$

2. The mantissas are multiplied, producing a 14 hexadecimal digit product:
    $$X'.21B93C'*X'.321AF6' = X'.0699BAF017A800'$$

3. The intermediate product is X'610699BAF017A800'. This number is normalized and the result stored in F0.

Upon completion of the instruction, F0 will contain X'60699BAF017A8000'.

Example 8.2.8 *Suppose that F2 contains X'A30014FA--------' and FACTOR contains X'2AB40619'. Consider the instruction*

> ME   F2,FACTOR

In this case, the value in F2 must be normalized before the multiplication can take place. The normalized value is X'A114FA00'.

The characteristics of the two numbers are X'21' and X'2A'. These values are added and the sum reduced by 64 to yield the characteristic of the intermediate product.

$$X'21'+X'2A'-X'40' = X'4B'-X'40' = X'0B'$$

The sign of the first number is '−' and the sign of FACTOR is '+', so the sign of the product will be '−'.

The two fractions are multiplied to 14 hexadecimal places.

$$X'.14FA00'*X'.B40619' = X'.0EC047E86A0000'$$

With the sign bit, the intermediate result is X'8B0EC047E86A0000'. The fraction is shifted left 1 position to normalize, and the result is stored in F2.

After the instruction has been executed, F2 contains X'8AEC047E86A00000'.

Example 8.2.9 *Suppose F0 contains X'AAB87FE364A034A8' and F4 contains X'BE467B892E400488'.*

Execution of

> MXDR   F0,F4

proceeds as follows.

1. The signs of both numbers are '−', so the sign of the product will be '+'. The characteristics are added and the sum reduced by 64.
    $$X'2A'+X'3E'-X'40' = X'68'-X'40' = X'28'$$

2. The mantissas are multiplied to yield a 28 hexadecimal digit fraction.

$$X'.B87FE364A034A9'*X'.467B892E400488' =$$
$$X'.32CC007D8AF651EA55CB4FEE9958'$$

3. The intermediate value is X'2832CC007D8AF651EA55CB4FEE9958'. This value does not need to be normalized. It is stored in the pair F0, F2. The leftmost byte of register F2 is not used. The contents of this byte are irrelevant.

After the operation, F0 will contain X'2832CC007D8AF651' and F2 will contain X'--EA55CB4FEE9958'.

Example 8.2.10

With F0 and F4 as in the last example, the instruction

        MDR   F0,F4

will perform the multiplication as above, however the product will be truncated to a long floating point number and stored in F0. After the execution of the instruction, F0 will contain X'2832CC007D8AF651'. The contents of F2 will not be affected.

The mantissa above is simply truncated. It can be rounded by using the pair of instructions

        MXDR   F0,F4
        LRDR   F0,F0

After executing this instruction pair, F0 will contain X'2832CC007D8AF652'. F2 will contain the rest of the product, X'--EA55CB4FEE9958'.

The division instructions are analagous to the multiplication instructions. The characteristics must be subtracted, but, in this case, the two 64's cancel each other, so the difference must be increased by 64. The fractions are divided. The result of this division will never have a leading 0, but it can be greater than 1, as the following decimal division illustrates.

$$.1\,5\,2\,\overline{)\,.2\,5\,1\,0\,0\,}\quad 1.6\,5$$

It may be necessary to shift the fractional quotient to the right one position and increment the characteristic.

In contrast to the multiplication instructions, the result is always the same size as the initial operands.

Divide

DER RR, Short operands.

      DER F_1,F_2

DE RX, Short operands.

      DE $F_1,D_2(X_2,B_2)$

DDR RR, Long operands.

      DDR F_1,F_2

DD RX, Long operands.

      DD $F_1,D_2(X_2,B_2)$

If necessary, the two operands are normalized. The characteristic of the divisor is subtracted from the characteristic of the dividend and the result increased by 64. This is the characteristic of the intermediate quotient. The mantissas are divided. The intermediate quotient never requires normalization, but the mantissa may need to be shifted right one position and the characteristic increased by 1. The result is truncated to the appropriate length and stored in F_1.

Condition Code: Unchanged.

Exceptions:

Access	Improper address for the second operand in an RX instruction.
Exponent Overflow	
Exponent Underflow	
Floating Point Divide	Division by zero.
Specification	Register operand not 0, 2, 4, or 6 for short or long operands. Register operands not 0 or 4 for long operands.

Expression Evaluation

The evaluation of expressions involving floating point numbers is essentially the same as the evaluation of other expressions. Assuming that all fields are in floating point form, we simply generate an appropriate sequence of floating point instructions to evaluate the expression using floating point registers and store the result in the appropriate field. We continue our practice of documenting the code with pseudocode assignment statements, assuming the usual operator precedence. Whenever the expression being evaluated involves constants, we can use a literal constant of the appropriate type.

Example 8.2.11 *Write instructions to implement the assignment $X = 7*Y^2 - (A+B)/Z$. Assume that all fields are type D.*

```
        LD    F0,Y              X = 7 * Y^2 - (A+B) / Z
        MD    F0,F0              :
        MD    F0,=D'7'           :
        LD    F2,A               :
        AD    F2,B               :
        DD    F2,2               :
        ADR   F0,F2              :
        STD   F0,X               :
```

E   X   E   R   C   I   S   E   S

For Exercises 1-3, assume that the floating point registers and fields contain the values indicated below.

```
F0     :    X'3D17A0004304AF00'
F2     :    X'8F19AF009D450000'
F4     :    X'4110000000000000'
F6     :    X'3DFFFFFFFFFFFFFF'
EWRD   :    X'5A368A13'
DWRD   :    X'C4D38090075F3291'
```

1. Give the contents of the target operand after each instruction.

   a. LE   F2,EWRD
   b. LD   F4,DWRD
   c. LER   F0,F6
   d. LDR   F2,F4
   e. STE   F2,EWRD
   f. STD   F6,DWRD
   g. LRER F0,F0
   h. LRER F0,F2
   i. LRDR F0,F0
   j. LRDR F0,F4

2. Give the value of the target field and the Condition Code after each instruction.

   a. LTER   F2,F0
   b. LCDR   F2,F6
   c. LNDR   F4,F4
   d. LPER   F4,F6

3. Give the value of the Condition Code after each instruction has been executed.

   a. CER   F0,F2
   b. CER   F0,F6
   c. CD   F2,DWRD

4. Suppose that the floating point registers and operand fields contain the values shown below.

F0 : X'317100009A34F900'
F2 : X'2D3010000100B000'
F4 : X'315A19F07A2B9000'
F6 : X'B15A16E5D516A100'

Give the contents of the target field after each instruction.

   a. AER   F4,F6
   b. AUR   F4,F6
   c. ADR   F4,F6
   d. AWR   F4,F6
   e. AXR   F0,F4
   f. SDR   F0,F2
   g. MER   F0,F2
   h. DER   F0,F2

5. Assuming that A, B, C, and DISC are all D-type floating point numbers, write the instructions to implement the following assignment.

   DISC = B^2 − 4 * A * C

6. Assuming that X, Y, Z, and W are E-type floating point numbers, write the code to implement the assignment statement.

   X = (5 * X − 2 * Y) / (7 * Z − 9 * W)

7. Assume that all fields are short-form floating point fields, write the instructions to implement the following algorithmic construct.

   IF A^3 < B
   THEN
        Z = X^2 − Y
   ELSE
        Z = A / B

8. Suppose that A, B, C, X1, X2, REAL and IMAG are D-type floating point fields. Assume also that there is a function ROOT that has a single non-negative D-type floating point argument and returns the square root of that number in F0. Write the code to find the roots of the floating quadratic polynomial

   $A*X^2 + B*X + C$

   using the quadratic formula

   $$X = \frac{-B \pm \sqrt{B^2 - 4*A*C}}{2 * A}$$

   If the roots are real, store them in X1 and X2. Otherwise, store the real part in REAL and the imaginary part in IMAG.

8.3 CONVERTING FULLWORD NUMBERS TO FLOATING POINT

In this section, we study the conversions between binary integers and floating point numbers. In the next section, we consider conversions between packed decimal numbers with an implied decimal point. Both kinds of conversions present new problems. For example, floating point numbers are stored in sign-magnitude form. When converting a signed binary number to floating point, we need to be able to adjust the sign bit of the floating point number. This requires a facility for changing a single bit in a byte without changing the rest of the byte. Similarly, in order to insert the characteristic in a floating point number, we need to be able to access a single byte in a register while leaving other bytes unchanged. Conversions from floating point to other types also require a facility for extracting individual bits or bytes from a fullword.

In this section, we introduce some special purpose instructions which allow us to perform the kinds of operations described above. These instructions include several logical operations and the insert-character instructions. These instructions are being covered here because this is the first time we have needed them. However, they have much wider application. For example, the ability to manipulate individual bits is often the rationale for writing particular programs or procedures in assembly language.

Logical Instructions

Recall that a logical AND operation is a binary operation on bits. It is described by the following table.

AND	0	1
0	0	0
1	0	1

The AND instructions perform a logical AND on the corresponding bits of the two operands. The result is stored in the first operand. This instruction is available in four formats: RR, RX, SI, and SS. The various formats are shown below.

aNd Register *NR RR*

NR R_1,R_2

Perform a bit-by-bit AND of the fullwords stored in R_1 and R_2 and store the result in R_1.

Condition Code:

0   Result is X'00000000'.

1   Otherwise.

Exceptions: None.

Example 8.3.1 *Suppose that R3 contains X'00217F5B' and R5 contains X'59A8652D'.*

The instruction

      NR   R3,R5

will AND these two fullwords, bit by bit, and store the result in R3. In binary, this operation proceeds as follows.

```
      B'0000 0000 0010 0001 0111 1111 0101 1011'
  AND B'0101 1001 1010 1000 0110 0101 0010 1101'
      B'0000 0000 0010 0000 0110 0101 0000 1001'
```

The value stored in R3 will be X'00206509'.

aNd *N RX*

      N $R_1,D_2(X_2,B_2)$

Perform a bit-by-bit AND of the fullwords stored in R_1 and the fullword designated by the second operand and store the result in R_1.

Condition Code:

0   Result is X'00000000'.

1   Otherwise.

Exception:

Access   Improper address for second operand.

Example 8.3.2

```
      N       R3,FWRD
      N       R3,TABLE(RA)
      N       R8,0(R4,R5)
      N       R4,=X'FF00FF00'
```

The last of these instructions will replace the second and fourth bytes of R4 with 0's, leaving the first and third bytes unchanged.

Example 8.3.3 *Suppose that R4 contains an E-type floating point number.*

The instruction

        N   R4,=X'7F000000'

would mask out the sign bit and the mantissa of the number, leaving the characteristic in the leftmost byte of R4.

Similarly,

        N   R4,=X'80FFFFFF'

would mask out the characteristic. The sign bit would remain in the leftmost byte of R4 and the mantissa in the other three bytes.

aNd Immediate *NI SI*

        NI $D_1(B_2),I_2$

Perform a bit-by-bit AND of the byte stored at the location designated by the first operand and the immediate datum designated by the second operand. Store the result in the first operand location.

Condition Code:

0   Result is X'00000000'.

1   Otherwise.

Exception:

Access   Improper address for the first operand.

Example 8.3.4

        NI   FLAG,B'00000011'
        NI   CODE,X'7F'

The first instruction will zero the first 6 bits of FLAG and leave the last 2 bits unchanged. The second instruction will turn off the leftmost bit of CODE. The remaining bits will not be affected.

Example 8.3.5 *Suppose that EWRD contains a short floating point number.*

The instruction

        NI   EWRD,B'01111111'

will set the first bit of the first byte of EWRD to 0. The rest of EWRD will be unaffected. This has the effect of replacing the number in EWRD with its absolute value.

aNd Character *NC SS-1*

NC $D_1(L_1,B_1),D_2(B_2)$

Perform a bit-by-bit AND of the two operands and store the result in the first operand location.

Condition Code:

0   Result is X'00000000'.

1   Otherwise.

Exception:

Access   Improper address for first or second operand.

Example 8.3.6

NC	FLAGS,MASK
NC	FLAGS,=X'F0F0F0F0F0'

The logical OR operation is described by the following table.

OR	0	1
0	0	1
1	1	1

The OR instructions work in an analagous manner to the AND. They perform a logical OR on the corresponding bits of the two operands and store the result in the first operand. There are four available formats, RR, RX, SI, and SS, as shown in the following.

Or Register *OR RR*

OR R_1,R_2

Perform a bit-by-bit OR of the fullwords stored in R_1 and R_2 and store the result in R_1.

Condition Code:

0   Result is X'00000000'.

1   Otherwise.

Exceptions: None.

Example 8.3.7 *Suppose that R3 contains X'00217F5B' and R5 contains X'59A8652D'.*

The instruction

> OR   R3,R5

will OR these two fullwords, bit by bit, and store the result in R3. In binary, this operation proceeds as follows.

$$
\begin{array}{rl}
& \text{B'0000 0000 0010 0001 0111 1111 0101 1011'} \\
\text{OR} & \text{B'0101 1001 1010 1000 0110 0101 0010 1101'} \\
\hline
& \text{B'0101 1001 1010 1001 0111 1111 0111 1111'}
\end{array}
$$

The value stored in R3 will be X'59A97F7F'.

Or O RX

> O $R_1,D_2(X_2,B_2)$

Perform a bit-by-bit OR of the fullwords stored in R_1 and the fullword designated by the second operand and store the result in R_1.

Condition Code:
0   Result is X'00000000'.
1   Otherwise.

Exception:
Access   Improper address for second operand.

Example 8.3.8

> O   R3,FWRD
> O   R3,TABLE(RA)
> O   R8,0(R4,R5)
> O   R4,=X'FF00FF00'

The last of these instructions will replace the first and third bytes of R4 with 1's, leaving the second and fourth bytes unchanged.

Or Immediate OI SI

> OI $D_1(B_2),I_2$

Perform a bit-by-bit OR of the byte stored at the location designated by the first operand and the immediate datum designated by the second operand. Store the result in the first operand location.

Condition Code:
0   Result is X'00000000'.
1   Otherwise.

Exception:

Access   Improper address for the first operand.

Example 8.3.9

```
        OI      FLAG,B'00000011'
        OI      CODE,X'7F'
```

The first instruction will turn on the last 2 bits of the byte indicated by FLAG. It will leave the other bits of this byte unchanged. The second instruction will leave the leftmost bit of CODE unchanged. The remaining bits will be set to 1's.

Or Character OC SS-1

```
        OC      D₁(L₁,B₁),D₂(B₂)
```

Perform a bit-by-bit OR of the two operands and store the result in the first operand location.

Condition Code:

0   Result is X'00000000'.

1   Otherwise.

Exception:

Access   Improper address for first or second operand.

Example 8.3.10

```
        OC      FLAGS,MASK
        OC      FLAGS,=X'F0F0F0F0F0'
```

Example 8.3.11 *The following instruction will turn on the sign bit of FPNUM. Its effect is to replace FPNUM with the negative of its absolute value.*

```
        OI      FPNUM,B'10000000'
```

Example 8.3.12 *Suppose that EWRD contains a short floating point number and that CHAR is a 1-byte field in which the leftmost bit is 0.*

The pair of instructions

```
        NI      EWRD,B'10000000'
        OC      EWRD,CHAR
```

has the effect of replacing the characteristic of the number in EWRD with the value from CHAR.

Insert Character Instructions

The two insert character instructions allow us to replace 1 byte in a register while leaving the other bytes in that register unchanged.

Insert Character *IC RX*

$$\text{IC} \qquad R_1,D_2(X_2,B_2)$$

The rightmost byte of R_1 is replaced by the byte at the second operand address. The other 3 bytes of R_1 are unaffected.

Condition Code: Unchanged.

Exception:

Access   Improper address for second operand.

Example 8.3.13

$$\text{IC} \qquad R2,=X'2A'$$

The rightmost byte of R2 is set equal to X'2A'. The remaining bytes of R2 are unchanged.

Insert Character under Mask *ICM RS*

$$\text{ICM} \qquad R_1,M_3,D_2(B_2)$$

Bytes from the address designated by the second operand are inserted in R_1 as indicated by the mask, M_3. The bits in the mask are numbered 1 to 4 from left to right. If bit *i* of the mask is 1, then the next byte from the storage operand is retrieved and inserted in byte *i* of R_1.

Condition Code:

0   No nonzero bits were inserted.

1   The leftmost bit which was inserted was 1.

2   The leftmost bit inserted was 0 and at least one nonzero bit was inserted.

Exception:

Access   Improper address for the second operand.

Example 8.3.14 *Suppose that, before each of the following instructions, R4 = X'01020304' and BYTES = 'AABBCCDD'.*

ICM	R4,B'0110',BYTES	will change R4 to X'01AABB04'
ICM	R4,B'1000',BYTES	will change R4 to X'AA020304'
ICM	R4,B'0010',BYTES	will change R4 to X'0102AA04'

Example 8.3.15 *Suppose that R3 contains a short floating point number.*

The instruction

```
ICM     R3,B'1000',CHAR
```

will assign the byte from CHAR to the sign-characteristic part of this number. The mantissa will not be affected.

```
ICM     R3,B'0111',MANTISSA
```

will change the mantissa, leaving the sign and characteristic alone.

Converting Binary Integers to Floating Point

We start with the problem of converting a fixed binary integer to short-form floating point. Suppose that the number to be converted is in a field named FNUM and the converted value is to be placed in ENUM.

Initially, suppose that FNUM contains a non-negative binary integer in which the leftmost byte is zero. In order to convert FNUM to a short form floating point number, we use the rightmost 3 bytes as the mantissa. The sign bit should be 0, so the only difficulty is the determination of the characteristic.

Example 8.3.16 *Suppose that FNUM = X'003A50F1'.*

Using the right 3 bytes as a floating point mantissa and representing the characteristic by X'hh', we will have a floating point number of the form X'hh3A50F1'. This would be interpreted as $X'.3A50F1' * X'10'^{X'hh'-X'40'}$. For this to be equal to X'3A50F1', the exponent must be 6.

As the characteristic contains the exponent in excess-64 notation, we have

$$X'hh' = X'06'+X'40' = X'46'$$

The floating point form of this number is X'463A50F1'.

As the example above shows, to convert a 3-byte non-negative binary integer to a short floating point number, all we need to do is to insert X'46' in the leftmost byte of the number. This can be accomplished with the following instructions.

```
L       R1,FNUM              R1 = FNUM
ICM     R1,B'1000',=X'46'    INSERT CHARACTERISTIC
ST      R1,ENUM              STORE IN ENUM
```

Now, let's generalize this by dropping the requirement that the number be non-negative. As floating point numbers are stored in sign-magnitude form, the mantissa must be the absolute value of the number in FNUM. We must determine the sign separately and insert the appropriate sign bit in the floating point form.

We use Load Positive Register to take the absolute value of FNUM. In order to determine the sign bit, we could compare FNUM with 0, or use the Load and Test

Register instruction, but a simpler approach is to extract the leftmost bit of FNUM and put it in the leftmost position of R1. In order to extract this bit, we put a copy of FNUM in R0 and AND R0 with a mask containing a 1 in the leftmost position and 0's in all other bit positions, X'80000000'.

```
L     R0,FNUM              R0 = FNUM
LPR   R1,R0                R1 = ABS(R0)
ICM   R1,B'1000',=X'46'    INSERT CHARACTERISTIC IN R1
N     R0,=X'80000000'      EXTRACT SIGN BIT
OR    R1,R0                PUT SIGN BIT IN R1
```

Note that, departing from our usual practice, we have made free use of literal operands in these instructions. This is because we will usually implement these instructions in macro definitions. The use of literals reduces the problems of defining storage area within a macro call.

In the conversion above, we assumed that the first byte of the magnitude of the number in FNUM was 0. This restricts the range of values we can convert. If we want be able to convert any fullword value to floating point, we must use the long form. In some ways, this apparently more general conversion is actually somewhat simpler to perform. If the final result is to be stored in short form, we can convert the number to long form, normalize the result then discard the rightmost 4 bytes of the mantissa.

We use a pair of general purpose registers to form the 8-byte floating point number. This allows us to put the entire fullword number in the second register as the mantissa. We will have to put the sign and the appropriate characteristic in the first register. In order for the floating point number to be equivalent to the original binary integer, the exponent must be 14, the number of digits in the fraction. The characteristic must be $64+14 = 78$, or X'4E'.

The instructions to perform this conversion are shown below. The number is loaded into R0. We use LPR to place the magnitude in R1. Then we eliminate all except the sign bit from R0 and insert the characteristic with an OR instruction. The result is then stored in DNUM.

```
L     R0,FNUM              R0 = FNUM
LPR   R1,R0                R1 = ABS(R0)
N     R0,=X'80000000'      ISOLATE THE SIGN BIT
O     R0,=X'4E000000'      INSERT CHARACTERISTIC
STM   R0,R1,DNUM           DNUM = R0,R1
```

Up to this point, we have not made any attempt to normalize the floating point number generated. If the number is to be used in a multiply or divide instruction, then normalization is not necessary, as these instructions normalize the operands before the operation begins. When normalization is required, we could write instructions to check the first digit of the mantissa and shift if necessary. However, it is simpler to make use of the automatic normalization of the floating point instructions. We can force normalization by adding 0 using Add Normalized. The instructions to normalize a short floating point number stored in ENUM are

```
        LE      F0,ENUM
        AE      F0,=E'0'
        STE     F0,ENUM
```

Similarly, to normalize a long floating point number stored in DNUM, we have

```
        LD      F0,DNUM
        AD      F0,=D'0'
        STD     F0,DNUM
```

As these conversions involve a large number of instructions, it is convenient to write macros to generate these instructions. An example of such a macro is

```
        MACRO
        CVTFD   &DNUM,&FNUM
.*
.*      CONVERT FULLWORD TO LONG FLOATING POINT
.*
.*      THE NUMBER IN &FNUM IS CONVERTED TO A LONG FLOATING
.*      POINT NUMBER AND STORED IN &DNUM. IT IS NORMALIZED
.*      WITH AN ADD INSTRUCTION.
.*
.*      REGISTERS R0, R1, AND F0 ARE USED FOR THE CONVERSION.
.*
.*      GENERATE CONVERSION INSTRUCTIONS
        L       R0,&FNUM
        LPR     R1,R0
        N       R0,=X'80000000'
        O       R0,=X'4E000000'
        STM     R0,R1,&DNUM
.*      NORMALIZE THE CONVERTED VALUE
        LD      F0,&DNUM
        AD      F0,=D'0'
        STD     F0,&DNUM
.*
        MEND
```

Converting Floating Point Numbers to Binary Integers

The conversion from a floating point number to a binary integer appears to be more difficult because we do not know in advance what the exponent will be. However, if we are sure that the number will fit into a fullword, we can force the exponent to assume the desired value using the unnormalized Add instruction. This is done by placing an unnormalized 0 with the desired exponent in a register and adding the value to be converted to that register. If the exponent of the normalized form of the second operand is greater than the desired exponent, then the conversion is impossible—the number is too large. Otherwise, the mantissa will be shifted right and the exponent increased until it reaches the exponent of the first operand. The digits shifted out represent fractional digits. This is illustrated by the following example.

Example 8.3.17 *Consider the following pair of instructions.*

```
LD      F0,=X'4E00000000000000'
AU      F0,DNUM
```

Suppose that DNUM contains X'473B10B4002A12B5'. The sign bit is B'0', the characteristic is X'47', and the mantissa is X'3B10B4002A12B5'. In fixed point hexadecimal form, this number is equivalent to X'3B10B40.02A12B5'. The Add Unnormalized instruction will shift the mantissa 7 digits to the right in order to increase the characteristic to the desired value, X'4E'. The value added to the 0 in F0 will be X'4E00000003B10B40'. This will be the result in F0. The rightmost fullword, X'03B10B40' represents the fullword binary integer equivalent of the magnitude of the floating point number in DNUM. The hexadecimal digits that were lost, X'02A12B5', represent the fractional part of the original number.

If DNUM contains X'C73B10B4002A12B5' the sign bit is B'1', the characteristic is X'47', and the mantissa is X'3B10B4002A12B5'. This is simply the negation of the number above. The mantissa will be shifted as above, and the result will be X'CE00000003B10B40'. In this case, the second fullword represents the absolute value of DNUM.

If DNUM contains X'493B10B4002A12B5', then the result in F0 will be X'4E000003B10B4002'. In this case, the characteristic extends left into the first fullword. The original number is too large to represent as a fullword binary integer.

Finally, if DNUM contains X'513A10B04672F781', the result will be X'513A10B04672F781'. The number in DNUM is too large to fit in a fullword.

Before using this approach, we must deal with the situation in the second example above when the value in DNUM was negative. In this case, the value in the second fullword represents the magnitude of the floating point number. When the value in DNUM is less than 0, the result must be negated. We could check the sign of the original value and negate the second fullword if necessary. However, there is an easier solution. Recall from Section 4.2, that, if k is a signed number which can be written in n-bit 2's complement form, its representation is the rightmost n-bits of $2n + k$. In this case, we want the 32-bit form of the number in DNUM, so $n = 32$. We need the rightmost 32 bits of DNUM $+ 2^{32}$. We can combine this addition operation with the instruction to force the desired exponent by adding DNUM to X'4E00000100000000', an unnormalized form of 2^{32}. We can extract the rightmost 32 bits of the sum as we did above by taking the second fullword of the result.

Assuming that DNUM can be written in 32-bit 2's complement form, we can convert DNUM to a fullword binary integer in FWRD with the following sequence of instructions.

```
LD      F0,=X'4E00000100000000'   F0 = 2^32 + DNUM
AW      F0,DNUM                   :
STD     F0,DWORK                  EXTRACT THE RIGHTMOST 32
MVC     FWRD,DWORK+4              BITS AND STORE IN FWRD
```

The conversion of an E-type floating point number to a fullword is similar. This and the provision of tests for overflow are left as exercises.

E   X   E   R   C   I   S   E   S

1. Suppose that R1 contains X'FF01007B' and R2 contains X'7FFFFFFF'. Give the result of each of the following instructions or instruction sequences.

   a. NR R1,R2
   b. OR R1,R2
   c. N R2,=X'3A210AB0'
   d. N R1,X'0000FFFF'
     O R1,X'55550000'
   e. IC R1,=X'00'
   f. ICM R1,B'1100',=X'5555'
   g. ICM R2,B'0101',=X'CDCF'

2. Suppose that BNUM contains the fixed binary number: X'FF9B15E4'. Write instructions to convert BNUM to a short form floating point number and store it in SFPNUM. Trace these instructions, giving the resulting floating point number.

3. Rewrite the code in Exercise 2 to convert BNUM to a long floating point number and store it in LFPNUM.

4-5. Write the additional instructions necessary to normalize the values stored in SFPNUM and LFPNUM of Exercises 2 and 3.

6. Rewrite the instructions for Exercise 2 to perform the conversion using a doubleword work area. Normalize the result before storing it. This allows us to remove the restriction that the magnitude of the number not exceed 3 bytes.

7. Suppose that DNUM contains a long floating point number. Write the instructions to convert DNUM to an integer in FNUM, dropping any fractional part. Include code to check the magnitude of DNUM. If it is too large and DNUM is positive, store X'7FFFFFFF' in FNUM. If DNUM is negative and will not fit in a fullword, store X'80000000' in FNUM.

8. Repeat Exercise 7, assuming the number to be converted is a short floating point number stored in ENUM.

9. Write a general-purpose macro, FLOAT, to convert a fullword binary number to floating point. The macro should check the type of the floating point operand to determine whether the result should be a short or long floating point number. Normalize the floating point number before storing it in the floating point operand.

10. Write a general-purpose macro called FIX to convert floating point numbers to fixed binary. Check the size of the numbers and store X'7FFFFFFF' or X'80000000' in the target field if the floating point number is too large to be converted.

11. Suppose we have two fullword fields, INT and FRAC, which contain, as their names imply, the integer and fractional parts of a number. Write the instructions to convert this number to floating point, normalize it, and store the result in DNUM.

12. Write the instructions to reverse the process described in Exercise 1-g. That is, take a long floating point number stored in DNUM and convert its integer part and fractional part to fullword binary integers. Store the results in INT and FRAC.

8.4 CONVERSIONS BETWEEN DECIMAL AND FLOATING POINT NUMBERS

We are now ready to consider the problem of converting fixed decimal numbers to floating point and back. We will begin with the conversions from packed decimal numbers to floating point numbers. These conversions are relatively straightforward. The conversions from floating point back to fixed decimal are more troublesome.

In order to make our treatment as useful as possible, we adopt the approach of writing a general-purpose macro for each type of conversion. However, these macros generate a fairly large number of instructions. It would not be good practice to write programs that used these macros over and over again. Instead, we normally use them in procedures that are called whenever a conversion is necessary.

Before considering our first conversion, we need to add a new instruction. In order to form the absolute value of a packed decimal number, we need to be able to put an X'C' in the rightmost hexadecimal digit. This requires a facility for changing one hex-digit in a byte without changing the other. This can be done with a pair of special purpose move instructions. We will use only one of them here, but we cover both for symmetry.

Move Instructions

Recall that the first hexadecimal digit in a byte is called the *zone portion* of the byte and the second is called the *numeric portion*. These terms derive from the corresponding names for fields on a punched card. The MoVe Zones instruction extracts the zone portion of each byte in the source field and places them in the zone portion of the corresponding bytes in the target field. The MoVe Numerics instruction performs the same operation, using the numeric part of the bytes in the source field.

MoVe Zones MVZ SS—1

MVZ $D_1(L_1,B_1),D_2(B_2)$

The zone portion of each byte in the second operand field is copied into the zone portion of the corresponding byte in the first operand field. The numeric portion of bytes in the operand field is left unchanged.

Condition Code: Unchanged.

Exception:

Access   Improper address for first or second operand.

Example 8.4.1 *Suppose that SOURCE contains X'CCCCCC' and TARGET contains X'F1F2F3'.*

The instruction

MVZ   TARGET,SOURCE

will set TARGET equal to X'C1C2C3'

MoVe Numerics MVN SS—1

MVN $D_1(L_1,B_1),D_2(B_2)$

The numeric portion of each byte in the second operand field is copied into the numeric portion of the corresponding byte in the first operand field. The zone portion of bytes in the operand field is left unchanged.

Condition Code: Unchanged.

Exception:

Access   Improper address for first or second operand.

Example 8.4.2 *Suppose that SOURCE contains X'C4C5C6' and TARGET contains X'F1F2F3'.*

The instruction

       MVN   TARGET,SOURCE

will set TARGET equal to X'F4F5F6'.

Converting Packed Decimal Fractions to Floating Point

Now we turn to the problem of converting a packed decimal number, with an implied decimal point, to a floating point number. The process is quite similar to the binary conversion covered in the last section. We first consider a sample conversion.

Example 8.4.3 *Suppose we need to convert the number PNUM to a long floating point number, DNUM.*

```
PNUM       DC      P'-48153.5891'
DNUM       DS      D
```

Note that we can represent PNUM as an expression involving only integers.

$$48153.5891 = -\left(\frac{481535891}{10000}\right)$$

We can get the floating point form of the quotient inside parentheses by converting the two integers to floating point, then using a floating point division instruction to evaluate the quotient. If PNUM is negative, as above, we can then insert a 1 bit at the left of the floating point number.

We assume that the numerator above can be converted to a fullword binary integer. This greatly simplifies the conversion, as it implies that the nonzero part of the mantissa can be placed in the second fullword of the floating point form. The first fullword will need to contain only the appropriate characteristic.

In this example, when 481535891 is converted to hexadecimal, it becomes X'1CB3A793'. If we use this as the second fullword of a long floating point number and represent the characteristic by X'hh', we have

              X'hh0000001CB3A793'

In order for this to represent an integer, the exponent must be 14. The characteristic must be 64+14 = 72 or X'4E'. This gives

              X'4E0000001CB3A793'

The conversion process for the numerator consists of the following steps. We convert the absolute value of PNUM to a binary integer in a register, say R1. If we then store X'4E000000' in R0, the pair R0,R1 will contain an unnormalized representation of the numerator. The instructions to perform this conversion are shown below. The absolute value of PNUM is formed by using MVN to put a C in the rightmost byte.

```
          ZAP     DWRK,PNUM                  DNUM = ABS(PNUM * 10**4)
          MVN     DWRK+L'DWRK−1(1),=X'0C' :
          CVB     R1,DWRK                    :
          L       R0,=X'4E000000'           :
          STM     R0,R1,DNUM                 :
```

Having formed the floating point form of the numerator in this fraction, we divide it by the floating point form of the denominator and determine the sign. The division is quite simple, we need only divide by the literal operand =D'1.0E4'. In addition to computing the quotient, this automatically normalizes the result. The result of this division is stored in DNUM. Finally, the sign of PNUM is checked. If it is negative, then a 1 is inserted in the sign bit of DNUM. The instructions to perform these operations are

```
          LD      F0,DNUM                    DNUM = DNUM / 10**4
          DD      F0,=D'1.0E4'              :
          STD     F0,DNUM                    :
IF00      EQU     *                          IF PNUM < 0
          CP      PNUM,=P'0'                 :
          BNL     ENDIF00                    :
THEN00    EQU     *                          THEN
          OI      DNUM,=X'80'                    DNUM = −DNUM
ENDIF00   EQU     *                          ENDIF
```

The following macro generalizes the operations in the example above. It uses the scaling attribute to determine the number of decimal places in &PNUM. It is capable of converting any packed decimal number to a long floating point number, as long as the mantissa will fit a single fullword.

```
          MACRO
          CVTPD1 &DNUM,&PNUM
.*
.*   CONVERT PACKED DECIMAL FRACTION TO LONG FLOATING POINT
.*
.*   THE NUMBER IN &PNUM IS CONVERTED TO A LONG FLOATING
.*   POINT NUMBER AND STORED IN &DNUM.
.*
.*   REGISTERS R0 AND F0 ARE USED FOR THE CONVERSION.
.*
          GBLB    &PD$DEF           THE WORK FIELD HAS BEEN DEFINED
          LCLA    &SCALE            SCALE OF &PNUM
```

```
.IF0        ANOP                              IF NOT &PD$DEF
            AIF     (&PD$DEF).ENDIF0
.THEN0      ANOP                              THEN
            B       PD$ENDEF
PD$DWRK     DS      D
PD$ENDEF    EQU     *
&PD$DEF     SETB    (NOT &PD$DEF)             &PD$DEF = TRUE
.ENDIF0     ANOP                              END IF
.*
.*
.*      THE INTEGER EQUIVALENT OF ABS(&PNUM) IS FORMED IN THE
.*      REGISTER PAIR R0,R1. R0 WILL CONTAIN THE CHARACTERISTIC
.*      AND R1 THE HEXADECIMAL EQUIVALENT OF &PNUM
.*
            ZAP     PD$DWRK,&PNUM
            MVN     PD$DWRK+L'PD$DWRK−1(1),=X'0C'
            CVB     R3,PD$DWRK
            L       R2,=X'4E000000'
            STM     R2,R3,&DNUM
.*
.****       DIVIDE BY 10**&SCALE      ****
.*
&SCALE      SETA    S'&PNUM             FIND SCALE OF &PNUM
            LD      F0,&DNUM
            DD      F0,=D'1.0E&SCALE'
            STD     F0,&DNUM
.*
.****       IF &PNUM IS NEGATIVE THEN INSERT A SIGN BIT IN &DNUM      ****
.*
            CP      &PNUM,=P'0'
            BNL     NDIF&SYSNDX
            OI      &DNUM,X'80'
NDIF&SYSNDX         EQU *
.*
            MEND
```

The restriction implied by the macro CVTPD1, that the mantissa fit into a fullword, is quite severe in that both the packed decimal format and the long floating point format can represent numbers with much more precision than is possible with a fullword. Packed decimal numbers can be used to represent integers with up to 31 digits. The mantissa of a long floating point number is equivalent to approximately 16 decimal digits. But, a fullword binary integer is equivalent to, at most, 10 digits. The following macro alleviates this restriction by converting the integer part and the fractional part of the number in two separate steps. This allows either part to have up to 10 digits and makes it possible to convert numbers, which will make use of the full precision available in the long floating point form.

```
          MACRO
          CVTPD2  &DNUM,&PNUM
.*
.*    CONVERT PACKED DECIMAL FRACTION TO LONG FLOATING POINT
.*
.*    THE NUMBER IN &PNUM IS CONVERTED TO A LONG FLOATING
.*    POINT NUMBER AND STORED IN &DNUM.
.*
.*    THE NUMBER OF FRACTIONAL DIGITS IN &PNUM IS DETERMINED
.*    FROM THE SCALING ATTRIBUTE.
.*
.*    REGISTERS R0, R1, F0 AND F2 ARE USED FOR THE CONVERSION.
.*
          GBLB    &PD$DEF          WORK FIELDS HAVE BEEN DEFINED
          LCLA    &SCALE           SCALE OF &PNUM
          LCLA    &FRBYTES         NUMBER OF BYTES CONTAINING FRACTION
.*
.*
.IF0      ANOP                     IF NOT &PD$DEF
          AIF     (&PD$DEF).ENDIF0
.THEN0    ANOP                     THEN
          B       PD$ENDEF
PD$PWRK   DS      PL16
PD$ENDEF  EQU     *
&PD$DEF   SETB    (NOT &PD$DEF)      &PD$DEF = TRUE
.ENDIF0   ANOP                     END IF
.*
.*
&SCALE    SETA    S'&PNUM          FIND SCALE OF &PNUM
&FRBYTES  SETA    1+&SCALE/2       FIND NUMBER OF BYTES CONTAINING
.*                                 FRACTIONAL DIGITS.
.*
.****     EXTRACT THE FRACTIONAL DIGITS    ****
.*
          ZAP     PD$PWRK,&PNUM
          MVN     PD$PWRK+L'PD$PWRK-1(1),=X'0C'
          ZAP     PD$DWRK,PD$PWRK+L'PD$PWRK-&FRBYTES.(&FRBYTES)
.*
.IF1      ANOP                     IF &SCALE IS EVEN
          AIF     (2*(&SCALE/2) NE &SCALE).ENDIF1
.THEN1    ANOP                     THEN
.*                                   MASK OUT ODD DIGIT
.*
          NI      PD$DWRK+L'PD$DWRK-&FRBYTES,X'0F'
.*
.ENDIF1   ANOP                     END IF
```

```
.*
.****        CONVERT TO BINARY AND INSERT THE EXPONENT        ****
.*
         CVB    R1,PD$DWRK
         L      R0,=X'4E000000'
         STM    R0,R1,&DNUM
.*
.****        NORMALIZE AND DIVIDE BY 10**&SCALE        ****
.*
         LD     F0,=D'0'
         AD     F0,&DNUM
         DD     F0,=D'1.0E&SCALE'
.*
.****        EXTRACT INTEGER DIGITS BY SHIFTING OUT THE FRACTION        ****
.*
         SRP    PD$PWRK,64-&SCALE,0
         ZAP    PD$DWRK,PD$PWRK
.*
.****        CONVERT TO BINARY AND INSERT THE EXPONENT
.*
         CVB    R1,PD$DWRK
         L      R0,=X'4E000000'
         STM    R0,R1,&DNUM
.*
.****        NORMALIZE, ADD TO FRACTION IN F0, STORE THE SUM IN &DNUM        ****
.*
         LD     F2,=D'0'
         AD     F2,&DNUM
         ADR    F0,F2
         STD    F0,&DNUM
.*
.****        IF &PNUM IS NEGATIVE THEN INSERT A SIGN BIT IN &DNUM        ****
.*
         CP     &PNUM,=P'0'
         BNL    NDIF&SYSNDX
         OI     &DNUM,X'80'
NDIF&SYSNDX     EQU    *
.
         MEND
```

There is nothing particularly special about the decimal point. The approach used in the last macro could be adapted to break a decimal number into two or three pieces, convert each piece to floating point, then add the pieces. In this way, it is possible to convert a full precision packed decimal number to an extended floating point number, without any loss of precision.

Converting Floating Point Numbers to Decimal

We conclude this section with a typical conversion from floating point to packed decimal. This is the most difficult of the required conversions. The general approach is similar to that used for the other conversions. We extract the mantissa and, treating it as an integer, convert it to packed decimal. We then examine the characteristic to determine the appropriate exponent. We compute the corresponding power of 16 as a decimal number and, using the decimal instructions, either divide or multiply the mantissa by that power. The number of fractional digits in the result can be determined by shifting before the last operation.

As with the other conversions, we first consider a specific example, then present a general-purpose macro to perform the operation.

Example 8.4.4 *Given the two definitions below, write the instructions to convert DNUM to PNUM.*

```
DNUM        DS      D
PNUM        DS      P'9999999.99'
```

We assume that the mantissa can be represented in 7 hexadecimal digits. This allows us to extract it by loading DNUM into a register pair and shifting right. We use an SRDA instruction to move the mantissa 24 bits to the right and leave the sign and characteristic in the first register. We then use a logical shift of 4 bits to make certain that the sign of the mantissa is plus.

```
        LM      R0,R1,DNUM      R0,R1 = DNUM
        SRDA    R0,24           R1 = MANTISSA
        SRL     R1,4            FILL LEFT OF R1 WITH 4 0 BITS
```

Note that the effect of these two shift operations is to truncate the mantissa on the right to 7 hexadecimal digits.

Next, we check the sign in R0. If it is negative, we complement the mantissa. This leaves a signed mantissa in R1, which we convert to decimal in a double word work area, DWORK. In order to have as much room as possible for the following arithmetic operations, we move the packed mantissa to a 16-byte packed work area, PWORK

```
IF00        EQU     *               IF R0 < 0
            LTR     R0,R0           :
            BNM     ENDIF00         :
THEN00      EQU     *               THEN
            LNR     R1,R1               R1 = −R1
ENDIF00     EQU     *               ENDIF
            CVD     R1,DWORK        DWORK = R1
            ZAP     PWORK,DWORK     PWORK = DWORK
```

Now, we examine the characteristic. As we have treated 7 hexadecimal digits of the mantissa as an integer, the characteristic must be decremented by 7. Thus, the true exponent is given by

EXPONENT = CHARACTERISTIC −7 −64 = CHARACTERISTIC −71

We can compute this value in R0 as follows.

```
        N       R0,=X'0000007F'    ELIMINATE THE SIGN BITS
        S       R0,=F'71'          :
```

This value may be negative or positive. We need to multiply the mantissa by 16^{EXPONENT}. But, an equivalent and simpler approach is to raise 16 to the absolute value of the exponent and then multiply or divide, depending on the sign. The following instructions compute this factor in the packed field named POWER.

```
            ZAP     POWER,=P'1'        POWER = 1
FOR00       EQU     *                  FOR R1 = ABS(R0) DOWNTO 1
            LPR     R1,R0              :
            BNP     ENDFOR00           :
FTEST00     EQU     *                  :
            MP      POWER,=P'16'       POWER = POWER * 16
            BCT     R1,FTEST00         :
ENDFOR00    EQU     *                  END FOR
```

Finally, we check the sign of the exponent in R0. If it is positive, we multiply by power and shift in 2 decimal places. If the exponent is negative, we divide by POWER, rounding the result to 2 places.

```
IF01        EQU     *                          IF R0 < 0
            LTR     R0,R0                      :
            BM      ELSE01                     :
THEN01      EQU     *                          THEN
            MP      PWORK,POWER                    PNUM = PWORK * POWER
            SRP     PWORK,64+2,0               :
            ZAP     PNUM,PWORK                 :
            B       ENDIF01                    :
ELSE01      EQU     *                          ELSE
            SRP     PWORK,64+3,0               :
            DP      PWORK,POWER                    PNUM = PWORK / POWER
            SRP     PWORK(L'PWORK−L'POWER),64−1,5
            ZAP     PNUM,PWORK(L'PWORK−L'POWER)
ENDIF01     EQU     *                          ENDIF
```

The following macro generalizes this process by using the scale attribute to determine the number of decimal places in the target field.

```
               MACRO
               CVTDP   &PNUM,&DNUM
               PRINT   GEN
.*
.*      CONVERT LONG FLOATING POINT TO PACKED DECIMAL
.*
.*      THE LONG FLOATING POINT NUMBER IN &DNUM IS CONVERTED TO
.*      A PACKED DECIMAL NUMBER AND STORED IN &PNUM
.*
.*      THE NUMBER OF FRACTIONAL DIGITS IN &PNUM IS DETERMINED
.*      FROM THE SCALING ATTRIBUTE.
.*
.*      REGISTERS R0 AND R1 ARE USED FOR THE CONVERSION.
.*
               GBLB    &DP$DEF         WORK FIELDS HAVE BEEN DEFINED
               LCLA    &SCALE          SCALE OF &PNUM
.IF0           ANOP                    IF NOT &DP$DEF
               AIF     (&DP$DEF).ENDIF0
.THEN0         ANOP                    THEN
               B       DP$ENDEF
DP$DWRK        DS      D
DP$PWRK        DS      PL16
DP$POWER       DS      PL8
DP$ENDEF       EQU     *
&DP$DEF        SETB    (NOT &DP$DEF)   &DP$DEF = TRUE
.ENDIF0        ANOP                        END IF
.*
.*
&SCALE         SETA    S'&PNUM         FIND SCALE OF &PNUM
               LM      R0,R1,&DNUM
.*                                     PUT MANTISSA IN R1
               SRDA    R0,24
.*                                     SHIFT 0'S INTO LEFTMOST BYTE OF R1
               SRL     R1,4
.*                                     IF R0 < 0
               LTR     R0,R0
               BNM     NIF0&SYSNDX
.*                                     THEN
.*                                         R1 = -R1
               LNR     R1,R1
NIF0&SYSNDX            EQU *
.*                                     END IF
.*                                     CONVERT MANTISSA TO DECIMAL
               CVD     R1,DP$DWRK
               ZAP     DP$PWRK,DP$DWRK
.*
```

```
.*                                     ISOLATE CHARACTERISTIC AND CONVERT
.*                                     IT TO AN EXPONENT
          N       R0,=X'0000007F'
          S       R0,=F'71'
.*
.*                                     FIND 16**ABS(R0)
          ZAP     DP$POWER,=P'1'
.*                                     FOR R1 = R0 DOWNTO 1
          LPR     R1,R0
          BNP     NFR0&SYSNDX
FTST&SYSNDX       EQU *
          MP      DP$POWER,=P'16'
          BCT     R1,FTST&SYSNDX
NFR0&SYSNDX       EQU *
.*
.*                                     END FOR
.*
.*                                     IF EXPONENT >= 0
          LTR     R0,R0
          BM      ELS1&SYSNDX
.*                                     THEN
.*                                         MULTIPLY DP$PWRK BY DP$POWER
          MP      DP$PWRK,DP$POWER
          SRP     DP$PWRK,64+&SCALE,0
          ZAP     &PNUM,DP$PWRK
          B       NIF1&SYSNDX
.*                                     ELSE
ELS1&SYSNDX       EQU *
.*                                         DIVIDE DP$PWRK BY DP$POWER TO
.*                                         &SCALE+1 PLACES AND ROUND
          SRP     DP$PWRK,64+&SCALE+1,0
          DP      DP$PWRK,DP$POWER
          SRP     DP$PWRK(L'DP$PWRK−L'DP$POWER),64−1,5
          ZAP     &PNUM,DP$PWRK(L'DP$PWRK−L'DP$POWER)
.*
NIF1&SYSNDX       EQU *
          PRINT   NOGEN
          MEND
```

In conclusion, we can see the advantage of creating macro instructions to perform the conversions above. However, these macros generate a fairly large number of instructions. It would not be advisable to write a program that invoked the same macro many times to convert fields of the same size. Rather, these macros should be called from conversion procedures. If the program includes fields of many different sizes, it might still be necessary to write a number of conversion procedures. However, most programs tend to deal with numbers of approximately the same size and precision. So, in actual practice, the number of such procedures would be relatively small.

E X E R C I S E S

1. Suppose that NUMS contains X'05020306' and ZONES contains X'C0D1E2F3'. Give the contents of the target field after each of the following instructions.

   a. MVN   NUMS,ZONES
   b. MVZ   NUMS,ZONES
   c. MVN   ZONES,NUMS
   d. MVZ   ZONES,NUMS

2. Suppose PKDNUM is a packed decimal number defined by

   PKDNUM   DC   P'37964.21735'

   Write the instructions to convert PKDNUM to long floating point form and store it in LFPNUM. Include any necessary symbol or storage definitions.

3. Use the following definition of PKDNUM

   PKDNUM   DC   P'7389.458'

   and trace through the macro CVTPD1 and show the results.

4. Repeat Exercise 3 using the macro CVTPD2.

5. Suppose that INT and FRAC are 5-byte packed decimal fields that contain the integer and fractional parts of a number. Write instructions to form the long floating point form of this number and store it in DNUM. Assume that INT and FRAC have the same sign.

6. Rewrite CVTPD2 as CVTPX, which converts a packed decimal number to an extended floating point number.

7. Given the following definitions

   LFPNUM   DS   D
   PKDNUM   DS   P'99999.9999'

   write the instructions to convert LFPNUM to a packed decimal number and store it in PKDNUM. Include any necessary symbol and storage definitions.

8. Suppose BIGNUM is a 10-byte packed decimal field that contains an integer. This number is too large to be converted to a fullword binary number. Write the instructions to separate BIGNUM into 2 pieces, convert each piece to floating point, then combine them to get the long floating point form of BIGNUM.

9. Suppose that FRACTION and EXPONENT are 5-byte packed decimal fields. Assuming that FRACTION has an implied decimal point at the extreme left, write the instructions to form the long floating point equivalent of

   FRACTION $*$ $10^{EXPONENT}$

10. Suppose that PNUM is defined by

    PNUM   DS   P'9999999.99999999 '

    and that DNUM contains a long floating point number. Write the instructions generated by the macro invocation

            CVTPD   PNUM,DNUM

11. Suppose that INT and FRAC are packed decimal fields and DNUM contains a long floating point number. Write the instructions to convert the integer part and the fractional part of DNUM to decimal and store them in INT and FRAC. Assume that FRAC has an implied decimal point at the extreme left.

8.5 SAMPLE PROGRAM

We conclude our examination of floating point instructions with a sample program that uses these instructions. We will use the macros developed in this chapter for conversions between floating point and other numeric types. We will also use the CALLD macro developed in Chapter 6 to implement procedure calls. This allows us to pass parameters from one procedure call as arguments to another call.

Problem Description

We will develop a program to print a table of the monthly payment required on a loan of a fixed principal and various interest rates and loan periods. Each row in the table will correspond to a particular interest rate and each column to a loan life in years. The user will enter the principal amount. There is no limit to the number of rows we can print, so we will allow the user to enter the interest rate to be used for the first row, the rate for the last row, and the increment to be used between rows. As the number of columns is limited, we will only allow the user to enter the loan life for the first column and the increment to be used between columns. The specifications for the input records are shown below.

Information	Columns	Format (Implied Decimal Points)
Rate Record:		
Starting Rate	1-4	.9999
Ending Rate	5-8	.9999
Rate Increment	9-11	.999
Life Record:		
Starting Life	1-3	999
Life Increment	4-5	99
Principal Record:		
Principal	1-7	99999.99

The output produced by the program will be a table with appropriate headings, which gives the loan payments. The monthly payment on a loan is computed according to the following formula.

PAYMENT = PRINCIPAL * ((RATE/12) / (1 − (1 + RATE/12) ** (−12*LIFE)))

As we don't know in advance how many lines the table will contain, we will check for page overflow before printing a new line. When necessary, we will start a new page and repeat the heading information.

Program Development

We will organize the overall program as follows: The main program will simply read the input records and call another procedure, PRNTBLE, to print the table. As we may need to print the headings several times, we perform this task in a separate procedure, PAGEHEAD. The evaluation of the expression above is fairly complicated, so this operation will also be performed in a separate procedure, CALCPMNT. A brief description of each of these procedures together with their parameters and types is shown below.

PRNTBLE   (STRATE,ENDRATE,RATEINC,STARTLF,LIFEINC,PRNCPAL)

STRATE	: Long Floating Point;
ENDRATE	: Long Floating Point;
RATEINC	: Long Floating Point;
STARTLF	: Fixed Binary;
LIFEINC	: Fixed Binary;
PRNCPAL	: Long Floating Point;

Print a table containing the monthly payment amounts for loans. The procedure calls PAGEHEAD to print page and column headings and calls CALCPMNT to determine the monthly payment.

PAGEHEAD   (PGNUM,LINECNT,STARTLF,LIFEINC,PRNCPAL,PRINTER)

PGNUM	: Packed Decimal;
LINECNT	: Packed Decimal;
STARTLF	: Fixed Binary;
LIFEINC	: Fixed Binary;
PRNCPAL	: Long Floating Point;
PRINTER	: Macro Label;

Start a new page and print the heading lines for the rate table of monthly payments. This procedure calls the procedure PRNTLIFE to print the column headings.

CALCPMNT   (PRNCPAL,RATE,LIFE,PYMNT)

PRNCPAL	: Long Floating Point;
RATE	: Long Floating Point;
LIFE	: Fixed Binary;
PYMNT	: Long Floating Point;

Calculate the monthly payment for the given principal, loan rate, and loan life. The payment is returned in PYMNT.

There are, in addition, several subsidiary procedures. In order to convert the input values to floating point, we provide two procedures, CONVERT2 converts a packed decimal number with two decimal places to a long floating point number. CONVERT4 performs the same operation on a packed decimal number with 4 decimal places. The procedure PRNTLIFE is used to print the column headings. Note that in this procedure as well as in PRNTBLE, part of the output line is manipulated as an array.

```
***************************************************************************************
*                                                                                     *
*      THIS PROGRAM PRINTS A TABLE OF MONTHLY LOAN PAYMENTS FOR A FIXED                *
*      PRINCIPAL AND VARYING INTEREST RATES AND LOAN PERIODS.                          *
*                                                                                     *
*      THE INPUT CONSISTS OF THREE RECORDS. THE FIRST CONTAINS THE                     *
*      STARTING INTEREST RATE, THE ENDING INTEREST RATE, AND A RATE                    *
*      INCREMENT. THE SECOND RECORD CONTAINS THE INITIAL LOAN LIFE AND                 *
*      THE INCREMENT FOR LOAN LIFE. THE THIRD RECORD CONTAINS THE                      *
*      LOAN PRINCIPAL.                                                                 *
*                                                                                     *
*      THE OUTPUT IS A TABLE WHICH CONTAINS THE MONTHLY PAYMENT FOR                    *
*      EACH COMBINATION OF INTEREST RATE AND LOAN LIFE.                                *
*                                                                                     *
***************************************************************************************
SAMPLE7   START   0                              START SAMPLE7
          PRINT   NOGEN                          :
          BALR    RC,0                           :
          USING   *,RC                           :
          ICM     R0,B'1000',=B'00001100'        :
          SPM     R0                             :
          LA      RD,SAVE                        :
          OPEN    READER                         OPEN INPUT FILE
          GET     READER,INCARD                  READ STRATE,ENDRATE,RATEINC
          PACK    DWORK,INSTRTE                  :
          CALL    CONVERT4,(DWORK,STRATE)        :
          PACK    DWORK,INENDRTE                 :
          CALL    CONVERT4,(DWORK,ENDRATE)       :
          PACK    DWORK,INRTINC                  :
          CALL    CONVERT4,(DWORK,RATEINC)       :
          GET     READER,INCARD                  READ STARTLF,LIFEINC
          PACK    DWORK,INSTRTLF                 :
          CVB     R2,DWORK                       :
          ST      R2,STARTLF                     :
          PACK    DWORK,INLFINC                  :
```

```
          CVB     R2,DWORK                      :
          ST      R2,LIFEINC                    :
          GET     READER,INCARD                 READ PRNCPAL
          PACK    DWORK,INPRNCPL                :
          CALL    CONVERT2,(DWORK,PRNCPAL)
          CALL    PRNTBLE,(STRATE,ENDRATE,      CALL PRINT__TABLE        X
                  RATEINC,STARTLF,LIFEINC,                               X
                  PRNCPAL)                      :
          CLOSE   READER                        CLOSE INPUT FILE
EOFADR    EQU     *                             :
          EOJ                                   END SAMPLE7
****************************************************************************************
*    SYMBOL DEFINITIONS                                                                *
****************************************************************************************
          REGEQU
*                                              LENGTHS FOR INPUT FIELDS
RATELEN   EQU     4                               STARTING AND ENDING RATES
RTINCLEN  EQU     4                               RATE INCREMENT
LIFELEN   EQU     3                               STARTING LOAN LIFE
LFINCLEN  EQU     2                               LIFE INCREMENT
PRINCLEN  EQU     7                               PRINCIPAL
****************************************************************************************
*    LITERALS                                                                          *
****************************************************************************************
          LTORG
****************************************************************************************
*    FILES                                                                             *
****************************************************************************************
READER    DTFCD   DEVADDR=SYSIPT,DEVICE=2501,EOFADDR=EOFADR                 X
                  IOAREA1=INBUF1,IOAREA2=INBUF2,WORKA=YES
INBUF1    DS      CL80
INBUF2    DS      CL80
*
PRINTER   DTFPR   DEVADDR=SYSLST,DEVICE=3203,BLKSIZE=133,CTLCHR=ASA,        X
                  IOAREA1=OUTBUF1,IOAREA2=OUTBUF2,WORKA=YES
OUTBUF1   DS      CL133
OUTBUF2   DS      CL133
****************************************************************************************
*    VARIABLES                                                                         *
****************************************************************************************
*
STRATE    DS      D                             STARTING INTEREST RATE
ENDRATE   DS      D                             ENDING INTEREST RATE
RATEINC   DS      D                             RATE INCREMENT
STARTLF   DS      F                             STARTING LOAN LIFE
LIFEINC   DS      F                             LOAN LIFE INCREMENT
PRNCPAL   DS      D                             BINARY PRINCIPAL AMOUNT
```

```
DWORK      DS     D                           DOUBLE WORD WORK AREA
*
***********************************************************************************
*     I/O WORK AREAS                                                             *
***********************************************************************************
INCARD     DS     CL80                         INPUT RECORD
           ORG    INCARD                          INTEREST RATE INFORMATION
INSTRTE    DS     ZL(RATELEN)                        STARTING RATE
INENDRTE   DS     ZL(RATELEN)                        ENDING RATE
INRTINC    DS     ZL(RTINCLEN)                       RATE INCREMENT
           ORG    INCARD                          LOAN LIFE INFORMATION
INSTRTLF   DS     ZL(LIFELEN)                        INITIAL LOAN LIFE
INLFINC    DS     ZL(LFINCLEN)                       LOAN LIFE INCREMENT
           ORG    INCARD                          PRINCIPAL INFORMATION
INPRNCPL   DS     ZL(PRINCLEN)                       PRINCIPAL AMOUNT
           ORG    INCARD+L'INCARD              END INPUT RECORD
*

           END


CONVERT2   CSECT
***********************************************************************************
*     CONVERT2 (PNUM,FLOAT)                                                       *
*                                                                                *
*     CONVERTS THE PACKED DECIMAL NUMBER IN PNUM TO A FLOATING                    *
*     POINT NUMBER IN FLOAT. PNUM IS ASSUMED TO BE 8 BYTES LONG                   *
*     AND TO HAVE TWO FRACTIONAL DIGITS.                                          *
*                                                                                *
***********************************************************************************
           PRINT  NOGEN                        :
           SAVE   (14,12)                       PROCEDURE CONVERT2
           BALR   RC,0                          :
           USING  *,RC                          :
           ST     RD,SAVE+4                     :
           LA     RD,SAVE                       :
           USING  PSECT,RA                      :
           USING  FSECT,RB                      :
           LM     RA,RB,0(R1)                   :
           CVTPD2 FLOAT,PNUM                    FLOAT = FLOAT(PNUM)
           L      RD,SAVE+4                     :
           RETURN (14,12)                       END CONVERT2
SAVE       DS     18F                           :
***********************************************************************************
*     SYMBOL DEFINITIONS                                                          *
***********************************************************************************
           REGEQU
```

```
*************************************************************************************
*     DSECTS FOR PARAMETERS                                                        *
*************************************************************************************
PSECT     DSECT
PNUM      DS      P'9999999999999.99'        NUMBER TO BE CONVERTED
FSECT     DSECT
FLOAT     DS      D                          FLOATING POINT FORM
          END

CONVERT4  CSECT
*************************************************************************************
*     CONVERT4 (PNUM,FLOAT)                                                        *
*                                                                                  *
*     CONVERTS THE PACKED DECIMAL NUMBER IN PNUM TO A FLOATING                     *
*     POINT NUMBER IN FLOAT. PNUM IS ASSUMED TO BE 8 BYTES LONG                    *
*     AND TO HAVE FOUR FRACTIONAL DIGITS.                                          *
*                                                                                  *
*************************************************************************************
          PRINT   NOGEN                      :
          SAVE    (14,12)                    PROCEDURE CONVERT4
          BALR    RC,0                       :
          USING   *,RC                       :
          ST      RD,SAVE+4                  :
          LA      RD,SAVE                    :
          USING   PSECT,RA                   :
          USING   FSECT,RB                   :
          LM      RA,RB,0(R1)                :
          CVTPD2  FLOAT,PNUM                 FLOAT = FLOAT(PNUM)
          L       RD,SAVE+4                  :
          RETURN  (14,12)                    END CONVERT4
SAVE      DS      18F                        :
*************************************************************************************
*     SYMBOL DEFINITIONS                                                           *
*************************************************************************************
          REGEQU
*************************************************************************************
*     DSECTS FOR PARAMETERS                                                        *
*************************************************************************************
PSECT     DSECT
PNUM      DS      P'99999999999.9999'        NUMBER TO BE CONVERTED
FSECT     DSECT
FLOAT     DS      D                          FLOATING POINT FROM
          END

PRNTBLE   CSECT
```

```
***********************************************************************************************
*        PRNTBLE (STRATE,ENDRATE,RATEINC,STARTLF,LIFEINC,PRNCPAL)                             *
*                                                                                             *
*        PRINT A TABLE CONTAINING THE MONTHLY PAYMENT AMOUNTS FOR                             *
*        LOANS. THE INITIAL PRINCIPAL IS PRNCPAL. THE TABLE                                   *
*        CONTAINS A ROW FOR EACH INTEREST RATE FROM STRATE TO                                 *
*        ENDRATE IN INCREMENTS OF RATEINC. IT CONTAINS 4                                      *
*        COLUMNS CORRESPONDING TO 4 LOAN LIVES BEGINNING WITH                                 *
*        STARTLF AND INCREMENTING BY LIFEINC.                                                 *
*                                                                                             *
***********************************************************************************************
                 PRINT  NOGEN                       :
                 SAVE   (14,12)                      PROCEDURE PRNTBLE
                 BALR   RC,0                         :
                 USING  *,RC                         :
                 ST     RD,SAVE+4                     :
                 LA     RD,SAVE                       :
                 USING  STSECT,R6                     :
                 USING  NDSECT,R7                     :
                 USING  INCSECT,R8                    :
                 USING  LSECT,R9                      :
                 USING  LINCSECT,RA                   :
                 USING  PSECT,RB                      :
                 LM     R6,RB,0(R1)                   :
                 OPEN   PRINTER                       OPEN OUTPUT FILE
                 CALLD  PAGEHEAD,(PGNUM,LINECNT,      CALL PAGEHEAD(PGNUM,LINECNT,X
                        STARTLF,LIFEINC,PRNCPAL,         STARTLF,LIFEINC,PRNCPAL,   X
                        PRINTER)                         PRINTER)
FOR01            EQU    *                            FOR RATE = STRATE TO ENDRATE
                 MVC    RATE,STRATE                    BY RATEINC
FTEST01          EQU    *                            :
                 CLC    RATE,ENDRATE                 :
                 BH     ENDFOR01                     :
IF01             EQU    *                            IF LINECNT >= PGLINES
                 CP     LINECNT,PGLINES              :
                 BL     ENDIF01                      :
THEN01           EQU    *                            THEN
                 CALLD  PAGEHEAD,(PGNUM,LINECNT,     CALL PAGEHEAD(PGNUM,LINECNT,X
                        STARTLF,LIFEINC,PRNCPAL,         STARTLF,LIFEINC,PRNCPAL,   X
                        PRINTER)                         PRINTER)
ENDIF01          EQU    *                            END IF
                 CVTDP  PKDRATE,RATE                 PRINT RATE
                 MVC    OUTRATE,RATEMSK              :
                 ED     OUTRATE,PKDRATE              :
                 LA     R5,OUTPMNT                   R5 = A'OUTPMNT
                 USING  PMTSECT,R5                   :
                 MVC    LIFE,STARTLF                 LIFE = STARTLF
```

```
FOR02      EQU      *                               FOR R2 = NUMCOL DOWNTO 1
           LA       R2,NUMCOLS                      :
FTEST02    EQU      *                               :
           CALLD    CALCPMNT,(PRNCPAL,RATE,         CALCULATE PAYMENT          X
                    LIFE,PYMNT)                     :
           CVTDP    PCKPMNT,PYMNT                   PRINT PAYMENT
           MVC      PAYFLD,PMNTMSK                  :
           ED       PAYFLD,PCKPMNT                  :
           LA       R5,L'OUTPMNT(R5)                POINT R5 TO NEXT COLUMN
           L        R3,LIFE                         LIFE = LIFE + LIFEINC
           A        R3,LIFEINC                      :
           ST       R3,LIFE                         :
           BCT      R2,FTEST02                      :
ENDFOR02   EQU      *                               END FOR
           DROP     R5                              :
           PUT      PRINTER,DETAIL                  PRINT DETAIL LINE
           AP       LINECNT,=P'1'                   LINECNT = LINECNT + 1
           LD       F0,RATE                         :
           AD       F0,RATEINC                      :
           STD      F0,RATE                         :
           B        FTEST01                         :
ENDFOR01   EQU      *                               END FOR
           CLOSE    PRINTER                         CLOSE OUTPUT FILE
           L        RD,SAVE+4                       :
           RETURN (14,12)                           RETURN
SAVE       DS       18F                             :
***************************************************************************************
*    SYMBOL DEFINITIONS                                                               *
***************************************************************************************
           REGEQU
*
RATELEN    EQU      4                               LENGTH OF INPUT RATE
PKDRTLEN   EQU      RATELEN/2+1                     LENGTH OF PACKED RATE
PKPMNTLN   EQU      4                               LENGTH OF PACKED PAYMENT
NUMCOLS    EQU      5                               NUMBER OF OUTPUT COLUMNS
MARGIN     EQU      20                              LEFT AND RIGHT MARGIN
COLWIDTH   EQU      (132-2*MARGIN)/NUMCOLS          WIDTH OF EACH COLUMN
***************************************************************************************
*    LITERALS                                                                         *
***************************************************************************************
           LTORG
***************************************************************************************
*    FILES                                                                            *
***************************************************************************************
*
PRINTER    DTFPR    DEVADDR=SYSLST,DEVICE=3203,BLKSIZE=133,CTLCHR=ASA,        X
                    IOAREA1=OUTBUF1,IOAREA2=OUTBUF2,WORKA=YES
```

```
OUTBUF1    DS     CL133
OUTBUF2    DS     CL133
*******************************************************************************
*     CONSTANTS                                                              *
*******************************************************************************
*
*     EDIT MASKS
*
RATEMSK    DC     X'402021204B2020'           INTEREST RATE
PMNTMSK    DC     X'4020202021204B2020'       PAYMENT
*
*     OTHERS
*
PGLINES    DC     P'24'                       NUMBER OF LINES PER PAGE
*******************************************************************************
*     VARIABLES                                                             *
*******************************************************************************
PGNUM      DC     P'0'                        PAGE NUMBER COUNTER
LINECNT    DS     PL(L'PGLINES)               LINE COUNTER
*
DWORK      DS     D                           DOUBLE WORD WORK AREA
*
RATE       DS     D                           INTEREST RATE
PYMNT      DS     D                           MONTHLY PAYMENT
PKDRATE    DS     P'9.9999'                   PACKED INTEREST RATE
PCKPMNT    DS     P'99999.99'                 PACKED MONTHLY PAYMENT
LIFE       DS     F                           LOAN LIFE
*
*
*
*******************************************************************************
*     I/O WORK AREAS                                                        *
*******************************************************************************
*
*     OUTPUT DETAIL LINE
*
DETAIL     DC     CL133' '                    DETAIL LINE FOR TABLE
           ORG    DETAIL+MARGIN+(COLWIDTH−L'RATEMSK)/2
OUTRATE    DS     CL(L'RATEMSK)                  INTEREST RATE
           DC     C'%'                        :
           ORG    DETAIL+MARGIN+(3*COLWIDTH−L'PMNTMSK)/2
OUTPMNT    DS     (NUMCOLS)CL(COLWIDTH)       PAYMENT ARRAY
           ORG    DETAIL+(L'DETAIL)           END DETAIL LINE
*******************************************************************************
*     DSECT FOR ACCESSING ARRAY                                             *
*******************************************************************************
PMTSECT    DSECT
```

```
PAYFLD      DS      CL(L'PMNTMSK)               SINGLE PAYMENT
****************************************************************************************************
*      DSECTS FOR ACCESSING PARAMETERS                                                            *
****************************************************************************************************
STSECT      DSECT
STRATE      DS      D                           STARTING INTEREST RATE
NDSECT      DSECT
ENDRATE     DS      D                           ENDING INTEREST RATE
INCSECT     DSECT
RATEINC     DS      D                           RATE INCREMENT
LSECT       DSECT
STARTLF     DS      F                           LOAN LIFE
LINCSECT    DSECT
LIFEINC     DS      F                           LOAN LIFE INCREMENT
PSECT       DSECT
PRNCPAL     DS      D                           PRINCIPAL AMOUNT
            END


PAGEHEAD    CSECT
****************************************************************************************************
*      PAGEHEAD (PGNUM,LINECNT,STARTLF,LIFEINC,PRNCPAL,PRINTER)                                    *
*                                                                                                 *
*      STARTS A NEW PAGE AND PRINTS THE HEADING LINES FOR THE                                     *
*      RATE TABLE OF MONTHLY PAYMENTS.                                                            *
*                                                                                                 *
****************************************************************************************************
            PRINT   NOGEN                       :
            SAVE    (14,12)                     PROCEDURE PAGEHEAD
            BALR    RC,0                        :
            USING   *,RC                        :
            ST      RD,SAVE+4                   :
            LA      RD,SAVE                     :
            USING   PGSECT,R6                   :
            USING   LCSECT,R7                   :
            USING   SLSECT,R8                   :
            USING   LISECT,R9                   :
            USING   PRPSECT,RA                  :
            USING   PRSECT,RB                   :
            LM      R6,RB,0(R1)                 :
            AP      PGNUM,=P'1'                 INCREMENT PAGE COUNTER
            MVC     OPGNUM,PAGEMSK              INSERT PAGE NUMBER MASK
            ED      OPGNUM,PGNUM                :
            CVTDP   PKDPRINC,PRNCPAL            INSERT PRNCPAL INTO HEAD1
            MVC     OUTPRIN,PRINMSK             :
            LA      R1,OPRNFRST                 :
            EDMK    OUTPRIN,PKDPRINC            :
            BCTR    R1,R0                       :
```

```
            MVI     0(R1),C'$'                 :
            PUT     PRINTER,HEAD1              PRINT HEAD1
            PUT     PRINTER,HEAD2              PRINT HEAD2
            ZAP     LINECNT,NUMHDLNS           LINECNT = NUMHDLNS
            CALLD   PRNTLIFE,(LINECNT,         CALL  PRNTLIFE(LINECNT,STARTLF,  X
                    STARTLF,LIFEINC,                 LIFEINC,PRINTER)           X
                    PRINTER)                   :
*
            L       RD,SAVE+4                  :
            RETURN (14,12)                     RETURN
SAVE        DS      18F                        :
*****************************************************************************
*     SYMBOL DEFINITIONS                                                    *
*****************************************************************************
            REGEQU
*
NUMCOLS    EQU     5                          NUMBER OF COLUMNS IN TABLE
MARGIN     EQU     20                         LEFT AND RIGHT MARGIN
COLWIDTH   EQU     (132−2*MARGIN)/NUMCOLS     WIDTH OF EACH COLUMN
PRINFRST   EQU     7                          DEFAULT POSITION FOR $ IN PRNCPL
*****************************************************************************
*     LITERALS                                                             *
*****************************************************************************
            LTORG
*****************************************************************************
*     CONSTANTS                                                            *
*****************************************************************************
*
*     EDIT MASKS
*
PAGEMSK    DC      X'4020'                    PAGE NUMBER
PRINMSK    DC      X'4020206B2021204B2020'    PRINCIPAL
*
*     OTHERS
*
NUMHDLNS DC        P'5'                        NUMBER OF HEADING LINES
*****************************************************************************
*     VARIABLE                                                            *
*****************************************************************************
PKDPRINC   DS      P'99999.99'                PACKED PRINCIPAL AMOUNT
*
*
*****************************************************************************
*     HEADING LINES                                                       *
*****************************************************************************
```

```
*     HEADING LINES
*
*                                              :
HEAD1    DC     CL133' '                        HEADING LINE 1
         ORG    HEAD1                           :
         DC     C'1'                            CARRIAGE CONTROL CHARACTER
         ORG    HEAD1+MARGIN+COLWIDTH/2-6  :
         DC     C'PAGE'                         PAGE NUMBER
OPGNUM   DS     CL(L'PAGEMSK)                   :
         ORG    HEAD1+MARGIN+(NUMCOLS+1)*COLWIDTH/2-18
         DC     C'MONTHLY PAYMENTS FOR '     TITLE
OUTPRIN  DS     CL(L'PRINMSK)                      PRINCIPAL
         ORG    OUTPRIN+PRINFRST               :
OPRNFRST DS     CL1                            DEFAULT POS.FOR $
         ORG    OUTPRIN+L'OUTPRIN              :
         DC     C' LOAN'                       :
         ORG    HEAD1+L'HEAD1               END HEADING LINE 2
*
HEAD2    DC     CL133' '                        HEADING LINE 2
         ORG    HEAD2                          :
         DC     C'0'                            CARRIAGE CONTROL
         ORG    HEAD2+MARGIN+COLWIDTH/2-6 INTEREST RATE HEADING
         DC     C'INTEREST RATE'                 :
         ORG    HEAD2+MARGIN+(NUMCOLS+1)*COLWIDTH/2-10
         DC     C'LIFE OF LOAN IN YEARS'      LOAD LINES HEADING
         ORG    HEAD2+L'HEAD2               END HEADING LINE 2
********************************************************************************
*     DSECTS FOR PARAMETERS                                                    *
********************************************************************************
PGSECT   DSECT
PGNUM    DS     PL1                            PAGE NUMBER COUNTER
LCSECT   DSECT
LINECNT  DS     PL2                            LINE COUNTER
SLSECT   DSECT
STARTLF  DS     F                              STARTING LOAN LIFE
LISECT   DSECT
LIFEINC  DS     F                              LIFE INCREMENT
PRPSECT  DSECT
PRNCPAL  DS     D                              PRINCIPAL
PRSECT   DSECT
PRINTER  DS     F                              PRINTER DTF
*
         END

PRNTLIFE CSECT
```

```
****************************************************************************************
*       PRNTLIFE (LINECNT,STARTLF,LIFEINC,PRINTER)                                    *
*                                                                                      *
*       PRINT THE APPROPRIATE LOAN LIFE AT THE TOP OF EACH COLUMN,                     *
*       AND INCREMENT LINECNT.                                                         *
*                                                                                      *
****************************************************************************************
            PRINT   NOGEN                   :
            SAVE    (14,12)                  PROCEDURE PRNTLIFE
            BALR    RC,0                     :
            USING   *,RC                     :
            ST      RD,SAVE+4                :
            LA      RD,SAVE                  :
            USING   LCSECT,R8                :
            USING   SLSECT,R9                :
            USING   LISECT,RA                :
            USING   PRSECT,RB                :
            LM      R8,RB,0(R1)              :
*
*       PLACE LOAN LIFE HEADINGS INTO OUTPUT LINE
*
            LA      R7,OUTLIVES              R7 = A'OUTLIVES
            USING   OLSECT,R7                :
            L       R3,STARTLF               R3 = STARTLF
FOR00       EQU     *                        FOR R2 = NUMCOL DOWNTO 1
            LA      R2,NUMCOLS               :
FTEST00     EQU     *                        :
            CVD     R3,DWORK                 PRINT LIFE IN R3
            ZAP     PKDLIFE,DWORK            :
            MVC     OUTLIFE,LIFEMSK          :
            ED      OUTLIFE,PKDLIFE          :
            A       R3,LIFEINC               R3 = R3 + LIFEINC
            LA      R7,L'OUTLIVES(R7)        :
            BCT     R2,FTEST00               :
ENDFOR00    EQU     *                        END FOR
*
            PUT     PRINTER,COLHEADS         PRINT LINE
            AP      LINECNT,=P'2'            LINECNT = LINECNT + 2
            L       RD,SAVE+4                :
            RETURN  (14,12)                  RETURN
SAVE        DS      18F                      :
****************************************************************************************
*       SYMBOL DEFINITIONS                                                             *
****************************************************************************************
            REGEQU
*
LIFELEN     EQU     3                        NUMBER OF DIGITS IN LIFE
PKDLFLEN    EQU     LIFELEN/2+1              PACKED LIFE LENGTH
```

```
NUMCOLS   EQU   5                          NUMBER OF OUTPUT COLUMNS
MARGIN    EQU   20                         LEFT AND RIGHT MARGIN
COLWIDTH  EQU   (132-2*MARGIN)/NUMCOLS     COLUMN WIDTH
*********************************************************************************
*    LITERALS                                                               *
*********************************************************************************
          LTORG
*********************************************************************************
*    CONSTANT                                                               *
*********************************************************************************
LIFEMSK   DC    X'40202120'                LOAN LIFE
*********************************************************************************
*    VARIABLES                                                              *
*********************************************************************************
*
PKDLIFE   DS    PL(PKDLFLEN)               PACKED LOAN LIFE
*
DWORK     DS    D                          DOUBLE WORD WORK AREA
*
*********************************************************************************
*    I/O WORK AREAS                                                         *
*********************************************************************************
*
COLHEADS  DC    CL133' '                   COLUMN HEADINGS
          ORG   COLHEADS                       :
          DC    C'0'                       CARRIAGE CONTROL
          ORG   COLHEADS+MARGIN+COLWIDTH+(COLWIDTH-L'LIFEMSK)/2
OUTLIVES  DS    (NUMCOLS)CL(COLWIDTH)      ARRAY FOR LOAN LIVES
          ORG   COLHEADS+(L'COLHEADS)      END COLUMN HEADINGS
*********************************************************************************
*    DSECT FOR ARRAY                                                        *
*********************************************************************************
OLSECT    DSECT
OUTLIFE   DS    CL(L'LIFEMSK)              LOAN LIFE
*********************************************************************************
*    DSECTS FOR PARAMETERS                                                  *
*********************************************************************************
LCSECT    DSECT
LINECNT   DS    PL2                        LINE COUNTER
SLSECT    DSECT
STARTLF   DS    F                          STARTING LOAN LIFE
LISECT    DSECT
LIFEINC   DS    F                          LIFE INCREMENT
PRSECT    DSECT
PRINTER   DS    F                          PRINTER DTF
*
          END
*
```

```
CALCPMNT  CSECT
***********************************************************************************
*       CALCPMNT (PRNCPAL,RATE,LIFE,PYMNT)                                        *
*                                                                                 *
*       CALCULATES THE MONTHLY PAYMENT FOR THE GIVEN PRINCIPAL,                   *
*       LOAN RATE, AND LOAN LIFE. THE PAYMENT IS RETURNED IN THE                  *
*       VARIABLE PYMNT.                                                           *
*                                                                                 *
*       THE FORMULA USED FOR THE CALCULATION IS:                                  *
*                                                                                 *
*       PRINCIPAL * ((RATE/12) / (1 − (1 + RATE/12) ** (−12*LIFE)))               *
*                                                                                 *
***********************************************************************************
              PRINT    NOGEN                      :
              SAVE     (14,12)                     PROCEDURE CALCPMNT
              BALR     RC,0                        :
              USING    *,RC                        :
              ST       RD,SAVE+4                   :
              LA       RD,SAVE                     :
              USING    PRPSECT,R8                  :
              USING    RTSECT,R9                   :
              USING    LFSECT,RA                   :
              USING    PMSECT,RB                   :
              LM       R8,RB,0(R1)                 :
              LD       F0,RATE                     F0 = RATE / 12
              DD       F0,=D'12'                   :
              LDR      F4,F0                       F4 = (1 + RATE / 12)
              AD       F4,=D'1'                    :
              LD       F2,=D'1'                    F2 = 1
FOR00         EQU      *                          FOR R2 = (12*LIFE) DOWNTO 1
              L        R2,LIFE                      :
              MH       R2,=H'12'                    :
FTEST0        EQU      *                            :
              DDR      F2,F4                         F2 = F2 * F4
              BCT      R2,FTEST0                    :
ENDFOR0       EQU      *                          END FOR
*             PRINCIPAL * ((RATE/12) / (1 − (1 + RATE/12) ** (−12*LIFE))) *
              LNDR     F2,F2                       F2=(1−(1+RATE/12)**(−12*LIFE)))
              AD       F2,=D'1'                    :
              MD       F0,PRNCPAL                  F0 = F0 * PRNCPAL
              DDR      F0,F2                       F0 = F0 / F2
              STD      F0,PYMNT                    PYMNT = F0
              L        RD,SAVE+4                   :
              RETURN (14,12)                       RETURN
SAVE          DS       18F                         :
```

```
*****************************************************************************
*     SYMBOL DEFINITIONS                                                   *
*****************************************************************************
          REGEQU
*****************************************************************************
*     LITERALS                                                             *
*****************************************************************************
          LTORG
*****************************************************************************
*     DSECTS FOR PARAMETERS                                                *
*****************************************************************************
PRPSECT   DSECT
PRNCPAL   DS    D                       PRINCIPAL
RTSECT    DSECT
RATE      DS    D                       INTEREST RATE
LFSECT    DSECT
LIFE      DS    F                       LOAN LIFE
PMSECT    DSECT
PYMNT     DS    D                       MONTHLY PAYMENT
          END
```

A sample input file and the corresponding output file is shown below.

Input:

085020000025
01005
4550000

Output:

PAGE 1   MONTHLY PAYMENTS FOR $45,500.00 LOAN

INTEREST RATE   LIFE OF LOAN IN YEARS

	10	15	20	25	30
8.50%	564.13	448.06	394.86	366.38	349.86
8.75%	570.24	454.75	402.09	374.08	357.95
9.00%	576.37	461.49	409.38	381.83	366.10
9.25%	582.55	468.28	416.72	389.65	374.32
9.50%	588.76	475.12	424.12	397.53	382.59
9.75%	595.00	482.01	431.58	405.47	390.92
10.00%	601.29	488.95	439.08	413.46	399.30
10.25%	607.60	495.93	446.65	421.50	407.73
10.50%	613.95	502.96	454.26	429.60	416.21
10.75%	620.34	510.03	461.93	437.75	424.73
11.00%	626.76	517.15	469.65	445.95	433.31
11.25%	633.22	524.32	477.41	454.20	441.92
11.50%	639.71	531.53	485.23	462.49	450.58
11.75%	646.23	538.78	493.09	470.83	459.28
12.00%	652.79	546.08	500.99	479.22	468.02
12.25%	659.39	553.42	508.95	487.64	476.79
12.50%	666.01	560.80	516.94	496.11	485.60

MONTHLY PAYMENTS FOR $45,500.00 LOAN

INTEREST RATE

LIFE OF LOAN IN YEARS

	10	15	20	25	30
17.00%	790.78	700.25	667.39	654.20	648.68
17.25%	798.00	708.32	676.06	663.23	657.92
17.50%	805.25	716.43	684.75	672.28	667.18
17.75%	812.53	724.57	693.47	681.34	676.44
18.00%	819.84	732.74	702.21	690.43	685.72
18.25%	827.18	740.94	710.97	699.53	695.01
18.50%	834.55	749.17	719.76	708.66	704.31
18.75%	841.94	757.42	728.58	717.79	713.63
19.00%	849.36	765.71	737.41	726.94	722.95
19.25%	856.81	774.02	746.27	736.11	732.28
19.50%	864.28	782.36	755.15	745.29	741.61
19.75%	871.78	790.72	764.05	754.49	750.96
20.00%	879.31	799.11	772.97	763.70	760.31

MONTHLY PAYMENTS FOR $45,500.00 LOAN

INTEREST RATE

LIFE OF LOAN IN YEARS

	10	15	20	25	30
12.75%	672.67	568.22	524.98	504.62	494.45
13.00%	679.36	575.69	533.07	513.17	503.32
13.25%	686.09	583.19	541.19	521.75	512.23
13.50%	692.85	590.73	549.36	530.37	521.16
13.75%	699.64	598.32	557.56	539.02	530.13
14.00%	706.46	605.94	565.80	547.71	539.12
14.25%	713.32	613.60	574.08	556.43	548.13
14.50%	720.20	621.30	582.40	565.18	557.17
14.75%	727.12	629.04	590.75	573.97	566.24
15.00%	734.07	636.81	599.14	582.78	575.32
15.25%	741.06	644.62	607.56	591.62	584.43
15.50%	748.07	652.47	616.02	600.48	593.56
15.75%	755.11	660.35	624.50	609.38	602.70
16.00%	762.18	668.26	633.02	618.29	611.86
16.25%	769.29	676.21	641.57	627.24	621.05
16.50%	776.42	684.19	650.15	636.20	630.24
16.75%	783.59	692.20	658.76	645.19	639.45

P R O G R A M M I N G   P R O J E C T S

1. The bisection method for finding a zero of a polynomial function, F, can be described as follows. Given an interval [a, b] such that F(a) and F(b) have different signs, let m be the midpoint of [a, b]. If F(m) = 0, unlikely with floating point numbers, then m is a zero. Otherwise, if the sign of F(m) is different from F(a), then F has a zero between a and m. If the sign of F(m) is different from the sign of F(b), then the zero is between m and b. In either case, we can replace a or b with m thus bisecting the original interval. This process can be continued until the difference is as small as desired.

Write a program which uses floating point numbers and the bisection method to find a zero of a function F. Read the initial values of a and b from an input record. In order to allow the function F to be changed easily, implement it as an external function which has a long floating point number, X, as a parameter and returns the value of F(X) in F0. Give the answer as an integer part and a fractional part of 9 digits each.

This program can make good use of the Halve instruction for floating point numbers. This instruction comes in two forms, HER for short operands and HDR for long operands. The instruction takes two floating point register operands. The number in the second register is divided in half and the result stored in normalized form in the first register.

2. There are a number of algorithms for numerical integration. The simplest of these divides the interval [a, b] into n subintervals of equal length, $(b-a)/n$. The endpoints of these subintervals are denoted $X_i = a+i*(b-a)/n$, for i = 0, 1, . . ., n. The integral $\int_a^b F(X)\, dX$ is approximated by the sum $\sum_{i=1}^{n} F(X_i)*(b-a)/n$.

Write a program which reads A, B, and N and performs a numerical integration using an external function F which accepts a long floating point number, X, and returns F(X) in F0.

3. The Taylor Series for sin(X) is

$$\sum_{n=0}^{\infty} (-1)^n \frac{X^{2n+1}}{(2n+1)!}$$

Write a function SIN which accepts a long floating point parameter, X, and uses the Taylor Series to find the sine of X. It should return this value in F0. The function should compute terms in this series, adding them to the sum, until the absolute value of the next term is less than .000001. (Do not attempt to evaluate $(2n+1)!$. Instead, compute each new term of the series from the preceding term. This reduces the possibility of overflow and yields more accurate results.)

Write similar functions COS and EXP using the Taylor Series for cos(X) and e^X shown below.

$$\cos(X) = \sum_{n=0}^{\infty} (-1)^n \frac{X^{2n}}{(2n)!} \qquad e^X = \sum_{n=0}^{\infty} \frac{X^n}{n!}$$

4. Write a program which prints a loan repayment table. The input for this program should be a record which contains the principal, loan life, and interest rate. Your program should compute the monthly payment using the formula given in Section 8.5. Print this amount, then print a table which gives the total payments, interest payment and principal repayment for each year in the life of the loan. Note that the formula in 8.5 assumes that the interest will be computed and paid monthly.

5. The Newton-Raphson method for finding a zero of a function F involves the computation of a sequence of approximations. Each approximation is related to the preceding one by the formula

$$X_n = X_{n-1} - \frac{F(X_{n-1})}{F'(X_{n-1})}$$

where F' represents the derivative of F. The method requires an initial approximation, X_0. We then compute succeeding approximations until F(X) is as small as desired or some predetermined maximum number of approximations is reached.

Write a function ROOT which uses the Newton-Raphson method to find the square root of a long floating point parameter, A. The function should return the approximation in F0. Limit the number of iterations to 15 and stop when the square of the approximation is within .00000001 of A. As a first approximation, use the number whose exponent is one-half the exponent of A and whose mantissa is 8. (In this case, F(X) = X^2-N and F'(X) = 2*X.)

Test this function in a program which prints the square roots of the integers from 1 to 50. Print the results with 7 decimal places.

A P P E N D I C E S

A. INSTRUCTION SUMMARY

B. CODES

C. SPECIAL PURPOSE INSTRUCTIONS

APPENDIX A

The table below gives all of the instructions covered in the text together with the most general assembly language form of the instruction using the following notation.

R   General Purpose Register
F   Floating Point Register
B   Base Register
X   Index Register
L   Length
D   Absolute Displacement
I   1-byte Immediate Operand
M   4-bit Mask

The operands D(B), D(L,B) and D(X,B) can be replaced by S, S(L) or S(X) where S is a relocatable expression.

The length value and index register can always be omitted; the assembler will supply defaults.

The table also gives the machine format and the opcode for the instruction. A "Y" in the last column indicates that the instruction sets the Condition Code.

Instruction Name	Assembly Language Format		Format	Opcode	CC
Add	A	$R_1,D_2(X_2,B_2)$	RX	5A	Y
Add Halfword	AH	$R_1,D_2(X_2,B_2)$	RX	4A	Y
Add Normalized Extended Register	AXR	F_1,F_2	RR	36	Y
Add Normalized Long	AD	$F_1,D_2(X_2,B_2)$	RX	6A	Y
Add Normalized Long Register	ADR	F_1,F_2	RR	2A	Y
Add Normalized Short	AE	$F_1,D_2(X_2,B_2)$	RX	7A	Y
Add Normalized Short Register	AER	F_1,F_2	RR	3A	Y
Add Packed	AP	$D_1(L_1,B_1),D_2(L_2,B_2)$	SS2	FA	Y
Add Register	AR	R_1,R_2	RR	1A	Y
Add Unnormalized Long	AW	$F_1,D_2(X_2,B_2)$	RX	6E	Y
Add Unnormalized Long Register	AWR	F_1,F_2	RR	2E	Y
Add Unnormalized Short	AU	$F_1,D_2(X_2,B_2)$	RX	7E	Y
Add Unnormalized Short Register	AUR	F_1,F_2	RR	3E	Y
And	N	$R_1,D_2(X_2,B_2)$	RX	54	Y
And Character	NC	$D_1(L_1,B_1),D_2(B_2)$	SS1	D4	Y
And Register	NR	R_1,R_2	RR	14	Y
And Immediate	NI	$D_1(B_1),I_2$	SI	94	Y
Branch and Link	BAL	$R_1,D_2(X_2,B_2)$	RX	45	N
Branch and Link Register	BALR	R_1,R_2	RR	05	N
Branch on Condition	BC	$R_1,D_2(X_2,B_2)$	RX	47	N

Instruction Name	Assembly Language Format		Format	Opcode	CC
Branch on Condition Register	BCR	R_1,R_2	RR	06	N
Branch on Count	BCT	$R_1,D_2(X_2,B_2)$	RX	46	N
Branch on Count Register	BCTR	R_1,R_2	RR	07	N
Branch on Index High	BXH	$R_1,R_3,D_2(B_2)$	RS	86	N
Branch on Index Low or Equal	BXLE	$R_1,R_3,D_2(B_2)$	RS	87	N
Compare	C	$R_1,D_2(X_2,B_2)$	RX	59	Y
Compare Long	CD	$F_1,D_2(X_2,B_2)$	RX	69	Y
Compare Long Register	CDR	F_1,F_2	RR	29	Y
Compare Packed	CP	$D_1(L_1,B_1),D_2(L_2,B_2)$	SS2	F9	Y
Compare Register	CR	R_1,R_2	RR	19	Y
Compare Short	CE	$F_1,D_2(X_2,B_2)$	RX	79	Y
Compare Short Register	CER	F_1,F_2	RR	39	Y
Convert to Binary	CVB	$R_1,D_2(X_2,B_2)$	RX	4F	N
Convert to Decimal	CVD	$R_1,D_2(X_2,B_2)$	RX	4E	N
Divide	D	$R_1,D_2(X_2,B_2)$	RX	5D	N
Divide Long	DD	$F_1,D_2(X_2,B_2)$	RX	6D	N
Divide Long Register	DDR	F_1,F_2	RR	2D	N
Divide Packed	DP	$D_1(L_1,B_1),D_2(L_2,B_2)$	SS2	FD	N
Divide Register	DR	R_1,R_2	RR	1D	N
Divide Short	DE	$F_1,D_2(X_2,B_2)$	RX	7D	N
Divide Short Register	DER	F_1,F_2	RR	3D	N
Edit	ED	$D_1(L_1,B_1),D_2(B_2)$	SS1	DE	Y
Edit and Mark	EDMK	$D_1(L_1,B_1),D_2(B_2)$	SS1	DF	Y
Exclusive Or	X	$R_1,D_2(X_2,B_2)$	RX	57	Y
Exclusive Or Character	XC	$D_1(L_1,B_1),D_2(B_2)$	SS1	D7	Y
Exclusive Or Register	XR	R_1,R_2	RR	17	Y
Exclusive Or Immediate	XI	$D_1(B_1),I_2$	SI	97	Y
Execute	EX	$R_1,D_2(X_2,B_2)$	RX	44	N
Halve Long Register	HDR	F_1,F_2	RR	24	N
Halve Short Register	HER	F_1,F_2	RR	34	N
Insert Character	IC	$R_1,D_2(X_2,B_2)$	RX	43	N
Insert Characters under Mask	ICM	$R_1,M_3,D_2(B_2)$	RS	BF	Y
Load	L	$R_1,D_2(X_2,B_2)$	RX	58	N
Load Address	LA	$R_1,D_2(X_2,B_2)$	RX	41	N
Load and Test Register	LTR	R_1,R_2	RR	12	Y
Load and Test Long Register	LTDR	F_1,F_2	RR	22	Y
Load and Test Short Register	LTER	F_1,F_2	RR	32	Y
Load Complement Register	LCR	R_1,R_2	RR	13	Y
Load Complement Long Register	LCDR	F_1,F_2	RR	23	Y
Load Complement Short Register	LCER	F_1,F_2	RR	33	Y
Load Halfword	LH	$R_1,D_2(X_2,B_2)$	RX	48	N
Load Long	LD	$F_1,D_2(X_2,B_2)$	RX	68	N
Load Long Register	LDR	F_1,F_2	RR	28	N
Load Multiple	LM	$R_1,R_3,D_2(B_2)$	RS	98	N
Load Negative Register	LNR	R_1,R_2	RR	11	Y

Instruction Name	Assembly Language Format		Format	Opcode	CC
Load Negative Long Register	LNDR	F_1,F_2	RR	21	Y
Load Negative Short Register	LNER	F_1,F_2	RR	31	Y
Load Positive Register	LPR	R_1,R_2	RR	10	Y
Load Positive Long Register	LPDR	F_1,F_2	RR	20	Y
Load Positive Short Register	LPER	F_1,F_2	RR	30	Y
Load Short	LE	$F_1,D_2(X_2,B_2)$	RX	78	N
Load Short Register	LER	F_1,F_2	RR	38	Y
Load Register	LR	R_1,R_2	RR	18	N
Load Rounded Long Register	LRDR	F_1,F_2	RR	25	N
Load Rounded Short Register	LRER	F_1,F_2	RR	35	N
Move Character	MVC	$D_1(L_1,B_1),D_2(B_2)$	SS1	D2	N
Move Immediate	MI	$D_1(B_1),I_2$	SI	92	N
Move Numerics	MVN	$D_1(L_1,B_1),D_2(B_2)$	SS1	D1	N
Move Zones	MVZ	$D_1(L_1,B_1),D_2(B_2)$	SS1	D3	N
Multiply	M	$R_1,D_2(X_2,B_2)$	RX	5C	N
Multiply Extended Register	MXR	F_1,F_2	RR	26	N
Multiply Halfword	MH	$R_1,D_2(X_2,B_2)$	RX	4C	N
Multiply Long	MD	$F_1,D_2(X_2,B_2)$	RX	6C	N
Multiply Long Register	MDR	F_1,F_2	RR	2C	N
Multiply Long to Extended	MXD	$F_1,D_2(X_2,B_2)$	RX	67	N
Multiply Long to Extended Register	MXDR	F_1,F_2	RR	27	N
Multiply Register	MR	R_1,R_2	RR	1C	N
Multiply Short to Long	ME	$F_1,D_2(X_2,B_2)$	RX	7C	N
Multiply Short to Long Register	MER	F_1,F_2	RR	3C	N
Multiply Packed	MP	$D_1(L_1,B_1),D_2(L_2,B_2)$	SS2	FC	N
Or	O	$R_1,D_2(X_2,B_2)$	RX	56	Y
Or Character	OC	$D_1(L_1,B_1),D_2(B_2)$	SS1	D6	Y
Or Register	OR	R_1,R_2	RR	16	Y
Or Immediate	OI	$D_1(B_1),I_2$	SI	96	Y
Pack	PACK	$D_1(L_1,B_1),D_2(L_2,B_2)$	SS2	F2	N
Set Program Mask	SPM	R_1	RR	04	Y
Shift and Round Packed	SRP	$D_1(L_1,B_1),D_2(B_2),I_3$	SS	F0	Y
Shift Left Double Arithmetic	SLDA	$R_1,D_2(B_2)$	RS	8F	Y
Shift Left Double Logical	SLDL	$R_1,D_2(B_2)$	RS	8D	N
Shift Left Single Arithmetic	SLA	$R_1,D_2(B_2)$	RS	8B	Y
Shift Left Single Logical	SLL	$R_1,D_2(B_2)$	RS	89	N
Shift Right Double Arithmetic	SRDA	$R_1,D_2(B_2)$	RS	8E	Y
Shift Right Double Logical	SRDL	$R_1,D_2(B_2)$	RS	8C	N
Shift Right Single Arithmetic	SRA	$R_1,D_2(B_2)$	RS	8A	Y
Shift Right Single Logical	SRL	$R_1,D_2(B_2)$	RS	88	N
Store	ST	$R_1,D_2(X_2,B_2)$	RX	50	N
Store Halfword	STH	$R_1,D_2(X_2,B_2)$	RX	40	N
Store Long	STD	$F_1,D_2(X_2,B_2)$	RX	60	N
Store Multiple	STM	$R_1,R_3,D_2(B_2)$	RS	90	N
Store Short	STE	$F_1,D_2(X_2,B_2)$	RX	70	N

Instruction Name	Assembly Language Format		Format	Opcode	CC
Subtract	S	$R_1,D_2(X_2,B_2)$	RX	5B	Y
Subtract Halfword	SH	$R_1,D_2(X_2,B_2)$	RX	4B	Y
Subtract Normalized Extended Register	SXR	F_1,F_2	RR	37	Y
Subtract Normalized Long	SD	$F_1,D_2(X_2,B_2)$	RX	6B	Y
Subtract Normalized Long Register	SDR	F_1,F_2	RR	2B	Y
Subtract Normalized Short	SE	$F_1,D_2(X_2,B_2)$	RX	7B	Y
Subtract Normalized Short Register	SER	F_1,F_2	RR	3B	Y
Subtract Packed	SP	$D_1(L_1,B_1),D_2(L_2,B_2)$	SS2	FB	Y
Subtract Register	SR	R_1,R_2	RR	1B	Y
Subtract Unnormalized Long	SW	$F_1,D_2(X_2,B_2)$	RX	6F	Y
Subtract Unnormalized Long Register	SWR	F_1,F_2	RR	2F	Y
Subtract Unnormalized Short	SU	$F_1,D_2(X_2,B_2)$	RX	7F	Y
Subtract Unnormalized Short Register	SUR	F_1,F_2	RR	3F	Y
Translate	TR	$D_1(L_1,B_1),D_2(B_2)$	SS1	DC	N
Translate and Test	TRT	$D_1(L_1,B_1),D_2(B_2)$	SS1	DD	Y
Unpack	UNPK	$D_1(L_1,B_1),D_2(L_2,B_2)$	SS2	F3	N
Zero and Add Packed	ZAP	$D_1(L_1,B_1),D_2(L_2,B_2)$	SS2	F8	Y

APPENDIX B

The table below gives the standard EBCDIC and ASCII characters for each of the possible 1-byte codes from 0 through 255. The last column gives the instruction mnemonic with the indicated opcode. Only those instructions covered in this text are included.

Code Hex.	Dec.	Character EBCDIC	ASCII	Instruction Mnemonic
00	0	NUL	NUL	
01	1	SOH	SOH	
02	2	STX	STX	
03	3	ETX	ETX	
04	4	SEL	EOT	SPM
05	5	HT	ENQ	BALR
06	6	RNL	ACK	BCTR
07	7	DEL	BEL	BCR
08	8	GE	BS	
09	9	SPS	HT	
0A	10	RPT	LF	
0B	11	VT	VT	
0C	12	FF	FF	
0D	13	CR	CR	
0E	14	SO	SO	
0F	15	SI	SI	
10	16	DLE	DLE	LPR
11	17	DC1	DC1	LNR
12	18	DC2	DC2	LTR
13	19	DC3	DC3	LCR
14	20	RES/ENP	DC4	NR
15	21	NL	NAK	CLR
16	22	BS	SYN	OR
17	23	POC	ETB	XR
18	24	CAN	CAN	LR
19	25	EM	EM	CR
1A	26	UBS	SUB	AR
1B	27	CU1	ESC	SR
1C	28	IFS	FS	MR
1D	29	IGS	GS	DR
1E	30	IRS	RS	ALR
1F	31	ITB/IUS	US	SLR
20	32	DS	Sp	LPDR
21	33	SOS	!	LNDR
22	34	FS	"	LTDR

Code Hex.	Dec.	Character EBCDIC	ASCII	Instruction Mnemonic
23	35	WUS	#	LCDR
24	36	BYP/INP	$	HDR
25	37	LF	%	LRDR
26	38	ETB	&	MXR
27	39	ESC	'	MXDR
28	40	SA	(	LDR
29	41	SFE	)	CDR
2A	42	SM/SW	*	ADR
2B	43	CSP	+	SDR
2C	44	MFA	,	MDR
2D	45	ENQ	−	DDR
2E	46	ACK	.	AWR
2F	47	BEL	/	SWR
30	48		0	LPER
31	49		1	LNER
32	50	SYN	2	LTER
33	51	IR	3	LCER
34	52	PP	4	HER
35	53	TRN	5	LRER
36	54	NBS	6	AXR
37	55	EOT	7	SXR
38	56	SBS	8	LER
39	57	IT	9	CER
3A	58	RFF	:	AER
3B	59	CU3	;	SER
3C	60	DC4	<	MER
3D	61	NAK	=	DER
3E	62		>	AUR
3F	63	SUB	?	SUR
40	64	Sp	@	STH
41	65		A	LA
42	66		B	
43	67		C	IC
44	68		D	EX
45	69		E	BAL
46	70		F	BCT
47	71		G	BC
48	72		H	LH
49	73		I	CH
4A	74	¢	J	AH
4B	75	.	K	SH
4C	76	<	L	MH
4D	77	(	M	
4E	78	+	N	CVD
4F	79	|	O	CVB

Code Hex.	Dec.	Character EBCDIC	ASCII	Instruction Mnemonic
50	80	&	P	ST
51	81		Q	
52	82		R	
53	83		S	
54	84		T	N
55	85		U	CL
56	86		V	O
57	87		W	X
58	88		X	L
59	89		Y	C
5A	90	!	Z	A
5B	91	$	[	S
5C	92	*	\	M
5D	93	)	]	D
5E	94	;	^	
5F	95	¬	—	
60	96	–	'	STD
61	97	/	a	
62	98		b	
63	99		c	
64	100		d	
65	101		e	
66	102		f	
67	103		g	MXD
68	104		h	LD
69	105		i	CD
6A	106	¦	j	AD
6B	107	,	k	SD
6C	108	%	l	MD
6D	109	–	m	DD
6E	110	>	n	AW
6F	111	?	o	SW
70	112		p	STE
71	113		q	
72	114		r	
73	115		s	
74	116		t	
75	117		u	
76	118		v	
77	119		w	
78	120		x	LE
79	121	'	y	CE
7A	122	:	z	AE
7B	123	#	{	SE
7C	124	@	¦	ME

Code Hex.	Dec.	Character EBCDIC	ASCII	Instruction Mnemonic
7D	125	'	}	DE
7E	126	=	~	AU
7F	127	"	DEL	SU
80	128			
81	129	a		
82	130	b		
83	131	c		
84	132	d		
85	133	e		
86	134	f		BXH
87	135	g		BXLE
88	136	h		SRL
89	137	i		SLL
8A	138			SRA
8B	139			SLA
8C	140			SRDL
8D	141			SLDL
8E	142			SRDA
8F	143			SLDA
90	144			STM
91	145	j		
92	146	k		MVI
93	147	l		
94	148	m		NI
95	149	n		CLI
96	150	o		OI
97	151	p		XI
98	152	q		LM
99	153	r		
9A	154			
9B	155			
9C	156			
9D	157			
9E	158			
9F	159			
A0	160			
A1	161	~		
A2	162	s		
A3	163	t		
A4	164	u		
A5	165	v		
A6	166	w		
A7	167	x		
A8	168	y		
A9	169	z		

Code Hex.	Dec.	Character EBCDIC	ASCII	Instruction Mnemonic
AA	170			
AB	171			
AC	172			
AD	173			
AE	174			
AF	175			
B0	176			
B1	177			
B2	178			
B3	179			
B4	180			
B5	181			
B6	182			
B7	183			
B8	184			
B9	185			
BA	186			
BB	187			
BC	188			
BD	189			
BE	190			
BF	191			ICM
C0	192	{		
C1	193	A		
C2	194	B		
C3	195	C		
C4	196	D		
C5	197	E		
C6	198	F		
C7	199	G		
C8	200	H		
C9	201	I		
CA	202			
CB	203			
CC	204	⌐		
CD	205			
CE	206	⊥		
CF	207			
D0	208	}		
D1	209	J		MVN
D2	210	K		MVC
D3	211	L		MVZ
D4	212	M		NC
D5	213	N		CLC
D6	214	O		OC

Code Hex.	Dec.	Character EBCDIC	ASCII	Instruction Mnemonic
D7	215	P		XC
D8	216	Q		
D9	217	R		
DA	218			
DB	219			
DC	220			TR
DD	221			TRT
DE	222			ED
DF	223			EDMK
E0	224	\		
E1	225			
E2	226	S		
E3	227	T		
E4	228	U		
E5	229	V		
E6	230	W		
E7	231	X		
E8	232	Y		
E9	233	Z		
EA	234			
EB	235			
EC	236	⊣		
ED	237			
EE	238			
EF	239			
F0	240	0		SRP
F1	241	1		
F2	242	2		PACK
F3	243	3		UNPK
F4	244	4		
F5	245	5		
F6	246	6		
F7	247	7		
F8	248	8		ZAP
F9	249	9		CP
FA	250	I		AP
FB	251			SP
FC	252			MP
FD	253			DP
FE	254			
FF	255	EO		

APPENDIX C

SPECIAL PURPOSE INSTRUCTIONS

There are several instructions in the 370 instruction set that perform highly specialized tasks. As such, they may not be used very often in general programming, but they are invaluable when the facility they provide is needed in a program. In fact the availability of these instructions is often the rationale for writing particular programs or routines in assembly language. They illustrate the power available to an assembly language programmer.

We cover a translation instruction, which is intended primarily to allow translations from one coding scheme to another. For example, it could be used to translate a string encoded in ASCII to EBCDIC. We also cover an instruction that allows us to scan a string for the first occurrence of a particular character or class of characters. Finally, we consider the Execute instruction, which allows us to manipulate fields of varying lengths.

The Translate Instruction

The Translate instruction performs a simple substitution of codes in the source string. It can be used for code translation and for rearranging fields in a record.

TRanslate *TR 1-Length SS*

> TR $D_1(L,B_1),D_2(B_2)$

The first operand represents a source string. The second operand represents a translation table. Each byte in the first operand is used as an offset into the table designated by the second operand. In this way, each first operand byte selects an entry from the table. Each byte in the first operand is replaced by the entry it selected from the table.

Condition Code: Unchanged.

Exception:

Access   Improper address for first or second operand.

Example C.1 *Suppose that STR contains X'02050A0A060B0D0D030F' and TABLE contains X'F0F1F2F3F4F5F6F7F8F9C1C2C3C4C5'.*

The execution of the instruction

> TR   STR,TABLE

will replace the first byte, X'02', in STR with the byte found at offset 2 from the beginning of TABLE, X'F2'. X'05' will be replaced by the byte at offset 5 from the beginning of TABLE. The new value in the second byte of STR will be X'F5'. In the same way, X'0A' will be replaced by X'C1', X'06' will be replaced by X'F6' and so on. The final value of STR will be X'F2F5C1C1F6C2C4C4F3C5'. Note that, in character form, this will be C'25AA6BDD3F'. Note also that TABLE could be defined by

```
TABLE      DC      C'0123456789ABCDEF'
```

If STR is any string of bytes in which each byte is less than or equal to 15, then the Translate instruction can use TABLE to translate the number in each byte to the corresponding character form.

Suppose we need to translate a string stored in INSTR from ASCII to EBCDIC. We construct a translation table, say ASC2EBC, which allows us to do the translation with the single assembly language instruction

```
         TR      INSTR,ASC2EBC
```

In order to simplify the construction of the table, we assume that the input string contains standard, 7-bit ASCII codes that have a 0 bit in the leftmost position. This means that the table needs only 128 entries. We also assume that we only want to translate printable characters. Any control characters should be replaced with a blank. Finally, we assume that lower case ASCII characters are to be translated to the corresponding upper case EBCDIC letters.

To construct the table, we first reserve space for the whole table. As a number of positions will be filled with blanks, we initialize all entries with the EBCDIC code for a blank. This can be done with the instruction

```
ASC2EBC   DC      CL128' '
```

We use an ORG instruction to assign other codes to positions corresponding to printable, nonblank characters. The first such character in the ASCII coding sequence is the exclamation mark, "!". Its ASCII code is 33, so we store the EBCDIC code for an exclamation mark at offset 33 in the table. This is done with the following pair of instructions.

```
         ORG     ASC2EBC+33     MOVE LOC CTR TO OFFSET 33
         DC      C'!'           STORE EBCDIC CODE FOR '!'
```

Referring to the ASCII coding sequence in Appendix B, we see that the next position in the table should be filled with the EBCDIC code for the double quote. The position after that should be filled with the EBCDIC code for the pound sign, "#", and so on. These assignments could be accomplished with the sequence of instructions

```
         DC      C'"'
         DC      C'#'
         DC      C'$'
          .
          .
          .
```

The same effect can be achieved with the single instruction

```
DC        C'!"#$.....
```

In fact, we can fill all the entries simply by writing DC instructions that use the type designator C and give the characters in their order of occurrence in the ASCII coding sequence. The assembler will insert the EBCDIC code for each of these characters in the order indicated.

The entire table can be defined with the following sequence of instructions.

```
ASC2EBC   DC     CL128' '                            ASCII TO EBCDIC TRANS. TABLE
          ORG    ASC2EBC+33                           :
          DC     C'!"#$%&"()*+,−./'                   ASCII 33 – 47
          DC     C'0123456789:;<=>?@'                 ASCII 48 – 64
          DC     C'ABCDEFGHIJKLMNOPQRSTUVWXYZ'        ASCII 65 – 90
          DC     C'[\]^_"                             ASCII 91 – 96
          DC     C'ABCDEFGHIJKLMNOPQRSTUVWXYZ'        ASCII 97 – 122
          DC     C'{ |}~'                             ASCII 123 – 126
          ORG    ASC2EBC+L'ASC2EBC
```

Notice that, in order to put a single quote in a string, it must be preceded by another single quote that is used as an escape character.

The Translate instruction can also be used to rearrange fields in a record structure. The source structure is given as the second operand. The first operand is initialized with a pattern indicating the location in the source string of the value to be copied into each byte. We illustrate this technique with an example.

Example C.2 *Consider the student record described by the following definitions.*

```
NUMLEN    EQU    6                          LENGTH OF STUDENT NUMBER
NAMELEN   EQU    20                         LENGTH OF STUDENT NAME
ADDRLEN   EQU    20                         LENGTH OF ADDRESS
CLASSLEN  EQU    4                          LENGTH OF CLASS DESCRIPTOR
CREDLEN   EQU    3                          LENGTH OF CREDIT HOURS FIELD
RECLEN    EQU    NUMLEN+NAMELEN+ADDRLEN+CLASSLEN+CREDLEN
LMARGIN   EQU    10                         LEFT MARGIN
COLSKIP   EQU    12                         SPACE BETWEEN OUTPUT COLUMNS
                 .
                 .
                 .
SOURCE    DC     C' '
STUREC    DS     XL(RECLEN)          STUDENT RECORD            COLUMN
          ORG    STUREC                     :
STUNUM    DS     ZL(NUMLEN)            STUDENT NUMBER             1
NAME      DS     CL(NAMELEN)          NAME                       7
ADDRESS   DS     CL(ADDRLEN)          ADDRESS                    27
CLASS     DS     CL(CLASSLEN)         CLASS                      47
CREDITS   DS     ZL(CREDLEN)          CREDIT HOURS               51
```

Suppose that we want to copy the information from STUREC into an output line, OUTLINE, with a left margin of LMARGIN spaces and COLSKIP spaces between columns. Assume that the information is to be reordered so that the student name is listed first, followed by the address, student number, class, and credit hours.

This could be accomplished with a sequence of Move Character instructions, but it can also be performed with the single Translate instruction

```
TR      OUTLINE,SOURCE
```

under the following conditions. First, we assume that the definition for STUREC is preceded immediately by the definition for SOURCE as shown above. Second, each position in OUTLINE must contain an offset from the beginning of SOURCE. Positions that should be filled with blanks contain offset 0. The positions that are to contain the student number contain the offsets of STUNUM from the beginning of SOURCE, 1 through 6. Positions that are to contain NAME are initialized to 7 through 26.

As the line itself may be used many times, we define a pattern in a separate field and move it into OUTLINE before each Translate instruction, as we would with an edit pattern. The required definition is shown below. When we define the pattern, the offsets need to be stored as 1-byte hexadecimal values. We could define them by using the X-type indicator, but this would require us to convert the offsets to hexadecimal ourselves. Instead, we can define them using the A-type address constant and an explicit length of 1. This allows us to give a list of values in decimal. The assembler will convert them to decimal and store each in a 1-byte field.

```
TRPAT     DC    133X'0'                   FILL TRPAT WITH 0'S
          ORG   TRPAT+COLSKIP         :
NMEOFFS   DC    AL1(07,08,09,10,11,12,13,14,15,16)   OFFSETS FOR NAME
          DC    AL1(17,18,19,20,21,22,23,24,25,26)
          ORG   *+COLSKIP             :
ADDROFFS  DC    AL1(27,28,29,30,31,32,33,34,35,36) OFFSETS FOR ADDRESS
          DC    AL1(37,38,39,40,41,42,43,44,45,46)
          ORG   *+COLSKIP             :
NUMOFFS   DC    AL1(01,02,03,04,05,06)           OFFSETS FOR NUMBER
          ORG   *+CLOSKIP             :
CLASOFFS  DC    AL1(47,48,49,50)                 OFFSETS FOR CLASS
          ORG   *+COLSKIP             :
CREDOFFS  DC    AL1(51,52,53)                    OFFSETS FOR CREDIT
          ORG   TRPAT+L'TRPAT    END TRPAT
```

The complete operation now requires a pair of instructions

```
MVC     OUTLINE,TRPAT
TR      OUTLINE,SOURCE
```

As an aside, we can even avoid listing the offsets using the following artifice. When the assembler encounters an A-type address constant with a duplication factor and an expression in parentheses, it reevaluates the expression each time it creates a new entry in the list of values. If the expression involves the location counter, then the resulting value will change, as the location counter value is adjusted after each item in the list is created. Thus, the definition

```
OFFS          DC          5AL1(*−OFFS)
```

will cause the value X'0001020304' to be stored beginning at OFFS. As each byte is stored, the location counter value will be incremented by 1.

Using this approach, we can create a definition for TRPAT that is shorter than the one above and that will be changed automatically if the definition of STUREC is changed.

```
TRPAT      DC     133X'0'              FILL TRPAT WITH 0'S
           ORG    TRPAT+COLSKIP        :
NMEOFFS    DC     (L'NAME)AL1(*−NMEOFFS+NAME−SOURCE)         OFFSETS FOR NAME
           ORG    *+COLSKIP            :
ADDROFFS   DC     (L'ADDRESS)AL1(*−ADDROFFS+ADDRESS−SOURCE)    OFFSETS FOR
           ORG    *+COLSKIP            :                                ADDRESS
NUMOFFS    DC     (L'STUNUM)AL1(*−NUMOFFS+STUNUM−SOURCE)       OFFSETS FOR
           ORG    *+CLOSKIP                                            NUMBER
CLASOFFS   DC     (L'CLASS)AL1(*−CLASOFFS+CLASS−SOURCE)     OFFSETS FOR CLASS
           ORG    *+COLSKIP            :
CREDOFFS   DC     (L'CREDITS)AL1(*−CREDOFFS+CREDITS−SOURCE) OFFSETS FOR CREDIT
           ORG    TRPAT+L'TRPAT        END TRPAT
```

The Translate and Test Instruction

In spite of its name, the Translate and Test instruction does not perform a translation. Instead, it scans a string under the direction of a table similar to that used by the Translate instruction. As in Translate, bytes from the first operand field are used as offsets into a table designated by the second operand. In the case of the Translate and Test instruction, the first operand byte is not changed. The operation continues, byte by byte, until the selected byte from the second operand is nonzero or the end of the first operand is reached. A complete description follows.

TRanslate and Test TRT 1-Length SS

```
TRT       D₁(L,B₁),D₂(B₂)
```

The first operand represents a source string. The second operand represents a table. Each byte in the first operand is used as an offset into the table designated by the second operand. In this way, each first operand byte selects an entry from the table. If the selected byte is 0, the operation continues with the next byte in the source operand. If the selected byte is nonzero, then the address of the current byte in the source operand is stored in R1, the byte selected from the table is stored in R2, and execution of the instruction terminates. If the end of the first operand is reached and no nonzero byte is selected, then the Condition Code is set to 0.

Condition Code:

0   All selected bytes were 0.

1   A nonzero byte was selected by one of the bytes before the last byte in the first operand.

2   A nonzero byte was selected by the last byte in the first operand.

Exception:

Access   Improper address for first or second operand.

In order to use the Translate and Test instruction, we create a table that has nonzero entries in the positions corresponding to the characters we are seeking. The table should have 0's in all other positions.

There are a number of instances in which TRT can be used. For example, suppose that we are processing free-form input records. We may need to scan a record for the first nonblank character. In order to search a string for a particular substring, we can use TRT to scan the string for the first character of the substring. If input records contain a combination of alphabetic and numeric information, we can use TRT to scan a record for the first digit or for a sign. We consider an example based on the second possibility to illustrate the use of the TRT instruction.

Example C.3 *Suppose that INREC contains a mixture of text and signed integers.*

We need to determine whether it contains a number. If it does, we want to store the starting address of the first number in a fullword field STARTAD. If it does not contain an integer, we store 0 in STARTAD. We store a sign for the number in a halfword field SIGN. In order to simplify this example, we assume that, if INREC does contain a sign, it will be followed by 1 or more digits. Thus, we will only need to scan the string once, looking for either a sign or a digit.

We create a table, DIGTBLE, which contains a nonzero entry corresponding to the characters "+" and "−" and the nonzero digits. (This allows us to ignore leading zeros.) The entries for these positions could be any nonzero values. However, we would like to use the value stored in R2 to determine the correct sign for the number. We will store X'FF' in the position corresponding to "+" and X'DD' in the position corresponding to "−". We will store X'FF' in the positions corresponding to nonzero digits. This will allow us to use the rightmost X'F' to supply a default + for numbers entered without sign.

```
DIGTBLE    DC      XL256'00'                   TABLE FOR NUMBER SEARCH
           ORG     DIGTBLE+C'+'                :
           DC      X'FF'                       CODE FOR '+'
           ORG     DIGTBLE+C'−'                :
           DC      X'DD'                       CODE FOR '−'
           ORG     DIGTBLE+C'1'                :
           DC      X'FFFFFFFFFFFFFFFFFF'   CODE FOR DIGITS
           ORG     DIGTBLE+L'DIGTBLE        END DIGTBLE

           LA      R1,0                        R1 = 0
           LA      R2,0                        R2 = 0
```

```
TRT     INREC,DIGTBLE          SCAN INREC USING DIGTBLE
ST      R1,STARTAD             STARTAD = R1
ST      R2,SIGN                SIGN = R2
```

The Execute Instruction

The length factor in all SS instructions is stored at the time that the program is assembled. This makes it difficult to manipulate strings of varying lengths. This difficulty can be alleviated with the Execute instruction. It allows us to postpone the determination of the length in an SS instruction until program execution.

EXecute *EX RX*

$$EX \qquad R_1,D_2(X_2,B_2)$$

The second operand is interpreted as the address of an instruction called the "target" instruction. If R_1 is not register 0, then an instruction is created by ORing the low-order byte of R_1 with the second byte of the target instruction. If R_1 is register 0, then the created instruction is the same as the target instruction. The created instruction is then executed.

Neither the value in R_1 nor the target instruction is changed by the action of the Execute instruction.

The target instruction may be any instruction except another Execute instruction. It must be located on a halfword boundary.

Condition Code: Unchanged unless it is set by the target instruction.

Exceptions:

Access   Improper address for second operand.

Execute   The target instruction is another Execute instruction.

Specification   The second operand address is odd.

While the target of an Execute instruction can be any instruction, it is most often an SS instruction. In this case, the second byte represents the length field. We can manipulate fields of varying lengths by placing the length factor in a register, other than R0, and specifying that register in an Execute instruction. The target instruction is usually identified by a label.

Example C.4 *Suppose that we are processing free-form input records that contain integers of different lengths.*

Assume that the starting address of such an integer is in a fullword field STARTAD and that its length is in the fullword field LENGTH. We create the code to pack this number into a field named PNUM.

The target instruction is a Pack instruction that specifies a packed decimal field as the first operand. The second operand will be specified by an explicit base register, R3, and offset 0. The length will not be determined until run time, but we put a 1 in the instruction for the use of the assembler. The instruction is identified by a label.

PKINST   PACK   PNUM,0(1,R3)

The code to execute this instruction places the address of the zoned number in register R3. The fixed length of the packed field is placed in R2 with a Load Address instruction. This length, which will not exceed 1 hexadecimal digit, is stored in the rightmost 4 bits of R2. It is shifted to 4 bits to the left with an SLL instruction. The rightmost 4 bits of R2 are filled with zeros. The length of the zoned number, also assumed to require no more than 1 hexadecimal digit, is placed in the rightmost 4 bits of R2 by ORing R2 with the field LENGTH. Assuming that the LENGTH represents the total number of digits in the zoned number, rather than the number of digits after the first digit, we must decrement the length before executing the Pack instruction. This is accomplished with a BCTR instruction.

```
L      R3,STARTAD       R3 = ADDRESS OF ZONED NUMBER
LA     R2,L'PNUM        LENGTH OF PACKED NUMBER IN RGT DIGIT OF R2
BCTR   R2,0             DECREMENT THE LENGTH BY 1
SLL    R2,4             MOVE LENGTH TO 7TH DIGIT OF R2
OR     R2,LENGTH        INSERT LENGTH OF ZONED NUMBER IN RGT OF R2
BCTR   R2,0             DECREMENT THE LENGTH BY 1
EX     R2,PKINST        EXECUTE THE PACK INSTRUCTION
```

The instruction identified by the label PKINST, along with any other instructions that will be invoked by Execute instructions, should be stored immediately after the EOJ macro if they are used in the main program. If they are used in a subroutine or a procedure, they should be stored immediately after the return instruction.

E   X   E   R   C   I   S   E   S

1. Write the definitions for a table to translate EBCDIC to ASCII.

2. Use the table defined in Example C.1 in a code segment to convert a fullword in register R2 to an 8-character string, HEXVAL, which gives the hexadecimal form of the number.

3. Alter the definitions in TRPAT to print the fields in order of their appearance in STUREC.

4. Write the definitions and instructions needed to scan a string in INSTR for the first nonblank character. Using the Execute instruction, write the code needed to left justify the nonblank part of INSTR in a field OUTSTR of the same size. OUTSTR should be padded on the right with blanks.

5. Suppose that a program is to manipulate variable length strings described by the following DSECT.

```
VSECT      DSECT
VARSTR     DS      CL256
           ORG     VARSTR
LENGTH     DS      CL1
STRING     DS      CL255
```

The length field will contain the current length of the string. This allows a null string to be represented by a record in which the first byte is 0. The characters in the string will be stored in the leftmost bytes of the STRING part of the record. Bytes beyond the length of the string should be ignored.

a. Write a function COMPARE(STRING1, STRING2) that accepts two variable length strings and compares them. It should return −1 in R0 if STRING1 < STRING2, 0 if the strings are equal, and +1 otherwise.

b. Write a function SEARCH(TARGET, SRCHSTR) that accepts two variable length strings as arguments and searches for the first occurrence of SRCHSTR in TARGET. If it is found, SEARCH should return the starting position of the substring TARGET, which matches SRCHSTR.

c. Write a procedure CONCAT(STRING1, STRING2, TARGET) that accepts three variable length strings as arguments. It should set TARGET equal to the concatenation of STRING1 and STRING2, truncating on the right if necessary.

INDEX